Dawson's Gift

Judith
Believe!.

Andrea Bell

Dawson's Gift

Andrea Bell

Odonata, LLC.
Novato, California

Body text is set in 11 point Bitstream Arrus and titles are set in Bitstream Ribbon 131. Book and cover design by Pete Masterson, Æonix Publishing Group, *www.aeonix.com*.

Old Rabbinic story from the Dr. Laura Schlessinger radio broadcast appearing on pages 124 and 125 appear courtesy of Dr. Laura Schlessinger and with express, written permission.

Reprinted quotes taken from the motion picture *Babe* appearing on page 421 copyright 2002 by Universal Studios. Courtesy of Universal Studios Publishing Rights, a Division of Universal Studios Licensing, Inc. All rights reserved.

Quotations from the motion picture *Forest Gump* on page 431 appear courtesy of Eric Roth and Paramount Pictures and with their express, written permission.

Story excerpt on page 548 taken from *Life Beyond Death* by Norman Vincent Peale Trust. Copyright © 1996 by The Norman Vincent Peale Trust. Used by permission of Zondervan.

Cataloging-In-Publication
(Provided by Quality Books, Inc.)

Bell, Andrea.
Dawson's Gift / Andrea Bell. -- 1st ed.
p. cm.
LCCN 2002091012
ISBN 0-9717206-1-4

1. Bell, Dawson. 2. Children--Death--Religious aspects--Christianity. 3. Bereavement--Religious aspects--Christianity. 4. Grief--Religious aspects--Christianity. 5. Heart--Transplantation--Patients--Biography. 6. Transplantation of organs, tissues, etc. in children--Biography. 7. Conversion--Christianity. 8. Spirituality I. Title.

BV4907.B45 2002

248.8'66'092
QBI02-701499

Odonata, LLC.
P.O. Box 1533   415-897-9957
Novato, CA 94948-1533   www.dawsonsgift.com

Printed in the United States of America.

This book is dedicated with love
to my daughter and to my mother.

*A woman is fortunate who shares a special closeness with her daughter,
but when that woman also has a mother with whom she has a special bond,
she is blessed.*

Table of Contents

Prologue

As far back as I can remember, I have cried on my birthday. Today is no exception. What were those silly things I had found to cry about in the past? When did I discover how trivial they were? I guess I've known for a long time now, but never more than I know it today.

Years ago I had some impossible expectations that my birthdays must be perfect days. Everything and everyone had to be just so. My daughter referred to me once as a "birthday brat." I thought that was cute. If only I could be that again.

My family accepted and indulged my notion that birthdays must be major events by making much of mine. Through the years I could confidently expect the people in my life to attempt to make my birthdays happy. One year, despite their pursuit of the perfect celebration, my mother, my father, and my then-husband, Bill, neglected to confirm who was to buy my cake. At the last minute, they feared the possibility that no one was getting it. That was the year I had three. Later, my boyfriend, Rusty, maintained the tradition. This ritual continued even though I had long been at that stage of life when most people stop making a fuss over their increasing age. My daughter, Claudia, understood and I could always count on her to remember to call and give me an affectionate card. And then there was Dawson, my somewhat unreliable son.

In recent years, it became evident that in order for my day to be happy I had to hear from Dawson. Dawson had touched my heart in a way that I could not explain nor understand. I had already experienced the feeling of a mother's love when I had my first child, Claudia, but with Dawson it was different. Not more, not less, just different. There was a sympathy I felt for him, almost a sadness, an undefined concern, a tug at my heartstrings, a love I knew had no limit.

Dawson was born when Claudia was nineteen months old. Claudia was a beautiful child with a sweet cherub-like face, soft peachy cheeks, dark curly hair and big brown eyes and was instantly liked by everyone she met. Dawson had big brown eyes as well, but his devilishly pointed eyebrows and somewhat flaring nostrils gave him a less friendly appearance. Later, these same attributes would contribute to his "bad boy" handsomeness.

I started Claudia in dancing school at an early age as my mother had done for me. Dawson would sit, sometimes patiently, on my lap as we watched her lesson each week. But when we were at home and she was showing her dad and grandparents what she had learned, Dawson would get out there with her. He would watch her every move and follow along, never taking his eyes off her. My aunt had once said, "Claudia will be a hard act to follow." She didn't mean her dancing, she meant it was going to be tough for Dawson to vie for attention with a sister so sweet and adorable.

Claudia was quite a good girl, even during the "terrible twos" and typically difficult teenage years. She had not caused me any serious problems and I knew she was on the right path. I wasn't so sure about Dawson. I always worried about him. So to hear from him on my birthday, or any other day, would comfort me and fill my heart as only he could.

Today, on my fifty-second birthday, I am remembering my last birthday, remembering how his call to me had changed my day. That morning I had locked myself out of my shop and a delivery-man was due to arrive. I had called the building manager, but he wouldn't be there with a key for another hour. I had to wait in the parking lot for fear of missing the delivery and I was quite upset. My birthday was off to a very poor start. Then my phone rang, the cellular phone Rusty had given me the year before so that Dawson could always reach me. "Hi. Happy birthday," Dawson said. "Are you driving?" he teased.

"No, I'm not," I said, with renewed lightheartedness.

He liked to joke with me about how poorly I drove while on the phone. He was riding with me once when I got a call and chuckled that it was "pretty scary." We talked for a long time, until the manager came. It was a nice talk. We laughed a little, as we usually did, and he sounded well. It was a happy birthday, that one last year.

This year's birthday, this one today, November 22, 1996, how can this one be happy? "Please let me hear from Dawson," I cry out as I have never cried out before.

I know he *wants* to wish me a happy birthday. Maybe that will have to be enough. I know in my heart that today he would say, "Hi. Happy birthday. I love you, Mom."

Part One

"In the beginning…"

—GENESIS 1:1

Chapter One

Monday morning, June 27, 1994: I awoke in a motel room. Alone. No luggage. No makeup. No change of clothes. No desire to get up, face the day, or to go home just a few blocks away. Home was a condo I shared with Rusty, my partner/boyfriend of seven years. He was a loving, caring, giving, generous man who took charge and took care of people, things, events, and me. He was attentive, considerate, angry and unreasonable. He could switch from compassionate to insensitive in an instant when something I said or did incited the anger in him that seemed to be ever simmering beneath his congenial demeanor.

Last night was one of those times. We had both been working very hard, very long hours. He was a firefighter and in addition to his twenty-four hour shifts at the firehouse, he worked at home on his computerized embroidery business. I helped with the business after my nine-hour waitress shift six days a week. We were tired, we were tense and we argued over little things. But why did an argument over something unimportant always turn into a major conflict? I hated the yelling and screaming, of which I did my share, and it never resolved our differences, it only widened the gap I felt growing between us. I was not afraid he would strike me in his anger, but the look in his eyes and the ugly words that came out of his mouth turned my stomach. I could not seem to reason with him when he got like that, so last night, out of intense frustration and fury, I fled. With my mind spinning, I grabbed my purse and ran out the door. "Where will I go? It's midnight. I can't go to my parents and upset them. They don't know how often or how bitterly we fight, but I don't want to sleep in my car and I don't want to go back in the house." I drove to a decent motel down the way and registered for the night. I was embarrassed and felt ashamed. I had been crying and I must have looked a mess. I spent a restless night and at 8:30 Monday morning, my one day off, I felt I had to go home. I was concerned about the reaction I would find there. Was Rusty still angry? More angry? Which one of us would speak first? What could we say to each other this time?

I walked in the door. Rusty was standing at the kitchen counter by the telephone, writing on a small, white pad of paper. When he looked my way, he spoke the words he had just written: "Dawson called."

"When? What did he say? What did he want?" Dawson was not inclined to call for no particular reason.

"He said he doesn't feel well and wanted to know if you could call a doctor for him. He's really hoarse and it was hard to hear him," Rusty answered, looking away.

I was immediately on the phone calling Dawson. "Hello," he answered, almost inaudibly.

"Dawson, what's wrong?"

"I don't know," he said. "I'm so hoarse and my legs and feet are all swollen."

"Do you want me to come down and take you to the doctor?"

"Well, I don't really have a doctor. I was hoping you could find me one and call for me because my voice is so bad. The doctor on my insurance records is that stupid Dr. Hooper. I don't want to go to him. He's that doctor that we went to when I was about ten years old, remember?"

"Yes, I remember." Dawson had a fever and I had taken him to see Dr. Hooper who had shrugged us off, saying there was nothing he could do. He said to Dawson, "You have the cruds." Dawson looked at me as if to say, "What do we do now, Mom?" I hadn't forgotten how unprofessional he seemed and we never went to him again. "I'll see if I can find a doctor who will see you today and I'll call you back. When did this come on you?"

"A couple of days ago," he answered.

"A couple of days? Does Dad know you're sick?"

"Yeah, he told me to call the doctor."

"O.K., I'll see what I can do and call you back." The argument Rusty and I'd had the night before that had seemed so monumental, now was quite trivial.

I proceeded to call nearby doctors, but none would see new patients on short notice. As a last resort, I called Dr. Hooper's office.

"We cannot squeeze a new patient in today," the receptionist said. Because it had been so many years since our last visit, Dawson was considered a new patient.

"But my son needs to see a doctor today," I pleaded.

"How about tomorrow?" she asked.

Suddenly, I remembered that I knew a woman who worked in that office. I had gone to school with her and had served her recently at the restaurant. "Is Rose there?" I asked.

"No, it's her day off."

When I hung up, I looked in the phone book, found Rose's number and called her.

"Hi, Rose? This is Andrea, the waitress at Tommy's."

"Oh, hi," she said, sounding slightly puzzled.

"I have a problem and I was hoping you could help. My son needs to see a doctor, but I can't find a single one in town who will take a new patient today. We had seen Dr. Hooper years ago so I thought maybe…"

"Andrea, give me your number. I'll try to get him in. I'll call you back."

When she did, she said the doctor would see him at 4:00 that afternoon. I called Dawson and told him the only doctor I could find was Dr. Hooper. Dawson said, "Fine."

"Do you want me to drive you?"

"No, that's O.K., I can drive. I don't know if I can put shoes on, but I'm all right to drive."

"O.K., if you're sure," I said. "Call me when you get back."

When it was getting on to 5:00 that afternoon, I began to wait for his call. As the minutes passed, I could do or think of nothing else.

Finally, the phone rang. "Dawson's in the hospital," Bill said.

"In the hospital? I'll be right down."

"No, no. There's no need for you to do that. They're doing some tests. You wouldn't be able to see him anyway. I'll call you when I know something. And if they let him come home, he'll call you."

"Oh, God, what is it? What is the doctor saying? I think I should be there."

"Don't panic. Stay put. I'll call you."

When Bill called later, he told me they were going to keep Dawson there. He said the doctors weren't saying much, just doing tests. He gave me the name and number of the doctor who was treating him and told me to call him. "You'll probably be able to get more answers than I will." When I spoke with Dr. Lee, the internist, he told me Dawson was experiencing congestive heart failure. "Heart failure?" I gasped.

He said it was treatable and they were giving him medication that would alleviate the swelling. "But what we need to do now," he said, "is find the cause. He's resting now and I'll see him tomorrow and follow up with more tests."

I thanked him and, immediately after hanging up, got out my Encyclopedia of Medicine. I read, "Although it sounds life-threatening, heart failure is usually a treatable condition and compatible with survival for many years."

O.K., I thought, the phrase congestive heart failure sounds worse than it is. It isn't good, but they can treat it. As I read on, the prognosis was sounding less optimistic. I called Bill to tell him what I had learned. I told him I would go by and see Dawson the next day after work.

On the phone the next morning, Dawson sounded a little better and he said he felt better, too. "They asked me if I were allergic to any medications. I told them I was allergic to penicillin. Is that true?"

"Well, yeah, I think so," I said.

"You're not sure?"

"Well, I never had anyone tell me, 'He's allergic to penicillin,' but I believe you had a reaction to it once. Do you remember? You were about eight years old, you had an infected throat and the doctor gave you penicillin. That night, you complained of your ears itching, deep inside. They were very red and you had a rash on your neck. I became alarmed, fearing anaphylactic shock, so I took you to the emergency room. They told me it might be a reaction to the penicillin. So the doctor said, to play it safe, we should switch you to a substitute. We never took a chance with penicillin again."

"O.K. I guess it was right that I told them that."

"I think so. O.K., well, I'll see you later, right after work. Call me if you want anything."

I was glad the restaurant was only minutes away from the hospital and when I got there, he was sitting up in bed. He was still quite bloated and seemed short of breath, but I could see he didn't want any fussing, and I knew he definitely wouldn't want me to show how worried I was.

On Wednesday, Dawson called me at work and asked me if I could bring him some things when I came by that afternoon. Over the phone, he gave me his list, toiletries, mostly, and some magazines. He seemed to be in a better mood and I stayed until Bill arrived. Before I left, a nurse came in and did an EKG, without comment.

When I was leaving, I said goodbye without so much as touching his hand. What I really wanted to do was hug him and cradle him in my arms, but Dawson had rejected hugs and kisses for many years. It had become a joke in the family how he would not let us hug him, and that only perpetuated his reluctance. He'd stand there, with his arms at his side, smiling sometimes, but trying to appear too tough for that sentimental stuff. My mother was never comfortable giving hugs, either, and she told me she and Dawson had an unspoken understanding. She said, "Whenever I'm saying goodbye to Dawson, it's funny. We look at each other and kind of awkwardly motion with our arms and shrug and smile. We know that it's O.K., we don't have to hug." I had never been one for hugs myself, but getting one from Dawson would have meant so much to me.

On Thursday, Dawson called me at work again. This time he said, "They know what's wrong with me."

"What is it?" I asked.

"It's my heart."

"What about your heart?"

"It's big," he said.

"What can they do for that?"

"I need a transplant."

"What?"

"Are you coming by today? The doctor wants to talk to you."

"Yes. Is the doctor there now? Should I see if I can get off work?"

"No, he said he'd be back later."

"O.K. I'll be there as soon as I can," I assured him.

When I got off work, I went right to the hospital and straight to his room. He was sitting in a chair at a small bedside table thumbing through a magazine. He looked at me and said, "Dr. Hooper was just here. He told me when you got here you should go to the nurses' desk and tell them you're here." Shortly after, Dr. Hooper came into the room. Dawson was still turning pages of a magazine and I was standing. Dr. Hooper approached me and said, "Dawson's heart is very bad. A healthy heart pumps like this," he explained, as he made a fist and repeatedly opened his hand fully and clenched it tightly. "Dawson's heart is pumping like this." He again opened his hand wide, then barely moved his fingertips, drawing them in only slightly and did not make a fist.

"What can you do for that?" I asked, trying to stay calm.

"Nothing," he said.

"What are you saying?"

"It's fatal," he answered matter-of-factly.

"What do you mean? What are you saying?" I pleaded, almost shouting.

Shrugging, as he had done those many years earlier, he answered casually, "Two days, two weeks, two months… I don't know."

I looked over at Dawson, still turning pages. When he looked up, the look on his face personified a phrase I had heard many times, but had never seen quite so literally, "keeping a stiff upper lip." His face was taut, his mouth tight, his eyes showed shock and fright. He appeared to be successfully holding back tears. I was unable to hold back mine. I looked at that doctor standing face to face with me. He stood there looking back at me. This couldn't be true. Was I hearing this right? I was in the middle of a nightmare and I wanted to scream, to wake up and have this not be true. How could this be true? How could this man be telling me this so nonchalantly? I would have thought he'd have suggested I sit down before telling me or have waited until someone was with me. This man had just told a mother that her only son, who appeared perfectly healthy less than a week earlier, might have only two days to live! And what was Dawson feeling hearing this? The doctor just stood there. He did not turn to speak to Dawson. He did not reach out to me. He did nothing but stand there staring into my face, saying nothing. I then motioned, gesturing wildly, with my hand, "Get out! Just leave!" I didn't know why he was still standing there, doing and saying nothing. I didn't know what he wanted from me. I just wanted him to go away. He finally turned and left. I looked at Dawson and went to his side and made a slight attempt to hug him, but he was typically unresponsive. He resumed his page turning and when he spoke, he said, "I'm not gonna die." The phone rang and he answered it.

He said to his dad, "The doctor was just here and Mom's here. I'll put her on, you can talk to her."

"What's up?" Bill asked. "Did you talk to the doctor?"

"I talked to Dr. Hooper," I answered. Then I said a phrase, an odd phrase, one I had not heard myself say in many years, "Bill, come home!"

When I got off the phone, I told Dawson I would be right back and quickly left the room. I went to the restroom and tried to compose myself. I thought it would be impossible. It was as though every fear and heartache I had ever experienced for Dawson since the day he was born had been leading to this moment. "Oh, God," I cried, "Please don't let this be happening! Not my Dawson, please not my Dawson! There must be something that can be done!"

When I went back to his room, a doctor came in and introduced himself as Dr. Burke, the cardiologist. He said, "Mrs. Bell, you've spoken with Dr. Hooper? He's explained Dawson's condition to you?" He then asked me if I had any questions.

"Yes," I said. "What is the condition called?"

"Cardiomyopathy. You've probably heard of an enlarged heart. That's what it is."

"And there's nothing you can do for that?"

"When the heart gets damaged and expands like this it loses its ability to pump properly."

"But the heart has some capability of repairing itself, doesn't it?" I asked.

"Yes, it does, to some extent, but when it is functioning as poorly as Dawson's, it is not likely."

"Isn't there any treatment for it?"

"What you are seeing now, with the swelling and shortness of breath, is a result of the diminished pumping capacity. Fluid is backing up and he's retaining it in his tissues. We can treat that. He is on diuretics and we will keep him on those to avoid this, as best we can. But beyond that, for the heart itself, the only corrective measure is a heart transplant."

"Then he could have a transplant," I said in desperation.

"Well, not necessarily. His liver may also be damaged. If that were the case, no, he could not get a transplant."

"What do we do at this point?"

"I'm letting him go home tomorrow. He'll remain on the diuretics and other medications to help his heart and I'd like to see him next week. He should take it easy and not do too much."

"He gets to go home?"

"Yes."

"Should someone be with him at all times?"

"Well, if someone could, it wouldn't be a bad idea. He should take it easy and not over exert himself. He has to watch his diet; eliminate salt, stay away from any packaged foods, avoid junk food and anything that has a lot of sodium."

Then I asked, "How common is this condition? What causes it?"

"It is not an uncommon condition, but for someone his age... well... and as far as what causes it, sometimes, we never know. The heart can become damaged for different reasons. It can be a virus that attacks the heart, it can be some kind of toxic poisoning, it can be alcohol..."

"Alcohol?"

"Yes."

I looked over at Dawson. His eyes widened.

"Anything else?" Dr. Burke asked.

"No, I don't think so. Thank you, Doctor."

"I'll set up an appointment to see you in my office next week, Dawson," he said, then left.

I went to his side and I said softly, "God, Dawson, why didn't you listen?" I hated uttering those worthless words, but did so out of absolute despair. I hoped he would show some emotion, that he would cry, that he would say, "Mom, I'm sorry." I hoped he would want me to hold him. He just looked at me.

Bill arrived soon after and I told him, briefly, what I had learned. Dawson was looking as though he didn't believe a word of it. I'm sure he thought, "I'm twenty-five years old! That's not going to happen! Die? Me? No."

Bill and I went out to the cafeteria's patio and I went into more detail about everything I had been told. He just kept shaking his head. He wiped tears from his eyes, as he asked, "How can this be? How can it be alcohol? Do you know how long some people have been drinking and how much and their hearts are fine? How could this happen? I can't believe this." He cried, "I really love that kid. I can't lose him!"

"I know," I said.

We sat quietly, our shock and distress shared in silence. As a breeze came through the little courtyard and shade fell upon us, I began to shiver. It was summer, but suddenly I felt very cold. I stood up, my arms folded tightly in front of me as Bill spoke. "He can come home? He's coming home tomorrow?"

"Yes," I said, still shaking.

"Maybe I'll see if my dad can come and stay at the house. He could be there all day with Dawson and he cooks, too."

"That would be good," I told him.

Dawson hadn't been very close to his grandfather, but that was partly because they hadn't spent much time together. Dawson liked him well enough. The only thing that might pose a problem was that Dawson wasn't going to like the idea of a "babysitter." But I would feel better knowing that he would not be alone.

We went back to his room. Bill told him that he was going to have Papa Tom come and stay. Dawson said he didn't need anybody, he was fine.

I noticed Dr. Lee at the nurses' desk and I left the room to go talk to him. I asked him what we could expect when we got Dawson home. He said, "He should take it easy. He could be all right for a while, but what we will be concerned with is arrhythmia."

"What is that?" I asked.

"Any irregularity in the heart beat."

"What if that happens?"

"He would probably die."

"If someone were with him and called for help, could he possibly be saved?"

"It's possible, but not likely."

"So the medication he's on, is that to help an irregular heart beat?"

"No, they're for the water retention and to help his heart pump a little better. He has to avoid salt, which adds to the water retention and he cannot have any alcohol. None. I told him that. A drop could kill him."

"You've told him all this?"

"Oh, yes," Dr. Lee said emphatically.

I went back to Dawson's room. His mood had not changed. When I left that night, I told him to call me at work in the morning and let me know what time he was going to be released. I went to the phone and called my mother to tell her I was leaving the hospital and going to her house. When she asked me if I were able to drive, I assured her I was.

During that twenty-minute drive, the words "It's fatal" played and replayed over in my mind. I could see Dawson disbelieving and trying to be brave as he heard those same words. Tears began to spill from my eyes. He was my child and we were living an unimaginable horror, an absolute nightmare, one in which your worst fears come true. I remembered having bad dreams from which I had awakened crying, my cool tears having brought a feeling of instant relief as I realized that I had only been dreaming. But this was not a dream, my tears could not soothe me and there was nothing that could rescue me.

When I arrived, my mother asked, "How are you?" She was concerned about me. After all, I was her child. I looked at her and cried out, "This is too big! I can't handle it! Mommy, what am I going to do? I'm so scared. Oh, God, you know, I always feared that someday I would experience sorrow over Dawson." It appeared that someday had arrived.

Chapter Two

Dawson had lived alone with his dad since I moved out seven years earlier, in July of 1987, six months after our divorce was final on January 1. I stayed on in order to help Dawson maintain his grades and to see to it that he graduated from high school that June. He had been sluffing off in school, but he always improved when I got serious and did more than my usual nagging. I should have done that more consistently over the years. Looking back now, I realize that I should have done more in many ways and that staying until he graduated was not enough. I should never have left. Had I stayed, things might have worked out differently.

Bill and I had been high school sweethearts and we had dated five years before we married, but we were still too young. Though we married without a clear and mutual understanding of what it took to be a strong family unit, in many ways I felt our life together was good. We loved each other, Bill had a good paying job, I was able to stay at home with my children, Claudia and Dawson, and they had a loving and close extended family of grandparents and cousins.

I volunteered in their classrooms and I was home when they came home from school every day, watching from the window for the yellow school bus that left them off at the corner. But I spent many days distracted and upset, upset with Bill. I knew there must be wives somewhere who would not have been as distraught as I was if their husbands were a little late getting home, but I just could not stand it and I had not expected it.

Often he was late because he was working overtime, but many nights when he could have been home for dinner, he had chosen to stop at a bar, instead, and have "a few beers with the boys." He did not seem to understand the negative impact it was having on his family. He saw himself as the hard working good provider he was. He gave me his entire paycheck each week and never questioned how I spent it. He was generous to the kids and me, but too often we were without him, too often we were waiting for him to come home. Surprisingly, when he did come home he never came home mean or looking for a fight. That seemed to be good enough to him and, in a sense, to the kids, too. But it was not enough for me. I wanted a man I could count on every day to be home on time and sober. His attitude of "what's the big deal?" was baffling to me. I had grown up with a father who walked in the door from work every day at 5:00 sharp. You could set your clock by him. My mother used to say that she could put the dinner on the table at 4:58 and not worry about it getting cold. And though I may not ever have expected Bill would be that punctual, I had not expected that he would be the husband and father he was.

When we first met, he had never even so much as tasted a drink, though most of his friends were already drinking. And by the time we were married, he still had shown no interest in alcohol. So when he began to drink regularly and enjoy it, I was astounded. I could not understand why he was choosing to behave so immaturely. How could he not see how much he was hurting the kids and me? Didn't he care?

Actually, Claudia seemed to be taking it all pretty well, and was more upset with me for my yelling than she was with Bill. It must have appeared to her that I was the cause of all the dissension because I was doing all the fighting and Bill never yelled back. My ranting did not seem to bother Dawson as much. He was more openly worried and quietly disappointed when Bill was late. He liked Bill and looked up to him. When he was very young he would put on Bill's gray-green work shirt and pretend that he was going to work. Dawson's admiration for Bill was undeniable in a drawing he did in the second grade. It showed a big Bill and a littler Dawson each of them wearing the green uniform shirts. And in the lines below the drawing, in his neat child's handwriting, Dawson wrote, "My Dad is an electrician and I am going to be one, too. My Dad is my best friend."

Dawson and Claudia were both sensitive children, but in different ways. Dawson seemed hurt when Bill was not home before he went to bed, whereas Claudia seemed unconcerned. Her sensitivity showed in other ways. At the age of four, she became emotional at the Ice Capades and cried because, as she had said, "It is so beautiful." And one day she was sad and cried as she told me she wanted to pick some pretty flowers, but would not "because they will die."

They were significantly different from each other in almost all ways possible; their temperaments, their attitudes, their likes and dislikes. They had different tastes in everything, including food. I could not cook a dinner that pleased them both. For if he liked it, she didn't and if she did, he didn't. But there was one thing I cooked they both felt the same about, though I did not discover the extent of their mutual dislike of Brussels sprouts until years later. They told me that whenever I cooked those sprouts they would wait until I was not looking and then they would hide them in their napkins and throw them away. They were both quite amused as they shared this confession to me. They thought it quite funny and seemed to delight in the fact that I had never caught on.

Claudia was definitely an easier child to raise than Dawson. My difficulties with him usually stemmed from a combination of two things: his immovable stubbornness and his unwillingness to talk about whatever was bothering him. As a very young child these characteristics made him seem bratty. But he was not a wild and disobedient child. In fact, he was more apt to be quiet and reserved. Not being openly excitable he showed his delight and enjoyment with his playful smile and little chuckle. But when he was upset, he was extremely difficult to reason with. Because of his unwillingness or inability to explain his feelings, I found it difficult to console him. And as a mother, I wanted to understand and help him when he was upset, but he did not often come to me for consolation. When he did, I opened my heart to him. One of those times I remember was when he and his cousin had found a tiny, baby jackrabbit trapped in a ditch. They rescued it and brought it home. Dawson found a small box and cut some grass and gently placed the little rabbit in it. He kept him in his room all night and when he awoke in the morning, the first thing he did was check on him. When he discovered that the baby rabbit had died during the night, Dawson came running into my room and threw himself on my bed, sobbing. I understood his tears and I was able to hold him in my arms and comfort him that day.

As he grew older, keeping his emotions to himself made him appear cold and unfeeling, though I had always seen a unique child, a sensitive boy, and eventually, a vulnerable young man beneath that aloof exterior.

Despite Dawson's stubbornness as a teenager, he was surprisingly good about checking in with me and getting home on time. Bill was a lenient father and made very few demands on him. In high school Dawson received a drunk driving charge, so I knew he was drinking, but I rationalized that it was just the "usual teenage partying." It was mandatory for minors who received that charge to attend a few sessions with a counselor. I drove Dawson to his meetings and on the last one, the counselor spoke with me. She said, "It appears Dawson's problem is that he has a very high tolerance for alcohol. What that means is that he is able to consume quite a bit before he is affected. Even then he can continue to drink more because he is still functioning; walking, talking and driving."

Although I had spent many days and nights talking to him about the dangers of alcohol, I received very little feedback from him. He had that "Yeah, I know, but I'm O.K." attitude. Out of all the times I talked to him, he only expressed one feeling. He had put his hands to his face, threw his head back, looked up to the ceiling, and said, "Mom, it's just so hard being me." I tried to get him to talk to me more about how he felt, but he would not. I asked him if he wanted to continue talking to a counselor, but he said he didn't want to and I let it go at that. But as the parent I should have forced him. Though I think I believed that if I couldn't get him to put his feelings into words, no one else could either. How arrogant of me.

I was so concerned about him, but perhaps my concerns were misplaced. Maybe I shouldn't have been so concerned with how he was feeling about things, maybe my concern should have been how he was dealing with things. Maybe he should have had stricter guidelines to follow; clear rules that were enforced and consistent standards of behavior that were demanded of him. But it wasn't that there was no structure. I had not ignored teaching and preaching about values, virtues and consequences. In fact, some of my friends thought I was too tough on the kids when they were little. And after all, Claudia had learned from the same "guidebook" and she had done well. She had been an honor student, never cut class, wasn't interested in partying and had respect for herself and others. I had never received any calls from school about her conduct, like the one I had gotten when Dawson had Crazy-Glued a girl's locker permanently shut. My disciplinary tactics and teachings had been enough for Claudia to learn from, but Dawson obviously needed more. So why hadn't I done more? Was I afraid to get tough with him? Was I unwilling to force Dawson to do something he didn't want to do for fear he would not like me? Had my affection for him turned me into a wimp? Had that "soft spot" in my heart that was filled with angst for Dawson led me to be less effective as a parent? So many interminable questions and maybes to torment me.

Over the years, I had tempered my worries by trying to convince myself that his teenage drinking was normal and that it did not have to turn into a serious problem. I had closed my eyes and crossed my fingers and hoped that fate would be kind to us. It's as though I believed I had no power to change what was to be. But there is no power in sitting back and simply hoping.

It was so unlike me to look the other way and give up. I considered myself a determined, persuasive person. No one could convince me anything was impossible. But by the time Dawson started drinking, I had already faced an obstacle I could not conquer. I had been unable to triumph when confronted with a husband who chose to drink. Alcohol was an adversary I could not defeat. I could not convince, cajole, motivate or threaten Bill to quit drinking, so I believed that I would not be able to convince Dawson, either. But because I had put all that energy and conviction into Bill and it had not worked, it did not mean I did not owe that same energy and conviction to Dawson. Why didn't I find the will to rise above those feelings of uselessness? Why did I leave his future to chance?

I guess I thought that everything would work out O.K., the same way I had thought, at one time, that everything would work out for Bill and me. Isn't that one of the reasons I had waited twenty years before I left? I wanted to be married, but I did not want my children to have a stepfather. I wanted them to have Bill. And I believed he would see it my way someday. And, eventually, he did seem to understand the extent of how he had hurt me, but it was quite late, too late for our marriage.

At the time I moved out, I had asked Dawson to come and live with Claudia and me, but he wanted to stay with his dad and stay in the house and town he grew up in. And so he did. All in all, my leaving Dawson, somewhat on his own, was probably a mistake. But he was eighteen and I believed he and his dad cared for each other, although they both seemed to have difficulty showing it.

After my move, I called him about once a week. It was the stereotypical mother and son routine, "Why don't you ever call your mother?" He did call me occasionally, but most of the time, I called him. We always got together on holidays and birthdays, which added up to at least ten times a year, but I wished I could see him more. He was hard to pin down, hardly ever home, always out and about. When I'd talk to Bill and ask how Dawson was doing, his usual answers were, "O.K." and "He's not home much."

Dawson had retained his desire to become an electrician like his dad. It seemed things were going well. A year after he graduated from high school, he took the Electrical Workers' entrance exam and finished in the top ten out of over five hundred applicants. He was then accepted into a five-year apprenticeship program. Bill was very proud. But Dawson was still doing a lot of partying, sometimes jeopardizing his apprenticeship. Bill pushed, prodded and supported Dawson through it all.

Finally, he was coming very close to completing his five years. With relief and joy I anticipated his accomplishment. I began seeing more of him because I had changed jobs and was working in a restaurant in the town where he lived. He started coming in with his girlfriend, Candace, for breakfast some weekends. She was cute, tiny, blonde and friendly. I liked her and he seemed happy. I was always glad to see him. It meant so much to me that he wanted to come in and see me. I could not explain to anyone why it was so inordinately special to me. And I didn't try. It was just good to look up and see him standing there, smiling at me with his one word greeting, "Hi." I enjoyed chatting with them about their plans for those sunny Sunday mornings. It does not seem like much for a mother to get excited about, but for me it was. Because I was still carrying around that place in my heart, that spot for Dawson labeled "Hope."

Chapter Three

The day after talking to the doctors, I went to work, but shouldn't have. As a waitress, you are expected to leave your troubles outside the door. Customers want cheerfulness served with their meals, but I was unable to fake even the slightest smile. I was unable to function. My customers were asking me what was wrong and I could not speak the words on my mind, "I've been told my son is going to die." A group of Friday-morning-regulars joked with me about why I looked so sad. "Did you have a fight with your boyfriend?" one of the men asked, teasingly. I was pouring coffee from two pots into two empty cups, a maneuver I had done a hundred times before. But this time, I was trying to respond to his question while holding back tears and thinking about Dawson. Completely distracted by my anguish, I poured the equivalent of about six cups of coffee all over the table. I didn't even know what I had done until my customer yelled, "Look what you're doing!" When I realized what had happened, I turned and ran to the kitchen, overwhelmed by it all.

My boss was very understanding and was not upset or angry, but suggested I take off work and go to Dawson. He said, "You should be there with him, not here. I don't know why you felt you had to come in today. No one would have expected it of you. We certainly would have understood."

I had always been a responsible employee, never taking time off, and I was trying to remain so, despite the staggering news I had received. Toni, the waitress who offered to cover for me, gave me a hug and said, "Dawson's going to be O.K. You take care."

As I drove to the hospital, I was anguishing over how his heart condition would affect his life. What limitations would it put on him? And how would he accept them? It would probably not be in the way most people would. I thought of how different Dawson had always been, even as a child.

We had encouraged him to play sports, thinking that having an interest and a focus would be good for him. Bill had played baseball as a boy and basketball in high school and had been good at both. When Dawson was very young, my cousin began extolling the benefits of Little League, so I signed him up. He was a little too young to play, but I was told he could get started on the team as a bat boy. He liked the idea. He would wear a uniform and Bill bought him a little mitt. They started practicing throwing and catching. Official team practice was held in the small park across the street from our house. On the first day of practice, I watched him cross the street alone, holding his new mitt. I watched with pride and joy and profound emotion. From our kitchen window, I saw him slowly approach the group of boys and the coach. I watched as the group broke up into smaller groups. I continued to watch as the boys and the coach started to throw and catch with each other as Dawson sat down on the bench holding his mitt. He was sitting there while the other boys played and laughed and ran after baseballs. "Why isn't Dawson playing?" I asked myself. I wondered if I should go over to the park and ask the coach. I resolved that I should not go running to his side, as much as I wanted to. This was one of Dawson's first steps out into the world. My heart continued to sink as I watched this unchanging scene. Finally, practice was over. Parents began arriving to pick up their excited little boys. Dawson came home, stopping to look both ways before crossing the street.

"How was it?" I asked him.

"O.K. I didn't have to go to practice, though," he answered.

"Why not?"

"I don't have to practice 'cause I'm the bat boy."

"But you could practice if you wanted to, though, couldn't you?"

"I guess."

He just seemed to accept that was the way it was. If it bothered him that he had been sitting there not playing with the other boys, he didn't show it. True to form, it was difficult to tell what he was feeling.

The following year, when he was old enough to play, we signed up again. He had a new team, a new uniform, a new coach and his mitt. Grandma and Papa, my parents, were invited to the Opening Day Parade and to watch him play. I had seen him at team practice and I knew baseball wasn't something he was thrilled about, but he was definitely excited about Opening Day. "Wouldn't it be something if I hit a home run?" he said with great enthusiasm and optimism. He looked so cute in his uniform as his team filed in and took their places on the bench. We were nervously anticipating Dawson's first step up to the plate. A couple of innings went by and he had not come up to bat. He had not gone out into the field, either. When he looked our way, I smiled and waved as my heart was aching. Other boys had already had more than one turn at bat and in the field. What was going on? Why wasn't he playing? By the last inning, I was getting very anxious. I was sure he was about to play at any minute. But then the game was over. He had sat on the bench holding his mitt through the entire game. And he had invited Grandma and Papa to watch him play. He didn't say much on the ride home, but I talked about next time.

This time I decided to call the coach and ask him about the policy of who gets to play and who does not. He told me that it was his decision and that he chose to have his best players play. I said, "On Opening Day, when family and friends are there and the kids are all so excited? These are little boys who have invited their families to see them! You mean that even by the last inning when the score wasn't even close, you could not have let Dawson get up to bat at least once?" It had taken everything I had to confront this man and question his judgment. Unfortunately, it took more than I had to control my emotions and my composure. My voice began to crack and I was unable to speak without crying. When I hung up the phone, I was embarrassed and mortified at my show of uncontrolled and almost childish behavior. I knew I had overreacted, but everything that had to do with Dawson tore at my heart.

Most of his team sports experiences were similar. He didn't get out there and hustle and he never looked comfortable playing. We tried different sports, different times, but he just didn't have an interest in it. This was unfortunate because it did seem that by the time they reached high school, the boys who had been involved in sports throughout the years were making better choices. They seemed to have less inclination to go astray.

Though he hadn't had an affinity for playing sports, he seemed to have one for riding motorcycles. He had a dirt bike when he was twelve years old and would spend hours "tearing up the dirt" on our property. That made me nervous, even though he had never gotten hurt and he seemed to be relatively cautious when riding it. But *driving,* that proved to be a different story. Within two weeks of obtaining his driver's license, at the age of sixteen, he received a speeding ticket. A week later, he demolished the right side of his car including its new tires. Luckily, this accident did not involve another car or person. When he was twenty, he was charged with "reckless driving" in his dad's truck. I read the police report and could not believe it. The report went on and on about how he went up this street and down that and sideways here and U-turns there! His lawyer later remarked to Bill that as I read it, all I seemed able to say was, "Oh, Dawson... Oh, Dawson... OH! DAWSON!"

I asked him, "What did you think you were doing? What were you thinking?"

He said, with that half-smile of his, "I thought I was Starsky an' Hutch."

I imagined that meant he thought he was "cool." Cool. Was that what everything was all about? Being cool? Had that been what had contributed to many of his difficulties? Had he been misguided by his sense of what "being cool" was? Had he seen with his young eyes that cool guys have a lot of fun? Cool guys take risks. Cool guys don't get hurt. And they definitely don't get sick...

When I arrived at the hospital, Bill was already there. He had taken off work. Dawson was *more* than ready to leave. Shortly after I got there, we were on our way out of the hospital, but he had refused the wheelchair. He was wearing a T-shirt and a pair of sweat shorts and I could see his legs were quite large. His tennis shoes were untied on his still pudgy, swollen feet. This did not hinder him from forging on ahead of us, giving him the appearance of being strong and determined. It was a poignant contrast to see this hefty young man, unabashedly toting the little gift bag brimming with the "goodies" I had brought him days earlier. He kept walking briskly and would not slow down. I said, "Dawson, just take it easy." He ignored my pleas. As Bill and I looked at each other, we just shook our heads. He was, obviously, going to be as stubborn as ever. Nothing had changed. He was always resistant to help from anyone and was unceasingly determined to do things for himself. I was reminded of the time when he was two and a half years old. We had given him a little motorized motorcycle for Christmas. It was easy to ride because it was designed for a child his age and size. But because of the large battery inside, it was extremely heavy. We took it outside and he was thrilled, riding it on the sidewalk in front of our house. When it was time to come inside, he attempted to ride it up the two small steps to the front porch. He tried and tried to make it go up the steps, but it would not. I told him I would help him. "No." Several more attempts at riding up the steps left him frustrated, angry and sweating. I explained to him he would have to get off the bike and we would walk it up the steps. "No." After a few more attempts, he threw himself off the bike, kicking and screaming with the bike landing on top of him. I said, "Dawson, get up and I'll help you."

"No!" he cried.

I said, "O.K., that's it. I'm bringing the bike in."

"No, I can do it!"

He tried and tried and could not push it up the steps. It was just too heavy and he was much too overwrought and hysterical to manage it.

He wanted to do it himself and did not understand why he was unable, but he was so determined. I let this scene go on much too long, until we were both angry and exhausted. When I finally picked up the bike and carried it in, he screamed and cried. I did not know how to help him and he would not let me.

Dawson rode home from the hospital with Bill. I followed them. I wanted to spend some time with Dawson and see him settled before going home myself. But when we went inside, I sat down at the kitchen table and Dawson went up to his room. I could hear him practically running up the stairs, then the sound of the bottles of pills he had been carrying, crashing on the steps. It was only pills, but to me the sound was so frightening, I jumped from my chair. I thought he had collapsed and dropped the pills in his fall. I ran to the stairs anxiously asking, "Dawson, are you all right?" As I reached him, he was continuing up the stairs and looked at me quite disgusted. *This is going be tough*, I thought to myself. All I wanted to do was take care of him. I could see he was going to have no part of that. He was not going to be babied.

He stayed in his room. I stayed downstairs a while then decided I should leave and went up to say goodbye. His attitude was better and he said a pleasant, "Bye, thanks." I told him I would call him the next day and that if he wanted anything, to call me.

When I got home, Rusty was there. He had gotten off duty that morning from the firehouse. He held me and I cried. He told me, "Everything's going to be all right." I prayed that was true. But how could it be, after what the doctors had said? "It's all up to Dawson," Rusty said.

I didn't want to hear that. "It's not that simple," I said.

"If he follows the doctor's orders and takes care of himself, he'll be all right."

"But will he follow orders? And, besides, that is no guarantee, either. He has a serious condition and even with the best of care, he could die. He could die two days or two weeks from now. That is what the doctor told me."

"I know, but Dawson will be fine," Rusty said with confidence.

I was not convinced. But I did feel that if anyone could overcome this, Dawson could. He always seemed to luck out in any of the situations he had gotten himself into and emerged none the worse for it. Could he do it again this time?

Rusty said, "You know, we don't have to go out to dinner Sunday night for my birthday. Let's just stay home. I'm sure your Mom and Dad and Claudia don't feel like going out, either."

I said, "No, that's O.K. It's your fiftieth. We'll still go."

What Rusty did not know was that it was not just my Mom and Dad and Claudia who were joining us for dinner. His mother, who lived across the country and had never been on an airplane, had let me in on the secret that she was coming out for Rusty's fiftieth birthday. And she wanted it to be a surprise! I was sure it would be. I had never told him she was coming. There was no way, even after all that had happened, I was going to spoil her plans to meet us at the restaurant and to surprise her son. But what a time to meet someone for the first time. And not only was I meeting Rusty's mother, but also, Claudia's new boyfriend.

Sunday, everything went as planned and we all met at the restaurant. Oddly, Rusty seemed only mildly surprised to see his mother there. He did not show much emotion, maybe because of all that we had been through that past week. Despite my sadness, I was happy to see Claudia with a nice young man. I hoped what I was feeling about Dawson's condition would not damper her happiness, so I was friendly and smiling when she introduced me to Tracy. He was, as she had described, tall and thin with light brown hair and his eyes were a nice shade of blue. He smiled a lot and seemed very at ease. They appeared comfortable with each other and I was pleased to see her looking so happy.

I had a difficult time getting into the mood of the celebration, but we talked of our plans for the next day, the Fourth of July. We were planning to go to the bocce ball party that our friends, John and Elaine, gave every year. I had already talked to Rusty's mother and she was excited about going and meeting his friends. John and Elaine's home was not far from Dawson's, so I planned to leave the party for a short while and go see him.

The next day, I went to the party, lacking in enthusiasm. I left shortly after and as I arrived at Dawson's, Papa Tom was arriving, too.

He said, "I understand we have a tough customer here."

"Yeah," I agreed. "Are you going to be staying?" I asked him.

"Yep."

"Oh, I'm glad," I said. "Thanks."

Bill's father was a friendly, easygoing man who liked to talk and tell old stories. He had not worked for many years and lived what appeared to be a very simple, unregimented life. He and Bill's mother had been divorced since I first met Bill over thirty years earlier. We had not seen much of his father over the years, but there had been no hard feelings.

Dawson seemed better, but tired. His friend, Matt came by to see him. I stayed a while and when I left I said what was going to become my oft-repeated, standard goodbye, "Call me if you need anything."

Dawson spent the next couple of days doing a lot of sleeping. Thursday, Papa Tom collapsed on the front porch. Bill was there when it happened and called for help. An ambulance came and took him to the hospital where Dawson had been the week before. Bill was quite upset, but sounded like he was bearing up under the strain when I talked to him that evening. A friend of Dawson's had seen the ambulance leaving the house and, of course, assumed it was for Dawson. I knew how relieved he was to discover it was not. Nothing significant was found to be wrong with Papa Tom. His fainting was attributed to overexertion in the heat. They stitched up the cut on his forehead and sent him home. The next day, Dawson had an appointment with the doctor whose office was next to the hospital. When Dawson told me the story of his grandfather with a bandaged head, driving so slowly, taking him to see the doctor, he laughed at what a pair they were. It was good to see and hear him laugh again. I was happy his sense of humor had returned.

Over the next few days, I went to see Dawson before or after going out with Rusty and his mother. His friend Matt was always there. I felt Matt was the nicest, most loyal guy I had ever met. I was so impressed with his concern and vigilance. He sat steadfastly by Dawson, sometimes on his bed, sometimes on the deck off Dawson's room. Most of that time, Dawson slept. When he was awake, he was often cranky and miserable, but Matt never let that deter him. I hoped that he would not get discouraged from going to see Dawson because it gave me comfort to know he was there with him. Also, it seemed as though Papa Tom might not be staying much longer. I had brought over some low-sodium cookbooks to help him with his meal preparations for Dawson, but Bill told me, many nights Dawson would not come out of his room for dinner. I understood how Papa Tom was beginning to feel unneeded and unappreciated. He left a week later.

Meanwhile, Rusty's mother, after her ten-day stay, went home. Although I was sure it had not been the exciting visit she had anticipated, she seemed to have had a good time none the less. She talked a lot about her late husband, Rusty's father, who had been dead for three years. She spoke of him and the things he said and what they had done in the 1940's, as though it were yesterday.

Dawson improved over the next few weeks. He was less tired and the swelling had diminished. But he wasn't able to return to work, and neither was I. I knew I would never be able to smile at another customer again and I felt I had to be available for Dawson anytime he needed me. With his increased energy, he was feeling almost normal and had started to go out with friends. He went away to the country one weekend, much to my distress. Twice he went to the drag races, finding it was strenuous walking to and from the track and the parking lot. He seemed to accept these limitations and his friends were understanding.

I worried every day that he was overdoing and not taking good care of himself. Rusty and I made him salt-free meals and I'd bring them to him. He would eat what I'd bring, but I was never sure how well he was following the diet when I was not there. I had begun to research his condition by reading books and articles. In the hospital's library, I was stunned when I found cardiomyopathy was sometimes referred to as "beer heart." Although alcohol was a common cause of this condition, anything that put a strain on the heart could cause it to enlarge. In Dawson's case, I, personally, had no doubt that alcohol was the primary factor. All of the information I read was disturbing, all stating the prognosis was very grim. A transplant seemed to be the only alternative, but even so, that was "a race against time."

He continued to see the doctor regularly and undergo more tests. An echo that was done on his liver seemed encouraging as it did not show anything significant. He called me when he got home from the procedure. He said when he was having the test done, the technician who was looking at the screen said, "So, why are you having this? You were just wondering how your liver was?"

Dawson said to me, "I told him the doctor thought I might have a problem. The guy just said, 'Hmm.'" We agreed it sounded good that the technician had not seen anything overtly disturbing.

Bill and I talked occasionally, usually when I would call for Dawson and he was not home. Bill would talk of how much he wanted to spend time with Dawson, how much he worried when Dawson was out late, how hurt he felt when he would ask Dawson to come home early and he did not. It reminded me of the *Cat's in the Cradle* lyrics and it saddened me. Bill said he finally understood what he had put me through all those years. He said he knew what it must have been like for me. He said, "If I could only make it up to you, Andrea, I would."

Chapter Four

Bill and I were third generation San Franciscans, born and raised. Most of the members of our family had moved to the suburbs, but had not ventured further than the San Francisco Bay Area. In 1977, Bill and I and the kids moved to Novato, twenty-five miles north of San Francisco across the bay by way of the Golden Gate Bridge. Claudia was the first of my immediate family to move out of state and it was something she had planned to do since the age of fourteen.

Claudia had always had a direction for her life. In her early teens, she had decided she wanted to be a meteorologist. She decided on the college she wanted to attend, the University of Colorado at Boulder. After she graduated from high school in 1985, she attended the local junior college, and then was ready to go off to Colorado. Rusty and I helped her move. Rusty drove his truck filled with all her belongings and she drove behind in her car. I took turns riding with her and then riding with Rusty. I was proud of her and felt she was quite brave for going to live so far away in a place where she knew no one. I could not imagine myself ever doing such a thing. But it concerned me there was no one there looking after her. I was relieved when she only stayed a year and then transferred to UC Davis. She was much closer to home. In 1991, she graduated from Davis with a Bachelor's degree in Atmospheric Science.

A month after graduation she was hired by the National Weather Service. Her first position was in a small town, Pendleton, Oregon, which seemed to me to be in the middle of nowhere. Again, she had made a move out of state to a place where she knew no one, but it was becoming evident this was not an easy thing for her to do. She had not been readily making friends and was spending most of her time alone. She was willing to make the sacrifices necessary to attain her goals. It was very commendable, but I was sorry it had to be that way. I would have liked her to be closer to her family and friends. It was ironic how she had become more solitary and Dawson had become more social, having many friends. It was a turnaround from the children they had been.

She called me on her first night in Pendleton, crying. She was feeling alone and scared. We talked for quite a while. I could imagine her overwhelming feeling of loneliness. I told her how admirable it was that she was willing to look past the discomfort of the moment for the greater achievements of her future. I was able to console her by telling her something very simple. I merely promised her that the sad and lonely feeling she was experiencing would not last. I understood that as she looked ahead to the upcoming year, all she could see was loneliness. But I confidently assured her that not every day would be like that. It was simple, but it comforted her and got her through that night and others. She stayed a year and a half and then was able to transfer to the office in Redwood City, which was only an hour away from me. What a pleasure it was to, finally, have her close to home. After a year and a half, she was offered a promotion and relocated to Sacramento. I was happy she was still in California, but her time in Sacramento was difficult. She and Tracy were far apart, her car was stolen and her new car vandalized. After only six months there, she applied for a new position and was quickly accepted in the Monterey office. She and Tracy now lived in the same town and were getting along well together. Monterey was a beautiful locale along the California coast two hours further away from me, but it was a positive personal and career move for her.

My waitressing career had come to an end the day after we had received Dawson's diagnosis. I had not waitressed a single day since that day I poured coffee all over the table. I had taken the week off while Rusty's mother was visiting and when she left, I made my decision not to go back. I could no longer cheerfully greet and wait on customers and I had to be available for Dawson. I did not want to have a work schedule conflict with anything I might need or want to do for him. It worked out well, for I was still very busy helping Rusty with the shop. Working both jobs as I had been doing had been quite exhausting, and being able to work full time at the shop was helpful, since we were overloaded with work and could barely keep up with our orders.

The fact that Rusty was a fireman gave us a specialized market in the embroidery field. Nearly one hundred percent of our orders came from firemen. I found firemen, on the average, to be a friendly, helpful group and the camaraderie Rusty had with them helped our business. Whenever I'd watch Rusty and the others sharing their fire stories, I thought how much he looked like a firemen. He looked much like one I remembered in my Little Golden Books from childhood. He had a thick, reddish moustache and curly, sandy-colored hair and big, pale blue eyes. Rusty's real attractiveness came from his self-confidence and sociability. He could be in a roomful of strangers and in no time would have engaged himself in several friendly and animated conversations.

As part of firemen's uniforms, they were allowed to wear navy blue T-shirts bearing their department logo. Every city had its own design. Conversing with other firemen, sharing stories and helping them decide on appropriate and accurate embroidered designs was a perfect job for Rusty. He had wonderful artistic abilities and was a great talker. But he found running the noisy, temperamental machines a rather nerve-wracking, tedious job. They often did not cooperate and, as Rusty would say, were known to "eat shirts." But he, alone, ran the embroidery machines and I did most of the bookkeeping, invoicing, ordering, inventory sorting, trimming, folding and packing. I was content to work seven days a week at the shop to get our orders out, knowing that I could just drop everything if Dawson needed or wanted me.

My life and priorities had changed completely. I made very few plans and had very little interest in a social life. All I cared about was helping Rusty with his business and being available for Dawson. Rusty would, from time to time, complain about the fact that we "had no life." He felt it was because I was just too concerned and depressed about Dawson to have any fun. He didn't seem to understand that a great deal of that had to do with our commitment to the business with its grueling schedule and work overload. Our lives had changed considerably since we first were together, but it was not entirely due to Dawson. Life had just been more carefree during our early years. We went out to dinner, dancing, to parties, and on short trips. But even before Dawson had gotten sick, I was feeling less like socializing. I took quite seriously the heavy weight of responsibility we had to the business. Its unyielding schedules and our monetary investments in it made my life and mood rather serious. The fact that Rusty and I disagreed on how to run the business just added to my concern and frustration.

Trying to discuss aspects of the business had become more and more difficult. There were things we needed to talk about; what bills should be paid, what jobs should go out, what orders needed checking into. But more often than not, when I brought a subject up, he became annoyed with me. According to him, it was because I had chosen the wrong time to discuss it. Those prohibited times were, specifically: when he just woke up, when he just got off duty, when he was eating, when he was on the computer, when he was on the machines, when he was on the phone, when he was relaxing watching TV, when he was driving, or when we were in bed. I did not know what time was left to talk of important matters and it made me extremely nervous knowing I had to find the perfect time to say what I wanted to say.

We tried to work out our problems, but it was not unusual for us to have a simple discussion escalate into a major blowup and potential breakup, as we both could be relentless in a disagreement. We'd talked many times about splitting up, but we cared a great deal for each other. Despite Rusty's discontent of my overwhelming concern for Dawson, he did seem to understand and accept that my priority was Dawson, and he supported me and my efforts to do for Dawson anything I felt was necessary and I was deeply grateful for that.

We got through the summer, but by the end of October, Dawson was not doing well. He was retaining fluids again, causing him to have trouble breathing and making him very tired. He asked me to drive him to his monthly appointment that November. I was more than willing. I would have gone to every appointment with him, had he let me. While in the waiting room, I asked if he wanted me to go in with him. I was not surprised when he answered "no," but I was feeling an urgency to hear what the doctor had to say about his present condition. After he was called to go in, I sat alone in the waiting room trying to figure out a way to talk to the doctor without Dawson knowing it. By a stroke of luck, his doctor came out from the back and was behind the desk, talking to the receptionist. I jumped up and went to him.

"Excuse me, Dr. Burke. Have you seen Dawson, yet?"

"No," he answered.

"I had some questions and…"

"Come around," he said, as he motioned to the door Dawson had entered and then he showed me to an examining room.

I said, "Dawson seems worse."

"Well, then, he probably is," he responded.

"What about the tests? What do they show?"

"Sometimes, the tests don't tell us as much as the symptoms," he said. "If he seems worse, he probably is," he repeated.

"What now?" I asked.

"We just have to wait and see. Right now, all I know is, he will die from this. I just can't tell you when."

I fought against reacting to his words and asked, "What about a transplant?"

"I don't know. I really don't think they'll transplant him."

"Who won't? Why not? What can we do?"

He seemed to ponder my questions, but without answering them he said, "I'll go in with him now and see how he's doing."

"Please don't mention that I talked to you."

I went back to the waiting room, hearing in my mind, "If he seems worse, he probably is."

"No," I thought, "I can't have him worse."

Dawson came out and set up his next appointment. When we were in the car, I asked, "What did the doctor have to say?"

"He said I'm retaining a lot of fluid. He could put me in the hospital or he could just try increasing the diuretics and see how that works. He asked me what I wanted to do."

"So, what did you tell him?"

"I told him I wanted to go home and try it. I don't want to go to the hospital."

"O.K. It's up to you. I guess if he thought it was absolutely necessary for you to go in, he would have insisted."

"Yeah," he agreed.

Later that afternoon Dr. Burke called me. I was stunned for a moment when I heard his voice. He had called to give me the name of a doctor in the transplant unit at a large hospital in San Francisco. "Call her tomorrow," he suggested, "and see if you can get an appointment before Thanksgiving. If you can't, call me."

When I next talked to Dawson, I spoke casually of Dr. Burke's call and of my phone conversation with him. If Dawson wondered, "Why'd he call *you*?" he never questioned it.

I called Dr. Thompson's office the next day. I told the receptionist that my son needed an appointment soon. I told her he was twenty-five years old and in the latter stages of cardiomyopathy. I had learned that with cardiomyopathy, by the time there are any signs, the condition has already reached that stage. I asked if there was any chance we could get in to see her before Thanksgiving. She said she had no openings available right away, but she would talk to the doctor and call me back.

When she did, she said, "She will see him this Monday, November 14th." She told me he needed to bring all his records from his regular cardiologist.

"Great, we'll be there. Thank you."

I picked up the copies of Dawson's medical records later that day. On the way home, in that slow, Friday afternoon commute traffic, I glanced over several times at the bulky manila envelope containing the facts of Dawson's health. It was both sealed and taped, making its contents inaccessible. When I arrived home with it, I held it close to me and prayed that within it there was something miraculous to be found that would save Dawson. "Please, dear God," I begged, "please help my Dawson." Several times over the weekend, I went through this ritual, praying for something in those records to inspire Dr. Thompson. I prayed there was something in them that would be encouraging. I prayed that Dawson would like the new, woman doctor and be motivated by her. I was praying for his life. I was praying as I had not prayed in years.

I had been raised Catholic. I had made my First Communion and as a child, I went to church every Sunday with my mother. Even though I had not been confirmed, Bill and I had been married in the Catholic church. Although I had seen to it that Claudia and Dawson had been baptized and had made their First Communion, shortly thereafter I stopped going to church. Over the years, I had gradually fallen further away from my religious upbringing. But from the first day Dawson became ill, I knew Dawson's heart condition was too big for me to handle, even with the help of my parents and Rusty. I needed something more and it seemed natural to turn to God. I bought a book on how prayers could heal and how it had been proven scientifically, and I began to say a rosary each night when I went to bed. Praying gave me hope.

Rusty drove us in to Dr. Thompson's that foggy Monday morning. Dawson was wearing sweats, his legs too swollen for jeans. He said the skin on his legs was pulled so tight it hurt. It made sitting and walking uncomfortable. Rusty left us off at the entrance. We were a little too early for our appointment, so we went into the tiny cafeteria off the lobby. Dawson wanted the ham and egg sandwich on an English muffin.

"Dawson," I said, "that has cheese on it. You know cheese has sodium and that ham is extremely salty."

"So? That's what I want."

"Dawson, you're already swollen, you can't have something like that."

"O.K., forget it," he said.

I suggested he have the egg on the muffin, no cheese and no ham and he complied.

When we finished, we went up to the fifth floor to Dr. Thompson's office. I watched him as he gave the receptionist his name and she gave him a form to fill out. He then sat down beside me. Despite the fact that I was so glad to be seeing this new doctor, I felt such sadness as I watched him. I was nervous but tried not show it. We saw a few women in white coats behind the receptionist's desk, busy coming and going. Dawson and I looked at each other, raising our eyebrows, wondering silently, *Is that her? Could that be her?* I hoped she would be attractive. I thought it might inspire Dawson to be good and follow her orders.

When they called his name, I asked him, "Do you want me to go in with you?"

"Yes," he said.

This time he said "yes." As simple as that, he said "yes." From that moment on I felt things were going to be different.

We were seated in an examining room. When Dr. Thompson entered, I was not disappointed. She was exceptionally attractive, tall and slender with thick, dark hair, perfect makeup and a down-to-earth attitude that I could see made Dawson feel comfortable immediately.

After she asked Dawson a few questions, she said, "What I've seen with patients with your condition is that some get a little better, some get a little worse, some get bad very quickly and some go on for a while staying the same."

"What contributes to such differences?" I asked.

"We really don't know, it's just the way it goes. A lot depends on how strong," she turned to look at Dawson, "how strong your will to live is."

I said, naively, "My will for him to live is strong enough for both of us."

She looked at me, not speaking the words I felt she was thinking.

I said, "Dr. Burke seems to feel that if your symptoms are worse, then you *are* worse. Is that always true?"

"Well, to some extent. But I'd like to do some tests and an evaluation on him," she said.

"That sounds like a good idea," I said. "Now as far as diet and such, it's important, isn't it, that he watches what he eats, sodium and everything?"

"It's critical," she answered emphatically.

I looked over at Dawson and nodded. He smiled and nodded back at me.

Dr. Thompson then said, "And no matter what the cause of the condition, I advise all of my myopathy patients not to drink alcohol."

Dawson nodded again.

"You've been told to watch your fluid intake, in general, haven't you?"

"No," we both said, as we looked at each other.

"You haven't? I can't believe how many doctors fail to instruct that."

I said, "Well, I guess they figure common sense ought to tell you, if you're retaining fluids, don't drink a lot of fluids, but I never thought of it."

"Neither did I," Dawson said.

I said optimistically, "Well, that's good. Now we know. That could really make a difference, huh, Dawson?"

"Yeah. I drink a lot of water and soda."

"It's understandable," Dr. Thompson said, "after all, the diuretics make you thirsty. So, what you can do is suck on small pieces of ice. It will help your thirst a little, without taking in a lot of fluid. Hard candy is good, too."

"That is really good to know. No wonder he's getting so swollen," I said, encouraged.

"He is quite swollen. We've got to get rid of that. If his skin stretches any more it could start to crack and get raw and infected."

Dawson and I looked at each other and grimaced at the thought.

"He probably is a candidate for a heart transplant, but I would like to have the transplant unit look at this report on his liver," she said, looking at me.

Then looking to Dawson, she said, "You know, if your liver has also been damaged by the alcohol we will not transplant you. But you need to know that with a heart transplant you would be trading one set of health problems for new ones. You would be completely tied to us. You'd have to come in regularly and be tested for possible rejection. That is done by inserting a probe in your neck and taking a sample from your heart to test."

Dawson really made a face at that one.

She continued, "You'd be surprised how you can get used to it. Though no one likes it, most, in time, are able to handle it. There will be a new method available for testing that will eliminate that procedure and it should be in practice in about five years."

I wondered if we would have that to look forward to.

"Now, if I can get you in today to see Dr. Steele of the Liver Transplant Unit, would you be able to? That would save you from having to come back into the city another day."

I said, "I'll call our ride and see if that would be all right with him."

I called Rusty. He said, "Sure, do whatever you have to do."

I told the doctor and she made her call to Dr. Steele. He could see us later. He was in another building, but we could get to it from "this floor" and "that corridor" and "some stairs." She gave us the directions and we started on our way, up and down and around. Dawson was getting out of breath, so I ran ahead to see if we were going in the right direction. That way he didn't have to take a lot of unnecessary steps. We were a little lost, but finally, we found the place and met Dr. Steele. He was very compassionate. He looked at the numbers and dismissed them as nothing to be alarmed about. The numbers were, more than likely, related to Dawson's poor heart function and a transplant would solve that. That was good news. He asked Dawson how much alcohol he drank on a regular basis before he had been diagnosed. Dawson's answers were somewhat vague and non-specific. Then Dr. Steele asked him how long it had been since he had a drink. Dawson responded that he had not had one since he had gotten sick. Dr. Steele talked to him about the relationship drinking had on his liver and told him that drinking in his condition could kill him.

"Do you know what I'm saying?" he asked Dawson.

"Yes," Dawson answered, as he sat with his legs dangling over the side of the examining table.

Dr. Steele said, "Tell me. If you drink…"

Dawson said, "I could die."

"That's right. If you think you'd need help to not drink, you know there are places like Alcoholics Anonymous where you can go to get help. You don't have to try and do it alone."

When we left the hospital, I felt better than I had felt in months. It seemed my prayers had been answered. Dr. Thompson had proved to be all that I had prayed she would be. Dawson liked her and seemed to respect her. He liked her advice and suggestions. She reinforced in him the need to weigh himself every day, so that he would know right away if he had started to retain water. He appreciated the fact that he would be able to start to treat the swelling before it got out of hand. And I liked it that she stressed to him that he could call her *anytime.* On the way home, we talked, almost excitedly, about the ways in which he would be able to have some control over his symptoms. He truly seemed to be inspired and encouraged by the new "woman doctor."

I printed out a chart for him that I had designed on my computer so that he could record his weight daily. He was able, in one column, to write his weight down and alongside it, connect the dots to form a graph that showed the fluctuations. He liked it and used it religiously. My mother gave him her ice crusher so he could have chips of ice to suck on. He was quite happy with that. He was closely watching his fluid and salt intake, as well. He was starting to read labels on all packaged foods and would remark to me, "Do you know how much sodium there is in...?" I was proud of him. He was accepting his condition and its restrictions quite well.

For my birthday get-together that month, I made a salt-free dinner and a salt-free dessert. It was not an elaborate meal, but that was of little importance to me. It was healthy for Dawson and I was just extremely grateful he was able to share it with us. It was the greatest birthday present I could have hoped for, just having him there. It was my fiftieth, but we kept it simple. Earlier in the year, before Dawson had gotten sick, my mother and father had told me of their plans to give me a fabulous party. I was thrilled with the idea and by June, I had my dress, my earrings, my shoes, the D.J., the restaurant and was in the process of designing the invitations. But after Dawson's diagnosis, the idea of a party no longer meant anything to me, in fact, it terrified me. I was not making any long-range plans, and certainly none so elaborate, involving so many. We canceled the whole thing shortly after.

Dawson and I kept in close contact and one day he called me and said he wanted to go Christmas shopping. This was a very rare desire, if not a first, for Dawson. For him to want to go shopping, Christmas shopping no less, and to want to do it with me, filled my heart with a joy for Christmas that I had not known for a long time. Over the years when I had not been going to church, the spiritual side of Christmas had been somewhat lost. The commercial side had always been fun for me; the shopping, the lavish decorating, the money spending. But with my busy work schedule and tight budget, it had all seemed rather pointless. I had seen what the Christmas Spirit looked like in the malls during the season; shoppers behind the wheels of their cars who would just as soon run into your car than to let you get their parking spot. Rusty thoroughly enjoyed the gift-giving side of the season, but was definitely "Bah, humbug" when it came to the Christmas-caroling-kind of Christmas. Yes, I had lost the Christmas spirit. But this year, I found it. Or, I should say, it was given to me. It was a wonderful gift from Dawson.

He did fairly well in the malls. I dropped him off at the door and then parked the car so he didn't have as far to walk. We walked slowly through the malls and stores, and sometimes I would go on ahead to see if that were the way we wanted to go. In case it wasn't, he wouldn't have to take those extra steps.

One day, while driving home from shopping, he told me, "I don't even feel like drinking anymore. Having a beer doesn't even sound good to me."

I asked him, "Is that unusual to have a beer not sound good?"

"Yeah," he answered, "I have never known a time when having a beer didn't sound good."

"Wow. That's great. That's really going to help, and watching your diet and your weight and taking it easy, it's all going to help you."

We had good times, good talks and some laughs on our shopping excursions. He neatly wrapped all his gifts and helped me with some of mine. He was very precise and joked about my hurried, less than accurate cutting, folding and taping. We had many funny stories to share with everyone that Christmas Eve at Grandma and Papa's. It was a Merry Christmas with many blessings for which to be thankful.

His doctor's visit that month was also a blessing. He called to tell me how it went. He said, "Dr. Burke said I'm doing really good. He said I seem better."

"Oh, Dawson, that's great! What is he basing that on?"

"I don't know, but he said he was pleased with how I'm doing. The nurse told me that it meant a lot coming from Dr. Burke. She said he usually doesn't say much and he doesn't say things like that unless he feels strongly about it. She said she was really glad to hear he had given me such a good report."

"Yeah, me, too. Keep up the good work, hon."

That winter, Dawson had been keeping pretty close to home and Bill had been cooking healthy dinners for him. Dawson kept busy watching TV, building model cars, and doing puzzles and crosswords. It had been raining quite a bit and he had been unable to ride his motorcycle. He missed riding his bike, a big Harley-Davidson. I, on the other hand, did not mind him not riding it at all. It always worried me and made me very nervous. I was glad when it was wet out and he couldn't ride. But it was something he loved.

After Christmas, with no more shopping to do, Dawson was getting bored. He had mentioned to me that he thought he'd like to have a dog. "Not a big dog," he said, "a heeler." We'd had a heeler before and they were a mid-sized dog with an average weight of fifty pounds. I told him he'd better talk to his Dad about it. When he found an ad in the paper for a litter of Queensland Heeler puppies, he and Bill went to look at them. It was the day after New Year's Day, 1995. Dawson called me when he got home. He had picked out a male. "He came right to me," he said.

"What did you name him?" I asked.

"Harley."

"That's cute."

"Guess when his birthday is. It's on your birthday. When can you come down and see him?"

"Well, I know Grandma will want to see him, too. I'll call her to see what day is good for her."

Harley was the cutest, funniest little puppy I had ever seen. And Dawson looked at him like he was so special. He was blue-gray with a black mask that went up to his black ears. He had a big black nose, short little legs, a bobbed tail and a crazy, friendly personality. It was great to see Dawson so happy and caring. The dog was good for him. Harley slept in Dawson's room in a little bed Dawson had made for him.

Dawson was now unable to sleep comfortably in a bed himself. He had a difficult time breathing when lying down. He had taken to propping himself up in bed, trying to get comfortable enough to sleep. Many nights he told me he would have to get up and just sit in a chair to breathe. He would stay awake thinking about the transplant and that "thing down the neck." He said he didn't like to think about it. My mother had told me that many nights *she* would wake up and be unable to get back to sleep just thinking of Dawson having to sit up, alone, in the middle of the night.

My father had a recliner-type chair that he knew, from experience, was comfortable to doze-off in. So he brought it down to Dawson for him to try. It was very cozy with soft-feeling upholstery. He was able to adjust it to three positions. Dawson really liked it, so Papa gave it to him. It was quite large for his room, but Dawson didn't care, he was able to sleep. We all slept easier knowing that Dawson was, too. He was so comfortable in his chair that Papa made him a wonderful table that fit right up to it. It was easily adjustable so that Dawson could use it for working on his projects and writing or eating or anything else he wanted to do and still be comfortable in his chair. Dawson really appreciated it and admired Papa's handiwork.

That month he started back to school to finish his apprenticeship classes. He went two nights a week. He seemed to be managing quite well, but his car was giving him problems. Although he had always worked on his own cars, he really wasn't up to it now. I worried that his car would break down some night on his way to or from school and he'd have to walk to a phone for help. I knew that would be too much for him. He called me one day and said he saw an ad for a truck in the paper and asked if I would go with him to look at it.

He said, "Maybe Papa could come, too. You know he's good at making deals and finding out stuff."

"Yeah, we're not. O.K., I'll ask him."

Papa seemed glad to go. Rusty, despite how busy he was, offered to drive us to the dealership. It was a bit far and in an unfamiliar area, so I was pleased how understanding he was and how generous with his time. When Dawson saw the truck, it was exactly what he wanted. It was a four-wheel drive, it was black, and it had "lifters" that made it high off the ground. The minute I looked at it I knew it was Dawson. Then we saw the price and knew, despite an adequate disability pension from the Electrician's Union each month, this truck was more than he could afford.

Papa said, "That's O.K., Dawson. Get it. I'll give you the money for the down payment."

Dawson's eyes opened wide as he asked, "Really? Are you sure?"

Papa said, "Yeah, I'm sure. I want you to have it. I'll make the down payment and you can make the monthly payments."

Dawson said, "Well, O.K., if you're sure."

My father worked out the deal with the salesman. Dawson was so happy. It was the first brand-new vehicle he had ever had. The payments were still going to be more than he had hoped for, but he felt he could manage them. He seemed very sure and he didn't seem worried.

When I talked to my mother later, I asked her if it was really all right for them to make the down payment for Dawson. "Are you sure Daddy doesn't mind?" I asked her.

She said, "He doesn't mind. He wanted to do it for Dawson."

Then she told me a story she had never told me before. She told me of a day when the kids were little and she and my father were babysitting them and they had taken them to the mall. At some point, they split up. Claudia went with my mother and Dawson went with my father. My father took Dawson into a toy store where Dawson saw a very big Tonka truck that he wanted. Dawson had many, many cars and trucks, but he asked Papa if he could have that one. He said to Dawson, "We'll have to ask Grandma." When they met up, my father asked my mother and she said, "No, we already bought the kids enough stuff today."

I knew Dawson didn't remember the incident, but my mother told me my father had never forgotten it. My father could not get over the fact he had turned Dawson down when he had asked him for something. Dawson had never asked him, personally, for anything before and the first time he did, he felt he had failed him. My father was filled with regret. After all, he said, he had the money in his wallet, he could have gotten it for him. All those years had passed, and yet he would still cry when he'd think of the day he said no to Dawson.

My mother told me that when my father came home from the dealership, he said with such emotion he could barely speak the words, "I got Dawson his Tonka truck." He was happy and I was grateful to my parents for their gift to Dawson that gave him such joy.

I was with Dawson when he received the payment book. When he saw the date of his last payment, he looked up at me.

"What?" I said.

He handed the book to me. Raising his eyebrows, he said, "It looks weird."

I saw, "JAN 29 00." I said, "Yeah, that does look weird."

We stood there looking at each other for a moment. The year two thousand. It seemed such a long way off. I wondered what that day and the future held for us. He looked like he was wondering, too.

Chapter Five

I was in awe of Dawson's ability to experience joy and I was frequently encouraged by his capacity to carry on. He would have his tired days, sometimes days at a time, but he'd sleep and rest and always recoup. I continued to pray and search for information. I was saying a rosary every night when I went to bed. I found it gave me great comfort and I was able to fall asleep, even when I thought I would not. My faith had been rekindled after having been put aside for many years. In my time of great need, I had turned to it and it was there for me. I wished I could share it with Dawson. I wanted him to feel the comfort faith was bringing me. But I knew he would just scoff at the notion, so I never mentioned it.

In my many prayers, I prayed that Dawson, along with getting well, would "see the light," find the right path to follow and be enlightened to do the right things in his life. I prayed that, on those nights when he was unable to sleep and stayed awake thinking, his thoughts would guide him in the right direction. Or that, after a night of blessed sleep, he would just awaken knowing what was good and right and what was best for him. He, perhaps, would not know where the message had come from, but I'd know. I prayed this insight would miraculously come to him. I had heard enough stories of how people had come to see the error of their ways, to know it often took a catastrophic incident to turn their lives around. I had heard of near-death experiences that had changed people's lives for the better. Near-death? I hoped that was not what it was going to take for Dawson, but I feared that it might and so I prayed.

Despite the fact he did seem improved and he did seem to be taking care of himself, I still worried because there were also those times it appeared he was taking his improved health for granted and not completely playing by the rules. So when I talked to him I tried to encourage, motivate, inform and pass on to him everything I learned about his condition.

One afternoon, I saw an Oprah Winfrey show featuring a support group called "Young Hearts" for young adult cardiac patients and their families. The group was in Chicago and I called the next day. I left a message on the recorder and, soon after, I received a response in the mail. I read the back-issue newsletters I was sent from cover to cover. One editorial by the founder, the young woman I had seen on television just a few weeks earlier, read in part, *"Everyone copes with problems and stress in their own way. I don't know how you personally work through problems, but as for me, my strength lies in my own religious position. It is here that I draw my strength, find my peace, and lay down my problems. People have many different ways of coping… Something upon which they rely to carry them through… I truly believe that God exists. I have seen it in the many wonderful things that have happened since we started this organization. So often, just when we realize there is some kind of need, be it a solid physical thing, or the support of someone who shares our experiences and feelings, they seem to be there for us. Right time, right place, right 'thing'… I believe we come as a 'gift' to one another, hopefully right time, right place and right 'thing.' God bless you all! Julie."* Then elsewhere in the newsletter it said, *"Yes, if a person continues asking, that person will receive. If a person continues looking, that person will find. And if a person continues knocking, the door will open for that person. Matthew 7:8."*

I was uplifted by what I read and so impressed with the literature "Young Hearts" had sent me, I immediately responded with a letter. I addressed it to Julie and thanked her for her prompt reply to my request for information and told her I found the complimentary newsletters informative and encouraging. I wrote of my need for this kind of information because I had a twenty-five year old son who had been diagnosed with cardiomyopathy seven months earlier. I went on to write, *"Your encouraging and enlightening words bolstered much of my own beliefs. That you have articles on new treatments that are 'on the horizon,' articles I have not found anywhere else, but felt must be 'somewhere,' furthered to make your newsletter a Godsend. Learning of your organization truly was a 'gift' at the 'right time' that had seemed to come quite by chance. The fact that I had tuned in to the program, that day... well... I guess it can only be explained (borrowing your reference to Matthew) as, "I was looking and I found." This gives me faith to continue 'asking, looking and knocking.' Thank you again. Sincerely, Andrea Bell."*

A week later, I was finishing the dinner dishes when the phone rang. I answered it and a female voice said, "Andrea?"

"Yes."

"This is Julie, from Young Hearts."

"Julie? I don't believe it."

"I received your letter and I wanted to call and thank you. I just had to tell you how much your letter meant to me. You know, it is so good to know, when we work so hard here, that we are appreciated. Your letter let me know that what I'm doing is worthwhile. It touched me and I wanted to let you know and to say thanks."

"Well, thank you. How nice of you to call me. I still can't believe it."

"Your letter touched me so much, I went out with my children today and bought a frame for it and hung it in my office. I've had this organization a few years now and your letter is only the third thing I have hung on the wall. It means that much to me."

"Julie, I can't tell you how much this call means to me."

We talked for nearly two hours. The conversation left me moved and inspired. I felt something glorious was in the works and I vowed I would never turn away from my faith again.

Despite everything, I felt I had a lot to be thankful for. Dawson and I were seeing more of each other and both of us were enjoying our times together. I no longer had to call him to talk to him, he was calling me. One day he called and asked, "Would you want to come down and help me with a jigsaw puzzle?"

"Yeah, I would," I said, without a moment's hesitation.

"A friend gave it to me. It's really hard. I think it would help to have someone to do it with."

"Dad likes puzzles."

"Yeah, but I showed him this one and he didn't want to do it. I think it made him sick. It is really awful. All the pieces look exactly the same."

"I wouldn't mind trying it."

"O.K. It's really bad," he warned, laughing.

We spent many hours working on that horrible puzzle and other puzzles, as well. I would go down and spend the day and cook him lunch and bring him snacks and be so thankful for every moment we shared. I didn't know how much the times meant to him, he never really said in so many words, but they meant everything to me.

The following month, Dawson had a pulmonary test done, ordered by Dr. Thompson. Rusty drove us in for the appointment. To have this test done, Dawson's fluid retention had to be more under control than it had been when she had seen him in November. This test, we were told, would help her in her evaluation of how he was doing and whether or not he was ready to be listed for a transplant. "You are advised to get listed when the chances are you will not survive a year without a new heart," she told us. We knew we didn't want to hear that time had come.

The test took over an hour and tired him out. When we were leaving, I asked the receptionist at the desk, "How long will it take to get the results?"

He answered, "Oh, they'll be ready for the doctor tomorrow. Then the doctor will call you."

"So I guess we should know something in a couple of days, then, Dawson," I said.

When he hadn't heard from Dr. Thompson by the next week, we decided he should call her. He did, but could not get to talk to her. He left a message, no response. Day after day, then week after week, he continued to try. Aside from my concern and annoyance, I was very disappointed in Dr. Thompson. I felt she had let Dawson down. He had trusted and respected her. He looked hurt when he would ask me why I thought she hadn't called him. He would say, "Remember how she had said I could call her anytime? Yeah, right!"

I told him I didn't understand it. And I didn't, at all. I asked him if he wanted me to try and call her. He said," Yeah, you can try." So I called and left messages along with him. Still, she did not return our calls. Then he just gave up trying to reach her. At some point, I think he decided maybe he didn't want to hear anything, anyway.

I was starting to worry more about him. He was still attending his classes, but didn't always come right home after them, as he had been. That worried Bill, too. We both asked him if he were taking care of himself and he assured us he was. I thought that he must be, otherwise, how could he be doing as well as he was?

On his twenty-sixth birthday, April 24, 1995, he seemed well and happy and was fun to be with. We all got together at Grandma and Papa's and had a salt-free dinner, a salt-free birthday cake and worked on a puzzle. He got tired and stayed later than he should have, but he seemed to be enjoying the evening.

After he left, my mother remarked about what a good time she'd had. She said, "He sure is funny. He's really got a sense of humor, a different kind of humor."

"I know," I said, "he always makes me laugh with the things he comes up with."

"Where'd he get that? Is it Bill?" my mother asked.

"Well, Bill does have kind of a dry sense of humor, but Dawson's is a little different. Bill told me that Dawson's friends call him The King of the one-liners."

The spirit of Dawson's spontaneous wit defied example. His humorous one-liners did not lend themselves to successful retelling by their very spontaneity. His clever remarks were the appropriate-to-the-moment, you-had-to-be-there type. And it's not just what he said or the timing, but how he'd matter-of-factly blurt out a clever remark. And it was his expression when he said them, his half-smile and raised eyebrows. When he'd laugh, it was almost a chuckle. It was catching because you knew he was thoroughly enjoying the moment. But his quips had a touch of cynicism, which were in keeping with his otherwise serious, standoffish nature.

"I never knew he was funny," my mother said with a reflective tone in her voice.

"His friends have always known it. I guess it's just that we're seeing more of him lately and actually getting to *know* him more, too."

"Yeah, I guess that's it. You know, not too many people make me laugh," my mother said.

I knew that to be true and I felt pleased my mother enjoyed being with him. I thought of how much I sincerely enjoyed his company.

"How remarkable," she said, "that he could find humor in anything, with all that must be on his mind."

The following month when we still had not heard from Dr. Thompson, I faxed her a letter. It read:

"May 22, 1995. Dear Dr. Thompson, As Dawson Bell's mother, I am concerned, as he is, as to why he has not been informed of the findings of the tests he had taken over two and a half months ago. We were told these tests would enable you to evaluate his condition and were very important in determining his

possible treatment. We are, therefore, unable to think of a reasonable explanation as to why our messages have not been acknowledged. Not hearing from you has left us worried and confused. When we have called your office, we were told you were either not in or that you were with a patient and to leave a message and you would return the call. As yet, that has not happened. It is going on three months since he took those tests and he has not heard from you regarding the results. At the time of the tests, you told him it could tell if getting him on the transplant list was imperative. Certainly you can understand that waiting to hear such information could cause some anxiety. He also was wondering about flying. He has a trip planned soon in which he will be taking a flight to Las Vegas. Is there any reason that would cause any problems for him with his condition and medications? I am hoping that you will talk to him today and answer these questions for him. Thank you, Andrea Bell."

We did not hear from her. On Dawson's next visit to Dr. Burke, he asked him if he had heard anything from Dr. Thompson regarding his test results. He had not, but said he would try to contact her. Dawson told me he forgot to ask Dr. Burke about flying.

He flew to Las Vegas on Friday, June 2, 1995. I hadn't wanted him to go. I wondered how he could go and not drink. He said he could, but I doubted it. I didn't think he was feeling as strongly about not drinking as he had. Thirty guys from the apprenticeship class were going to celebrate their completion of the five-year program. They were now full-fledged journeymen electricians and Dawson was one of them. This should have been one of the happiest times for all of us, but it was not. After all, we knew that Dawson would probably never work a day as a journeyman electrician. And he must have known it, too, yet he wanted to be part of the celebration. How could I, or at least some small part of me, not want that for him, too? But the thought of that trip filled my heart with yearning for what might have been and clenched my heart with terror for its consequences.

Dawson arrived back home late the following Monday night. On Tuesday morning, my mother and father and I were driving down to Monterey to spend a couple of days with Claudia. Claudia had invited us down to see her new place. I was looking forward to visiting her.

In the car on our way down, my cell phone rang. It was Bill. He told me Dawson had gotten home from Las Vegas the night before and he looked bad. He said it was obvious to him he must have partied pretty hard. I was upset, but I tried not to let on to my mother and father because I did not want to spoil their time. How terrible that I should have this on my mind while away. I wanted so much to see

Claudia and enjoy our stay. It would not be fair to her to let Dawson spoil our visit.

She was pleased to have us there. The weather was perfect and the surroundings relaxing. I confided my concerns for Dawson to her, without telling the details of Bill's phone call. She made me feel better when she said, "Mom, just because he goes off this one weekend, that doesn't mean he can't get back on track." Claudia was confident that Dawson would "luck out" as he usually did.

As soon as we got back from our trip, I drove down to see him. It had been four days since he had returned home. He was alone and sleeping. I woke him up when I knocked on his door and he let me in. He was exhausted and miserable. His appearance confirmed what I already knew. He'd had a destructive weekend, but he did not admit it. I was unable to get much conversation out of him and I left extremely upset.

The trend continued. He was spending more time with his friends and staying out late or not coming home at all. I asked him what kept him out all night. I told him that I worried when I heard of his late hours. I said, "When I hear that you haven't come home all night or that Dad hasn't seen you in a couple of days, the only reasons I can think of are that you are drunk or dead."

He said, "Mom, those are not the only reasons."

"They're not?"

"No."

"Dawson, it seems like you are a totally different person in summer than you are in winter. You take such good care of yourself in the winter and come summer you get crazy."

"Yeah, I know. I hibernate in the winter," he said, smiling.

"Oh, is that it? Just like a bear."

"Yeah," he said.

He *was* like a bear, sometimes like a grouchy, growling, very sleepy big ol' bear that just wants to be left alone. And, sometimes, like an awkward little bear cub, stumbling and falling and playing, seemingly without a care in the world. I was reminded of a tale I had seen on television as a child. It was the story of a mama bear and her cub. It showed how the mama bear would leave the baby, safe in a tree, when she went in search of food. She did this day after day. But when the time had come for the baby bear to be on his own, she would leave him in the tree, as she had done so many times before, but this time, she would not return. She knew she must leave her baby so that he would learn to take care of himself. But the baby bear did not know that. He did not understand why his mother did not come back. He waited and waited and waited for her. As a child, it broke my heart to watch that baby waiting all night and crying and calling out for his mother. My mother had explained to me, as we were watching, that it was because the mama bear loved her baby so much that she must let him go. We watched as he waited up in the tree, like a good little bear, until the following morning. When his mother still had not come back for him, he bravely ventured down and was, forever, on his own. The thought of that story touched me even deeper than it had so many years earlier and I wondered if that time had come for my baby and me.

Dawson's behavior continued the same through the remainder of the summer. He had been enjoying himself, out and about. Then he started retaining fluids again and Dr. Burke prescribed extra doses of the diuretics. They worked, but the quick loss of water that resulted, brought on the most painful leg cramps he said he had ever experienced. His entire leg would cramp and twist up. He said it would happen a lot in the morning when he was alone in the house and he would just scream out in pain. Sometimes, he said, he would just pound on the muscle that was all gnarled, but with no relief. He asked me to get him some ointment that my father had told me about. But there were times when he was unable to rub it on his legs and feet because his arms and hands would cramp up, as well. Despite it all, he still appeared to be doing well, even after having the flu and a couple of colds.

After more than three months, Dr. Burke finally obtained the results of the pulmonary tests. Dawson was told that everything was as they had expected. There was no significant change in his condition. Sometime in his future, he was going to need a transplant and he was told he should be thinking about it. Well, Dawson didn't want to think about it. He felt he was doing fine. He was certainly managing and he was even riding his motorcycle. I marveled at that.

I asked him, "Doesn't it take a lot of energy and strength to ride your bike?"

"Yeah, I guess, but it doesn't bother me."

Although I was encouraged by his ability to continue to ride, it made me uneasy to know he was out on his bike. I was sure most mothers would worry about their sons on a motorcycle, but I didn't just start worrying when he began riding motorcycles. I worried about him when, as a child, he began riding horses. Bill felt I was unduly concerned, especially when he thought with a name like Dawson Bell, he just might become a rodeo rider someday.

When Dawson was born, we had not yet picked out a boy's name. We could not agree on a name that started with a "D." I had decided it had to be a "D" because we were going down the alphabet, "A" for Andrea, "B" for Bill, "C" for Claudia, and "D" for Dierdre, if I had a girl. But I had a boy! He was two days old and we still could not agree on a name for him. The hospital was getting quite impatient, but Bill did not like any of the "D" names I had suggested. Then I remembered when I was about ten years old, my older cousin had a friend named Dawson.

I said to Bill, "How about Dawson?"

To my delight, he said, "O.K., I like it. Dawson Bell. I can just hear it, 'Dawson Bell, ridin' Buckin' Bronco outta shoot number five!'"

I liked the sound, too. "Dawson, Dawson Bell." No middle name, just Dawson Bell.

I came to love the name and I hoped Dawson would, too. When he first learned to talk and was asked his name, he would answer, "Boy named Dawson." We did not know how he had come by this phrase, but it was so amusing we asked him often, "What's your name?" He would always answer, "Boy named Dawson." When he got a little older, he just wanted his name to be Jim. But as a young man, he seemed to appreciate the uniqueness of his name. He liked the idea that everyone who knew him knew only one Dawson.

I was glad to see the cooler weather coming on in October, knowing Dawson would want to get comfortable in his sweats and warm, cozy room and work on his indoor projects. "Hibernate." And, sure enough, he did.

Chapter Six

A week after my birthday, Dawson had to be admitted to the hospital. It was December 1, 1995. He had a cold with a persistent cough. He was retaining fluids, causing him to have difficulty breathing. Extra doses of diuretics were not helping. Dr. Burke admitted him, diagnosing him with bronchitis. He went in quite willingly and was in good spirits. The next morning he called me and asked if I could get him a new robe and slippers. I was glad to hear there was something I could bring him. I found it gratifying to find things that could make him comfortable. I was getting quite good at it. That hadn't always been easy to do, especially when it came to his clothes. He was so particular, but not in the sense of being style-conscious. He simply had definite ideas about what he would and would not wear. He wouldn't wear any button-down shirts, ties, dress pants, sweaters, bright or pastel colors or patterns. Almost everything he owned was black. I hoped I would be able to find a robe and slippers that he liked.

He had always been adamant about what he would not wear, to the extent of refusing to even try something on if he didn't like it. I had experienced that with him countless times over the years. "Dawson," I'd say, "just try it on," to no avail. It was next to impossible to get him to do something he didn't want to do. It was during those incidences that his stubbornness would always show itself, almost to the ridiculous. My persistence only added to the absurdity because the more he felt he was being pressured or coerced, the more obstinate he became. Bribing and coaxing simply fueled his stubbornness.

While driving to the mall to buy him a robe, I was reminded of his first robe, the little blue and white terry cloth one I had given him for his second birthday. As he opened the present and took it out of the box, I said, "Let's see it on you, Dawson. Try it on."

"No."

"Bring it here. I'll help you."

"No."

"Come on, Dawson, please."

"No."

I went to him and picked up the robe and put it on him, against his will. I tucked it around him and tied the tie around his waist. He was so upset, he just fell to the floor. Amused, I went to him and told him how cute he looked in his new robe and told him I wanted to take his picture. He finally got up, I snapped the picture, then I helped him off with it and said, "O.K. Let's open your other presents." He opened toys and a wool hat. We lived in a foggy, windy area, at the time, so I always had the kids wear their knit hats when they went outside. When he opened the box and took out a forest green hat, Claudia said, "Dawson, put it on."

"No."

Well, Claudia wasn't going to try and talk him into putting on the hat. She grabbed it and stuck it on his head. He tried to get it off, but she pulled the little earmuffs down over his ears and fastened it under his chin. After the struggle, he just stood there with a disgruntled and slightly bewildered expression on his face and the hat on his head. That was Dawson, then.

As I arrived at the mall, my thoughts returned to Dawson, now. The stores were decorated for Christmas. I felt everyone was doing their Christmas shopping, except me. I was shopping for Dawson to the sounds of Christmas carols while he was in the hospital. The words to the familiar carols were not going through my mind, anguished questions were. *Will he be all right? How will he be for Christmas? Will he be O.K.?* I was hurrying through the stores. I wanted to get to the hospital as soon as I could. I knew he wanted company. I felt quite lucky when I found a robe and slippers I was sure he'd be happy with. The robe was soft fleece in a low-key dark charcoal color and the slippers were an inconspicuous navy blue. I bought him some puzzle books and brought those to the hospital, too. He was feeling fairly well when I got there and was very pleased with his gifts. He put the robe and slippers on and as we worked on the puzzles together, he told me about one of the night nurses who had been very nice to him. He said they had known each other from high school. She had brought him some magazines and had stayed a while in his room talking. I thought maybe when he got out of the hospital he could bring her some flowers to thank her. I had always hoped he would find a nice girl who would make him want to settle down. I was thinking, *who knows?* Perhaps, this could be that girl. And who would be better than a nurse to understand his needs?

The next day when I was visiting he said to me, looking concerned, "I think Dr. Burke is going to say the tests they took show I'm getting worse. I think he's going to tell me something bad."

I could see he was getting apprehensive about seeing the doctor and I was glad I was there with him when Dr. Burke came in to the room.

I said, "How is he?"

He said, "He has bronchitis."

"What about his overall condition?"

"Umm, about the same."

Dawson looked at me. He looked relieved, but I knew what he was thinking and I knew the specific question that was on his mind. I thought for a moment and then decided to take the chance and ask the question outright.

"Then, he is not worse?"

"No. He isn't any worse."

Dawson looked at me again, this time he smiled at me with a look of distinct relief and gratitude for having asked the question he had been reluctant to ask. His condition, thankfully, wasn't any worse.

Later, we walked to the courtyard and sat where Bill and I had first discussed his diagnosis a year and a half earlier. I was thinking back to that day, that day that seemed like a lifetime ago. I was remembering the doctor telling me Dawson might only live two days… two weeks… two months… and here we were, coming up on two years. I was thankful, yet fearful. *The more months that go by, does that mean the better he is? Or the more months that go by, does that mean the closer…?* I stopped myself from asking that question.

It was a little cool, so I changed seats with him so he would be in the sun. I tucked his robe in tighter around his chest so that the collar protected his neck from the December breeze. He did not mind my fussing. I thought to myself, *We surely have come a long way since his first time here.* I wanted to hug him, but we hadn't come that far. I smiled at him and he smiled back at me.

He stayed in the hospital a few days and then was released. Dr. Burke started him on a new diuretic that worked well for him. He was soon feeling much better and wanted to start Christmas shopping.

He called me one night at the shop as Rusty and I were getting ready to leave. I stayed on the phone and talked for a long time, ignoring the fact Rusty and I had been about to go home just before he called. Everything stopped for Dawson. Perhaps it wasn't right to be so focused on him, but that was the way it was.

I so enjoyed talking to him and I was so gratified I was able to be there for him to talk to whenever he wanted. I was exhilarated, also, by the fact, *I* was the one he wanted to talk to. It was incredible how good I felt when I spoke with him. I knew Rusty could see it and I never tried to hide how important Dawson was to me and how much I cared about him.

Whenever I talked to him, I felt I could tell if he were taking care of himself. He would call more, yes, but it wasn't only that. It was that I could hear contentment, almost gladness in his voice. I knew he was happy with himself when he was being sensible. And, somehow, I knew it gave him a good feeling to know he could call me and could tell me, honestly, he was behaving himself.

Most of the time when he called, he would just say, "Hi," then pause. Then I would start talking and going on and on and then, finally, I'd say, "Oh, I'm sorry. I didn't let you tell me why you called."

"Oh, nothing much," he'd say. But then we'd end up talking for an hour.

That night when he called, he got right to the point. He said, "Hi, what size shoe do you wear?"

I said, "A six."

"Oh, that's what Grandma said."

"What's up?"

"Well, I decided to go out today, for no particular reason. I went down Grant Avenue and went into a sports shop. I had never been in there before, but I went in today. I saw a pair of those boots, those Uggs, the ones you wear all the time. They were the only pair they had and they were black and a size five. They looked small, but I thought they might be your size. They were on sale for thirty dollars. They're normally over a hundred, aren't they?"

"Yeah."

"I bought 'em for you," he said.

"You did?"

"Yeah, but I guess they won't fit, huh?"

"Well, I don't know. The ones I'm wearing are a size six and they fit me when I first got them, but they really stretched out. They're huge on me now."

"So, you think they might work? I just couldn't pass them up. I didn't even know why I went in that store, but when I saw those boots, it seemed like that was the reason. I want to give them to you. I'm sorry it won't be a surprise, but I was worried about the size and after I asked Grandma and she told me she thought they'd be too small, I had to ask you."

"Oh, that's O.K., I don't care about a surprise. I'm just happy you were thinking of me and I'm sure they'll fit after I break them in."

"But I want to give them to you before Christmas so you can try them on. I just want to know they'll be all right."

The following week we got together at Grandma and Papa's for my mother's birthday and Dawson brought my Uggs. I said, "Oh, Dawson, I didn't know you were going to wrap them. I thought you were just bringing them for me to try on."

"This is your Christmas present. Of course I'd wrap it."

"Maybe I should just wait until Christmas to open it. It looks so nice." The wrap was black with shiny red and green holly and a big green bow.

"No, no. Open it now. I want you to have it now. I want to know if they fit."

They were very tight, but I managed to pull them on. I said, "If it weren't for the fact that my other ones had stretched so much to where they are too big for me now, I would think these were too small. But I know they will work. They'll be great. Thanks, hon." He seemed very pleased and so was I.

The next time I talked to him, he told me he was feeling so well, he was able to sleep lying flat with no trouble breathing. He no longer needed to sleep in his chair. He had been sleeping on his futon, but it wasn't very comfortable. He said, "I told Dad I'd like a bed."

"What did he say?"

"He said we'll go look."

"Great. Do you know what you want?"

"I think so. Not a small one."

"You mean not a twin size?"

"Yeah, I guess. What's the next size?"

"A double."

"And then?"

"A queen size."

"That's probably the size."

"Really? I think a double should be fine. With all your workshop stuff in your bedroom, I don't know if you could fit bigger than a double."

"Oh, yeah, I could fit it. I can work it out."

"You should measure the space. When are you and Dad going to look?"

"I'm not sure, maybe tonight. Dad was saying maybe we should look at those adjustable ones. That way I could sit up if I wanted to."

"That would be good."

"Yeah, we'll see," he said, sounding excited.

When we got off the phone, I was filled with mixed emotions. On the one hand, I was intensely grateful he was feeling so much better that he could want a bed and, on the other hand, so saddened by the circumstances that made him excited just to get a new bed. I told Rusty, "Dawson wants a bed for Christmas. Bill's going to get him one. That would be so good if he could sleep in a bed again. He sounded kind of excited to go look." I cried, "God, that doesn't seem like too much to ask, does it, that he be able to sleep comfortably in a bed?"

My thoughts turned to the day he got his first bed, when he had progressed from a crib. I recalled how happy he was with it and his new dresser. I remembered tucking him in, gently rubbing his eyebrows and kissing him good night. I could still see his sleepy brown eyes looking up at me. I had gotten into a routine of stroking Claudia's eyebrows to get her to sleep. She never wanted to go to bed and would always fight it and get upset and cry at bedtime. I found rubbing her eyebrows seemed to relax her and put her to sleep. Although Dawson never had any trouble sleeping, I would rub his eyebrows in the same way. And I thought of the Christmas when he was eleven years old and he got his bunk beds and how thrilled and surprised he was with them. I was thinking of the Christmas coming and I wanted to tuck him in, rub his eyebrows and kiss him good night.

We started our Christmas shopping together again, as we had done the year before. He was in better condition than he had been then. This was starting to look like a tradition, Dawson and me shopping together. We spent many hours on the phone discussing what to get and where to get it. I was thoroughly enjoying it. My attitude was no longer, "Bah Humbug!" We spent Christmas Eve at Grandma and Papa's and as usual we had a good time. We found so many things to laugh about. I had bought my father a golf hat with earmuffs for his break-of-dawn tee-times. He looked so silly in it, we couldn't help but laugh. We were all in such good spirits. Dawson kidded Claudia about her strict Christmas ritual: All presents were to be opened one at a time, each person was to have their turn based on the number of presents remaining in their stack, and there was to be no going out of order! She was lenient when anyone asked, "Which one should I open?" "Any of them," she'd say. But, inevitably and predictably I would say, "No! Not that one!" The guys thought we were crazy, but good-naturedly went along with it.

A couple of months earlier, Rusty had bought Dawson a large model kit of an old pumper-style fire truck. Rusty's embroidery business had grown so much we had moved the equipment out of our condo and into a shop/warehouse. I wanted Dawson to make the truck for me because I had the perfect place to display it. Well, Dawson had completed it, but hadn't told me. He wanted to surprise me with it. It was wrapped in a cardboard box he had made that fit the model perfectly and held it securely. He had constructed the inverted box and wrapped it in such a way so that as I lifted the lid the model was fully revealed. The truck was built with great detail, many tiny pieces, and he had done a beautiful job. I loved it and he knew it. We smiled at each other with the spirit of Christmas in our hearts. After opening all our presents, we worked on Claudia's *Gone with the Wind* puzzle. It was a huge puzzle and we worked on it for hours. We enjoyed the time, finding pieces while Dawson interjected the witty one-liners we had come to expect from him. This year we had so much to be thankful for. Christmas was fun again.

Christmas Day, Dawson called to tell me his Dad had given him power tools. He had told Bill he was going to be doing some woodworking projects, so Bill bought him the tools he thought he could use. He was very happy with them.

Dawson had always been very adept at drawing and working with his hands. He had the patience and precision it took to work on those small model cars and it was obvious he could apply that to other projects, as well. Rusty had been telling me Dawson needed and would benefit from a *serious* hobby. The models were fun, Rusty said, but it would be good for him to have some projects that gave him a sense of accomplishment and even earned some money. I agreed. Rusty thought woodworking or woodcarving would be something Dawson would like. I talked to Dawson about it and he seemed interested. I bought him some magazines on the subject and he was very enthusiastic. He went out and bought himself some carving tools. But now, with his new equipment, he could do much more. After the first of the year, he started getting into his newfound pastime. It was wonderful to see him so excited.

I began collecting fire memorabilia for the office in the shop and I had the idea of something I wanted Dawson to make for me. I called him and said "I'd like you to make me a shadow box with little fire-related items. Do you know what I mean?"

"I don't know," he said.

"Well, a shadow box hangs on the wall and has little sections where you put figurines or artifacts or things like that. I want to put little fire things, shapes cut out of wood. Do you think you could do it?"

"Yeah," he answered, sounding quite interested.

"O.K., I'll have to draw up the idea. I'm not sure of the sizes and all the particulars. I think it would be so cute. I'm going to hang it here in the shop in my office."

The next time we talked, he asked me if I had drawn up my idea so that he could see it. I told him I was working on it. He was getting very anxious to get started. What a bonus that was for me. He not only was going to do it for me, but he was looking forward to doing it. When I had it worked out, I brought it down to show him. He liked the concept and took to the whole idea instantly. I had some ideas for some of the little figures, but wasn't sure about others. He said he might have an idea or two of his own. We began to talk almost every day. He called sometimes several times in one day, telling me of his ideas. He came up and showed me his drawings of the project. They were very good. He made organized, detailed lists of the materials we needed and together we shopped for them. We were having such a good time, sharing and creating.

All the while, I looked forward to the arrival of the latest "Young Hearts" newsletter. There was a section in the publication that was devoted to letters from members. Members would write of their experiences dealing with their particular heart condition. I was hoping there would be a letter from a young woman in our area. I thought it was possible, perhaps not likely, but possible. I felt it could be wonderful for Dawson to meet a nice young girl who would understand his condition. They could support each other in so many ways. I wanted to see him with someone he really cared about and who cared about him. I was more optimistic that in one of the issues there would be an article on a remedy for cardiomyopathy, something "new on the horizon." And, sure enough, there was. At last, in that long-anticipated newsletter, there was a letter from a member with cardiomyopathy telling of her experiences living with the condition. She wrote of a drug that had helped her and mentioned the drug by name. I was ecstatic. It was just what I had been waiting for. A twenty-seven year old woman had cardiomyopathy for almost three years. It had been confirmed by four doctors that she needed a transplant. She was put into a case study and was given Carvedilol. In a matter of months, her ejection factor went from nine to twenty-five and her heart actually shrunk twice. She was then taken off the transplant list.

I told Dawson about it and told him to ask Dr. Burke about it during his next visit. After his appointment with the doctor, Dawson called me.

"Burke thinks I'm worse."

"What! Why?"

"I don't know, but I think it's just because I've been sick a few times."

"Did he do any tests?"

"No."

"Did you ask him about that new drug, Carvedilol?"

"Yeah."

"What did he say?"

"He said it wouldn't do anything for me."

"Why not?"

"I don't know."

"Did he know of the drug?"

"I guess so."

"Did you tell him all the good things we heard about it?"

"No."

"Oh, Dawson. Why not?"

"I don't know. He said it wouldn't help me anyway. He said he thinks I should see Dr. Thompson to see what she thinks about a transplant."

"Really?" I said, suddenly feeling quite nervous. "O.K. Then we could ask her about the new drug. Let's make an appointment. Make it anytime you can get it. Rusty will drive us, O.K.?"

"Yeah, O.K."

His appointment was set for January 24, 1996. Rusty drove us in again. Without even questioning it, I went into the examining room with him. There was no longer any doubt that he would want me to. We were in this together.

Dr. Thompson never mentioned my letter and neither did I. She made no apologies or explanations about why she had not responded. She said, "Dr. Burke thinks you are slipping. He thinks you should be put on the transplant list. What we will need to do is have you come in to the hospital, stay overnight and we will run a battery of tests on you. We will find out everything we will need to know for transplanting you."

Dawson and I looked at each other.

I said, "Are these tests going to tell you whether or not he is ready to be listed?"

"No. They will tell us what we need to know for the time of the transplant."

"These tests are not to evaluate his condition?"

"No."

"Well, how do we know he's worse? How do we know he's ready?"

Dr. Thompson answered, "If Dr. Burke thinks he is, that's good enough for me."

Dawson and I looked at each other, again. That wasn't what *we* thought. We wanted further tests. We wanted Dr. Thompson to confirm he was worse from what she saw.

She said, "Decide when you can come in, but I want you to wait until you are completely over your cold."

Then I asked her about Carvedilol. She said she knew of it, in fact, she knew a doctor who was in on the study. She had heard very good things about it, recalling that some patients had been removed from the list after its use. I said we were quite interested in finding out all we could.

She said, "I'll see about getting him on it."

"That would be great," I said.

I knew Dawson was extremely reluctant about a transplant. He would not submit to the idea until he was absolutely sure it was necessary. A new drug was much more appealing to him, and to me, as well.

The thought of them removing his heart was horrifying. But, if it would save his life, of course, it would be wonderful. I knew he could not stand the thought of the doctor calling him one night, when he was feeling fine, saying, "Come in, we're taking your heart out tonight." He told me he would always wonder, "Could I have lived without having had this done?" It was going to be a difficult decision to make and he had to make it for himself. I knew it would not be right for me, even if I could, to coerce him. And I did not know which was the best decision. Dawson's ability to "luck out" led me to trust we would find the right road to take. I had to have faith that whether it was a new drug or the transplant or whatever, we would be led in the right direction. I felt, surely, my finding out about Carvedilol must be a "gift" from somewhere, at the right time. I had to pursue it.

I was very skeptical, from my past experience, that we would hear promptly from Dr. Thompson. I decided to find out what I could for myself. After a few calls, I spoke to a woman who gave me the name and number of the pharmaceutical company that had submitted the drug for testing. I called and talked to a very helpful, considerate and informative man. He told me it was approved only for use in treating high blood pressure, but all the clinical tests were done on its treatment of cardiomyopathy and had been submitted to the FDA for approval. Approval was expected in about seven or eight months. He said there was a packet of information and a toll-free number for patient enrollment requirements for individual participation in the compassionate use study. It was available to physicians only and he advised me how my doctor could obtain the needed information. I told Dawson what I had learned and told him to call Dr. Burke and tell him.

He said, "I'd rather talk to him in person. Write it down for me. I'll take it to him."

"O.K. As long as I'm doing that, maybe I should write a letter and explain how you feel about a transplant and the tests and everything."

"O.K."

When it was completed, Dawson came up and we worked on it together, changing some things to Dawson's specifications. He wanted me to change the phrases, "before my bout with bronchitis," and "my bout with the flu," removing the word, "bout." He said, smiling, "What's with this bout?"

I laughed and said, "You don't like that? O.K."

It read in part:

January 28, 1996. Dr. Burke, I appreciate your concern that I might be "slipping" and I understand your feeling I need to be placed on the transplant list before I "run out of time." I know I have not shown any significant improvement in the year and a half since I was diagnosed, but as you said when I was hospitalized with bronchitis in December, I "was no worse."

I realize there is justification for a transplant, but my concern is that Dr. Thompson is ready to put me on the list without any further evaluation to confirm your thinking. I know she feels it is sometimes impossible to "come back" after an illness, but I am already feeling much better.

I then went on to explain the favorable things Dr. Thompson had heard about Carvedilol and the status of the drug in regards to its testing, approval and availability.

I closed by writing, *Because you have been so considerate and helpful, I am asking and hoping you will obtain this information for me, evaluate its possible benefits and share your thoughts with me.*

I would like the opportunity to try this alternative before being placed on the transplant list. I have not given up the idea I still might improve. I would like to discuss my options with you. I would prefer not to wait until my next scheduled appointment. I would hope we could do it soon. Thank you, Dawson Bell.

Two days after we composed the letter, Dawson called me, describing excruciating pain in his big toe. He told me he was barely able to walk.

He said, "It hurts really bad. I'm getting these sharp pains shooting through my toe."

Concerned, I said, "I think you should call the doctor."

He reluctantly said, "Yeah, maybe I will."

Later, when I talked to my father about Dawson's pain, my father said it sounded like the gout. Again, I went to my Encyclopedia of Medicine. This time, I looked up and found "gout."

It read: "An acute attack of gout usually affects a single joint, most commonly the joint at the base of the big toe..."

"That's it," I thought.

I read further, "The intensity of the pain is such that the person may not be able to stand on an affected foot or even tolerate the pressure of bedclothes on it." It surely sounded like what Dawson had described. I wondered what caused it and why he would have it. I continued to read on, "Gout may be associated with kidney stones and ultimately may lead to kidney failure." I thought, *The effects of the*

diuretics on his kidneys must be the connection, the reason why he would get this.
I called Dawson and told him what I had learned.

He said, "Yeah, that sure sounds like it. I have the gout?"

"I think so. You should call Dr. Burke."

"It's kind of late now, I think I'll just go by his office tomorrow and then I can give him the letter."

When Dawson called me the next day, he told me I was right.

He said, "Dr. Burke said it was the gout and it's common for anyone on diuretics. He gave me a prescription for it."

I closed my eyes. I imagined that the anguish I was feeling was nothing compared to what he was going through. *Dear God,* I thought to myself, *this is just too much. God, why does he have to go through all this?* At his young age, he was experiencing such discomforts and so many limitations. He had ailments one usually does not have to deal with until old age, if then. I could not have anticipated the variety of painful effects he would have to endure as the result of his heart condition. It was breaking my heart. But Dawson, true to form, seemed to accept it all. He actually kind of chuckled at the sound of having the gout. He had looked it up in the dictionary after he had talked to me the night before.

He read it to me over the phone, "A disease of metabolism characterized by inflammation of a joint, as of the great toe..." He said, with a hint of whimsy in his voice, "I have gout in my *great* toe."

"Oh, Dawson," I said, "are you having a bout with the gout?"

He laughed and so did I.

"Well, it should be starting to get better," I said. "My book says the pain reaches a peak level of intensity within twenty-four to thirty-six hours."

"I guess it's already reached its peak then," he said with relief. "That's good."

In a few days, sure enough, he was over it. The book had also said it was recurrent. I hoped it would not come back too soon.

Chapter Seven

Dawson continued working on my shadow box project and we were talking daily. He called often to discuss his ideas. He began getting quite creative with the simple designs I had given him. One of my designs was a cutout of a fire hydrant, just the outline of the shape.

He called and said, "I've got an idea of how I'd like to do the hydrant. I'm going to do it differently than you had it, not just a flat piece of wood cut out in the shape. Is that O.K.?"

"Sure, however you want. My plans were just to give you the idea, to get you started, but you're the one making it. I think it's great you're putting so much of yourself into it. I can't wait to see your designs. When can I see them?"

"Well, I'd kind of like to wait and show it to you completely done, but then, I would like you to see the things I've done so far," he said, sounding quite proud of what he had accomplished and seeming very anxious to have me see his work.

One night he called when he was working on the miniature ladder. My plans showed an ordinary ladder. He called and wanted to know the particulars of an extension ladder, the kind firemen used. I asked Rusty and then relayed the information to Dawson, until it became too technical for me. I put Rusty on the phone and he gave him all the details, including that the top legs should be painted white and the bottom legs painted black. These were things Dawson and I hadn't known. They were small details, but Dawson wanted it to be accurate.

I wanted the outside of the shadow box to look like brick. We got together many days to try and figure the best way to accomplish that effect. Rusty thought we should use a brick-patterned stamp and Dawson and I explored that possibility. Dawson made a pattern of what we would want and we took it to show a stamp maker. We got an estimate, but we weren't convinced that was the way we wanted to do it. I thought it should be stenciled, Dawson agreed. After much shopping around, I found a stencil of brickwork I thought might work. I bought various materials and paints that might simulate the texture of brick and brought it down for Dawson to try. He was enthusiastic about trying it out. He then showed me the wooden pieces he had been working on. The fire hydrant was cuter than I could have imagined. He had made it out of dowels and pegs that he had cut to varying sizes. It was three-dimensional, not flat. He painted it a bright, shiny red with gold details and a chain attached from the caps. He was so pleased with it and so was I. He could see my genuine appreciation of his diligent work and my excitement over what he had done for me.

The extension ladder had tiny rungs of cut wood, smaller than toothpicks, which he had glued one by one into the minute holes he had drilled into the side rails.

The real surprise was the fire extinguisher. He had come up with the idea and the design all on his own. He had carved it out of a dowel, painted it red and attached a tiny black hose to the silver-painted, hand-cut nozzle. It was perfect and I told him so. Everything he had made was terrific. I couldn't wait to have him complete the other pieces and the box itself so I could hang it in the shop and see it every day. I looked forward to proudly showing it to everyone who entered. I told Dawson, "Maybe you could sell these if you wanted to make more, after I get mine."

"Maybe," he said.

Dawson seemed well and optimistic, but I could not stop worrying. Most days and more nights, I was extremely nervous just thinking about his condition. Rusty's fire department schedule kept him at the firehouse twenty-four hours at a time while he was on duty. On those days, I went to visit my parents and would stay for dinner and play cards afterward. I didn't want to be home alone for too many hours. I liked staying late because then I could go right to bed when I got home, say my rosary for Dawson and, usually, go right to sleep.

I was driving home late one night after one of my visits, when my cell phone rang. It startled me, but when I answered it and heard Dawson's voice sounding so cheerful, I was instantly relieved and happy.

He said, "I tried that stuff you brought to make the bricks."

"How did it work?"

"Pretty good, I think."

"Really? Great. Was it hard to do?" I asked.

"Well, you should see the mess I've got here," he said with a laugh.

"I can imagine."

"I doubt it. I've been working on it for hours, adding and mixing all that sand and paint and that powder stuff. It's everywhere," he said, laughing out loud.

"Do you think you would be able to mix that again, knowing how you did it this time? You know, if you wanted to make another one with the bricks, could you?"

"I don't know. I was kind of mixing like crazy," he answered, still amused.

"Yeah, I know what you mean. I've done things like that. So how far did you get with it, how much did you get done?"

"I finished all the bricks on both sides," he said, sounding very pleased.

"You did? Great."

"That's part of why it took so long, 'cause I waited 'til the one side was dry, well almost dry, and then I was able to work on the other side."

"How does it look? Do you like it?" I asked.

"It looks pretty good. I'm happy with it."

To hear Dawson express such pleasure in what he had accomplished thrilled me. "I can't wait to see it. When can I?"

"There's a few more things I want to do, then I'll show you, O.K.?"

"Sure, you let me know."

Our conversation lasted my entire drive home. We were still talking as I got out of the car, went up the stairs and into the condo. At that point, I said, "I'm home. I guess we should get off the phone. It's pretty late. But I'm so glad you called. You let me know when I can see what you've done. I can't wait. You have a good sleep, hon. Good night."

The next day he called and asked me, "Do you think you could come down tomorrow and see the things?"

"Yeah, tomorrow would be good."

When I arrived the next morning, I expected to go up to his room and see some completed pieces on his worktable. But, instead, the entirely completed shadow box with all the objects placed in their designated sections was sitting on the kitchen table, waiting for me to see. He was standing by the table, smiling.

"It's done!" I said with surprise.

He nodded, "Yeah."

"You didn't tell me it was finished."

"I wanted to surprise you. I finished it late last night."

"Dawson, it is so darling," I cried as I examined it closely. "I love it. You did a great job. The bricks look great. Everything does; the alarm box, the dalmatian, the turnout coat and boots, the helmet, the axe, the hose, the bucket, I love them all." I was amazed at the level of detail. "Oh, the fire truck!" I exclaimed. "You did a fantastic job on that, with the bell and hose and *everything*. What detail!"

"If I do another one for anybody else, though, the truck won't have as much detail as this one. This one is special 'cause, you know, I made it for you. You'll have the only one like this."

"It is so terrific. Wait until Grandma sees it. And Papa."

He stood there smiling.

I thought, *"What a gift!"*

"Look at the back," he urged.

I turned it around and read, "Hand Crafted by Dawson Bell." He had used the electric wood burning iron I had given him to burn those words into the wood like a branding iron. I had special-ordered the iron from a catalog. It was a perfect final touch to a beautifully hand crafted work of art.

Despite the fact we no longer had to discuss or shop for the shadow box project, Dawson continued to call almost every day, sometimes more than once. I wouldn't have thought it possible to enjoy any calls more than I had enjoyed the ones discussing our project. Surprisingly, our new conversations were even more enjoyable and meaningful. He would call with some little question and we would end up talking for hours. Sometimes, we would do crosswords together over the phone. He liked the *TV Guide* puzzles and would call me when there was reference to an old-time show.

He had a curiosity about so many new things. He had opinions on subjects that, previously, I had not heard him express. During one of our more profound conversations, he impressed me with his insight. I said, "Dawson, you're pretty smart."

"Yeah," he said, like it was something he had known all along.

"You really are smart," I said, again, sounding surprised.

"Yeah, I know," he said, sounding pleased that I knew it, too.

"Then why have you done such stupid things? I thought, at times, you must just be stupid. Now I'm finding out, more and more that you're not stupid at all." He responded with a chuckle.

He seemed to have a newfound interest in everything around him, in things that would not have interested him in the past. It was wonderful to see and to be a part of.

He and his dad had gone to a dinner dance and he called me the next day to tell me about it. It was a casual crab feed at a private club and they were invited by close friends. Dawson told me he knew he shouldn't eat too much crab, so he had salad and some French bread with butter. He told me who had danced and how. He said the friend's daughter had tried to get him to dance, but he wouldn't.

Then he really surprised me. He said, "I think I'd like to learn how to dance."

"Really?" I said, excited and shocked. "I'd love to teach you. I tried to teach you a long time ago, but you would have no part of it, remember? I think it would be great for you to learn."

I had been a dance instructor when Dawson was thirteen years old. I had tried to coax him, many times, to let me teach him to dance. I remembered saying, "Dawson, come here and just try these steps. Just try it. Please."

"No."

I told him that girls always like boys who dance. I managed, once, to get him to stand up. That was as far as he would go. He would not try the steps I was showing him. So, to hear him say, "I think I'd like to learn how to dance," was quite exciting. I knew then we really had come a long way!

One day he called, telling me of something he had seen on a late-night TV program. He said there was "some guy" on who had written a book about "hair carving."

"Hair carving?" I said. "What's that?"

"I'm not sure, but I think it's tiny, tiny carvings on hair. Intricate, detailed carvings of all kinds of things, Napoleon, Snow White, all kinds of stuff. You just can't imagine. It's kind of unbelievable what this guy was saying. I'm not even sure I heard it right. I didn't get the name of the book, but it was something about... a needle... or something. The guy who did this stuff is dead. He had a weird, long name. I didn't catch it. I don't know."

The next day I did some searching and found the book and bought it. It was called *The Eye of the Needle: The Unique World of Microminiatures of Hagop Sandaldjian.* I researched further and found that the miniature works were on display at a museum in Southern California. I thought maybe Rusty and I could take Dawson there. I surprised him and brought the book down to him. He was very impressed and appreciative. He was glad to know that what he had thought he had seen and heard on TV was, for the most part, true. The pictures were unbelievable. One showed nine carved, exotic, colorful birds standing on a strand of hair from the artist's three-month old son. Another picture showed the tiny sculpture of a Spanish dancer with her castanets. She was wearing a scarlet dress and was shown standing in the eye of a needle. There was picture after picture showing these incredible microscopic works of art. Dawson was fascinated and, frankly, so was I.

He was watching quite a bit of television, but more educational programs than he ever had. He would tell me about the programs he had seen. Sometimes he would suggest I watch a certain program, too. Then we would discuss them the next day. But his standard nightly program was still David Letterman.

He called one day and asked, "Where do you get postcards? Not the picture kind."

"The post office, I think."

"David Letterman is coming to San Francisco and they're having a drawing for the tickets. They said to send a postcard, only one per person."

"We could send in cards with my name and Rusty's and Claudia's and Dad's and Grandma's and if they got picked, they'd give you the ticket. Do you want me to get them for you?"

"O.K., if you want to."

"Yeah, I can do that. Do you want me to write them out?"

"O.K. I'll give you the address."

That day I went to the post office. The next day Dawson called and said they had given a new address for where to send the postcards.

"I'm glad I hadn't written them out yet."

He said, "They changed the address because they had already been flooded with so many cards, they couldn't handle them all."

"They got that many already?"

"Yeah."

"I'll get these out today."

Over the next few days, he continued to give me an update on the overwhelming response the Letterman people had received. They had cards stacked out in the hallways and everywhere. They had received thousands and thousands of cards.

I said to him, "Dawson, do you realize the odds of them drawing your card?"

"Yeah."

"The chances of getting drawn…"

"Yeah, I know, but I think I could get picked. I'm pretty lucky."

I was so struck by this comment. After all he'd been through, he still thought of himself as "pretty lucky." Pretty lucky. That's why he never walked around with a "poor me" attitude and never complained. Only once did I hear him ask the usual question, "Why me?" and even then it was asked very matter-of-factly, without a hint of whining.

"I'm pretty lucky," I had heard him say. What a testament to his power to see beyond adversities, I thought to myself. What a testament to Dawson, my son.

Chapter Eight

Several months earlier, Bill's father had been diagnosed with cancer. He had been undergoing radiation treatments and seemed to be doing fairly well. But on Tuesday, February 20, 1996, his seventy-ninth birthday, he was rushed to the hospital. Dawson called me and told me.

"What happened?" I asked. "The cancer?"

"I think so. Dad went to see him. I'll know more when he gets home."

"Will you let me know how he's doing when you find out?"

"Yeah. I'll call you tomorrow."

When Dawson called the next day, he said Papa Tom was quite ill. He had been bleeding internally. Evidently, he had bled during the night and was too weak to call for help. A friend who lived close by and had been checking on him every day found him in the morning.

"Is there anything they can do for him?" I asked.

"I don't think so. The doctors are saying he has six months to live."

On Friday, Dawson went with his dad to see Papa Tom. He called me after his visit and told me he didn't look well and was very weak.

Bill went to see him almost every day. Bill's only sister, Bev, who didn't drive, visited her dad on Saturdays. She would get a ride with a friend of Papa Tom's. One day, Bev needed to take care of some things at her dad's apartment and had no way of getting there. Dawson volunteered to pick her up and drive her to the apartment and then take her home. It was a total of about two hundred and seventy miles. I thought it might be too much for him, but I was pleased he had chosen to help his aunt.

"Did Bev ask you to drive her?" I asked.

"No, I offered," he said.

"That was really nice of you, Dawson. Did you get tired?"

"No, not really. I didn't get home 'til late, though. But it was O.K. I'm glad I did it. Bev really appreciated it."

We continued to have our good talks on the phone, but they were less frequent. When I didn't hear from him for a few days, I'd worry. Was he behaving himself? Was he taking care of himself? Rusty would try to assure me that Dawson would not do anything to jeopardize his health. "He's learned," he would say to me. I could not be convinced because I knew Dawson. He seemed sensible now and appreciated it when he felt well and he enjoyed his hobbies and our relationship. But I knew there was that part of him that could still decide to just forget everything and want to party just like everyone else. I prayed he wouldn't do that, but I feared he would. I prayed the day would come when he truly would not want to take the chance and drink or do anything that might make his condition worse. I knew when that day came, there would be no one who could talk him into doing otherwise. That would be when his stubbornness would be a virtue.

The phone rang. It was Dawson. "Hi," he said, "I'm going on a vacation."

"Where?" I asked with surprise and apprehension.

"Hawaii."

"Hawaii? How'd that come about?"

"Matt's getting married over there and a lot of his friends are going."

"Really? How long will you be there?"

"A week."

"A week? That's kind of a long time, isn't it? To have to watch what you eat and everything."

"No, I can do it. We're staying in a condo with a kitchen. So I can eat at home a lot. That will help. I'll be O.K."

"Oh, Dawson, I don't know. You really want to go, huh?"

"Yeah."

"You're not worried?"

"No."

"Gee, I don't know. It just seems like it will be hard for you, a whole week."

"I'll be O.K."

"Yeah, I know, but you know me. You know how I worry."

"Yeah, but I'll be fine."

"When is it?"

"April."

"April? That's soon."

"Yeah, kind of."

"Is Matt the friend that always came by and stayed with you when you were first sick? He was there a lot right after you got out of the hospital that first time. Is that him?"

"Yeah."

"He seemed really nice. He's a good friend, huh?"

"Yeah."

"What's his fiancé like? Is she the same girl he was going with back then?"

"Yeah. She's really nice. They get along really good. I've never seen them fight."

"So, I guess you're going to need to go shopping."

"Yeah."

"Well, if you want, call me and I'll go with you."

"Yeah, I would like that. That would be good."

When we got off the phone, I tried to think of ways I could plead with him, or even, bribe him not to go. But knowing Dawson, I knew he could not be talked out of anything he had decided to do, and I was so worried. How could he go to Hawaii and not party? How could he stay on a salt-free diet? How could he handle running around in the heat? Why did this have to come up? Why did he have to go? Should I try to talk him into going for just the weekend or just a few days, even though I knew there was really no hope of changing his mind? The only thing good about the trip was his attitude. He wasn't worried. He was excited. He was confidant. He was looking forward to it with so much enthusiasm. I admired that about him, his continued ability to live life. But I was so scared. I decided I had to talk him out of going. That was, until he called and said, "Matt asked me to be his Best Man."

"Really, Dawson? That is such an honor. Matt must feel very close to you."

"Yeah, we've been friends a long time," he said.

"Well, there's no way you could not go now."

"Oh, I'm going."

"I know. It'll be fun," I said, resigned to the idea.

"Can you come shopping with me? I don't know what to get for a present."

"Sure, I'll get their list from the bridal registry. We can look it over before we go and that will help give you some ideas."

When I got their list, I called Dawson and read a few things to him. I said, "The crystal candle holders would be nice, especially from the Best Man."

"I can't give them that."

"Why not?"

"Matt doesn't want candle holders."

"It's on their list," I said.

"He doesn't want that," he said emphatically.

"If it's on their list…"

He interrupted, "I can't give Matt crystal candle holders. What else is on the list?"

"The usual. Towels, silverware, appliances."

"I can't give him things like that. I want to give him something fun, like tools."

"They're not on the list," I said.

"So what? I want to give him something that he'd like."

"But if he doesn't have any tools on the list, how would you know what tools he wanted?"

"Any tool is good."

"Yeah. And I'm sure Jenn would like it, too. Well, I guess we'll just have to go look."

The next time I talked to him he said, "I asked Matt what he wanted."

"What did he say?"

"He said, 'Anything is fine.'"

"See, whatever is on the list would be good," I told him.

"Nah."

"Dawson!"

He laughed at the silliness of it all. "Matt told me they got an espresso maker and he said that was a fun gift. I said to him, 'Yeah, right.'"

"Well, it probably was. Maybe you could get him nice cappuccino cups to go with it."

"Hmm... I don't think so."

"Oh, this is going to be tough. We'll just have to go and look, I guess."

When we went shopping, he bought what he needed to wear in the wedding and some summer stuff for his stay. He still did not want to get anything on the bridal list as a gift. He said, "Can't I just give them money? I want to give them enough, though."

"Well, yeah. I'm sure they'd like it. Everyone can always use money. I feel a lasting gift would be more appropriate, but if that's what you want to do, then I guess why not. Let's go look at cards." We found one he thought was perfect, a money-enclosure card with no frills and no mush.

We talked that day of the importance of taking care of himself while away. He said, "Yeah. I thought about how terrible that would be if something happened while I was there."

"Really, think of Matt. He obviously cares a lot about you to ask you to be his Best Man. You owe it to him to do what's right."

"I know. I've been thinking about that."

"With the people that are going, do you mind making an issue about what you can eat and drink?" I asked.

"No, I don't care about that."

"That's good. Because if they are your friends, they'll understand. And if they don't, they're not worth being your friends."

"I don't have a problem with that."

I said, "Dawson, I want to tell you something. It's kind of abstract. You'll have to bear with me. It's a thought I had." Dawson often joked with me about how I could come up with some of my ideas. He blamed it on what he called my thought process. "Man," he'd say, "that thought process of yours..." and just roll his eyes.

I said, "Picture yourself in Hawaii. You're disregarding everything. You're eating and drinking without any concern for what's right. You make it through the week, but when you get home, you start to feel the effects of your behavior. Maybe you even have to go back to the hospital, you're doing so poorly. You feel really bad. You are filled with regrets for not having been sensible and for not having taken care of yourself. You are so sorry you did not just appreciate the fact that you were able to go to Hawaii, and be there for your friend. You wish you had just been thankful for that, had a nice time, and not pushed for more. You are so afraid you're going to hear your condition is worse as a result of what you did in Hawaii. You are lying in the hospital, thinking to yourself, 'If only I could do it over. If only I could go back and keep my promise to myself and to my mom that I would not do anything stupid. If only I could go back to that day one week before my trip. I would make that promise and keep it. I wish I could go to Hawaii and do it over.' Well, you know what, Dawson? Your wish came true. You *are* here, one week before you go to Hawaii and you do have the chance, you can do it right."

He looked at me, thinking and nodding. He took my preaching in stride, as he always did.

I said, "I know it sounds odd the way I put it, but right now you have the choice. Please do what's right."

"I will."

"I'm sorry, Dawson. It's just that I worry so much about you. And you know how awful it is to be worried. I remember you told me about that night Harley didn't come home. You told me how you called and called for him and he didn't come. Remember? You went to bed, but couldn't sleep because you were so worried and you kept getting up all night, calling and whistling for him and he didn't come. You were sure something had happened to him. Remember? You told me it made you feel sick. You said it was a horrible feeling. Don't make me feel like that, please. I hope I will hear from you at least once while you are away." Though I knew he would do what he wanted, he seemed to understand my heartfelt intentions were pure and would forgive me my nagging.

He smiled at me and said, "I'll be O.K. and I will call you."

The night before his flight, I brought him some salt-free snacks to take on the plane. He was very excited about his trip and I was glad for him, despite my fears. He did keep his promise to call me. I heard from him on the second day.

"Hi. I'm here."

"Dawson, hi! How's it going?"

"O.K. The condo is really nice. I've got the master bedroom and bath."

"That's nice, how'd you manage that?"

"My roommate here, Will, said I could have it."

"That was nice of him. How was the flight?"

"Fine. They served lasagna. I didn't think that would be too good to have, so I didn't eat it. I had some of my snacks."

"Great! It sounds like you're off to a good start."

"We saw some whales. They are huge."

"Were you out in a boat?"

"No, you can see them from the beach, but we are going on a fishing boat. Maybe I'll see them even closer. Everyone went to the beach again today, but I'm hanging out in my air-conditioned condo."

"That sounds like a smart thing to do. Did you have rehearsal for the wedding?"

"No, Matt said it's really informal."

"So, what's the name of your condo?"

"Kihei Akahi."

"Would you care to spell that for me?"

"No," he laughed.

"O.K., I get it. You don't want me to track you down. 'Don't call me, I'll call you?'"

He laughed again.

I said, "I'm really glad you called, hon. I guess I should let you go. You have a good time. Take care. Call me anytime."

It was a very long week. Finally, he was home. I went to see him and he seemed none the worse for the excursion. He told me about the wedding, the luau, and the fishing expedition. It turned out, he said, that you could see the whales better from the beach than you could from the boat. He told me about riding around in the golf cart at a very expensive golf course. He seemed to have enjoyed himself and had felt well while he was there. For that, I was very grateful and I was happy the trip was behind us. Now we just had spring and summer to get through. These always seemed the hardest for me. They meant he was out more, with his friends more, riding his bike more. The warm seasons gave me more to worry about. That's when he came out of hibernation.

It was April 24, 1996, his twenty-seventh birthday. We all got together the week after he came back from Hawaii to celebrate. He looked well and was in very good spirits. He talked about his trip and told some funny stories. We had dinner at Grandma and Papa's and I baked weird little salt-free cakes. Everyone was getting very used to my salt-free experiments, by now, especially Dawson. Over the past couple of years, I had made him many unusual things. He was always good-natured about trying everything. Once he asked if I had made a batch of cookies with bubble gum. He liked the dried fruit I had found at a specialty store where they had an abundant variety. I would always try to keep him well stocked with those.

He was very pleased with his birthday presents. Rusty and I gave him some wood and supplies for a project he had seen. It was a model of an old pickup truck. It would be the first model he ever made out of wood. The plans looked very involved, but he wanted to try it so I sent for them. Grandma and Papa gave him a unique machine that was designed for tiny woodworking. Claudia gave him a gift certificate from the craft store. He was looking forward to getting started.

For the past few months, he had been helping a friend of his who was building a shop for a new business and Dawson spent many hours there, working. This kept him from getting started on his new projects and kept him out more than I thought was good for him.

He called me on Mother's Day, but asked if it would be all right if he didn't come up to see me because he was really tired. He had worked late with Tony the night before and had started early that morning. They still had some things to do and when they did finish he just wanted to go home and go to bed. I was disappointed, but I understood and I certainly didn't want him to drive up overly tired to see me. I would rather he stayed home and went to bed. I did not know if he actually did go home and go to bed, but I was glad he called.

I wasn't hearing from him as often as I had been and when I'd call him, he was usually out. When I did talk to him, he assured me he was doing all right. And I would say to him, "Dawson, please be good. You know I'll find out if you're not taking care of yourself because it will catch up with you. Please, don't let that happen."

I'd get off the phone and express my fears to Rusty because I could not hide my anguish. Rusty felt he should be able to console me and he would try. His method of trying to calm my fears was to tell me that he *knew* Dawson was going to be all right. He would state it as though it were an absolute fact and I was required to believe it. "Dawson's not stupid," he would say. "Dawson's learned his lesson. He's strong, he wants to live. Dawson will live." When I could not be comforted by his words, he would get upset and act as though I was unreasonable. My fears were not unreasonable, they were real. What I was living was a reality.

Rusty often accused me of "being negative." It was not as though I let my fears keep me from being hopeful. I was always searching for promising information and was encouraging and supportive of Dawson in every way I could, as was Rusty. If I were being negative, I would have been saying, "He's going to die, I know he is, there's nothing I can do." But I wasn't. Yes, I was terrified he might die, but I always had hope and faith we would find a way to make him well. I felt my attitude was an absolute contradiction of Rusty's description. That I believed he could die and yet never gave up on my faith in God, Dawson, or my ability to find a way seemed to me to be quite positive. That I felt pain and dread seemed perfectly understandable to me. How could a mother not feel what I was feeling? How could Rusty expect his words, though filled with sincere concern and love, to wipe away those real fears? Even if Dawson took *perfect* care of himself, the prognosis was still frightening. The doctors had said, "He will die of this" and "A transplant is probably in his future." They did not say, "If he *does not* take care of himself..." these things will happen. It seemed likely they would and it was terrifying.

I did not expect Rusty to be able to make me feel unafraid. I appreciated his efforts, but it was too hard for him to watch my pain and not be able to console me. He wanted his efforts to change my outlook. When they did not, he felt ineffectual and that made him angry with me. Then I would get upset with him. He acted as though I was upset because he hadn't helped me when, in fact, I was only upset that he was angry. It was becoming a vicious circle.

So he was understandably disappointed in me when I could not look forward to events and occasions. We had plans to go on a four-day trip to Reno on May 27, but I was not excited. I hated to make plans, for fear of "something" happening. But I tried to put my worries aside and when we went, I tried to have a good time. It was a golf/gambling bus trip that my father had organized for his club. Rusty and I had gone the year before and it was important that we go because I helped my mother serve refreshments on the bus and Rusty helped my father with the golf scoring and prizes.

Rusty was looking forward to the awards dinner on the last night. My mom and dad and I went down to the banquet room to check on things. Rusty was to come down a little later. When he did, he peeked in the room and motioned to me to go out to the hallway. When we were away from the doorway, he said to me, "My mother's dead."

"What! Oh, my God, no! Rusty, what happened?"

"A friend of hers found her when she went to pick her up for Bingo. The friend called the police. It looks like she had a heart attack. She was dressed, sitting in a chair."

"God, I can't believe it. How did you hear?"

"My mom had my phone numbers written down and the police found them. When they couldn't get me at home, they called my firehouse number. They found out where I was staying and the lieutenant called and told me. I'm going to see about getting a flight out of here tonight, go home, and get the earliest flight I can to Michigan. Don't tell your dad. I don't want to upset him and spoil his night."

"What should I tell him? He will think it's pretty odd when you do not arrive. How can I not tell him?"

"I don't know, but I think hearing this will upset him too much."

Rusty was unable to get a flight out that night, so he was there for the awards and dinner. When it was over and we were back in our rooms, he told my father what had happened. He flew out the next morning and the rest of us went home on the bus that same day. We were all stunned. I felt so bad for Rusty. He had been looking forward to this trip so much. Who could have imagined it would have ended like this? He had received the phone call I feared I would get. So it was true—people do get those dreaded calls. They do.

He stayed in Michigan a month to take care of his mother's affairs. He learned that his mother was found holding his father's death certificate. It appeared she knew and, perhaps, was even content, that she was going to join her beloved husband.

In June, I heard of a program on television that had reported on a new surgical treatment for enlarged hearts. I called the station and was faxed a transcript. A doctor in South America was having encouraging results with his controversial methods. He had discovered he could improve the condition of and prolong the life of patients with enlarged hearts by "simply" removing part of the heart, literally making the heart smaller by cutting away part of it. He was working under less than ideal conditions, yet he was having some success. His accomplishments had come to the attention of doctors here in the United States. Most were skeptical, but interested. A few American cardiologists were planning to try the unconventional techniques under optimum conditions, expecting more promising results.

Dawson called that afternoon after his visit with Dr. Burke. I told him what I had learned about this possible new treatment that sounded better than a transplant. "But," I said, "it is still experimental. How did you do at the doctor's today? What did Dr. Burke have to say?"

Dr. Burke had disappointed me when he had responded quite nonchalantly to Dawson's letter. He told him that getting on the transplant list was strictly up to Dawson. We already knew that. And as far as the new drug, Dr. Burke had maintained his opinion that it would not help him. He gave Dawson the name of a doctor at another transplant facility in the city that could answer some questions for him, for we had not heard from Dr. Thompson.

Dawson answered, "He asked me if I was going to go see that other doctor so he could explain to me why Carvedilol will not work for me. That just seems dumb."

I said, "I know, but it wouldn't hurt to hear what he has to say. Not just about the drug, but the transplant, too."

"But I feel too good."

"Too good to bother about seeing another doctor?" I asked.

"Yeah."

"I'm glad that you're feeling so well, but..." Then I let it go. I knew I was not going to be able to talk him into going.

It was late July before I brought it up again. "What about making an appointment with that doctor?" I asked.

He said, "I don't know. It's just that it doesn't seem like the time 'cause right now, I wouldn't even know I have a heart problem."

"So you don't think it would be a good idea, at least, to see him? I'm glad you're feeling that well, but..." Then I let it go, again. I didn't argue with him. I didn't tell him that it didn't matter he didn't feel like he had a heart problem, he *did* have a heart problem. I didn't tell him, "Go see that doctor." I didn't tell him, "Get on the list." Was that because there was a part of me that still hoped and believed there was a better alternative? In any case, I believed I would not be able to talk him into going. It was going to have to come to him on his own. I hoped he would not put it off too long. It was wonderful he was feeling so well, but I feared it was causing him to neglect his condition.

When I got off the phone, I told Rusty how my conversation with Dawson had gone. Rusty responded with many of the same things he had told me before. He said, "Well, maybe Dawson knows. He knows best how he feels. I've told you, Dawson is taking care of himself and he knows what he has to do. It is all up to him. I believe in that kid. Stop being so negative. If Dawson were doing everything you think he is, he'd be dead."

I knew that Rusty, as always, was saying these things out of sincere concern and love for me and Dawson, but he would never be able to relieve my fears. It was not his fault. It was an impossible task.

Chapter Nine

It was nine o'clock Wednesday evening, August 7. Rusty and I were at the shop working when the phone rang. It was Dawson.

"Hi," he said.

It had been almost six months since Papa Tom had gone into the hospital with the grim prognosis and in the last week, his condition had worsened considerably. "What is it?" I said, expecting to hear him say, "It's Papa Tom…"

But that was not what he said. "I'm not feeling well. I'm going to the hospital."

"What's wrong?" I asked.

"I'm having a hard time breathing."

"Are you swollen?"

"A little."

"Is Dad there? Is he taking you? Did you call the doctor?"

"Yeah. I'm ready to go, but I wanted to call you and let you know."

"Well, I'm glad you did. Do you want me to come down?" I asked, trying to stay calm.

"No, that's O.K., I'll call you later or Dad will."

"O.K., hon. Take care, you better go." I hung up the phone and screamed, "Rusty! Dawson's going to the hospital!"

"What happened?"

"I don't know. He said he's having a hard time breathing."

"Well, it's probably just water retention. They'll give him the diuretics like they've done before. He'll be O.K."

"I don't know. It seems different. I don't think he's even that swollen."

"Now don't start painting ugly pictures. You'll just have to wait and see what happens. Is he going to call you later?"

"Well, I guess, or Bill will. Oh, God, I'm so scared."

"Andrea, you don't know anything right now. There is no sense in panicking. Just stay calm. He'll be all right."

"I don't know. I don't know. Maybe I should go down there."

"Andrea, relax. Wait until you know something."

"I'd better call my mother," I said. When I told her what had happened, she just moaned. Then she was silent for a moment. "Well, he'll be all right," she said. "You know Dawson."

"Yeah, but I'm scared. I better get off the phone. We're still at the shop and I want to go home. I'll call you later if I hear anything."

We left the shop and went home to wait. It wasn't long before Bill called. He said the doctor had looked at Dawson and felt the difficulty he was having was just due to anxiety.

"Anxiety? Don't they know he suffers from congestive heart failure?"

"I'm only telling you what they told me. They're doing tests, so I'm sure they'll know."

"What is Dawson saying? How is he feeling?"

"He says he doesn't feel right, but he's laughing and joking with everyone."

"Maybe I should come down."

"No. Just wait. I'll call you later. I'm going back in to see him now."

"O.K. Call me as soon as you hear anything, please."

When he called back, he informed me they were going to send Dawson home.

"What?" I shrieked. "They can't send him home. Dr. Burke always told him, 'If ever you don't feel well, sign yourself in to the hospital.' That's what he's trying to do and they won't let him?"

"I don't know. They said they can't find anything wrong."

"Well, something's wrong. Dawson knows it. What's he saying?"

"He doesn't think he should go home."

"Then don't let him."

"They told me he has an upset stomach, it might be the flu. They said I should go out and buy something soft for him to eat at home."

"Bill, that sounds crazy. Do you know if Dr. Burke has been called?"

"I don't know."

"I'm getting off the phone and calling him."

"O.K. I'm going to the store to get some stuff for Dawson. I'll call you back."

The first call I made was to the hospital. I told them who I was and that I wanted to know about Dawson's condition. They told me because he was not a minor, they couldn't tell me anything. I asked to speak to the doctor who had seen him and I was told she was too busy. When I hung up, I called Dr. Burke and reached his service. Dr. Burke was not on call that night. Would I like to leave a message for his associate?

Dr. Grossman returned my call promptly. He was very considerate and attentive as I explained my concern. I had to tell him Dawson's history, which he had not known. I said, "Dr. Burke had always told Dawson to sign himself in to the hospital if he didn't feel well. Well, he doesn't and they're sending him home. I don't know that he's having the same discomforts he's had before, but he had always been treated with diuretics when he was there. What ever it is, I don't think he should go home. Dawson is not an alarmist. If he felt bad enough to go into the hospital, he must have been feeling very ill. I want them to keep him, but no one at the hospital will talk to me."

The doctor said he would check in on him, find out what was going on and call me back. When he called, he said they were doing more tests. When Bill called, he told me that when he had gotten back to the hospital after grocery shopping for Dawson, they told him they were going to keep him there, after all.

"Thank God," I said. "I guess Dr. Grossman must have had something to do with it."

"I don't know. I think they just hadn't completed all the tests."

"Well, then why did they tell you before that you could take him home?"

"I don't know."

"Well, it doesn't matter. At least they are going to keep him. I feel better about that. I just didn't want him to go home if he wasn't all right."

"Yeah, I guess it's good."

"O.K. I'll go down to see him in the morning. But call me if you hear anything."

I was relieved they were keeping him, but so afraid. I thought of all that he was going through. I tried to stay calm despite my fears and I decided to go to bed. I planned to get up early in the morning to go to the hospital. I said my rosary and fell asleep. I awoke several times during the night thinking of Dawson. Each time I would say a prayer and fall back to sleep.

At 4:30 A.M., I awoke to the phone ringing. "Oh, no!" I cried. It was Bill. "Oh, God! What is it?"

"The hospital just called. They're taking him into intensive care."

"Why? What happened?"

"I'm not sure. I'm going to get ready and go over there."

"O.K. I'll be there as soon as I can."

Rusty was now awake and starting to get ready for work. He was going on duty that day and suggested he drive me to the hospital on his way to work in the city. "I don't think you should drive," he said.

I didn't know whether I should or not, but it sounded good not to have to drive myself. I was beginning to panic, trying to get ready as fast as I could, murmuring, "Oh, God... Please God... No, God... Please!" I was rushing and moving as fast as I could, but it felt like frenetic slow motion, the way one looks under a strobe light; frantic and rapid yet slow and hesitant, getting nowhere. Rusty was trying to help me, asking if I needed this or that. I didn't know. I couldn't think beyond Dawson. Then I shouted abruptly, "Let's just go," and we rushed out the door. The sky was still dark as we got into Rusty's truck. Rusty was talking to me, but I could not respond to what he was saying. My mind was racing, my heart pounding, and my stomach churning. I started a rosary, saying it aloud. I could hear my voice as if it were echoing in my ears from some far off place, "Hail Mary full of grace, the Lord is with thee..." over and over and over. I stopped frequently in the middle of reciting my prayers to cry out, "Oh, Rusty!... Rusty!... he has to be all right!"

We were about twenty minutes from the hospital when my cell phone rang. "No!" I screamed. I knew it was Bill. He said, "The hospital called again. They told me to get over there right away. I'm leaving now."

"Oh, no!" I cried. "What is it? What did they say?"

"I don't know. I'm going. I just wanted you to know."

"Yeah, O.K. O.K., I'll be there. I'll be there. Oh, God!" I hung up.

"Andrea, what is it?" Rusty asked.

"They told Bill to get over to the hospital right away! That means it's bad! Oh, no. What's going to happen? Am I going to make it there in time? Oh, God, please! Rusty!" I was trying not to get hysterical, but my panic was building. "No! Dawson! Please, Dawson, I'm on my way, I'm coming, hon. Oh, God!"

"Andrea, stay calm," Rusty said.

I could not. My God, could this be true? Could this be it? I had to be there with Dawson. I had to get there. I had to see him. We weren't moving fast enough. My legs were quivering, my heart and my mind were racing on ahead of me. I felt constrained by my body and confined by the truck I was riding in and bound to the freeway we were on, restricted by everything physical. They were holding me back from being with Dawson. I wanted to jump out of my skin, out of the truck, out of this horror of not being there with him when he needed me. I was shaking so badly, I thought perhaps my soul could be jolted beyond my body to transcend time and space. If it could, I could be there with Dawson in an instant. I wished to be there with him in that magical instant.

I looked toward the predawn sky and tried to calm myself. I prayed silently. I focused my eyes on the headlights passing in the opposite direction and the red taillights streaming up ahead. I stared out the window at the commuters heading off to work and I prayed for a miracle.

At last we were there. I bolted out of the truck and ran into the emergency entrance. I told the woman at the desk who I was and she took me into Intensive Care. There was so much going on around him, but all I could see was Dawson. He was lying there with Bill standing by his side. Bill looked so frightened. I went to Dawson's side. His eyes were partially open. I said, "Dawson, I'm here." He seemed to blink as if he heard me. I held his hand and squeezed it. He weakly squeezed it back. He knew I was there! I said, "You're going to be O.K., hon."

Through my tears, I looked around the room. The scene looked like something I had seen on television. The monitor was beeping with corresponding green lines moving across the screen, there was the sound of oxygen being forced through a large corrugated plastic tube and so many little tubes running from clear bags hanging by the bed and they were all attached to Dawson. The nurse was looking concerned and smiled at me with compassion. I looked at Bill and he just shook his head.

"Dawson," I said. "Mom's here. It's going to be O.K." I rubbed his arm and squeezed his hand. He squeezed back.

I had never seen anyone on a respirator before. It was horrible to see that tube going into Dawson's mouth and taped to his lips. I stood there holding his hand and praying. A nurse came to my side and put her arm over my shoulder. She said he was doing a little better, he was more stable. I was so relieved to hear that. I was not sure what had happened. If they were telling me, I wasn't hearing it. All I knew was that he was alive and I was there with him. And there was hope.

Slowly, I began to understand what I had heard. Evidently, Dawson had some irregular heartbeats early that morning. That was when they put him into intensive care. Then it seemed he must have gone into cardiac arrest. That's when they called the second time to tell Bill to get right over there. I understood they had managed to stabilize his heart and the respirator was making it easier for him to breathe. I focused on the words, "He is stabilized." Then it hit me. If he had gone home, as they had originally planned, he would have died. I asked the nurse if that were true. "If he had been home when all this happened," I asked, "could he have survived?"

"Not likely," she answered. "I doubt that he could have gotten here in time for us to save him." I knew then God must have been watching over us.

Bill said he was not going to go to work, but he had to go back home to do a few things. I told him that was fine. I would be there with Dawson. Before he left, I called my mother and father and my father said he would be right down.

Then Bill left, and for a short while I was alone with Dawson. I said to him, "I love you, Dawson. You're going to be O.K." I prayed and prayed and held his hand.

When my dad arrived, he was visibly shaken by what he saw. He went immediately to Dawson's side and rubbed his arm and held his hand. He said, "It's Papa, Dawson." My father looked at me and said, "He squeezed my hand."

"Yeah, he knows we're here," I responded.

When Bill returned, we continued to stand by Dawson's side. Several times, Bill seemed to be overcome with emotion and left the room. Five hours passed while I continued to stand by Dawson's bedside, holding his hand, talking to him and praying. I had not seen any of the doctors, but the nurses were there continually. They were very supportive and kind and they tried to encourage me to take a break. I was reluctant, but my dad suggested we step outside for a while. When I did, it occurred to me I did not have my car and, for some reason, I felt I should. I also felt I would probably not be going home that night and should have a change of clothes for the next day. My dad said he would drive me to pick up my car. When I asked the nurses and Bill what they thought about my leaving for a short time, they assured me it would be fine. It had been almost six hours since I had arrived that morning. It was now going on noon. I went to Dawson and I told him, "You're doing good, Dawson. You're going to be O.K."

My father and I left and went out to his truck. It was a sunny, warm summer day. He drove me home and I packed some things I thought I might need, shoving them into an overnight bag. I then drove quickly down to my parents' house. When I got there, my dad asked me if I'd had anything to eat.

I said, "No, I'm not hungry."

"You should have something," he said, concerned. "How about a banana?"

"Let's share one," I answered. "My stomach just feels too nervous and I want to get back to the hospital."

"O.K.," he said, as he cut the banana in half.

I wanted to eat it quickly and hurry and get back to Dawson, but I thought I should take a minute and try to calm myself before getting back in the car. I took the banana and went outside on the deck and sat in the sun. Whenever I had sought out a sunny spot to sit in, Rusty would always say to me, "Energizing yourself?" Maybe that is what I felt I needed to do. Instead, as I took one bite of the banana, the phone rang. It startled me and I jumped up and ran into the house to answer it. It was Dr. Burke. He said, "Mrs. Bell?"

"Yes," I said, taking a deep breath.

"This is Dr. Burke. I understand that you were here at the hospital earlier. Why did you leave? You'd better get back here right away. We're losing him."

I heard those words, those words that I had prayed I would never have to hear. "I'll be right there!" I said. I hung up the phone and screamed, "Daddy, we have to go! That was Dr. Burke. He said they're losing him!"

"Oh, God, no," he cried. "Let's go. I'll drive."

I was gone such a short time! I was told it would be all right for me to leave! Now they were telling me I was going to lose him? I can't lose Dawson! God! I can't lose Dawson! He was stabilized! Here I was again trying desperately to get to his side. I said another rosary on the way to keep me from screaming out in anguish. Daddy was asking me questions, but I could not answer him.

When I arrived back at the hospital and entered Dawson's room, I could hear his labored breathing. Every breath was a gasp. The beep on the monitor was noticeably weaker. The nurses looked considerably more concerned and Bill looked terribly frightened. He looked over at me and, again, he did not say a word, he only shook his head.

I went quickly to Dawson and held his hand and said, "Dawson, I'm here. Mom's here, Dawson. You're going to be O.K." The nurses looked at me with sympathetic eyes. I said, "He's going to be O.K." One nurse looked at me with a very sad smile and I said it again, "He's going to be O.K." I leaned over to Dawson and I said, "Can you hear me, Dawson?" He weakly nodded his head. "See. He's going to be O.K.," I cried.

Dr. Burke came in and said, "It doesn't look good. It doesn't look like there's anything we can do for him."

Bill and I could not speak. We just stood by Dawson's bed, staring at our son as he struggled and gasped for each breath. Dr. Burke left the room. My father said he was going home to get my mother and they would be back. Bill and I continued to stand by Dawson's side. Bill looked at Dawson with obvious pain and love in his eyes and he occasionally looked over at me as I spoke to Dawson and as I prayed out loud. Bill had a look in his eyes that seemed to ask "Can you do it, Andrea? Can you get your prayers answered?"

I prayed as I had never prayed before. My prayers came from a place so deep in my being that, before this time, I did not know that place was there. I was begging for something powerful. I was pleading for something more powerful than this doctor, this doctor who had told me there was nothing he could do to save Dawson's life. Strangely, I felt I had more power than Dr. Burke. I felt my power was in my prayers and my inexhaustible love for Dawson. I felt an energy running through me that I wanted to transfuse to Dawson through my touch, so I did not let go of him. I stood, I prayed and I held on to him.

When Dr. Burke returned, he said they were going to do a test, so that he could better evaluate Dawson's condition. It involved sticking a probe down Dawson's neck and we were asked to leave the room. I did not want to, but we had to. Bill and I sat outside the Intensive Care Unit.

As we waited there, a priest came by and asked us if we were the Robertson family. I said, "No, but, Father, my son is in there and he's very sick, please pray for him."

He said, "What is his name?"

"Dawson, Dawson Bell."

"I will remember him in my prayers."

"Thank you, Father," we said.

Bill looked at me as if to say, "That was something." It was like a TV program where the angel arrives in the hospital waiting room disguised as a hospital worker... or... maybe as a priest. Even though it appeared the priest was there for another family, I felt sure he was really there for us.

My mother and father arrived, looking distressed. I hated to tell them Dr. Burke said Dawson had about a 20 percent chance of surviving. They were quite shaken by the news. It seemed to be taking longer than Dr. Burke had anticipated to do the test, and when he finally came out, he said they were having trouble inserting the probe. It had something to do with the vein in his neck, but they were still trying. He went back in and I began to pace.

When he came out the next time, he said they had succeeded in getting it in. We were all seated and he stood in front of us as he spoke. We remained seated and looked up at him as he informed us of the results of the test. He said, "I'm sorry I don't have something better to tell you. It looks very bad. It is not likely he will make it through this." His words cut through me. We sat silently, listening as he went on, "I think his chance of surviving is, actually, less than I had said before. I feel very bad. It's been a couple of years now that I have known Dawson and I care about him. I know I can't feel what you're feeling, as his family, but I am very sorry."

"There's nothing you can do?" I pleaded.

"I'm afraid not. We've done all we can. You can go in and see him."

We went back in, helplessly despondent. We all spoke to him and touched him. His eyes were open, staring up to the ceiling. The nurses said he was quite sedated, but his eyes looked awake. He looked aware and trying, trying to breathe. The air being forced through the tube now no longer seemed to be flowing smoothly. He had to struggle to get each breath, with an audible gasp. It was excruciatingly painful to watch his efforts and be incapable of helping him. The sound of each gasp was both horrendous and glorious, for as horrible as it was to hear him struggling, it was, nonetheless, the beautiful sound of him breathing. As long as he still had a breath, there was hope.

The beep on his heart monitor had become torturously slow. Earlier, it had been, "BEEP...............BEEP...............BEEP." Now it had become, "beep. . . . . beep. . . . . beep. . . . . beep." It was getting longer and longer between those beeps, making the waiting to hear the next one seem like an eternity. And I was waiting, waiting to hear Dawson's heart still beating. It was getting so long before his heartbeat registered each time, it seemed each beat I had heard had been his last. Just when I would be about to collapse at the thought and dread, almost miraculously, I would hear another beep and I would thank God. I would say to Dawson, "You're doing good Dawson, it's going to be O.K. Mom's here."

The nurses came to my side, each with an understanding smile. I told each one of them that Dawson was going to be O.K. They just smiled kindly. One told me, "He's very, very sick."

"I know," I said, "but he's going to be O.K."

"He's very sick," she repeated, with an unmistakable sadness in her eyes. Over the next few hours, I heard this said many times to me as I stood there by Dawson's side, praying and talking to him. "He's very, very sick." They were trying to prepare me for what they believed was the inevitable. I knew it appeared he could not possibly hold on much longer, but I would not give up hoping and believing he could, somehow, pull out of this. One nurse, Bonnie, talked frequently to him. She asked him how he was feeling, she assured him she was there to help him, she told him to hang on.

My mother looked more frightened than I had ever seen her. She sat in the room, appearing horrified and petrified. She had never witnessed anything like this in all her seventy-five years. She looked at me and could say nothing. She wanted to help Dawson and she wanted to help me, but there was nothing she could do. She had always been able to fix things for me when I was upset, but this was too big, even for Mommy. I wanted to collapse and cry, but, instead, I reminded myself that I was the Mommy and that my son needed me. So I stood there and, not for one minute, did I give up my faith in God or in Dawson.

We continued on like this. We talked to Dawson and he nodded, weakly. We held his hand and he faintly squeezed ours. The nurses, several of them, came and went, all looking at me with the saddest eyes. It seemed to everyone to be just a matter of time. I called Claudia and told her what was happening. She said, "Mom, do you want me to come up?"

"I don't know, Claudia, I don't know what to do."

"I'll be there. Let me see what I can do. I'll call you back."

Then I called Rusty at the firehouse. He said he was going back home to pick up some orders that he had to deliver. In our urgency that morning, he had not taken the time to load the truck. "Since I'm going home, is there anything I can get for you? I can bring it to you on my way back to the city," he said.

"Yeah, my Uggs. Thanks, Rusty. I'll see you later then."

I went back to Dawson's side. It was 6:00 P.M. Twelve hours had passed. Dr. Burke entered the room. He stood at the foot of Dawson's bed and he said, "There is one very small chance we have, if you want to try. It is very risky and I do not know that it will work."

A chance? Do I want to try? I thought. *Of course, we will try anything. A chance to save his life!* I asked, "What is it?"

He said, "We could try to get him to the city to see if there is something they can do for him there. They have equipment and methods in their facility that we don't have here."

"Yes! Let's get him there!"

"It is very risky in his condition."

"But, if there's a chance, we have to try!"

Dr. Burke turned around and looked at Bill and asked, "Does he still have his insurance?"

Bill, astounded by the question, answered an emphatic, "Yes."

Dr. Burke leaned over Dawson and said, "Dawson, do you want to try and get to the city?"

Dawson, showing more strength and energy than he had in hours, vigorously nodded his head, "Yes!"

He must have understood. He must have been aware! Sedated or not, he had responded. "Dawson," I said, "we're going to go to the city. You're going to be O.K."

Dr. Burke left the room and I thought, *My prayers are being answered.* I anticipated that within minutes they would be rushing him off in an ambulance, taking him to a hospital that would save his life. I said, "Dawson, we're going to go. It's going to be all right, hon."

When Dr. Burke returned, he said, "He will have to be transported in a Critical Care ambulance. In his condition, it is the only way. Even at that, the move is very risky. I want you to understand it is quite possible that he will not survive the ride. The other problem is, there are only a few of these specialized ambulances in the area. The closest one right now is two hours away."

"Two hours! My God! Can we make it two more hours?" It seemed unbelievable that anyone would expect us to. It seemed unimaginable. It seemed impossible. Could we do it? Could Dawson continue to gasp for air for two more hours? Would his heart be strong enough to struggle to beat for two more hours? Could I carry on my vigil for another two hours? I did not know if I could endure another second, let alone two hours. I was ashamed to admit that I did not know if I could do it. I did not know if I could withstand another two hours waiting for our miracle. It was as though every minute fiber of my entire body, mind and soul had been called upon and had reached its limit. I did not know how long I could sustain that peak of intense will before collapsing. I was so afraid and I was trying so hard to survive each moment, both mentally and physically. I looked at the clock and prayed we could hold on until eight o'clock. "Maybe it won't take as long to get here as they think," I said, desperately.

One nurse nodded, another one shrugged her shoulders, as if to say, "Maybe."

I pleaded, "He could last two more hours, couldn't he?"

She answered, "He's very sick. I don't know."

"But he *could*, though, couldn't he?" I cried.

"He could," she answered softly.

"Miracles can happen, you know. Even in hospitals," I said, wanting to believe my own words. "Dawson, you can do it," I said leaning closer to him. His eyes were still open, looking to the ceiling. He looked aware. "You can do it, Dawson. We're here with you every step of the way." A nurse came around to tend to him from the side of the bed where I was standing. I grabbed her arm and held on to her for support. I laid my head on her arm and cried, "He can do it. Dawson can do it." When I let go, she looked at me in such a way, I felt she knew my suffering.

Dr. Burke came in and said, "You have a choice. You can leave before the ambulance gets here or you can wait for it. If you leave before, you will be at the hospital when he arrives. If you wait for the ambulance and leave at the same time they do, you will arrive later because you must not try to keep up with it. So it's up to you."

I said, "I am not going to leave him. I am going to wait with him. We will leave when he leaves."

Dr. Burke said, "Fine, but I'm telling you, don't try to keep up with them." Then he left the room.

Bill said, "Maybe I should have Glen come and drive us." Glen was a fellow electrician who had come out from Connecticut to work and was staying with Bill and Dawson.

"O.K.," I said. I told my mother and father they should probably go home when we left and I would call them. It had been a very long day. I felt it would be best for them and they agreed.

I went on to pray, sometimes silently, and sometimes aloud. I looked around the room at Bill, my mother, and my father. I felt they were looking to me to stay strong. I felt Dawson needed me to stay strong. Dawson needed to know I believed in him. I looked at him and I assured him, "You're going to be O.K., hon." I had not lost my faith in him nor in God.

Everyone was quiet. The only sounds were Dawson's long gasps for air and the agonizingly slow beeps of his heart. His heart was valiantly continuing to beat, however weak. I looked at the clock. It had been an hour. Time was passing and we were enduring.

"We're going to make it, Dawson. Help is on the way. They're going to be here soon. It's O.K. It's O.K. You're doing good." I stood by his side and held his hand and thought, *Another hour more? Please, hurry!*

Dr. Burke came in and asked us to leave the room. He said they had to prepare him for the move. One of the most compassionate of the nurses, Bonnie, said she would be making the ride with Dawson. I asked if I could ride in the ambulance, too, but she said there was no room with all the critical-care apparatus. Also, his grave condition required they give him constant attention. I understood and was glad Bonnie would be going with him. She had been so encouraging to him and he seemed to respond when she spoke her supportive and comforting words to him.

We were waiting in the hallway when I decided to walk outside through the side door that was close by. When outside, I saw a large ambulance arriving with the words, Critical Care Unit, in big letters on the side. "It's here!" I said out loud. They had made good time. They were twenty minutes early! *We made it, Dawson,* I thought to myself. *We did it!* I ran back in to where everyone was waiting. "I think the ambulance is here!" I cried.

With that, the paramedics walked in. They were angels wearing navy blue uniforms with a bright yellow "EMT" emblazoned across the back. I followed them into Dawson's room. They quickly began to work on preparing to move all the paraphernalia that was hooked up to Dawson. They asked me to step outside to sign an approval to transport him. Bonnie then informed me she would not be going with him, for they had their own critical care nurse. I said to Bonnie, "But she won't be as good with Dawson as you are. He needs you."

She said, "Oh, these are very qualified people. They are trained to deal with patients in critical condition. They'll talk to him and encourage him. They will be good to Dawson."

"But he's used to your voice and I won't be there," I said.

"It'll be O.K. They'll take good care of him and he is very sedated."

"O.K. I know. I'm sorry."

"It's O.K.," she said and hugged me.

As they were about to wheel him out to the ambulance, Dr. Burke came to me and said, "Good luck. You understand he may not make it to the city."

"He'll make it," I said. I looked over to Dawson as they wheeled him out, looking so pale and still. Tears flowed from my eyes and I sobbed out loud. Each nurse, one by one, came up to each one of us and hugged us and gave us their sincere good wishes. It felt like they were almost cheering us on. They stood back and waved and shouted, "Good luck," as we triumphantly went through the door to the outside world. I watched as they wheeled him into the ambulance, surrounded by apparatus and attendants. Rusty drove up at that moment and rushed to the door of the ambulance. He looked in and said, "Hang in there, Daws." I yelled, "We're with you, Dawson," as they closed the door. I said goodbye to my mother and father, then I went to Rusty's truck. He had brought me my Uggs so I would be comfortable. I put them on, my Christmas present from Dawson. I quickly thanked Rusty and said goodbye.

Bill and I got into Glen's truck. The red lights began to flash on Dawson's ambulance as it moved through the parking lot. We pulled up right behind it. As it exited the parking lot, the sirens began to blare. My Dawson was in there, my Dawson was fighting for his life. We were able to stay behind him all the way to the freeway. We all sat silently, staring ahead at this vehicle carrying Dawson. Dawson! Please, God! Although we did not say a word, I knew we were both thinking of Dr. Burke's words, "He might not make it to the city." That was the reality facing us. We might get to the hospital and they could inform us he had not survived the ride. His death could come at any moment as we unknowingly made our way through the traffic to be by his side. I thought, *I may never feel his hug, I may never hear him say, "I love you."* I tried not to think about that and I reminded myself that we had already witnessed a miracle. And I was so thankful. Could there be another? Could he hold on? Or, God forbid, would we arrive to hear that the unthinkable had happened to our son, our Dawson?

We rode voiceless, suffocating from the fear and dread of what lay ahead.

Part Two

"I cared for you in the desert, in the land of burning heat."

—Hosea 13:5

Chapter Ten

It was a terrifying and perilous road I had to travel, but there was no other way. It was paved out before me, each stepping stone being a moment in time. I was heading for the unknown, certain of only one thing; there was no turning back. I had to take each step, thus live each moment, no matter how painful it might be. There was no skipping over the rough stones, nor lingering on the smooth ones. I was being pushed forward by a force that had no regard for what it was thrusting me toward. I had no choice but to continue down that frightening and lonely path: time.

I could see people going about their lives, inhabitants of a normal, routine world, of which I was not a part. I was aware, yet somehow removed. Aware of the traffic, the pedestrians and the declining sunshine glaring in the window of Glen's truck. I watched as the cars up ahead pulled to the side of the road to let the ambulance pass. I felt worlds apart from the passengers of those cars who were experiencing a day like any other day. How could that be? How could Dawson be dying and the whole world just going about its business? It did not seem possible that this horror could be happening while life-as-usual was going on around us. I felt distanced from everyone and everything and so far away from Dawson. I had never felt so desolately helpless. I was alone in the middle of an immense, unyielding universe and so afraid.

My mind was becoming my enemy, for it was taking my thoughts to the outer limits of fear. I knew that fear could overpower me. But for Dawson's sake, I knew I could not let myself succumb. I had to rein those fears in and lock them away. I knew that in order to do that, I had to, somehow, concentrate only on mundane matters. Engrossing my thoughts on some kind of trivial figuring usually worked to avert my brain from panicking. *But can it work this time? What can I possibly find to focus on? What? Maybe figuring out how far it is to the hospital, how long it will take the ambulance to get there. And just how long will it take us?* It seemed we were not going fast enough. Glen was driving way too slowly. I knew we were told not to keep up with the ambulance, but I thought we should at least be in the fast lane. We should have been trying to get there as quick as we could. I wanted to scream, "Can't you go any faster? What are you thinking, don't you know we're in a hurry?" I wanted to scream at him, but mostly I just wanted to scream. For I was, yet again, in a race against time to get to Dawson's side.

I knew I had to continue to try to fight the panic and find a way to stay calm. I tried to talk myself back into rational thinking. *Glen is driving safely, that's important. We certainly can't have anything happen to us to delay us from getting to Dawson. So how long should it take us to get there? About forty minutes? Forty minutes? God, more than two thousand tortured seconds to try to live through. How can I? Tell me, God, how can I do it?*

So far, nothing was helping to ease my anxiety. I tried reminding myself, again, that my prayers were being heard. After all, Dawson had clung to life long enough for the ambulance to get to him and that surely seemed like a miracle. For that reason alone, I knew I must continue to pray and, moreover, there was absolutely nothing else I could do. Finally, I found quiet comfort in prayer and by reminding myself of how fortunate we were to be on our way to get help. I started a silent rosary and settled into a quiet, sheltered world of my own, hearing and seeing nothing around me, immersed in my desperate prayers of hope and thankfulness.

I believe in God, the Father Almighty, Creator of Heaven and Earth ... Glory be to the Father, the Son and the Holy Spirit, as it was in the beginning is now and ever shall be, world without end. Amen. Was it a coincidence that at the very moment I finished my unspoken rosary, I heard, "There it is. That's the hospital..."? Emerging from my silent world where I had been alone with my prayers, I heard Bill's voice, "You can leave us off right there."

We had arrived. We had made it. Had Dawson? *Dear God, did Dawson make it? I cannot hear that he did not. I can't!*

I'd had the strength to get me through this day, but did I have enough strength to face this moment?

I had been unaware that night had fallen as we were riding in. Now, hearing Bill's words seemed to bring everything into focus. I was looking at the hospital, the same building where Dawson and I had gone to see Dr. Thompson, but it seemed strangely unfamiliar to me in the dark of night. I looked at the entrance where Bill was pointing and saw what appeared to be the lobby, but I had no sense of ever having been there before. I sat reluctantly for a moment as Bill jumped out of the truck. Then he looked back at me and shouted, "Let's go!" I quickly got out and followed him as he ran to the entrance doors. We frantically tried to open them as we peered inside. All the doors were locked, the lights were dimmed and we saw no one.

I looked at Bill in horror as Glen drove off. "This isn't the right place!" I shrieked.

Bill said, "I know, there must be another entrance."

"No!" I yelled. "I mean this isn't the right hospital!"

"What? What do you mean?"

"It doesn't look the same as when Dawson and I came here before!"

"Andrea, this is the hospital, it's just the other side of it. You must've gone in from another entrance. C'mon, let's go this way!"

The chilly darkness seemed to encircle me as we started to run down the dimly lit street. As we ran, the sound of our urgent footsteps echoed in the quiet. Running past the shadowy shrubs, I was thinking how frightened I would have been, under other circumstances, of the possibility of someone lurking in the darkness amongst the bushes. But tonight my fear was of what was waiting for us inside this darkened, foreboding hospital building. We ran until we came to the end of the block. As we turned the corner, a huge, brightly lit sign suddenly illuminated the street. It read, in giant red letters, "EMERGENCY." Below the sign was the ambulance garage and just inside the entrance, there was one ambulance. It appeared to have been hastily parked.

Bill said quickly, "We can go in here!"

"We can?" I said somewhat out of breath. It didn't seem like the proper entrance, but I followed.

We ran down the driveway and into the garage. I was glad I was wearing my Uggs. They made it much easier to run and I was running as fast as I could down the grade.

Bill said, "That's the ambulance. That's Dawson's ambulance!"

"Yeah! It is!" It was larger than a standard ambulance and there was no mistaking the words "Critical Care Unit" on the side.

As we quickly looked around, we saw two doors on opposite sides of the garage. *Which one do we take? Do we know where we are going?* One door read "Emergency." I followed Bill through that one and we found ourselves in the Emergency's busy waiting room. We hurried up to the desk and a young woman asked if she could help us.

Bill said, "My son just got here. We're trying to get to him."

I added, "He arrived in that ambulance out there." Then, I thought, *Oh my God, she probably knows something. What is she going to say to us?*

She said, "What is his name?"

"Dawson Bell."

As she shuffled through sheets of papers, I held my breath. Then she looked up at us and said, "He's in Room 301."

He's in Room 301? He's in a room? He's in a room! He made it! He made it! Oh, Dawson, you made it! Thank you, dear God.

She said, "You can go through this door," as she motioned to the door behind her. She then gave us directions, but I was not absorbing them. We went through the door and, this time, found ourselves in a corridor. As we were searching for the elevator, a hospital worker, a large man in a brown suit, approached us and asked us if he could help. He was so kind as he escorted us to the elevator and rode with us to the third floor. He walked us to the entrance of the Intensive Care Unit and asked us to wait there as he entered the double doors. In a few minutes he returned and said, "Someone will be out to talk to you in a minute." We thanked him for his help and he smiled and left. *Did he know something? Had someone inside told him something? Did this kind man in the brown suit know something about Dawson that we had yet to hear?* Bill and I stood there waiting, waiting to hear something, waiting for that "someone" who would be out to talk to us. We looked at each other and at the doors that were keeping us from Dawson. Bill had a look of terror on his face that I imagined resembled my own.

At last, the doors opened and a young woman came out. She was wearing a navy blue and white-checkered dress with a navy blue cardigan sweater, not the usual hospital attire. She looked stern, but when she spoke, her eyes showed a kindness I had not anticipated.

"My name is Lacy," she said. She looked at Bill and said, "Mr. Dawson?"

"No," I answered, "It's Bell."

"Oh, I'm sorry, we have another patient who arrived tonight, his name is Ralph Dawson. You're Mr. Bell, of course, you're Dawson Bell's father, I'm sorry."

Bill smiled and said kindly, "Oh, that's O.K."

I did not smile as I was thinking, *I don't like mix-ups. They can be dangerous.*

She went on to say that Dawson had arrived in very serious condition, "But," she added, "he is still holding on." She said the doctors were tending to him and were evaluating his condition and would be out to talk to us. "You can have a seat in the waiting room," she said. "I'll show you where it is." We followed her down the hallway. The room was a relatively short distance and directly across from the elevator we had just come up on. As she headed back, she said, "I'll tell the doctors where they can find you."

I noticed two pay phones beside the elevators and I said to Bill, "I'm going to call Mommy." I called my mother and father and told them we had all arrived and we were waiting to talk to the doctors. I then called Rusty at the firehouse and told him the same. When I got off the phone, I joined Bill who was alone in the waiting room. It was a very small room with no windows to the outside, but with a window to the hallway. Bill was sitting with his back to the window and I sat across from him, facing it.

I asked Bill, though I knew he did not have the answers to my questions any more than I did, "What are they going to tell us? Is there something they can do?"

"I don't know. I hope so," Bill responded.

Hope so. Yes, hope. There was some hope. In the small community hospital where Dawson had just spent the last twenty-four hours, we were almost devoid of hope. But here, yes, thank God, we could hope.

"Dr. Thompson! Bill, it's Dr. Thompson." She was out in the hall and I could see her through the blinds on the window. I jumped up and went out to her and Bill followed me.

"Hi," she said. "Well, it's very serious. He's in very bad shape." She looked at Bill.

I said, "This is Dawson's father. Bill, this is Dr. Thompson." They shook hands as I asked, "Is there anything you can do for him?"

She looked down the hall toward two men who were walking our way. One was wearing slacks with a shirt and tie and a white doctor's coat. The other was in green scrubs.

She said, "I'll have Dr. Hunt explain to you what we're going to do." When the two men reached us, she said, "This is Dr. Hunt and this is Dr. Harris."

Dr. Harris was Head of the Intensive Care Unit. Dr. Hunt was the surgeon wearing the scrubs. He had sharp features, convincing blue eyes and he spoke rather straightforward with a hint of a Canadian accent. He said, "Dawson's condition is, as you know, very serious. His heart is barely functioning. What I am going to do is put him on a bypass machine. The machine will do the work for his heart, but it is only a temporary measure. We cannot leave him on it longer than a couple of days, but it will give us a little time. We'll see how he responds and then we'll consider him for a transplant. If he survives this, he is going to need a transplant. There is no other option available to him. But first, we have to get him on the bypass. I am going to do the operation and I hope to start by ten o'clock. It will take a couple of hours and I'll come and talk to you when it is over."

We shook hands and thanked him and both doctors turned and left.

I asked Dr. Thompson, "What time is it now?"

"A little after nine."

"So it will be almost an hour before they operate?"

"Well, they have to prepare things," she answered.

"How risky is this operation?"

"Well, there is a great deal of risk, especially for Dawson in his condition. You probably have no idea how risky it was for him just being transported here. But without this operation, he has no chance of surviving and Dr. Hunt is very good." As she turned to leave, she said, "We'll have to just wait and see."

We'll have to just wait. Yes, I knew about having to wait. The dictionary defines "wait" as: *1. to hold oneself ready for an arrival or occurrence 2. to be in expectation or hope of something.* That was what we were doing, holding ourselves ready for an occurrence and in hope of something. But that does not nearly describe "wait" as I'd come to know it.

Bill and I stepped back into the waiting room and sat down. I was thinking, *His heart has to hold on almost another hour before he will have the help of the machine. God! Please, God!* Here I was, living through yet another torturous increment of time, just "holding myself ready for an occurrence." My life had become an endless series of insufferable time slots, periods of time in which to wait. It started with the almost unendurable two-hour wait for the ambulance, then the unbearable forty-minute wait until our arrival at the hospital, now the wrenching one-hour wait for the surgery to get underway and then there would be the two-hour wait for the operation to be over. I was living for the moment when we would hear the doctor say, "He's O.K." But the haunting reality that each passing minute could be bringing me closer to hearing otherwise never left my mind.

Bill broke into my thoughts, saying, "I like that Dr. Hunt. He seems so confident. He is so calm. How could he be so calm? Man, what a handshake, he's got some strong hands. I guess a surgeon would."

"Yeah, I guess. I like him, too, and Dr. Thompson said he's very good. We are so lucky to have made it here. You know, maybe Dawson is going to be all right."

Bill said, "Yeah, he will be. I feel good about this doctor."

"I do, too. And, after all, Dawson survived until the ambulance got to him and he survived the ride here. You know, my prayers are being answered. These are miracles!"

Lacy came into the waiting room and told us there was a cafeteria on the lower level. It was not open, she said, but they had vending machines and tables and we could wait there if we wanted to. She said, "At least it will be a change of scenery for you." She said we could also wait in the lobby and they had a television there. We did both, waited in the empty lobby and in the quiet cafeteria. It was a strange feeling to be in these large deserted areas, so vacant and so alone.

But time was passing and, finally, ten o'clock arrived. I looked at the clock and thought, *O.K., he must have made it to surgery. He had hung on. Dawson, you did it! They are going to help you now. Your heart is going to get a rest.*

We would now begin to wait our next agonizing increment of time, "a couple of hours." A couple of hours! To have to wait another two hours before we could see him and know how he was seemed impossible to endure. I hoped the surgery would go quicker than Dr. Hunt had anticipated. But then I dreaded the thought of seeing the doctor come out of surgery too soon. That could mean Dawson had not survived the operation! *Dear God, please, you've brought us this far ... God, what is going to happen? Can he get through this?* I wondered just how many more unanswered questions I could ask myself while I waited for the next two hours to pass.

Time was passing slowly as we watched the clock and waited. We took the elevator down to the cafeteria, bought two hot chocolates from the vending machines and sipped them there as we waited. We went back up to the lobby and stared blankly at the television and waited. And waited. I was becoming numb with fear as I pleaded, *Please, God, let Dawson be all right.*

We had estimated he could be out of surgery around midnight. When the clock in the lobby said eleven-twenty, I said to Bill, "Let's go up." I knew there was no clock or television in the small waiting room on the third floor, but I felt we had to be there, waiting for Dr. Hunt. Bill agreed, so we went up and continued our wait. Because I hadn't worn, nor even felt the need to own a watch in many years, I didn't know what time it was getting to be. And I did not know how much longer I could wait in this state of controlled terror.

"I haven't seen my dad in two days," Bill said, breaking the silence, "and I had been going every day to see him. You know, he's really bad."

"Yeah, I know. Dawson told me."

Bill said sadly, "He looks really terrible. When I saw him last, he looked like he was … not there." I could see the pain in Bill's eyes as he continued, "It won't be long, I know that and I know I should be there with him, but what can I do now?"

Suddenly, Dr. Hunt appeared in the doorway. He entered the room and sat next to Bill and across from me. He said, "Well, he made it this far."

"Oh, thank God." Bill and I both gave an audible sigh of tremendous relief.

"I'd like to explain to you what we did. We inserted catheters into his femoral artery and vein and then connected them to the bypass machine which substitutes for the function of the heart and lungs. His blood is being pumped out of his body, then through the unit where oxygen is added to his blood and then returned. It is going to give him some needed time. Do you have any questions?"

"How is he?" I asked.

"He did O.K. His heart is very large. It's enormous." Sensing my next question, he said, "That doesn't mean anything at this point, it's not bad, it's not good, it's just big. He's on the bypass machine now, so it is doing the work of his heart. Now we'll just have to see how his body responds. His organs have all suffered from the trauma. With his heart barely functioning, his kidneys and liver took quite a hit. The next twenty-four hours will tell us something. They are critical."

"Tell me, what should I hope for?" I asked.

He turned to look directly at me. He seemed surprised by my question, and that surprised me. I did not think it was an odd question, but I could see that he seemed to think it was. Was it possible he had never been asked that before? He must have been in a situation like this many times and wasn't it the logical question? Other than the obvious hoping for recovery, wasn't it natural to want to know what to hope for along the way?

He then gave me a slight smile and said, "Well, we must hope he does not get an infection, we must hope his kidneys start functioning and we must hope he does not get a blood clot."

"O.K. What is the likelihood of any of these things happening and what can be done if they do?"

"We've got him on antibiotics to help alleviate the chance of an infection, he's on dialysis to get his kidneys working, and he's on a blood thinner to lower his chances of a clot. If he gets a clot there's nothing we can do."

Now I knew what hurdles we might have to face. Now I knew what to hope for and what to pray for. "Can we see him?" I asked.

"Yes, but he's very sedated, you understand."

"Of course. But we just want to see him," I said.

Bill put his hand out to Dr. Hunt and said, "How can I ever thank you?"

As he shook Bill's hand, Dr. Hunt responded, "You don't have to. This is just what we do."

He looked toward me as he stood up and I simply said, with infinite gratitude, "Thank you, doctor."

We then followed him out of the waiting room, down the hallway through the double doors into ICU. We walked through a short entrance area and turned the corner. He stopped at the first room on the right. The room's walls were large panes of glass, from floor to ceiling, covered by light blue curtains. When we entered, I saw what seemed to be dozens of doctors and nurses surrounding the bed. They looked up at us and stepped aside. There was Dawson, lying flat on his back on a very narrow "bed" with his arms outstretched and strapped to two extended "boards." He still had the respirator inserted in his mouth, but his breathing was no longer labored. He was breathing so peacefully and the monitor was beeping in perfect rhythm as he slept. In addition to all the bags of fluids hanging around him and the tubes inserted in his arms, there were two machines sitting on the floor. One was about two feet tall with tubes running from it to his body. I could not see where they were attached to him, as they went up under the sheet that was covering him from his chest down. The machine had a pumping action and the tubes were obviously carrying blood. I thought, *That must be the bypass machine, the machine that saved his life.*

We were told that if we wanted to get closer to Dawson, we would have to step around the bypass and dialysis machines to get to the other side of the bed. Bill and I stepped, cautiously, over the tubes and wires laying across the floor and went to Dawson's side. Despite all the apparatus, he looked so comfortable. It seemed like it had been an eternity since I had seen him restful. Tears of awe filled my eyes.

I quietly said, "Mom's here, Dawson. You're going to be O.K."

Bill did not speak as he gazed down at Dawson and gently touched his hand.

We stood there for a few minutes until the nurse asked us if we were going to be staying or going home. Bill and I looked at each other. We knew we could not go home, even if we had wanted to, for we had no vehicle. I said, "We're not going home."

She said, "You can sleep in the waiting room or even in the lobby, if you'd like. I can give you a couple of pillows and some blankets."

I looked questioningly at Bill and he responded, "Yeah, I guess. We've got to get some sleep."

She gently coaxed us out of the room as she looked at me and said, "Dawson is being monitored and I will be watching him." As she sat down at a little table placed right at the entrance to his room, she said, "I am assigned to him and I will be staying right here."

She must be a mother, I thought. *She must know how hard it is for me to leave him.* But she also knew she could do a better job of taking care of him without us in the way. She said compassionately, "If we need you, we know where to find you. But he'll be O.K., so don't worry. Now you need to get some rest, too. You can come back in to see him whenever you want to."

"Really? I can? Oh, O.K., thank you," I said gratefully.

She went to a rack of supplies that was nearby and handed us some blankets and pillows.

I said to Bill, "Let's go to the lobby because I doubt that I will be able to sleep and I can watch television there."

"O.K.," he said, "It doesn't matter to me. I can sleep anywhere."

"Wait. Here, hold these," I said as I handed him my bedding, "I want to look in on him once more before we go."

I went back, just to the entrance of his room and said silently, "I love you, Dawson. Good night, hon." I stood there for a moment, watching him breathe so effortlessly. It was truly a blessed sight.

As I left his room, I thought to myself, *Is there any wonder how a doctor can fall prey to thinking of himself as God?*

Chapter Eleven

I t was almost one o'clock in the morning when Bill and I went down to the lobby, taking our borrowed bedding with us. Bill settled on one of the many couches, with his legs draping over the armrest. I pulled a chair up closer to the television and put my blanket, pillow and tote bags on it. Bill fell asleep almost instantly and I went to the telephones to call my mother. She had said, "Call me when Dawson comes out of surgery. I don't care how late it is."

When she answered the phone, she sounded as if she had been asleep and her hello had a tone of trepidation. I said, "He's out of surgery and he's doing pretty well. We got to see him. He was sleeping, but he looked good. They're saying the next twenty-four hours are critical, but right now I feel like I witnessed a miracle."

My mother sounded so relieved. She just kept repeating, "Oh, that's good, oh, that's good." She asked, "Are you going to call Claudia? She's working the midnight shift tonight, so she'll be up. Well, actually, she's at work already. But she said you could call her there. It'll be O.K. She wants to hear."

"I'll call her as soon as we get off. I wish I could call Rusty, too, but it's too late to call him at the firehouse. I'll have to wait until morning."

"What are you going to do now?" she asked.

"Well, we don't have a car here, but I don't want to leave anyway. Bill and I are going to stay here in the lobby, the nurse gave us some blankets and pillows."

"Do you think you can sleep?" she asked, sounding concerned.

"I don't know. I'm going to try. But I'm still so worried."

"I'm sure. Well, try to take it easy. We'll be down tomorrow."

I called Claudia and told her Dawson had made it through the surgery. She had been anxious to hear from me and her friend, Sally, had helped ease her wait by staying with her until she left for work. She said Tracy was going to take off work the next day and they were coming up. "That's good. Thanks, hon. I'll see you tomorrow. Good night."

After the calls, I made an attempt to get some sleep, curled up in the chair, staring at the television. Watching television usually worked to put me to sleep by distracting my fearful thoughts. I hoped it would work this time and, amazingly, it did. But not for long. Bill was still sleeping soundly when I awoke a short time later. Sitting there, unable to get back to sleep, I was thinking about going up to Dawson's room. After all, the nurse had said I could go in anytime I wanted. And I did want to, very much. So without waking Bill, I left and walked through the deserted lobby to the elevator and rode up alone to the third floor. I thought how good it was we had been somewhat forced to stay at the hospital, for it would have been unbearable to be home. At home, I would be lying awake just wishing I could be with Dawson, but here, he was only an elevator ride away. As I reached the doors of the ICU, I became almost overcome with apprehension. *Should I be doing this? Is it really O.K. for me to walk in at this hour? And what if he's not all right? Can I bear to see that? Should I just go back to the lobby and try to sleep?* I stood there, about to turn around and leave. *No,* I thought, *I have to see him.* So, trembling, I pushed the doors open and entered the unit. I turned the corner to his room and as she had promised, the nurse was sitting at the small table, watching Dawson. When she looked up and saw me, she smiled, "You're back."

"Yeah, is it O.K? I couldn't sleep."

"Sure."

"How is he?"

"He's doing O.K. But," she said compassionately, "you must understand that his condition is very critical. It is hard for me to say he's doing well. At this point, anything can happen. But he is holding on."

I looked in on him and he looked just as he had when I said good night to him a few hours earlier. I stood there for a few moments, then the nurse said, "You can get closer if you want, you know, you can go around to the other side of the bed."

"Oh, yes, thanks."

I was by his side, right where I wanted to be. I touched his hand and was so thankful for this moment. I looked at the nurse and she smiled at me. I said quietly, "O.K. I think I can get a little more sleep now."

"That would be good. I know it's been a very long, hard day for you."

"Yes," I said, as I looked back once more at Dawson and left the room. When outside his room, I said to her, "Thanks, I'll probably be back later."

And I was, a couple of times. Each time, the nurse was right there watching over Dawson and each time she saw me she was kind and understanding. I'd then go back down to the lobby so grateful for everything and be able to fall asleep, if only for a short time. Bill had given up on the too-short couch and had, evidently, decided the floor was a better option. He seemed to be sleeping quite well, despite it all.

The long night was nearly over and I went to the ladies' room carrying the tote bags I had hastily packed the day before. I washed my face, redid my makeup, combed my hair and changed my clothes. It felt strange to be doing these things in a public place, even though there was no public there at that wee hour. It was the sheer emptiness that contributed to the strangeness. After I freshened up, I went back to my chair in the lobby and wrapped myself in my blanket and waited for daybreak.

Having worried through many a dark night, I knew the comfort the light of day could bring. "Making it through the night" seemed to portend that all would be well. Everything was somehow less frightening in the morning.

I had always found the dawning of a new day to be a quiet declaration of hope and solace. I had never been able to appreciate a sunset the way I could a glorious sunrise. For a sunrise is not only what you can see, it is the feeling of warmth and hopeful anticipation of a promising new day. I needn't be at the perfect vantage point, watching the sun come up over the horizon to appreciate its arrival. I could be anywhere. Today, anywhere was the quiet hospital lobby. It was here that I watched through the window as the light of day slowly appeared. I watched as the dark night sky turned light, light with potential and promise and hope.

Shortly after dawn, Bill awoke. I told him I had been up to see Dawson a few times during the night and that he seemed to be doing all right. Bill said, "You did? And he was O.K.?"

"Yeah. I really didn't sleep much, but I'm so glad we stayed."

"Let's go up."

"O.K. Let me get this stuff together."

I began to fold the blankets. This simple task was to me an unspoken acclamation to the long-awaited dawn and a visible affirmation that we all had, in fact, made it through the night.

Dawson was still sleeping when we looked in, while activity was going on around him. The nephrologist, an Asian woman with thick, shoulder-length, black hair introduced herself to us. She said her specific field was in the treatment of kidney disorders. Then she said, smiling, "He likes this machine."

"Really? He does?" I asked.

"Well, his body does. His kidneys are responding quite well."

"Oh, what good news!" *See,* I thought to myself, *that was one of the things I was told to hope for and one I had prayed for! My prayers are still being heard and answered.*

We stayed in his room until the nurse told us we had to leave. It was time for the nurses' shift change. We were informed that when the nurse goes off duty she recaps her shift's activities to her replacement. In ICU, everything was recorded continuously, hour after hour. His blood pressure, temperature, heart rate, oxygen level, urine output, and various other things were all noted. The two nurses went over these records together, so the nurse coming on knew everything there was to know about her patient. No visitors were allowed at that time, so we left and went down to the cafeteria. It was no longer vacant and quiet. It was now bustling and noisy and had the aroma of breakfast cooking. It was an entirely different place where we now sipped our hot chocolates. I was feeling cautiously optimistic as I faced this new day, Friday, August 9.

Bill said, "I have to figure out a way to get my truck. I don't want to go get it, but I think I should have it here. I don't like being without it. I'm not sure what to do. What are you going to do?"

"I'm not going anywhere. I'm not leaving him," I said emphatically.

"O.K., well, I'm thinking that Carlos might be getting an early start up to the country today. If I could get hold of him, he could swing by here on his way and drop me off at the house. I could get my truck and come right back. What do you think?"

"That sounds like a good idea. I think you should try."

"I'll call him right now," he said, as he got up to leave the table. "I should call my mother and sister, too, and let them know about Dawson."

"You can use my phone to call them if you want."

"No, that's O.K. I'll just use the pay phone."

"Well, give them my cell phone number, just in case they want to call you here."

When he was through making his calls, he came back to the cafeteria. He said, "O.K., I talked to Carlos, he can do it. He said he'll be here around eight-thirty. I'll have to be looking for him from the lobby, so we should go up there pretty soon. I hope I can go in and see Dawson again before I leave."

"Did you call your mom?" I asked.

"Yeah. She and Bev are going to try and come by later."

It was going on eight o'clock, a good time to call Rusty. He would be getting off duty at eight. I figured he would be up and expecting my call. My cell phone didn't seem to be working very well, so I went to the pay phones and called him and told him how things were going. He asked me if I needed anything.

He said, "I brought the laundry in and washed it here yesterday, so if there's anything you want for a change of clothes, I could bring it to you."

"O.K." I said. "What time do you think you'd be here?"

"Well, I have a few things to do. It will be in about an hour, say around nine o'clock."

"O.K., I'll be in the lobby. It's not the one where you dropped Dawson and me off for his appointments, though."

"I know where it is. It's the hospital lobby, not the office-building lobby. It's around the corner from where I've dropped you off before."

"Right," I said. "Bill is having Carlos pick him up and take him home to get his truck. And Claudia is coming up, but I have no way of knowing right now what I'll be doing later, I mean, if or when I'll be home."

"I know. Don't worry about it, I understand. What time is Carlos picking Bill up?"

"About eight-thirty. He said he would be gone a couple of hours."

"O.K. Well, I'll be there about nine. See you later, babe."

Rusty was so caring and he seemed to understand this would not be a good time to meet up with Bill. They had never met face to face and I always felt if and when they did, it would be a very unpleasant confrontation. If that were true, this certainly would be the absolute worst time for it. Dawson's fight for survival was all my mind could handle and I was sure it was the same for Bill, so I greatly appreciated Rusty's consideration.

Carlos was right on time. When Bill left, I was struck by how much more nervous I was feeling. I began to pace up and down the lobby waiting for Rusty. When I saw his truck go by, I ran out to the sidewalk. He didn't see me and kept on going. I waited, unnecessarily frantic, until I saw him come back the other way. He had spotted a perfect parking place right across the street. I ran out to him and he jumped out of his truck and quickly came to me and put his arms around me. It was a warm, engulfing, comforting hug. With the side of my face against his chest, I broke into tears. He stroked my hair as he assured me Dawson was going to be all right. As he gently let go of me, he said calmly, "O.K., now, what clothes do you want, in case you stay here tonight?"

"I don't know. What's here?" I looked through the neatly folded, clean clothes. I couldn't seem to focus on what I would want or need. I fumbled through the bin again and finally pulled a couple of things out and tried to stuff them into my small red bag.

Rusty said, "Put them in the bigger bag."

"No!" I said impatiently. "I think I'd like to get rid of that bag and just keep the small one. It would be much easier for me. I've lugged both these bags up and down too many times now."

Rusty, seeing my distress said, "O.K., O.K." Then, with his help, I did some consolidating of the contents from each of the bags, putting the things I felt I wouldn't need into the bigger one and told him to take that one home.

He said, "Are you sure you have enough?" As he pulled out a shirt from the bin of clean clothes, he said, "Here, how about this? It'll fit in there."

"No, this is fine, really. Thanks. I have enough." I stood there in the morning sun and closed my eyes for a moment as he put the laundry bin and my bag into his truck and locked it. Then he took my hand and we quickly crossed the street and went into the lobby.

He said, "Have you eaten anything?"

"No, but I had some hot chocolate."

"You should eat. Do you want to go to the cafeteria and get something?"

"No, I don't think so."

He said, "O.K., wait here, I'll be right back."

He went into the gift shop and came back with a small bag and handed it to me. Inside were lifesavers, gum and three energy bars. He said, "You need your strength. You probably haven't slept, either, have you?"

"I'm O.K." I looked at the clock. It was now after ten. Bill had left at eight-twenty. He said he would be back in a couple of hours. That meant he could be back about ten-thirty. He could be arriving any minute, but I was fairly sure he would be gone longer than he thought. I wanted Rusty to see Dawson, so I said, "Would you like to go up and see him?"

"Yeah, I would," he said appreciatively.

As we turned the corner to Dawson's room, I saw his new nurse standing at the table outside his room, holding a large clipboard. She was a young woman with short, dark hair and dark eyes. She was wearing a black T-shirt, green scrub pants and white clogs. She looked over at us when we stopped at Dawson's room and greeted us with an unpretentious, "Hi." I liked her immediately. When she spoke, she made me feel comfortable, although she simply said, "I'm Cara. I'm Dawson's nurse today. He's doing pretty well." She had a natural manner and spoke matter-of-factly in a low-pitched voice and seemed confident, capable and compassionate.

Rusty and I moved to the entrance of Dawson's room. I looked at Rusty and watched him as he stood there looking at Dawson. Rusty was not moving to enter the room. Despite his usual invulnerable, I-am-fire-department-I've-seen-everything manner, he appeared undeniably struck by the sight of Dawson lying there so still and encumbered.

I said, "He looks so much better than he did yesterday."

Rusty did not respond to my words, nor did he take his eyes off Dawson. He stood there, uncharacteristically silent and motionless.

Several doctors gathered outside the room, as well. Cara looked at us in a way I felt meant we should leave. So I said to Rusty, "Maybe we should go. I'm glad you got to see him."

"Yeah, me too," he said quietly with an unmistakable look of sadness in his eyes.

Cara said, "You can come back in about an hour, O.K.?"

We went back down to the lobby and Rusty said, "Have one of those energy bars."

"O.K.," I said obediently. "Do you want one?"

"No, babe, they're for you."

As I was unwrapping the bar, Rusty said, "I guess I'll get going. Are you going to be O.K.?"

"Yeah." I looked at the clock. It was ten-forty. "I'm so glad you saw him. Thank you, hon, for everything. I'll call you later," I told him and kissed him goodbye. When he left, I went up to the third floor waiting room, hoping Bill would be getting back soon.

I passed the time looking through magazines, but with no clock in the room, I didn't know exactly how long Bill had been gone. It seemed he should be back. I wanted to go in to see Dawson, but I decided to wait a little longer for Bill to arrive, feeling the need for emotional support. Growing apprehensive, I tried to console myself with the fact we had made it halfway through the twenty-four-hour critical period. But we still had another twelve hours to go! At the end of that period, would he no longer be critical? No one had said that. My thoughts were starting to run away with me, again.

My cell phone rang and startled me. It was Bill's sister. She said, "Hi, Andrea. This is Bev. Is Bill there?"

"No, he went home to get his truck. He should be back any time, though."

"Oh, I need to talk to him." Pausing, she said, "Dad died this morning."

"Oh, Bev. I'm so sorry to hear that! Are you all right?"

"Yeah, I'm O.K., but will you have Bill call me when he gets there?"

"Oh, yes! I will."

"How's Dawson?"

"He's very serious, but one of the doctors told us his kidneys are working better. That's one good thing. We're so lucky to have gotten him here last night. I'm hoping to know more after I talk to the other doctors." Sighing, I said, "I hope that will be soon."

"Well, we're going to try and come by later."

"That would be nice. Claudia will be here later, too."

"Good, well, just have Bill call me."

"I will. Take care."

"Thanks."

Hanging up the phone, I sat there, stunned. I knew Papa Tom's death was imminent, but the timing was devastating. *Will Bill be able to handle this? Just how much can a person take?* This seemed to be too much. He was living with the harrowing fear of Dawson dying and now his father was dead?

Then a chilling, ghastly fright swept over me. I tried to dismiss the gripping fear by telling myself the astronomical odds of what I was imagining, made it an impossibility. I tried to convince myself it couldn't happen. A man could not lose his father and his son on the same day under totally unrelated circumstances. *It couldn't possibly happen! It could not, dear Lord, could it?*

Chapter Twelve

Is he always this calm?"

Bill and I were standing just inside Dawson's room when Dr. Harris questioned us. "I've let Dawson come out of the sedation," he went on to say, "and he seems to be doing extremely well. I'm quite amazed." The doctor was, in a way, seeing Dawson for the very first time. I, on the other hand, was seeing the Dawson I had prayed I would see again.

Bill had arrived shortly after I had gotten off the phone with his sister. As soon as he had entered the waiting room, and before I had a chance to tell him of her call, he asked, "How's Dawson?" I told him he seemed to be doing all right and that I had only seen him for a short while. I told him how I had to leave when a group of doctors came by.

I said, "I haven't gone back yet. I've been waiting for you."

As I was about to tell him about his father, he said, "I think something happened to my dad." Taken by surprise, I merely nodded. With a questioning look in his eyes, he said, "It's true? I thought so. How do you know?"

"Bev called," I said.

"Oh. I knew it. There was a message at home from the convalescent hospital. They just asked me to call them, but I knew."

"You didn't call them?"

"No, I didn't. I knew what they were going to say. I decided to wait and talk to Bev first. I planned to call her when I got here. What did she say?"

"She said it happened this morning."

"And I wasn't there," Bill said, shaking his head. He sat silently for a few minutes then he stood and said, "I guess I'd better go call her."

When he came back from the phone, he said, "Let's go see if we can get in to see Dawson."

It was then that we had arrived to Dr. Harris' question and to the unexpected sight of Dawson awake. His eyes were wide open, he was looking right at us and he knew we were there! It was incredible to see him awake and looking so aware. It was not so much that he had awakened, it was as though he had returned, returned from that place we had seen him slip off to just the night before. He had, undoubtedly, gone alone to the brink of death, but now had come back and rejoined us. I was understandably joyful and surprised, but not as surprised as I should have been. Despite the fact there had been a chance he would not survive the night, a part of me had truly believed if anyone could overcome the odds, it was Dawson. And, yes, I could have bet he would be calm about it, too.

So I answered Dr. Harris' question with an emphatic, "Yes." I said, "He really takes everything that comes his way and just rolls with it."

Dr. Harris, with a quizzical look on his face, unfolded his arms and placed one hand on his chin as he continued to observe Dawson. He stood there as if pondering what it was he was seeing.

As Bill and I moved in closer, Dawson's eyes followed us. "Hi, hon," I said. Dawson lifted his hand. He could not speak, as the respirator was still in his mouth assisting his breathing. Bill took his hand and held it. I said, "You're doing good, Dawson." Continuing to look right at me, he nodded.

Bill said, "Hey, Dawson, you're looking good." Dawson responded by slowly closing his eyes and opening them again, this time looking at Bill.

When Dr. Harris spoke again, he voiced the thoughts he had evidently been mulling over in his mind. "I'm considering taking him off the respirator," he said. "I have never taken a patient off a respirator this soon. It hasn't even been twenty-four hours since he was put on the peripheral bypass, but I'm getting the feeling that Dawson will be able to handle it."

"Really?" I said. "Why don't you normally do it this soon?"

"Well, usually, I can't. In order to successfully get a patient off the respirator, the patient must be both calm and alert. Ordinarily, that is a difficult combination to come by."

"Why is that?" I asked.

"To be able to remove the respirator the patient must be alert, and to be alert he cannot be sedated. And if the patient is not sedated, under these circumstances, he can become quite anxious. It is a rather vicious circle. You cannot remove the respirator if the patient is experiencing anxiety. So if you sedate him for the anxiety and he becomes calmer, he is no longer alert. But as you can see, Dawson is doing very well. He's very alert and aware, yet seems quite relaxed. That's so unusual. I can honestly say I have never seen this before this soon."

That's my Dawson, I thought to myself.

Dr. Harris continued, "That's why I was asking if this apparent calmness was usual for him."

"Well, yeah, it is. He does take things as they come. He doesn't get real excited."

"O.K. I think I'm going to do it," Dr. Harris said, enthusiastically. "Dawson, I'm thinking of removing this breathing tube. I bet you'd like that, huh?"

Dawson nodded.

"O.K.," he said, looking at Bill and me, "I am going to do it. You'll have to leave the room, but you can come back in a little while."

Looking into Dawson's eyes, I said, "We'll be back, hon. You're going to be O.K." Bill and I walked quickly out through ICU's double doors and into the hallway. As I was saying to myself, *Oh, Dawson, I knew you could do it,* and feeling unbelievably lucky, Bill suddenly stopped in the hallway and leaned up against the wall.

"Are you all right?" I asked.

He turned to face me, leaning his back against the wall. He said, "Can we just wait here? I don't feel like going back to that waiting room." Looking down, he said, quietly, "I just can't believe I wasn't there with my dad. I mean, I hadn't been there for two days! I'd been going every day! Why today? Why, when I wasn't there?"

"I don't know, I don't understand why it had to happen like this.

I do understand how you must feel, but there's nothing you could've done, Bill."

"I should've been there."

"How could you have?"

"I know, I couldn't. I had to be with Dawson."

"Bill, you really did. Don't do this to yourself, please. I know how you wish you'd been with your father these last few days, but you did all that you could've done. You'd been there for him every day these past months when he knew you were there. If he were aware that you were not there with him today, he knows now why. He understands."

Bill sighed, "I don't know, I guess. But I feel so bad that I hadn't been there to see him on his last days."

"I know, I know." After a long silence, I said, "Bill, can I tell you a story?" Unfortunately, Bill had never cared for my stories, finding them too long and drawn-out. While he would motion to me, impatiently, to get to the point my solution how to make a long story short had always been to just talk faster. I imagined that his feelings about my stories had not changed over the last nine years, but I wanted him to hear this one, so I asked permission again. "Can I tell you a story?"

Shrugging his shoulders he said, "Yeah, I guess. Go ahead."

"Well, there was this great flood. The water was covering miles of land and was rising up to the treetops. Way up in one of the tallest trees, three baby birds were stranded. They were too young to fly, so would surely perish when the water reached their nest. The daddy bird was going to try to save his babies, carrying them across the raging waters to dry land. He could not carry the three baby birds at once. He had to take them one at a time to safety and try to get back to the next baby before the floodwaters reached him.

He picked up the first baby bird and started to fly with him over the stormy waters. The daddy bird said, 'Baby bird, baby bird, when I am old, will you take care of me like I am taking care of you now?'

The baby bird said, 'Oh, yes, Daddy, I will.'

Daddy bird said, 'No matter what?'

'No matter what, you'll come first. I promise you,' the first baby bird said.

With that, the daddy bird dropped the baby bird into the floodwaters and flew back to rescue the second baby bird. Picking up the next baby bird he asked him the same question, 'Will you take care of me when I am old, the way I am taking care of you now?'

'Of course, I will. I promise, you will always come first. I will always take care of you, Daddy,' the baby bird said.

With that, the daddy bird dropped the second baby bird into the turbulent waters below and flew back to the nest through the wind and rain. He picked up the last baby bird and asked him, 'Baby bird, when I am old, will you take care of me like I am taking care of you now, no matter what? Can you promise me that?'

The baby bird said, 'Daddy, I promise you, I will take care of *my* babies the way you are taking care of me now, no matter what.'

The daddy bird, holding that baby tightly, flew over miles of violent water through the strong winds and carried that baby to safety."

I had to stop several times in the telling. When I came to the part where the baby bird said he would take care of *his* babies the way his daddy was taking care of him, I was so choked with emotion that I could not say that line without my voice cracking and my eyes filling with tears. So I stopped, took a breath and tried again. And again.

After a few such attempts, Bill said, "You know, if I couldn't tell a story, I don't think I'd try." Not surprisingly, it looked as though Bill's attitude toward my stories had not changed at all.

"Yeah, yeah, I know," I said, regaining my composure. I was then, finally, able to finish the story, saying the line, "Daddy, I will take care of *my* babies the way you are taking care of me now." I continued, "Bill, your father understands. You had to be with *your baby.* He knows you had to put your baby first, before him. He understands." Bill looked at me with an expression I did not recall ever having seen on him. He appeared to be moved by what I had said and somewhat consoled, as though I had confirmed what he had already known, there had been no other choice he could have made. He knew he had to take care of his baby. And I knew, at that moment, Dawson would always be *our baby,* no matter how old we all lived to be.

I went to the phone to call my mother and father and let them know how well Dawson was doing. My mother told me they were getting ready to come down to the hospital. By then, we felt enough time had passed, so we went back to Dawson's room. The curtains were open and we entered to find Dawson still lying flat, but with the respirator removed. He gave us a smile when he saw us. We quickly moved to his side, stepping over the now-familiar tubes and cords strewn across the floor. "Hi, Dawson," I said. "How're you feeling?"

"O.K.," he said, in a slightly hoarse voice.

Cara came over to us and said, "He's doing really well."

I looked at Dawson and he was smiling, again. No one could have convinced me I was not witnessing a miracle.

Cara said, "He can have some ice from a cup, but he must remain flat. He is not allowed to even raise his neck. He must stay completely flat because he has a probe in his neck that runs down to his groin and it must not get bent or twisted. You can feed him some ice from a spoon, but don't let him sit up or raise his head, O.K.?"

As she handed the cup to me, I said, "Dawson, do you want some ice?"

"Yeah."

"Do you understand that you have to stay flat?"

"Yeah," he said, showing slight annoyance at my question.

Oh, oh, I thought, *I guess that revelation I had been waiting for had not come to him during those critical moments, as I had thought it might.* He still was capable of showing his I'm-fine-don't-fuss-over-me attitude.

As I gave him the ice, he tried to raise his head and almost sit up. "Dawson!" I said. "You can't do that. You have to lie flat! This is important."

He looked at me like, "Yeah, yeah."

Bill said, "Come on, Dawson."

He laid back down and I gave him more ice. He smiled and said, "That is really good. I'm so thirsty."

"Yeah, I bet. You had that tube down your throat for two days."

"Really?" he said, sounding surprised.

"Do you remember coming here last night in the ambulance?"

"Ambulance?"

"Yeah. Do you know where you are?"

"Novato Hospital?"

"No, you're in the city."

"Really? What happened?"

"You do remember going to Novato Hospital. Well, you needed more care than they could give you, so Dr. Burke recommended you come here. This is the hospital where Dr. Thompson is. They brought you here in an ambulance."

"I don't remember that."

"You were pretty sedated. I'm not surprised you don't remember and it's just as well. Anyway, they put you on this machine and now you're doing really well."

"Oh." Then, as if unconcerned, he asked, "Can I have some water?"

"I don't know. I'll have to ask the nurse."

Cara had heard us and said, "You can have some water, but just sips from a straw." She went to the sink and got a cup of water and a straw and handed them to me.

I held it for Dawson and, actually had to remind him, again, to stay flat. When he finished sipping, he said, "That is so good."

We took turns giving him the ice and the water. He was becoming a little demanding, but Cara was very good with him, no-nonsense, yet friendly.

Not long after, my mother and father arrived. When Dawson saw them, he smiled and said, "Hi, Grandma. Hi, Papa." Dawson had a funny way of saying, "Hi, Grandma." My mother and I had talked about his way of addressing her and we both had found it endearing. He *always* said it the same, whether in person or on the phone. He never just said, "Hi," as he did to me. He never said any variation like, "Hi, how are you," or "Hi, it's Dawson," or anything else. He always greeted her with, "Hi, Grandma," and he always said those two words as though they were one. He spoke them with a slight lilt in his voice and his particular phrasing and pleasant tone combined to reveal a sweetness, an almost childlike innocence, which was a side of him he did not often show. He had a way of touching our hearts when we'd hear him say, "higrammah."

My father went right to his side and held his hand. My mother said, "Hi, Dawson, how are you doing?"

"O.K.," he answered.

"Oh, that's good," my mother said. She looked at me as if she wanted to say, "This is really hard to believe."

I said quietly, "He is something, isn't he?"

Only two people were allowed to be in his room at a time, so each of us took our turn staying with him. We did that until Cara reminded us that it was the nurses' shift change and that we would all have to leave. While we were in the waiting room, Claudia and Tracy arrived and joined us.

Claudia asked, "How is he?"

I said, "Good."

"Really?"

"Yeah, they took him off the respirator and he's talking and drinking and looks good."

"Wow."

"I know. It's pretty amazing. Even the doctor thought so."

"Really?"

"Yeah, is this typical-Dawson, or what?"

"Yeah," Claudia agreed. "So, can we see him?"

"Yeah, but the nurses are changing shifts right now, so we have to wait a little bit."

"I wanted to buy him something, I just wasn't sure what. I decided to bring him this bear. A friend sent it to me when I was all alone in Pendleton to cheer me up. I thought maybe it would do the same for Dawson."

"It's cute." It was a small, light brown bear with a sweet face and moveable arms and legs.

"I brought you some puzzle books. Do you think you'd want them?"

"Oh, that's nice, yeah, I'll take them. I've tried reading, but there were times when I just couldn't concentrate. But we do a lot of waiting, so I'm sure these will be good to have. Thanks, hon. Bill, do you think we can go in now?"

"Yeah, probably."

"They really don't want more than two visitors at a time in his room," I told Claudia. "So, Bill, why don't you go in with Claudia and I'll wait here."

I stayed in the waiting room with my mother and father and Tracy, my feelings fluctuating from guarded joy to lingering apprehension. When Bill and Claudia returned to the waiting room, I quickly asked, "How's he doing?"

Bill answered, "Good."

I sighed and said a private thank you to God, whom I was sure must be watching over us. My father and mother took their turn to go in to see Dawson. As Claudia sat down next to me, I said to her, "He looks pretty good, huh?"

"Yeah," she said hesitantly.

From her response, I realized what looked good to me probably looked far from that to her. He was, after all, still hooked up to ominous-looking equipment and still in such serious condition. I said, "He just looks so much better. You didn't see him last night, you just can't imagine how awful it was."

"I know, it sounded pretty bad."

"We almost lost him. I mean, he came so close."

"Oh, Mom," Claudia said, as she touched my hand. She looked at me as though she understood my anguish. With a hint of astonishment in her voice, she said, "When I was leaving his room, I said, 'I love you, Dawson.' Mom, he said, 'I love you, too.'"

"Really?" My heart was instantly uplifted by her words.

"Yeah, he's never said that to me before."

"Oh, Claudia, maybe something in him *has* changed. You know, I had been thinking that this might be the experience that would help him "see the light," though it hadn't really seemed like it. But, you know, maybe it is."

"Yeah, maybe."

"You know, a person could not get any nearer to death than he was. If we had not come here…"

"I know, Mom. He's very lucky," Claudia said. "I think he liked the bear. He put it on his chest and was kind of playing with it, you know, moving the bear's arms and legs."

"I'm glad he liked it," I said and I was reminded of the documentary I had seen of Coco, a gorilla who had learned to communicate with the researchers. I had been touched by the scene that showed this large, fierce-looking gorilla gently holding a little, gray kitten to its massive chest. As it cuddled it and affectionately played with it, it showed a tenderness that was quite unexpected. It seemed it would be impossible for anyone not to have been as captivated by the sight as I was. And imagining the sight of Dawson holding the little bear to his chest captivated my heart, as only Dawson could.

I said to Tracy, "You can go in and see him, if you want."

Bill and Tracy left the waiting room. When they returned, Bill was smiling. He said, "When we went in, Tracy went to the far side of Dawson's bed, carefully stepping over all the wires and tubes on the floor." Bill had a sudden burst of mischief. When he saw Tracy stepping near the cords, he shouted, "Tracy, you're standing on his air tubes!" Dawson, without a moment's hesitation, obviously not wanting to miss the opportunity of a good prank, opened his mouth wide and began to fake gasping for air. Tracy, with a look of horror, jumped straight up and frantically leaped clear of the lines. Bill was laughing as he said, "You should've seen Dawson and the look on Tracy's face." Bill thought it was hilarious and Dawson had been predictably amused, but I failed to see the humor in it. Claudia thought it was funny and so typical of Dawson. It certainly wasn't something you would have expected from someone in Dawson's condition, but then this wasn't just someone, after all, this was Dawson.

By late afternoon, everyone had left while Bill and I stayed. The new nurse was helpful and informative and we continued to help Dawson with the ice and water.

Between sips, Dawson said, with a hint of a grin, "A few nurses came by and looked in on me. They all said the same thing, like they were really surprised, 'Dawson? Is that you?'"

His nurse smiled and added, "They come by, look in, and do an obvious double-take. They all are amazed when they see it's Dawson. They can't believe how good he looks. One nurse said he looked like Charlie Sheen."

Raising his eyebrows and smiling slightly, Dawson looked at me and asked, "Just how bad was I looking?"

"Dawson, pretty bad."

"Oh."

"But you're looking good now."

"Can I have something to eat?"

The nurse said, "You're feeling hungry?"

"Yeah!"

"Well, I'll see if we can get you something. We'll have to start light, though."

"Whatever, I'm starving."

"O.K. You're going to have to stay flat when you eat, too."

"All right."

When his food arrived, the nurse asked me if I would help him. I was happy to. I was always happy to help Dawson, but under the circumstances, this duty gave me absolute joy, though helping him proved to be not an easy task. The nurse had positioned him on his side. He wanted to feed himself, but was unable to in that position. When he was convinced he wasn't able to eat on his own, he let me help him. I tried to spoon the food to him in a way that he would not have to raise his head and we managed fairly well. Despite his frustration about being unable to sit up and eat like he wanted, he enjoyed his meal immensely. If yesterday, I had been told that today I would be watching him enjoying dinner, I would have found it almost impossible to believe.

It was time for the doctors' rounds. Bill and I had to leave, so we went down to the cafeteria. When enough time had passed, we took the elevator back up to the third floor. As we were getting off the elevator, a nurse whom I did not recognize, but who recognized us from the night before, stopped us. Smiling broadly, she said, "Mrs. Bell, have you seen your son today?"

"Oh, yes, we stayed all night."

She was so excited, saying, "I couldn't believe it when I saw him today, he looks so good! I was here when they brought him in last night! He's doing great."

"Yeah, I know, thanks. It's a miracle." I wanted to cry with joy and pride. She appeared to be beaming and I could only imagine the extent that I must have been, too. I wanted to shout, "That's my Dawson!"

When we got back to his room, the nurse told us he was getting tired. We felt we should probably leave and let him get some sleep.

Dawson said, "How come there's no TV in this room? There isn't even a phone."

"I guess it's because it's Intensive Care. But maybe you can get a TV, I don't know, I'll find out." I asked the nurse and she said there was a portable one. She said if no one were using it, she'd get it for Dawson. She left to find the television and she came back wheeling it. We both thanked her and I turned it on. He seemed pleased to have it despite the fact he could not see it that well from his prone position. I was very glad he had it because I knew he was a lot like me, in that he fell asleep easily while watching television. With him settled, Bill and I decided it was time for us to leave.

As I touched his hand, I wanted to say, "I love you, Dawson," in the hopes he would say, as he had said to Claudia, "I love you, too." But I did not want to take the chance that he might not. I would be content knowing he had said it to her and I would continue to pray for the day I would hear him say it to me. Now, more than ever, it did seem possible. So I just said, "Goodnight, hon. We'll be back in the morning."

I had Bill drive me to my parents' house where I had left my car the frantic day before. When I got there, my mother said, "Dawson called."

"What? He called? Is he all right?"

"Yeah, he sounded fine. He said to have you call him when you got here. I couldn't believe it when I heard his voice."

"I guess not. What a surprise." I called him immediately.

"Hello."

"Dawson! You got a phone!"

"Yeah, they brought it to me right after you guys left."

"I can't believe you!"

He gave me his little chuckle and I could see in my mind how tickled he must look at my astonishment. He said, "When you come tomorrow, do you think you could bring some of that dried fruit you buy for me?"

"Sure, any particular ones?"

"No, I like them all. How about some fresh fruit, too, maybe nectarines? That sounds good."

"O.K. hon, I will. That store doesn't open until ten, though, so I'll be a little later getting to the hospital than I planned. Dad will be, too, because we're coming in together. Is that O.K.?"

"Sure. That's all right."

"Is there anything else I can bring you?"

"No, that'll be good, thanks."

"Well, if you think of anything, you can call me in the morning." I could barely believe I had actually received a phone call from Dawson, giving me a grocery list, no less! "Well, you should try to get some sleep now, hon, I'll see you tomorrow." I said to myself, *I love you, Dawson.*

"O.K. Good night."

This day that I had prayed for had, indeed, arrived and now was coming to a more glorious end than I could ever have imagined. I had said if anyone could come through this, it would be Dawson. Yet I went to bed astounded at his triumph, for even I marveled at the calmness with which he had done it.

Chapter Thirteen

I was out of bed and preparing to face the unknown challenges of the day when Saturday morning dawned bright and sunny. I was hoping to get to the hospital as early as possible. I planned to go to the market, buy the nectarines Dawson wanted and be at the gourmet food store shortly before ten o'clock. The doors of the inviting shop were already open when I arrived and I quickly gathered up bags of the dried fruit that were in bushel baskets arranged against the wall. I knew where everything was and I quickly picked out blueberries, strawberries, cherries and banana chips. When I placed the bags on the counter, the friendly clerk cheerfully said,

"Oh, these are so good, have you had them before?"

As I watched her ring up my purchases, I answered, "Yes." I could have stopped there, but, instead, I continued, "I buy them for my son, he really likes them. He's in the hospital in Intensive Care and he called me last night asking me to bring him some. I'm on my way to see him now. He needs a heart transplant." I blurted out those painful words to that total stranger, not stopping to question why I felt she had to be told. But it just seemed everyone should know that this was not an average, sunny day, that I was not an average woman out shopping, and that my son was not an average, carefree young man.

I did not stop to question why this woman should know or even if she should.

"Oh, God," she said, retaining her lighthearted tone. "I sure wish him well. Good luck to you." She handed me the small shopping bag filled with the treats for Dawson and I hurried out to my car.

Bill was almost ready when I arrived at the house and we left for the hospital a short time later. Though traffic was light and we were making good time, I was growing fretful at how late in the morning it seemed to be getting. Arriving at the hospital and seeing him would be such a relief from the night long, nervous anticipation. It must have been close to noon when we arrived at Dawson's room.

Eyeing the bag I was carrying, he asked, "Did you get nectarines?"

"Yeah, and the dried fruit, too."

"Oh, good, thanks. Can you give me a nectarine?"

I asked the nurse if he could have one and she said, "Sure."

"Do you need to turn on your side, Daws?" I asked.

"No," he said, emphatically. "The nurse turned me on my side this morning and it really hurt."

"Are you sure you can eat it like that?"

"Yes," he said quite insistently. "You know, they didn't even bring me breakfast this morning. I was so hungry and I had to ask the nurse for something to eat. When it finally came, she helped me with it, but I didn't like it when she moved me. I would have rather just eaten it like this."

I rinsed off a nectarine in the sink and handed it to him, while he remained flat on his back. As he bit into it, the thick juice spilled out and ran down the sides of his mouth and his neck. "Ummmm, ummmm," he said, closing his eyes in absolute delight. He looked almost blissful as he savored the flavor and juiciness of the ripe, fresh fruit. It seemed that nothing could have satisfied him more, nor could anything have given me more pleasure than watching him. When he finished it, he handed me the pit and I handed him a dampened washcloth. He wiped his face, neck and hands and said, "Man, that was good!" He was looking content and sleepy and soon dozed off.

The nurse informed us he was doing fairly well, but was still considered in "guarded" condition, which was upgraded slightly from his original "critical" status. He'd had some problems during the night with bleeding from the insertion site and had required units of blood. She said, "The doctors are going to want to talk to you about what they'll be doing next." I had not forgotten that the bypass was only temporary, so I was not surprised to hear the time was nearing when we would have to face the next step. She continued, "You knew he would only be on the ECMO a couple of days, right?"

"Yes. Are you referring to this bypass machine?"

"Yes."

"What did you call it?"

"ECMO. It's short for extracorporeal membrane oxygenation. Did the doctors tell you anything about what comes after it?"

"Not really, just that it was temporary and that when they take him off of it they'll have to put him on something else until he gets a transplant."

"They'll either put him on drip medication or the VADs. Well, the doctors will explain all that to you. They'll talk to Dawson, too."

I was wondering if Dawson realized it had come down to this, the transplant was his only option. He would have to accept the reality of it now. I was glad the doctors were going to explain this to him because I did not want to be the one to do it. Still, I did not want them to tell him just yet. I thought they should give him a little more time to adjust to the idea of the machines.

I noticed blood was starting to seep onto the sheet covering him. The nurse noticed it, too, and lifted up the sheet and looked under it. "I'm going to have to change the dressing," she said. "You'll need to leave for a little bit."

Back in the waiting room, Bill and I talked about our fears, our hopes, his dad. We talked about our schedules and how we would plan our time to be at the hospital as much as we could. I deliberately mentioned Rusty whenever it was appropriate, though I had never talked of Rusty to Bill before. Previously, we both seemed to avoid saying his name. But, with as much as I was going to be seeing Bill now, I felt it was necessary to establish an openness in regards to my relationship with him. I did not want to continue to feel Rusty's name could not be mentioned or that I could not acknowledge his existence. After all, he was a major part of my life. So I mentioned him nonchalantly, avoiding any talk of feelings or any telling of anecdotes. Our conversations, as such, seemed to be going fine. That was a welcome relief, one less thing to worry about, however small. And it was small, in light of what was going on. Dawson's life and death struggle made everything else quite trivial.

"Hi. How're you doing?" I asked Dawson when we went back to his room.

"O.K.," he answered. Then, rather seriously, he looked at me and asked, "Why now? I wonder why this happened now?"

"I, I don't know, Dawson. I don't know why now."

Quietly, with a sad look of resigned acceptance, he said, "I guess it was just going to happen sometime, huh?"

I answered slowly, "Yeah. I think so. That is probably the best answer there is. It was just inevitable."

"Well, you're sure looking good, Dawson," Dr. Harris said as he entered the room. "How are you feeling?"

"All right."

"I hear you've been eating pretty well."

"Yeah."

"That's good. Dawson, you know this machine we have you on is temporary. In a couple of days we're taking you off of it and putting you on something else."

"O.K.," Dawson responded, characteristically accepting.

That afternoon in the waiting room, we had a family reunion, of sorts, when Bill's mother and sister, my mother and father, and Claudia and Tracy came to visit Dawson. It was the first time we had all been together in many years. I suppose it should have felt strange or somewhat emotional, but it did not. I could feel no other emotions beyond those that were entirely consumed by and focused on Dawson. And what could feel strange to me, anyway? I was living an unreal existence, as it was. Spending time with Bill's family was not at all awkward, but was surprisingly comfortable. We were all there for the same reason, to show our love and support for Dawson. He was our common bond and we each took our turn spending precious time with him.

While I was in the waiting room, I noticed Dr. Harris in the hallway. He was standing alone at the elevator, so I went out to the hall and approached him. "Hi," I said, "how is he doing?"

"Fairly well, actually. We're going to have to make a decision soon about which route to take from here."

"I know there are a couple of choices. What do they involve?"

"The drip medication is given through an IV, but the VADs require surgery."

"What are the VADs?"

"The VADs are, literally, a Ventricular Assist Device. It's a pump that is surgically attached to the heart. The device remains outside the body and is attached to a power source."

"But there's a chance that he might not need that? He could get by with just medication?"

"It's possible. We're going to have a meeting, Dr. Hunt, Dr. Thompson and I, to discuss the options. We'll evaluate his present condition and decide upon a plan. But either way we go, he won't be able to leave the hospital until he gets a transplant. The fact is, he will not be leaving here until he gets a new heart."

The reality of his words, though not a surprise, jolted me. It was horrific to know that when we were ready to leave here to take him home, the heart that he was born with, the heart that was, at that moment, beating inside him would no longer be a part of him. Trying not to show how shaken I was by the disturbing facts of our future, I calmly asked, "How much longer do you think you will be leaving him on the ECMO?"

"Well, hmm, let's see, this is Saturday, probably until Tuesday or Wednesday. I'll keep you posted."

Tuesday or Wednesday, that would give us a few days to see him recover a bit from his ordeal. That was good. And it would give him a few days of feeling better before he had to face the next step. I hoped that step would be getting him on the drip medication, but I had the apprehensive feeling the next step was going to be the VAD surgery. *Oh, Dawson,* I thought to myself, feeling utterly helpless, *how are we ever going to get through this?*

I saw Bill's mother and sister coming down the hall. Bev was smiling as she approached me. "He looks really good," she said.

"Yeah, it's like a miracle."

"God, I guess," Bill's mother said, looking away.

Bev said, "We're going to leave, he's getting tired."

As we hugged each other, I said, "Thanks for coming, it was good to see you."

"You, too. Take care and if you need anything, please let us know. And let us know how he's doing."

"We will. And you can call us, anytime. You still have my cell number, right?"

"Yes. Thanks," she said, as they got on the elevator.

My mom and dad left a short time later. After I helped Dawson with his dinner, we had to leave his room because of doctors' rounds. Claudia and Tracy went down with Bill and me to the cafeteria. I hadn't had much of an appetite the last few days, I had been much too tense, but Claudia being there helped to ease some of that tension.

Claudia said, "After we eat we'll go back up to see Dawson and then I think we'll leave, O.K.?"

Bill said to me, "What time do you want to leave?"

"I don't."

"Well, what time do you think we should?"

"I don't know. I'd like to stay as late as they'll let us."

"O.K., that's fine with me."

When we returned to Dawson's room, I waited outside. From where I was standing, I could see Claudia move in close to Dawson's bed and I could also see the nurse sitting at her table at the entrance to his room. Becky, his evening nurse, was a soft-spoken woman with pale, sleepy eyes and medium brown hair pulled back into a short ponytail. She was sitting with her elbows on the table and her chin resting in her hands as she watched brother and sister. It was a touching sight for me, to see Claudia having come to Dawson's side with concern and love and to see Dawson genuinely appreciative of her. Becky continued to gaze at them with a tender, almost misty-eyed expression and I wondered what she was thinking. I was thinking how Claudia and Dawson appeared to be close, yet it was just yesterday that he had said "I love you" to her for the very first time.

Claudia and Tracy soon said good night and left. Bill and I stayed and I tried to find something on television that Dawson liked, but wasn't having much luck. I could see he was tired, so I said, "Dawson, I think you'll be able to sleep, you seem pretty sleepy now. We'll be back here tomorrow. We're coming in the morning, a little earlier than today."

"O.K.," he said.

Bill said, "Take it easy, Dawson, get a good night's sleep," as he gently stroked his arm.

"Good night, hon," I said.

On the ride home, I reminded Bill of our earlier discussion about my riding in with him again the next day. "So, it'll be O.K.?" I asked. It was very important to me to make sure our arrangements were settled. I had always hated to drive to the city, even under the best conditions, and had refused to do so in the last several years. It made me extremely nervous to drive there, to the point of having a panic attack once while driving over the Golden Gate Bridge. I knew someday I should conquer that fear, but I certainly did not think this was the time to try. I had enough real fears facing me each day, I did not need to add to them. Just to be sure Bill understood that he did not have to drive me in if he did not want to, I told him I could ask my dad. I said, "He's probably going in anyway. I know he wouldn't mind."

Bill said, "No, that's all right. We might as well go in together."

When we got to his house, he asked, "So, what time will you be here tomorrow?"

"I'll be here at ten."

I got into my car and drove home. When I arrived, Rusty seemed relieved to see me. I had called him throughout the day to let him know how things were going and I had called him before I left the hospital to tell him I was on my way. He greeted me at the door and was concerned and comforting. He put his arms around me and as he held me, he asked, "How is he?"

"I don't know, he seems pretty good, but I'm so scared."

"I know, but he'll be all right."

I wondered if that were true.

Later, when I went to bed, I prayed that Dawson's night would be better than the night before. Above all, I hoped he would not be worse and that I would not get a call from the hospital during the night. That was my worst fear upon going to bed, that I would be awakened with horrid news. I prayed to God to help us through another night. I said my standard rosary and fell asleep hoping I would not wake up before morning.

My prayer that night was answered. No frightening call came. But I awoke several times, feeling as though I had never been fully asleep. Each time, I looked at the clock and was grateful for every hour that was passing without news. Luckily, I was able to fall back to sleep quickly. Finally, I was awakened by Rusty's alarm. Morning had arrived. Rusty was going to work and I got up when he did, apprehensively anxious to start another day.

Bill and I arrived at the hospital at eleven o'clock. I was walking ahead of Bill toward Dawson's room when a nurse approached me. In a low voice she said, "Hi, I'm not Dawson's nurse today, but I wanted to ask you, is Thomas Bell Dawson's grandfather?"

"Yes," I said.

"So did Dawson's grandfather just die?"

"Yes."

"I read it in the paper, but I couldn't believe it. It said, 'Father of William and grandfather of Claudia and Dawson Bell,' so I figured it had to be, but it just seemed so incredible. I can't imagine what Bill must be going through, his son so serious and losing his father at the same time."

"Yes, it's pretty horrible. It happened the day after we got here."

"How awful. I'm so sorry. Had he been sick?"

"Yes, it was expected, but this is such an unbelievably terrible time. We haven't said anything to Dawson, yet."

"Oh, sure, I understand."

Bill came up beside me and the nurse smiled at him. As we went into Dawson's room, we saw his new nurse. She was a small, young woman in loose-fitting navy blue scrubs. She had a sallow complexion, dark, almond-shaped eyes and long, jet-black hair. Except for a few strands of bangs over her forehead, her shiny-clean hair was pulled back away from her face and cascaded over her shoulders in large, loose, glistening black curls. She greeted us warmly as she introduced herself.

"I'm Cindy," she said and as she glanced over at Dawson, she said, "We like those banana chips." She smiled at him and he gave her a little smile back. "They're my favorite, huh, Dawson?" she said, still smiling at him. He nodded.

"I'm glad to hear that you're enjoying them. That's good. How's he doing?"

"He's been tired, but he is so easily awakened, he really hasn't gotten much sleep."

"How was his night?"

"We had to give him some units of blood, again, because he is continuing to ooze from his right groin."

"Is he O.K., though?"

"Yes, he's tolerating everything fairly well."

Suddenly, alarmed by the sight, I asked, "What is wrong with that machine?" I couldn't believe what I was seeing. The ECMO that was sitting on the floor in the middle of the room was leaking! There was a foam-like substance flowing out of it and spilling onto the floor. Its base was wrapped in towels to absorb the fluid.

"Oh, it's just oxidizing. It's O.K. We've adjusted the settings. It'll be all right."

It's all right? I thought. *How could it possibly be all right that the machine your life literally depends on is malfunctioning?*

I looked at Bill and he, too, looked appalled.

Cindy said, calmly and with, what seemed to be, sincerity, "Don't worry, it's O.K."

"It can't be good," I said. But Dawson did seem to be doing fine. He didn't seem to be affected by it. So I told myself maybe Cindy was right that it was nothing to worry about. Putting my concern about the looks of that machine aside, I asked, "Have you heard whether they are going to be putting him on the drip or the VADs?"

"No, I haven't heard. Dr. Harris is here today, so he'll probably be talking to you."

Dr. Harris oversaw every patient in the Intensive Care Unit, all with their varying conditions. He seemed quite confident in handling such an enormous responsibility. Understandably, he was quite serious, but it was in a rather nonchalant sort of way. I liked him, although I did not feel totally comfortable with him. He was not particularly friendly and was, actually, somewhat intimidating. But I did like and appreciate that he was tolerant and attentive when I asked my unsophisticated questions and he took care in answering each one of them. That was as vital to me as his competence as a doctor. I was surprised to find out he had held this position for several years. I thought he must have been rather young when he took the post, although I did not know his age. He may just have appeared younger than he was in his colorful, tailored shirts that were perfect complements to his ties. His coordinated shirts and slacks were always worn under a crisp, white coat and I wondered how he managed to maintain his well-groomed appearance throughout the long, busy days.

Dawson was sleeping off and on and was requiring his dressing changed periodically, so Bill and I spent a good deal of time in the waiting room and the cafeteria.

"I don't like the looks of that machine," Bill said.

"I know, neither do I. But the nurse assured us it wasn't anything to worry about and he seems to be doing all right."

"Yeah, I know, but I don't like it."

"It does look really bad. I mean, wet towels all around it on the floor? It seems so unsanitary. I don't know, but I guess it's O.K."

"I guess."

As we sat there, we were often silent. At times, we tried to talk of things other than hospital matters. Our conversations seemed to be going smoothly as I continued in the same mode as before, mentioning Rusty whenever appropriate.

Amidst one of the silent moments, Bill spoke. With a disturbing look on his face and an intense frown, he said, "You know what bothers me?"

"No, what?"

"That you were seeing Rusty while we were still married."

"What?" I was taken aback. I thought to myself, *Are we really going to get into this now?* I answered, "That's not true, I was not."

"Yes, you were. You were seeing him when we went to that wedding. You knew he was going to be there."

"I did not. I swear I did not know that." That was the Almighty truth, though it was incredible how I just happened to see him there. I understood why it was so hard to believe.

"But you knew him."

"Yeah, I knew him, but I had no way of knowing he was going to be there and I certainly had not been seeing him. That is the honest-to-God truth," I continued, intent on setting the record straight. "I met him four years earlier, one night when Dixie and I went out. You and Dan had gone hunting and she called me and said, 'Are you doing anything? Since the guys are away, do you want to get together?' She said she had heard about a country-western bar that had just opened up and she'd like to see it. She was in the process of decorating her Circle D Deli and thought she might get some ideas to help her with it. As you should remember, she and I both hated country music and neither one of us drank. We weren't going there for any big night out. We sat at a table by ourselves way in the back and watched the dancers. I had always disliked that music, but I had not been aware, until that night, that it was quite danceable. This was back when the Urban Cowboy fad had just gotten started. You know I love to dance, so when I was asked, I accepted. The man who asked me was Rusty. Right off, I told him I was married. I wasn't trying to hide anything or play any games. I had no sordid intentions, it was just innocent fun. I'm sure you never did anything like that, or worse, while we were married, huh?

Looking back, I realize it wasn't right, I should not have been there. But I assume, and I certainly hope, we both have grown up and learned a lot in these last fifteen years. But it was fun and, at the time, I felt I wasn't doing anything wrong. Because we had such a good time, Dixie and I decided to go there again. We went one more time and, by chance, he was there. I danced with him and that was it. I had not had an affair with him and I was not 'seeing' him. That is the truth. I swear to you, nothing was going on with him when I saw him at that wedding. We didn't get together until after you and I were going through the divorce."

"I don't want to hear any more. I don't care, anyway."

"Fine! It certainly isn't important now, but I would like you to know the truth. I had no idea he would be at that wedding. I hadn't even seen him or spoken to him in four years and, before that, I had only seen him a couple of times. I didn't even know his last name. It just wasn't the way you think it was. It was really a fluke that we saw each other there."

"Whatever." Looking infuriated, he suddenly stood up and quickly left the waiting room.

I knew what I was telling him was hard to believe. Bill and I had not been getting along for quite some time when he received the invitation from a fellow-electrician. He had asked me if I were going and I said, "No, we are not a couple." He said, "Good, because these people know how to have a good time and you don't." I thought that was the end of the discussion and I never gave it another thought until the week of the wedding when Bill asked me again, "Are you going to the wedding?" "No," I said. He said, "I have to work that day, I'll be going there right from work, so you couldn't go in with me anyway, even if you wanted to." It didn't matter, I had no intentions of going. What made me decide to go on the night before the wedding, I'll never know. But on the spur of the moment, I called friends of ours who were going, and asked if I could ride in with them. Suddenly, it was important for me to go, but I didn't know why. When I found out later that Rusty had not been planning on going to his best friend's brother's wedding until the night before, either, it seemed that something big, like fate, must have been at work. Whatever it was, it was something far beyond my doing. I was genuinely surprised to see him there and even more surprised he remembered me. I called my cousin, Dixie, the next day to tell her who I saw. "Remember Rusty, that guy I danced with at the North Dallas? He was at the wedding!"

Had it not been for that wedding, it is likely I would never have seen him again. At the time, he had already quit the fire department and was moving back to Michigan. But it took living through only three winter months there for him to realize how much he preferred California. He returned and was immediately reinstated into the fire department. By that time, Bill and I were going through with our divorce, but Rusty would never have known this, had we not happened to see each other before he moved. When he and I finally got together, it seemed that had been the ultimate purpose of our fateful re-meeting, our predestined reason for having gone to that wedding. But that meeting definitely had not been planned by me.

As I sat alone in the waiting room, I felt ill. This was what I had been hoping to avoid. My plan to speak casually of Rusty had been my way of testing the waters and, more importantly, easing into them. I needed an understanding of Bill's tolerance of Rusty. I needed to know whether or not it would be a difficult situation if Bill were to see Rusty and me together at the hospital or Rusty, alone, for that matter. Seeing Bill's intensity on the subject, I concluded I had my answer. I had been hoping I was just being paranoid to think it might be as bad as this. My stomach was turning from Bill's unsettling reaction. My heart sank at the prospect of what it meant and how it was going to affect me and Rusty and my seemingly friendly relationship with Bill and, ultimately, Dawson. It seemed sickeningly obvious to me if Bill saw Rusty at the hospital it was going to be a problem. I didn't need any more problems to upset me. I was barely holding it together as it was. And I certainly didn't want Bill upset, either. After all, on top of his concern for Dawson, he had just lost his father two days before.

What should I do? I sat there trembling, feeling so alone and sick to my stomach. This hospital was a horrible place to feel alone. I thought of Dawson and how alone he must feel. In order for me to help Dawson feel as secure as possible, it was necessary for me to be stable within these surroundings and with everyone in it. It was a very fine line I was walking, between sanity and hysteria. I had been managing to maintain my sanity, but I felt the slightest breeze of contention could cause me to topple to the other side. This turmoil with Bill felt like a strong, hostile wind and I was becoming almost too unsteady to hold on, but I knew I had to. I had to for Dawson. I just wasn't sure how or what I should do to remedy this unfortunate situation.

I stood, walked out of the waiting room and looked down the hallway. I could see Bill leaning against the wall facing the ICU doors. Despite how upset I was with him, I could not help but notice how striking his full head of white hair and full white beard was.

His hair and beard had turned nearly all white by the time he was forty-five. He had started getting a few gray hairs when he was only sixteen, soon after we had met. I used to joke that it was only a coincidence. Certainly, I had nothing to do with him going gray!

I thought back to that time. I had always thought he was cute, but I just thought he looked cute to me because I liked him. I soon realized other girls felt as I did. But he never encouraged attention, perhaps because he didn't have to. That he did not have a conceited attitude added to his attractiveness. He was so unassuming and rather shy.

As he grew to a young man, he was movie-star-handsome. He had good features, thick, brown hair, nice hazel-green eyes, but for me his appeal was the twinkle in his eyes. Perhaps that was one of the things I disliked most when he drank. The twinkle was gone and he'd look at me with either a blankness or what I referred to as his meany-face. I hated both.

As I continued to look down the hall at him, I was thinking how his angry look today could not compare to those of years ago, but nevertheless, I needed him to get over it. I wanted to make it right. I decided to walk to where he was standing. As I approached the doors, I could see the "Doctors' Rounds" sign was posted, which meant we were not allowed in at that time. So I stopped and stood there, awkwardly silent and uncomfortable. Bill, still frowning, did not speak, nor did he look at me. I moved to the adjacent wall where I waited through a long, tense and unfriendly silence until the doors opened. When we were finally allowed to enter the unit, I walked behind him to Dawson's room. Dawson's dinner had arrived and he asked if I could help him with it. We were both getting a little better at it and when we finished, I left the room, so that Bill could have some time alone with him. Also, I did not want Dawson to feel the tension. When I returned, Dawson seemed quite tired. Bill said, "Dawson, I think we should go, but I'm going to stop by and see you on my way to work in the morning. It'll be early, like before seven. O.K.?"

"O.K.," Dawson said, sounding pleased.

"I'm going to take the bus in," I said. "I'll be here about eleven."

"O.K"

"You have a good sleep, hon."

Bill walked quickly to the elevator and with even more quickness out to the truck. His angry expression had not changed and he was still not speaking. This expression of what looked like contempt was going on much too long. As I rode with him in the truck, the tension was so unbearable for me that I leaned against the passenger door and closed my eyes. The sun had not yet set and was shining in the window, which I hoped would make me drowsy, as it usually did. But I was too upset to sleep and neither of us uttered a single word the entire ride home.

It was unlike me to stay silent, but I had said my peace and I had told the truth. Normally, I would have told Bill how unwarranted and destructive I thought his behavior was. But I did not have what it took to further express how I felt, for it would take energy and spirit; and all of mine were saved for Dawson. I had none to spare. It was as simple as that. I had to take the quiet way out. So I, too, spoke not a word.

We had talked earlier in the day of our schedule for the next day. Bill thought it would be all right for him to stop by at 7 A.M. and see Dawson for a few minutes before going on to work, although it was too early for visitors. I was going to take the bus in and we had agreed Bill would give me a ride home. Now, I didn't know what to think. It looked as though I would have to forget that plan. I certainly wasn't about to ask him if he were still going to be giving me a ride.

When we arrived at the house, I hoped he would mention something of our plan, but he did not. He simply said, coldly, without looking my way, "See ya."

All I could say was, "Yeah." But as I got into my car, I was thinking, *God, I don't need this!*

Because Rusty was on duty at the firehouse, I was going to spend the night at my parents' house. Driving there, I asked myself, *Could I have avoided this? If so, how? Was there a way, was there something I could have done to have it not come to this?* I didn't have an answer and it didn't really matter anyway. It was behind me, now. I decided what was more important was to learn from it and, above all, to try to keep the situation from escalating. To do that, I would need Rusty to help me. I had to count on him to be understanding of my predicament. He had to be the calm in the storm, for I had no choice but to try to weather the disturbance with Bill. I was not going to fight with Bill, for any argument with him would be senseless, irrational, unproductive and, worst of all, damaging to the time I would be spending in the hospital with Dawson. We were under so much stress and it was important for us to remain a strong front for Dawson.

Rusty understood so many things about people and their need to just do what they had to do. And this was one of those times and one of those things I felt I just had to do. I had to avoid any further confrontations with Bill. I had to eliminate any chance of adding to his contempt. One way I thought I could do that was to have Rusty not go to the hospital. It seemed like a simple solution, but I knew it probably was not. But it could be, if Rusty put his own feelings and personal dislike of Bill aside and tried to understand the precarious position I was in and the strain I was under. I knew it was a lot to ask. I would have to be Rusty's priority as Dawson was mine.

I needed him to accept that I would be seeing Bill there every day and that it was important to me that Bill and I not be at odds. I had to have Rusty look beyond his own needs and indulge me in mine at this most desperate time in my life. But I was worried how he would take such requests, for he had already started looking at me questioningly, as if I were dressing up for someone, when I was merely dressing for my long days at the hospital. I had to ask him to allow me to go to Dawson, however and whenever I needed to and to be able to do it free of any unwarranted guilt.

I just don't want to make Rusty mad, I said to myself. *I hope he won't be angry with me.*

Continuing my solitary conversation, I asked, *When should I tell him?* I answered, *He'll be at the firehouse until the morning and I will be talking to him on the phone tonight, but I don't want to discuss this with him until I see him. But I should say something to him tonight because his firehouse is so close to the hospital he could decide to go by when he gets off duty in the morning and that could be bad. Wait, no, that should be O.K. Bill will be going by earlier than Rusty would be. It's not likely they will run into each other.*

I was driving to my parents' house, but I was also driving myself crazy. This was just the kind of thing I didn't need to be worrying about. I was becoming overwrought just imagining the what-ifs: What if Rusty gets mad, what if Bill stays mad, what if there's a confrontation, what if Dawson sees it?

Stop this, I said to myself. *Just wait and tell Rusty your honest feelings when you see him at home tomorrow. Tell him you think it best he not chance going to the hospital just yet, and maybe he will be understanding. Maybe he will accept that, for now at least, as unreasonable as it seems, this is the way it has to be.* I hoped Rusty would realize the whole situation was potentially explosive due to the tension we were under. And, hopefully, the pressure would be subsiding soon, as Dawson's condition improved.

I tried to convince myself I was just over dramatizing the situation, but I was beginning to feel overwhelmed by my circumstances, caught in the middle, weak and vulnerable. It was all just too much. Pleading out loud, I begged, "No more, God. Please, no more."

Chapter Fourteen

I gave myself an excessive amount of time to catch the 8:21 A.M. bus. I could not subject myself to the anxiety and fear that I might miss it. Simply running late would have thrown me into an unnecessary state of panic. My nerves were such that I had to take care in everything I did in a deliberate attempt to avoid any upsets. I was aware that, at any given moment, I could become too distraught to handle even the slightest predicament.

I was not certain where the bus depot was located, but I had a general idea and, thankfully, found it easily. Yet, despite all my precautions, I was feeling panicky as I drove into the large parking lot. The lot seemed full and I nervously asked myself, *Where am I going to park? What if there are no available spaces?* My anxiety was starting to build as I drove to the far end of the lot. It was a distance from the ticket depot, but I was relieved to find plenty of spaces there. I hurriedly parked and got out of the car, ridiculously worrying, *Is it getting late?* I tried to assure myself that I couldn't possibly be late. I had allowed plenty of time for getting lost, parking, and any unexpected delays. Nonetheless, I began to walk quickly, almost running, feeling slightly frantic. *For God's sake, calm down! Taking the bus shouldn't be this unnerving. Why is this so unsettling? Would everyone feel this uneasy in an unfamiliar bus stop or is it just me? Or is it just the circumstances under which I'm traveling?*

Whatever the reason, I found myself unable to shake my nervousness as I boarded the empty bus. I continued to question my every move and hesitantly chose a seat. *I hope this is the right bus, it did say Number Eighty, didn't it?*

When the driver got on a few minutes later, he looked at me sitting alone in the back of the vacant bus and smiled and said, "Good morning."

I responded, "Good morning." Getting up from my seat and moving to the middle section of the bus, I said to the friendly driver, "I'm going to California Street, do you stop there?"

"Sure do," he said.

O.K., I thought, taking a breath, *maybe I can relax a little, now.*

After he placed a small duffle bag behind his seat and had filled the token box with change, he stepped off the bus. I guessed that I must have been very early and I wondered how long it would be until departure. I took out the morning paper from my tote bag and started to look through it. Maybe I could do a crossword puzzle. Maybe not. I was distracted by my thoughts of Dawson, Rusty and Bill. One minute I could see Dawson smiling, the next all I could see was the life-support equipment to which he was attached. As for Rusty, I was fretting over the fact I had not told him of the dissension that had built up between Bill and me. It was important that he know soon, for it was going to impact on his plans of visiting Dawson. And what was Bill's attitude going to be when I saw him later that day? Would he, with his scowling silence, continue to show his anger with me? Would he make me feel as uncomfortable as he had the day before?

The driver at last returned, settled into his seat and started up the bus' noisy motor, letting it idle for a few minutes before proceeding out of the depot. As we slowly moved out onto the street and into the sunlight, I sighed. *O.K, Dawson, I'm on my way. Mom's coming to be with you.* The thought of him waiting for me filled me with both joy and fear. What a blessing to be able to visit him. How lucky I felt that he was there, waiting! Yet, how afraid I still was, knowing that anything could happen at any moment. Still, I knew I could never be as frightened as I had been when we were on our way to the hospital last Thursday with Dawson in that ambulance.

What was that, five days ago? I had lost count. *Let me think. Yeah, that's right, this terrifying nightmare began last Wednesday night when he went to the community hospital. That was six days ago. My God, it's been almost a week!* Feeling the weight of those spent days, I slowly slouched down in my seat. I stared out the window and as the bus made its stops for passengers, I wondered with envy where the bus was taking them. I was going to visit my son in Intensive Care. This had become how I defined myself, as a mother whose son needed a new heart. In doing this, I had set myself apart from everyone. I felt as though there was no one living through what I was, no one who could know the fear and anguish I was feeling.

The bus was full by the time we made the last stop before crossing the Golden Gate Bridge. As I looked out over the bay, for one quick moment I thought, simply, *What a pretty day.* It was a picturesque sight, the San Francisco skyline emerging from the sparkling water. But in a blink, my thoughts returned to the matters at hand as I focused on the road ahead. As we neared the city, I worried I would not recognize my stop. Would the driver tell me when we were there? Maybe, but I thought it was unlikely. Yet, after we got into the city, he started calling out the names of all the stops. I was so relieved when I heard, "California Street." I quickly stood up and pulled the buzzer. Still afraid of missing my stop, I made my way to the front door weaving from side to side while the bus was still moving. I was standing alongside the driver's seat when we came to a halt. As I stepped off, I said, "Thank you," to the driver and he responded, "Have a nice day." I thought, *A nice day. That sounds so simple, like it shouldn't be too much to ask. "Have a nice day" … was that a command, as if I had some control over the events of my day? Or was it meant kindly as in, "Hope you have a nice day?" If so, could this stranger's nonchalant wish for me have some unsuspected power? Could it come true, could I have a nice day?*

I walked up the steep hill to catch the city bus that would take me to the corner several blocks away. From that corner, I hurried down the block to the hospital and was out of breath when I reached the entrance. I wasn't sure how much of my panting and thirst was from actual physical exertion and how much of it was sheer anxiety. I entered the hospital lobby, took the elevator up to the third floor and walked into ICU. It was the first time I had arrived there alone. I was realizing how much more frightening that was. Before I rounded the corner to Dawson's room, I was aware of the sound of labored breathing, though not labored in the same way I had heard Dawson breathing before. This was different, it wasn't gasping, more like panting. It was audibly rapid and definitely unnatural and it seemed to be coming from his room. *Please, God, no,* I thought. As I entered his room, my hopes were shattered to see it was Dawson who was breathing so strenuously.

"What's wrong?" I asked the nurse.

"It's not as bad as it sounds," she said. "It's the oxygenation of the ECMO. He really doesn't have to breathe fast, but his brain is telling him that he does."

I thought, *What the Hell does that mean? He looks like he must feel terrible. What is happening to him?* Although thoroughly frightened and dismayed, I tried to smile and said, "Hi, Dawson."

"Hi," he said, in a strained voice.

I looked at the nurse, pleadingly. She smiled and tried to reassure me. "He's doing O.K.," she said. I was glad his nurse was Cara because I liked her and trusted her from that first day he was here. She said, "Dr. Harris wants to talk to you."

"Where is he? I need to talk to him, too." I had to hear what he could tell me about Dawson's changed condition.

"Oh, I'm sure he'll be by."

"Dawson, you're O.K., hon. The nurse says it's nothing to worry about, but how do you feel?"

"Ummm," he groaned, frowning.

"That's too bad, hon. Well, I'll see what the doctor has to say." I touched his hand, mustered up half a smile and left his room in search of the doctor. He was at the nurse's station just outside Dawson's room. He saw me approaching and came out from behind the desk to meet me. He raised his eyebrows and gave me a knowing look in anticipation of my unasked question.

"Well, he's obviously having some distress," he said. "We've readjusted the ECMO, but it hasn't helped much, so we want to get him off that machine. We could put him on another ECMO, but, you know, it would be just temporary, anyway. So, inasmuch as he was going to be coming off of it in a couple of days, we think we might get on to the next procedure, though it is a little sooner than we had planned. Since he is having these difficulties, we are going to have to make some decisions soon."

"So you don't know whether you'll be putting him on the VADs or when you'll be taking him off this ECMO?"

"No, I'm not sure yet. We're going to meet later today to decide."

"Is it true that he looks worse than he is? I mean that breathing?"

"Yes, he's just uncomfortable. Well, I'll let you know when we make a decision."

I stood there for a moment as he turned and left, my mind absorbing the fact that we were approaching the next step. What would it be? What was waiting ahead for us? I hated the thought of them putting Dawson through surgery. How much better it seemed if a medication could work for him, but I did believe the VADs were what he needed. I could only pray that, whatever the procedure, it would be successful and Dawson would get well. I went to the waiting room and called Rusty to tell him of the latest development and he tried to comfort me. I went back to Dawson's room and found him looking exhausted. I could see it would be a strain for him to speak, so I sat quietly by his bedside. Cara said she had been told it would be a couple of hours before we would know what the doctors had decided. She said, "They're in a meeting."

I sighed nervously, "I know. We'll just have to wait."

She seemed to want to help me and asked, "Do you know what the VADs are?"

"Yeah, kind of. I know they are pumps and that they would be attached to him and that lines attach them to the power source."

"Do you know what they look like?"

"No."

"Do you think you'd like to see one?"

"Can I?"

"We have a patient on one, so I could show you. Wait here." When she returned just minutes later she said, "I'm not so sure I should take you into her room, so I won't be able to show you the pumps themselves. But I can show you the power unit, there's one that isn't hooked up. It's a backup unit out in the hall." As I followed her out of Dawson's room, she said, "It kind of looks like a washing machine." She went on to explain, "For every patient on the VADs, there is a backup. If Dawson goes on one, there'll be two backups." She stopped walking. "This is it," she said. There was the unit I had passed every day on my way to Dawson's room, unaware of what it was. She was right, it was about the size and shape of a washing machine, but it was slightly taller and it wasn't flat on top, it was slanted. On the slant there were gauges and buttons and dials. It was greenish-beige in color, had wheels, and a handle across the front with which to push or pull it. Cara said she'd had patients that did so well on the VADs they were able to get up and walk around, pushing it. It seemed that would be quite an accomplishment, for she said it weighed about three hundred and fifty pounds. Cara showed me where the hoses from the pumps attached to it. She looked at me and asked, "Do you have any questions?"

"How do the VADs differ from the ECMO?"

"The ECMO can only be used for a short period of time, preferably only for a few days. Its function is to oxygenate the blood as it bypasses the heart and lungs. The VADs are meant to sustain a patient for several months, even up to a year, as it assists the heart's pumping function. Tubes from the pumps are attached to the heart through the abdomen. The pumps remain outside the body and rest on the stomach. Lines come from the pumps, attaching them to the power unit."

O.K., I thought, *I've become accustomed to seeing Dawson with tubes and lines, even the ones that were visibly carrying his blood to and from his body. I can handle this.* We went back to his room and I began to wait and to think. Earlier, I had been so concerned about how unfriendly Bill was going to be when he arrived that afternoon. Now, that was no longer important. My only concern was Dawson. As I sat quietly at his side, I wanted to cry out, "Please, somebody, tell me he's going to be all right."

An hour or two had passed by the time Dr. Harris came in and checked on Dawson and motioned to me to step outside of his room. He said, "We have decided to put him on the VADs. His heart is shot, there is no way he could manage without them."

"That's what I expected."

"We're going to do it today, around four o'clock."

"Today? Really?"

"Yes, we don't want to wait. I'm going to tell Dawson what we are going to do, but I'm not sure how much he will comprehend. I've had him slightly sedated to make him a little more comfortable."

"I know the VADs are a 'bridge to transplant.' Are you going to tell him that? I don't know if he really knows that he has to have one. Can we wait to say that?"

"All right. I'm going to talk to him now."

I went to the waiting room and paged Bill. It was proving to be true, you just never know what's going to happen from one minute to the next. You can imagine this and imagine that, prepare for this and that, but it really doesn't mean anything. That morning I had been so worried about Bill's mood and his attitude toward me. I had imagined I would be nervously anticipating his arrival after work, wondering if he would speak to me, imagining I might have to make the uncomfortable decision to speak first. I had not imagined this, that I would be calling him at work, telling him they were going to put Dawson on an artificial heart in just a few hours.

Shortly after I had paged him, my phone rang, "Hi," Bill said. "What is it?"

"They're going to put him on the VADs this afternoon."

"What? Why?"

"It's that ECMO. It's still not right. He's having trouble breathing. Dr. Harris said they want to get him off of it. They're not going to wait, they're planning on doing it about four o'clock."

"O.K., I'll be there. I'll be as quick as I can."

"Good, thanks. I'll see you." There was no more attitude, no more petty mood, there was only our love and concern for Dawson.

When I returned to Dawson's room, he was sleeping. His breathing was still so rapid it was painful to see, yet I sat in the chair beside his bed and watched him. I prayed and I worried and I waited.

A woman entered the room and introduced herself as Joyce Toohey, a social worker with the heart transplant unit. She had short brown hair, a friendly face, and was dressed in a tan skirt and print blouse. She was smiling a sympathetic smile. "Mrs. Bell, I'm here to answer any questions you might have and to help you understand what to expect if Dawson gets a transplant. Would you like to talk?" I looked at Dawson. He was sleeping, so I stood and nodded to the social worker and followed her out into the hall. "Let's go to the waiting room," she said. As we exchanged questions and answers, I found her to be very easy to talk to. She was understanding, knowledgeable and extremely informative. She told me of patients she knew who had been on the VADs. She explained what was involved with them and further, about recovery, rejection, and medication after a transplant. She said she conducted a support group for transplant patients and their families. "We meet once a month and we're meeting this Saturday. I think it would be beneficial for you to attend. You'd meet some of our patients who have had heart transplants and you could see how well they're doing. It's a little discussion group. Do you think you would like to come?"

"Yes, I would. Where is it?"

"Right here in the hospital, on the first floor. Do you think Dawson's dad would like to attend? Here, I'll give you a flyer."

"I don't know, I'll ask him. Thank you so much."

She reached out and shook my hand. "I know how difficult this is for you. My number is there. Call me anytime if you have any questions."

I thanked her again, feeling so grateful to her and the many caring, competent and helpful people I had met that week.

I was back in Dawson's room when Bill arrived. He entered the room, his eyes asking, "What happened?" I just shook my head. He went directly to Dawson who was still panting and visibly exhausted. Dawson acknowledged him as Bill touched his hand. Then he sleepily closed his eyes. It was so painful to see Dawson having relapsed, especially after we had experienced such joy at seeing him smiling just the day before.

Bill and I went out into the hall. "I knew that ECMO was bad yesterday!" Bill said. "What were they doing about it? How could they have left him on that when it wasn't working right? That's why he's having this trouble now!"

"I know, but they're going to take him off of it. Maybe this is one of the reasons they don't leave anybody on that ECMO for more than a couple of days. They said it degenerates the blood or something. Maybe this is just the normal course of things. He was going to have to come off of it, anyway. This is just a little sooner than it would've been." I relayed to him all that I had learned about the VADs and I showed him the one in the hallway. I told him we should expect the operation to take about six hours. He appeared to wince at the thought of a six-hour wait. I knew how he felt and I wondered how we would endure it. I told him at least Dawson was probably not aware of what was going on. He had been quite drowsy when Dr. Harris explained to him what they were going to do. I was glad for that. It spared him the anxiety. There was nothing that could spare me. I knew I had to keep my thoughts and fears under control, but could I? How would I manage to do that, yet again? Could it be possible the events of the week had helped to make me stronger, actually strengthening my ability to endure this extreme fear? Or had the stress of it all only weakened my capacity to endure another minute? Had I, in fact, reached my limit? And what if I had? What would that mean? I had no answers to my tortured questions. All I knew was that I was just so afraid and had been so for what seemed like a very long time.

We went back to his room and I began to watch the clock. When it was getting close to four o'clock and it did not appear any preparations were being made, we were informed that the surgery was going to be delayed. On one hand, I was glad to have the extra time with Dawson,

just to be close to him, to look at him. Yet, on the other hand, I hated
the delay, for it lengthened our wait and prolonged that minute when
he would be out of surgery. And, oh, how I wanted that surgery to be
behind us. Oh, to see him breathing peacefully again.

We sat waiting and then watching as activity surrounding Dawson
increased. And then it was time for them to take him in. Although he
was quite sedated, I held his hand and said, "Everything's going to be
all right, Dawson. We're here, we're right here. We'll be waiting." They
wheeled him out, tubes and lines draped around him. It was close to
six o'clock when Bill and I walked silently from his empty room.

Out in the hall, Bill asked, "Where do you want to go? The
cafeteria?"

"I guess so. I'm going to make some calls, first, though. Are you?"

"Yeah, I'll call my mother."

I went to the waiting room and called Rusty and my mom and
dad and told them Dawson had been taken into surgery and that he
would be in there for about six hours. Midnight! God, this was so
terrifying. I reminded myself we were so lucky and though this was a
nightmare, it was also a miracle. This surgery was not even available
a few years ago and without it he could not survive. But the dreadful
fact was that even with it, he still might not! *Dawson, I can't lose you!
Please, God, please, don't let that happen!*

Bill and I moved to the lobby for a change of scenery and to watch television. But it didn't help. The wait was agonizing. At about eight o'clock,
as we sat quietly in the empty lobby, suddenly Bill said, "That's Matt!"

"Who? Where?"

"Matt. He's at the door. He can't get in."

"Dawson's friend, Matt?"

"Yeah," Bill said as he rushed to the door. The doors were locked,
both from the inside as well as the outside. Bill motioned to Matt to
go down the outside stairs, then turned toward me. "C'mon," he said.
I quickly got up and followed him as he hurried to the elevator. We
took it down to the cafeteria level and rushed past the cafeteria to
an outside entrance where there sat a stern-looking guard. He was
talking to Matt, telling him he could not enter.

Bill said, "He's with us. Bell."

The unfriendly guard checked his computer screen and said, "O.K.,
but you can't go up, you have to stay here."

Matt, looking at me as he entered said, "Hi, this is Jenn. I don't
think you've met."

"Hi, no, we haven't." I looked at her and, strangely, felt an instant kinship. She reached out her arms and we hugged each other. Matt was saying to Bill, "What happened? I just found out tonight that he was in the hospital."

Bill said, "He wasn't feeling well last Wednesday, so we went to Novato Hospital. While he was there, we almost lost him. They didn't think he was going to make it and they rushed him here."

I said, "They're operating on him right now. They're putting him on an artificial heart."

Matt looked pale and shocked, Jenn looked concerned and sad. Bill went on to explain how Dawson had been quite good for a couple of days and how this was going to buy him some time until he got a transplant.

"He's going to need a transplant?" Matt asked.

"Yes," I answered.

Matt looked down, slowly shaking his head. When he looked up, he asked, "How long is this surgery going to take?"

I said we were not expecting him to be out before midnight. Matt looked at Jenn and she moved closer to him. I sensed the love they shared for one another and for Dawson.

We stood there in the corridor talking for a long time. It was good for Bill and me to have someone else to talk to aside from each other. It was after ten o'clock when Matt said, "I guess we should go. Will you let me know how he is?"

"Yeah, I will," Bill said.

I said to Jenn, "I'm so glad we met. I just wish it had been under better circumstances."

She nodded in agreement.

Bill and I went back to the lobby to continue our wait. We were alone again in the quiet when I heard footsteps approaching. A wave of panic rushed over me. Knowing it was too soon for the surgery to be over, I feared it was someone coming to tell us the worst had happened. I sat frozen, my heart pounding, as the footsteps came closer. A large man in a maroon uniform-jacket came into view. As he passed us and went on to check the locked doors, I sighed in relief. He made this round several times and each time, when I realized the footsteps were his, passing us by, I said a silent prayer of thanks. A few times he smiled over at us. I was able to smile back because I was aware I had just lived through a moment when the dreaded had not happened, no one had come to tell us what I most feared.

Those moments of relief were linked to tense minutes that added up to agonizing hours spent waiting.

Those hours finally passed and it was time to go up to the waiting room where Dr. Hunt would meet us after surgery. Was it possible that those last few minutes of waiting could be more torturous than the past several hours combined? It felt that way. *Please, God, help us through this, let everything be all right!*

While in the lobby, Bill had managed, from time to time, to doze off in a chair, but here we were both nervously awake when Dr. Hunt came through the door. He was still in his scrubs and as he entered, he stopped and casually removed the light blue booties covering his shoes. He tossed them, stained with Dawson's blood, into the wastebasket. He said, "Well, he did fine."

"Oh, thank you!"

"Now, we'll just have to see how he does from here. Hopefully, he won't have any complications before we transplant him. But at least we don't have to worry about his heart now."

"Can we see him?"

"Not yet. The nurse will let you know when they're ready for you. I should tell you, he doesn't look too good."

"What do you mean?"

"We had a problem with the line in his neck. He has a hema-toma."

Alarmed, I said, "What's that?"

"A bruise."

"Oh. We just want to see him," I said.

"I know, I wanted to prepare you," Dr. Hunt said. He shook Bill's hand and left.

I thought, *A bruise? That doesn't sound that serious. How bad could it be to see a bruise after all we have been through? And he is O.K. He lived through the surgery! This moment has finally arrived, the surgery is over and he made it! That's all that matters.* Bill and I sat there grateful, relieved and quiet.

Shortly after, a man wearing navy blue scrubs came in and said, "Mr. and Mrs. Bell?"

"Yes."

"My name is Bill. I'm Dawson's nurse. Would you like to see him?"

"Oh, yes!"

"O.K., come with me." As we followed him down the hall, he said, "He has a large hematoma on his neck."

"Yes, Dr. Hunt told us." Again, I was thinking, *How could that matter? Just to see him! Alive! And breathing peacefully! Why is everyone making such a big deal out of a bruise? He will look beautiful to me!*

We followed him into ICU and passed the empty room where Dawson had been. He was now two rooms down. Bill entered and I followed, a few steps behind. I was not prepared for what I saw. He lay under the glare of several harsh fluorescent lights, completely bare except for a sheet that was draped across his thighs and groin and there was a shocking, overall paleness to his skin. He was strapped down flat, with his arms outstretched, giving the ghastly appearance of a naked body laying atop a table. Enormous, round machines were mounted to his stomach. An extremely large, ruddy-purple lump protruded from his neck. Huge tubes were everywhere on his body. There were two main tubes sutured directly into his abdomen. Large bandages surrounded the wound. A horrific sound of clanking and sloshing filled the room. As I slowly moved closer and closer, I focused on the source of that horrendous sound. The pumps, attached to the tubes inserted in his abdomen, were clear, hard plastic, exposing the valves inside them that were opening and closing, noisily pumping his blood through his body. I had walked into Dr. Frankenstein's horror chamber. The walls and the deafening sounds began to loom over and surround me. I grabbed hold of Bill's arm, then reeling, I ran to escape from the room's clutches. I ran down the hall and when I finally stopped, I leaned my head against the wall. *Oh, Dawson! Dawson! What have they done to you!* The nurse rushed to me, put his arm around me and said, "Are you all right?"

"What will he do when he wakes up and sees that?" I cried.

In a strong voice he said, "Are you all right? You're not going to faint, are you?"

"No. No, I'm not going to faint. Can't they cover those?"

"No. They have to stay uncovered."

"How is he going to take that? And that noise?"

"Most people adjust quite well. You'd be surprised."

"Oh, my God. I thought I could handle it."

"You will."

I cried, "I'm sorry, I'm sorry."

"It's O.K."

"I have to go back in."

"Are you sure?"

"Yeah. I have to. It's Dawson."

"O.K. I'll go with you." He walked me slowly back to his room and, cautiously, to Dawson's side. Bill was standing close to Dawson, looking at him adoringly. He looked over at me, a frown crossing his face. He said, "What's wrong with you? He's O.K."

"I know. I just …"

Bill's expression softened and in a hushed tone he said, "Andrea, he's O.K." He slowly turned his head back toward Dawson, quietly coaxing me to look and see for myself and, gently, he repeated, "He's O.K."

I looked at Dawson lying there. He looked peaceful, despite everything. What more could I ask for?

The nurse asked, "Are you all right?"

"Yes, I'm sorry."

"That's all right." He stood by my side for a few minutes then said, "He's quite sedated. He'll be out for a while. You should probably go home and get some sleep yourself."

"I know. Thanks."

Bill said, "We should leave, I guess."

"Yeah, I guess so." Knowing it was time to go I said, "Dawson, we'll be back in the morning."

The nurse was now sitting at the entrance as we left the room. He said, "Are you going home? I want to make sure that we have your phone numbers." He must have seen the look of alarm on my face because he said, reassuringly, "He's doing fine, but I always like to make sure I have all the information."

As we approached the elevator, I said, "I have to make some calls." The pay phones were there and I was finding them more reliable than my cell phone, which often cut out on me when I used it here. I would be absolutely unable to cope with that if it happened to me now.

I called Rusty and my mother and father. I cried hysterically when I described what I had seen and I expressed my concern for Dawson. They assured me Dawson was going to be fine. My mother said, with great conviction, "Dawson will be able to accept it. Anyone else and I wouldn't be so sure, but Dawson will handle it, I know it."

Yet, on the ride home, I continued questioning it, saying to Bill, "How is he ever going to accept that thing?"

"It's not that bad, he'll be all right."

"Really? It seemed horrible," I cried.

"Andrea, get a hold of yourself. He's alive! Don't you remember last week? If we hadn't gotten here … and without those VADs … do you know what we'd be doing today, how we'd be feeling? Don't forget, we would've lost him! That's a fact. Think about it. Just think about how we'd be feeling today. Andrea, we're so lucky. Don't forget that. This isn't that bad compared to what it could have been."

"Yeah, you're right, you're right. We are lucky. I'm just thinking of what it will be like for him."

"Well, he didn't have any better choice. He'll have to understand how lucky he is."

When we arrived at Bill's house, my father was there waiting. I jumped from the truck and ran into my father's arms as I had not done in almost fifty years. I sobbed, "Daddy, it's awful, it's so awful."

He said, "It's O.K., Sweetie. He'll be O.K." He opened the car door and I got in. He went to Bill and patted him on the shoulder. They spoke briefly and then Bill turned and walked to the front door as we drove down the road. I put my face in my hands and cried. Daddy was concerned and he tried to console me, but my heartache for Dawson went beyond anyone's reach. As he drove, he asked me questions and talked hopefully of Dawson's recovery. I said very little. I was remembering how apprehensive I had felt that morning driving my car to the bus depot where I had left it. Now, on my way to pick it up, there were no words to describe what I was feeling.

Daddy said, "Why don't I just drive you home and Rusty and I can go and get your car?"

"No, that's O.K."

"Are you sure you can drive?"

"Yeah, it isn't that far." I appreciated that he wanted to make things easier for me, but nothing could help. "I'm O.K. Thanks."

"Well, I'll follow you home from the depot."

It was almost three o'clock in the morning when we arrived at my condo. As we walked up the stairs, Rusty opened the door to greet us. He reached out to me and I sobbed in his arms. "Babe, c'mon. He'll be all right," he said. He led me to the kitchen table, where I sat, weak and broken. He and Daddy talked a short time, standing in the kitchen. When my father was ready to leave, he came to me, leaned over and gave me a reassuring hug. I watched him as he went to Rusty and shook his hand. "Thanks, Frank," Rusty said, as he walked him to the front door. I was thinking, how awful this must be for Daddy and for Rusty, too, to see me so upset. Rusty, coming toward me said, "Babe, you should go to bed, you've got to get some rest."

"I don't know if I can sleep," I said, not moving from the table.

"You will. You must be exhausted. And you'll be able to handle this better in the morning."

"I don't know. This is just too much for me. I can't handle it."

"You have to," he said, as he coaxed me to stand. "You have to."

I knew he was right. I did have to. I had to be strong for Dawson … for Dawson, and for all those who loved us both.

Chapter Fifteen

Must every good thing we hope for come to us with a price tag attached? Was there no such thing as pure, untempered pleasure? Certainly, the joy of seeing Dawson on a miraculous lifesaving device had been nearly obliterated by the sight of the very thing which brought us that joy. Was that the way life was, with everything having both an upside and a downside? Assuming this was so, one could say then that though every pleasure was tempered, so every pain was soothed. If every good thing came with a price tag, every *bad* thing must come with a *blessing*, if not conspicuously attached, then tucked somewhere inside. No wonder the old cliché about those dreary clouds with their bright linings endured. Trite as it was, its message was surprisingly profound.

The challenge was in trying to see the positive side in life's negative experiences, for often in those situations, only one side was visible at a time. With a coin, we simply flip it to view its hidden side. Can we, somehow, do the same with our experiences? Can we choose which side to dwell upon, to react to? Given that possibility, all of life's experiences may merely be subject to one's own perspective.

I did not know what I was dreading or fearing most as I walked hesitantly toward Dawson's room. Was it to see him looking as he had the night before, lying motionless with that horrifying contraption mounted to his body? Or was it to find him awake and upset, unable to cope with his new circumstances? Was it too much to hope for, to find him awake, alert, yet calm and accepting that machinery as a necessary part of his body? If only I could see him looking, however slightly, as though he were on the road to wellness. I felt it imperative we get a quick, strong start down that road. It seemed vital to our ultimate success that we embark at once and then proceed forward each day without hesitation. I was so afraid of any obstacles that would cause delays.

Although wishing one a "speedy recovery" and to "get well soon" was in no way unusual, what I was feeling was. It was not just that I wanted Dawson to get well as soon as possible, but it was that it seemed a dire necessity he do so. My feelings of urgency stemmed from an unexplainable sense that he had a limited amount of time to accomplish it. It was as though there was some predestined time frame allotted to him in which he must get well in order to survive.

My body tensed as I saw he was just as we had left him, in a seemingly deep sleep, unaware of anything around him. For a moment I wondered if perhaps he had already been awake, maybe he had seen the VADs and had gone peacefully back to sleep. But his nurse soon informed me he was still sedated and that they had tried to let him come out of the sedation, but were unable to for he became much too agitated. He had tried to pull on his lines when he was coming to, so they felt it best to keep him sleeping, for now. She said they would try again later. "It is not unusual for someone coming out of surgery to be anxious when they wake up," she assured me.

"Oh, I know," I said. "I was told how *un*usual it was when Dawson came out of the first surgery so calm."

"Then you know, also, we cannot take him off the respirator until he is relaxed."

"Yes, I do. We were so lucky the first time." I knew, more than ever, just how lucky we had been and I was frightened at the prospect of our luck running out. *God, no, that can't be,* I thought. *We need all the luck and blessings possible to get us through this very important step.* It was crucial we make steady progress and it was frightening to think that we had been stalled even so slightly.

Dawson started to squirm. The nurse said, "He can hear your voice. You can get closer and talk to him."

As I anxiously moved nearer to him, I kept my eyes focused on his face, avoiding looking at the VADs. "Dawson," I said. "I'm here, hon." His legs slowly started to move, then suddenly he was kicking wildly. His head turned quickly toward me, his eyes opened and he looked right at me. But his eyes showed fright and confusion and, unable to speak, they pleaded with me, "Mom, help me, get me out of here!"

I said, "It's O.K., Dawson, it's O.K."

He started to throw his head back and forth and began to choke and gag. I was shaken by his startling reaction, but the nurse calmly came to us and in a loud and confident voice said, "Dawson, relax now. You're all right." He continued to thrash about. She looked at me and said, "I'll give him something to quiet him down." I'm sure she could see the terror on my face and said, "It's very common for patients to react strongly to family members."

"It seems like he wants me to help him," I said. Distressed by the fact I was unable to, I moaned, "He wants me to help him." I could see why they had to keep him sedated and how unready he was to get off the respirator, but it was with tremendous anguish that I faced the reality of this delay.

In an upbeat tone, she said, "We'll try again later. He's just not up to it yet. It isn't anything to worry about, it's very common."

But I wondered what was making him react so differently this time, so differently than he had when he had awakened from the ECMO surgery. Was it because he had not been sufficiently informed about what was going to happen? No, that didn't make sense, he hadn't been aware of what was happening the first time, either. What was the difference? Why was he not the Dawson-that-takes-things-as-they-come this time?

I moved to a chair in the corner of the room and watched as the nurse busily attended to him. When he was quieted down with the help of the medication, she turned to me and said, "I understand you had a difficult time last night."

"Oh," I said, taken by surprise. I had not expected my reaction from the night before would have been relayed to the day-shift nurse. "You mean when I first saw him on the VADs?"

"Yes, I heard it was very hard for you. Are you O.K. now?"

"I think so." Disappointed in myself, I said, "I was very bad last night, though. I thought I was prepared, but it was just too awful."

She smiled kindly at me and nodded. Her expression made me feel there was no need to be ashamed. She then took her post at the table right outside Dawson's room. As he slept, I took the time to slowly get acquainted with the sight and sounds of the VADs. The more I looked at them, the less frightening they became. The longer I sat there, the less aware I was of them. In the hours that passed, I was amazed at how much smaller and quieter they seemed. Maybe our luck had not run out, after all. I had so wanted to see him off the respirator, but could it actually be a blessing that he had been kept sedated a while longer? Eventually, he would have to face the VADs, but maybe I needed this extra bit of time before he did. The extra time had given me the opportunity to adjust to the machinery first, and I believed my accepting it would help to make it easier for him to do so. I was stronger for the delay and certainly my strength could only be of benefit to Dawson.

Dr. Harris and Dr. Hunt came by. They examined Dawson, spoke with the nurse and then came and stood by my side. They were quite casual about Dawson's agitation. Dr. Harris said, "We can't get him off this respirator yet, but we'll try again later. If there are no complications, he could be listed for transplant soon."

"How soon?" I asked.

Dr. Harris answered, "Mmmm, ten days?"

Dr. Hunt added, "Maybe sooner."

"We'll get him listed as soon as we can," Dr. Harris said, "and then you know, he could get a heart the next day."

Theoretically, he could have a new heart in a week. He could be on his way to real recovery in just over a week! He could! But would he? Would he, really? Would we be that lucky? There were no answers, no promises, no guarantees.

"How long does it usually take to get a heart after you're listed?" I asked.

"Since he will be listed Class One, a couple of months."

"Oh, that's not bad," I said, but I was imagining the anxiety involved in that wait. Then I was thinking, what would that be like, to get word that a heart was available for him? And the waiting through that surgery while they removed his heart and replaced it with someone else's, what would that be like to live through?

"We'll just have to wait and see," they casually agreed as they left. So many things yet to wait for, yet to live through.

They stopped outside of Dawson's room and spoke briefly to a woman with curly, dark hair in a white lab coat before she entered. "Hi, Mrs. Bell?" she said. "I'm Nina, with the VAD team. I'd like to talk to you and maybe help you understand some things about the VADs and answer any questions you may have."

"Oh, I'd appreciate that."

"Do you want to go to the waiting room?"

"Yeah, that would be good."

As we sat talking, I was awed by how at ease I was with this stranger. I felt as though I were talking with an old friend. Although she was clinically descriptive as she explained to me the workings of the VADs, she showed such compassion and consideration. It was apparent she'd had much experience with the cold, hard facts of a ventricular assist device, yet she responded warmly to me. I was confiding in her my utmost fears and she was listening with such interest and understanding. I wondered how I could have been so lucky to have met someone so helpful and comforting at a time when I needed it so. Since the beginning of this heartbreaking ordeal, it had seemed just when I needed it, someone would be there to show me kindness and give me strength. I wondered, *How many angels has God sent to me this week?* We talked for a rather long time, until I could see she was feeling the need to get on to her other duties. I apologized for taking so much of her time and she graciously assured me not to worry. I was pleased to hear she would be following Dawson's case and would be coming by regularly to see us.

I called Rusty and shared with him the details of my day and he thanked me for keeping him posted. Bill called to find out how Dawson was doing. He had been asleep when Bill had stopped by to see him earlier. I told him Dawson was still sleeping and they had tried to get him off the sedatives, but he was, what they were calling, "agitated." I told him what had happened when Dawson had heard my voice. He thought that sounded terrible, but seemed confidant that the next time they tried to wean Dawson off the sedatives, he would do fine. I hoped he was right. I started to tell him of my meeting with the woman on the VAD team, but he interrupted asking, "Are you going to be there this afternoon?"

"Yeah, I'm staying."

"O.K., good, I'll see you then. I've got to get back to work."

I went back to Dawson's room to discover they had attempted to bring him out of the sedation and, again, he was quite upset. He had pulled out his air tube, so they had restrained his arms by tying them to the bed sidebars. I could have cried at the sight. *Dawson! Dawson, you're O.K. Mom's here. Please, Dawson. Please, God.*

What was going on? Again, I was realizing how the things you think you have to worry about often turn out not to be the problem, after all. I had been so worried about him waking up and discovering what had been done to him, that I had been actually dreading to see him awake. Now, with all my heart, I was praying for it.

Dawson still was not awake by the time Bill arrived. He went to Dawson's side and said softly, "Dawson." Immediately, Dawson had the same reaction to Bill's voice as he had to mine: squirming, kicking, trying to free his arms, throwing his head back and forth, and choking. It was a frightening, heart-wrenching sight. It was unbearably painful to see him so distraught and be unable to help him. We were again assured that often this did occur and that it was quite common. But it was extremely hard for us to accept that he was so scared and that there was nothing we could do to help him.

We stayed by his side for hours, seeing no change in him. Feeling utterly helpless, I called Rusty and told him I would be leaving for home shortly. It was obvious Dawson would not be waking up soon and that our being there was of no benefit to him.

I told Bill I had taken the bus in and had left my car at the bus stop near his house. I said, "I was hoping to get a ride back with you."

"That's fine," he said.

On the ride home, I was still concerned about Dawson's reaction to the VADs, but I was encouraged by my own newly found tolerance of them. Now, Dawson's uncharacteristic agitation had become my primary concern, giving way to an aching need to see him awake. I longed to see Dawson, the real Dawson, the old roll-with-the-punches Dawson. I wistfully imagined seeing him finally waking up and surprising everyone by nonchalantly accepting the mechanism attached to him. It could happen. It could. Dawson could do it. My mother had said Dawson could do it and I had always believed her. I prayed she was right and that he would do it and soon.

When I arrived home to Rusty, he was eager to hear about everything. I was appreciative of his interest and comforted by his common-sense approach to the situation. He assured me it all sounded within the realm of normal. And he believed what I could only hope and pray for, that Dawson was still Dawson, the guy who could handle whatever life had to offer. "You'll see," Rusty said, "tomorrow will be better."

It wasn't. Dawson was intermittently sedated and agitated throughout the long day. It was a continuous cycle, watching him going from a drugged sleep to a terrified awakening and back again. I stood by his bed, but was reluctant to speak, for when I did he awakened and cried out silently to me with his eyes, "Mom, please help me!" It was strange and frightening, how he was looking right at me, but when I responded to him, it seemed he had not seen me at all. He appeared aware, yet he seemed far away. He frowned intensely as if he were trying so hard to get me to understand what it was he wanted to say. Yet when I spoke, it was as if he could not hear me. I wanted him to know I understood and wanted to help him. I tried to console him, but all my reassuring did not get through to him. I could not help him, calm him, nor comfort him.

I talked to Rusty at the firehouse, I talked to my mother, I talked to Bill and expressed to everyone the pain of feeling so helpless and the fear of impending events that were far beyond my control. The doctors were becoming slightly concerned, but did not seem alarmed. "It happens sometimes," they said. But why was it happening to Dawson at this time? It wasn't supposed to go this way. This was Dawson. The same Dawson everyone had marveled about days before saying, "Have you seen your son today? He looks great!" God, I needed to hear that again, but no one could say it. Have I seen my son today? Yes, yes I have, but it seemed that he could not see me.

Bill arrived right after work, desperately hoping to see Dawson awake and calm. Bill was as bewildered as I was about what was happening. That magic combination of alert, yet relaxed was beyond our reach. When Dawson heard Bill's voice, he pulled his restraints to their limits trying to reach out to him. He had that same desperate, pleading expression on his face when he turned toward Bill's voice as when he had turned toward me. To Bill's dismay and mine, he was no more able to ease Dawson's anguish than I had been.

In great despair, I stepped outside of his room. I was standing there alone with my troubled thoughts when a tall, slender woman in a long, black coat approached me. She had pale skin and short, shaggy, dark hair. In a New York accent she said, "Mrs. Bell, I'm Laura Bernstein, the psychologist assigned to Dawson's case. How are you doing?"

I just sighed and shook my head.

"I know, I know," she said. "I see Dawson is still sedated."

"Yes."

"That's too bad. I was hoping to talk to him. I've tried a couple of times these last few days, but I obviously can't talk to him while he's on the respirator." She went on to explain that interviewing him was a routine procedure for anyone needing a transplant. Looking at her note pad, she said, "So he's been here a week now."

"Yes, that's right, we were rushed here last Thursday. They didn't think he was going to make it. He was very bad," I said, my voice trembling.

"I know, I know," she said, again, in an understanding tone. She paused, then asked, "So how was he doing before he was admitted?"

"Really well."

"Is that why he hadn't been listed for a transplant before?"

"Yeah, he said he felt too good."

"He was taking care of himself, was he?"

"Yeah, pretty much, but I worried all of the time that he might not be."

"Did you have any reason to think he wasn't?"

"Well, I know Dawson and I knew it was possible, so I worried. But, of course, as his mother, the only way I could have felt his care was good enough would have been if I were taking care of him myself twenty-four hours a day."

"Sure, sure. Did he drink?"

"He had."

"Since he'd been diagnosed?"

"I don't know. I worried that he did."

"Did you ever see him drinking?"

"No."

"Does he live close to you?"

"Not too far. He lives with his dad."

"Oh?" she responded, sounding alerted. "You and his father are divorced?"

"Yes."

"How long have you been divorced?"

"About ten years," I said, feeling surprisingly ashamed.

Bill came out from Dawson's room and I introduced him to the psychologist. As they shook hands she said, "So you and Dawson live together."

"Yes," Bill said with a frown and an expression that showed he did not want to talk.

Disregarding this, she asked him, "Has Dawson been taking care of himself?"

"Yes," he said, flatly.

It was obvious Bill was not interested in continuing the conversation. She said apologetically, "I am going to have to talk to Dawson sometime. I'll check back another time. Take care, now."

When she left, Bill said to me, "What did you say to her about Dawson?"

"What do you mean?"

"Did she ask you about him taking care of himself?"

"Yeah."

"What did you say?"

"I don't know, just that I always worry about him."

"Did she ask you if he drank?"

"Yeah."

"So what'd you say?"

"I said I worried about it."

"You really shouldn't be talking to her."

"What do you mean?"

"These people can decide whether or not they want to give him a heart. That's why she was asking about his drinking. If they think he's been drinking, maybe they won't let him have a new heart."

What! I felt like I had just been stabbed! Wounded, my mind cried out in disbelief, *No one would not let him have a new heart, would they? God, after we had come this far, someone might just say no?* I stammered, "Well, I just told her the truth. I really don't know anything for sure, only how I feel and that I worry that he might drink."

"Yeah, but I know you, you can go on and on."

"But I really don't know anything for sure. The truth is, I never saw him drink and there were times when I felt that he was taking perfect care of himself. But there were also times when I wasn't so sure. I really don't know, so I don't know how much it matters what I say."

"Well, I'm just telling you, think about it."

I felt disturbed by Bill's attitude. This woman had seemed concerned and sincere. She seemed like someone I could talk to. I could not explain it, but I liked her. And now he was telling me to be wary. It didn't come naturally for me to think before I spoke. I had always spoken straight out, unafraid of telling the truth about what I thought and felt. How could that hurt Dawson? How could the truth spoken out of my love and concern for Dawson be used against him? And, after all, I hadn't really said anything, anyway. *But, oh, my God, when Dawson awakens, were there truths that he, himself, could say to her that would hurt him? Were there facts about his behavior that could deny him a last chance at life? Could that be possible? Oh, God, was this actually something else to fear?*

The day had not been filled with gallant strides forward, as I had so desperately hoped, but, instead, had been wracked with delays and disappointments and now, with mounting worries. I prayed tomorrow would bring with it a blessing and I prayed for the insight to recognize it, however well hidden it may be.

Chapter Sixteen

H i, are you at the hospital, yet?" Rusty asked.
"We're just driving into the parking garage now," I answered into the cell phone.

Rusty responded with a hint of excitement. "Today is going to be a good day," he said. "I was there at the hospital to see Dawson earlier this morning."

"You were? You saw him?"

"Yeah, that's what I'm saying, I saw him and he's waking up!"

"Really, and he was O.K.?"

"Yeah!" Rusty said.

My dad pulled into a parking space as I anxiously asked Rusty, "Did he know you were there?"

"I think so. He squeezed my hand."

"Oh, God, really?" I said, my hopes soaring. I stepped out of the car, walked through the garage and across the street while continuing our conversation. "Did you see his nurse?" I asked.

"Yeah, she said he had a good night."

"Oh, that's great! O.K., I'm in the hospital now, I'd better go. Thanks, hon. I'll call you later."

Rusty had worked his twenty-four-hour shift at the firehouse the day before and had gotten off duty that morning. I had spent the night at my parents' house and my father had driven me to the hospital in the morning. We were just arriving when Rusty called. After I hung up, my father had asked, "Was that Rusty?"

"Yeah, he saw Dawson this morning. He said he's waking up!"

It was with great anticipation I entered Dawson's room, though from what I could see, everything looked the same as it had the day before. I promptly asked Cindy, his nurse, "How is he?"

"Well, he had a pretty good night and he had a visitor this morning, a fireman."

"Oh, yes, I know, I just talked to him and he told me Dawson was waking up."

My father had moved to Dawson's side and touched his hand. He said, softly, "It's Papa, Dawson, it's Papa." Dawson did not respond.

"He's been sedated," Cindy said, almost apologetically.

"No!" I cried. "Why?"

"Well, we had him off the sedatives for a while, but when we tried having him breathe on his own he became so anxious his heart and respiratory rates went up too high. He then became increasingly agitated over the next few hours. I had to sedate him to protect him from pulling out his lines."

"Why is he doing this?" I asked, my voice straining and my mind and heart pleading for someone to help me understand why this was happening.

She appeared unable to give me an answer. "It just happens sometimes," she finally said.

That was not an answer, at least not the answer I needed. I stood there, confounded and suffering from the letdown. My father motioned to me and we stepped outside the room. "Are you O.K.?" he asked. "Do you want to go to the coffee shop for a little bit?"

"I don't know," I sighed. "I really want to talk to the doctor."

"Oh, O.K. Well, maybe I'll go down and get a cup of coffee. Do you want me to bring you anything?"

"No, I don't think so. Thanks." I glanced around the unit looking for a doctor to talk to. I saw none, so I went to the waiting room where I had a view of the elevator. This gave me a good vantage point from which to spot one of Dawson's doctors. When I saw Dr. Harris, I quickly went out to him. "Have you seen Dawson today?" I asked.

"Yes, I have. He's still quite agitated," he said matter-of-factly.

"I know, but what does it mean?"

"Well, he does have a fever. That could be playing a part."

"A fever?"

"Yes, but it's only slight. Otherwise, he's doing fine. In fact, his kidneys and liver are responding very well."

That was a tremendous relief, for that had been one of the major concerns. He could not survive the wait for a heart if his other organs were not functioning. "But why would he have a fever?" I asked.

"Patients on the VADs have been known to run this low-grade fever with no obvious reason, but if it goes up, we will do some routine cultures looking for a source of infection. In the mean time, we will continue to try to get him to breathe on his own."

"O.K.," I sighed, "so we just continue to wait and see, hope for the best and try to get him off the sedatives and the respirator. I guess he cannot be listed until then, right?"

"Yes, but we're working toward that and as Class One, he'll be at the top of the list. His blood type, A, isn't rare, so it should not be too long after he's listed before a heart becomes available for him."

I saw this moment as my opportunity to bring up a subject that had been nagging at me for the past couple of days. "Nina told me that a heart is chosen not only by blood type, but by size, as well. She said that Dawson needs a big heart."

"That's right, he's a big guy."

"That's exactly what she said, but it's not true. He's not a big guy." Dr. Harris looked skeptically at me. I said, "I know his weight is up right now, but he's really not a big person, he's only five-foot-nine."

"The heart transplant people know his height and weight," he said, appearing unconcerned over what I had said. If he were annoyed by what must have seemed like my lack of confidence, I saw no sign of it.

"Yes, I know," I answered, "but he is just not what I would describe as a big man and I'm afraid it could make a difference." Dr. Harris said nothing. Finally, with a sigh of feigned resignation, I said, "I guess they know more than I do." He nodded, with barely a hint of a smile. But neither the doctor nor Nina had eased my doubts.

During the conversation I'd had with Nina a few days earlier, I had said to her, "So if something happened to me, and my organs could be donated, you're saying that even though Dawson and I are the same blood type, he could not get my heart?" She had answered, "Right. He could not. It would be too small for him." Questioning this, I had told her of a story I had read. It was about a man who was waiting for a heart when his teenage daughter was in a serious automobile accident. When it became apparent she would not recover, her heart was offered to him. She had been a registered organ donor, yet he was hesitant to accept it. He eventually did, for he knew his daughter would want him to have it. I had seen a picture of the father and he did not appear to be a small man, so after having told Nina that story, I had asked her, "How can you explain that? Wouldn't you think his daughter's heart would be too small for him?" She had shrugged her shoulders saying, "Yes, I would." With some insistence, I had concluded with, "But they gave it to him and he did very well, so I'm just not convinced that Dawson has to have a big heart."

She had not known the facts about that case, but I told her I remembered that story very well because Dawson and I had discussed it. I had said to him, at the time, "I should have it documented somewhere that if anything happens to me, you get my heart!" Then I had said, "You know what would be even better, is if we could just trade hearts! I'll take yours and you can have mine." Dawson, smiling, had said, "Well, at least you'd know the diet you had to follow and you know all about having cardiomyopathy." He had made me smile. "That's true," I said. When I had told Nina of that conversation, she had responded with a little laugh, "I know we wouldn't do that! But," she added, more seriously, "I'm sure that your heart would be too small for him anyway. I know the size heart I want for Dawson. I know you don't believe it, but he is a big guy."

In spite of her assurances, this "big" description continued to disturb me. I could not shake my uneasiness, not simply because it was a description of Dawson I did not agree with, but because I feared it could become the crux of his recovery. I had this vivid picture, a clear vision of myself one day saying, "If only you hadn't thought of him as big!" I worried about why I should see that scene so clearly. Was I looking for things to worry about, as though I didn't have enough? Or was I just going crazy? After all, no one else saw what I saw. Wasn't it foolish of me to continue to make an issue of this? And what would I have to do to make my point? I had already voiced my opinion, told my stories, and expressed my feelings. Was there any more I could do, or should do? And what if someone actually listened to me, and I were wrong?

The only thing I could do was to put my faith in God that this assessment would, miraculously, work in our favor. For it was out of my hands and, also, I did not need to add this to what had become my ever-growing list of worries.

I had delayed calling Rusty until after I had talked to the doctor. I hoped it would help to have some explanation to give him for the disappointing news I was about to deliver. "Hi!" Rusty said, with excitement after he heard my voice. I hated to have to tell him the day had not gone favorably, as he had expected. When he heard, he was stunned. He said, "But he seemed so calm. The nurse even said he was."

"I know," I said, equally baffled. "He had been more alert and calm during the night than he had been in days, but he grew progressively agitated throughout the morning, and they don't really know why."

"What are they saying?"

"It could be because he has a slight fever."

"Well, they can manage that."

"I guess, but I just can't stand this, it scares me so much. I just want him to wake up. I want him off that respirator. I want to be able to talk to him. I want him to start getting well."

"He will, it's just going to take a little more time, that's all, but he will."

When my father returned, he said he'd like to go in to see Dawson.

"O.K., you go. I'll wait here, all right?" I was feeling nervous, confused and scared. Now a fever? Every hour something new and dreadful.

A short time later, I saw my father pass the waiting room window, appearing upset. My heart began to race, and when he walked past the door and did not enter, I jumped from my chair and went out to him. He was shaken and could barely speak. Terrified, I said, "Daddy, what is it?"

He said, his voice shaking, "He was asleep, I touched his hand and I said, 'Dawson...'"

"And what happened?" I interrupted.

My father put his head down and spoke slowly, swallowing after each word, "I said, 'It's Papa, Dawson.' I guess I upset him. He started kicking and grabbing and squirming."

"No, Daddy, it wasn't your fault. That's exactly what's been happening every time he wakes up. He did that with me and Bill, too. I know how awful it is to see him like that, but you didn't cause it. Oh, God, this is too terrible!" We stood silent for a few moments before I decided to go in and see him.

My father said, "I'll be in in a little while."

I went to Dawson's room and he was sleeping quietly. The nurse said, "I've had to sedate him again. Even with his arms restrained, he was moving his body so vigorously that his main line was pulled out. I've warned him several times about moving around and I've cautioned him against biting his air tube. We just can't have him doing that, so I had to put a bite guard in his mouth."

I shuddered, but calmly asked, "Does he understand when you talk to him?"

"I think so. He seems to respond."

I knew Dawson to be stubborn, even downright obstinate, and I wondered if that could be all this was. Was he just refusing to listen, refusing to do what he was told? It couldn't be that simple, could it? No, it looked as though there was something much more going on here. He was fighting something. *Oh, Dawson, what is it? Why can't I help you? How can this be happening to us?*

My father entered the room and saw that Dawson was calmed down. He said, "Now that he's sleeping, do you want to go down and get something to eat? You really should."

"Oh, I don't know."

"Maybe you could just get a soda."

"I don't know. I don't know what to do."

"Well, we can just go down for a little bit. You know, you really should eat something."

"Yeah, I guess. All right." As we left the room, I said to Cindy, "We'll be back, we're just going down to the coffee shop."

I looked at the menu, but I had no appetite. My stomach was in knots and I could not stand to be away from Dawson for too long. All I could manage was a cup of hot chocolate and I drank it quickly and said to Daddy, "Let's go back up."

After we had been in Dawson's room for some time, my father asked if I were ready to leave for home. I said, "No, but, it's O.K. for you to go. I don't want you to get in all that commute traffic over the bridge. I think I'm going to stay. I'll get a ride with Bill later. I just can't go yet."

"That's O.K. with Bill?"

"Oh, yeah, he won't mind."

"O.K., then I guess I'll go, dear."

"Thanks for coming in with me. When Mommy gets home, tell her I'll call her tonight. I'm going to go call Rusty now."

I told Rusty that things were still the same, no change. I said, "Daddy just left, but I'm staying. I just can't leave."

"I know. Are you going to get a ride with Bill?"

"Yeah, I'll call you later, O.K.?"

Bill arrived a short time after. He looked at me as though he could not believe there still had been no progress. He went to Dawson's side and stared sadly down at him. He rubbed his arm gently and I knew how badly he wanted to wake him. Though we both desperately wanted to let him know we were there with him, we were hesitant to try and rouse him. We were sitting solemnly by his side when Laura Bernstein, the psychologist, entered the room. She was disappointed to discover Dawson was still sedated. She looked at us as if she could only imagine our disappointment. She said, "I guess I won't be able to talk to him today, but I am going to have to submit a report. Could I, possibly, interview both of you? Would you be available now?"

Bill and I looked at each other, shrugged our shoulders and I said, "I guess so."

She said, "Let me see if there is a place where we can talk. I'd rather not go to the waiting room. I'll be right back."

When she left, Bill turned to me looking concerned, his expression cautioning me. I said, "I'm just going to tell her what I know."

He said, "I hate this. I don't feel like talking to her."

"I don't mind. I want her to know Dawson. All she has seen of him is how he is looking and behaving now. You know, she hadn't seen him when he was himself, laughing and joking after the ECMO surgery."

She hurried back in and said, "O.K., we can use the small meeting room, follow me." The three of us sat at the large, round conference table with several chairs to spare. She took out her notebook and in a sympathetic voice said, "This must be so hard for you."

"It's terrible," I said.

"I know, I know," she responded. Although I was beginning to realize this was a phrase she used often, it did not diminish its meaning for me. She began the interview by asking, "So how has Dawson been handling his heart condition?"

I said, "I think he took it unbelievably well. He just seemed to accept it. He never complained, he remained enthusiastic and he never lost his sense of humor. He really didn't let his condition restrict him much, either, though he knew his limitations and was not ashamed of them. Nevertheless, I worried about him overexerting himself. I got him started on woodworking. It was great for him, not physically strenuous, yet creatively stimulating. He made some wonderful things for me and he really enjoyed it. He loves tools and takes pride in working with his hands. He's good at it, too, very neat and precise." When I stopped talking, I realized how much I must be sounding like a typical mother.

She asked me how involved I'd been with his health problems and I told her of the research I had done right from the beginning. I told her how he recorded his weight religiously on the monthly charts I had made for him to watch for any sudden weight gain that would indicate water retention, and how he began reading food labels for sodium content.

We talked, in greater depth than we had the first time we met, of his reluctance to get listed. I explained to her how he couldn't stand the thought of, while feeling fine, getting a call one night to "come in, we're taking your heart out." I confided to her that although I had felt he should get listed, there was a part of me that had secretly trusted his decision. I did not know whether it was a trust in God or in Dawson himself, but something had made me feel, whatever he decided to do would turn out to be for the best. "But I'm not so sure about that now," I said. I continued, telling her how he had said he would always wonder if a transplant had been necessary and if, perhaps, he could have lived without having had it. I said, my voice trembling with emotion, "At least now he will have no doubts. He will know."

Bill spoke of how Dawson had been living a relatively normal life and how he loved to ride his Harley and was still quite able. Laura responded to this, saying she liked to ride, as well. When Dawson had first gotten his motorcycle, he had told Bill he could borrow it any time. Bill told Laura he had not ridden it for fear he'd want to buy one. "And," he said with a slight smile, "a bike is the last thing I need." He told her he'd had a motorcycle many years earlier, "But," he added, "I didn't ride like Dawson. He can really ride that thing." Laura smiled in response to a father's obvious pride.

She asked if Dawson had a girlfriend and Bill told her he did not. "Is this by choice?" she asked.

Bill said, "Yes, he's had many girlfriends, but he's never gotten serious."

"But what about Candace?" I said. "I think he really cared for her." Bill nodded.

She then asked at what age Dawson had started to drink. "I was aware he was partying on the weekends during high school and I knew he was drinking," I answered, though I was ashamed to admit I had allowed it. I was grateful she did not seem to judge me, for I was bearing enough guilt of my own. When she asked how much he drank as a teenager, I had to say I did not know the quantities. When she asked, "How much has he been drinking in recent years?" I said I did not know that, either. That was the truth. She asked us if we drank. Bill said he drank socially, and I said I rarely drank and when I did, I drank very little.

She told us that after the heart transplant, Dawson would need twenty-four-hour care for the first month. "Who would be able to be with him?" she asked. Bill said he could take some time off work and I said I was available for whatever he needed, day or night.

The interview lasted for quite a while. I felt it had gone well and that my instincts had been right. After getting to know her, I still liked her and continued to feel she was sincere and concerned. Surprisingly, Bill seemed to like her, too. We stood, shook hands and she said, warmly, "I'm looking forward to meeting Dawson. I can hear from both of you what a very special young man he is."

I arrived home later that evening with Laura's tender words still with me, echoing my own biased, yet deeply felt sentiment, "What a very special young man he is."

When I awoke the following morning, I threw the covers back in search of the rosary beads I had taken to bed with me the night before. Before Dawson had gone into the hospital, upon finding them, I would have put them into their case and placed them on my night stand. But now I immediately put them in the pocket of the jacket I was going to be wearing that day, so I would not leave the house without them. I might need them to hold on to for strength and comfort at any time. Many days I had said a rosary on the bus, in the hospital lobby, or in the waiting room, and all the while I had managed to keep the beads concealed in my pocket. I had reached in, felt for the crucifix and upon finding it, held it tightly between my fingers and silently begun, *In the name of the Father, the Son ...* The beads, a high school graduation present from my Aunt Elmy, were unusual in that they were not round, but were large, brilliant crystals in the shape of cut diamonds. With the rosary hidden in my pocket, I had prayed, blindly moving my fingers from one triangular bead to the next. Why had I kept them from view? Would I have been embarrassed or ashamed to have someone see?

Dawson's Gift

I arrived at the hospital a little early for visiting hours, so I went into the small, familiar waiting room. There was a woman there, sitting alone, and I sat down slightly across from her. There was something about her that brought to mind my childhood.

When I was a child, we had lived in a neighborhood where many Italians had settled. Quite a few of those families had their elderly parents, most often their mothers, living with them. I was told they had come over from the "old country." The women dressed in black and wore black "ol'lady" shoes and dark print scarves on their bowed heads. They looked very old, I suspect, older than their years. I found it curious how they all looked so much alike, yet I never saw them together. They appeared to be living solitary lives. I would see them as they walked to and from the grocery store carrying their shopping bags. They looked lonely and sad to me, as if their lives had been full of sorrow. I was just a child, walking to school or running to meet a friend, but whenever I saw one of those ladies I would stop and wonder what it was that made her look so sad.

When this woman in the waiting room looked over at me, there was no mistaking the sadness in her eyes. She looked at me and did not speak or smile, nor did I. She looked away and as I watched her, I saw her hands clutching her rosary beads that were lying in her lap and she appeared neither embarrassed nor ashamed. A man, younger than she, entered and sat beside her. I was not surprised when they did not speak English. As they talked, the woman began to cry. This was the first time I had seen this, though I had encountered many family members in this waiting room over the past several days. No one had shown this kind of emotion before. Most of the families had been waiting for a loved one to come out of surgery and they were anxious and nervous, but shortly, the surgeon would come in and say that all had gone well. They would leave and I would not see them again, for their loved ones soon would have been moved out of intensive care and into a regular unit on the next floor. What a joy that must be. Up to that point, I had not seen anyone who seemed to be feeling as upset as I was or anyone appearing to be in a more dreaded situation than I was in. My heart was reaching out to them in their obvious pain, but I tried not to watch them. Not understanding their language, I had no way of knowing what their circumstances were. I concluded he was her son and they were there for her husband, his father. When the man got up and left the room, she looked over at me again, and this time, I smiled sympathetically.

She responded with, "My daughter has lupus."

"Oh," I said, surprised to have her speak in English to me and surprised to hear she was there for her child, "I'm here for my son."

"Oh," she moaned, "what is wrong with him?"

"His heart. He needs a heart transplant."

She quietly moaned again. "My daughter has had lupus for many years and it is very bad. She has been in the hospital many times before, but this time..." She took a handkerchief from her pocket and wiped her eyes, "this time there is nothing they can do."

"Oh, no," I said, my heart breaking for her. "I'm so sorry." Then I did something I could not remember ever having done before. I stood and went to this stranger and placed my hand over hers. There was nothing I could say, but I wanted so badly to comfort her.

She began to tell me about her daughter and told me the man who had been sitting next to her was her daughter's husband. She said her own husband of many years was dead and that she had five children. "But it does not matter how many children you have," she said softly, "you cannot bear to lose one." She wept as she said the words, "I am going to lose my daughter."

All I could do was hold her hand and listen. When her son-in-law came back, I got up and left and went to Dawson's room. All the while I was thinking, will that be me? Would I be sitting there one day knowing I was about to lose my child? And would I, having reached that point, be shamelessly holding my beautiful rosary beads in plain sight, visibly praying without embarrassment? I put my hand into my jacket pocket and I entered Dawson's room.

The report from his nurse was not good. She had to keep him sedated to protect his tubes and airways. "He pulled out his chest tube," she said.

I felt I could crumble to the floor. Dr. Harris entered and I wanted to scream and cry, "Why can't you do something!" The doctor looked more serious than usual as he said, "He goes into respiratory distress when we take him off the respirator."

"What does that mean?"

"We cannot take him off yet."

"But why?"

"I don't know, but I don't think it is physiological. It seems he is just going through a lot of anxiety."

"What can you do?"

"Just keep trying."

"You mean it could just suddenly work?"

"It could."

"Why is this happening?"

"He's just too agitated."

"But why?"

"It could be the fever."

"He still has a fever?"

"Yes. We're doing some cultures."

"Has his fever gone up?"

"A little."

The situation seemed no longer to be the oh-this-happens-some-times-scenario. It seemed different. It appeared Dr. Harris thought so, too. Afraid, I asked, "How serious is this?"

"His condition is still quite serious, of course, but as far as getting him extubated, we're just going to keep trying. I'm not going to try again today though. I want to give him a rest. He really gets worked up. *Extubated?* I thought. *Oh, yes, I remember the nurse using that word. It means taking him off the respirator. While he is on it, he is intubated.*

Because Dawson was going to remain sedated, I spent most of the day in the waiting room. I called Rusty and my mother. It was with great dismay I relayed the doctor's report to everyone. His recovery was not progressing according to the schedule I had prayed for and I was feeling helpless, frightened and alone. The woman I had met that morning was no longer sitting there, most likely she was by her daughter's side, but she was in my thoughts and I was reminded to be thankful I still had hope.

However, this was the most horrendous ordeal I could ever have imagined living and I did not know how I could get through it. The fear of losing Dawson was overwhelming, the agony of imagining what he was going through was devastating, and the desperate need to stay hopeful was crushing me under its own weight.

I did a lot of thinking during those hours I spent waiting. I thought about Bill arriving in the afternoon and how I hated to have to tell him they still could not let Dawson wake up. Bill had been arriving each day hopeful that perhaps this would be the day Dawson would be smiling again, the day he would arrive to find Dawson waiting for him. I was a witness to Bill's daily optimism turning to anguish and frustration when I had to sadly shake my head, "No," to the question in his eyes, "Is he awake?" I wanted to help ease his pain, but there was little I could do, except to share it.

Sitting alone in the waiting room, I wondered if anyone could possibly imagine the total, single-minded focus it took to hold on to the hope that gave me the courage to face each day. I considered it vital I not allow other concerns to distract me, for I believed they would weaken me. I told myself, *You must find a way to survive these anxious days and find peace and strength.*

I was feeling stressed about not having told Rusty of my concern over him coming to the hospital. I knew I needed to settle the matter to eliminate that worry. But every time I planned to talk to him, I found myself unable to do so. I didn't want to say the things I felt I had to and the timing never seemed quite right to do it. The day before, I was so happy Rusty had seen Dawson slightly awake and calm, I had not wanted to take away from that. I did not even ask him what time he had been there, although I had wondered. He must not have run into Bill and that was all that mattered. I was thinking we might not be as lucky the next time, if I did not talk to Rusty soon.

I had already expended too much energy thinking about it, but wanting to be sure I was clear about what I wanted to say to him, I led myself through my own familiar maze of questions and answers. *What was it about Rusty coming to the hospital that concerned me?* Having seen the extent of Bill's long-held resentment for him, whether justified or not, led me to believe Bill's attitude was going to cause me problems. Worrying about how I would handle them had already begun to distress me.

Was that enough reason to ask Rusty not to come? My gut feeling was, yes, it was. But it was far more than just to avoid a few uncomfortable moments. I believed Bill's moody reaction to Rusty being at the hospital would make all my days there more tense than they already were.

How could I possibly tell Rusty not to come? I knew how much he wanted to see Dawson and how much he wanted to be with me, to console and encourage me. He would want to ask questions, be informed and be a part of Dawson's care. I would have wanted that, too, but as I sat in the waiting room and imagined it, I did not feel comforted. In my mind, I saw Rusty having an unfavorable reaction to seeing Bill since I was now on friendly terms with him. I felt nervous and panicky. Those were exactly the feelings I was trying desperately to avoid. Unlike the many situations I had no control over and could not change, this one was within my power.

As I ran the potential conversation with Rusty through my mind, I knew it was going to be difficult to explain everything and I knew it would anger and hurt him. I hoped it would help if I told him how much it meant to have his emotional support through this ordeal. I wanted to explain to him I understood how he must feel, but I felt no man in Bill's position should have to deal with anything else other than standing vigil by his son's bedside.

When I imagined myself telling Rusty how seeing him would upset Bill, I saw him asking me, "Don't you think I'm upset?" I didn't want to have to say, no matter how much he cared for Dawson and me, there was no way he was going through what Bill was. Nothing in this world could compare to watching your child day after day fighting for his life. Nothing. I would have to tell Rusty I was not going to do anything that would add to Bill's pain. That meant I would not put Bill in the position of having to think about facing Rusty, or confronting him, accepting him, or even, simply, avoiding him; the man he blamed for stealing his wife. I hoped Rusty would see he was in the position to be charitable and I wanted to ask him to do that for me, not for Bill, but for me. The important thing was not that I was trying to spare Bill's feelings. I was primarily trying to spare my own.

Could I make Rusty see there was some consolation, however bittersweet, that Dawson was unaware of who was there and who was not? Couldn't I tell Rusty it was possible when Dawson's condition improved, there would be a change in attitudes and everyone could become more reasonable? I could explain to Rusty he would be merely waiting to see Dawson until he could truly visit and talk and laugh with him.

I wished I could simply say, in one intelligible sentence, what the issue was, for I knew from past experiences the more I tried to explain everything to Rusty, the greater the potential there was for getting into an argument. Our long discussions always had a way of escalating. The fact that Rusty was at his most confrontational when his feelings were hurt added to my fear of where our talk might lead us. I could not afford to let it get out of hand, for I was in no condition to engage in any exhausting, heated and emotional dispute. Furthermore, the points I had to make were non-debatable. The bottom line was, for the moment, my life was at the hospital with Dawson and nothing else compared or mattered.

I hated to say all this to Rusty, but I believed I had no other choice. I was trying to avoid a disaster. Something powerful had been telling me there would be consequences and that they would be far-reaching. I could never have imagined in what way or to what extent that would be true.

Chapter Seventeen

Undoubtedly, we all know of families who have stood vigil, waiting and praying for a loved one's emergence from a coma. Those tragic stories are not unheard of, nor, I suppose, was Dawson's situation unprecedented, but I had never heard of anything like it.

Dawson was not in a coma, yet we stood there waiting and praying for him to awaken, as though he were. His condition was more frustrating and perplexing than a coma. He was not unable to wake up, he just could not do it calmly. His deep sleep was not his body's involuntary reaction, it was intentionally induced by the doctors. The fact it was deliberately inflicted upon him made it all the more difficult to accept. If he were being sedated for the purpose of relieving pain that would have been understandable, but he was not. The nurses routinely asked him if he had any discomfort and he consistently shook his head, no. Yet in the next minute he would be thrashing about so violently they had to medicate him. Dawson just could not tolerate being awake, and no one knew why.

The scenario should have been simple: he is taken off the sedatives and he wakes up. He would then open his eyes and see me. He would hear me telling him how much I loved him and how everything was going to be O.K. and that I was there with him every step of the way.

How I yearned to live that scene, not just imagine it. It was time. In fact, it was way overdue. He should already have been placed on the transplant list. He should just be waiting for a heart. It seemed the doctors and nurses thought so, too, and were almost as confused as we were as to why he was not ready. *Is he ever going to be? Will I ever see him awake again? God, will the day come when I see his smile? Oh, to hear his voice, his laugh, to see that look in his eyes as I delight in his clever wit. Dear God, forgive me if I am asking too much. Forgive me if I sound ungrateful. For though I am unable to talk to him and hold him, I am truly thankful to be able to hold on to hope. God, I do know how lucky I am he is alive.*

After all my ruminating over the points I had wanted to make and all my planning on how best to approach Rusty on the topic of his potential visits, by the time I arrived home from the hospital, I still had not decided exactly how to bring up the subject. I had been home over an hour, Rusty and I were sitting at the kitchen table talking amiably, yet I had continued to stall. I was thinking of the things I needed to say, but I was not saying them. I sat there, dreading to speak it, but trying to come up with my opening line.

When Rusty got up to get a cup of coffee, I went into the bathroom, and when I returned to the kitchen, he was standing at the table looking through some papers. I went to my chair and remained standing beside him while I placed one knee on the chair's seat. It was a casual pose that I had taken, perhaps it was a subconscious attempt to appear nonchalant. He was still looking down when I began to speak. The words that came out of my mouth were, "Well, Bill is still being a jerk about you ..." Immediately, Rusty snapped his head up to look over at me, his eyes instantly glaring.

Rusty had often talked of the feeling he had as a child when his father would get angry. He said his father was a gentle, kind man, but there were times when Rusty knew not to cross him. He knew those times by the look in his father's eyes. He remembered his eyes as turning a cold, steely-gray with a menacing red dot in the center. He said he never tangled with his father when he got that look.

I cannot say Rusty's blue eyes actually changed color, but I can say the look that flashed from them was like a shot from a stun gun, halting my words mid-thought. I knew, at once, I had cause to fear that the conversation might turn ugly. I was afraid my next words, whatever they might be, would further that possibility. But how could I just leave it at that? After all, there was so much more to say. The next look Rusty darted at me before he turned his back, clearly said,

"Don't you dare! Don't say it! I don't want to hear it! Don't!" He looked so angry with me. I knew from experience anything I said would fuel his anger and, furthermore, he appeared to have grasped the meaning behind my feeble words. I stood there silent, leaning into my chair, while my thoughts clashed in my mind.

What should I do? I wish I could say something to smooth things over. Shouldn't I say something more? Shouldn't I do something?

No. I must let it go! The point was made.

But is that good enough? I could try to explain it better, I should explain.

No, he doesn't want to hear it. Nothing I could say right now is going to make it any better. I cannot risk a blowup, I just can't, and he knows that, too. I must leave it alone!

I believed the more I said right then, the worse it was going to get. If I started trying to qualify my statement, God only knew where the inevitable chiding back and forth would lead us. I decided not to take that chance. So with some regrets and cowardice, I retreated into silence, dumbstruck. After all my going over and over in my mind about what I wanted to say and how I should say it, I could not believe that was it, "Bill is still being a jerk about you." Bill is still being a jerk about you? What was that to say? I had wanted to condense everything into one intelligible sentence, but that sentence was hardly what I'd had in mind!

I slid limply into my chair. Without a word, Rusty left the room. I remained seated at the kitchen table, alone, feeling as though I should say something, but convinced it would be wise to take my cue from him and say nothing more. Although his choice to become uncommunicative left me feeling unsettled, I found the consolation I needed by telling myself the important thing was that Rusty, now, did know that coming to the hospital would mean a very unpleasant confrontation with Bill. However crudely, the point had been made. And Rusty and I, however awkwardly, had avoided a quarrel. So this was the way it was going to be and I had to be satisfied with that and had to let go of the turmoil that churned inside me.

Nothing more was said on the subject the remainder of the evening or the following morning. I was grateful and relieved everything was as usual between us when Rusty left for work, and I readied myself for my day at the hospital which included the transplant meeting that morning. I was glad Bill had agreed to go, for I preferred not to have to go alone.

We easily found the small meeting room on the first floor. Joyce was sitting at the head of a long table. A woman and two men were sitting at the far side of the table facing us as we entered. Joyce smiled at us and said, "Oh, I'm so glad you both made it. How's Dawson today?"

I answered, sighing, "The same. They still can't let him wake up. We were with him all morning and nothing has changed."

She shook her head and motioned to us to have a seat. As others continued to arrive, she engaged in some small talk with them while Bill and I sat silently. We had been quiet most of the morning. It had not been an awkward quietness, but more of a quiet, unspoken apprehension. What had there been to say, anyway? Just to ask each other the same unanswerable questions, "Why is Dawson so agitated? Why can't they get him off that respirator? Why can't he wake up? Why? Why? Why?" There was no point in our questioning each other. I had also decided that there was no point telling Bill of my talk with Rusty.

The meeting started and I squirmed in my chair when Joyce began by saying, "It's good to see all of you here. We have a couple of new people here with us today, so we should all introduce ourselves as we go around. O.K., let's start over here. Ernie, you can go first, introduce yourself to the group and maybe tell us a little bit about how you're doing."

Oh, no, I thought, *I hate this!* I had always dreaded the first day of a new class for this very reason, anticipating the instructor saying something like, "We'll just go around the room, and you can tell us why you're here and what you hope to get out of this class." It was quite a common format in classes I had attended through the years and I suppose I could have anticipated it at this type of gathering as well, but I had not. How I hated to have to speak in front of a group for it always made me extremely nervous. *God, do I need this today?*

I listened as Ernie, a small, black man told how he had been feeling a little tired in the past few weeks. He said he had not been able to do as much as usual, but Joyce gave him some encouraging words reminding him he could be getting his new heart any time. He smiled and appeared hopeful as he told of his plans for after his transplant.

Next, a middle-aged man and his wife told of their wait for his heart. While waiting, he had been hospitalized on the medication they had considered for Dawson. The wife told us of the day she received the call at home, "Can you come in to the hospital? Your husband's getting his heart!" She told of the emotions and excitement she had felt that day. He watched her as she spoke and he looked healthy and so grateful to be alive.

Then the tall, muscular, middle-aged black man who was sitting next to me introduced himself. Smiling, Joyce interjected, "You'll have to tell everyone, Charlie, what happened to you last month."

With a chuckle, he leaned back in his chair. He, too, looked quite well. He was dressed in a neatly-pressed denim shirt and jeans and was jovial as he told his story. A few weeks earlier he had been mugged and had been shot. He appeared quite proud and pleased with his new, strong heart that had survived the ordeal. I listened, knowing I was going to be next to introduce myself and I was thinking if only we had proceeded in the other direction around the table, Bill would have spoken before me. Then I would only have had to say my name and not have had to say much more, for Bill would have already told everyone our reason for being there.

When Charlie was through, Joyce looked at me, nodded and smiled encouragingly. I started speaking, my voice noticeably shaky, "My name is Andrea Bell ... and ...," my lip began to quiver and my eyes filled with tears. With the vision of Dawson in my mind, I was barely able to speak my next few, painful words, "we're here because our son needs a heart." At that moment, I found myself sitting there with tears spilling from my eyes. Though I had dreaded speaking and had feared appearing uncomfortably nervous, I had not expected I would have had such an overtly emotional reaction. I also could not have expected Bill would come to my rescue. I was quite surprised when, immediately, he picked up where I had left off, saying in a soft, but clear voice, "Our son has cardiomyopathy and he's here in intensive care waiting for a heart."

Joyce added, "Their son is on the VADs." Then looking over at us, she asked, "How long has it been now?"

Embarrassed that I had not controlled my feelings, I quickly composed myself and I was able to answer her question unemotionally, "He's been in the hospital eleven days and on the VADs, six."

I knew exactly how long it had been because Nina had just told me the day before that she recorded her notes, not only by date, but by, "Days on VADs." She had said, "Today is day number five." She explained she had become accustomed to keeping her records in that way when the VADs were in their trial stages. She said she was no longer required to keep extensive notes, but she still preferred to do so. I admired that about her and I liked that I would be able to ask her any time, "What day is it?" and she would be able to tell me in numbers.

Joyce said to the group, "They've been having a pretty rough time. Their son has remained intubated since he was put on the VADs. He's been too agitated to be taken off the respirator and he has a fever." All sympathetic eyes turned toward us as Joyce continued, looking at Bill and me, saying, "We have a lady who comes to our meetings sometimes who had been on the VADs before she got her heart. I'm sorry she isn't here today. She's doing very well and it would have been good for you to talk to her."

The introductions continued around the table to an Asian man who also had cardiomyopathy and was reluctant to get listed. He was concerned about his allergies to medications. That was something that concerned me, too, about Dawson. Penicillin was the only medication we suspected him to be allergic to, but with the number of medications he was on, and would continue to be on forever, I felt it quite possible he would have an adverse reaction to at least one of them. I watched this man's wife and daughter as he spoke and I could see and feel their concern.

There was an Hispanic man sitting next to him who was being considered for a transplant, and then a woman who had undergone hers with minor complications, and a man who had received a heart Joyce said was "as close to a perfect match as you could hope for." She said, "He has never had to be treated for rejection, not even one time." I learned most recipients have to go through signs of rejection at least once, and usually more. Increasing the dose of medication is quite common and generally takes care of the problem. To discover if there are any early signs of rejection, recipients must have a procedure done regularly, the one that Dr. Thompson had told Dawson and me about where a probe is inserted in the neck. Some at the meeting spoke of having become used to having it done. I remembered Dawson hating the sound of that, but compared to what he had been through at this point, it seemed minor.

I had already known it, but I could now see clearly we would never be completely "home safe" even after he received his heart. Nonetheless, I was praying for that day.

Joyce said, "I have the pictures from our annual dinner. Oh, here, here's a picture of Kim, the lady I was telling you about who had been on the VADs. She really went through a lot, too. She was put on the VADs shortly after having a baby. Can you imagine that! But she's doing great. See, this is her here," she said as she pointed to a smiling, attractive woman surrounded by many smiling people. I thought about the possibility of us being there at that dinner with Dawson next year, celebrating. I knew without a doubt if we were there, we would be smiling, too.

When the meeting came to a close, we all wandered out into the hallway and everyone approached us. One by one, showing their compassion, they all wished us well. Some hugged me and others said they would pray for Dawson. Bill and I thanked Joyce and as we got into the elevator to go up to see Dawson, I felt encouraged by having seen heart transplant recipients looking so well and by having seen people whose prayers had been answered. I was glad we had attended.

Putting my hand into my jacket pocket, clutching my rosary beads, we entered Dawson's new room. We had been told, when we were there to see him earlier that morning, they would be moving him to a room on the other side of the nurse's station.

When Dawson had been alert and feeling well in those early days in his first room, he had said to me, "Why is this room so dark? It's like a dungeon!" The nurse had told us, then, that he would be moved to one of the rooms with windows when he was better. He was glad to hear that and was extremely anxious to make the move, but today they had moved him while he slept, unaware. He was in his new, light, sunny room, where he had wanted to be, but he did not know it. If only he were awake! As I stood by his bed, I stared out the window at the view of the sky, wishing Dawson were seeing it, too, and fought back tears. Despite all the very serious things that were going on each day, it was the little things that could bring me down, the little things that tore at my heart.

Though his room was changed, his condition was not. The nurse, almost resolutely, shrugged her shoulders and said, "We tried C-Papping him again, but he failed." I had come to learn when they tried letting him breathe on his own, it was called a C-PAP trial. They gradually lowered the amount of oxygen he was given through the ventilator to test how well he was able to breathe without it. He was monitored and evaluated throughout the procedure. He had to go a certain length of time without distress and, evidently, he was still unable to do so.

Sad and disappointed, Bill and I left his room and went down to the cafeteria to wait for Claudia. She and Tracy were coming to visit sometime in the afternoon. The cafeteria was quieter than it had been in the last few days. There was less activity because of a diminished weekend staff. Bill and I had what was getting to be our standard cups of hot chocolate. Surprisingly, for all the hours we had spent in the cafeteria, we had eaten very little there. We were generally too upset and nervous, but the hot chocolate seemed to offer some needed comfort.

Dawson's friend, Matt, who had been coming to the hospital faithfully every night since that first night he had found us in the lobby, would not be coming that day. He was going to be away for three days to celebrate his birthday. It was a trip planned before Dawson had been hospitalized, and he said now he almost hated to go because he wanted so much to be there when Dawson woke up. He had been waiting with as much anticipation as Bill and I to see Dawson awake. But we assured him it was good for him to get away and relax and enjoy himself and we told him we would be sure to tell Dawson, should he wake up, that he had been there every day to see him. It had been good for Bill and me to have Matt's company and though he looked sad and concerned when he was there, he seemed optimistic. He was not talkative, mostly discussing electrical work with Bill, but he listened intently when I gave him the report of the day, frowning and slowly shaking his head as I spoke. I was deeply touched by his concern for Dawson. At times, Bill and I would stay in the waiting room while Matt would spend some time alone in Dawson's room. It was always comforting to know someone who loved Dawson was with him, whether it be Matt or my family or Bill's. The rules of the intensive care unit were that only family members were allowed in, but Matt had said to us, "I'll just tell them that he is my brother." The look in his eyes told me he felt that to be true, that Dawson, in his own special way, was his brother.

As Bill and I sat in the quiet cafeteria, I wondered if it would happen that way. After all the days that Matt was there waiting, would Dawson wake up when he was not there? Although Matt would be disappointed if it should go that way, I knew what exciting news that would be for him to return to. I hoped we would be able to say, "He's awake," the next time we saw Matt.

I had hoped to be able to say those words to Claudia when she arrived. Though I could not, I tried not to show how despondent I felt, enabling us, despite everything, to have a pleasant visit. She seemed to have such confidence in Dawson, or his strong will, his lucky star, or something. I held my personal fear and dread inside me as best I could.

When they were getting ready to leave, Claudia took me aside and said, "Rusty's at work today, right? I was thinking, since it is so close, maybe Tracy and I could go by his firehouse when we leave here. Tracy said he'd like to see it. Do you think Rusty would mind?"

"No, I'm sure he would like it. I'll call him and tell him." Rusty seemed very pleased Claudia would be coming by and he was more than happy to give them a tour of his firehouse. He gave me directions to give her and said he would try to be outside looking for her to show her where to park. As she left, I gave her a hug and thanked her for coming.

Not long after Claudia and Tracy left the hospital, Bill asked me if I would mind if we did not stay late. He had things at home he needed to attend to, having been at the hospital so many days and nights. I agreed reluctantly. It was not that my being there made any real difference to Dawson's welfare or that it made me feel any better, it was just that it was always so painfully difficult to leave him.

When I arrived at my parents' house, I was slightly surprised to find Claudia was not there yet. When she had left the hospital, she'd said, "I'll see you at Grandma's." Despite her plan to stop at the firehouse on her way, I had expected she would get "home" before me. I called Rusty to let him know I was at my mother's. I sensed an edginess to his voice and our conversation seemed strained and tense. Something was obviously wrong. Was his attitude a carry-over from the previous night's conversation? If so, why had he seemed fine earlier?

The only thing I could imagine was that he might be questioning why I had not ridden home with Claudia, why I had stayed and chosen to ride home with Bill. So, though he had not asked, I volunteered the information, saying, "I guess I could've left with Claudia, but I just wasn't feeling ready to leave that soon." When he was silent, I felt it necessary to explain further. I said, "When Claudia left, I didn't know then Bill was not planning to stay late." I shouldn't need to explain. And was it going to make any difference to him whatever I said? Or was he just too incensed by the idea of my spending time with Bill, especially when he could not be there with me, himself?

If it were the other way around and he and his ex-wife were sharing so much time together, I would not like it. What was there to like? But couldn't he understand how important and painful my every minute with Dawson was? Didn't he know all my minutes, all my days, wherever I was and whomever I was with were all agonizing? All that mattered to me was my time with Dawson, not my time with anyone else. Under ordinary circumstances no one would be expected to accept this situation, graciously or otherwise. But these were extraordinary times and they called for extraordinary deeds.

When I hung up the phone, I began pacing my mother's kitchen while I was questioning myself, speaking aloud, "Should I have waited to call Rusty until after Claudia got home? That way it would have looked like I had stayed at the hospital longer. Would Rusty have been less annoyed that way? Or should I have called Claudia at the firehouse from the hospital when I realized I would be leaving soon? In case she had not left there yet, I could have asked her for a ride. Is that what I should have done? Or should I have left with her? Had I upset Rusty? Was there something I should have done differently?" My mother, who ordinarily easily understood me, was looking at me like I was crazy. She had never looked at me quite like that before. Her expression showed confusion about why I was so frantically second-guessing myself over something that seemed so trivial. What I was saying did not seem to be making sense to her, so she finally asked, "What's the matter with you?"

What was the matter? I was concerned Rusty was upset with me, but I was already so overwrought, was it possible I might be making something out of nothing? Maybe I was just imagining there was something wrong. I thought perhaps my mother was right to look at me like I was crazy, maybe I was. Yes, I might be crazy, but did anyone stop to question why? At that moment, it seemed no one understood! *Dawson could die!* My heart cried out, *Please don't anyone question me! Don't you know? Dawson could die!*

Did anyone know what it was like for me, watching Dawson struggle for his life while being unable to help him? I understood how painful it was for Rusty to watch me in despair, unable to help me. But his frustration over his helplessness was adding to my despair.

I did not talk to him again until the following day when I called him from the hospital. Thankfully, our conversation was far more amicable. Unfortunately, Dawson's condition remained unchanged. Everyone was becoming extremely frustrated and even Dr. Harris was beginning to appear baffled. I told Rusty of my utter dismay and he was consoling and encouraging. I was quite relieved the tension between us had disappeared.

Matt had been away Saturday, Sunday and Monday, and when he

came to visit Dawson after work on Tuesday, there was no good news to report. Dawson continued to fail the C-Pap, he continued to have a fever and the doctors continued to appear perplexed by his anxiety. At that point, he had been on the VADs nine days and sedated for as many. That was, by all accounts, an unusually long time to remain sedated after surgery. According to the doctor's original estimate, he could have been listed in that time. At the very least, he should have been awake. This was not the way it was supposed to go. Dawson, if he were being true to form, would have been the patient that surprised everyone with how quickly he was getting well. We were not following his normally-charted course. *Oh, my God, is this, then, his destined-charted course? Lord, I'm afraid to ask where it is going to take us.*

On the VADs nine days, and he had gone into the hospital five days before that, which meant this was our fourteenth day. Two weeks had passed. The days were adding up. Frighteningly, the days were progressing, but we were not.

Describing Dawson as "sleeping" or "sedated" could evoke an inaccurate image of peacefulness. Though at times he did appear to be restful, most often he appeared uncomfortable. It was a sight that broke my heart. The respirator tube was held in place by a wide piece of white tape pulled tightly across his mouth. He coughed frequently, gagging, turning red, his eyes watering. And when he coughed, a nurse would stick an implement down his throat that noisily suctioned out bloody phlegm as he struggled and tried to pull away. There were tubes inserted into his neck that pulled at his skin. He was retaining fluids and was quite swollen. Bill had become upset when, on more than one occasion, we arrived and saw that his arms had fallen limply between the side bars of his bed and deep indentations had formed in his puffy arms and hands. Bill propped pillows alongside his arms to protect them, as he had seen one of Dawson's early morning nurses do. He wanted to make him comfortable, but at best it was not a peaceful sight and always there was the incessant sound of oxygen pushing through the breathing tube and the ever-present clicking of the VADs.

Dawson's temperature was rising above the low-grade-fever stage. Cultures had been analyzed and so far they had been negative which made the doctors unable to confirm infection as the source of his fever. There seemed to be a correlation between his anxiety and his fever. When his temperature was low, he was less combative, but never completely calm for any length of time and he was at his worst when his temperature was up. It seemed his progress toward extubation was dependent upon finding the source of and eliminating the fever. But that was proving to be a difficult task.

Rusty and I were having only slight ups and downs. He was cranky with me at times and loving at other times. Though I sincerely did not want to do or say anything I thought would upset him, I did nothing to alleviate his disappointment in me. That was the best I could do under the circumstances and to avoid making myself sick over it, I resigned myself to the fact I could do no more than that.

I was falling behind in my work at the shop, only managing to spend an hour or so there in the morning before going to the hospital. This week was better for us, both business-wise and personally. Rusty was on his five-days-off schedule which enabled us to have more time together. On Rusty's days home, the mornings were spent working. We'd get up early and go down to the shop around seven. I'd do my office work and leave around nine-thirty to meet my dad or to catch the bus to take me to the hospital. I'd call Rusty a couple of times throughout the day and I'd get home around nine or ten at night, weary and frightened. That schedule repeated itself until Rusty went back to work at the firehouse on Friday. That was Dawson's "Days-in-Hospital: Number Seventeen," and "Days-on-VADs: Number Twelve."

After I arrived at the hospital and had seen Dawson, I called the firehouse and asked to speak to Rusty. When he came to the phone, he sounded cranky. "Are you busy?" I asked apologetically. He answered with a curt, "No." I asked him if anything were wrong and, sounding irritated, he said, "It's just that I get worried when you call." I was taken aback. I had thought he felt it considerate, in fact almost mandatory, for me to call him regularly and let him know how Dawson and I were doing. *What is this?* I thought. *Am I damned if I do, damned if I don't?* I could understand his apprehension, but to actually sound annoyed that I was calling? What did he want from me?

The next morning, despite his attitude, I felt it was necessary for me to call again. I had spent the night at my parents' house while he was on duty, so I called to tell him of my plans for the day which, of course, involved my going to the hospital. I had decided to ride in with Bill. It was Saturday and Bill did not have to go to work, so he was able to be there when visiting hours started. My mother and father were going in, as well, but somewhat later. I wanted to be there as early as possible, which made my decision to go with Bill an easy one. Though I assumed Rusty would rather I did not ride with Bill, I certainly believed I should tell him I was. It was out of the question for me to lie about it, so I matter-of-factly told him of my plan and we talked for a short time. I left soon after and arrived at Bill's on schedule. Harley, who was no longer a puppy, came running to meet me. He was still quite cute and friendly and loved to romp. I was reminded of how happy I had been when I had seen Dawson running and laughing and playing with him. My heart ached to see him like that again.

That day seemed so far away, far off in some mythical future, as I stood by Dawson's bedside, his condition still unchanged. Bill and I had arrived to find his nurse completing yet another unsuccessful C-PAP trial. Was this the beginning of another disappointing day? I hated to have to tell my parents when they arrived that Dawson was still being kept sedated. I hated to see the letdown on their faces and the questions in their eyes, for which I had no answers. I could see how hard all of this was for them, and I tried to appear optimistic.

We again took turns being with Dawson and when my mother and I were in the waiting room I said to her, "I called Rusty this morning from your house before I left, but I haven't called him since I've been here. But there is just nothing to report, really, and since he was on duty last night, he might be trying to get some sleep today. I would hate to wake him up, just to say I have nothing to say."

My mother said, "Oh, I wouldn't call him and take the chance of waking him."

"And he told me it scares him when I call. If Dawson's fever were gone, if he were calm, if he were awake, if he were off the respirator, if he were any of those, I would take the chance and call him, but the way it is, what can I tell him? And after all, he can always call me."

"Yeah, I wouldn't call him."

"I guess I won't. I could call him later, but sometimes he doesn't go right to bed, he goes to the shop for a few hours and then goes home in the afternoon and lays down. So I don't know, I guess I'll just wait and see how it goes here."

My mom and dad left in the early afternoon. Bill and I stayed in Dawson's room although there was no change in his condition. About four o'clock, when the nurse told us they would not be trying another C-PAP until the following morning, I deluged her with my tormented questions. "Do you have any idea why he can't pass the C-PAP? What is it going to take for him to do it? It's been almost two weeks since the VAD surgery, what is happening? And what can happen to change things? How's he ever going to get off that respirator?"

"We're just going to keep on trying," was the nurse's answer.

Bill said, sadly, "Andrea, we're not going to see him awake tonight."

"I know."

"Maybe we should go. What do you think?" Bill said as the nurse left us alone.

I did not respond right away, but stood there looking at Dawson. I said finally, "Yeah, I guess so." I wanted to hold Dawson's hand, but was hindered by the tube inserted into it, so I touched his arm, softly, so as not to disturb him. I quietly said, "I love you, Dawson, it's going to be O.K., hon."

Bill went to the other side of the bed and put his hand, palm up, under Dawson's and with his thumb he gently stroked the top of Dawson's hand. Bill said, "I'll see you in the morning, Buddy."

We walked outside the hospital to a sunny afternoon, a definite change from the early evening darkness that had been greeting us during the week. I had not called Rusty yet, but I thought, *Well, at least, I'll be home early and he'll be so glad to see me.*

On the ride home, Bill said, "Do you want to get something to eat?"

We had not eaten all day and I thought it considerate of him to offer me dinner, but I said, "No, I don't think so, I want to get home. But thanks." I was thinking it was likely I would be home before Rusty had dinner and how pleased he would be if I could suggest we go out to eat and spend some time together. I thought to myself, *Getting home early will be good, we'll have a normal night. Rusty will be so pleased.*

Bill drove me to my car and I drove directly to the shop, assuming Rusty would still be working. I walked into the shop anticipating Rusty's pleasant surprise at seeing me. He was at the computer with his back toward me and I said, "Hi, hon."

He spun around in his chair and his expression was neither pleasant nor one of surprise. Nor was it a look of alarm. What I saw in his eyes was unmistakable anger.

I said, "What's wrong?"

He did not answer me.

"I'm early, huh?"

He still did not answer.

My heart began to pound. I asked him, "What's the matter?"

His expression unchanged, he sprang from his chair and shouting at me said, "What do you think I'm going through when I'm here and I don't hear a word from you? What do you think that's like?"

"I didn't call because I had nothing new to report. Unfortunately, there was no change."

"Well, couldn't you have called?"

"I thought you might be sleeping."

"Sleeping?" he said, sounding incredulous.

"Yes, you know you do sometimes when you've had a busy night at the firehouse."

"Oh, yeah, like I could sleep."

"Well, I thought you might and I hated to call you and startle you out of a sleep just to tell you nothing was changed. Then, when I was leaving early I knew I'd be getting home much sooner than you were expecting me. I thought you'd be glad."

"Don't you understand what I'm going through when I don't hear from you? I have no idea what is going on!" he said, raising his voice, anger flashing in his eyes.

"Well, you could've called me."

"Oh, yeah, I'd call you there!"

"You have before. You know you can call me anytime."

"I'm not going to call you. I think you should realize what it's like for me not being there."

"I'm sorry, but I didn't think …"

"Yeah, right, you didn't think. What am I, just some outsider?"

"Don't say that. Please. C'mon, that's not true."

"Oh, it isn't?"

"No, please, please don't do this to me."

"To you? You don't care what you've done to me! I'm treated like a nobody, yet I'm the one who has seen you through these past two years!"

"I know that, and I appreciate it, you know that. I know all you've done for us, please!"

"Please, what?" His anger had turned to rage. Pacing, pointing his finger at me, he shouted, "Lady, I've been here for you!"

"Don't do this to me!"

"Do this to you? Fuck you!"

"Don't say that! I told you not to ever say that to me again!" I screamed at him, "How could you pick a time like this to do this? How could you?"

He shouted questions at me. What time had I left for the hospital, what time had I arrived at the hospital, what time had I left for home. His words ripped through my already torn-apart heart and I cried out in absolute disbelief at what I was hearing, "What are you trying to say? What are you doing? I don't believe this is happening. Please, don't do this!"

"Don't do this? After all I've done for you and Dawson, you treat me like this?"

Shouting at him, I cried, "Treat you like what? I'm here! I'm early! I thought you'd be glad. Where do you think I've been? What do you think I've been doing? Don't you know what it's like for me watching Dawson? What do you think, I was out having fun somewhere while Dawson was lying in that hospital? What is wrong with you?"

"What is wrong with me? You didn't have five minutes to make a call?"

"I told you, I had nothing to report and I thought you might be sleeping."

"I've supported you and Dawson through this whole ordeal. Don't you think I have a right to know what's going on? Don't you think that maybe I'd want to be with him now?"

I was stunned for a moment. I realized I had hurt him deeply by the decision I had made. "Yes, I know, I know, but please just don't do this now. Please, Rusty, please, not now."

"Get out of here!" he shouted.

"Please, don't say that, I need you."

That enraged him even more and he screamed at me, "You need me? I have been here for you for two years! And you need me now?"

"Yes, so why aren't you here for me now?" Then I was screaming, "Why not now, when I need you the most?"

"Shut up!" he yelled.

"Answer me," I screamed. "How could you do this to me, now?"

"Shut up! Keep your voice down!"

Then I was screaming louder, "Why are you doing this now? Tell me, why now?" I could not believe he was turning against me. How could a man who loved me as much as Rusty did, do this to me? For it was true, he had been there for me. Even more than just being there, he had shown his support in the most loving and thoughtful ways. How could he care so much for me and yet lash out at me so viciously at this most terrible and neediest of times?

I felt as though my world had split open beneath me and there was nothing to hold on to, nothing to grab hold of that could spare me from an inescapable Hell. I was screaming from the top of my lungs to the pit of my stomach, "Please, Rusty. Please!" Completely out of control and out of my mind I was screaming, "Why are you not here for me now? Why not now? Why not now? Why not now? You are the cruelest man I have ever known!"

That hit a chord in him and he shouted, "Me? I'm cruel? Lady, the cruelest man you have ever known is your ex-husband!" He walked quickly to the front door. I followed him, crying hysterically. When we were outside, he locked the door and went to his truck. I thought, *We're going home, maybe he'll say he's sorry for having said the things he did, maybe he'll hold me.* I went to my car and, still crying, I drove home, two minutes away.

I ran up the stairs, hurled myself on the bed and cried like I had never cried before. I was crying convulsive tears, tears of fear of what was to become of Rusty and me, tears of anguish from an overwhelming sense of aloneness and I was crying openly for every heartbreaking moment I had spent in the hospital holding back those tears.

When time had passed, and Rusty still had not arrived, I realized he had deceived me into thinking he was leaving the shop and coming home with me. Locking the shop's door, and walking to his truck had been his way of getting me out of there, and it had worked. I had thought he would be following me home, but he, obviously, was not ready to make any amends. That realization only contributed to the emptiness I was feeling.

The world had become too big for me and I felt so alone in it. I was terrified, as terrified as I had been on a day long ago. I was a child and my mother had taken me shopping with her in a large downtown department store. We were in the toy department and I was fascinated with an elaborate train set on display. My mother said I could stay and watch it while she went down an aisle to get something. She told me, "Stay here, I'll be right back." I watched to see where she was going and continued to look back and forth between her and the train. When, in my next glance up, I did not see her, I panicked. I ran to where she had been, and terror overtaking me, I continued to run up and down the aisles searching for her. I was growing more frantic with each minute. The store had instantly grown into a surreal vastness and the sounds had become nearly deafening. I was so frightened and everywhere I turned I saw strangers. The world was so big and scary and I was so small and helpless. That was the way I felt now. I remember that day and that feeling from almost fifty years ago so clearly. I remembered hysterically running up to the counter, sobbing out the ridiculous words, "H-h-have … you … s-s-seen … m-my …

Mother?" My mother heard my terrified voice and came running to me.

The thought of losing Rusty made me feel like that lost child, alone in a frightening immenseness. I reached for the phone and called my mother. When she heard the pain in my voice, she became alarmed. "What is it?" she asked, sounding worried.

"Rusty's mad," I sobbed.

"What? What do you mean?"

"He's furious at me because I didn't call him today!" I said, starting to cry again.

"No! Oh, Andrea, no."

"Yes. He is so mad! He was yelling and screaming at me. He said I treated him like an outsider! Oh, I don't know what to do."

"I don't understand how he could do that!"

"You know how he is when he gets that mad and that hurt."

"Yeah, is he there?"

"No, he stayed at the shop. And I thought he was going to be so happy to see me when I got there because I was home early."

"Oh, Andrea, how awful."

Heartbroken, I cried, "How could he do this to me now? I'm already so afraid I'm going to lose Dawson, I don't think I deserve this."

"No, it's not right. Gee, and I told you not to call him."

"It's not your fault."

"What are you going to do?"

"I don't know," I cried. "I don't know. Oh, God!"

"Do you want to come down here? Do you want your father to go and get you? What do you want to do?"

I said slowly, "I don't know. I don't know what to do." Feeling weak and crushed, I said, "I'll call you later, O.K.? Thanks, bye."

When night came and Rusty had not come home, I called my mother again to tell her I was going to bed. I said, calmly, "I'm hoping I can sleep. I don't want to be exhausted when I see Dawson in the morning." Although I had not eaten all day, I went to bed without dinner. I was too upset to eat.

I awoke much later to hear Rusty's key in the front door. Shortly after, he entered the bedroom and came to bed. I lay there awake, thinking, *He'll reach over to me and say he is sorry and I will tell him I am so sorry, too. He will tell me how terrible it is to feel left out by someone you love and I will tell him I honestly understand. He will tell me he knows what I must be going through and that he did not want to hurt me. I will tell him I forgive him and ask him to forgive me, for I had not wanted to hurt him either.*

But he did not reach out to me, nor I to him. He did not speak those words, nor did I and I lay awake a long while, my heart aching.

I had a restless night's sleep and when I awoke in the morning, I heard Rusty getting ready. I stayed in bed, waiting for him to come to my side and say the words I had hoped to hear the night before, "Andrea, I'm sorry." But no words came. He left without speaking. When I heard the front door close, I got out of bed. I watched him from the window as he walked to his truck. Then I showered and dressed for the hospital and packed a small suitcase. I did not know it at the time, but I was never to spend another night in that house.

Chapter Eighteen

Sunday, August 25....Days in Hospital:19....Days on VADs:14

His rash is spreading!" I said.

"Yes, it has a little," the nurse agreed. "And his fever is up."

Raising my voice, alarmed and frustrated, I said, "It's obvious he's having an allergic reaction! Has the doctor seen him today?"

"Yes."

"What did he say?"

"He said he thinks it is related to his medication."

"I knew that three days ago!" I cried out. On Friday, I had seen a few tiny, red dots on Dawson's right side. I had become concerned and had called nurse Cindy's attention to it. "I'll go tell Doctor Harris," she said as she headed out the door. When she returned to tell me of his response, I'd gotten the distinct impression he had taken the report rather lightly. Later that day, I approached him in the hallway. "What do you think about Dawson's rash?" I had questioned him. "It's very slight," he responded. "But do you think it's a reaction to his medication?" I pressed. He answered quite casually, "It could be." "Is there something you can do about it?" I continued. He said he was hesitant to try anything because Dawson was on so many medications and he needed all of them. "Do you have any idea which one he might be reacting to?" "I can't be sure," he said, "but there are a couple I would suspect." I asked about the possibility of taking him off of them, but he shook his head. I understood that Dawson needed his medications, but continuing to give him something that was causing a negative reaction frightened me. The doctor responded emphatically, saying, "I will be watching him. There is just nothing else I can do."

Now, with the rash having gotten worse, what would he do? Was there anything he could do? I looked at Bill. He was frowning, but he did not seem to be feeling quite as upset as I was. It was unlikely he had spent days contemplating the possibility of this happening and the possible consequences of keeping him on a medication he was allergic to.

Realizing I had not yet checked Dawson's monitor, my eyes quickly moved to the familiar screen. I had become accustomed to watching the blinking green numbers that told me of Dawson's ongoing fever. Despite the fact that the nurse had just told me his fever was up, I was startled by what I saw. It was a number I had not seen on the monitor before. His temperature was registering 40.0. His fever had climbed to one hundred and four degrees.

I had so desperately needed a positive day after the traumatic night I'd had with Rusty, that I wanted to scream out loud, "God, why is this happening? How much more do you think I can take?" Instead, I calmly asked the nurse, "Where's the doctor? I need to talk to him."

Bill and I waited quietly in Dawson's room while she went to find him. Earlier, it had been hard to dismiss from my thoughts the horrible scene I had lived through with Rusty the day before. Now I had no difficulty putting it aside. I was mindful that there would come a time when I would have to give it serious thought, though I had no idea when that would be or what I would eventually do about it. At the moment, none of that mattered, and beyond the fact that I was not going home to Rusty that night, I had made no plans for dealing with that part of my life.

When the doctor came into the room, he went to Dawson and leaned closer to examine him, then turning to us he said, "His fever is dangerously high. I'm getting concerned. I'm considering discontinuing an antibiotic in an attempt to identify the source of this." He went on to explain, "I hadn't wanted to take him off the Vancomycin, but I have to try something. His fever is just too high and has gone on much too long. We have to find out what is going on here. If we take him off of the Vanco and it is what he's been reacting to, his fever should go down. It would take about twenty-four to forty-eight hours for that to happen, then, at least, we would know something."

I was wishing he had done this days ago and hoping that this action would prove to be the answer to my prayers. *But will there be dreadful consequences to face from stopping an antibiotic that he needs?* My mind was going in circles. Yet I knew the doctor was right. Something had to be done. I believed if and when Dawson's temperature were normal he would be, too, so I had to welcome any decision that might bring that about. After all, we had proof that when his fever was lower, he was calmer. On one such day he had lasted seven hours C-PAPping, but as his fever had increased so had his agitation. Eventually, he had become unmanageable, thrashing and kicking. Sedating him had been the nurses' only recourse.

I had seen what he was like when he was deliriously out of control. It was a terrifying sight and I had become fearful of witnessing it again. One morning, before we had realized the extent of Dawson's agitation, his nurse had said to me, "You can talk to him, you know. He'll hear you." When she left his room and I was alone with him, I spoke softly to him saying, "Dawson, Mom's here, hon." His feet started slowly moving, then his legs, slowly bending. Then with one, quick, thrashing movement, he flung both of his legs over one side of the bed's metal railing. He grabbed his VADs and hooked his thumbs around the strings attached to his wound dressing. He was violently and with deliberation wrenching his way down to the bottom of the bed with his legs still over the side. I had visions of him crashing to the floor, pulling the IV stand to which he was attached right down with him. I yelled for the nurse and grabbed his hands. I tried to release his hold, but could not. His fingers were clenched tightly around the VADs' tubes. I could not pry them loose and I was terrified he would rip them out from their incision. I frantically begged him, "Dawson, please let go. You're all right, Dawson. I'm here with you, hon. Dawson, please don't pull on these, they are beautiful things, they're helping you. They are a miracle. Dawson, please let go!" The nurse came rushing in and gave him a shot, then calmed him down and checked to see if there had been any damage done. Thankfully, there had been none, but I was quite shaken and I had not been able to rid the experience from my mind.

Since that day, especially when I would arrive alone, I'd stand outside his room awhile, afraid to enter. I would stand where, if he were awake, he would not have been able to see me, yet where I had a view of his uncovered feet. Watching his feet, I'd hope they would remain still. That way I could be assured he was calm. At times he seemed to get overly restless merely by the sound of my voice as I talked to his nurse outside his room, so I'd stand there quietly.

Every day's arrival was filled with hope and dread and fear of what I might find, but nothing could have kept me from being there. I had not missed a day of seeing Dawson, nor had Bill. In addition to spending each evening at the hospital, he checked in on Dawson on his way to work early every morning. I was very grateful when he began calling me each day to give me that morning's report, telling me how Dawson's night had been and updating me on his latest condition. I came to rely on his eight o'clock calls to start my day, for Bill's reports were, more often than not, encouraging and optimistic. Most mornings he'd say that his fever was lower. "Today might be the day," he'd say, meaning the day Dawson's fever would finally be gone. But so many days, by the time I arrived at the hospital just three hours later, his fever had gone back up.

Monday, August 26....Days in Hospital:20....Days on VADs:15

It had been almost twenty-four hours since Dawson had been taken off the antibiotic when I arrived at the hospital the next day. Bill, on his morning call had sounded happy when he told me Dawson's fever was "definitely coming down." I felt truly hopeful, anxiously anticipating the possibility of seeing Dawson awake and calm without that fever. I had imagined walking into his room unafraid, yet as I approached his room, I hesitated for just a moment and with great anticipation I asked his nurse, "How is he? Is his fever still down?" Her answer was, "No." That blunt word was to my heart like a quick blow would be to my stomach, almost taking my breath away and I audibly moaned. I put my hand to my chest, immediately halted, too disappointed and, once again, too frightened to enter his room. I was so ashamed that I was letting my fear keep me from going in. I despised myself for being afraid to see him and I struggled with my feelings, *How can I be frightened of Dawson? Now, when he needs me? When he, himself, must be so frightened?* I said to myself, with great scorn, *How dare you not go to his side. How can you be so weak?* I prayed to God, *Please grant me the strength I need.* I took a deep breath, slowly entered his room, and tried to think optimistically. I reminded myself that, after all, it hadn't been a full twenty-four hours since taking him off the antibiotic, and the doctors had said it might take up to forty-eight to see any improvement. I convinced myself of the real possibility that this, still, could be the day that I would look into his eyes and not see that awful terror in them.

I stood silently by his bed, thinking, *If only I could do something for him.* I looked at the numbers on the screen of the monitor, focusing on the numbers representing his temperature. They were bouncing back and forth between 39.5 and 39.7, I stared intently at them, trying to will them down. Never taking my eyes off of those numbers I prayed, believing that with faith and sheer will, I could help his fever to go away. I stood there for over an hour staring and praying that I would see a miraculous 37 or 38, but the lowest it went was 39.3. And though it did not stay there, I tried to console myself that it was still early and at least it had not gone back up to that horrible one hundred and four. But it was a long way from normal and I knew, all too well, how such small signs of improvement could be fleeting. I had been reminded of that fact almost daily. This day was proving to be no different from so many others.

In addition to calling me in the morning, Bill had gotten into a routine of calling me from work to hear the latest report from me. He was always shocked and dismayed when I'd tell him, "His fever is up again." I had to tell him that, again this day and when I did, he just cried out in frustration, "It was coming down, I saw it, it was lower than ever! Why would it go back up? What is this? Andrea, what is going on?"

"I don't know," I said. "God, I don't know."

We both needed the updates, but following the constant ups and downs of Dawson's condition was quite painful for us. It might seem that having Bill tell me in the morning that Dawson was better would only make it harder for me when I arrived to find him worse. Though it is true the resulting letdown was overwhelming, I needed his encouraging morning calls. They were truly a blessing, for they helped me to enter the hospital, ride up in the elevator, and walk into Dawson's room a little less apprehensive than I would have without them. And I needed that, for these simple tasks seemed to be the hardest things I'd ever had to do.

Though I had managed to maintain some optimism at the twenty-four-hour point, when thirty-six hours came with no signs of improvement, it took everything I had to remain hopeful. Progressing slowly or progressing not at all had been bad enough, but this, this seemed to be a dreadful step in the wrong direction.

His condition seemed to be taking him down a road to a place I feared, while at the same time, my faith was heading me down a road of my own. Although we were on separate paths that appeared to be taking us in different directions and further away from each other, I wondered, at times, if it were possible that we were actually heading for the same destination. That destination being like that imaginary vanishing point in the distance where parallel lines ultimately converge. If that were so, where was that point where we would eventually meet, what was it and when would we reach it?

My prayers were obviously not being answered in precisely the manner in which I had hoped, but despite that, my faith was not waning. That was partly because I was just too terrified to let go of it, but also because, ironically, there were things happening to me that were helping to bolster my faith.

While waiting at the bus stop one morning, a young woman approached me and began talking to me about face cream. She told me about a product she was selling, reached into her bag and handed me some samples. I thanked her but told her I really was not interested. She smiled and proceeded to chat about other mundane things. When my bus came, I got on with her following right behind me. Seating herself next to me, she returned to the conversation of the benefits of skin care. I said, "I'm sure your products are good, but at this time there is nothing I could be less concerned about than taking care of my skin. My son is in intensive care. He needs a heart transplant. I'm on my way to see him."

"Oh, I'm so sorry," she said, sounding sincere, "I'll say a prayer for him."

I was impressed by her gesture and said, "That would be very nice, thank you."

"In fact," she said, "I'll have the whole congregation pray for him." Then she took a small laptop from her bag, asking, "What is his name?"

"Dawson," I said, looking at her rather mystified. "Dawson Bell."

"D-A-W-S-O-N?"

"Yes."

"Bell. O.K." Then she proceeded to type and slowly speak the words as she typed them. "Dear Lord, we are praying to you today for Dawson Bell. We are asking that you take care of him. He needs a heart and he needs your help. Please answer our prayers. Thank you, Lord. Amen."

I was moved by her expression of compassion, yet I could not help but think that what she had done had made her seem to be somewhat of a kook. But my mixed emotions about this stranger and the fact that it all seemed rather bizarre, did not lessen the sincere gratitude I was feeling for her thoughtful prayer. In fact, the unusual circumstances surrounding it, only added to its meaningfulness. For I had to ask myself, *What are the odds of meeting someone on the bus who would use their laptop to compose a prayer for you on-the-spot? A woman who is selling cosmetics. How odd. Really, how many people can say that they have had that happen to them?* I thought there must be a reason why I had met this woman and the reason was clear to me. It was God's way of telling me not to give up on my prayers. I could not explain how else I could have happened to meet a stranger on the bus who would do this for me.

"I will give this to my pastor," she said, "and we will all say it in church on Sunday."

"Thank you," I said and I turned away, blindly looking out the window, for tears were blurring my vision as I imagined the touching sight of a church full of people praying for Dawson. She got off the bus shortly after, long before my stop and I thanked her again, from my heart.

"Would you like to come with me to church one day?"

I had answered, "Yes, I would. I would like to very much." I had been talking to a woman in the waiting room whose husband was suffering from leukemia. She said he had been diagnosed only a short while before, but that he now was in the hospital in very serious condition. She told me of the trip to England they had planned to make very soon. She lowered her eyes as she said, "He talks of how he's looking forward to our wonderful trip, but I know that all he really wants to do is just come home." Sadly looking up at me she said, "That's all I want, too." "I know," I said, nodding, understanding just how she felt. She told me of a church a few blocks away from the hospital that she often walked to. She said, "I'm not Catholic, but I find comfort there. It's a beautiful, peaceful place."

"What church is it?" I asked.

"St. Dominic's. Are you Catholic?"

"Yes, I am."

Our schedules had not enabled us to go together, but because I had been made aware that there was a church close by, I felt I must go. I asked my dad if he would drive me there and we went one afternoon. My dad held the large, heavy wooden door open for me as I entered. The church was empty and quiet. As my eyes moved about the church, I was awed by its magnificence. It was immense and ornate with massive stone columns and archways, glorious stained glass windows and a lofty, domed ceiling above the altar. It had been a long time since I had been in a church for the sole purpose of praying, and this church was as splendid as any that I could remember. Its imposing size could have made it seem cold and unfriendly, but, on the contrary, its grandeur was a symbol to me of something so great and powerful that I felt strangely comforted. As I walked slowly down the center aisle, the sight of hundreds of flickering candles came into view, and their warm light and inviting scent welcomed me home. There were more candles than I had ever seen and I knew I must light one there for Dawson. Kneeling before Saint Jude, I prayed for Dawson's recovery. My dad knelt beside me. When we stood, I motioned to him to enter a pew. We knelt, again, bowed our heads and my father quietly wept.

Learning of this church seemed to be another message from God, this one also clear. This one was to let me know He was with me to comfort me and to give me hope.

When I told Bill that I had gone, I was surprised and quite pleased when he responded by saying he would like to go sometime. I felt fortunate when he suggested we go together the very next afternoon. It proved to be an inspiring experience for both of us and we began going often, lighting candles each time we went. It was emotionally stirring to pray within the sanctified surroundings, and reassuring to know there was a candle burning there for Dawson. We learned that there was a five o'clock mass in the small side altar each evening, referred to as the Saint Jude mass. When we attended, we discovered there was a time during the mass when the priest asked for "intentions." We did not know, at first, what that meant, but soon saw it was an invitation to those congregated there to ask that a significant prayer be said. Anyone could randomly speak out. Bill and I looked at each other, but neither one of us was ready to do that, just yet. We sat through many masses listening to others' intentions. I did not know if I would ever be able to speak aloud there, but one day Bill said that he was ready. And when the time came, his voice rose from our back pew, "Please pray for our son, Dawson, who is very sick and is in the hospital." Those gathered responded in resounding unison, "Lord, hear our prayer." Bill looked at me as tears rolled down my face and I nodded to him, "That was good." I put my hands to my face, knelt and bowed my head on the back of the pew in front of me, begging silently from my heart, *Dear, God, please make Dawson well.*

As we filed out of the pew, a young woman I had never seen before stopped and nodded to me. Bill and I continued on out, walked to his truck and drove back to the hospital. As we got into the elevator he said, "Do you want to go to the cafeteria before we go back up?"

The doors closed, and I said, "O.K.," as I pushed the button marked "two," just in time. The doors immediately opened and I was utterly astonished to see the young woman from church standing there. As we exited the elevator, this woman took a step toward me, reaching out to me with her hands. As she held my hands, our arms outstretched, she said, "I was so touched by your husband's request, I am going to pray for Dawson every day."

"Oh, thank you," I said, moved by this unexpected act of kindness. "Are you visiting someone here in the hospital, too?"

"No, actually I'm on my way to a meeting here, but I think I am on the wrong floor."

I asked her where she was going and when she told me I said, "You are not only on the wrong floor, you are in the wrong building." Astounded, I said, "It's pretty amazing that we would run into each other here, especially when this isn't even where you are supposed to be."

She nodded, saying, "St. Dominic's isn't even my church, I had never been there before and had no plans of going, but I passed it on my way here and I was drawn in."

"Really? And because of that, more prayers will be said for Dawson."

"Let's say a prayer for him now," she said.

We were standing just to the right of the elevator as people came and went. I stood holding hands with this stranger as she closed her eyes and began reciting a spontaneous prayer for my son, whom she had never met. Dawson was somehow inspiring these strangers' prayers, and though I had said many times before in other instances, "If anyone could do it, Dawson could," could there be any doubt where these inspirations were truly coming from?

These unexpected prayers uplifted my spirit, awakened my faith and inspired me to recognize every small favor as a blessed gift.

Bill's early morning visits were giving him the opportunity to meet the late-night nurses, for the late shift was eleven P.M. to seven A.M. Bill was his most optimistic when Scott had been Dawson's night nurse. Bill admired him and appreciated his special care. He said to me, "Scott is so nice, he's really good to Dawson. Dawson always looks better when Scott has been his nurse. You should see him. He washes his hair and has him looking so comfortable. He props pillows up all around him, his arms resting on them, and with the bed in almost a sitting position, Dawson looks like he's just sleeping in his chair." When Bill spoke of Scott, I could hear the gratitude in his voice and each night when we'd leave Dawson, Bill would say to me, "I hope he has Scott tonight." Though I had not met him, I hoped so, too. I appreciated what he was doing for Dawson and, in turn, for Bill. And, too, he was good about giving Bill detailed information, information that Bill would pass on to me when he made his morning call.

Because Bill called me on my cell phone, he had no idea where he was reaching me, which was good because I had not wanted to have to explain why I had not been home for several days. I still had not told him anything about what Rusty and I had gone through, for there was no need for him to know. Furthermore, I simply did not feel like talking about it to anyone, not even to Rusty. On the first night that I had not gone home, Rusty had called my mother. When I had arrived at her house that night, she said to me, "Rusty called, he said to call him if you want to. Do you think you will?"

"I don't know," I'd said at first. But after giving it some thought I said, "I guess I will. I'm sure he wants to know about Dawson." When I spoke to him that night, we talked only of Dawson's condition. We never mentioned "us." That was the way I wanted it, for I had not been ready to discuss "us" or, for that matter, give "us" any thought.

Wednesday, August 28....Days in Hospital:22....Days on VADs:17

Sitting in the waiting room, my stomach churning, wrought with nerves, I was anxious to talk to the doctor. I had so many questions going around in my mind. Forty-eight hours off the antibiotic and Dawson's fever was still raging and showing no signs of breaking. *Does this mean that he's not having a reaction to that particular drug? Can we be sure? Is there another medication that he could be taken off of? Will they try that? And how will that affect him? And that's another forty-eight hours before we know? Or do we just assume that an infection is the source? But if so, why doesn't anyone know where the infection is and why aren't the antibiotics helping? Dear God, what are we going to do now?*

I had been told that his blood and urine cultures were still coming back negative, but the doctors had also informed me of sputum cultures showing "pan-sensitive staph" one day, "candida from sputum" on another day, and something that was "growing gram-negative rods," whatever that meant. *Could these be considered as the source?* I was confused about all that was going on and I tried to understand as best I could. But, at times, I still did not fully comprehend the details of his condition, though I had been asking endless questions. I was grateful that the doctors had continued to answer them without showing any annoyance, for now I had more questions to ask of them. *Where is the doctor today?* I wondered as I glanced at my watch.

I now had a watch. A few days before Rusty and I had our confrontation, he had handed me a small bag. Inside, wrapped in tissue paper, was a watch. Rusty said, "It's so you will know what time it is when you are in the waiting room." "Oh, how nice," I said, and I put it on. But its fixed, silver band was too big, so Rusty insisted we go right back to the store to exchange it. I was appreciative of Rusty's thoughtfulness, but part of me was balking at the idea of getting a watch and I was having a difficult time finding one that was just right. The band had to be small enough to fit, but I wanted the face to be big enough so that I could read it easily without my glasses. He could sense my reluctance and was becoming slightly aggravated with me when I was not accepting any that I saw. I couldn't tell him why I was resisting finding the right one because I knew he would get angry with me, for my reasoning would sound absurd. I could not tell him I was afraid that having it would prove to be for naught, afraid that my hospital visits would abruptly come to an end. It was a ridiculous way of thinking, but I knew so well how things go. You get all prepared for something and then it doesn't happen. I could get all set for a long stretch in the hospital and then the next day, it's all over. I knew how stupid it would sound to say such a thing, after all, if it did go that way it would not be because I had a watch! I knew enough not to say anything to Rusty about how I was feeling, but he could see something was wrong and had become impatient with me, but it was not unusual to have his thoughtfulness countered by his impatience and annoyance. Realistically, I knew his idea of a watch was a good one and, eventually, I found one that I accepted. It had a very cute, adjustable bracelet-type band made up of silver links and fancy hearts, Xs and circles and it had proven to be very nice to have.

As I looked at it today, feeling terribly nervous, I thought of Rusty and the extremes of his personality. He took such pains to do thought-ful things for me, and he had the ability to make me feel so loved and cared for. Yet, so often, he was capable of saying and doing things that were unnecessarily contentious and extremely destructive, though he never hurt me physically. The worst thing was not that he often became angry and showed his temper, but it was that his temper did not pause for anything. When he was angry, he was angry and that was that. Nothing stood in its way. We had many horrible fights on special occasions, occasions that I would have thought were important enough to put disagreements aside for. But he, obviously, had not. And those events that I remembered with bitterness were numerous. They included three weddings, a Father's Day, an Easter, two Christmas parties, a birthday party and one very special wedding anniversary. Because there had been so many special occasions along with countless ordinary days that had turned ugly, and because I now had this last episode to add to the list, I saw clearly that his anger held nothing sacred. That he had not controlled his temper with me at a time like this, made me realize there would never be a time, nor a person, nor anything more important to Rusty than his own anger. It was now so obvious. All his wonderful traits—understanding, generosity, compas-sion, helpfulness, intelligence and integrity—were entirely under-mined by his overt defensiveness, which often went beyond reason.

I was thinking how he had grown increasingly irritable with me over the past year. Perhaps it was simply due to the many hours we spent working at the shop together, but that alone should not have caused the rift between us. The fact that we disagreed on so many facets of running the business was the prime cause, yet it was not so much that we disagreed. For me, the problem was that we could not discuss our differences. It appeared he did not want to hear what I had to say and took almost every suggestion I made as a direct insult to him and took the questions I asked as a sign of a lack of confidence in him. There were things we needed to talk about, but he said I always chose the wrong time to do it. Many days, I sat there in the shop, my stomach in knots as I struggled to find the right way and the right time to say something like, "So-and-so called and wants to know when he can expect his order or such-and-such bill is due this week." God forbid, if I questioned the correctness of an order!

But I can say, without a doubt, if I told him that I needed him to do something for me or Dawson, Claudia or my parents, he would willingly drop anything and everything to come to our assistance.

And he had done so, many times, in a generous, giving way. I admired that quality about him, it endeared me to him and it made me feel special and important to him.

As I continued to sit alone in the waiting room, I realized that the nervous feeling I was experiencing was all too similar to the way I had felt so many days working at the shop. *I've been as nervous in the shop as I am in this hospital waiting room!* I nearly jumped to my feet from the revelation and almost speaking out loud, I uttered to myself, *It is understandable that I am feeling so nervous today. I have every reason to be upset. I could not expect to be anything else. My son is in critical condition, his fever is out of control and no one knows why. Of course I am nervous. But that I should have been equally as tense in the shop over pathetic nonsense is outrageous. Yes, today I have to live with this feeling, I have no choice and I truly have reason to be distraught. But from this day on, I vow I will never, ever again allow anyone to put me in a position to be this nervous when I do not have to be. I will always distinguish between the important matters in my life and the worthless ones. I will forever know the difference.*

That night when I talked to Rusty, I said to him, "No one could possibly go through what I am going through and not be changed by it. No matter what happens, I will never be the same after this."

"Oh, yeah, I know," he said with sarcasm, "you're going to church." I had mentioned I was going, during a previous night's conversation, and I had said to him, at that time, that it was giving me comfort and a renewed faith, which I so desperately needed.

Now, in answer to his scoffing remark, I tried to explain, "I don't mean I'm different because I'm going to church or because I pray ..."

"Yeah, right," he interrupted, "*you* pray to God. But, Andrea, when was the last time *God* talked to you?"

"Rusty, don't, please. I really don't want to get into this with you."

"Yeah, fine," he said abruptly, and hung up.

I sat there a moment with the receiver to my ear, not having informed him that, indeed, quite recently in fact, God *had* spoken to me.

Chapter Nineteen

Thursday, August 29....Days in Hospital:23....Days on VADS:18

A nurse's aid was in Dawson's room when I arrived. She smiled at me, as she had done many times, but this time there was a seriousness in her expression that I had not seen before. I wondered if it were simply due to the fact she'd seen him lying there for so many days. Or more likely it was due to the sight of him with a raging rash that was now covering 80 percent of his body. She gazed soulfully at him and, though she had never spoken to me before beyond a quiet "good morning," this day she did.

She looked at me and asked, "Are you his wife?"

Despite my distress, I could not help but smile momentarily and I answered somewhat proudly, "No, I'm his mother."

She looked surprised and slightly embarrassed and she said, apologetically, "Oh, I didn't know."

"That's O.K.," I said, imagining Dawson would have seen the humor in that question and definitely have gotten a chuckle out of it. But first, I'm sure he would have rolled his eyes and smirked, showing the sardonic side of his personality. I, myself, did think it quite absurd, but I was flattered. But far beyond having received a compliment, what meant more to me was that I had been given the chance to tell her who I was. I was glad to tell her, for I believed she would then know the full depth of my concern and love for this young man, my son. That is not to say a loving wife would not be filled with much the same emotions, but mine were combined with and amplified by a mother's instinct to protect and an inherent desire to make everything "all better." Certainly, it was not necessary this woman know all my feelings, yet I felt surprisingly grateful I had been given the opportunity to express to her the full extent of my heartache, and I had said it all in four simple words, "I am his mother."

I had thought my relationship to Dawson was obvious, but what was not as obvious, was my relationship to Bill. Though we had been asked all our statistical information at the time of Dawson's admittance, it seemed that only the nurses who had been assigned to Dawson during his first days there knew that Bill and I were divorced. And as time went on, there seemed no reason to announce that fact to each new nurse we met. We were simply Mr. and Mrs. Bell to them, Dawson's parents. Therefore, some nurses knew that we were not married and some did not. One day, one of the nurses who did not know, told us that if we did not want to drive home late or we did not want to be far away from Dawson, we could talk to the social worker from the transplant unit and she would arrange for us get a room close to the hospital to spend a night or two. We knew that the transplant services had apartments available for that purpose and when the social worker had asked us if we might be interested in getting a room, Bill and I had looked at each other and said, "No, probably not." Bill and I had talked about it later, and he'd said, "Maybe you could stay sometime, if you wanted to." I told him that, depending on the circumstances of Dawson's condition, I might, but that I really preferred to stay at the hospital or go home. So far, there had been no urgency to take advantage of their considerate offer, but perhaps a time would come when I would. I knew, also, that any transplant recipient who lived more than fifty miles away, as Dawson did, could move with his family into the apartments when released from the hospital, and I imagined the possibility of Dawson and I doing that when that wonderful time came.

As the nurse's aid was leaving Dawson's room, Dr. Harris entered. His expression, too, was more serious than usual. He was frowning as he said, "His fever went up to 40.1 last night and, as you can see, his rash has gotten much worse. I think this all could be due to a drug reaction, but I am still not comfortable ruling out infection as the possible source of his fever. So in an attempt to locate it I'm ordering a CT scan, and I've asked to consult with the infectious disease department in the event that he has some uncommon infection that we are not detecting."

"Do you think he has something unusual?"

"Not really, but we must get control of this fever soon, so I'm going to try everything I can."

"With his fever so high, I guess there isn't much chance of getting him off the respirator today then, is there?"

"Well, we're certainly going to try. I'm thinking that if we can only get him off of it maybe he could tell us something that would help lead us to the problem. He cannot go on like this much longer. It's just too hard on him. We're now having trouble maintaining his blood pressure." He looked quite concerned and his words caused a new fear to rush over me. *Trouble maintaining his blood pressure? My God!* Terrifying scenes I'd seen on many television shows invaded my mind, where a frantic emergency room doctor is shouting, "His blood pressure is dropping! We're losing him!" I had seen that drama played out countless times on TV and the image of that happening to Dawson left me unable to respond to his statement and he continued on. "Dr. Wiviott from infectious disease is extremely efficient and very thorough. I hope to talk to him today." And as he left he said, "We're trying."

I spent most of the day in Dawson's room and, as far as I could tell, no new doctor had come by. When Bill arrived that afternoon, I told him that I was quite sure that the infectious disease doctor had not been to see Dawson yet. I said, "But Dr. Harris said that he was going to consult with Dr.," I paused, "Dr. whatever-his-name-is. So maybe he's been here and they discussed Dawson, but I just haven't seen him."

"Did they try to have him breathe on his own today?"

"Yeah, he didn't do well."

During doctors' rounds, Bill and I went down to the cafeteria, but did not stay long. I found it too noisy and uncomfortable, yet neither the quiet lobby nor its soft couches helped me to relax. As I sat on the edge of the chair thinking of the struggle Dawson was going through and his unexplained fever, I noticed Laura coming our way. She was wearing black pants and a fuchsia satin blouse, carrying her coat over her arm. She was walking quickly as though she were in a hurry, looking somewhat frazzled. I thought that if I did not know her, I would not have guessed that she was a psychologist. If her appearance had a touch of unsophistication, it was probably that very quality about her that I appreciated most. She was so down-to-earth, natural, and real. As I had liked her from the first time I met her, my fondness for her had grown the more I had gotten to know her. She had continued to come by often to see Dawson in the hopes of talking to him and when she had found him sedated and still on the respirator, she seemed truly saddened and listened to my laments with compassion. Today, though obviously in a hurry, she stopped to acknowledge us. "Hi, how're you guys doing? I haven't seen Dawson today, but I'd guess that he is still intubated."

"You're right," I nodded, "he is. They tried, but still, no."

"I thought so. You don't look like parents whose son has been extubated. I'm so sorry. Well, maybe tomorrow."

"Yeah, maybe. I hope so. It's just so hard."

"I know, I know," she said. "Take care now. I'll check in on you guys next time I'm here."

Soon after, we returned to the ICU and I noticed a doctor who I had never seen before sitting in the nurses' station talking on the telephone. I stopped, reached for Bill's arm and whispered to him, "That might be him." Then I motioned to Bill to go on ahead to Dawson's room while I stayed back to listen. I could not hear everything he was saying, but I grasped bits and pieces, words here and there. I could make out, "He was transferred to this medical center for consideration of … upon arrival he appeared quite ill with … and near complete … and recent history of significant arrhythmias and … slowly improved … with fever … we must consider the possibility that … true pulmonary infection." It wasn't much, but it was enough. I believed it was Dawson he was speaking of and I did not want to hear any more. I could eavesdrop no longer, for I was convinced that he was Dr. "Whoever" and I did not think that I could bear to hear his diagnosis. I knew it seemed a little too soon for him to make one, but I was afraid he might have come to a preliminary opinion there was infection around Dawson's heart. That had been mentioned to me earlier by Dr. Harris, somewhat off handedly, but I had the impression it would be very serious if that were the case. I could not have handled hearing that, so I stopped listening and went to Dawson's room. I said to Bill, "I think it is him."

"What was he saying?"

"I think he was dictating into the phone, and every other word was a medical term, I just couldn't catch it all. I didn't hear him say Dawson's name or mention the VADs, but from what I could understand, I do believe he was talking about Dawson. I heard something about pulmonary infection."

"What does that mean?"

"I don't know, infection around the heart or lungs, I guess, I don't know. But if it is his lungs, maybe that is why he can't get off that respirator. Maybe he gets agitated because it hurts or it is hard for him to breathe. But I would have thought they would have detected that. They'd know if he had pneumonia or something, wouldn't they? I just don't understand. Infection around the heart, I believe that would be really bad. Oh, but I shouldn't be trying to guess. We'll just have to wait to hear what he has to say. Maybe when he gets through and he sees us in here, he'll come and talk to us."

But the next time I looked over to where he had been, the doctor who had indeed sounded quite thorough on the phone, was gone. *Perhaps it's just as well*, I thought. *It's late and I don't know if I'm up to hearing anything bad tonight.*

Friday, August 30....Days in Hospital:24....Days on VADS:19

I followed Dr. Harris into an area past the ICU where I had not been before. He clipped an X-ray onto the illuminated board on the wall and I thought, *God, what am I about to see?*

"There appears to be some inflammation in his sinuses," he said.

"Could that be what's causing his fever?" I asked.

"It could be. That sure would be something if it turns out to be as simple as that. But sometimes it goes that way. You're looking for something obscure and it's something quite common. I sure hope that this is it. I was afraid he might have an infection around the VADs. Well, I still can't rule out that possibility, but let's hope it is his sinuses."

"If it is that, and the antibiotics aren't working, what can you do?"

"I'm considering surgery."

"Operating on his sinuses?"

"Yes. Ordinarily, I wouldn't think it necessary, but his overall condition is so serious, I feel we have to take aggressive action. His fever went up to 403."

"How high is that?"

"It's about a hundred and four and a half. We can't have it get any higher than that. I'm going to consult with an ENT about the possibility of doing it today. I'll need your consent."

"Well, if you think it's necessary and could help him."

"I do and I'm afraid to wait on it."

"O.K.," I agreed.

"I'll schedule it for as soon as possible."

I had not dismissed the fact that Dr. Harris had said he could not rule out the possibility of an infection around the VADs, so I had to ask, "If it isn't his sinuses and it *is* the VADs, I mean, what if there *is* an infection around the VADs, what then?"

He looked into my eyes, and speaking slowly and seriously, he said, "That would be a disaster." I took a deep breath and felt my legs trembling at the enormity of the word, disaster. There were no more questions I could bear to ask.

When I returned to Dawson's room, I spoke silently to him, *I'm with you, hon, and I'll be with you every step of the way. Dear God, please let it be something simple and please let him wake up soon.*

Dr. Hammond, the ENT, came into Dawson's room shortly after Bill arrived that afternoon. He introduced himself and informed us that he was going to do the surgery that evening. He was an affable, nice-looking man. He looked so sympathetically at us, I thought it likely he had children of his own. He said, "Your son's condition is quite grave and his fever is really wearing him down. I don't ordinarily operate on Friday nights, but Dr. Harris feels we cannot afford to put this off. So we're going to start getting him ready. Were you told of the risks involved?"

"No, not really."

"Well, he is on Heparin."

"I know that is a blood thinner," I said.

"Yes, so he could have excessive bleeding. But we'll deal with that if it becomes a problem. The surgical procedure involves going into the sinuses, breaking open the little pockets and draining them. The membranes are very fragile, almost like potato chips, which makes collapsing them very easy. But the risk is that, where they are located there is the possibility of pushing too far and hitting his eyes or his brain." His words had hit *my* brain and I thought, *Can I bear up under the fear of anything more?*

"The chances of that happening are slight, but you must be aware of all the risks."

"I know. I do understand."

"I'll talk to you when we are through."

Bill and I were asked to leave and we went to the waiting room to, of course, wait. The surgery, we were told, should take about an hour and a half. That would be one of our shorter waits, but I was aware that it would only be leading us to yet another anxious wait for that elusive sign of Dawson's improvement, his fever coming down. Dr. Harris had told us if Dawson's sinusitis was the cause of his fever, it would be gone soon.

When Dr. Hammond appeared in the doorway a little over an hour later, smiling, I sighed with relief. "It went well," he said. "He did fine. A little bleeding, but we packed it and he's O.K."

"Oh, good. Thanks. So do you think his sinuses have been the problem?" I asked.

"I don't know, but he certainly did have a significant amount of purulent discharge in the left side. We'll see."

Wanting some kind of absolute, definitive explanation, I asked, "Do you think that what you found could have caused his fever to be so high?" I wanted to hear an unequivocal, yes. That way, perhaps, I could rest believing that he did not have that terrifying, disastrous condition surrounding his VADs.

But his answer was, "Well, um, it's possible."

"If his sinuses were the cause, when do you think his fever would start to come down?" I knew the answer already, the all-too-familiar and so-far-disappointing twenty-four to forty-eight hours, so I added, "A day or two?"

"I would think so," he said.

"O.K. Thank you, doctor," I said as Bill shook his hand.

"He's sleeping now, but you can go in and see him. I'll be in to check on him tomorrow."

Dawson appeared peaceful when we looked in on him, quite sedated from the surgery. We stayed a few minutes, standing close to him, holding his hands, unafraid of touching him, for we knew there was no way we might awaken or disturb him.

"Good night, Dawson," I said, also unafraid of the chance of him hearing my voice. But in the hopes that somewhere in the depths of his unconsciousness he could feel my words, I said, "I love you, baby."

Bill patted his arm as he gazed down at him and we left him in the nurse's care.

Saturday, August 31....Days in Hospital:25.....Days on VADs:20

When Bill and I entered Dawson's room in the morning, Nina was examining him. She had a flashlight held close to his VADs. It was a routine check that the VAD technicians performed and I was accustomed to seeing it done. As I understood it, they were checking the "flash," a way of assessing the workings of the valves. I was always glad to see Nina and pleased that she came by often. Most often her visits were on the weekdays, before Bill had arrived and I always barraged her with questions. This morning as Bill and I arrived together, he smiled at her, nodded a silent, "Hello," and I proceeded, as usual, with my many questions for her. She was characteristically patient with me and I was grateful for her thoughtful and knowledgeable answers. Glancing over at Bill I could see he appreciated her insights, as well, though I knew he was slightly embarrassed by what he most likely thought was my badgering.

Nina was head of the VAD team and I had great confidence in her. The team consisted of Nina and the VAD technicians. The technicians were conscientious, compassionate young men and women who came by individually at scheduled intervals around the clock. They would come by, check all the connections and lines and tubes to the VADs, examine the valves, record the numbers off the unit, and chat a little with Bill and me. Jim, a short, muscular young man with a black goatee and hair even darker than Dawson's was one of the first techs we met. He was quite friendly and talkative and asked us, "Does Dawson like baseball or football?" When Bill answered that he did, Jim said, "Oh, good, then we will be hanging out in Dawson's room watching the games with him." At that time, I had no reason to believe that Dawson would not be waking up soon, but it was also at a time when I was especially tortured by the possibility of him being upset when he did. But Jim and his upbeat attitude and encouraging smile had managed to lift my spirits with that wondrous image.

But today, when he arrived to do the routine afternoon check, he too, appeared more serious than I had seen him. It was becoming more and more evident to everyone that Dawson's condition was becoming quite fragile. And to those who had seen his ongoing struggle, it had been a long time, too long, with no signs of improvement.

But Dr. Wiviott, who was new to the case, entered with fresh optimism. He came into Dawson's room and with a hearty handshake he said, "I'm Dr. Wiviott of Infectious Disease."

He was the doctor I had seen and heard dictating into the telephone and I responded, "Yes, I know. How do you say your name, again?"

"Wivv ee ott. It's spelled W-I-V-I-O-T-T."

"When Dr. Harris said your name, I just couldn't catch it. It's a very different name. I've never heard it before. Wiviott. O.K., so what do you think is going on with Dawson?"

"There is a distinct probability he is having a drug reaction. But in addition, his cough and sputum volume has increased and being ventilator-dependent as he is, there is a strong likelihood of infection. The first step I'm taking is to recommend some changes in his medication. I'm concerned with the continued use of gentamicin because it can be harmful to the kidneys, so I'm substituting that with something that I feel is less likely to cause a serious side effect or allergic reaction. And I am going to resume the Vancomycin, at least until we get the results back from his latest cultures, because I am concerned with the significant possibility of staph. But I am trying a lighter dose, for I suspect that the Vanco could be what he is reacting to."

"Do you mean the Vanco could be the cause of the rash?"

"We have the skin biopsy results and they are consistent with a dermal hypersensitivity to a drug and, yes, I suspect that it might be the culprit."

"I knew it. I know that they are all necessary, but I knew that all these medications could be bad for him. You know he's allergic to penicillin."

"Yes, I know."

"And his cardiomyopathy, that itself, is his heart's reaction to something toxic to his system. That's what is happening to him now. I know it. This is too much."

"Yes, I know, but I am changing the medications. We'll see how that works."

"But aside from the rash, which is probably an allergic reaction, you don't think the fever is part of the reaction, too? You do think an infection is causing his fever?"

"Well, the VADs, themselves, have been known to cause a fever, but usually not this high. And there have been some cases where we were never able to find the specific cause. Then when the patient got off the VADs and received their heart, they were fine. But in Dawson's case, I feel we cannot take the chance of assuming that this would be true for him and not try to find a source of his fever. I feel that we must rigorously pursue all possible sources in case there is a true infection. So..."

I interrupted him, asking in horror, "Could he be having an allergic reaction to the VADs?"

He thought a moment. "I suppose," he said, "that is a possibility, but in Dawson's case we cannot risk not trying to find another reason and to get control of this fever. So in addition to some changes in his medications and a topical treatment for his rash, he'll have an echocardiogram and abdominal ultrasound."

"When will that be?"

"Today, I think. Dr. Harris is scheduling that."

"The echo and ultrasound would detect an infection?" I asked.

"Yes, they could show evidence of it."

"What about his sinuses? Do you think that could've been the cause of the fever?"

"It is possible. His fever has come down slightly. I'm open to all possibilities and agree with Dr. Harris that we must be aggressive. We're going to try everything. If we don't find anything in the echo or ultrasound, there are other tests we can do."

When he left, I said to Bill, "He is very efficient and thorough, just like Dr. Harris had said and he seems confidant and hopeful. I like him."

Bill said, "Yeah, I do, too. I trust him."

I watched him as he walked to the nurse's station and I saw Dr. Thompson, who I had not seen in a while, approaching him. I watched them as they talked and when they were through with their discussion, she turned and was coming my way. I met her outside Dawson's room and asked her, "What do you think?"

"I don't know. This really is something. He's been on the VADs now, what, three weeks?"

"Yes, just about. Is this really unusual?"

"Yes, it is."

"So, what do you think?"

"Well, I'm thinking of ordering a pericardial tap."

"What is that?"

"There is some indication that he has fluid around his heart. We would go in and draw that out and check for possible infection."

Oh, no, I thought, *no, not that! Not infection around his heart!*

"I'm only considering it as a possibility. I'll let you know. In the meantime, maybe his fever will go down from the sinus surgery. That is still a possibility."

Yeah, I thought, *it is, it has been just twenty-four hours.* But there we were again, just like I had dreaded, in the middle of a long, likely-to-be-disappointing forty-eight hour wait. We'd been there before. I felt frightened and frustrated, for it seemed as though his sinuses had not been the problem. His fever was not dropping dramatically as I had hoped it would. *Why,* I wondered, *if his fever were going to be gone, why wouldn't we have seen real signs of it by now? Couldn't we have been spared this agonizing wait? If his fever is going to go, couldn't we just know it today? And all those other possibilities, fluid around his heart, drug reaction, VAD allergy or VAD infection, or infection somewhere, but where? Why, God, why is it going like this?*

Though his fever was slightly lower, he was still quite agitated throughout the day, continuing to pull on his vital lines requiring the nurses to keep the restraints on his arms and legs. Because of his anxiety, Bill and I were reluctant to touch him or to speak to him. And when it came time for us to leave him, I could only whisper, "Good night, Dawson." His room was very quiet and though I thought it might sound stupid to say, I said to his nurse, "Could you turn the TV on? Dawson is like me, the TV relaxes him. Maybe if he wakes up anxious, it would calm him down by distracting him from what it is that's been upsetting him so."

His nurse, Bonnie, a very attractive woman with blonde hair and the most beautiful blue-green eyes, smiled and said, "Sure." She went to the TV and clicked it on and turned to me and said, "I have a son about his age."

"Really?" I said, thinking that I would never have guessed that she was old enough. She went back to her post in the doorway and I whispered to Dawson, "I'll see you in the morning, hon, good night." On my way out, I paused at Bonnie's table, and from one mother to another, I nodded my thanks to her and I knew she understood my heartache. She smiled slightly and I saw her pretty eyes fill up with sympathetic tears before she looked away. *She'll be kind to Dawson,* I thought. *If he wakes up scared, I know she'll be nice to him.* I looked back at him as we left. *Good night, Dawson, good night.*

Chapter Twenty

Attending the small evening masses at St. Dominic's continued to be comforting and inspiring, but our first Sunday morning mass went beyond that. Unlike the daily masses, the Sunday service was offered at the large main altar. There, beneath the towering blue stained-glass window and a dome that arched nearly one hundred feet above, the High Altar with its white marble spires and golden tabernacle seemed to be a glimpse of Heaven itself.

The brilliant reflections before my eyes joined with the angelic hymns coming forth from the choir and enlivened my soul. Prayers burst from the depth of my heart with such fervor that I had no doubt they were reaching the Kingdom of God.

Almighty Lord, the giver of life, I am on my knees before you. I believe in You, I know You hear me. I'm asking You, please, with Your power and mercy, please let Dawson get well. Please do not take him from me. I'm begging You, please.

Tears poured down my face. Wiping my eyes, I looked at Bill and I shrugged, *I'm sorry, I can't help it.*

He nodded that he understood. I knew that he did, for, undoubtedly, we were sharing the same vision and the same prayer.

As mass ended, the priest and his procession walked slowly past us down the aisle. Bill's eyes expressed such awe as he turned to me and said simply, "This church is so beautiful."

"Yes, it is," I agreed, "and it was such a beautiful mass."

"Yeah, but it sure is a lot different than I remember it," he said.

It was true, there had been many changes in the mass since we had attended years earlier. The most obvious was Communion and it looked so different to see those receiving it walk up to the priest or lay person and be handed the holy bread. In the past, we were never allowed to touch the Eucharist, in fact, we had been instructed that while we knelt at the altar we were to tuck our hands under the pure white cloth draped over the rail. The priest, and no one other than the priest, came to us and placed the Host upon our tongue. I thought it would be strange to receive it in this new way, but I imagined that it would be quite a while before I would be participating in this, the most sacred part of the mass. Receiving communion required being in a state of grace that could only be achieved by going to confession, and I was not ready to do that. That was something I had always dreaded, even when I had been going regularly. Now, with it having been so many years since I had made a confession, I did not know what it would take for me to decide to go.

We did participate, however, in a new ritual that had been added, shaking hands with those around you, expressing, "Peace be with you." We had even been somewhat uncomfortable with that at first, but we were slowly getting used to it.

Though mass was now being said in English, Bill said, "I can't seem to follow along. I feel like I need to know what I'm supposed to say and when, so I could participate better. I don't even know some of the prayers they're saying."

I understood, but I had not been concerned about it myself. I suppose I was less aware of my own interaction, or lack thereof, with the priest and his words, for I had been immersed in my one-on-one conversation with God.

"Maybe there is a book or something we could get," Bill said.

"Yeah, maybe." I decided I would check into that for him.

When we arrived back at Dawson's room, his nurse greeted us, saying, "I'll be right back, I'm just going to look for the fan." I knew what fan she meant. I had often seen it in his room and it had always struck me as looking out of place. This ordinary, old, household fan sitting on the bed table amidst the roomful of high-tech equipment was used to help bring Dawson's fever down by simply blowing cool air on him. The nurse looked back at us as she hurried off saying, "I guess someone borrowed it, but they shouldn't have. Dawson needs it."

Her consideration for Dawson made me smile, despite my disappointment at discovering that his fever, obviously, was up. I was relieved when she returned carrying the fan, for I was concerned that if she had not found it she might have resorted to using the cooling blanket on him. The cooling blanket was just that, a frigidly cold vinyl sheet that they laid over him to lower his temperature. I did not know how successful it was, but it was something they did try from time to time. I had never seen him with it on, they mainly used it during the night, but I had heard how he hated it. I could imagine how awful it felt to have that freezing cold thing covering him and nurses had told us how he fought them when they tried to put it on him. One nurse, Elizabeth, a very tall, blonde English woman had told me he had kicked her across the room. She had said, "He is still very strong. He got me with those tree trunk legs of his." It was that kind of behavior that made it understandable why they kept his legs tied to the bed. I had apologized to her for him and she had said, "Oh, it's all right, he doesn't know what he's doing."

What does he know? I wondered. *Does he know where he is and what is happening to him? He is so frightened and with his hands and feet tied he is like a trapped animal. But is it really only his temperature that is driving him wild? Or could this constant fever and onslaught of drugs have caused damage to his mind? God, is this something new to add to my list of worries? If they ever get his fever down is he going to be normal?*

Any questions I had went unasked, for it was the usual weekend in the hospital, quieter with significantly fewer doctors around. That was immaterial, I suppose, for there was no one who could tell me what I wanted to hear. Church seemed to be the only place I received the answers I needed. Pray. Have faith. Trust God.

After leaving the hospital early that evening, Bill drove me back to his house to pick up my car. From the driveway, I could see something on the doorstep. I thought it was probably for Bill because his birthday was the next day. But as I was about to get into my car Bill said, "Andrea, wait, this is for Dawson."

"What is it?" He handed me a piece of poster paper, rolled up and secured with a rubber band. I unrolled it to see a big, multi colored sheet of shiny paper with several large, handwritten messages addressed to Dawson. My heart aching, I said "If only Dawson were awake we could bring this to him." I began to read it. "He's really loved," I said. The messages, in part, were: *We love you and miss you, please, come home soon … Awesome Dawson … Think positive and hang in there … You've got a lot to live for … Hang tough, Dawson … We can't have one of the world's greatest people sick … Keep the faith … With love and respect … You are in my prayers and in my heart … I love you … Don't deprive the people who care for, love and respect you of your presence in this life … You are more man, real and true than most of us could ever be …* There was also one that made mention of, *All the times we partied …* and one that said, *We're all clean and sober now!! Life is wonderful straight. So great times are still to come!!*

Yes, Dawson, great times are still to come. You are so loved. Everyone is praying for you, hon. So yea, "hang tough," Dawson, "hang tough."

Monday, September 2....Days in Hospital:27....Days on VADs:22

Though I had not gone back home to Rusty, I continued to help at the shop, going there while he was at the firehouse. When I had offered this plan to him, he had gratefully accepted it and had thanked me for whatever time I could manage. He desperately needed my help and I felt an obligation not to let him down. I certainly did not want to jeopardize the business, yet I knew I was greatly compromising it by not being there every day. But that was the way it had to be.

Knowing this was one of those mornings when Rusty would not be there, I went to the shop to try and catch up on the bookkeeping before going to the hospital, and I also went by the house and picked up some clothes as I had done a few days earlier. I chose a couple of things and packed them into a bag. I was taking my belongings the way I was living my life, a little bit at a time. It was a strange way to live, unable and unwilling to plan or think past a single day.

This being Labor Day, Bill had the day off, so I rode with him to the hospital, my mother and father planning to go later. On the ride, Bill said, "Maybe his fever will be down for my birthday. That would be the best gift I could get."

Unfortunately, the minute we got into his room I knew his fever was still high, seeing the fan turned on, the fan that now had a piece of paper taped to it that read, "Dawson Bell's fan." His nurse, Dana said, "Now, no one else can take it. It is only for Dawson."

I had to smile, but I said sadly, "It's Bill's birthday, we were hoping his fever would be down. What a nice present that would've been. I actually thought it might happen."

"Well, it still might," Dana said.

I liked Dana. She was forthright and affirmative and I thought she was rather good-looking: tall, with dirty-blonde hair and a strong build that matched her personality. Whenever Dawson had gotten out of control with her, she had been able to handle him, both physically and verbally, which gave me great confidence in her.

She was not what I would call talkative, but we conversed easily and I told her about the card for Dawson that had been left at the doorstep. She said, "Oh, bring it in. Tack it up on his bulletin board. He'll see it when he wakes up."

"That would be nice," I said, "but it's pretty big." Bill and I had already discussed how much we wished he could see his friends' loving card, but Bill had said he wasn't sure he wanted the doctors to see it. He thought we should not advertise the partying side of Dawson. He thought the doctors would take it to mean that Dawson did a lot of drinking. But, of course, they already knew that. Also, there was mention of being clean and sober. That sounded good to me, but Bill felt it highlighted how seriously he and his friends were into alcohol and, possibly, drugs. Bill was concerned and I understood he was trying to protect Dawson. And it was true, it was too big for his small bulletin board, so we decided to wait until he was awake to bring it in to him.

After we had spent the entire morning in Dawson's room, Dana asked, "Do you guys ever go out to eat? Or do you only eat in the cafeteria?"

"We never leave the hospital once we're here, well, except to go to church," I answered.

"Oh, you really should get out more. How long has Dawson been here now?"

"Almost four weeks," I answered.

"You've got to get out," Dana said, "especially today. Bill shouldn't have to eat cafeteria food on his birthday and there are some pretty good restaurants around here. Dawson will be fine. You should go. Do you like Mexican food? There's a restaurant just down the street."

I asked Bill if he'd like to do that and he was very congenial, saying that it was up to me. Shortly after my mom and dad arrived, we left, walked across the street and down the slight hill to the brightly painted Mexican restaurant on the corner. It was a strange feeling to be out, the four of us like old times, while in reality nothing was at all like the old times. *My God, Dawson is lying there in the hospital fighting to live and we're out to lunch like we have something to celebrate.* We ordered our meals and I felt uncomfortably far away from Dawson. We even ordered appetizers and soon after they arrived, I looked up to see someone familiar. She was a woman I'd met through Rusty. She worked for the fire department in charge of uniforms and she stocked and sold the embroidered shirts that Rusty made. I had gotten to know her because I had often gone with Rusty when he delivered the shirts to her and she and I had spoken many times on the phone. It had not occurred to me that she had come to the restaurant to see me. That was the farthest thing from my mind. So when she came over to our table and said, "The nurse told me you might be here," I thought, *The nurse?* "You were at the hospital?" I asked.

"Yes, I have something I want to give you."

"Really?" I was slightly bewildered by her unexpected visit. Dorothy did not know Dawson well, but had met him on a couple of occasions when he had taken the ride with us to the city. I asked her, "Did you see Dawson?"

"No," she answered, "not really."

"You know he's sedated," I said looking up at her as she stood beside me.

My dad pulled a chair over for her and she smiled and thanked him. "I didn't go into his room," she said as she sat down next to me. Then, taking something out of her purse she said, "I want you to have this." She showed me a small, oval-shaped, silver medal. "This was Mother Theresa's."

"Really?" I said, astonished, but I did not ask her how she had come to have it.

"Two friends of mine borrowed it from me when they were very sick and it saved their lives. I want you to have it while Dawson is sick. You can keep it as long as you need it." She took my hand and placed the medal in my palm and looking directly at me she said, "But you must accept God's will, *whatever* it is."

The gratitude I had been feeling was almost all but swept away in that instant as I thought, *No, do not ask that of me. Accept God's will whatever it is? No, not if His will is that Dawson is to die! I cannot accept that, My God, I can't.* For a minute I almost thought that I could not accept her well-intended gift, not with those conditions. Why should I have to accept those conditions? After all, hadn't she said that it had saved her friends' lives and wasn't that what it was going to do for Dawson?

She went on to say, "You must keep it with you at all times. Pray with it always. It saved my friends. Have faith." Letting go of my hand she said, "Andrea, trust in God."

I looked long at the medal and then, slowly closing my fingers around it, I said, "I will. I will," I said again, submitting myself to God.

Tuesday, September 3....Days in Hospital:28....Days on VADs:23

Dr. Thompson was coming out of Dawson's room as I was arriving. She said, "We've decided not to do the pericardial tap."

"Really, why?" I wondered if this were good news or bad.

"The doctor I had consulted for an evaluation is disinclined to do anything at this time," she said. "He feels the risks involved with the exploration and drainage outweigh the potential benefits. I tend to agree."

"He doesn't think that there is infection around his heart?" I asked.

"He feels that the likelihood of that is rather low. And whenever you go in like that you run the risk of introducing infection. We certainly do not want to take the chance of that happening, especially if this procedure is not absolutely necessary."

I was relieved they were not going to put Dawson at risk and I understood what she was saying. But there was a small part of me that had been hoping that they would try it, just to rule out infection around his heart, just to get a definite answer, to be able to stop guessing. If they had discovered there was infection there, at least, it would have given the doctors something tangible to fight. But overall I thought it *was* good news.

"And he feels that the presence of any pericardial fluid does not appear to be compromising his overall status," she added.

Well, that was, undoubtedly, good to hear. With a sigh I said, "O.K., so now what?"

"Dr. Wiviott will be evaluating the latest cultures. I will be talking to him and discussing our other options. I'll let you know," she said as she walked away.

Bill had teased me that the doctors must hate to see me coming. "I'm sure they try to avoid you," he had said jokingly, but I knew he had meant it. That didn't stop me from making a pest of myself with them and it only seemed to add to Bill's appreciation of my efforts. Many days, confused and frustrated, he had said to me, simply, "Andrea, find out," and he knew I would do my best to do just that.

I noticed Dr. Harris and went to him. The look on my face was one I was sure he was getting accustomed to seeing. Before I had a chance to ask him anything about Dawson, he said, "Well, his fever is still high, but it does seem to be trending down. His blood pressure is holding, his white blood count looks good and renal functions are improving. He had a short C-PAP trial, only three hours, but he initially tolerated it quite well and the rash is subsiding. All in all, things are looking a little better."

God, could this be the turnaround I have been praying for? Now, if his fever could just go away, perhaps, just as mysteriously as it had persisted.

I shared the promising report with Bill when he called at lunchtime. When he arrived later that afternoon, I was in the waiting room and I stood to greet him as he entered. His first words were, "How's he doing?"

"About the same," I said as we walked out into the hallway and started toward Dawson's room.

"He's still sedated, huh?"

"Yeah. He is a little calmer, but not enough to take him completely off the sedatives, yet. But if his fever is coming down, maybe by tomorrow ..."

Bill immediately went to Dawson's bedside and touched his arm. He did not respond. And though he remained sedated and unaware that we were there, we stayed in his room until we were asked to leave when the doctors were about to make their rounds. We went to the cafeteria and had frozen yogurts from the machine. Bill said, "This is pretty good. Dawson would really like it."

"Well, maybe we will be able to bring him some soon." My heart just leaped at the thought; to see him awake, to see him smiling, to see him enjoying something, even something so simple as ice cream.

Bill said, "I can't wait to be able to do things for him again."

"Me either. You know, I was thinking of something I wanted to do for him. I mean when he comes home."

"What's that?"

"I'd like to tie a hundred ribbons on every tree and fence post along the road to the house to welcome him home."

"OK. We can do that. We can put up some ribbons for him."

"Not *some* ribbons, Bill. A *hundred*." As he nodded that he understood,

I could feel the emotion welling inside me at the thought of such a wonderful moment and I wanted to be with Dawson. "Are you ready to go back up?" I asked.

"Yeah, let's go," he said. We stayed a while in Dawson's room before we said good night to him. We left, optimistically looking toward tomorrow and the day when we would tie a hundred yellow ribbons for Dawson's homecoming.

As we drove down the main street of town to where I had parked my car that morning, I read to myself the words on the huge banner that was suspended across the street from one side to the other. It was not the first time that I had read it, in fact, we had driven under it many times. Every time I read, *"FARMER'S MARKET THURSDAY EVENINGS,"* I had the same thought, *When Dawson wakes up, I'm going to shop there for some fresh fruit for him.* I'd imagined how happy I would be shopping there for Dawson and bringing what I bought to him the next day. It had seemed like that day was never going to come, but newly encouraged by the day's report, I said, "Maybe this Thursday I'll be able to go there and get something for Dawson."

"Go where?" Bill said.

"The Farmer's Market here in town. You know, it's here every Thursday. I was just reading that sign. I'm going to get Dawson some fruit there. Remember how much he enjoyed what I had brought him when he was first on the ECMO?"

"Yeah," Bill said, obviously remembering that day with almost as much emotion as I was.

"I'm thinking, well, I'm hoping that maybe I'll be able to do that this week," I said. Then, unexpectedly, I started to cry.

Bill, reaching for my hand said, "C'mon, he's going to be all right."

"I know, I know, I pray he will be," I said. "It's just ..." It was just that I so desperately wanted him well and I was still so scared.

As I drove home to my mother's, I was thinking how prayers had become such a part of my life. I did not know what I would be doing without faith, for even with it I was still so close to falling apart, and I was thinking how surprising it was that Bill could reassure me with his words.

By the time I had arrived at my mother's house, I had decided that I would try and find a book for Bill like he had said he wanted, one that could help us with the procedures and prayers and changes in the church. I wasn't sure where to begin. I doubted that a bookstore would carry what I was looking for. That was unfortunate for that would have been the easiest way, to just go into a store and buy it. I decided that making a call to a church was where I should start. There were two Catholic churches listed in the phone book in Bill's town and I deliberately called the one that was farthest from his neighborhood. My naive thinking was, I know Bill is not ready to involve himself with a church, so it would be best not to call his parish. How silly, as if that could make a difference and if it could have mattered, then maybe I should have called a church far out of town.

The phone rang several times and I was about to hang up when a woman finally answered, "St. Anthony's."

"Hi," I said, "I wonder if you could help me. I'm looking for some books or literature that explain the mass and have the prayers, like, maybe, a catechism book?" *Do they still call them that?* "Do you have anything like that?" I asked.

"Well, not really. Are you a member of our parish?"

Uh, oh, I thought, *Here I am taking up this woman's time, I don't want to tell her that I do not even live in her town.* The fact was, I did not know where I lived. All of my things were still at Rusty's, yet I was sleeping at my parent's house every night, living out of unpacked boxes, bags and suitcases. Where was my parish, where was my home?

So I stammered, "Um, no. I've been away from the church for quite a few years. I've just gotten back and have discovered there have been quite a few changes. I was hoping that there was just something I could read that would help me."

"We really don't have anything like that, but we do have an RCIA group starting."

"What is that?"

"RCIA stands for The Rite of Christian Initiation of Adults. It is a program designed for adults who are converting to the Catholic faith and it meets once a week. You would get the answers to all your questions. Would you like to register for that?"

"Uh, well, no, that's not really what I had in mind. I just thought I could read something."

"Have you been confirmed?"

"No."

"Well, this class would be perfect for you. You would learn what you need to know and then you would be able to make your confirmation, as well."

"Oh, I don't know. This is really not a good time for me ... with my schedule ... my son is in the hospital, he is in critical condition needing a heart transplant, I am at the hospital with him every day and every night."

"Oh, I'm so sorry."

"His dad and I have been going to a church near the hospital and it has been so comforting. But there have been so many changes."

"Yes, that is true. I'm so glad that you have decided to come back to the church. What is your name? I'll have Deacon Joe give you a call."

"Oh, uh, Andrea, Andrea Bell."

"And your phone?"

I hesitated a moment and then gave her Bill's number. Because I was never at his house except for Saturdays and Sundays to drop my car off and pick it up, I added, "He can ask for Bill." I knew Bill was not going to like it that I had gotten him personally involved, but, *after all,* I thought, *he's the one who has all the questions. Oh, but he is going to be mad when I tell him someone is going to be calling him. He'll think that he is going to be pestered. So who was it that she had said would be calling, Deacon Joe? Deacon Joe?* I did not recall any deacons in the Catholic churches I had attended in the past. Why was that? And, if there were, I doubted they had been called by their first name. *Joe? Deacon Joe.* Yes, things certainly had changed.

Wednesday, September 4....Days in Hospital:29....Days on VADs:24

"I'm not God."

No kidding! I thought.

My mother and I looked at each other like, *What the Hell kind of a stupid thing is that to say?*

Dawson's fever had gone back up and, distraught, I had moaned, "What is going on? Is there anything you can do? Is he going to be all right?" In her English accent, the nurse Elizabeth had responded to my laments with her, "I'm not God" answer. I suppose, it only meant that his recovery was in God's hands, which it was, but I did not need to hear it from her.

Perhaps, it was not as ridiculous and inconsiderate a response as it had seemed to be at the time. Was it true that doctors have been known to write on patients' charts, "GOK"? Didn't that mean, "God only knows?" I didn't know if they really did that, but I imagined there does come a time when He is the only one who knows. So why should her answer have upset me? Hadn't I promised to submit myself to God's will?

But I needed to see that God was taking my prayers into consideration as He carried out His plan. I still believed He was listening to my prayers and I had not given up on their power. I continued to carry my rosary beads with me every day and now I carried the little medal, as well. In addition, I wore a scapular.

I had met a woman in the waiting room whose husband was in the cardiac unit of the ICU. Over the past several days, I had often talked to her and her daughter. They were going through much of the same heartache that I was, as he was on a similar up and down course as Dawson. I sometimes saw her praying, and on one of Dawson's discouraging days she had given me this scapular, but I did not know what it was at the time. It was a long, brown satin ribbon and attached to each end was a small, brown fabric rectangle with a medallion-like design. She had said, "If you can, put it over your son's shoulders." That did not seem possible to do with all the tubes and wires that were attached to Dawson, and I was too embarrassed to try it. I did not want the doctors and nurses to think I was some kind of religious fanatic. My faith and rituals were personal and I doubted anyone could understand what they meant to me. At times, I did not fully understand them myself. She had said, "If he can't wear it, then you wear it or, at least, keep it with you." Many days I did wear it under my shirt, and when I did not, I carried it in my pocket. At night, I wore it to bed, following her instructions by always having it with me.

Today, I arrived at the hospital concerned for her and her husband. The day before, while we had received that good report on Dawson, her husband had experienced a set back. The first time I spoke to her today, I was quite surprised and relieved to find out that her husband was doing much better, and I knew she sincerely sympathized with me when I told her that Dawson was not. This was the opposite of the way I had expected the day would be. She asked me if I were praying with the scapular and I told her I was. What I did not tell her, or anyone, was how fully armed I was with my rosaries in my jacket, the scapular over my shoulders, the medal in the watch-pocket of my jeans and a St. Jude prayer card in my purse.

It was rather appropriate to be fortified with these particular items, for I was soon to discover just what it was that I was battling.

By the time Dawson's evening nurse came on duty, his fever had unexpectedly reached an alarming all-time-high of 40.6. It had spiked to over a dangerous one hundred and five. As I walked through the unit with his day nurse who was now off-duty, she told me something that she had heard the doctor say. She said, "Dr. Harris just cannot believe Dawson's fever. He says he has never seen anything like it. He calls it The Fever from Hell."

I thought, *My God, is it? Oh, but certainly I have the right ammunition to fight it. I, alone, must be carrying enough of an arsenal to protect the whole ICU.*

I said goodbye to her in the hallway and hurried back to Dawson. I touched his hand, his arm, his forehead. He was burning hot. What was this inferno that he was engulfed in? I stood there, my heart searching for solace, my eyes roaming aimlessly about the room. Then, they suddenly stopped at the sight of his bulletin board.

Before Dana had told us that we could put Dawson's card up there, I had assumed the board was for hospital staff. Knowing now that we could use it, I reached into my purse and took out my St. Jude card. On one side of the card was a prayer and on the other was a picture of St. Jude. He was cloaked in white against a blue-green background of sky and sea. I walked over to the board and tacked it in the upper right-hand corner with the picture side visible. Remembering Dana's words, referring to his friends' card, "He will see it when he wakes up," I questioned myself about what I was doing. I was worried, *If he does see this when he wakes up, what will he think? What will his reaction be?*

It was possible that he would not respond to it the way I hoped he would. In fact, it was more than possible, it was quite likely. What I hoped for was that he would be comforted by the sight of St. Jude and that he would understand and appreciate that I had placed him there to watch over him. How could I even imagine such a response from Dawson? How could I hope for that? It seemed so impossible.

Dawson was not religious. Dawson did not seem to be even remotely spiritual. He was so matter-of-fact, so anti-anything-mystical. He was down-to-earth, interested in the here and now. It seemed he could not be bothered with some ethereal, far-off time or place. *If he wakes up and sees a picture of a saint tacked on his wall, he could easily give me a look that says,* "Mom, do you really think that is going to help me? Do you think going to church and saying prayers means anything?"

It would tear me apart if I had to see him look at me like that. I thought, *If I cannot share my faith and hope with him I'm afraid of what that will do to me. I must be able to give him this gift. But how will it ever happen that he will open his heart and soul to accept it? Dawson? I don't think so.*

That evening at the St. Jude mass as I prayed for Dawson's recovery, I also prayed for something else, something as important. It was incredible to me to discover that anything could be equally as important as his recovery. Yet I found this to be. But it seemed to be even farther from my grasp than his getting well. It felt absolutely unattainable.

I lifted my head and spoke directly to God,

Please let the day come when I see Dawson awake. Please let me see his eyes, again, please let me hear his voice, and please, dear God, let him accept our prayers. Please, dear Lord, if You see to it that Dawson awakens, please let him embrace the presence of You in our lives. Please let me see him comforted when I tell him we have been going to church. Please let him know what is in my heart.

I knew Dawson could so easily dismiss the power and beauty of God and my prayers. He could scoff, he could roll his eyes, he could smirk when I tell him we had been going to church. When I tell him of all the people who were praying for him, he could shrug it all off with an attitude of, *Yeah, sure, that's great.* I knew that it could go that way and at that moment I felt that would be the worst thing that could happen to me. But how could I be thinking that? If Dawson were to die, was that not the worst thing that could happen to me?

As much as I wanted to see him awake, and there is no one in this world who could ever have wanted anything more, I knew that I could not bear to see him wake up and reject the faith that was sustaining me. *My God, what am I saying? That I would rather have him never wake up than have him wake up and turn his back on our God?*

I longed to share my faith with him, to have him feel the hope, the comfort, the love that it had brought me. I had to have the opportunity to share it with him. I begged God, please.

It seemed too much to ask for and too much to hope for. I could imagine him getting well easier than I could imagine him getting religion. Was I now asking for the truly impossible? And what was I asking for, not just to have him awake, but to have him reborn?

Chapter Twenty-One

Thursday, September 5....Days in Hospital:30....Days on VADS:25

Another morning. Another night behind me. Another day to face.

And another bus ride.

And the first elevator ride of the day.

So many days living with this awful fear and uncertainty. Would I ever have a morning when I could feel calm? Would there ever be a day of joy? Or would there be one of unimaginable sorrow? I dared not think of such a moment. I had this moment to live, another day's arrival into Dawson's room.

What will his fever be? What will the doctors do for him? What will they say? And which of Dr. Wiviott's words will touch our lives today?

Days earlier, my mother and I had been sitting in the waiting room when Dr. Wiviott peeked in the doorway. He said, "Oh, Mrs. Bell, good, you are here. I was hoping to talk to you."

He sounded rather upbeat, so I was not too uneasy about what he wanted to talk to me about, though this seemed to be his general nature. I had told my mother about him, but she had never met him, so I said, "Oh, I'd like you to meet my mother. Mom, this is Dr. Wiviott."

"Hi," she said, giving him a timid smile.

In a friendly, respectful manner he said to her, "Oh, I am so pleased to meet you. You have such a nice family." He sounded quite sincere, shook her hand and sat next to her on the couch. Facing me, he said, "I wanted to tell you that I've made some changes in Dawson's medication." He went on to explain what they were and he told me of his expectations. He sounded quite optimistic. I nodded to everything he said, looked to my mother and she nodded her approval. Everything he said sounded hopeful. "There are still other things I can try, as well," he said. Then, with no change in his voice or manner, he added, "But that may not always be the case."

What? I was thinking, *Do I really need to hear this?*

Evidently he had thought that I did, because he continued. "What I am saying is that right now we are still trying, but considering the seriousness of your son's condition it is possible that there could come a time when we cannot try anything more. But as of right now there are still things I can do and I feel hopeful that they will work. I really think we can get control of his fever. So I am doing everything I can, but I want you to understand that someday we might have to stop trying. Dawson is going through so much and we could get to where I just cannot put him through any more."

I was stunned. *How could he say that? There can never come a day when we will stop trying. No.* I looked at my mother and she looked like she was in shock. Her expression was strained and her face pale.

"But I am not at that point," he said reassuringly. "I am going to do everything I can. I am not ready to give up. So let's see how these changes work over the next couple of days."

I tried to be reassured and in a sense I was. He was still allowing me hope. "Thank you," I said. And I was thankful, for he was trying, he was doing something, he had the knowledge and he had, what seemed to be, a sincere desire and determination to get Dawson well.

When he left, my mother and I looked at each other. She was the first to speak. Her words surprised me. She said, "I don't care for him."

"You don't?" I said. "I really like him. Bill does, too."

"I know you've said that, but he scares me."

"What do you mean?"

"The things he said … I guess it's that he is just too blunt."

"Well, yeah, I know. That was pretty awful, but he said he is not at that point yet. He is still trying."

"I know, but … really. I guess it just sounded too terrible. I hope we never get there. I don't ever want to hear him say those things …"

"Those things." I did not want to ever hear him say them either, so whenever I had spoken with him since that day, I had been doubly grateful when he'd tell me of the new remedies he was trying.

I continued to appreciate his openness and his sincere concern and I was impressed with his assistant Sheila, also. She was a young woman intern who worked closely with Dr. Wiviott and came to see Dawson regularly. If Dr. Wiviott were thorough, she was even more so. She took extensive notes and always spent time listening to my fears and my questions. There were times when she felt she had not answered me to her satisfaction and she had made it a point to inform me more fully the next day. She made me feel that I could ask her anything, which I really appreciated, for I worried about being annoying and sounding dumb to the doctors with the things I said and asked.

So this morning I was extremely glad to see her arrive, for Dawson's fever had gone back up, having reached as high as 40 degrees again overnight. I knew I could express my concerns to her and she would understand.

She had listened intently and had responded compassionately, then, she said, "Dr. Wiviott will be coming by later."

Oh, God, I thought, *don't let this be that day that he had spoken of, that hypothetical day when he will do no more for Dawson.*

My thoughts were already leaping ahead when I heard her telling me of their plan for the day. Their plan for the day? I was so relieved to hear that, yes, they had a plan, they were still trying. She said, "Considering that his fever is still extremely high even after the changes we made in his medication, we just cannot rule out an infection somewhere. So we are going to do another test today."

"What kind of test?" I asked.

"An idium scan."

"What is that? What does it involve?"

"We inject him with isotopes and then we put him under a special scanner and the tags will light up. We will see where they have collected. They will gather in infected areas."

"So it will show you right where his infection is?"

"Yes."

"Well, that sounds good." *See?* I thought to myself, *There is still hope. No one is giving up. They will find the source of his fever.* I wondered why they hadn't done this test sooner. "You're going to do that today?" I asked.

"Yes, I hope so. Well, we'll inject him today and then take him to nuclear medicine tomorrow to do the scanning."

"I've seen that, Nuclear Medicine," I said, remembering having read it on a sign, and having wondered what that was. I had not imagined that Dawson would be taken there. "It's on the second floor, isn't it?" I asked.

"Yes, it is. It's too bad that we have to move him. You know, it is going to be quite an ordeal. We must have the VAD technicians help us and fitting the ICU bed and all his equipment in the elevator is going to be quite tricky."

I asked her how long the procedure would be, if they would know the results immediately or would it take time to evaluate them, and who would be doing it.

She answered everything I asked her. Then smiling, she said, "You ask very good questions. In fact, that is just what I said to Dr. Wiviott this morning, 'Mrs. Bell asks all the right questions.'"

"Wow, that's something," I said. She could not have known how much it meant to me to hear her say that. I had become so accustomed to Rusty getting annoyed with my questions, I had become slightly reluctant to ask them. I said, "Thank you for telling me. I'm usually told I ask too many."

"No, not at all," she said, "and they are always very good ones."

We walked out of Dawson's room together, through the unit and out into the hallway, talking as we went. I discovered where some of her compassion may have come from as she told me of her aunt who was on the waiting list for a liver transplant. She said, "I know some of what you are going through." We rode down in the elevator together until I got off at the cafeteria.

I stayed longer than usual there, reading the paper, having a snack, talking on the phone, and daring to feel a little relaxed and a little hopeful.

When I returned to Dawson's room, the nurse said, "Had you heard about the lady who was put on the VADs right after she had a baby?"

"Yes," I answered, "Joyce told me about her."

"She's here today having a checkup. She heard about Dawson and came by to see him."

"Really? I missed her? How long ago was she here?"

"She just left. She might still be around."

"I really would have liked to talk to her."

"C'mon, let's see if she's still here." Then to a nurse close by, she said, "I'll be right back. I'm going to be outside with Mrs. Bell for a minute."

We hurried out of the unit. "Oh, good, she's there at the elevator." We rushed down the hall and when we reached her, the nurse said to her, "This is Dawson's mother."

"Oh, hi," she said, smiling.

The nurse said, "I've got to get back," and hurried off.

I said to Kim, of the-lady-who-was-put-on-the-VADs-right-after-she-had-a-baby fame, "I am so happy to meet you."

"I'm glad to meet you, too. This is my mother and my daughter." The small child reached her arms up to her wanting to be picked up. Kim nodded to her mother to help her. I could see Kim had a bandage on her neck and I thought, *Ooh, she must have come in for that probe they insert down the neck.* But beyond that, I noticed how perfectly well she looked. "I was in to see your son. I had been hoping that I could talk to him," she said.

"That would have been nice, but he is still sedated."

"Yes, I know. That is too bad."

"It is bad, very bad. He has not been awake since he got on the VADs a month ago. He's really having a rough time."

"Oh, I did, too," she said.

"You did?"

"Oh, yeah."

"This is so hard," I said.

"Yes, I know how hard it was on my mother, too."

I looked at her mother. I could see she had not forgotten just how very difficult it had been, but as I looked at her I saw the luckiest woman on earth. Her child's heart transplant was behind her. Looking back to Kim I asked her, "What kind of problems did you have?"

"Oh, all kinds of things."

"But he can't even get off the respirator," I moaned.

"Oh, I had that. I mean I had to go back on it after I had been off of it. That was awful."

"You did?"

"Oh, yeah. My blood had become acidotic."

"What is that?"

"I don't know, but they told me there was nothing they could do and I was going to die if it didn't balance itself out."

"God. So what happened? It just got better?"

"Yes, but it was scary … and my mother was taking care of my baby … oh, it was horrible."

"God, I guess. So then you got your heart?"

"Yeah."

"How lucky. I was wondering," I said, "did the sound of the VADs bother you?"

"Yeah, somewhat. I used to put a pillow over them. It helped a little." Her eyes turned away from me and she looked toward her mom holding her daughter and I could see this conversation was bringing back painful memories for them. Although it looked to me like this mother was in a wonderful place, a place where I would have given anything to be, I realized that it was still very hard for her. After all, they were there to have that probe done. What was that for, to check for her body's possible rejection of her heart? How scary must that be? I knew her mother's concerns for her daughter were not over and, in fact, that they probably never would be.

For the first time in a long while, I wished for the truly impossible. I wished that Dawson had never gotten sick.

Friday, September 6....Days in Hospital:31....Days on VADs:26

I watched as they wheeled Dawson out of his room. I was thankful he was sedated and did not have to feel apprehensive about where he and his entourage were going, what was going to be done to him, and what the results would show.

I prayed that the results would lead to a simple solution to his fever. Simple solution? God, any solution would do. Even a result that gave some insight to the cause of his fever would be good.

It was Dr. Harris who informed me: The idium scan showed no evidence of any active inflammatory disease.

What? That, ordinarily, would be good to hear, but with us so desperately needing to know something, the lack of a diagnosis was hard to take. I thought I might just crumble to the floor, weak from disappointment and frustration. "What does this mean?" I asked him.

He shook his head. "Unfortunately, the idium scan was not helpful."

"We don't know anything more than we did before?" I asked. "What do we do now?"

He shrugged his shoulders. "Well, there are still some cultures pending ... "

I'd heard that before, many times. *What does that mean, that the cultures could show he has an infection that the scan could not find? How could that be? What is this mysterious source that is keeping Dawson from us? How can it remain so elusive?* I could not bring myself to ask these questions even if they were good ones, even if they were the right ones. I was so discouraged, for there seemed to be no right answers.

He went on, "We're considering doing a transesophageal echocardiogram to assess a possibility of a cardiac source to his fever."

"And what does that involve?"

"We go down through his esophagus, get pictures and actually look at what is going on around his heart."

I was feeling painfully disillusioned, but I asked, "So when would you be doing this?"

"Hopefully, today. I'll let you know. You will have to sign a consent form."

"O.K.," I sighed, thinking, *How many of these forms have I signed so far?* As I walked to the elevator and got on, I was remembering the yellow form I had signed that gave my permission to transport Dawson here. That seemed so long ago.

Instead of getting off at the cafeteria, I rode down to the lobby to the coffee shop. This was where I usually went with my mother and father when they came to visit. I had never gone there alone. But today I needed ... what? The waitresses there were friendly and I guess I thought I needed a sympathetic listener. They all knew about Dawson's ordeal and had seemed very interested and concerned. I ordered a cup of hot chocolate from the elderly, red-haired lady who had offered weeks ago to make a milk shake for Dawson when he woke up. "You could bring it to him," she had said. "Do you think he'd like that?" "Oh, yes," I had answered emphatically, "he sure would." I had longed for that day to come, but I had to face the fact that today was not going to be it.

"How's your son today?" she asked as she handed me the hot cup of chocolate.

"Oh, the same," I said. "Still the same," was all that I could say. A sympathetic stranger is not what I needed after all.

As I was riding back up in the elevator, Nina got on at the second floor. "How're you doing?" she asked.

"I don't know," I answered. "I just don't understand what is happening. This constant up and down, the hope, and the utter fear. I feel like I'm living in a made-for-TV-movie. This is just unbelievable. Sometimes I think I could write a book. But when I think about it, it terrifies me … because I can't stand to think about how it might end."

"I can imagine how you must feel." We got off the elevator together and she walked with me into the waiting room. We sat down and she said, looking quite serious, "You must know, not every VAD patient goes on to a transplant."

I felt my heart quicken. Of course I had known that had to be true, but I did not like hearing it. I said, "I know. You mean the VADs are not always the life saving solution?"

"Right, unfortunately, they are not. But I can tell you, no one has ever died of a fever."

"Really? Well, what do they die from?"

"Usually, it is multi-organ failure."

"So things just stop working?"

"Yes, but Dawson is still doing pretty well in that regard. He's had periodic problems, but he has always bounced back from them."

"I know. Do you think he has an infection?"

"I don't know. But if he does, we have to find it."

"Why can't we?"

"I don't know." She paused, then with some hesitation, she said, "I've thought … I don't know … what should we do … call in a psychic?" She looked slightly embarrassed by her words and smiled as if to let me know that, professionally, she was not really considering such a thing.

But I responded, "You know, I've thought of something like that, too. Not exactly that, but I've thought about, maybe if I were to lie down beside him, close my eyes, hold his hand, and somehow get in touch with some greater power. A power that could transmit from him to me … something that I could feel in the exact place on my body where the source of his problem is. I know it sounds crazy. Actually, I like the idea of the psychic better."

"I guess we are getting desperate, aren't we?"

I signed the consent form for the transesophageal echocardiogram, which the doctors referred to as the TEE, for short. They began to prepare Dawson and I called Bill and my mother and told them. Then I waited alone in the waiting room. I passed the time looking through magazines until Dr. Harris entered.

"Are they through?" I asked.

"Oh, yeah," he answered.

"How did he do?"

"He did fine. No complications."

"Oh, good. So? The results?"

"Underwhelming."

Underwhelming? I did not think that I had ever heard that word before. And I doubted if I could ever have imagined it producing such an *over*whelming feeling in me.

"It showed no abscesses and no vegetation to speak of."

That sounded good, but my legs were trembling. "So we don't know anything?" I asked.

"I'm afraid not."

Taking a deep breath I said, "O.K., are we back to the, there's-no-infection-so-it-must-be-a-drug-related-fever theory?"

"Well, I am still reluctant to positively rule out an infection."

"I know, I understand, but I don't think he has an infection. I think he is reacting to the medications. I really do. I think it's the Vancomycin. He's back on that, isn't he?"

"Yes, but I'm going to be discussing all of this further with Dr. Wiviott," he said.

As it turned out, that afternoon I was able to discuss it with Dr. Wiviott myself, in great lengths as he explained his thoughts and theories to me. He said he was extremely concerned with the fact that Dawson's fever was continuing to spike to 40 degrees and that his rash was looking worse. He said his concerns were that it was wearing Dawson down considerably and would most probably begin to affect the function of his other organs. *My God, would that mean multi-organ failure?* And he felt that his body just could not go on trying to fight it for much longer. "I am very worried," he said, "but I have a suggestion."

Oh, thank God, I thought, *he isn't about to tell me he is giving up, he is saying he is going to try something.* "What is it?" I asked.

"Well, it is not without controversy. I have suggested it to Dr. Harris and Dr. Thompson and they are against it. I can understand why, but we must give Dawson some relief."

"What is it?" I asked again.

"A steroid. It will not help us find the source of his fever, it will not treat any infection, it would only eliminate the fever."

"Eliminate the fever?"

"Yes, it is very likely that it would do that. It would inhibit his body from reacting to whatever it is that is causing his fever, whether it is an infection or an allergic reaction."

"His condition would remain the same, except that he would not have a fever?" I asked, disbelieving.

"Yes, exactly. His body would just stop reacting to whatever it is he has been reacting to."

"His fever could be gone?" I asked, incredulous.

"Yes, most likely."

"Tell me, why is everyone against it?"

"Well, it is not a good idea to be on it when one would be undergoing a transplant, due to the high dose of immunosuppressants that are required at that time."

"But he is not ready for transplant yet."

"That's my feeling, as well. And I believe he never will be if we don't give him some relief from this fever."

"Are there any other reasons why they object to it?"

"They know that it will not cure the problem, it will only mask it and it can possibly increase susceptibility to infection. But their main concern is the need for immunosuppressants at the time of the transplant, so it is just not advisable to be on a steroid now. I understand their reluctance, but I feel if we put him on it for a very short time, just long enough to get that fever stabilized, it would be beneficial. I'm hoping that they will agree to that. Would you?"

"I trust you and I feel, too, that he cannot go on like this. It's too much for him, I know it, such a high fever for so long."

"So you would agree?"

"I think so. Of course I'll have to talk to Bill."

"Of course, and I'm sure Dr. Harris will talk to you, too. Everyone will have to be in agreement. I just wanted you to understand and I needed to know how you felt about it."

"Thank you, thank you very much."

"But we're not going to do anything now. I will be on duty all weekend, so I'll be watching how he does in the next day or two. If we decide to start him on it, I will be here and we'll be able to do it then. Well, think about it. I will see you tomorrow."

Would this prove to be the right thing? I knew it was not the answer, but could it really be possible that it could take away his fever? And if so, would that mean that he would be calm, he would be Dawson? Although this could not be the ultimate answer to my prayers ... could it be the start?

Saturday, September 7....Days in Hospital:32....Days on VADs:27

I could see the concrete sidewalk rapidly coming closer and closer. Then with the impending disaster inevitable, I felt the solid impact of my face hitting the street. I stayed there a moment face down, my arms outstretched ahead of me, one hand still holding my red tote bag.

"Get up," Bill said.

"Is she all right?" the passenger in a passing car asked.

"Yes, I'm fine," I said as I gathered myself to my feet. I looked at Bill and we began to laugh. I could not believe it. I had actually fallen flat on my face on the street. We had just gotten out of Bill's truck and had started walking quickly toward the hospital when I caught my foot on a ridge in the sidewalk. The momentum from the weight of my bag had hurled my hands forward and I could not use them to break my fall. There I was, laying on my face outside the hospital.

I said to Bill, "Am I bleeding?"

"No," he said.

"Is my face scraped?"

"No, well there is a small scratch on your forehead."

"How about my nose, is it scraped?"

"No."

"Are you sure? It felt like my face was being dragged across gravel."

"Well, you look fine."

"Oh, my hands are cut, but not too bad."

"Let's see," Bill said, chuckling.

I looked at him as he looked at my hands, and laughing at myself I said, "How can falling down be so funny?"

"I don't know. You could've gotten hurt."

"I must've really looked stupid. How'd I do that?"

"The root of that tree buckled up the sidewalk."

"Oh, and I guess this bag didn't help," I said as I handed it to him.

"What do you have in here? It weighs a ton."

"I know. Oh, magazines and stuff."

"Man!" Bill said laughing as we shared a moment of childish amusement. Wishing that I could share the lighthearted moment with Dawson, I said, "I'll bet Dawson would have thought it was funny, too. I'd like to be going in to tell him. I can see him chuckling."

"Hey, maybe we will," Bill said.

"Yeah, maybe, huh?"

"Well, if Dr. Wiviott puts him on the steroids, yeah, we might. So are you O.K.?"

"Yeah, hey, what better place to fall than in front of a hospital? At least if I needed first aid, I sure wouldn't have far to go."

On the ride in, Bill and I had been discussing the idea of starting Dawson on the steroids and Bill felt that if Dr. Wiviott recommended it we should agree. He trusted him implicitly. And I felt it would be very difficult for me to turn down a remedy that might eliminate his fever and give him some relief. But the decision would depend upon his condition this weekend. If he should start to show any improvement, perhaps it would not be necessary.

"How is he today?" I asked his nurse.

"Still febrile," she answered. "His fever is quite high and he's very agitated. I had to put a bite guard in his mouth to keep him from biting his line."

"No!"

Bill went to his side. Dawson was flushed with fever and the overall rash.

God help us, I prayed. *Guide us to do the right thing.*

"Good morning," Dr. Wiviott said.

"Oh, hi," I said. "He's not looking good."

"I know and we're having trouble keeping his blood pressure up."

"So what are we going to do?"

"We changed his catheter tip and we're waiting to see if that's going to help."

"So we're waiting?"

"We'll know more tomorrow."

"Can we afford to wait until tomorrow?" Seeing Dawson so obviously burning with fever, I felt that we could not. I wanted help for him immediately.

"We're going to keep a close eye on him today."

And Bill and I were, as well. The only time we left him for any length of time was to go to church. I prayed my usual prayer along with the one I had added days earlier. *Please, dear God, make Dawson well. Take away his fever. Let him wake up and please, dear Lord, help him to accept my prayers for him.* Since the first day that I had asked God to help Dawson embrace the fact that Bill I were going to church, I had included it in my daily pleas.

He remained febrile the entire day and became more agitated as evening approached. We stood outside his room and I watched him fighting a demon. I leaned against the doorway, feeling exhausted. "What must it be like for him?" I groaned.

The nurse could see my obvious torment. She said reassuringly, "He won't remember any of this."

"He won't?"

"Oh, no. The sedative he is on is an amnesiac. He will have no memory of what he is going through."

"Really?" I was only momentarily consoled, for I did not see how that could help him now. He still was going through Hell at that moment.

"Yes, he won't remember any of this," she repeated.

"Maybe I should be on that drug," I said, "then maybe I wouldn't have to remember this either," because I was thinking, *I know I will never forget the pain of what we are going through. Never, ever will I forget.*

The early years

Engagement, September 1964

Wedding, May 1965

New parents with baby Claudia, November 1967

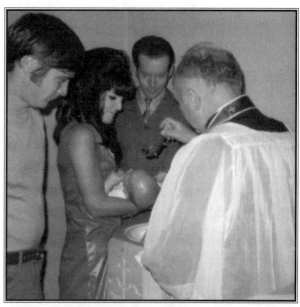

Dawson's Christening, Bill and Godparents, August 1969

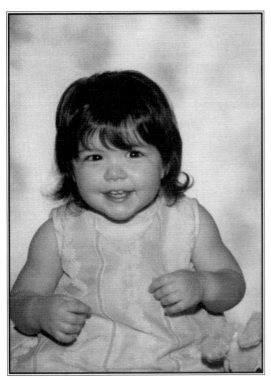

Claudia, 1½ years, March 1969

Dawson 1½ years, Claudia 3 years

Dawson's Gift

**Dawson's 2nd birthday,
April 1971**

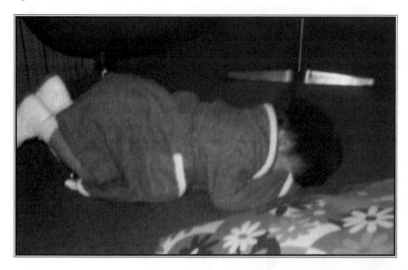

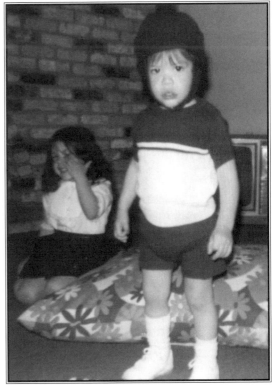

Dawson 2½ years, Claudia 4 years, September 1971

"Me Cowboy. Me Dawson." October 1971　　*Dawson's first motorcycle, December 1971*

Dawson Batboy, April 1977

Hobo and Dawson, 1978

"Like father, like son,"
Easter 1980

Dawson 18½ years, Claudia 20 years, September 1987

Dawson and me on my happy 44th birthday, November 1988

Part Three

"Awake, awake! Rise up..."

—Isaiah 51:17

Chapter Twenty-Two

I was lying awake in the snug, twin-sized bed that had been mine when I was young, but was now the guest bed in my parents' spare bedroom. I was thinking about the circumstances in my life and in Dawson's that had brought me here, and like so many mornings that I had awakened here these past weeks, I found myself restlessly waiting for daylight to show through the white-curtained windows.

At the first glimpse of light I was up and out of bed. It was rather early to be getting up, considering that I was not going to the shop, nor did I have to catch the bus. I was going to be riding to the hospital with Bill and it was hours before I would be meeting him. But, as usual, I had been unable to sleep. As a result, I was ready early and I decided to call Bill. He said that he was ready, too, and when I arrived twenty minutes later he had already put Harley in his pen and was waiting by his truck. We both got in and he said, "There was a message on my phone when I got home last night."

"Who was it?"

"I think he said Deacon Joe."

"Oh, Deacon Joe."

"Who is he?"

"He's the deacon from the church. Remember I told you I had called to ask about getting a book?"

"Oh, yeah. He left his number and he said to call him back, but I'm not going to call him. I don't know what to say to him."

"But you had all those questions," I said reminding him.

"Yeah, I know, but you should be the one to talk to him. You call him."

"Well, I guess I could if you want me to." I was surprised that Bill was not annoyed with me about getting a call from the deacon, but his reluctance to talk to him did not surprise me. That was simply Bill being Bill. He had never been very talkative, in fact, years ago a friend of mine had dubbed him, "Man of few words."

Because Bill had not changed in that respect, I knew he liked it that I did all the questioning of the doctors. But when we arrived at the hospital and saw Dr. Wiviott, Bill did not hesitate a moment before asking him the question, "How is he?"

"He is not any better," Dr. Wiviott answered. "Although his white blood count is down slightly, other important factors are still grave. His temperature went up to 40 degrees again this morning and his rash is looking worse. His fever is between 38 and 39 right now and we're still having to continue a near maximum dose of Neo to keep his blood pressure up."

Bill asked him yet another important question, "Are you going to put him on the steroids?"

Dr. Wiviott, motioning toward the waiting room, said, "Let's go in here. I want to talk to you about that. I feel a trial of Medrol is reasonable at this time and I am definitely recommending it."

Bill said firmly, "Well, that's good enough for me."

Dr. Wiviott looked to me for my response and I said, "I guess we have to do it, huh? I was just hoping that we wouldn't have to. I want to see him get over this fever, but I want to know that it's because he's getting well. Doing it this way is scary to me."

"I understand how you feel," Dr. Wiviott said. "I wish it could have worked out that way, too, but I believe this is our only option now. This could give us the break we need by giving us time to try and find the source of his fever. Without this break, well, I just don't think we'd have a chance. I'm afraid we'd simply run out of time. I do understand how difficult this is for you." He paused a moment, then continued, "Dawson's situation is very grave, such that I feel there is an immediate need to modify the course of action. I mean, immediate."

Realizing he was saying that without a break in his fever Dawson was not going to survive this, I wanted to scream to God, "Why are you not answering our prayers?"

"Mrs. Bell, what do you think?" Dr. Wiviott was asking.

In that instant, my thoughts had changed from outrage at God to thinking, maybe God *was* answering our prayers, maybe this drug was His answer. Hoping that it was, I said, "Did you want to start it today?"

"Yes."

"O.K.," I said, "do it."

"I will prescribe a substantial dose initially and will be following him very closely."

"You really believe his fever will come down?" I asked.

"Yes, I do."

"How long do you think it will take?" I asked and with a touch of frustration and cynicism, I added, "Twenty-four to forty-eight hours?"

"Oh, no," he said, "I think we could see it dropping sooner than that."

"Really?" *Could this be true? Would this finally be the time when we would see a prompt sign of improvement without that agonizing two-day wait?* With newfound optimism I said, "I know that 40 degrees is a fever of about one hundred and four, and I've been watching it in the high thirties for weeks, but I've forgotten, what is actually normal? I want to be sure I recognize it when I see it."

"Oh, around 37. All right, I'm going to get this ordered so I can start him on it as soon as possible." We shook hands and thanked him. When he left, Bill and I stood there looking at each other, not knowing what to say. I did not even know what to feel. Thankful? Afraid? Hopeful? What did I feel? All of the above? Yes, and more. But mostly I was excited, inwardly excited. The thought that in less than a day Dawson's fever could be gone filled me with such delight that I did not dwell on the disturbing fact that the cause of his fever had not been resolved. The possible repercussions of all this worried me, but I took comfort in the fact that Dawson could soon be getting some relief from that awful, burning fever and that, at last, we could be seeing him awake and calm.

We went to his room, stood by his side and I prayed for God's help. Doctors came and went, checking on Dawson and talking with us. Nina came by, too. She said, "We're going to do the steroids, huh?"

"Yes, what's your feeling about that?" I asked her.

"Well, I think we had to do something," she said. "Let's hope it works."

Bill and I were alone with Dawson when his nurse came in. "O.K.," she said, "it's here. We can get him started." I watched as she hung the large plastic bag of clear liquid onto the standing rack that was already heavily laden with similar type bags. She then inserted the line into Dawson's IV. This insignificant-looking fluid was about to enter his body. I looked at my watch. It was noon. I looked at the numbers on his monitor. His fever was 38.6.

Two hours passed. The number remained at 38.6.

But an hour later the number was 38.1. Was it happening, was it working?

By four o'clock in the afternoon, it read 37.3. Bill and I kept looking back and forth at each other and Dawson and that incredible number. *God, it is working. It is actually working.* We were not experiencing that usual disappointing wait. We were, finally, on the side of success. *Oh, Dawson. Thank you, God. Thank you, Dr. Wiviott.*

Then, a mere five hours after having been given the Solumedrol, Dawson's fever was 37. Normal! Normal. My God, it was normal.

Every other time a new remedy had been tried, we had been told that it may take forty-eight hours to see his fever drop. I had, nonetheless, become discouraged when there were no signs of that happening after just twenty-four hours had passed. I had always felt that if it were going to happen, it would happen right away. Perhaps my expectations had been unrealistic those other times, for these circumstances and this remedy were far different from anything that had been tried before. But this was the way I thought it would be, seeing an indication within hours. Yet now that it was actually happening, it was positively unbelievable. This was quicker than I had ever imagined possible.

No doubt I had witnessed a miracle, albeit, a miracle of modern medicine. This drug, this miracle-like drug, had done what no other had been able to do thus far.

As word spread throughout the unit that Dawson's fever was down to normal, several nurses came by to see us. I had not realized how much the nurses had been hoping for this, or how unanimous their collective hope must have been, for there had only been a couple of nurses who had shown or expressed their personal feelings to me before this.

A couple of weeks earlier, one male nurse, Manuel, had been assigned to Dawson for three days straight before he was to leave for his vacation. Dawson's fever was at its lowest on Manuel's last day and it had looked as though it was about to reach normal. When Manuel got off duty he was so excited he made that motion with his fist like golfers do when they make a great shot, shouting, "Yes!" Then he high-fived another nurse saying, "We did it! Now I can go on vacation knowing Dawson's fever is down." Unfortunately, he had returned a week later to discover that Dawson's fever had returned, as well. And there was another nurse, Suzann, who had never been Dawson's nurse, yet frequently talked to Bill and me. That was unusual, for most of the nurses that we were acquainted with had been assigned to Dawson. We both liked her. She was so natural and easy to talk to. She was small and blonde and there was just something about her that made her cute, but not cutesy. One night Bill said to her, "I wish you'd get Dawson sometime. How come you've never had him?" "Oh," she said, "I don't know, but I don't want him." I was quite taken back by what seemed like such a cold, insensitive response, but she went on to explain. "I don't want to care for Dawson because it is just too sad. I feel so bad for him. He is so young to be going through all of this."

It was apparent now that it had been more than just those two nurses who felt sympathetic toward Dawson. One nurse who came by said, "We are so happy his fever is down. We have all been rooting for Dawson to beat this thing."

"You are all so great," I said. "I don't know how you guys do what you do day after day. It must be so hard on you."

Soon after we were alone again with Dawson, Dr. Harris came by. "This is really something, isn't it?" I said to him.

"It certainly is, but you know that I do have my reservations about this."

"Yes, I do and I understand why. But it is so good to know that he is not fighting that fever."

"Yes, it is. He really needed this break. Next, we'll try C-PAPping him and get him off that respirator."

Not long after he left, Dr. Wiviott entered. So in awe of these incredible results, I was unable to hide my excitement when I saw him. "This is so amazing!" I exclaimed.

"Well, he definitely will be feeling much better."

"Oh, he must be feeling better already," I said, so grateful to this doctor who had made this possible.

"We'll start slowly weaning him off the sedatives late this evening and see how he does."

"Do you think he will be calmer than he had been before?" I asked.

"Yes, I do."

"I do, too. Then, maybe, he will be able to get off this respirator."

"Well, that's certainly what I'm expecting," he said.

Dawson's temperature continued to get lower and by nine o'clock that evening it was 36.1. "Is that all right?" I asked the nurse. "Is that too low?"

"It's fine," she said. "He was given quite a large dose of the Medrol today, but I'm sure we will start tapering it down a bit. I've been able to lower his dose of Neo, too, so that's good."

I had been aware of the juggling that had been going on with Dawson's medication over the past few weeks. I had often been told by the doctors how they were going to add a dose of this, and discontinue that, and cut back on another while increasing something else and substituting this one for that one. After watching all of this, I had come to the conclusion that medicine was not an exact science. It was more like an art form, adding a splash of this color here and a dab of that tint there and a mixture of shades and hues all brought together to create the perfect balance, to create something beautiful to behold.

In the way that a work of art, a masterpiece, is unveiled, was Dawson about to be? With his veil of fever now being removed, were we on the eve of beholding something beautiful?

Monday, September 9....Days in Hospital:34....Days on VADs:29

Will I see Dawson awake today? I could barely wait to find out. In the wee hours of the morning, between short periods of sleep, I almost called the hospital. But I decided not to, fearing that I might not hear what I was hoping for.

I was so glad when morning finally came. My wait would soon be over and all of the previous night's questions could soon be answered. *Will he really be awake? If he is awake, how will he be? Will he be calm? Will he be Dawson?*

My mother came into the kitchen where I was sitting at the table having a cup of hot chocolate. I was dressed and ready to go. "Hi," she said.

"Hi," I responded, giving a big sigh.

Making herself a cup of tea she said to me, "You look good."

"You're kidding. I do?"

"Yes, I had been thinking that it is something, how every day you manage to get yourself going and looking nice."

"Really? I can't imagine how I can even look halfway civilized. I'm not sleeping well and I feel like I must have aged fifty years this past month."

"I'm sure with all you've been through, you could feel like that."

I did feel that I must be looking terrible, despite that I was trying my best. I always had my make-up on and did my hair, such as it was. But I felt like I had a permanent grimace on my face, and my body was always tense, my stomach continually churning and this morning my mind was unable to focus. I kept looking at the clock. Bill usually called when he got to work around eight o'clock, and it was only seven-twenty. I was wondering how I could bear to wait any longer to hear from him. I was thinking that maybe I should just call the hospital myself when my phone rang. My heart jumped. It had to be Bill, but it was so early! *He must still be at the hospital,* I thought. *What is he going to say?*

I rushed to get it. "Hello?"

"He's awake!" he said. Bill had wasted no time in telling me. He did not even bother with hello. He just said, "He's awake!"

"He is? He really is?"

"Yeah, he is!"

"How is he, I mean, is he O.K.?"

"Yeah, yeah, he is."

"Like what? Is he looking at you like he knows you?"

"Yeah. He's trying to ask me something."

"What?"

"I don't know. He's still on the respirator. He can't talk."

"Why do you think he's asking you something?"

"He's making some motions with his hands."

"Like what?"

"I don't know … kind of like, oh, I don't know."

"Well, how does he seem? He doesn't look scared like he did?"

"No, he looks good."

"His eyes, they're not looking frightened?"

"No. Andrea, he looks so good."

"Oh, Bill, I can't believe it. He's awake and calm?"

"Yeah. I know. I can't believe it either. I'm going to go back in and see him before I leave, but I just wanted to call you and tell you."

"Oh, I'm so glad you did. I was going to call there, but I decided to wait to hear from you. God, I can't believe it! O.K., I'll let you go. Tell him I'm coming down, O.K.? Thanks, Bill, I'll see you later."

"O.K. I'll call you."

"Mom! He's awake!" I cried as I hung up.

"How is he?" my mother asked.

"Bill said he seems good. He said he's trying to ask him something. I wonder what it is. I better get going. I'm still going to the shop before the hospital, but I might not spend as much time there as I had planned. Maybe I'll be able to catch an earlier bus."

While I was at the shop, hurrying through my work, Bill called. "Dawson wants a mirror," he said. "Do you think you could bring him one?"

"A mirror? Like a small compact mirror?"

"No, bigger than that, I think."

"What does he want it for?"

"I don't know. He was trying to write something. It was really hard for him and I could barely read it. I could only make out the word, mirror, and I asked him, 'You want a mirror?' and he nodded that he did."

"O.K., I do have one here at the shop I can bring. So he's still like normal?"

"Yeah, he is, but he didn't know why he was in the hospital. He thought he must have been in an accident and wrecked his bike."

"Really? Did he write that?"

"Yeah. He was worried. He was relieved when I told him that his bike was fine. I told him that he was in the hospital because of his heart. He looked like he was glad to hear it was his heart and not his bike."

"Oh, God. That's Dawson. I can't wait to see him. I'm just finishing up here and getting ready to leave. I'm glad you caught me before I left. I'll bring the mirror. Did you tell him I was coming?"

"Yeah, I told him. He looked glad."

"God, I just can't believe this. O.K., I'll see you later. Thanks, bye."

I found the mirror, put it in my bag and locked up the shop. I drove to the bus stop and was on my way, on my way to see Dawson, to really see him. I had waited so long for this day. He was awake and calm. God, awake and calm! I thought, *So it was true after all, his agitation had been entirely due to the fever. If he had not had that fever he would have been awake right after the VAD surgery. How many days ago was that? God, how many days have we lost?*

I dismissed those thoughts, for I was too full of joy to waste any time lamenting over what could have been. With my mind so absorbed in anticipation of seeing Dawson, the bus ride went quickly and I soon arrived at my stop. I stepped quickly off the bus and hurried down the street while looking up at the hospital windows. Every time I had walked from the bus stop I had done this, wondering which window was Dawson's. And again like I had done so many times before, I imagined the day that I would look up and see Dawson standing in his window waiting for me. Today, with Dawson finally awake it seemed possible that one day that would happen and in my mind I saw us waving at each other. The joy in my heart was magnified by that image as I thought, *I could live that someday, God, I really could.*

I walked through the lobby doors to the elevator, up to the third floor, down the hall, through the ICU doors, around past the nurses' station toward Dawson's room. The nurse sitting at her post outside his room saw me and smiled. I smiled back, but did not say a word. I did not ask my usual question, "How is he?" Instead, I peeked into his room to see for myself.

And what I saw was that beautiful sight I had been waiting for. Dawson was sitting up, and his eyes were wide open. He was awake, awake and so calmly sitting there. I had waited so long to see this. God, the moment had finally arrived. "Hi, Daws," I said. He nodded to me and lifted his hand. I went to him. "Oh, Dawson," I said as I put my hand on his, "it's been an unbelievable wait." I could not believe that, just as I had prayed for, I was looking into his eyes.

The nurse said, "He's very alert this morning. He's still a little sleepy and dozes off, but when he's awake he watches everything."

"It's wonderful," I said, smiling at Dawson. His mouth still had the respirator taped to it, so he could not smile back at me, but I saw a smile in his eyes.

"Good morning, Mr. Bell," Dr. Wiviott said to Dawson as he entered.

I said, "Dawson, this is one of the doctors who has been treating you. This is Dr. Wiviott."

Dawson nodded as Dr. Thompson entered. "Hi, Dawson," she said.

The room seemed rather crowded and Dr. Wiviott motioned to me that he'd like me to step outside with him. I said, "Dawson, I'll be right back, O.K.?" I followed Dr. Wiviott out past the nurse's station.

He said, "I just wanted to talk to you and tell you how things are going. I read over Dawson's chart earlier this morning. No doubt, he clinically looks a lot better."

"He looks really good," I said. "It's incredible to me how he can look fine just because he doesn't have a fever even though whatever it is that caused it is still there. I always felt he would be calm without that fever, but it is really something to see that it was true."

"Yes, his mental status is greatly improved. And while it is quite obvious that the Medrol brought his fever down, it is possible the antibiotics may be having a positive impact on his condition, as well, which would be very good. We really can't be sure just how much at this point. In any case, his blood pressure is holding and his white blood count is normal. This is quite significant because, typically, the steroid could have a tendency to bring the white count up, so to see it down to normal is especially noteworthy. Did you notice that his rash looks better, too?"

"Yes, I did. It's all so incredible."

Dr. Wiviott went on to say in a more serious tone, "I talked with Dr. Thompson earlier and she wants to get him off the steroids ASAP. In some respect I agree with her that it would be desirable, but I am inclined to suggest that we keep him on them for at least three to five days more. I want to see him more improved and stable before we taper off completely."

"Well, I trust your judgment," I said.

"Thank you," he said. "I'll be talking to you."

I went back to Dawson's room. Dr. Thompson was gone and Dr. Harris was there. "He sure looks good," Dr. Harris said.

"He sure does," I agreed.

"You're doing very well, Dawson," Dr. Harris said. "I'll be checking back with you later." My phone rang and I answered it. It was Bill. He said, "Are you with him?"

"Yeah, I am."

"How is he?"

"Good," I said smiling as I looked over at Dawson.

"Did you give him the mirror?" Bill asked.

"No, actually I haven't had a chance. We've been pretty busy. The doctors have been here. Dawson," I said, "I brought a mirror. Dad told me you wanted one."

He nodded. Bill said, "I really can't talk, but I just wanted to hear how he was doing. I'm going to try and get out of here early today."

"That would be good. We'll see you later." Dawson raised his eyebrows and pointed to the pen and paper. I handed them to him and he tried to write something, but was having a difficult time. His fingers could barely hold the pen and his hand was quite shaky, so he put them down. "Do you want the mirror?" I asked.

He nodded and I took it out of my bag and handed it to him. He pulled his hospital gown aside with one hand and held the mirror up to the VADs with the other. *Of course,* I thought, *of course that is what he wanted the mirror for! He wanted to see the VADs.*

I said, "I guess you wanted to see that, huh?"

He raised his eyebrows and nodded a definite, "Yes."

"Did they explain anything to you about them? They are called VADs and that stands for ventricular assist device. They are helping your heart to pump. When you came to this hospital, you were in pretty bad shape. You don't remember that?"

He shook his head. "They put you on a temporary machine, not this one, a different one. You were awake after that. You don't remember?" I was telling him things that had happened right after the ECMO surgery. I thought he would have remembered, but he shook his head again.

I thought, *That nurse must have been right about the sedative being an amnesiac.* She had told me that he would not remember this past month's ordeal and what he had been through. I had been slightly skeptical, but I now knew it to be true. I said, "After that machine, they put you on these VADs. It was like a miracle, Dawson."

He put the mirror down, his eyes wide with a look of wonder, but in the next moment they drowsily closed and he fell peacefully asleep.

He, unknowingly, had given me the answer to my tortured question, "What will he do when he sees those VADs?" Well, he had boldly looked at them and had calmly accepted them. And in doing so, he had answered another one of my many questions, "When he wakes up, will he be Dawson?" The answer was, yes, he was definitely Dawson.

I stayed in the room awhile watching him sleep then left and went to the desk. I asked Lacy, "Do you have Post-its?"

"Yes," she said, "here," as she handed me the yellow note pad.

"May I take the whole pad?"

"Sure," she said, "I have plenty."

I took it with me to the waiting room. The note paper was larger than I was expecting, but I figured that I could make them work. I proceeded to write the alphabet on the paper, three letters apiece. When I finished, I took out my tiny fold-up scissors that Rusty had given me and cut the pieces of paper into twenty-six squares, each having one letter on it and one sticky edge. I went back to Dawson's room. He was still sleeping.

The nurse said, "He's been resting comfortably. Oh, I think he just woke up. How are you feeling, Dawson?" she asked. He nodded in response to her question.

"Hi," I said to him. "You had a nice nap and while you were sleeping, I had an idea. It seemed kind of hard for you to write, so I made these letters. You want to try them?"

He nodded enthusiastically. I showed him how he could use the letters to spell out what he wanted to say. I put them one by one in alphabetical order on a sheet of paper that was on his bed table. He took one letter off and tried to stick it onto another piece of paper, but even this was difficult for him to do. He had a hard time grasping the paper square and pressing it down, so I held the sheet of paper for him and helped him stick the letter T on it. Then he pointed to the H. I took that and stuck it on the paper next to the T. Then the A. I said, "I guess we don't even have to stick the letters down. This is kind of silly, huh?" I saw a twinkle in his eyes that would have been a chuckle as he agreed with me. "You can just point to them and I'll spell it out," I said. "T, H, A." He then pointed to the N, the K and the S. "Oh, you're welcome, Dawson," I said. "You are so very welcome." He lifted his hand and I took it. He squeezed my hand and I said, "It is so good to see you, Dawson. You just can't imagine."

He nodded and closed his eyes. The nurse came in. "It's time for our shift-change," she said, "I'm sorry."

I said, "Dawson, I'll have to leave for just a little bit. They do this every time the new nurse comes on duty, but I'll be back." He frowned as if to say, "I wish you didn't have to leave," then resolutely nodded.

While I was in the waiting room, Bill arrived. He was early, just like he said he would be. I was glad to see him and share my joy with him.

"How is he doing?" he asked.

"Great," I said.

"I want to see him. Do you think we can go in?"

"Yeah, probably. Let's go. They'll understand how anxious we are to be with him."

Dawson's day nurse was just leaving and his night nurse said, "We're going to try C-PAPping him a little later and see how he does."

Oh, God, I thought, *he has to do all right. If he does well, he could be off the respirator soon. We've come this far … God, it has to work.*

"Hey, Dawson, how you doing?" Bill said. Dawson lifted his hand and Bill held it. "You're looking good," Bill said. Dawson raised his eyebrows and looked at me.

I said, "Yeah, you do."

His nurse said, "We've been reorienting him, you know, telling him where he is, what day it is, things like that."

I said, "So Dawson, you know it is September, huh?"

He nodded that he did, but then shrugged his shoulders as if to say that it was hard to believe.

I said, "I know it must be strange to find out that so much time has passed. I can't imagine what this is like for you, Dawson. This has really been something for us, too, but now to see you awake is so wonderful."

Bill said, "The nurses have been taking good care of you. They are all pretty nice here." The monitor started beeping and Dawson's eyes darted toward the sound.

I said, "Oh, that's just to tell the nurse it's time to check on your medications. It's O.K. She'll just change one of the empty bags hanging there. That beep used to scare me, but now I'm used to it. Hey, look who's here, Dawson."

Dawson turned his head and looked toward the door to see Matt entering. Matt had continued to come by almost every day after work hoping to see Dawson awake, and today, finally, he could. Matt went right to Dawson's side and they grabbed each other's hands.

"Matt's been here every night," I said. Bill motioned to me and I said, "Dawson, we'll be right back."

When we got outside his room, Bill said, "I thought Matt would be more comfortable talking to Dawson alone."

"Yeah, that's true, I'm sure he would. I'm glad you thought of that."

We went down to the cafeteria and soon after, Wes, one of Bill's friends, came by to see us. He had been coming by every so often to keep us company and to help lift our spirits. He was a longtime friend, but before my seeing Wes here in the hospital, I had not seen him in many years. Bill and I had first met him when he started to work for Bill. At that time, he was a young, single guy and Bill and I had been married for a few years. Claudia and Dawson were very young and Wes, in his funny way, used to call them "little rug rats." I had never heard that phrase before and thought it was cute. The kids liked him because he joked around with them and I liked him, too. He was pleasant, polite, always in a good mood and I found him enjoyable to talk to. In fact, years later it became a joke between Bill and Dawson. If the phone rang and I answered it and talked for quite a while before saying, "Bill, it's for you," Dawson, with a deadpan expression would just say, "Dad, it's Wes." Bill found Dawson's remark amusing because he was always right.

Wes was happy to hear our good news that Dawson was awake. He stayed only a short while, saying, "I'm sure you want to get back to him." We thanked him for coming. Bill said, "Maybe next time you come, you can go up and see him."

"Sounds good," Wes said, "sounds real good. I'll see you guys. Take care."

Later that evening, they tried C-PAPping Dawson, but the trial only lasted an hour and a half. He was having difficulties and became anxious and his heart and respiratory rates went up. He was given some mild sedatives for his anxiety and the nurse assured us this was all understandable because it had been quite a day for him. She said, "He'll have a good night's sleep and we'll try again tomorrow. He'll do fine."

"How long does he have to stay on C-PAP before you decide that he's ready to be taken off the respirator?" I asked, though I thought I knew the answer.

"We'd like him to go all day."

"That's what I thought, but I was hoping that maybe it could be less. O.K., well, now I know what to hope for tomorrow."

Bill said, "Andrea, it has been a big day and he's sleeping now. Maybe we should go, and I'll be here very early in the morning."

"O.K.," I said, "it has been a very good day and tomorrow should be even better. He could be off the respirator." I said to the nurse, "We're going to leave. Maybe later you could turn David Letterman on his TV, O.K.? If Dawson wakes up, it would be good for him to see and hear something familiar."

"Sure, I'll do that," she said. "Now don't worry. You get a good night's sleep, too."

A good night's sleep? Is that possible? With all the excitement of today and the anticipation of tomorrow … could I sleep?

Tuesday, September 10....Days in Hospital:35....Days on VADs:30

To my surprise, I slept quite well, better than I had in a long while. Seeing Dawson looking so like himself had calmed some fears. I awoke with the excitement of seeing him again and, perhaps, even talking to him. This very well could be the day that he would get off the respirator. So not only would I be able to talk to him again, but he would be able to talk to me. I could not wait to hear his voice and to see a smile, not just in his eyes, but on his lips. What a glorious day this could be.

While I was getting ready for this hopefully momentous day, and before I had even begun to wait for Bill's morning call, my phone rang. *It's Bill!* "Hi," I said, excited to hear this morning's report.

"He's sedated!" Bill said. "Andrea, he's sedated!"

"What? What do you mean?"

"He's sedated! He's out! They have him sedated again! I just went crazy!"

I had never heard Bill so upset. "Bill, what do you mean? You know they sedated him a little bit last night."

"No, Andrea, it's not like that! He's sedated like he was before! His fever is back!"

"Oh, God! No! Why? Why? What happened? What are they saying?"

"I don't know! No one would tell me anything!"

"Did you talk to Dr. Harris?"

"No, he's not here, it's too early, but I have his number."

"Did you ask what time he'll be there?"

"Yeah, but they're not telling me anything. I think they think I'm a madman. But, Andrea, you can call him."

"I can't believe this. How could this happen?"

"Call Dr. Harris."

"I will, but I'll have to wait until he gets to the hospital. God, Bill, can't you find out something now? You're there."

"But this number I have, you can call it now."

"What do you mean?"

"I think it's like an emergency number."

"Dr. Harris' emergency number? You mean like his answering service?"

"Or his home, I don't know."

"What? Who gave it to you?"

"I got it off that big board. I'll give it to you. Just call him."

"Are you sure it is his number?"

"Yes, it said Dr. Harris above it."

"O.K. O.K., give it to me." I wrote it on the back of a piece of paper on my mother's kitchen counter and said, "Call me back in a few minutes." I was thinking, *Can I really call Dr. Harris at home, I mean, if that is what this number is?* Well, I had to, so I nervously called the number and to my astonishment, he answered. "Dr. Harris?" I said, "I'm sorry to bother you. This is Andrea Bell. Bill was in to see Dawson this morning and his fever is back up and he's sedated. No one could tell him what was going on. I just needed to know what happened."

"I haven't seen him yet this morning," he said. "Let me find out and I'll call you back. Give me your number."

I gave it to him, thanked him and when I hung up, my phone rang. It was Bill. "Did you get a hold of him?" he asked.

"Yeah, he didn't know anything about it. He's going to call me back, so I shouldn't be on the phone. I don't know how long it will take for him to get back to me, so maybe I should page you after I hear from him, O.K.?" My mind began racing, *What could have happened to Dawson? Were the steroids no longer working? Had yesterday been just a fluke? Would I ever see him awake again?*

When Dr. Harris called, he said, "We had lowered his dose of the steroid last night and evidently it was too low. We're going to give him more this morning."

"O.K." I said. "Well, thank you." I paged Bill and when he called me I told him what Dr. Harris had said.

"Are they stupid or what?" Bill said, sounding angry and disgusted. "Don't they know what they're doing?"

"I don't know. I know they wanted to taper it off as soon as they could, but I wouldn't have thought they would have done it this soon. Dr. Wiviott wanted to keep him on it for at least three days, but Dr. Thompson wanted him off of it right away. I don't know exactly what happened. I'll know more when I get there. I better get going. Daddy's going to drive me in. I'll talk to you later."

"O.K., I'll call you."

As we were arriving at the hospital, I saw Dr. Wiviott across the street. It appeared he had just come from there. I said to my dad, "There's Dr. Wiviott. I've got to talk to him!" and I ran to catch him.

"Oh, good morning, Mrs. Bell," he said as I nearly charged him.

"Did you see Dawson this morning?" I frantically asked.

"No, I had planned on seeing him when I get back. I want to see him when I have more time. I won't be gone long."

"Then you don't know?"

"Know what?" he asked.

"Dawson's fever is back!"

"What? No, I did not know. Well, I'm not going to wait. I'll go up there right now."

"Thank you," I said as he turned and hurried back toward the hospital doors.

When my dad and I arrived at Dawson's room, Dr. Wiviott and Dr. Harris were talking outside. When they were through, Dr. Harris walked away and Dr. Wiviott came to me and said, "Dawson's been given a dose of the Medrol this morning. He'll be fine. I have to go now, but I'll be back later and I'll see you then."

"What happened?" I asked.

"We cut the Medrol back too far, but he's back on it now. But we're not giving him as large a dose as the first one we gave him yesterday, so it will take some time to work, but he will be fine. Don't worry. I will see you later. I must go now."

"Thank you," I said.

I then told my dad that I was going to find Dr. Harris and when I did, I asked him how this could have happened. He said, "We do not want him on a high dose of these steroids for any length of time. You know that we really need to be able to get him off of them before he gets transplanted. That is why we lowered his dose. We are trying to find the minimum that will get that fever down and keep it down. He had some other problems last night, too."

I could not stand to hear what they were and I did not want to hear that he'd had, in any way, an uncomfortable night, but I asked, "What kind of problems?"

"He was uncontrollably agitated and he was very wide-eyed and shaking."

Shaking? *He must have been having some kind of a reaction*, I thought. "That sounds like withdrawal," I said, "is that possible?"

"Yes, I believe part of that was due to withdrawal, most likely the Fentanyl."

"That's one of the sedatives, isn't it? He's been on such a heavy dose of those for so long. Yesterday was his first day off of them, right?"

"Yes, I'm sure that was part of it and, of course, the fever."

"With his fever shooting right back up like it did, it must mean that whatever was causing his fever is still there. Without the steroids, his fever would not have dropped at all."

"That is true," he agreed.

"Dr. Wiviott thought that perhaps the antibiotics, along with the steroids, could have been a factor in his fever coming down. I guess that is not so."

"No, it isn't."

"Then how is he ever going to get off the steroids?"

"We are going to continue to try and find the source of the fever and then we'll treat it."

"I know, and that will have to happen soon, so he won't have to be on the steroids too long."

"Exactly."

"And we have to find and get rid of any infection because he will not be listed for transplant until then."

"Right."

"What if it is a drug reaction? Will you be able to list him?"

"If we can positively rule out infection, yes, we will list him."

"Is he back on the Vanco?"

"Yes, we cannot discontinue it at this time."

"So the Vanco still could be the drug that is causing his fever," I said.

"Yes, but his white blood count is up, so that could mean infection."

"But it could mean it is up because of the steroids, couldn't it?"

"Yes, that's a possibility, too."

I went back to Dawson's room overwhelmed by the complexity of his condition. When my dad asked me, "What did the doctor say?" I could only manage a shrug.

Dawson was still sleeping, so my father and I went down to the coffee shop. There was no change in Dawson's condition or his fever when we returned to his room. My dad stayed a short while, then left for home and I went to the waiting room where Joyce, the social worker, found me deep in thought.

She said, "Andrea, hi, how are you? I heard that Dawson's fever was down yesterday. I had thought that I was going to be able to talk to him today."

"Me, too," I said. "I can't believe this."

"So the steroids brought his fever down."

"Yes. God, it was so amazing, but I guess they are trying to keep the dose down to a minimum. I don't know."

"I can imagine how hard this must be for you."

"It is awful. Just when we saw him get some relief, just when we thought he'd be getting off the respirator. We were so close. He was awake and calm. It is really something how without that fever he was not agitated, he was not fighting or kicking. The nurses said he was actually cooperative."

"Yes, I heard. I was really looking forward to seeing him like that."

"You know, all that fighting he was doing, it just wasn't him."

"I know."

"I can't stand the thought that he had a scary night last night. This is just so terrible. He looked so good yesterday."

"Yes, I heard that he did."

"Did you know that I met Kim the other day, the one who had been on the VADs? She told me she'd had a really hard time, too, when she was on them. She said she had lots of problems."

"Oh, but nothing like this," Joyce said.

"Really? She told me that she'd had all kinds of trouble. She said she went through a lot."

"No, not really. Well, she did, but nothing like what Dawson is going through and this has been going on for so long. How long has he been on the VADs now?"

"Thirty days today," I said.

"Really? Thirty. That is a long time. Not for the VADs, but for being sedated and on the respirator."

"Tell me about it," I said. "I am really worried. I don't know how all these problems are going to get resolved. I'm so scared. And just when I had some hope. It was so wonderful to see him awake and looking good. I knew the steroids were not the answer to all our problems, but they seemed to be a start. I do worry about why the doctors want him off of them. Is it because the anti-rejection drugs wouldn't be as effective if he's already been on a high dose of steroids? If that's true, that would be serious, but I don't know. I don't understand. It is all too much. I just don't know how it can all work out."

"Well," Joyce said, "his fever will be coming back down now."

"I know. Tomorrow could be a much better day. This is the way it's been going. You know, one day up and one day down and every day never knowing what might happen. That's just the way it is here. It can be really awful. I saw a family in the hallway a couple of days ago. They were crying. Then their minister arrived carrying his bible and they all went into the cardiac ICU. When they came out, there were several people sobbing. I knew what must be happening. God, I hated to see that. It made me have to think about ... what I would do. I mean ... what would I do if ... oh, I can imagine myself just wanting to jump out the window. I know that sounds stupid, I just don't know ... maybe I would fall to the floor screaming like a woman I had seen on the news a while back. I will never forget her. There had been a plane crash and I watched as they showed the families who had been waiting for their loved ones to arrive. This woman I saw, they said her son had been on the plane. I saw her fall straight backwards to the ground as she lay there in the middle of the airport screaming and writhing in the unimaginable pain of having lost her child. God, I just don't know what I ... oh, Joyce, I can't lose him."

She reached over and took my hand. "They're doing everything they can and tomorrow will be better," she said. "His fever will be down and," sounding optimistic, she added, "I'll finally get to interview him."

"Oh, wouldn't that be nice," I said, sighing. "We sure have waited a long time for that."

"Yes, we sure have. You must take care of yourself, Andrea. You know you can call me anytime and I will come by and see you tomorrow."

It helped to talk to her and I knew she understood my fears, but there was no way for anyone to alleviate them. Only time could tell us how this would all work out. And time was exactly what we needed. Would it hold out long enough for us to find the cause of Dawson's fever? This was not the way the day was supposed to go. Yesterday was so beautiful. Today should have been even more so. But I should not have been surprised, for this was life in the ICU.

This constant up and down, the inevitable swing between hope and dread was not just something that was happening to us and to Dawson. I had seen other families going through similar days and nights, though no one had been going through it for as long as we had.

For the past several days I had been seeing two young women in the waiting room and we had shared our stories with each other. I found the women to be very nice and I had learned from them that they were from the Middle East and that their mother had come to the United States to wait for a kidney transplant. She was hospitalized after suffering complications from a fall. Since being in the hospital she had contracted an infection. She had been on and off the respirator, which to me seemed somewhat better than what we were going through, but not much. There were days when she seemed improved only to take a turn the next day. Her daughters were understandably frustrated by the things that had happened and frightened over the things that still might.

Oh, there were those families in the ICU who it had worked out for, but there were more for whom it had not.

The husband of the lady who had given me the scapular recovered and went home.

An Asian man whose large family was on the verge of having to make a painful decision, suddenly made a turn for the better.

But the man who had leukemia whose wife had told me about St. Dominic's took a serious turn for the worse and I never saw her again.

And the mother whose daughter was dying of lupus never returned after that day we spoke.

And the African-American family whose minister came, had spent their last day there.

Yes, this was life in the ICU or, more accurately, this was life and death in the ICU.

"Does he still have the fever?" Bill, predictably, asked when he arrived.

"Yes. They're saying that it will be coming down, though."

But we sat for hours in his room and his fever stayed between 38.1 and 38.3. That was not terribly high, something like 100.5F, but it was showing no signs of dropping. We were told that we should not worry, for he would be getting his next dose of the steroid at nine o'clock that evening. They assured us that his fever would be down by morning.

Bill said, "Do you want to stay until they give him his next dose or do you think we should go?"

It was only seven-thirty and Dawson was sleeping under the sedation, but I did not know what I wanted to do. I said, "If he were going to be awake I definitely would stay."

"Well, of course, so would I," Bill said emphatically.

"I know, of course we would, but he isn't going to be awake tonight," I said sadly.

"And you know, Andrea, I will be here to see him early in the morning," Bill said. We both knew that it made sense to leave and I was aware how hard this schedule must be for Bill. He looked very tired and I knew he must have been getting up quite early each morning, for he had been arriving at the hospital around six-thirty. He had been doing this so that he could have about forty-five minutes with Dawson before he went to work, even though Dawson had not been aware that he was there. Then he'd work all day and come straight to the hospital every afternoon. We had been staying until seven or eight in the evening, so he was not getting home sometimes until nine o'clock at night. He had been doing this every day for the past month and I knew it must be rough on him.

"O.K., I guess we could go," I said. After having spent the previous day with Dawson so aware and happy to have us with him, it was heartbreaking to be back to this.

Bill said, trying to sound encouraging, "His fever will be down again in the morning and he will be awake. Tomorrow will be a good day."

"I know," I said trying to convince myself. Then with my voice barely a whisper, I said to Dawson, "We'll see you in the morning, hon. We'll see you in the morning. You have a good night. I love you, Dawson." Hoping that Bill's words would prove to be true, and in an attempt to reaffirm them I said them out loud, "Tomorrow will be a good day, Dawson."

Bill and I walked slowly out of the unit. We rode down in the elevator with the two young women whose mother was waiting for a transplant. "How are you doing?" I asked them.

They shrugged their shoulders, slowly shaking their heads. "How are you?" one of them asked.

"Oh, you know," I said.

They both nodded that they did know, for they, like us, had spent another long day within the wearisome walls of intensive care.

Chapter Twenty-Three

I doubt if my heart could have been pounding any faster or if my mouth could have been any drier. I had become accustomed to experiencing these discomforts, but today they were extreme. I felt out of breath as if I had been running, running in fear. I understood these physical reactions were merely a result of the mental torment I continually put myself through, but there seemed no way that I could avoid it.

Excitement, when joined with apprehension, was just too powerful a combination to overcome, so the expectation, the uncertainty and fright grew more intense the longer I stood waiting for the elevator that would take me up to see Dawson.

I should not have been so nervous, for Bill had given me a wonderful morning report. As of eight o'clock this morning, the good news had been that Dawson's fever was down. He was awake, alert and calm, the perfect combination, and they were going to start C-PAPping him. I could not have expected to hear anything better than that. If he could stay with it for several hours, perhaps by evening the respirator could be removed. But the nearer I got to Dawson's floor, the more nervous I became thinking about how important it was for him to do well on the C-PAP trial. I was feeling overly desperate, as if this would be the only opportunity we would ever have to get him off that respirator.

By the time I reached his room, all my hopes and fears were at their peak in anticipation of what I was about to see. I began to look for signs in the nurses' faces of what was in store for me. The first nurse I saw outside his room smiled at me. The nurse coming out of his room was also smiling. I felt that he must be doing well, but I was afraid to believe it.

I did not hesitate a moment. I walked straight into his room with high hopes of seeing him doing well on the respirator. When that was not what I saw, I stopped short and stood there staring at him. *Oh, my God,* I thought, *am I seeing right? Could this be true? God, yes. Yes, it is.* The respirator had already been removed and he was breathing on his own! Breathing on his own and smiling. Smiling and looking right at me. And looking right at me, he said, "Hi." A simple, little "hi," the most wonderful word I had ever heard. His voice was low and hoarse, but I heard it. I heard it. Just as I had prayed for, I heard his voice.

"Dawson, I can't believe this! Oh, hon, you look so good." My words burst forth, high-pitched and rapid in contrast to Dawson's one little word, so soft and low. I went to his side and turned to the nurse who was smiling broadly. "How did this happen so quickly?" I asked her. "This is unbelievable. I thought he had to go all day on C-PAP before you could take him off the respirator."

"Yes, ordinarily that is true, but Dr. Harris ordered it removed."

"Had he been on C-PAP at all today?" I asked, smiling at Dawson.

"Yes, for a little while."

"How long was he on it?"

"Only for an hour and a half."

"An hour and a half? That's all?" I said, totally amazed. "Was it all right to take him off so soon?" I questioned.

"Well, Dr. Harris thought so. He came in and said, 'Let's get him off that thing.' I was pretty surprised myself when he said it."

"It is so incredible! I just can't believe it!" I was aware that Dawson had been watching me as I was talking to the nurse, and when I turned back to him, I saw this look in his eye, this expression on his face that was not quite like any I had ever seen on him before. It was a tender, unmistakable look of caring, unfeigned and unguarded and it took me by surprise. He smiled sweetly at me and I said, "Dawson, do you know how glad I am to see you?"

"Yeah," he said. His expression told me he was as glad to see me.

"How are you feeling, hon?" I asked.

It took a moment before he answered and when he did, his speech was unusually slow and breathy. "I feel all right," he said, "but my hands are itchy."

"Oh, they're itching from the rash," I said. "The rash is from your medication. It's looking a lot better than it did, though, but they are kind of dry."

"The nurse gave me some hand lotion," he said in a soft voice that was almost in a monotone. His speech was so slow and his manner of speaking was so odd that it concerned me, for I had worried about the possibility of the fever and drugs affecting his brain. Aside from his manner of speech, he did seem quite alert, which consoled me.

"That was nice," I said. "That will help. Wait until Dad hears that you're off the respirator!" I said, showing my excitement.

"Yeah," he said, giving me a smile that told me he knew how good the news would be for his dad. "Can we call him?" he asked.

"I could page him, but I'll bet he will be calling soon. He calls every day from work to see how you are."

As if on cue, my phone rang. "How is he?" Bill asked.

"Good," I said, "can you hold on a minute?" Looking at Dawson, I silently mouthed the words, "It's Dad," and handed him the phone.

"Hi," Dawson said. I knew what a wonderful surprise it would be for Bill to hear that beautiful word. I wanted him to hear it just as I had.

One of the first things I heard Dawson say to Bill was, "How's Papa Tom?" and I waited for his next response, which was, "Oh, no, that's too bad." They continued to talk and I spoke quietly to the nurse. I told her again how astonished I was to see Dawson off the respirator and how absolutely wonderful it was to see him looking so well. I said, "I was sure I was going to have to spend the entire day afraid, afraid he'd fail the C-PAP."

She said, "Dr. Harris knew that. I think that's one of the reasons he took him off when he did."

"Really? Why do you say that?"

"I don't know, it just seemed that way to me. You usually get here around the same time every day, and he was so anxious to get him off of it right then. He did it just before you got here."

"Well, I can't tell you how great it was and how scared I had been."

"I can imagine," she said.

I looked back at Dawson and he said, "Dad wants to talk to you," and he handed me the phone.

Bill said, "I can't believe this."

"I know. I couldn't believe it either when I got here. When I came into his room and saw him off the respirator, oh, God, it was so good. The nurse told me Dr. Harris was really anxious to get him off of it, so he just did it."

"That's great."

"Yeah, it is."

"It sure was good to talk to him. Well, I better get back to work. I'll see you guys as soon as I can. I can't wait to see him!"

When I hung up, I said to Dawson, "Dad said he can't wait to see you. He's really excited."

"Me, too," Dawson said.

Dr. Harris came in and looking at me he said, "He looks good, doesn't he?"

"He looks fantastic," I said. I was absolutely gushing as I thanked him for everything and every part that he had played in getting us to this moment.

"Dawson," he said, "would you like some ice to chew on?"

"Yeah," Dawson said. "That sounds good. I am thirsty."

"I'd like to start you on a little ice before letting you have some water."

"O.K.," Dawson said, "that's fine." Dr. Harris nodded to the nurse and she left her post. She returned with a paper cup filled with small ice chips and handed it to Dawson and he thanked her.

Throughout the remainder of the morning, several nurses stopped in to see us and I told Dawson how they all had been taking such good care of him. When nurse Cindy came by to say hello, I said, "Dawson, you probably don't remember Cindy, but she knows you very well. You shared some of your banana chips with her. She was one of the first nurses you had here. She's been taking wonderful care of you since the beginning."

"Thank you," he said, smiling at her. He was friendly to her, as he had been to all the nurses who had come by and he thanked her with the same obvious sincerity as he had the others.

When we were alone, I said to him, "It must be very strange for you not to know these people when they know you. It is understandable, though. You were quite sedated when they were taking care of you. One of the nurses told me that you wouldn't remember anything about that time."

"I do remember some things," he said.

"You do? Like what?" I had so often wondered what he would remember about his experience and because he had come so close to death, I wondered what, if anything, would be his memory of that. Might he have had a so-called near-death experience that he would recall? If so, would that explain why something about him seemed changed? But what was it that was different about him? I could not find the exact word for it, but there was a warmness, an openness, a genuineness that he had not shown as readily before.

He said, "I remember a lot of people running around me. They were hurrying."

"That must have been when you were rushed here, when they were preparing you for the emergency surgery."

He did not respond to what I had said. He appeared lost in his thoughts and he had a far away look in his eyes as he said, "They had me pinned to the ceiling."

What? Could this be that near-death, out-of-body experience that I had wondered about? Perhaps, but I did not interrupt him to ask him exactly what he had viewed from up there. I wanted to let him continue sorting out his thoughts in his own time, so I let it go. But I found it quite interesting that he had actually said something I could interpret in such a way.

"They were poking me, but I escaped through the ceiling." Then his expression changed and he smiled and said, laughing, "I was a quarterback for the L.A. Rams."

"What?"

"We were playing on a field in the middle of a gas station."

"You weren't a 49ER, huh?"

"No." His expression turning serious again he said, "I had lots of dreams." He tilted the paper cup to his lips and tapped the bottom to shake the ice into his mouth. "This sure is good."

"I'll bet it is," I said, thinking about how long he'd had that respirator tube down his throat and how good that cool, wet ice must feel going down. He was still very hoarse and speaking very slowly, but after all, it had been a very long time since he had spoken.

It was turning into quite a busy day, with doctors and nurses continually coming by. Despite that the visits and procedures took away from my alone time with Dawson, I was excited when I saw Sheila coming into the room.

"Hi," I said. "Look at Dawson."

"Oh, I know," she said, "doesn't he look great? I was here earlier when they extubated him. I was able to talk to him a little, but I had to leave."

"Oh, I guess I just missed you. I got here soon after," I said.

"I am really impressed," she said. "He is remarkably alert and lucid."

"You know, I'd forgotten for a moment that you had never seen him awake. You were not on his case when he was on the ECMO. So this is the first you've really seen him."

"Yes, and it is very nice to meet you, Dawson," she said shaking his hand.

"Thank you," Dawson said, "it is nice to meet you, too."

I was continuing to notice how Dawson was unusually gracious and appreciative to everyone he met and I was struck by how easy and natural it seemed for him. That impressed me because in the past Dawson had often appeared uncomfortable and hesitant, almost embarrassed, when he had expressed his thanks or gratitude. *Something is different,* I thought, *something is definitely different.*

Alone again, Dawson said to me, "I thought I had wrecked my bike."

"I know. You thought that was why you were in the hospital, right?"

"Yeah. I was really worried. You know what I thought?"

"No, what?"

"I thought these VADs were part of my bike."

"Oh, God, really?"

"Yeah. Not after I woke up, but when … oh, I don't know … it was when I was dreaming I guess … or something. I don't know, but I could feel all this metal inside me. I really thought it was my bike."

"Oh, Dawson. That sounds awful."

"Yeah, it was."

"Is that why you wanted to see them?"

"Yeah, kind of."

"Well, you're O.K. now, hon. Everything's going to be O.K."

"I know," he said and I reached over and took his hand in mine and he squeezed it.

The nurses' afternoon shift change came much too soon. I hated to have to leave him. "Mom, do you have to go?" he asked.

"Yes, but I will be right outside in the waiting room," I said, "and as soon as they are finished, I will be back. O.K.?"

"O.K.," he said.

Bill arrived while I was in the waiting room and for the first time in a long while, he was not frowning and I did not have to say, "Dawson's fever is up," or "Dawson is sedated." I could say, "Dawson is awake and talking and smiling and eating ice." I had so much more to say and I was telling him of Dawson's dreams when Joyce joined us in the waiting room.

She said, "I finally got to talk to Dawson."

"Isn't it amazing?" I said.

"It sure is, but I'm going to have to talk to him again. He seemed a little confused. He was telling me he had played for the Rams and that he was in a motorcycle accident."

"Oh, he had been talking to me about that, too, but he seemed to know it wasn't true. He said they were dreams, but I think they did seem different to him than ordinary dreams."

"I'm sure they were. Being in and out of various levels of sedation would make it hard to distinguish between what was real and what was a dream. To add to that, so much time has passed. It might take a little while for him to sort things out. He's been through quite a lot."

"I know."

"But his spirits seem good and he's very congenial," Joyce said.

Smiling, I said, "Not at all like he was, huh?"

"No, not at all. So you guys must be feeling much better, too."

"Oh, yes," Bill said.

I said, "Yes, this is wonderful, but I am still concerned about how and when we will be able to take him off those steroids and get him listed."

"Well, at least, we have some time to work that out now."

"I know and, believe me, I am very grateful for that."

"You guys have waited such a long time for this. I'm so happy for you. Well, I'll be back to talk with Dawson in the next couple of days. I still have to complete my evaluation report."

"Yes, I know. And you have waited a long time for that."

When she left, Bill said, "What does she want to know from him?"

"I don't know, but I'm not going to worry about that now. I can't imagine that after all he's been through and how hard they are trying to get him well enough to get listed that he could say anything that could change their minds."

"Yeah, true. Let's go see him."

I walked into Dawson's room ahead of Bill. "Dawson," I said, "look who's here."

"Hey, Dawson," Bill said. "You look great."

Dawson was smiling a happy grin. "Hi, Dad," he said.

"How you doin'?" Bill asked.

"Good," he said as he looked toward me. Then looking past me, he said, "Hi."

Bill and I turned around to see Matt. "How about this?" I said to Matt. "Can you believe it?"

I had never seen a smile on Matt like the smile he was giving Dawson as he went around to the far side of his bed. The three of us gathered around Dawson, but we were all silent, as if we were at a loss for words. I suppose in a sense we were, for there were no words worthy of this long-awaited moment.

I was the first to speak and in a deliberate attempt to lighten things up I said, "Dawson, some of your friends left a card for you at the house. It's really big and quite a few people signed it."

"Who?" he asked.

"I don't know if I can remember any of the names, let me think. Oh, Mike and Anita? Does that sound right?"

"Yeah," he said, nodding.

"I don't remember the other names. We'll bring it in for you to see."

"I think I know who else could have signed it," he said. "Yeah, I'd like to see it."

"They all miss you very much and want you to get well. Someone wrote about how much fun he had partying with you and how you always made him laugh."

I could not have imagined what Dawson's reaction would be to my statement. I was stunned when I saw that his eyes filled with tears. Bill and I looked at each other, wondering what this meant. I thought that it must be that he was feeling sad because he could not be partying with his friends and I was sorry that what I had told him had upset him. As the tears spilled down his cheeks, I said, "Dawson, what is it, hon?"

He said slowly, "I did this to myself." Then he quickly wiped his eyes, looked at Matt and said, "Hey, man, I'm sorry."

Matt clasped Dawson's hand and said, "It's all right, Dawson. It's all right."

When they let go of each other, Dawson took a sip of melted ice, then with his eyes down he said, "What else did they say?"

I thought for a moment and then I deliberately chose to tell him, "Some said they are praying for you. Dawson, you are in their prayers."

He lifted his head and turned to face me. He looked directly at me with an unmistakable expression. It was quite readable, spontaneous and honest. I will never forget the gentleness in his eyes. He was looking at me as if I had told him that someone had just given him a most generous, unexpected gift. He looked awed and appreciative.

"What do you think about this guy?" Dr. Wiviott said cheerfully as he entered the room.

"I think this is a miracle," I said with conviction, knowing that another prayer of mine had just been answered.

"He does look quite good, doesn't he?" he said. "How are you feeling, Dawson?"

"Good," Dawson answered. "Am I going to be able to get out of bed?"

"Oh, sure. You will need to get some strength back in your legs, though. You haven't used them for a while."

"Except to kick the nurses," Bill said, jokingly. Matt laughed and Dawson shook his head.

"Oh, that's right," Dr. Wiviott said smiling. "We'll have to get you started on a physical therapy program, Dawson. Dr. Harris can tell you when you can start that."

"O.K.," Dawson said, "I'll ask him about it. I would really like to get up." Watching him as he talked to the doctor, I found it astounding to see him so eager and energetic after all that he had been through.

Although his speech was still slow and his voice hoarse, he was talkative and expressive. He was anxious to share the memories of his experiences with us. And we were quite interested in everything he had to say. We stayed later than usual, but no one told us we had to leave. Everyone knew this had been a very special day for all of us.

As hard as it had been to leave him before, seeing the look in his eyes tonight made it harder than ever. He looked so happy to have us there with him it was difficult to tell him we were going to go. Bill said, "I'll be here early in the morning, Dawson, before I go to work." Dawson looked glad to hear that.

"I'll be here around eleven," I said as I took his hand. "I'll see you in the morning, hon."

"O.K.," Dawson said, "Bye."

That morning, I could not have dreamed that the day would hold such wonders, and that I would have such precious moments to relive. When I got into bed, I went over in my mind all the prayers I had been saying and all the things that I had pleaded to God for. "Please bring Dawson's fever down, please let Dawson wake up, please let Dawson be calm, please let me see him smile, please let me hear his voice" and my latest, earnest prayer, "please do not let Dawson scoff when I tell him that prayers are being said for him." Up until now, my prayers had all been "Please, God this" and "please, God that," but not tonight. Tonight they would not begin with "please," but with, "thank you."

Thank you, my dear God. Thank you for Dawson's fever coming down, for him waking up, for his smile, for his voice and for his obvious and astonishing appreciation of our prayers.

I lay awake only a short while, but just long enough to say my new prayers and, as that old song goes, "I fell asleep counting my blessings."

Thursday, September 12....Days in Hospital:37....Days on VADs:32

I got out of bed and knelt beside it, the way I had been taught to say my prayers as a child. I was on my knees to praise and to humbly thank God. I thanked Him again for all the prayers He had answered and for the gift of faith that he had bestowed upon me.

As I went about getting ready for the hospital, I thought about what it meant to me to have received this gift from God and I remembered a sermon about faith from a few weeks back. I had listened with great interest as the priest spoke from his pulpit. I found the pulpit itself quite interesting and impressive. It was a small balcony to the side of the magnificent altar and he appeared through an archway. From this exalted position he told how faith was a gift from God and how blessed those were who had received it. I had listened, but had not realized until days later that faith was not a gift in the way I had thought. It was then I concluded that God had not given me faith. God had not handed faith to me. The gift he had given me was the choice to believe or not. It was my free will that was his gift, my opportunity to make my own choice and I had chosen to believe. I had made a conscious decision to have faith, but the irony of it was that it *was* a gift from Him waiting for me, and all I had to do was accept it.

It seemed to me, therefore, that one should not wait until a miracle happens before one will believe, for if one believes … what? The miracles will happen? I could not say that, but I did know something had happened to Dawson that I believed could not have happened without the help of God.

So far, all the improvements in Dawson's condition that I had prayed for and that had come true could be explained by the wonders of medicine. But Dawson responding in the way he had when I mentioned someone was praying for him, could only be explained to me as a blessing from God.

I knew it was only a look that I saw on Dawson's face. He, in fact, had said nothing that told me he was grateful and thankful for our prayers, but his expression had been undeniable. His look had been so clear and obvious to me, I'd had no doubt what I was seeing. Though today I found myself wondering and I began questioning myself. *Had I read more into Dawson's expression than was there? Would I see that look in his eyes again? What will he say today? And what, if anything, did that mean when he said he had escaped through the ceiling?* That did seem to be just a remembrance from his delirium. And, too, hadn't he said that he had felt them poking him? Didn't that mean that he must have still been in his body, not above looking down on himself? It seemed to me that he had not had the classic near-death experience, or at least not one that he was recalling, but I could not deny that whatever he had experienced seemed to have had a profound impact on him.

For many reasons, I was anxious to see what his demeanor would be today. *Will he still be open with his thoughts and feelings? Will he still be warm and caring?* And I was anxious to hear his "Hi" again. I was thinking how remarkable it was that after months of being away in that other world of fever and sedation he had greeted me with his simple little one-word greeting just like he always had. Some things about him hadn't changed and that was as amazing and special to me as those things that had.

My dad drove me to the hospital and when we walked into Dawson's room, Dawson immediately gave us a smile. "Hi, Papa," he said. My dad went over to him and appeared choked up for a moment, for he did not speak. He just smiled and patted his arm.

I said, "How do you feel, Daws?"

"Pretty good," he said, "but I can't hear very well."

"Did you tell the nurse?"

"Yeah, and the doctor, too."

"What did they say?"

"A doctor is going to come and see me."

"That's good. You're hearing me O.K., aren't you?"

"Yeah, I can hear, but it's hard."

My father said, "Dawson, Grandma said to say hello. She's coming to see you on Saturday."

Dawson smiled at him. "O.K., good," and looking at me he said, "The nurse gave me some popsicles last night."

"That must have been a treat."

"Yeah, it was. They said I might be able to start eating today, but I felt kind of sick this morning."

"Oh, that's too bad."

"But I feel better now. The nurse gave me something for my stomach." Holding up his hand, he said, "Look at my fingers. They're all peeling. Look, Papa."

My dad took Dawson's hand and said, "Do you have any hand lotion?"

"Yes," Dawson said. "It's there on the table."

"You should put some on," my dad said. "Your legs are very dry, too. Do you want me to rub some on your legs?"

"O.K.," Dawson said, raising his eyebrows and smiling at me.

Dawson and my father had a nice visit and when my dad was ready to leave for home, I walked him to the elevator, thanked him for driving me and he gave me a hug. "Bill's coming tonight, right?" he asked. "You'll get a ride with him?"

"Oh, yes," I assured him, realizing how confidant I was that Bill would be there. I never worried that he would be late or not show up or let us down in any way. That was quite a realization to come to considering our past, and if there ever was a time I needed to know I could count on him, this certainly had been it.

I went back to Dawson's room and I said to him. "Oh, I want to tell you what happened to me last week. Dad and I had gotten out of the truck and were walking toward the hospital." With a light-hearted tone in my voice I said, "You should have seen me, I tripped on the sidewalk and that fifty-pound bag I carry went flying out in front of me and I landed flat on my face on the street and just lay there. All Dad did was stand there and say, 'Get up.'" I was smiling as I told him the story, but to my surprise, Dawson was not. I had been sure he would see the humor in such a sight, but instead of the usual glint of amusement in his eyes, I saw something else. It looked like concern.

"Were you hurt?" he asked.

"Oh, no," I said, "just a little scrape on my forehead and my hands."

"You could have gotten really hurt," he said frowning.

"Yeah, I know, but it was the perfect place to have it happen, right outside the hospital."

"That's true," he said, quite seriously, "but I'm glad you didn't get hurt."

"Me, too," I said somewhat stunned by his obvious concern for me. It left me wondering more about the apparent change in him.

When Dawson's evening nurse came on duty, she introduced herself, for we had never met her. She did not know Dawson, though she had been briefed on his case. She said, "You've been here quite a while, Dawson."

"Yes," he said.

"Over a month," I said.

"You came here for a transplant?" she asked.

We had not yet talked to Dawson about the inevitable transplant, and I looked at him to see his reaction. He raised his eyebrows and gave me a nod and a little smile that said, "I know."

I said, "Well, he was not listed before he came here. He came here under emergency circumstances. He had gone to the community hospital not feeling well. They were going to send him home. Then his heart got very weak … and they knew there was nothing more they could do for him … and then after several hours, his doctor decided to ask if he could come here." My lip was beginning to quiver as I said, "When we were told they would take him here and would try and save him, it was like a miracle, but they didn't know if we could get him here in time … he was so close to … God, we came so close."

I looked over at Dawson and again I was surprised by what I saw. Tears were flowing from his eyes. He looked at the nurse and with tremendous emotion and sincerity he said, "I know I could never have made it without my mom and dad." Then he looked at me. Undeniably, there was a look of love and gratitude in his eyes and though he had not said the words, I knew them. That knowledge warmed my heart and comforted me in a way that nothing ever had.

Later that evening, while in the cafeteria, I told Bill of Dawson's gratitude to us. "Don't you think something is different about him?" I said.

"Yeah," Bill agreed.

"What do you think it is? Do you think he could just be realizing how close he came to dying and is so thankful to be alive?"

"Yeah, I guess."

"I had thought that maybe he'd had a near-death experience when he was talking about being pinned to the ceiling, but he didn't say he saw himself as he looked down."

"Yes, he did. He said that."

"What? He said what? When?" I asked astounded.

"When he told me about being on the ceiling. That's what he said."

"What's what he said?"

"That he looked down and saw himself."

"Are you sure he said that?"

"Yeah, well, that's what it sounded like to me."

"I didn't hear that, so I don't know, but one thing I do know is that he is changed."

Because of that change in Dawson, when I said good night to him later that evening, I almost said, "I love you." I believed he would be open to hearing that and would even say those words back to me. As much as I had longed for that, I did not say it. It was precisely *because* I had waited so long to hear those words from him that I held back. I suppose that it should not have mattered who said the words first, but they were too special to me to have them said as a casual, programmed response. I did not want them to be the obligatory, "I love you, too." He had to feel it from his heart and I was content in the belief that we were closer than ever to the day when that would happen. Having seen the love in his eyes was as meaningful to me as hearing the words.

Friday, September 13....Days in Hospital:38....Days on VADs:33

After telling me how well Dawson was doing and how good he looked when he saw him in the morning, Bill said, "Deacon Joe called again yesterday. I got his message when I got home last night. He said something about wanting to talk to you about making your confirmation."

"What? Oh, that's it. That's why he's calling. That lady I talked to at the church had asked me if I had made my confirmation and when I told her I hadn't, she told me about a class. I guess that is the message she passed on to the deacon. Now, *I* don't want to talk to him. I don't want to have to explain why I haven't been to church in so many years and about being divorced and all that and I'm not about to be making my confirmation. I haven't gone to communion or anything in so long and I don't want to have to explain all that."

"Yeah, whatever. Well, I just wanted to let you know that Dawson's doing good. I better go. I'll talk to you later."

Arriving at the hospital was a little less scary than it had been. I was rather confidant that I would see him sitting up in bed waiting for me. The surprises and the blessings continued to come. I entered Dawson's room and found him sitting up waiting for me, but he was not in bed. He was sitting in a chair! He looked so happy and so proud. His expression said, "Hey, Mom, look at me!"

"Dawson, you're up! That's great," I said.

"Yeah," he said with a look on his face I will never forget. He looked so pleased with his accomplishment and he appeared so happy to share it with me.

The nurse confirmed my feelings when she said, "He's been so anxious for you to get here. He could hardly wait for you to see him."

"You look so good, Dawson," I said.

The nurse went on to say, "He wanted so much to be out of bed before you got here. He is not able to get up on his own yet, but we worked it out by using this special chair. It made it easier for him." Taking a better look at the padded, green vinyl chair he was sitting in, I could see that there was something different about it. She said, "The way this works is that it folds out flat. We place it right next to the bed and then we slide him over onto it while he's lying down. We strap him in and then we crank it into a sitting position with him in it."

"Pretty ingenious," I said looking at Dawson. He nodded his agreement. The fact that I had heard of the effort it had taken on everyone's part for him to be sitting up in a chair to greet me, did not seem to take away from his pride, but it tugged at my emotions. He looked thoroughly happy and pleased with himself and I was so happy for him.

The nurse said, "You two have a nice visit. If you need anything, Dawson, let me know."

"O.K.," Dawson said. "Thanks." Looking at me he said, "They are so nice to me."

"I know."

"I mean they really try to help me, everyone here does." He had that expression in his eyes again, that look of awe and appreciation. It was the expression that I had wondered if I would see on him today. Well, I did not have to wonder very long.

"They are very nice here," I said, which was an understatement compared to what he was thinking.

He said, "I've watched them everyday helping me and others. It is really something to see how they spend their days taking care of people."

"I know, I've thought about that, too," I said. "It must be so hard to do this day after day."

"Yeah, it makes me think. You know, in all my twenty-seven years I've never done anything for anybody."

"Oh, Dawson, I don't know if that's true."

"Really, Mom. Yeah, I've done things for my friends and stuff, but I mean, you know, just helping other people who need it."

"Yeah, I know what you mean. I have felt so grateful to these people for their knowledge and compassion and dedication. It does make you think."

"Things are going to be different," he said in his low, breathy voice as he wiped tears from his eyes. "I am going to be different."

"I know, Dawson, I know it and I believe it." I did believe it for he was already different. I had not been wrong about that. It had not been my imagination. Later when a nurse who stopped by to say hello said, "Dawson, what a turnaround you've made," he looked over at me and gave me a knowing smile, for we knew how true her words were.

"He is so grateful to all of you," I said. "He appreciates everything you all have done for him." I was speaking those words as Suzann came into the room. She was the nurse who had told me she hadn't wanted to be assigned to Dawson because it was too sad.

Smiling, and giving Dawson a wink, she said, "Oh, he is just in the euphoric stage."

Euphoric Stage? Is that true? Is that what this is? Is this just a temporary phase of happiness and gratitude that he is going through? No, I decided. I knew there may have been some validity to what she was saying, but I believed what I was seeing went far beyond that.

Chapter Twenty-Four

Saturday, September 14....Days in Hospital:39....Days on VADs:34

W hat is that?" Dawson asked, looking in the direction of the bulletin board on the wall across from his bed.

I had wondered when the time would come when he would ask that question and now that the time was here, I was surprisingly at ease about answering him. I believed I was about to learn something, and because of the changes I had seen in Dawson, I was rather confidant of what that something would be. I walked over to the bulletin board, pointed to the upper right-hand corner and said, "Is this what you mean?"

"Yeah. What is that?"

"It's Saint Jude," I said. "It's a picture of Saint Jude."

"Can I see it?" he asked, obviously interested and not at all irreverent.

"Sure," I said taking it off the board. *So far, so good,* I thought. *He wants to see it.* So I added, "We got it at the church down the street." I handed it to him, saying, "Dawson, Dad and I have been going to church."

"Really?" he said.

"Yeah, it's a very beautiful church and they have a Saint Jude shrine there. That's where we got this card." He held the card and looked a long while at Saint Jude's picture, then as he turned it over to look at the back, I said, "That's one of the prayers we've been saying for you."

After reading it, he looked up at me and I saw the look of gratitude in his eyes that told me what I had hoped for; he, undoubtedly, had accepted and welcomed our prayers.

Bill said, "There are hundreds of candles at the shrine. We always light one there for you."

I said, "You know, Dawson, many of our prayers have been answered."

Dawson nodded in agreement, then looked down again at the picture of Saint Jude in his hands. "Here," he said, handing it to Bill, "would you put it back up there. I don't want to lose it." Bill took it and tacked it back up on the board. "That's good," Dawson said, speaking in a low voice. "I can still see it and I'll know where it is. I like it there."

"I'm so glad, Dawson," I said and I could not have meant those words more.

"I sat in the chair again last night," he said. "I couldn't sleep, so I asked if I could get up. The nurses helped me."

"You sat in the green chair?"

"Yeah."

"How did you feel?"

"Good. I feel better sitting up. The nurse said that the physical therapist is going to come by today and that I'll probably be able to get up in a regular chair."

"Oh, that'll be good."

"Yeah, but I wonder when she's coming," he said. "I hope she gets here soon."

The doctor on the weekend staff walked in. "Hello, Mr. Bell, I'm Dr. Brown. I'm taking over for Dr. Wiviott this weekend. How are you feeling?"

"Good," Dawson replied.

"Dr. Wiviott told me that when he saw you yesterday, you looked the best he's ever seen you." Dawson responded with a smile.

As Dr. Brown examined him, a young Asian woman in a white lab coat peeked into the room. When she saw that Dawson was busy with the doctor, she turned and left. I followed after her, thinking she might be the physical therapist, which she was. I said to her, "I'm Dawson's mother. He's really anxious to see you. Will you be coming back today?"

"Oh, yes," she said, smiling. "Tell him that I'll see him later."

"Oh, good. He'll be so glad to hear that. Thank you."

When Dr. Brown was gone, I said to Dawson, "Did you see that woman in the white coat who looked in here? She's the physical therapist."

"I wanted to see her!" he said.

"I know. I told her that. She said that she would be coming back."

"When?"

"I don't know. She just said that she would be back."

"I hope so," he said. For the next couple of hours he appeared to be on the lookout for her, anxiously awaiting her return. Then he said, "Mom, is that her? I think I just saw her go by! Go see."

"Dawson, if it is her, she'll be here. She said she would be back."

He said, "Please, Mom, go get her." I went outside his room and saw her about to enter a door two rooms down. "Excuse me," I said as I approached her, "will you be coming to see Dawson? He saw you go by and he's so anxious to see you. He was afraid he would miss you again."

"Oh, no," she said sweetly. "I'll be there. Tell him not to worry. I will see him."

"Thank you so much," I said, feeling embarrassed for being so pushy and grateful that she had been so nice about it.

Shortly after, she came into the room and in her sweet tone she said, "Dawson, I understand you wanted to see me. I'm Pamela, your physical therapist."

"Hi," he said, "I want to be able to get out of bed."

"Good. That's what we'll be working on. So, Dawson, you've been up in the green chair, right?"

"Yeah."

"How did you feel?"

"Fine."

"O.K., well, you will be getting up to a regular chair, but probably not just yet. But you can start working on that while you're still in bed, O.K.? I want you to flex your feet for me, Dawson. Can you do that?" He tried bending his feet back and forth at the ankles and seemed surprised at how difficult it was to do. She said that some of that was due to the swelling and that exercise would help the swelling to go down. She then instructed him to raise his heels off the bed and lower them and then to bend and straighten his legs. He had to do the same bending and straightening with his arms. It all appeared to be quite an effort for him, but she encouraged him to stay with it. When these tasks were completed, she said, "That's great, Dawson. Do these several times today and I will be back to see you tomorrow."

When she left, I said to him, "That was a good start."

"Yeah, but I wanted to get up."

"You will, Dawson," I said.

"I know, but I want to be able to get up to go to the bathroom. I don't want to have to use the bedpan again."

"Oh. Well, yeah. I can understand that."

Bill said, "Don't worry about it, Dawson. Just do what you have to do."

"Yeah, but I don't like it," he said.

They had started him on light foods in the morning, and he had eaten fairly well. He tried everything on his tray and had a milkshake-like dietary supplement. But throughout the morning he'd had to use the bedpan. He seemed quite concerned about it and I told the nurse and I was now wondering if that was why he had eaten very little of his lunch. She said she had given him some Imodium and thought that should help.

When his dinner came, he barely touched it. Bill and I tried to coax him to eat more, but his evening nurse assured us that what little he had eaten was enough. She said that it sometimes takes a while to get a full appetite back and that, in general, she felt that he was doing well. In fact, she said that he seemed to be even "more energetic" than he had been the day before. She told him she thought he would be able to get up to a chair, and that she would help him. He was extremely pleased to hear that. She helped him to sit on the side of the bed to dangle his legs. She checked his blood pressure and heart rate and saw that he was doing fine. So while he sat there, she prepared the big salmon-colored vinyl chair that was in his room by placing pillows and a lightweight blanket and a sheet on it. She called for another nurse to assist her in getting him out of bed and asked that we leave for a short time while they had him stand and move to the chair.

Bill and I went to the waiting room feeling encouraged with Dawson's progress. It was wonderful to see, but the thought of that unidentified infection still haunted me. In addition, I knew they had started to wean him off the steroids and I had noticed his temperature was slightly up. I had not been told, nor had I asked, just when they expected that the steroids would be stopped all together and I worried, *What will happen then? Will his high fever return?*

All such fears, doubts and questions were put aside when we returned to his room and I saw him contentedly sitting up in a regular chair. A regular chair. Such joy. He was so happy. He looked so good. He was smiling. Under these circumstances, little, ordinary things had become extraordinary events.

"How do you feel?" I asked him.

"Good," he said. "The VADs feel better when I'm in this position and I feel like I can breathe easier."

"That's great, Dawson. You look so good."

"Thanks," he said. "Dad, could you bring me my slippers from home?"

"Sure," Bill said. "I'll bring them tomorrow."

God, this was real progress, wonderful, blessed progress and how wonderful it was to have my mother and father arrive to see Dawson looking so happy.

"Higrammah. Hi, Papa," he said.

"How're you doing?" my father asked.

"Good," Dawson answered.

My mother went to Dawson and stood beside him as I said to my dad, "He looks good, doesn't he?"

As he was about to answer me, my ears suddenly tuned in to what Dawson was saying to my mother. I heard, "Grammah, I want to thank you for everything."

My mother responded, "Oh, Dawson, you know that if you ever need anything ... you can always ..."

"I know," he said. "Thanks. Grammah, I'm sorry."

"Oh, Dawson, it's O.K., you don't have to be sorry," my mother said. "I understand."

"But I just wanted you to know how sorry I am and how much I appreciate everything."

"I know, Dawson. It's O.K." They looked at each other for a moment and I knew that, in their unique way, they had shared a moment of closeness that went beyond a hug.

My father then went to Dawson and Dawson reached out his hand to him. My father took Dawson's hand and cupped it between both of his. Dawson was looking up to him from the chair as he spoke. "Papa," he said and he began to open his heart to him in the same way he had done with my mother.

My mom and dad left before dark, having spent a pleasant and memorable time with Dawson. He spent another couple of hours in the chair before he said that he was ready to get back into bed, and his nurse was quite pleased with how well he had tolerated sitting up. We stayed in the room while the nurses helped him from the chair and he settled comfortably back into bed. I knew that it was now time to say good night. I gently stroked his forehead. He slowly closed his eyes as I whispered, "Sleep well, Dawson. I'll see you in the morning." Bill said good night and we left. When outside his room, I stopped and turned to look back at him and saw that he was watching us walk away. I blew him a kiss and he blew one back to me. I stood a moment looking at him, then turned and left, filled with love and heartache for this child of mine.

Remembering how he had gazed at the picture of Saint Jude as he'd held it in his hands earlier in the day, I prayed, *Please, Saint Jude, please watch over Dawson. Please comfort him and keep him safe.*

Sunday, September 15....Days in Hospital:40....Days on VADs:35

I had thought that a time might come when I would want to go to communion, but I could not imagine what it was going to take for me to decide to go to confession. I had not known what would bring me to this point, but here I was. I had made the decision to go to confession and I decided that I would go today. I checked the schedule in St. Dominic's bulletin, and on the ride to the hospital, I told Bill of my decision.

"You're really going to do it?" he said. "I don't think I can."

"That's all right. You don't have to. This is just something that I feel I have to do. So many of my prayers have been answered. Seeing Dawson awake, seeing him smile, seeing him so enthusiastic, it is all like a miracle. But, most of all, it is his reaction to our prayers and his interest in the fact that we have been going to church. Did you see how he looked at Saint Jude? Bill, I prayed for that exact thing and I saw it happen. There is no doubt that was a prayer answered. I know God must have heard my prayers and I have to give Him thanks. I've decided the best way I can do that is to confess my sins and receive Holy Communion. Believe me, I am terrified to go to confession. I am dreading it and I wonder how I can even do it, but when I tell myself, 'Look what God has done for you,' I know I must try to show my gratitude and faith in some way. I've decided this is the way to do it."

"Wow," Bill said, slightly exaggerating his response, but obviously impressed with the sincerity and bravery of my gesture.

When we arrived at Dawson's room, he was in the chair and looking well. He said again how much better he felt in a sitting position and how much easier it was for him to breathe. That was important, for since he had been extubated, he had remained on some amount of oxygen that he was receiving through a nasal cannula. It was merely a narrow, clear tubing that went over his ears and had small prongs that fit at his nostrils. He could take it on and off as he needed it and when up in the chair, he did not need it. The cannula was a far cry from the respirator, but it would definitely be a step in the right direction to have him off of it, too.

I asked the nurse if he had eaten in the morning and she said, "A little bit." She said he'd had a moderate appetite, but had felt slightly nauseous. He could not drink the milkshake supplement and the dietician was unhappy with that, for he needed the added nutrients. They had tried several varieties, but he said they all made him sick. His stomach problems had persisted and the Imodium had not been helping much. The nurse said, "But despite it all, his spirits remain high and he's very pleasant and cooperative with everyone."

Bill said, "I brought your slippers," and I said, rather matter-of-factly, "Dawson, Dad and I are going to church today. We're going to the five-thirty mass, but we have to be at church by five o'clock, because I am going to confession." Then I said, with a look of mock-terror, "Do you believe that?"

"You're going to confession? Really?" he said seeming to understand the magnitude of what I planned to do.

"Yeah. Do you know how long it has been since I have been to confession? I mean, it has been ages."

"I can imagine," he said.

"But I really want to do it."

"That's good," he said.

"Yeah, but am I nervous. I'm going to try to get Father Cassidy to hear my confession. He is the priest that says the Saint Jude mass that we go to. He is really nice. I'm going, Dawson, because I prayed so hard that I would see you looking well, and I have to do something to thank God for making it happen. He did answer my prayers, you know."

"I know," he said, and I was sure that he did.

Bill and I left his room at four-thirty and arrived at church before confession had started. On the way, Bill had been joking with me about how scary it was going to be to confess a quarter of a century worth of sins. But I felt much of that would depend upon which priest I had, so the first thing I did when inside the church was to check the names of the priests on the doors of the confessionals. Then I told Bill, "Let's sit here." Motioning, I said, "That is where Father Cassidy will be and if I sit right here, I can be first in line. I want to get it over with." As soon as I saw the light go on over his door, I looked at Bill and said, "O.K., here I go." I got out of the pew, walked to the door, opened it and entered the tiny cubicle. When I closed the door behind me, I was surprised to find it was not as dark as I had remembered confessionals from my past. I knelt down and by the time Father Cassidy slid the shutter open and I saw his silhouette through the screen, I was so nervous I thought I might panic and leave. I took a deep breath and not sure if there were a new protocol for saying a confession, I proceeded in the only way I knew. I said in a hushed voice, "Bless me Father, for I have sinned. It has been at least twenty-five years since my last confession. I have come back to church because my son is very ill. He is in the hospital nearby. I have been praying for him to get well. It has been a great comfort for me to be in church and I know that my prayers have been heard. My son has improved, but is still in very serious condition. He needs a heart transplant. To say thanks to God and to profess my faith, I am here to confess my sins. I don't know where to start. I am divorced … I have not been living a Christian life … I am very sorry for all my sins."

"My child," he said, "God has led you back and He welcomes you. May I hear you say an Act of Contrition?"

"Oh, my God, I am heartily sorry," I said, remembering those words from so many years ago. I continued, hesitating only slightly near the end then finished with, "and I firmly resolve with the help of Thy grace to sin no more and to avoid the near occasion of sin."

"God has forgiven you," he said. "Your sins are forgiven."

"Thank you, Father," I said tearfully.

"How old is your son?" he asked.

"He is twenty-seven," I answered, my emotions brimming over.

"What is his name?"

"Dawson Bell."

"I will pray for him. God bless you. Go in peace."

"Thank you, Father. Thank you." I made the sign of the cross and

I did feel a sense of peace that I had not felt in a very long time. As I stepped out of the confessional, I saw Bill looking toward me as if he had been anxiously anticipating my emergence from the inner sanctum. Tears were streaming down my face as I slid into the pew next to him.

"Hey, looks like that went well," he said, opening his eyes wide and looking at me with an amusing expression of exaggerated terror.

I had to smile, myself, and I said, "Yeah, it did. It really did. You should do it."

"Yeah, right," he said.

I sat through the mass anticipating my first communion after so many years. I prayed that I was worthy of receiving the Holy Spirit and deserving of all the blessings I had received. As those in our pew filed out, I followed. I walked down the aisle, my heart pounding. I took the Eucharist in my hand, placed it in my mouth and was overwhelmed with a feeling of closeness to a power greater than I could imagine, a power that I knew had touched Dawson.

Monday, September 16....Days in Hospital:41....Days on VADs:36

The days were starting to move quickly, in contrast to those long, slow days I had spent waiting. Now my time was filled with moments shared with Dawson, and I tried to hold on to every precious one, savoring them and reliving them. One consolation to them passing almost too quickly, was the belief that there would be many more to share.

Dawson's nurse today was new to me. She was a tiny, older woman with kind eyes and an unusually soft-spoken manner. She was tending to him when I arrived in the morning and she greeted me by saying, "Dawson is doing very well today."

"That's good to hear."

"This is my mom," Dawson said.

"Hi, I thought so," she said. "I'm Elissa. It's nice to meet you. I've been seeing you here. Do you come every day?"

"Yes, I do," I said.

"Dawson has been very anxious for you to get here today."

I looked to Dawson, questioning if there were a particular reason why. He grinned and shrugged his shoulders as if to answer, "No, no particular reason. I just wanted to see you."

"He's been up in the chair all morning," Elissa said. "He does better sitting up. The VAD output is excellent in that position."

"Is that why he says he feels better sitting in the chair?" I questioned.

"Oh, yes. I'm sure it is. The VADs do seem to function at their best when he is up." She went on to say, "Dawson and I have talked about his decreasing need for oxygen, and we're trying to get by without it as much as possible. He really does fine when he takes it off, but he is still a little dependent on it." She looked at Dawson as she continued, "But we've talked about it and he seems motivated to go without it as much as he can."

"Oh, good," I said. "That sounds like real progress."

"Dawson," she asked, "should I take this tray away? I don't think you're going to eat any more of this, are you?"

"No, you can take it," he said. "Oh, wait. I'll keep the straws for my mom."

She looked at me and I explained, "I have a sensitive tooth that hurts when I drink anything cold. If I drink through a straw, I can avoid it somewhat."

Still in their paper wraps, Dawson handed them to me saying, "Here, Mom, you can put them in your bag. That way you'll always have one when you need it."

"That's a good idea. Thanks."

"Sure," he said, giving me a smile and Elissa smiled, too, as she left with his tray. She seemed to be a very caring, competent nurse and I could see that Dawson liked her. It looked like the feeling was mutual.

Later in the day when Dawson had fallen asleep, I left his room to call my mother to give her the day's report. When I returned to his room, Elissa said in her quiet voice, "He's still sleeping. He didn't sleep very well last night, but that should start to improve."

"I hope so," I said, "but I think that was somewhat his schedule before he came here. Before going to the hospital, he said he was having trouble sleeping at night and sometimes he'd still be awake when he'd hear his dad get up for work. I suppose that some of that was just because he wasn't feeling well, but I think he preferred that schedule. I know he stayed up very late when he was working on projects for me, and then he'd sleep all day."

"Well, maybe he will be able to sleep better at night when he gets more comfortable here. He is still a bit anxious."

"I know," I said, sadly.

Softly, she said, "He is a very nice young man."

Her comment took me by surprise. Though I had always felt he was, I had never known that anyone else could see it. This was a different experience for me. "How nice of you to say," I said. "He is quite special to me."

"I can tell," she said. "You know, I have seen many patients who had been quite ill and their family members had stayed by their sides for days, just as you have. Then when the patient improves, he can be quite cranky and miserable to his loved ones who have been there. It happens often. I have seen patients treat their concerned families rather poorly." *Her words could have described Dawson a few years back,* I thought. "But Dawson is not at all like that with you," she said. "It is so obvious how much he appreciates you being here with him and how much he cares for you."

"Really?"

"Yes, I can really see what a fine person he is and he told me that he owes everything to his caring family."

"Really?" That was all I could say, as I was so struck by her words.

She could not have had any idea just how much these words meant to me. She probably could not have imagined that Dawson had not been inclined to express such feelings until now. Though she may not have known all this, I sensed that she did know how much I loved Dawson and how special he was.

Tuesday, September 17....Days in Hospital:42....Days on VADs:37

All the worrying I had done about the possibility of Dawson's fever returning when they lowered his dose of steroids, had not prepared me for it actually happening. Perhaps that was not entirely true, for in a sense, I was prepared. My worry and anticipation had lessened my shock upon hearing the news, but what it had not done, however, was lessen my anguish.

"His temperature spiked last night to 38.7," Dr. Harris said as he stopped me on my way to Dawson's room.

"Oh, no," I cried. "No."

"But it is down now," he said encouragingly, "and he's doing fine. Even during the night when his fever was high, he had tolerated it quite well."

"Oh, God," I sighed. "So he didn't get agitated or anything?"

"No."

"Has he been off the steroids? Is that why his fever came back?"

"We've been doing a slow taper and he'd had a very low dose yesterday."

"I thought so. I had seen that his temperature was running slightly higher than it had been." I guess I knew this was coming, but Dawson had seemed so well, I had simply chosen not to dwell on the negatives. I had not let my concerns interfere with my time with him. These past few days were too special to me to let anything take away from them and after all, the doctors were taking care of his medical needs. I felt it was up to me to take care of his emotional ones, so I had deliberately not looked as much at his monitor to assess his condition, but looked, instead, directly at him. I could look into his eyes and see everything I needed to know. But now, I asked Dr. Harris, "When are you planning to stop the steroids entirely?"

"He received his last dose this morning at ten."

"Oh. So what do you expect will happen now?"

"Well, he has been on such a low dose for days and he's tolerated that well. The fever has returned somewhat, but … we had to get him off them in order to get him listed. We're considering listing him on Thursday."

"You are? This Thursday?"

"Yes. Well, we're going to wait and see, but we are considering it."

That news stunned me, but it was not the kind of news I'd had to prepare myself for. I was elated that they thought he was ready. I had waited a long time to hear that. "Thank you so much," I said and proceeded on my way.

I had not gone far when I saw Dr. Wiviott. "Good morning, Mrs. Bell," he said.

"Hi. Dr. Harris just told me that Dawson might get listed this week."

"Yes. He's off the steroids now."

"But what about the fever?"

"We did get a positive culture from the tip of one of his lines, so we're thinking that may have been the cause. Hopefully, now with its removal, his temperature will go down. I must say he is continuing to look quite well clinically. Actually, not only clinically, but in all ways. He is looking very bright and alert."

"I know. I'm still amazed." When I finally made it to Dawson's room, I was startled to find his curtain drawn. I looked for his nurse and saw she was with the patient in the next room. I waited for her and when she came out, she said, "He's fine. I just helped him to the commode."

"Tell him I'll be back," I said. *That's good*, I thought. *Being able to get up is going to calm some of his anxiety.* I left and when I returned, I discovered that was not the only progress he had made. His blood pressure had been holding steady without the need of medication, so in addition to the bags of Solumedrol and dietary supplement that had already been removed from the IV stand, today the bag of Neo had been removed, as well. The nurse told me they were weaning him off of the IV Heparin, the blood thinner, so soon that bag would be removed, too. The IV rack that had once been over laden with bags of medication was now starting to look a little sparse. He was not coughing as much, he no longer had the red rash, just the peeling effects from where it had been, and his desire to share his feelings and thoughts continued to flourish.

"Maybe you could get a big tablet of paper," Dawson said. "Bring it in and I can tell you some things I remember about my dreams. You could write them down for me, O.K.?"

"Sure, I can do that. Are you remembering more things about when you were sedated?"

"Yeah. There was one dream I had. It was like an old-time black and white Western movie."

"Oh, how funny," I said, but I saw that his expression was quite serious.

He said, "It was weird how it looked like an old movie. I was in this house and these people were keeping me there. I wanted to leave and get to Dad, but they wouldn't let me. They put me in this room and I could look out the window, but every time I did, I saw Dad leaving. He would be riding away on a horse, just like in an old Western. This kept happening. I'd fall asleep in that room waiting for him to come back and then when I'd wake up and think that I might see him, he'd be riding off again."

"Oh, how terrible, Dawson," I said.

"Yeah, it was. I had lots of dreams like that. There was one where I was trying to get to a phone to call Dad and I just couldn't make it. I could see a phone booth in the distance, but I couldn't get there."

"Oh, Dawson." My heart was breaking for him.

"There was another one. I was like a P.O.W. They had me tied down. They poked me and hurt me. I tried to get away, but couldn't."

"God! But I could understand how you could have a dream like that. It was true! All those things were happening to you. You were tied down and they were sticking you. A nurse told me that you were not going to remember what you had gone through! I see now that wasn't true."

"No, I remember and it was awful," he said.

"I thought that it had to be. It looked like it was. But I tried to tell myself that while someone's sedated, there is no concept of time. So what I had hoped for was that maybe that month of sedation could have felt like it was only one day to you."

"No, Mom," he said with tears in his eyes, "it was not a day. It was a year."

"Oh, Dawson," I said, "how terrible. I knew it was bad for you. I knew it. And I couldn't do a thing to help you."

"It's O.K., Mom, it's O.K." Then still looking at me, he said, "You know, I learned a lot."

"You did?"

"Yeah. Mom, I think what I learned could help other people."

"I bet you're right, Dawson, I bet it could."

He looked so serious and so sad as he said, "I wish I could tell my friends what I learned. I know it could help them. But I know they wouldn't listen. I wouldn't have listened before, either. Mom, I want everyone to know my story. I know it's going to help someone."

"It will, Dawson. I know it will."

"I just feel like I want to tell everyone."

"You know what, Dawson? I had told Dad that I wanted to write about what I was going through this past month. It felt like something so big was happening to me that I wanted to tell it, but you've gone through even more."

"You wanted to tell your story?" he asked.

"Yeah, in a way. I felt that so many things were happening, amazing things and changes in me and just big stuff. Hey, maybe we can tell *our* story. We'd tell the same story, in a sense, but from our two different perspectives."

"Yeah. Will you get a tablet to write on?"

"I'll see if there is some place around here where I can get one. I'm sure there is."

"O.K., good. Thanks. We'll do that, O.K.?"

"Yes. We will do that, Dawson. We definitely will."

By the time Bill arrived in the afternoon, Dawson and I had a lot to tell him. I had learned so much of Dawson's thoughts and feelings and to hear that he wanted to tell his story in order to help others went beyond what I could have imagined hearing him say. Dawson was anxious to share the stories of his dreams with Bill. As he told them in great detail, he managed to put a little humor in some of them. He sat in the chair most of our visit and seemed to truly enjoy himself.

As it got late and was getting close to the time for us to leave, he said, "My nurse last night helped me lie on my side. She put pillows around me and it was really comfortable. Before you go, I want the nurse to do that."

"O.K., do you want to tell her now?" I asked.

"Are you getting ready to leave?"

"Yeah, pretty soon," Bill answered.

"Will you tell her?" Dawson asked, looking at me.

"O.K.," I said. Susan was his nurse and I was not entirely comfortable having to tell her what I wanted her to do because I knew she liked to do things in her own way. It was obvious she was very meticulous in the way she wanted things done because whenever she came on duty, she would straighten all of Dawson's lines, tubes and wires and rearrange everything the nurse before her had done. Dawson liked that about her, and so did I, because he hated it when his lines were tangled and his room cluttered. Knowing that she had definite ideas about how things should be done, I said, with some reluctance, "Susan, we're going to be leaving soon and Dawson wants to get back into bed. He said his nurse last night had positioned him on his side and it was really comfortable. She put pillows all around him. He was wondering if you could do that before we leave."

"Sure," she said, getting up from her post. She did not seem to mind and I greatly appreciated that. "Dawson, you're ready to get back into bed? You want to try it on your side?"

"Yeah," he said. "It was pretty comfortable."

"O.K. I can do that." She helped him stand and slowly take the couple of steps to his bed. He turned and backed up to it and she and Bill helped him in. Then she left to get more pillows.

Dawson said, "Mom, could you give me that Saint Jude card?"

I went to the board, took it down and handed it to him. Susan came back with the pillows and he held the Saint Jude card in his hand as she turned him to his side and propped the pillows all around him.

"How's that?" she asked him. He said it was good and she went back to her table.

Dawson was now lying on his left side, facing the window, his back toward us, so Bill went around to the other side of the bed. Dawson said to him, "Dad, could you tape this card here on the side of the bed so it will stay there where I can see it?"

Bill looked across to me. His eyes were saying, "Wow! What's going on here?" He turned around to the supply table and took a roll of tape that the nurses used for Dawson's wound dressing.

Dawson said, "Dad, put it so I can see the prayer side," and Bill did, taping it to the bed's metal side rail. "That's good," Dawson said. "Thanks, Dad."

I was awe-struck, but tried not to show it in my voice as I said, "Oh, that's good, Dawson. You're all comfortable now and you can say your prayer before you go to sleep." I then went around to the other side of the bed and said good night to him. Bill told him he'd see him in the morning and we left. I stopped and looked back at him the same way I had done before, but tonight was much different. Tonight, he was not watching me, as he was lying facing the other way, but I stood there watching him. He was gently touching the Saint Jude card in such a way I knew there was no need to say the prayer I had said before, *Please, Saint Jude, please watch over Dawson, please comfort him and keep him safe,* for I could see Saint Jude was already taking care of him.

Bill and I had a wonderful night with Dawson, talking and laughing with him, and on the ride home, we relived the things Dawson had said and we marveled at his enduring sense of humor and his newfound spirituality.

Soon after I arrived home at my mother's, her phone rang. It was ten-thirty and it startled us both. I answered it and it was Dawson. He said, "Mom, I have to talk to you."

"Are you all right, Dawson?"

"Yeah. Yeah, I'm fine. I just have to talk to you."

"What is it?"

"Mom, when I read that Saint Jude prayer tonight, it seemed like it was written just for me."

"Oh, Dawson! It was."

"Mom, I know things. I know things I never knew before. I feel things, things I never felt before. I have to tell you, Mom. I have to tell you how I feel. I have to thank you and Dad. I have to talk to him, too. I'm so sorry for everything. I know it's late, but I want to talk to Dad tonight. Mom, I told the nurse I want to talk to a priest. I told the nurse I had to get out of bed."

"Dawson, are you O.K., really?"

"Yeah, Mom, really. I feel good. I mean, I feel really good. I just have a lot to say and I wanted to tell a priest. I told the nurse and she said a chaplain would come and see me. Oh, she's here! I'll call you back, O.K.? Will you call Dad and tell him I'm going to be calling him later?"

"Sure. I'll talk to you later, Dawson."

When I hung up, my mother said, "What was he saying?"

"I'm not sure," I said, as I sat down on her couch staring through her.

"Is he all right?" she asked.

"He said he was. He sounded like he was, a little excited, but O.K. He said he felt really good."

My mother was looking bewildered. I suppose that was because I must have been looking that way myself. I said, "He said he wanted to talk. He said he feels things he never felt before. He said that he knows things. He's going to talk to a priest. He said he felt like the Saint Jude prayer was written just for him. Something really big is going on here. This is really something."

"What do you think it is?"

"I don't know, some kind of an awakening, an epiphany. It's what I prayed for. God heard me, Ma. He heard me!"

I called Bill and it was obvious I had awakened him. I said, "Dawson called. He wanted me to call you to tell you he is going to be calling you later, O.K.?"

Still sounding half asleep, he said, "What? Why? What did he say?"

"He said he feels things he never felt before and he wants to tell you and thank you."

"How did he sound?"

"He sounded good, I guess. I don't know. So he's going to be calling you. I'd better go."

"O.K. I'll talk to you tomorrow," Bill said, still sounding a bit dazed.

Not long after, the phone rang and it was Dawson. He said, "I talked to the chaplain. She was really nice. I told her all the things I was feeling. It was really good."

"I'm so glad, Dawson."

With obvious emotion, he said, "I told her how much I owe to my family and how thankful I am for all you've done."

"Oh, Dawson."

"I wanted to tell you, Mom … I love you."

"Oh! I love you, too, Dawson! You know that, hon."

"Yeah, I do. I really do know it. I'm going to call Dad now. Did you tell him I was going to call?"

"Yes, I did."

"What did he say? Did he say it was O.K. to call him so late?"

"Sure. I'll let you go. Call him now. I'll see you in the morning. I'm so glad you called. Thank you, hon. Good night, Dawson."

"Good night. I love you, Mom."

"I know. I love you, too, Dawson, very, very much."

I hung up the phone. My mother and I talked a little before I went to bed. As I lay there staring up at the ceiling, tears ran freely from the corners of my eyes and down my temples, drenching my hair. My body was motionless while my mind, my heart and my soul were bursting with energy. They were fueled by awe and love and wonder. My mind surged as I relived every word of my astounding conversation with Dawson. My heart was ignited by the love we shared and my soul soared in homage to a Lord so magnificent.

Chapter Twenty-Five

Dawson had never been one to get sentimental and anyone who knew him knew that he would never say anything nice just because he thought it was something you wanted to hear. In fact, he had told me that he could not give a greeting card with a message that he did not feel. This made buying greeting cards a major ordeal for him and he had called me once to tell me that he had just spent "a day" at the card shop. He had been looking for several Christmas cards and he said he had looked at "every single mushy one" and had not found any that he could buy. They were all "just too much." He had managed to see some humor in his futile attempt and had me laughing that day, but he had added quite seriously that he would rather give no card than to give one that said things that did not sound like him.

I respected this and I never took it for granted that I would receive a birthday or Mother's Day card from him. When I did, they were quite special to me. Believing that the sentiments of the cards he had chosen for me were undoubtedly sincere increased my appreciation of them. I remembered those special cards that said things like ... *I may not often express ... my feelings may go unspoken ... sometimes I can't find the words … I do love you.* They had touched my heart and had given me such joy that I could only have imagined what it would feel like to actually hear him say the words.

I had waited a long time for that day and there had been many days over the past several years when I had been sure that I was going to die without ever hearing Dawson say that he loved me. More recently I had thought *he* would die never having said those words. Thank God, I had been wrong. Though I had believed that the greatest thing about hearing Dawson say "I love you" would be how wonderful it would make me feel, I had been wrong about that, too. I had discovered that my greatest joy was in seeing how wonderful it had made *Dawson* feel.

His heartfelt excitement had added to my own and had made the moment that he had opened his heart to me more extraordinary than I could have thought possible. Somehow I had not anticipated the extent of what this experience would mean to Dawson and I thanked God that I had waited to hear his words come not from prompting, but from his heart. Had I become impatient, I would have deprived us both of that special moment.

Wednesday, September 18....Days in Hospital:43....Days on VADs:38

I placed a cup of hot water into the microwave and looked at the clock. I was thinking that Bill should be calling soon when my phone rang. My first question to him was, as always, "How's Dawson?" and after hearing that he was "good," my next question was, "Did he call you last night?" When Bill said that he had, I then asked him what Dawson had said to him.

"He thanked me for being with him through everything," Bill answered, "and he said that he was sorry and that he loved me."

"It's really something, Bill, isn't it?" I said.

"Yeah, it is. I talked to Scott this morning. He was Dawson's nurse last night. He said that Dawson told him that he wanted to write some things down, so Scott gave him some paper."

"Did he write anything?"

"Yeah."

"Did you see what he wrote?"

"Dawson showed it to me, but I really couldn't read it."

"You have no idea what it said?"

"No, not really. His writing was very shaky. He'll show it to you. You'll probably do better with it than I did."

"Maybe. Was Dawson able to read it to you?"

"It didn't seem like it."

"So how was he today?"

"Good," Bill said again.

"What I mean is, was he saying the same kind of thing that he had said last night?"

"Yeah, a little bit." Then Bill was quiet for a moment before he said, "Andrea, you know I love that kid."

"Yeah, I know you do and now Dawson knows it, too."

Bill was quiet again and when he finally spoke, all he said was, "I'd better go."

"Yeah, me, too. I have to get ready for the hospital. I'll talk to you later. Thanks."

I looked over at my mother who was just coming into the kitchen. "I have a sore throat," she said. "I guess I'm coming down with a cold."

"Oh, no! That's awful. I can't afford to get it and expose Dawson to it. That's all he needs. If I get it, I won't be able to go see him. I can't have that. I can't get it! What am I going to do?"

"Well, we'll have to keep away from each other. We really haven't had that much contact anyway. You usually go right to bed when you come home and you don't eat here. It's not like I'm handling your food or anything."

"I know, but … I just can't be here … knowing there are cold germs around. It would just be too terrible if I got a cold."

"What are you going to do?"

"I don't know. Why did this have to happen?" I had to think of a way to avoid getting this cold and by the time I was ready to leave for the hospital, I was thinking that I might just stay there for the night. I packed a few extra things in my bag, just in case that was what I decided to do.

I was on my way to ICU when I saw Laura, the psychologist, coming down the hall. She stopped and we stepped aside, moving out of the way of others walking by. She said, "I just saw Dawson."

I was glad to hear that, but she had an unusual expression on her face that made me concerned and I asked her, "What's wrong? Is he all right?"

She put her hand to her lips, as if to hide her emotion, but I saw that her eyes held tears. She spoke slowly and softly. With a look of what appeared to be reverence for what she had just witnessed, she said, "He is a changed man."

"You saw that?" I said, sounding surprised. But I was not as surprised by her statement as I was by seeing her so visibly moved.

"There is no doubt in my mind that he has undergone a kind of inner transformation."

"I believe that, too. What did he say to you?"

"He expressed his gratitude for the care he has received and he seems awed by the profound difference he sees in himself. He appears to have gained a deep sense of connection with others that he had not had before. He spoke of his lifestyle before he came here and of his dreams while he was sedated and how he now feels that he is ready for what he called his next step, the transplant. He is quite optimistic about it."

"That is so good to hear," I said, appreciating her sharing her insight with me. I really liked her. I had liked her from the first time I met her and now I could see that she liked Dawson. This meant so much to me. "I know he appreciates being able to talk to you," I said.

"Well, he's very appreciative of everyone on the staff. They are all heroes to him. He is so grateful for the care they have given him and he is so happy to be alive." It was obvious that she had been touched by her encounter with Dawson as she repeated, "He *is* a changed man."

"I know. I know he is. He told me things I'd never heard him say before. You know, all along, I knew something monumental was going on here. It was not my imagination."

"No, definitely not." Speaking in a more professionally detached tone she said, "He appears to benefit from sharing his thoughts and feelings, so I will be continuing to visit with him."

"Thank you," I said. "Thank you so much. I better get in to see him. He kind of waits for me to get here."

"Oh, I know. He'll be glad to see you. His spirits are very high today and he's feeling strong and very optimistic."

"Oh, that's great. Thanks again."

To my surprise, there was a woman visiting with Dawson when I arrived at his room. She was a tall, black woman in a brown print dress whom I had never seen before.

Dawson looked over at me and I could see that his eyes were misty. He smiled and said, "Hi. This is Juana, the chaplain."

"Oh, hi," I said as I put my hand out to her. "I'm so glad to meet you. I'm Dawson's mother." I saw that she looked teary-eyed, too.

She smiled at me and said, "I was hoping I would meet you. Dawson told me how you are here with him every day."

"There's nowhere else I'd rather be," I said. I looked at Dawson and he smiled at me and there was no doubt this was the only place in the world for me.

"Dawson and I had a beautiful talk last night," she said. I looked at Dawson and saw that he was watching her as she spoke, gazing, as if at an angel.

I said, "Oh, I know. He called me last night after he'd talked with you. It sounded like it must have been incredible."

"Yes, it was," she said. "I have never experienced anything quite like it." They looked at each other and it was obvious they shared a unique and special bond. She stepped closer to Dawson and took his hand and said, "I must get going now, Dawson, but I will see you again soon." She came to me, shook my hand and said with sincerity in her voice, "Your son is very special."

"Thank you," I said. "Thank you for everything."

After she had gone, Dawson said, "Mom, it really was something when I was talking to her last night. It was like I was talking to, oh, I don't know, I can't explain it, but I am so glad she came to see me. And last night I slept really good for the first time since I've been here."

"Oh, Dawson, that's great. You know your call last night made me very happy. You do know how much it meant to me." He smiled and nodded. I said, "Dad told me you wrote some things down."

"Yeah, I did. It's over there, but it's really hard to read."

I went to the table and picked up the sheet of white paper. Written straight across the top in black ink was *Old West, BW, Cowboy, Dad.* These were the only words written in a straight line and it appeared the page must have moved after he had written that first line, for all the other entries were written at an angle diagonally across the page. They were written in groups of words and were extremely shaky and mostly unreadable. From these, I could only make out the words, *LA Rams.* There were almost fifty other words written on the paper that I could not read at all. I said, "I see you wrote down the old black and white Western movie that you told me about and the Rams, but I can't make out the other words, can you?"

He looked at the paper and chuckling as he spoke, he said, "No."

I smiled at him and said, "Oh, well. It looks like it might have been interesting."

Still smiling he said, "I guess you'll have to write the things down for me that I want to remember, O.K.? Oh, I have an idea about this foam thing that they put under my VADs. I wanted to draw a picture of my idea, but I guess it would be better if you drew it for me."

"O.K.," I said, "I can do that." The pieces of blue foam rubber were something that the nurses used to prop up the heavy round pumps that rested on Dawson's stomach. They made them more comfortable for him by keeping the metal off of his skin, plus they kept the tubes from kinking. The left tube, in particular, had a tendency to get flat in one spot, which was something that they definitely did not want to happen. It was vital that there not be any interruption of the flow to and from Dawson's heart. In fact, whenever there was, the unit would beep. It was louder than the beep from the monitor or IV unit and the nurses responded quickly to it. Dawson had been made aware of this and had found that he only needed to change his position or straighten out the line to correct it. "So what's the idea you have?" I asked him.

"Well, this foam is O.K., but something could work a lot better. I think it could be more flexible. See what this block of foam does when I press it down? Well, it should be able to compress more on the edges. It should be something like … well … draw a short cylinder … but the sides should not be straight … draw zigzags instead."

As I finished drawing, I looked at him and he said, "That's it."

"It looks like … something," I said. "Do you know what?"

"Yeah."

"Oh, I know, too," I said. "It's like a pump you'd use to inflate an air mattress or something. You know, they're rubber and they are attached to a tube and you squeeze it to pump air."

"Yeah, that's the idea, only these wouldn't have the air tube, of course, and they would be the same size as the VADs. They'd fit perfectly under them and have a stickum that would hold them there, so they wouldn't keep falling out like this foam. They should be made of, or covered with, a material that would be comfortable against the skin. I don't have it exactly, but that's kind of the idea."

"Sounds like a good one, Dawson."

"I have an idea about hospital gowns, too. The way they try to run all these lines through the neck or sleeve and even this slit doesn't work very well. I have an idea about how it would work better. And I know a way to keep these lines from getting all tangled up."

"Hey, you've been busy."

"Yeah," he laughed.

Elissa, his nurse today, who had been in and out of the room as Dawson had been talking, said, "Dawson is quite enthusiastic today, isn't he?"

"He sure is," I said as she left again.

She was out of earshot when Dawson said, "She is so tiny you wouldn't think she was very strong, would you? But she is. She can really handle me. She helps me up all by herself. At first, I was worried and told her that she would need to get someone to help her, but she said she could do it alone and she did. She is really good. You know, every day they change the bandage where the VADs go in. She does it the best. They all do it a little differently, but she mixes the solutions exactly the same each time and cleans it really good and tapes the gauze neat and tight. It feels so much better when it is done like that. She does it the best."

"Did you tell her?"

"Yeah! I wish I had her every day. She's so nice, too."

"I know. I like her. I can tell she likes you."

He smiled, looking pleased. He said, "She's even smaller than you, Mom."

"I know. I feel like a monster next to her." He laughed and I was thinking of the many times he had stood next to me and had playfully patted me on the top of my head and said, "My little Mom." Oh, to live that again someday, to see that playful glint in his eye and have him standing straight and strong next to me.

When Elissa came back in, she said to me, "You and Dawson are so fortunate that you are able to be here every day."

"Oh, I know. I am very lucky," I said.

"You don't work?" she asked.

"No. Well, I have a business. I guess I should say, I *had* a business. I kind of gave it up when Dawson came here. I just had to be with him. He is more important to me than anything."

"I know," she said in her soft voice, "I see that." She seemed to understand the love I had for Dawson and the heartache I was going through. Then she smiled at me and asked, "Are you a dancer?"

"What?" I said, quite surprised by her question. "Well, I was," I answered. "I mean, I do dance. I always have. I haven't done much of it lately, but I was a dance instructor a while back. What made you ask?"

"You just look like a dancer to me. It's something about the way you move."

"You're kidding. I can't imagine how I could look like that now."

"Oh, but you do."

"Wow. I just would not have thought so."

"What kind of dancing did you teach?"

"Ballroom. Social dancing."

"Oh, that sounds like fun."

"Yeah, it was. I enjoyed it. My claim to fame is that I was George Lucas' dance teacher," I said, embarrassing myself with my obvious name-dropping. I looked at Dawson and he was smiling, but he was rolling his eyes like, "Oh, Mom."

"Star Wars' George Lucas?" Elissa asked.

"Yeah. He's really a nice guy. It surprised me how polite and considerate he was. When he was going to be late or unable to keep his appointment, he'd always have his secretary call me at home. I just hadn't imagined celebrities being like that. I know it's unfair to make such an assumption, but I would have expected him to keep me waiting or just not show up and not even bother letting me know. But he never did that. He was just a nice guy. I enjoyed teaching him because he took the lessons seriously, yet he could see the silliness of some of it, too. I liked him." I took a deep breath and sighed. "Gee, that was a long time ago."

Everything in my life that had happened before Dawson had been diagnosed with his heart condition seemed a long time ago, a long time ago in another kind of world. Everything was so different then, before he was sick. But I pondered the past only momentarily, for I knew I had far greater things to live for in the days to come.

Bill arrived after work right on schedule. I said nothing to him about my dilemma until we went to the cafeteria while the doctors were with Dawson. I said, "I have been staying at Mommy's for the past few weeks."

"Yeah?" Bill said without much interest.

"Yeah. Rusty and I had a big fight and I haven't gone back there except to get some clothes. I've talked to him on the phone because he still wants to hear how Dawson's doing and I go to the shop now and then to do book work, but that's it. I have not seen him."

Bill, now appearing more interested in what I was saying, said, "That's too bad. You sure don't need that happening at this time. You've got enough to worry about."

"Yeah, really. That's for sure. But I guess it was kind of my fault. I did something that really hurt him. I knew he really wanted to see Dawson, but I made it clear to him that I thought you wouldn't like it. That made him furious with me."

"I never said he couldn't see Dawson," Bill said.

"I know. I never asked you if he could, either. I just knew that you'd rather not have him here and I decided that it would be best for me if I did not have to worry about it. I know it wasn't a good thing to do, but I had to do it. I knew I could not handle the tension worrying about what could happen if you two met here."

"Well, he could've come when I wasn't here."

"I know, but it got bigger than that and it's too late for that now. He got so angry with me that I can't forgive him for the way he treated me at a time like this. But I've got another problem now. I've been staying at Mommy's and this morning she told me she's coming down with a cold. I can't afford to get it and risk giving it to Dawson. I don't know what to do."

"You could stay at the house if you want."

"Really? It would be O.K.?"

"I don't have a problem with it."

"O.K. I could just sleep on the couch in the family room?"

"Yeah, that's where Dawson was sleeping for a few nights before he went to the hospital."

"Well, that would be fine with me."

"Too bad Glen has Claudia's old room. You could've slept there."

"That's O.K. I don't mind the couch. I can stay tonight?"

"Yeah, that's fine," Bill said.

I called my mother and told her of my plan. When Bill and I left the hospital, he drove me to my car as he had been doing every night. But tonight, instead of going home, I drove to his house. Bill was already in the house when I arrived, but the front door was open. Soon after I entered, he headed up the stairs to get me some bedding. I said, "Just a blanket would be fine. I don't need sheets or a pillow."

"Are you sure?" he said.

"Yeah, that'll be fine."

He brought a couple of blankets down then headed back up the stairs to his bedroom. "Good night," he said.

"Good night. Oh, Bill? I was thinking maybe I'd ride in with you in the morning, O.K.? What time do you leave?"

"Quarter to six. You'll be ready?"

"Yeah, getting up early is not a problem for me. But what about the hospital? Do you think they'd mind if I got there that early and stayed?"

"I don't think they'd mind. If they do, you don't have to stay in his room. And I'm sure Dawson would like you there."

"O.K., I'll see you in the morning."

Thursday, September 19....Days in Hospital:44....Days on VADs:39

It was so much easier arriving with Bill. I was still apprehensive about how Dawson would be when I saw him for the first time, so I lagged behind and let Bill go in ahead of me. When I heard Bill say, "Hi, Dawson," I knew everything was all right. "Look who's here with me," Bill said.

"Good morning, Dawson," I said. Dawson looked pleased and surprised. "I rode in with Dad today. I'm going to stay all day."

"Really?" Dawson said. "That's good."

"Yeah, if the nurses don't mind."

As it turned out, the nurses were very nice and did not seem to mind my being there and Dawson seemed quite happy to have me there. I straightened things up in his room, helped him with his breakfast and we talked and watched TV.

It was midmorning when Dr. Harris came in the room saying, "Well, Dawson, how would you like to move to a big, new room?"

"What?" I asked as I looked over at Dawson. Dawson's eyes were wide with interest.

"I'm thinking that he's doing well enough to be moved to the Transitional Unit," Dr. Harris answered.

"Really?" I said. "When?"

"Maybe today or tomorrow."

I knew this was a big step, a wonderful step in that all-so-important-right-direction, but my first reaction to the news was one of uncertainty and I almost asked the doctor, "Are you sure he is well enough to be moved out of Intensive Care?"

Dr. Harris must have read my thoughts, for he went on to say, "He really is doing quite well. He will be off the remaining IV today, so there is no reason why he should have to stay in ICU, and he will still be monitored." He looked at Dawson, saying to him, "It is a very big room. You'll be able to walk around there and you'll have your own bathroom. You'll like it. It's a nice room with a great view. In fact, it used to be my office."

Knowing that we were quite lucky to have come this far I said, "Sounds pretty nice, Dawson. This is great. You're really making progress!" Dawson raised his eyebrows and nodded, but he looked as though he were experiencing the same mixed emotions that I was.

Dr. Harris' next words were, "We have come to the conclusion that his fever was caused by an allergic reaction and that if there is an infection, it is around the VADs."

"So what does that mean?" I asked him.

"We have made the decision to put him on the transplant list. He will be listed as Status One."

My God, how long had I waited to hear those words? "Oh, that's great!" I said. "That's good, huh, Dawson?" He smiled and nodded, but I knew that mixed emotions went along with this news, as well. Undoubtedly, getting listed was what we had been striving for. It was our only answer. It was our goal, but this did not change the fact that it was a very frightening event to look forward to. I was so glad that Laura had told me how Dawson was feeling optimistic about the transplant. I was grateful that this day had come at a time when he felt ready for it. "Are you going to list him today?" I asked.

"Yes. We all met this morning and agreed."

I had to have faith the doctors were right to think Dawson was strong enough to undergo the transplant. I had to believe this in order to alleviate some of my concern. For what concerned me was that there were those disturbing aspects of his condition that had not been resolved. His fever was ever-lingering on the edge of tolerable, all the while threatening to spike. His stomach problems were not improving, making it necessary for him to have to get to the commode several times throughout the day and night. He was periodically feeling nauseous, getting sick to his stomach and he was still unable to tolerate the necessary supplemental milkshakes, which greatly concerned the nutritionist.

Having just heard from Dr. Wiviott that he was going away for the next ten days no doubt contributed to some of my uneasiness. Although he had assured me that he would be in contact with the hospital and that they would be able to reach him if they needed to, it was not the same as having him there. I relied on him and Dr. Harris, as they were so familiar with the ins and outs of Dawson's condition.

On the bright side, and there definitely was a bright side, Dr. Harris seemed confidant that Dawson was ready to make this move and he felt that the problems Dawson was having would be resolved when the VADs were removed and he received his new heart. It was incredible to think that it could happen any day now, now that he was finally on the transplant list. Whenever it happened, he would truly be on his way to getting well and on his way to coming home. God, it could happen. It could really happen. All we had to do now was wait for a heart.

When Bill called at noon, I told him the exciting news, "They're going to list Dawson today!"

"Oh, that's great!" Bill said.

"Yeah, and he's going to be moved to a new room in the Transitional."

"What's that?"

"You know the sign we see that says TICU with the arrow pointing down the hall past MSICU, where we are now? That's the Transitional. There won't be a nurse at his door, but they feel he's well enough and he'll have a nice big room and his own bathroom."

"Sounds great."

"Yeah, we are coming along, aren't we? He's going to be O.K."

"Of course he is," Bill said. "Are they moving him today?"

"Maybe, but it might be tomorrow." I added in almost a whisper, "I hope they wait until tomorrow." *I know it's a good move, but somehow I don't know if I'm ready …*

Chapter Twenty-Six

Friday, September 20....Days in Hospital:45....Days on VADs:40

It was around midnight of my second night on the couch when Bill yelled down to me, "Are you going to keep that TV on all night? If you are, maybe you could lower it." I was startled and surprised that it was loud enough for him to hear. I certainly had not wanted to disturb him, so I quickly lowered it, but did not turn it off because I needed it to keep me from doing too much thinking.

By morning, my restless thoughts and apprehension from the night before had mellowed into cautious anticipation. Those thoughts that had been filled with uncertainty about Dawson's readiness to take this next step were put aside. What had taken their place was the reasonable expectation of the day's move, a move I felt would mark our entrance into a new phase of Dawson's recovery. The fact that the unit into which he would be moving was called "The Transitional" was significant in ways that I was yet to discover.

We left for the hospital in the early morning darkness and I was feeling grateful that I had been given the opportunity to spend some extra hours with Dawson. On the ride in, I was thinking of the quirks of fate that had brought these circumstances about. Had it not been for my mother's cold and the conflict I'd had with Rusty, I would not have thought to do this. It was interesting that as horrible as that day with Rusty had been, it had come with quite a blessing. Now I was able to come and go and stay with Dawson as long as I wanted without having to explain or answer to anyone. I contemplated continuing on this early schedule even after my mother was over her cold.

Bill stayed at the hospital only about twenty minutes before he left to go to work. As he was leaving, he said to me, "I'm sure glad you're here with Dawson."

"Me, too," I said.

"It's been hard leaving him these mornings, but now that you are here with him it makes it a little easier." No doubt this was a blessing for all of us.

I received my morning report firsthand again, but was disappointed to hear that Dawson had not slept well during the night. The nurse said, "He was having some anxiety. He could not seem to relax."

"Oh, I hate to hear that," I said. "I wonder if, maybe, just learning that he had been listed for the transplant could have had something to do with it. I'm sure he was thinking about it."

"Oh, that's possible, and he is moving out of ICU today, too, I understand."

"Yes, I think so," I said. "Dr. Harris said it was going to be yesterday or today. They didn't do it yesterday, so ..."

"Yeah, I'm sure it'll be today. Do you know what room he'll be in?" she asked me.

"Dr. Harris said it was his old office."

"That's the room he's getting? That's great. Oh, Dawson, you'll really like it." Then looking back at me, she said, "You should go see it."

"Could I?"

"Sure. You just go out, turn right and then go straight down the hall, as far as you can go. It's the last room on this side, in the corner. It's at the end of the building and has large windows on two walls with a great view."

"Should I go now?" I asked, looking over at Dawson.

The nurse said, "Yeah, sure. Go now," and Dawson nodded his agreement.

"O.K., I'll go check it out," I said enthusiastically. "I'll be back."

As I exited the ICU doors, Juana, the chaplain, was entering. We both responded with pleasant surprise. I said, "I want to thank you again for visiting with Dawson the other night. It meant so much to him."

"It meant a great deal to me, as well," she said. "I'll never forget it."

"Really? I knew it was a big event for him, but I didn't know ...'"

"Oh, it was big for me, too," Juana said. "I have wanted to tell you about it. That night, as I was talking with him, he appeared ... how can I explain it ... enlightened ... almost aglow." I was so awed by her words I could not respond. Hearing this from the chaplain had confirmed all the feelings I'd had about that evening, that it had been a truly extraordinary event. She went on to say, "I have never experienced anything like it. I will always remember the way he looked at me with those big, brown eyes of his. If I never minister another day for the rest of my life, I'll know that the time I had with Dawson ... " she paused, "I know I ministered that night and it was so beautiful. I mean it. I will never forget it."

"I knew something special was happening that night," I said. "I'm so glad that you were there to share it with him. I can't thank you enough."

"Just take care," she said. "Take care of yourself. You need your strength, too."

"I will. I'm on my way to see Dawson's new room. He's moving into the Transitional."

"How wonderful. I'm on my way to see him now."

"Oh, good. He'll be very happy to see you."

I proceeded on my way and when I found the room, I walked in. An orderly was mopping the floor. *Getting it ready for Dawson,* I said to myself. The room was everything that everyone had said it was. It was big. It had a bathroom with a shower. And it did have quite a pretty view through the large expanse of windows. They looked out across the bay with a glimpse of the Golden Gate Bridge. Yes, it was nice and as I stood there looking around at our new surroundings, I found myself wondering what events might lie ahead for us here in this new room.

When I returned to Dawson, Dr. Harris was there and he asked me, "Did you take a look at the room?"

"Yes, I did."

"What do you think?"

"You were right," I said, then looking at Dawson I said, "It's nice."

Dr. Harris said, "We're going to be moving him shortly. I've called for the VAD tech." Whenever the VADs were unplugged, they switched automatically and without interruption to battery-operated emergency power. I imagined that if anything went wrong when that transfer was made it was vital to have a tech there.

In the past, during the time that Dawson had been sedated, he had been taken out of his room a few times to have procedures done. Today would be the first time he would be awake outside of his room. That alone made this move momentous, but I had not anticipated the depth of emotion that it would stir.

One nurse gathered up his lotions, toothbrush and other toiletries and put them into a plastic hospital bag. I packed a box with the magazines, games, tapes, and other things we had accumulated over the past weeks. The bear that Claudia had given him went in, too. Another nurse came in with a wheelchair. Dawson said, "Mom, could you give me my robe?"

"I guess we are ready to get going, huh?" I said as I helped him on with it. It was the same charcoal fleece robe I had bought him two years earlier while he was in the hospital. It was the robe that I had snuggled around his shoulders that breezy afternoon in the community hospital's patio. I remembered how worried I had been that day about our future and here we were today. The future was now.

The VAD tech arrived, Chris, a tall, thin, blonde, young man with sharp features. He was always very nice to Dawson. "Hey, Dawson," he said, "where we goin'?"

Dawson smiled, raising his eyebrows, "New room," he said.

"We're moving to the Transitional," I added.

"Great," Chris said. "That's great, Dawson."

Two nurses helped Dawson from his bed to the wheelchair. The tech unplugged the VADs. One nurse, carrying our box of stuff, left the room. The other nurse stepped behind Dawson and wheeled him out. I followed them, then walked beside Dawson. The tech, pushing the VAD unit, followed behind us. Dawson was looking around, taking everything in, seeing for the first time what had been his surroundings for more than a month. We wheeled past the other ICU rooms where the nurses were posted at the doors. Each nurse we passed stood in acknowledgment of Dawson. They gave us smiles, waves and high-fives and called out, "Way to go, Dawson!" I was so touched by the warm and caring response to him as he made his way on through. What special people these nurses were. I felt such admiration for them and pride welled up inside me for Dawson, who had come so far and who it seemed had touched so many hearts along the way.

Outside in the hall, I pointed things out to him, saying, "There's the elevator we come up on and there are the waiting rooms where we've spent a lot of time." We then entered the Transitional Unit and proceeded down the hall to his new room. The room was inviting with late morning sun shining in through the large windows.

"Well, what do you think, Dawson?" the nurse asked.

Dawson smiled and said, "Yeah, it's pretty nice." The nurses placed his belongings in the room and the tech plugged in the VAD unit and checked its readings. They all wished Dawson well as they left.

His new nurse came in. "Hi, Dawson," she said. "Welcome. I'm Sharon, your nurse today. I'm going to get you settled into bed and then I'll explain all about how things work here in this unit, O.K.?"

Dawson said he preferred to sit in a chair, so she prepared the one by the window for him by putting a sheet and pillows on it. She helped him to the chair as she said, "You're pretty steady, Dawson. You've been seeing the physical therapist, right?"

"Yeah," Dawson said.

I added, "He does some exercises in bed like bending and flexing his arms and legs. She also has him standing and marching in place."

"Good," she said as she brought another chair over and sat facing us. "The therapist will continue to work with you here and eventually you will be able to walk completely on your own. The lines attached to the VAD unit are long enough that you'll be able to reach the bathroom. In the meantime though, you can still use the portable commode. When you get stronger, you can walk anywhere. Someone can walk with you and push the VAD unit and eventually you will be able to walk and push the unit by yourself. You will be getting stronger," she said. "We had one man on the VADs who rode a stationary bike in his room."

"I had heard about that," I said. "That's pretty amazing."

The nurse went on, looking at Dawson, "The longer you are here, the stronger you will get. That is one advantage if you have to wait a while before you get your heart. But you never know when one will become available for you. It could be only a few days. You just never know, but this is where you'll be until that time. This is your room." She turned to me and said, "You can bring pictures he'd like to put up on the walls. You can bring projects or hobbies that he'd like to work on. Dawson, be thinking of what you'd like your mom to bring. There is plenty of room here for whatever you want."

"That's great. Hey, Dawson, we can bring your power saw in and you can do your woodworking here," I said.

"Yeah," Dawson said. "That would be great."

The nurse smiled, "You do woodworking?" she asked. "Dr. Hensley does that, too."

"Dawson, you'll have to talk to him about it," I said. We had met Dr. Hensley a few times. He was one of the transplant team of doctors.

The nurse continued with her information, "You understand that you are wearing a portable monitor. It is registering at the nurses' station, so you don't have to worry that there isn't a nurse right outside."

"That's good to know," I said, but I was thinking that I liked it better when we could see the nurse and she could see Dawson. I knew that I should not even be thinking like that, for this was progress.

"Dawson," she said, "I see that you did not sleep much last night. Are you tired now?"

"No, not really," he said.

"You don't want to get into bed?"

"Maybe later."

"O.K. Do either of you have any questions?"

Dawson and I looked at each other, shrugged our shoulders and I said, "No, I guess not."

She said, "If you need me, you can buzz me," and she left.

I said, "Well, Dawson, what do you think?"

"It's nice," he said, looking out the window.

It really was a nice room, as hospital rooms go, and if all went well and Dawson got better and stronger and we brought in puzzles and stuff that he'd like, well, this just might be a very nice room in which to wait for his heart. "Nice view, huh?" I said, breaking the silence.

"Yeah," he answered. Pausing, then turning to look at me and speaking rather slowly, he said. "Mom, do you think I could be home by Christmas?"

His question took me by surprise and tugged at my heart. "Well, yeah, sure. That would be possible. They told me that the average wait for a heart is about two months. Let's see. This is, what, September twentieth? Three months until Christmas? Sure, you could definitely be home. You could even be home in time for us to do our shopping together. Hey, do you remember what I told you I wanted for Christmas? A small tool box?"

"Oh, yeah," he said, smiling.

"Hey, you might even be home in time to get it for me for my birthday. How about that?"

"That'd be really great," he said and he looked happy thinking about that possibility. Then he was frowning, "Does Dad know my new room number?" he asked.

"No, I guess not, but don't worry, he'll find us. In fact, he'll probably call." And sure enough, he did. "We're in our new room," I said to him. "It is Room 337." We talked a little and then Bill and Dawson talked.

When Dawson hung up the phone, he said, "I think I want to get in bed," then sounding nervous he said, "but first, I have to go to the bathroom. I'm going to call the nurse." When the nurse came, I left the room.

When I returned, Dawson was settled into bed looking comfortable, but the nurse seemed concerned with how often Dawson was having to go. She said that they were going to start him on a new medication to try to slow things down. Why had none of the medications helped so far? Was it because this was his body's way of ridding itself of all those drugs? If so, then what could control it? How would anything ever? I kept these worrisome questions to myself and I let the nurse leave without bothering her with them.

Dawson and I were now alone. The room was bright and warm with sunlight shining in. I was looking at him sitting up in his bed and I wondered if he were asking himself the same questions I was. It appeared he was not, for though he looked deep in thought, he did not look concerned. He actually looked content. He was quiet for a long while, intently gazing out the window. The expression on his face did not change as he turned his head and looked at me. "Mom," he said, "I think I might get my heart tonight."

He looked so innocent and, yet, so knowing, all in that one moment. "Dawson. Really? Do you think so? That would be wonderful. It is possible, hon."

"I know," he said. Then he looked away, looking out to the view beyond his window.

Could he be right? I thought. *It seems like he knows something. God, is he going to get his heart tonight?*

It was possible. He *was* listed and they were gathering all the pertinent information that they needed. They had started a twenty-four-hour urine check, getting samples to determine his creatinine level. I did not know what that meant, but it was something that they would need clearance for at the time of transplant and I was reminded of the day that we had been in Dr. Thompson's office. At that time, she had suggested that he come in and stay in the hospital to do all the data gathering that was necessary before the transplant. When we found out that the tests were not to assess his *need* for a transplant, but merely give them the information they needed *for* transplanting him, he had opted not to do it. I could not help but think how different today would have been had he decided to go for it then. I now wished that I had tried to encourage him to do it. At the time, the idea of him having to spend a night in this hospital seemed awful, but compared to the forty-plus nights he had spent here under these conditions, that would have been easy.

The urine sample collecting sounded like a simple enough thing to do, but it turned out that it was not. Because the VADs were cumbersome, Dawson found it difficult to get into a position that enabled him to reach around and over the VADs to hold the hand-held urinal in a way to catch the sample. He had resorted to calling the nurse to help him.

While the nurse helped him, I stepped out of the room. On one such time, I saw Nina. I told her how Dawson had said that he thought he was going to get his heart that night.

"Oh, I hope so," she said. "I'm on call tonight for organ retrieval."

"You actually go get the organs?"

"Yes."

"I didn't know that."

"Yeah. I'm hoping that I am on call when Dawson's heart comes. I want to be the one to get it for him."

"Oh, I hope you are."

"I was just on my way to see him. Can we go in?"

"Yeah, I think so."

"Oh, wait, I want to check his chart first. Oh, oh, his fever is up today."

"It is? Without the monitor in his room, I don't know his numbers anymore. I don't like that."

"Well, maybe it is easier for you if you don't know," she said.

"No, I have to know what's going on. What about this fever? Do *you* think it's from an infection around the VADs?"

"Well, there is an infection that attaches itself to foreign matter."

"So when he gets his new heart and they remove the VADs, the infection will go with it?"

"That is the thinking, so the type of antibiotics that he is on should keep it contained there. Let's go in and see him." Nina talked with him and examined the VADs and the VAD site. "Everything looks good," she said. "Take care, Dawson. I'll be seeing you." She smiled at me as she left. Was she thinking what I was thinking, that she might be seeing him tonight bringing him a new heart?

Sharon came in to tell us she was going off duty and that the evening nurse, Tammy, would be coming in soon. Not long after, Tammy did arrive. She rushed in, her voice bubbling with enthusiasm. "Dawson," she said, "I'm Tammy, your nurse tonight." She looked like someone who, under other circumstances, Dawson would have been interested in. But as his nurse? I didn't think so. I knew I was being judgmental, forming an opinion of her abilities based only on her appearance, but she just did not look like a nurse. I knew that nurses' attire had become far more casual than it had been in the past and it made sense for them to be comfortable and less starchy and white, but Tammy's outfit looked inappropriate. Most of the nurses wore loose-fitting cotton pants and tops with comfortable-looking shoes or clogs. With her green cotton pants, Tammy was wearing a tight, scooped-neck, black tee shirt, earrings, a necklace and bracelets. Her shoes were black sling-backs with a mid-height heel. Her blonde hair was piled loosely on top of her head with straggling locks falling around her face. Dawson was frowning at her as she rambled on to him. If this were what being in the Transitional was going to be like, I had been right to think that we were not ready for it.

The remainder of the afternoon passed without much incident although Dawson seemed restless and unable to get comfortable. He had been in and out of bed, the chair, and the commode and I was very happy to see Bill when he arrived. "Hey, nice room, Dawson," Bill said. Dawson looked as happy to see Bill as I was. When Dawson's dinner came, I suggested to Bill that we go right then to the cafeteria and get something to eat and bring it back up so we could have dinner with Dawson. Bill and Dawson both thought that was a good idea. In the cafeteria, Bill said, "I'm going to bring Dawson one of these frozen yogurts."

"We've been talking about doing this for such a long time. I can't believe we finally can," I said.

"Yeah, I know," Bill said. "I think he'll like it."

Dawson did not eat much of his dinner and ate only a little of the dessert we had brought him. Either he did not have much of an appetite or he was trying to avoid having to go to the bathroom again. At least, having to urinate into the plastic bottle was not as much of an ordeal, for now Bill could help him. How good it was for me and for Dawson to have Bill with us.

When evening came, the view outside the large windows seemed to change instantly to one of sparkling lights and stars against a clear black sky. When nurse Tammy came in to check on Dawson, she asked me, "Are you going to be staying?"

"Oh, for a little while," I said.

"You don't want to stay the night?" she asked.

"What? Well, I hadn't thought about that. I didn't know that I could."

"Oh, yeah. You could stay. I can bring a cot in for you."

"Really?" I looked at Dawson and then at Bill.

Tammy said, "You can think about it and let me know. I'll be back."

Bill said to me, "You should stay."

"What do you think, Dawson?"

"It's up to you, Mom. If you want to, I'd like that."

Without much hesitation, I said, "O.K. I think I will," but I was thinking of how I had always hated hospitals and I could not believe that I had voluntarily decided to spend the night in one. On top of that, I did not sleep well in strange places, but none of that could matter now. Dawson was spending his first night in a strange room with no nurse close by and I had been given the opportunity to be there with him. He would not have to be alone and he would not have to watch us leave. I was glad to be able to do this for him.

Tammy wheeled in a folded cot and left to get some linens. Bill opened it out for me and set it up in the far corner, saying, "I wish *I* were staying." When Tammy returned with a set of sheets, a pillow and a heavy, rose colored blanket, Bill said, "I guess I should get going. Remember, I'm working this weekend, so I'll be here tomorrow morning on my way." I could not have forgotten that Bill was working the whole weekend, for I was wishing that he didn't have to. I had been looking forward to the weekend thinking that he was going to be with us all day. I felt I needed him there to share my concern and lessen my fright. *Why did it have to go like this?* "I'll see you guys in the morning," Bill said and as soon as he walked out, fear came over me. I felt like a child who had been left alone in a scary place. I had to remind myself that I was there to allay Dawson's fears. I was a mother, not a child. This was not about me, it was all about Dawson. I had to be strong, so I went to him and smiled encouragingly and touched his hand as if to say, "I'm here for you, Dawson."

When Tammy returned, she was carrying dressing supplies and a manual. She said, "Dawson, I'm going to change your VAD dressing now. I brought these instructions so I can read how to do it."

I cringed and I saw Dawson looking aghast. "You don't know how to do it?" he asked, sounding horrified.

"Oh, no, it's not that. It's that I just want to be sure. It's been a while since I've done one."

Dawson looked over at me, frowning, and looking quite disturbed. Trying to smooth things over, I said, "Oh, but you have done it before."

"Oh, yeah, and it is just changing a dressing. I've certainly done enough of those."

"That's good," I said, nodding to Dawson that it was going to be O.K.

She proceeded to open the book and read it. Then she lowered the bed and Dawson told her that he could not lie flat. He said, "I can't breathe like that."

She looked slightly annoyed as she raised him up. Then she put gloves on and a mask and removed his old dressing. She opened two bottles of solutions and poured some from each into a container and began to dab at his wound.

Dawson said, "No! That's not right!"

Startled, she asked, "What? What do you mean?"

"That is not the right mixture. It should be exactly equal parts."

"That's not what it says here," Tammy said.

"Well, I've watched this enough times and I know how it's done and I know which way is best."

"Well, it says here that this is the way to do it. If it is done a little differently than you are used to, it won't make a difference." She continued dabbing and I could see that they were both quite upset and I was not sure that I should have been there to witness it. She then went on to tape the gauze. He said, "It has to be tighter." She did not acknowledge what he had said and as she placed the final tape and tied the strings, he said, "It is too loose." She stood, gathered her equipment, removed her gloves and mask and left. As she walked past me, I smiled apologetically to her and she looked down.

Visibly upset, Dawson said, "Mom, it's not right. It doesn't feel right. When they are not held tight, they pull on me. She didn't do a good job. Mom, she didn't even know what she was doing. I know she didn't mix the solution right either."

I said, "Well, she did go by the book. It is probably O.K."

"No, Mom, it isn't right."

"O.K., Dawson, let me see what I can do. I'll be back." I walked out of his room and stood there a moment in the unfamiliar corridor wondering just what it was I planned to do. Was there someone there who would listen to me and understand? Someone who would care about our concerns and not dislike us for overreacting and being too demanding? I felt so alone. I started to walk toward the nurses' station. It seemed that the nurses there had seen me coming and had looked away, so I stopped, turned around and proceeded in the opposite direction down the hall and out of the TICU. I found myself walking into ICU where our old nurses greeted me warmly. I went over to Diane, who had always been very nice to us. I said, "We're trying to get settled into the transitional, but we're not feeling very comfortable there. We miss you guys. Dawson's nurse tonight seemed unsure of how to change the VAD dressing, so Dawson did not have any confidence in her. And he knows how it has been done and how he likes it done. He upset the nurse when he told her she wasn't doing it right. Anyway, he's really uncomfortable with it the way it is. I know it is not your problem and I feel stupid to have come here to tell to you but, I don't know, I just needed to talk to someone, someone who knows us. I don't know anyone over there."

"Oh, it's O.K." she said, "I'll go and see what I can do."

"Would you? I would really appreciate that. Thank you so much. I'm really sorry to bother you with this. You have your own patients. It's just …"

"I know," she said.

"I know I should have talked to the nurses over there, but … "

"Don't worry about it. It's all right. I'll be there in a minute."

"Thank you," I said. I was feeling so appreciative and yet so ashamed of the cowardly way I felt I had handled the situation. I went back to Dawson, grateful that I could say, "Diane's going to come and see you." In minutes she was there.

"How're you doing, Dawson?" she said.

"I don't know," he said. "I'm not happy with this bandage."

"I know. I'll be right back." When she returned, she said, "Someone's going to come in and take a look, Dawson, O.K.? Take care." He thanked her and she smiled at me and left.

Soon after, a nurse came in. She said, "I'm Pat, the Head Nurse here. I understand you are not happy with your dressing."

"The other nurse didn't do it right," he said.

"Well, there can be different ways of doing it."

"But I know how it feels best," Dawson said.

"Well, that's probably true, but it does not mean that it is wrong."

"It is wrong if it doesn't feel good."

"What do you mean when you say 'doesn't feel good?'"

"They feel loose."

I sat silently on the cot as they talked. Appreciating how she was letting Dawson explain, I stayed quiet.

"The VADs feel loose?" she asked.

"Yes," Dawson said.

"How do you mean?"

It appeared he felt he had been asked enough questions and he said, showing his annoyance, "I mean when the gauze and tape are not put on tightly the VADs move around."

Trying to console him, she said, "But they *are* all right. It is O.K. for them to move. They will not go anywhere. I mean they can't pull out."

"Fine. But what I am saying," he said, trying to hold back his emotion, "is that no one knows what it is like to have these things attached to your body. I do. This is my body they are hanging out of. I know how they feel best. I know how Elissa did it. She mixed the solution perfectly and she used all of it and cleaned around the VADs really good. It felt really clean. Then she put the gauze and tape really tight. All I'm asking is that it be done like that. I'm telling you, you don't know what this is like."

God, it's true, I thought, *we don't know. It must be horrible. This is too awful for anyone. And it's Dawson that is having to go through this.*

The nurse said, "You're right. Let me look at it, Dawson. I'll fix it for you. Tell me how you'd like it."

"Thank you," he said.

She let him tell her everything he wanted every step of the way. She did what he said, while disagreeing with him on some points, telling him that doing it another way really was not *wrong,* adding, "but if you *prefer* it this way … " She looked slightly perturbed with his attitude, but when she was through, she sat at the edge of his bed and talked with him, listened to him, explained things and comforted him. He thanked her again and so did I. Then she left.

"Does it feel better?" I asked.

"Yeah," he said. "You know it's true, Mom, no one can imagine what it is like to have these things hanging out of your body."

"I know, Dawson, it is hard to imagine."

"Thanks for getting the nurse. I'm really glad you're here."

"Me, too." I was so very glad I had stayed. "Should we try and get some sleep?"

"You must be tired, huh?" he said.

"A little. But I'm thinking of you. You've had a big day."

"Yeah. Are you going to make up your bed?"

"Yeah, kind of. I don't think I'll put both sheets on, though, because I'm going to stay in my clothes and just throw the blanket over me."

"Mom, I have to go to the bathroom. Just pee. I really don't want to bother the nurse. You know how Dad held the bottle for me? Do you think you could? Would you mind?"

"Sure, I'll help you," I said, but I was thinking that this was going to be strange. I certainly had not been so familiar with Dawson since he was a young child. But we had been through a lot together these past days, things that had brought us so close that we were beyond modesty. I discreetly managed to help him and I said, "O.K., now let's try to get some sleep. Oh, would you like to say a prayer first?"

"The Saint Jude prayer?" he asked.

"Yeah, would you like to?"

"Yeah. Bring it over here and we can read it together, O.K.?"

I got a chair and pulled it up close to the side of the bed. Holding the Saint Jude prayer card so that we both could see it, we began, *"St. Jude, glorious apostle, faithful servant and friend of Jesus, the name of the traitor has caused you to be forgotten by many. But the Church honors and invokes you universally as the patron of difficult and desperate cases. Pray for me who am so miserable. Make use, I implore you, of that particular privilege accorded to you to bring visible and speedy help where help was almost despaired of. Come to my assistance in this great need that I may receive the consolation and help of heaven in all my necessities, tribulations and sufferings, particularly"* (on the card it says, "here make your request,") and I said, *"please make Dawson well,"* and Dawson added, *"please, not just for me, but for my family, so they won't have to worry."* Together we continued, *"and that I may praise God with you and all the elect throughout all eternity. I promise you, O blessed Jude, to be ever mindful of this great favor. I will honor you as my special and powerful patron and encourage devotion to you. St. Jude, pray for us and for all who honor and invoke thy aid."*

"That was beautiful, Dawson."

"Mom, I'm really different than I was before. From now on, everyone is going to be able to count on me. It might take time for them to see the difference in me … No, that's not true … I think from the very first time someone asks me for something, they'll know."

"I already know," I said. He smiled and nodded. "Do you think you can sleep, hon?"

"I don't know," he said. "How about you?"

"I don't know. Are you going to leave the TV on?"

"Yeah," he said, "unless you want it off."

"No, I'd like it on."

"Me, too. O.K., good night, Mom." He laid his head back on his pillow.

I stood and reached over to him and touched his face. "Good night, hon," I said. Then, as I had not done since he was a child, I placed my hand on his forehead and with my thumb and fingers, I stroked his eyebrows and he peacefully closed his eyes. I went to the cot and laid down. I looked over at him. He was looking at me and I waved to him. He waved back and I smiled at our innocence.

I was feeling tired, but not sleepy. He looked like he was feeling the same. I lie there quietly with my eyes closed hoping that he would fall asleep. From time to time, I took a peek at him. Each time, I saw that he was still awake. He looked wide awake staring at the TV or looking out the window. He looked over at me, as if checking to see if I were asleep. I said, "You're still awake, Dawson?"

"Yeah, you, too? Mom, you have to sleep."

"Dawson, so do you."

"I know," he said and we both kind of laughed. It reminded me of kids at a slumber party, waiting and watching each other, wondering who would get to sleep first. I remember that I was always the last one, lying there wide awake for hours. I imagined that was the way it was going to be tonight, but I did not care for myself. I only cared about Dawson and I had hoped that having me there would have helped him to relax.

"I hope my being here isn't keeping you from sleeping," I said.

"No, Mom, it's not. I'm really glad you're here, but I want you to get some sleep." I was concerned for him and he was concerned for me. Wasn't that just the best way it could be between a mother and a son?

"Let's try this again," I said.

"O.K. Good night, Mom."

"Good night, Dawson."

Saturday, September 21....Days in Hospital:46....Days on VADs:41

It turned out to be quite a long night for both of us. The nurse had come in often to assist Dawson to the commode and to give him his medications. I was still awake when all of this was happening and I talked with the nurse about what was going on. Dawson was having to go to the bathroom so frequently that they decided to insert a tube so that he would not have to worry about getting up to go. It was in the wee hours of the morning when she told me this, saying, "This will be better for him. He's exhausted. Hopefully, now he'll be able to get some sleep. And you, too."

I did finally sleep for an hour or so and awoke a little before six. I looked over at Dawson and saw he was asleep. I did not want to disturb him, so I lay there until six-fifteen, then I quietly got up and left the room. The hospital was very quiet at this hour as I walked down the empty hallway. I went out to the elevator just as Bill was getting off. "What timing," I said.

"How's it going?" Bill asked.

"We didn't sleep much. He was having to go to the bathroom a lot. They finally put a tube in so he won't have to worry about it. He was sleeping when I left, though."

"Maybe I shouldn't go in now. I don't want to wake him," Bill said.

As we stood talking at the elevator, we heard voices coming from down the end of the quiet hall. Bill and I looked in their direction. Beyond the open double doors marked, "No Admittance," we caught a glimpse of Nina. Bill and I quickly looked at each other, for what we had seen was Nina walking fast, carrying a small, red and white ice chest. "Oh, my God," I said, "Someone's getting a heart! Oh, Bill, why couldn't it have been Dawson?"

"I guess it wasn't a match," Bill said.

"Why not? Wrong blood type? Oh, Bill," I moaned.

"Maybe it wasn't even a heart. It could have been something else," Bill said.

"I know, I know, but he thought ... he thought he was going to ... last night ... oh, God, why? ... why couldn't that be his?"

"Don't worry, Andrea. He'll get one."

"Bill, do you think that maybe he really isn't ready yet? I mean, maybe it will be better for him if it takes a little while, huh? ... so he'll be stronger?"

"Yeah. I think so," Bill said. "I've got to go see him."

"O.K., you go. I'll be there in a minute. Don't say anything to him about someone getting a heart, O.K.?"

Dawson was awake when I went back to his room and Bill said he had been awake when he got there, so he must not have slept very long. Bill could only stay a short while, for he had to get to work. When he was leaving he said, "I'm hoping to get back here a little earlier than usual."

"That would be good," I said.

"Yeah, Saturdays are different, so maybe. We'll see."

When Bill was gone, Dawson said, "Did you get any sleep last night, Mom?"

"A little. You didn't get much, did you?"

"Not really. I don't feel tired, though," he said.

"How could that be?"

"I don't know. It's like I don't need to sleep."

When we had moved here, I had taken the small, tan bear that Claudia had given him weeks earlier and placed it on the table at the foot of the bed. Dawson was now looking at it. He said, "Mom, in the Saint Jude prayer, is the word determination there? Does it say something about thought and determination?"

"I don't think so, Dawson. No. Why?"

"Well, those words keep coming to my mind. I thought maybe it was from the prayer."

"Thought and determination?"

"Yeah. Mom, look at the bear's face. Look at his expression. He looks deep in thought, doesn't he?"

I went and took a closer look at the bear and was surprised to see that he did have a rather serious expression on his face. "Yeah, he does look like he's thinking."

"Giving something great thought, huh?"

"Yeah," I agreed.

"Determination," Dawson said. "That's what he's thinking about. It's almost like he's telling me that it's going to take determination from me. I thought it had something to do with Saint Jude, though."

"Well, maybe it does. Maybe Saint Jude sent you the message

through the bear." I actually said that, knowing that I was sounding a little weird, a little out-there or whatever one would call it. We were both talking oddly, but it did not matter. And it did not matter where this came from; lack of sleep, over-medication or whatever. We were sharing something and there was something so unmistakably special about it that it made the bond that had grown between us seem even stronger.

"Yeah, maybe," he said. "Mom, would you come here?"

"Sure, what is it?"

As I stood by his bed he said, "You know, Mom, how you always asked me for something. And I never gave it to you. I'm so sorry." He reached his arms out to me.

"Oh, Dawson." I reached out to him and he hugged me tight.

"Mom, I'm sorry I never gave you a hug before."

"That's O.K., Dawson."

"No, Mom, it isn't O.K. I should have." We held on to each other for a long time. When we let go, he looked at me and said, "Mom, you'll have this hug forever."

"Oh, Dawson," I said as tears rolled from my eyes. We hugged again and I did not want to ever let him go. When I did, I saw that he was looking so sleepy and he slowly closed his eyes. I gently brushed his hair back with my hand and kissed his forehead. I whispered, "I'll be right back, Dawson, maybe you can get a little sleep."

I dried my eyes and quietly left the room. As I was on my way down the hall, I saw Nina standing by the elevator.

"Nina!" I said as I hurried to catch her before an elevator came. When she turned around and saw me, she walked to meet me. I said, "Did someone get a transplant this morning?"

"Yes."

"Was it a heart?" I asked, afraid to hear the answer.

"Yes, it was a heart." She said, "I was asleep when my beeper went off and I said, 'Oh, my God, Dawson was right! He said he was going to get his heart tonight!' I couldn't believe it. I was so excited."

"So what happened? It was the wrong type?"

"No, it was his type, Type A, but it was too small."

"What? No! Nina, no!" I cried. I had envisioned this nightmare and now it was actually happening. My God, it was just too much to bear. My legs went limp and I pressed my hand against the wall, leaning into it for support. Feeling all hope was gone, I gasped, "Nina, he didn't need a big heart! He's not that big. I knew this would happen!

I knew it was bad that everyone was saying he needed a big heart! Nina, that should've been *his* heart! He knew it was coming!"

"No, Andrea. Believe me. It was too small. Please trust me. I know the size heart I want for Dawson. That's one of the reasons why I want to be the one to get his heart for him. I know what he needs."

"But it could have worked."

"No. I know the heart I want for Dawson and I will know it when I see it. Please trust me."

"I'm sorry. It's just … I was so afraid of this happening."

"I know, but because he is on the VADs, his heart can hold on for a long time. That gives us the advantage of not having to settle for a heart that is just O.K. for him, we can wait until we find one that is best."

"I know, but I'm worried about the fever, the infection, the drug reaction and his stomach problems. You know, that is not getting any better. They had to put a tube in last night. It was just too much for him to try to keep up with it and it was making him nervous. Nina, I'm really worried. I wanted to be so happy that we were making this move into the Transitional, but I can't help feeling apprehensive."

"I can understand, but try not to worry too much. We'll get him his heart."

"O.K. Thanks," I said. The elevator doors opened and as she got on, sadness and confusion rushed over me. That should have been Dawson's heart and somehow Dawson had known it. It *was* his. So why did he not get it? I could not understand how this could happen. After all our prayers had been answered, why hadn't this one? I was going over these questions in my mind as I walked slowly back to Dawson's room. When I got there, his nurse was tending to him. She said he had asked to get up in the chair, but his blood pressure was too low. She wanted him back in bed.

Was this my answer as to why he had not gotten that heart? Was he not well enough? Was he not strong enough? Was he just not ready? I had to believe that it was just a matter of time and he *would* be ready and he *would* get the perfect heart. I had to believe our day would come.

Sunday, September 22....Days in Hospital:47....Days on VADS:42

"Our day" could be today. Now that he was listed, every day had that potential.

We had spent another nearly-sleepless night, although Dawson had fallen asleep quite quickly. I had sat by his bed and began to read to him in the hopes of making him sleepy. The book I had chosen, though not one that would be considered a bedtime story, had worked as perfectly as any good bedtime story should. It was apparent that any book would have done the same, for he fell peacefully asleep before I had finished the first page. Unfortunately, he had not stayed asleep for very long and we ended up spending a night too similar to the night before.

But when morning dawned and Bill stopped by, all seemed better. Again, Dawson did not look tired, but he did choose to stay sitting up in bed, not in the chair that he usually preferred. He looked comfortable and relaxed. When Bill left, I used Dawson's bathroom to comb my hair and put my make-up on. Looking in the mirror, I could see that, though Dawson was not looking tired, I certainly was.

Dr. Hensley came in to examine Dawson and said that he had requested a consultation with a gastroenterologist, who would be in to see him later that morning. When the new doctor arrived, he had already received a full blood workup on Dawson. So in addition to noting all his vital signs, i.e., temperature, blood pressure, respiratory rate, oxygen, and so forth, he seemed to know everything else he could possibly need to know about him. He read off the nearly fifteen medications he was currently on, and the several others that he had been on, and his white blood count, his electrolytes, triglycerides, volume output, and on and on. There seemed nothing more that he could need to know, but he did have one question. He asked, "Dawson, have you been camping recently?"

"Camping?" I said. "He's been *here*."

"So you have not had any well water to drink or mountain stream water?" he asked.

"No," Dawson said.

I said, "He's been *here* for over a month. Whatever he has, he got it here!"

"O.K.," he said, "I had to ask. I'm just trying to find the source of this diarrhea."

"I know. I'm sorry. I am just so frustrated. They've been trying to find the source of his fever for weeks, then the rash and now this. They can't find anything."

"I understand," he said. "What about all that soda water?" He was looking at a large cooler of sodas in the corner of the room. "That's a lot of fluid."

"Oh," I said, "he isn't drinking all that."

"Well, some of those are citrus based. That could contribute to his condition."

"I don't think the little bit that he is drinking could do much."

"Perhaps not, but I would take him off the citrus."

I realized that what he was seeing was quite a large assortment of soda, but Dawson was barely drinking any of it. We had brought it in because he had gotten it into his mind that he wanted to have it. We had brought the large cooler in along with a small one that he kept by his bed. It was almost obsessive how he just wanted it there though he hardly drank it. It was as if it gave him some security, something that he felt he was in charge of as he counted and checked the selection. Dana, an ICU nurse had explained to me how people in situations like Dawson's, where everything in one's life is out of his/her control, it was common to become obsessive.

"I'm going to change his medication. I'm going to try something else. We're going to get you strong for your new heart, Dawson," the doctor said, confidently.

"Thanks," Dawson said and I shook the doctor's hand before he left.

I was sorry that I had shown my concern and my frustration in front of Dawson and I said to him, "He seems pretty confident. That's good. I really think he's sure he can make you better and get you ready for your heart."

"Yeah, he seems O.K.," Dawson said. He was looking unconcerned and quite relaxed. In a soft voice, he said, "Don't worry, Mom, the day is already set and it will be perfect."

My heart felt like it had stopped for a moment. What was he saying? I went to his side. "Dawson, what do you mean? The day of your transplant is set?"

He turned to look at me and looking me in the eye with a most contented expression, he shrugged his shoulders and said softly, "Whatever."

"Dawson, what do you mean, hon?"

"The day is set and it will be perfect."

"Dawson!"

"Mom, there is this light. It comes down." With his hands he was making a motion as if forming a large ball. He said, "It comes down and goes around and around and around until it is perfect and when it is, it takes you up to a beautiful place up past the sun."

I could not hold back my tears. This was the most beautiful, astounding and alarming thing I had ever heard, but I could not fully comprehend what I was hearing. "Dawson!"

"Don't worry, Mom, whenever it is, it will be perfect."

"When you get your heart, Dawson?" I said, needing to hear him tell me that.

"Maybe," he said. "Mom, remember when I called you that night to tell you I was going to the hospital?"

"Yes."

"I had been downstairs. I went up to my room to call you. Going upstairs to call you, that was the first step of my journey." I had never heard Dawson use the word "journey" before. "I did not know it then, that it was my first step," he said, "but I know it now. I've learned a lot here, Mom."

"I know you have. I have, too, Dawson." Tears were streaming down my face. He knew things. I knew things. We did not put a word on what it was we knew, we did not need to. We just knew. There was something between us that made an explanation unnecessary. My heart had been opened and tears poured forth. "Dawson, we are so very lucky."

"I know," he said.

"No one would believe it if they saw us now. They would not understand how we could feel lucky. You in that bed and me ... standing here crying ... "

"But, Mom, we are."

"I know. You are so fortunate, Dawson. You know things at twenty-seven that some people at seventy-seven don't even know."

He was looking at me with an expression in his eyes that I will never forget and I said again, "You know things, Dawson, that other people just don't know."

His eyes looked into mine and they were so knowing. He looked wise far beyond his years as he said softly, "Oh, but they will." He was telling me that the things he knew today, everyone would know when that day came for them. I was in awe. This was my son who knew these things. I had a son I was so proud of and I was remembering the day he was born. They told me, "You have a son. It's a boy!" The words came back to me, but today they were, "You have a son. He's a man!" Was this not the rebirth I had prayed for?

Dawson said, "Mom, I know this is going to sound odd and I hope you won't mind, but would you wash your face and take all your eye makeup off?"

That was odd, but I said, "O.K." and I went into the bathroom, looked in the mirror and saw that I had cried some of it off already. But I took the soap and washed my face and rinsed and dried it.

I went to him and stood by his bed. Tears began rolling down my cheeks. He took my face in his hands and wiped my tears with his thumbs. He held my face close to his and as he looked into my eyes and into my heart and soul, he said, "Mom, you have the darkest eyes I have ever seen. I wanted to see them just as they are without any makeup. Did I ever tell you, Mom, how much I love you?" And then he kissed me, a sweet little kiss followed by a gentle hug. With his arms around me, he said, "I do love you, Mom."

"And you know I love you, Dawson, so much."

Those roads I had imagined? Those roads leading us to a common destination. Had we reached it? It seemed as though we were truly in the same place, on the same plane. It was a place from which I knew we would never travel separately again. We would forever be together, no matter what.

A nurse peeked in and saw me standing there crying then walked away. A short while later, a young woman came in. She introduced herself as a chaplain from the hospital's pastoral ministry. I said, "Oh, we know Juana. Dawson has spoken with her several times."

"She is not here today," she said. "The nurse called and said that Dawson might want to talk to me."

I said, "Do you want to talk to her, Dawson?"

"O.K.," he said.

I left his room and right outside, I saw Chris, the VAD tech. I suppose I was looking and sounding like I was hysterical when I said, "He saw a light!"

Chris had no idea what I was talking about and he looked at me like I was nuts. "What?" he said.

"Dawson spoke of a light, you know, a light. A light that will lead him to a place up past the sun." I began to cry and a nurse came over to me. "He knows something," I said to her. "He knows."

"What do you mean?" she asked.

"He said the day is already set. It's like he knows."

"What do you think he knows?"

"That he is going to die." I began to sob. "He looks so at peace that it's like God told him. How can I argue with God? If the doctors told me, I could say they were wrong, a miracle could happen, but if it is God who is saying it …"

The nurse said, "I'll go in and see him." When she did, I watched from outside his room. He was still sitting up and looking so at peace. The chaplain came out to me.

Calmly, I said to her, "He seems so peaceful."

"Yes, he is," she said.

"Does he know something? Do people know these things before-hand? Have you ever seen this? This peace that has come over him, does it mean something?" She seemed unable to answer my questions and I was wishing Juana had been the chaplain on call. She could talk to Dawson. She would know. The nurse came out and said to me, "He's actually doing O.K. He's quite fine."

"I've got to call his dad," I said.

She said, "You can use the phone here at our station, if you'd like."

"O.K.," I said, slightly dazed. I thanked her as she led me to a chair behind the desk and I called Bill at work. "What's wrong?" Bill asked.

"Dawson's talking about a light."

"What do you mean?"

"A light that will take him up past the sun. He said the day is already set. Bill, he knows something."

"Andrea, what do you mean? What does he know?"

"I don't know, but it is like God told him that he is going to die and he is so at peace with it."

"Do you want me to leave now and get over there?"

"I don't know. I know you're busy. I just felt I had to tell you. Bill, I'm so scared."

"Well, how does he seem?"

"The nurse said he is fine."

"Well, that's good. O.K., I was just finishing things here. I'll be there as soon as I can."

When I got off the phone, a woman came over to me and introduced herself. I had been vaguely aware of her watching me while I had been talking to Bill. "Yes," I said, "we have met." I knew who she was now. She was on the team of psychologists with Laura. I had never really spoken to her, but I knew she had a part in evaluating Dawson. I said, "Are you here to talk to Dawson?"

"No, actually I'm here to see you. How are you doing?"

"I don't know," I said, speaking almost in monotone. "Something is going on with Dawson."

"Like what?"

"I don't know. Like he knows something. It's hard to explain."

I guess she got the idea that I really did not want to talk to her because she said, "Would you like me to have Laura come and see you?"

"O.K.," I said, "I have to go back and see Dawson now." I went into his room and he was still sitting up in bed looking calm and relaxed. "How are you doing, Dawson?" I asked.

"Good," he said.

I sat in the chair next to his bed and suddenly felt very tired. I thought that I might actually fall asleep. I suppose I did, for the next thing I knew, Bill was there. The events of the day had obviously overwhelmed me. Bill and Dawson talked and watched television as I sat quietly watching Dawson. I was glad to see that he seemed to be feeling well and he was not saying anything odd, but from time to time I could see a faraway look in his eyes. I said to him, "Dawson, Dad and I are going to have to leave soon to get to church."

"O.K.," he said, "what time will you be back?"

"Oh, about six-thirty." On the way to church, I told Bill more of the things Dawson had said.

Bill said, "But he seems fine, now."

"Yeah, I know. Bill, I know how hard it would be to imagine what it was like. You would have had to see the look in his eyes. He knows something. God talked to him. I have to talk to God." In church, I did just that. In addition to praying to God about what I feared Dawson knew and praying that it was not true, I said, *Dear Lord, I know You have heard my prayers. I know Dawson has been blessed by You. I know this day was a gift to me. I know that every day I have shared with Dawson has been Your gift. I thank You, Dear Lord, and I pray that You will let him live ...* and then I used a phrase that I had never used before ... *but, no matter what happens, I promise You that I will be forever grateful for these days.*

These days could only have happened by the grace of God and I believed that *no matter what happened,* I could never forget the beauty of the love Dawson and I had for each other. I had to be forever grateful that we were given these special days to share. I knew I had truly turned our fate over to Him when I was able to say those words. It was all in His hands and I trusted Him.

There was no doubt in my mind that my prayers for Dawson's recovery *could* be answered, for I had felt the power, beauty and mercy of His hand upon us. He *could* make Dawson well and I would continue to pray for that along with the vow to be forever grateful. No matter what.

By the time Bill said good night to us, I was exhausted. Dawson seemed quite tired, as well, and his fever was up again. Were they going to have to resort to putting him back on the steroids? With Dr. Wiviott still away and Dr. Harris off, there was no one I could ask.

Dawson said, "You look really tired, Mom. You shouldn't have to stay here with me anymore after tonight. I should be able to stay alone. It's not right for you to have to do this. And Dad, too. He looked tired, working all weekend and then having to come here."

"Dawson, we don't come here because we have to. We're here because we want to be."

"But you guys have to have a life."

"Dawson, you are my life. This is where I want to be, with you."

"I know, Mom, and I want you here, but it's too hard for you to spend this much time here. You'll have to get some sleep tonight."

"I know. I think I will. I am very tired." We said our prayer, and tonight when Dawson said good night to me, he added, "I love you, Mom." With all my heart, I knew it was true.

I laid down on the cot, pulled the blanket over me, looked over at Dawson, closed my eyes and fell instantly asleep. It was not a deep sleep, for I became aware of activity going on in the room. I was half-asleep the entire night, hearing footsteps and nurses' voices all night long. It was strange how I never got up to inquire about what was going on. I just lay there, still and quiet. It was so odd how I had been able to do that. My God, how could I have managed to lay there seemingly unconcerned?

Monday, September 23....Days in Hospital:48....Days on VADS:43

When I fully awoke in the early morning, the first thing I did was look over at Dawson. When I did, I sat up quickly. I saw that he was asleep, but he had an IV! And oxygen! *What had happened? Why was he needing that? God! Why didn't I wake up to be there for Dawson when he obviously needed me?* I got right up and went out to the nurses' station. Dawson's nurse came over to me.

Before I asked her what had happened she said, "Dawson was having some problems last night."

"I saw that. What is it?"

"Well, his blood pressure had dropped quite low and his heart rate was high. His fever had spiked, causing him distress."

"Oh, no," I moaned.

"He is doing better this morning, though."

"Oh, that's good," I sighed, "but I should have been there for him."

"He did fine. Really. With all the problems he was having, the only thing he was worried about was that we were going to wake you. He's quite a son. He was telling us, 'Please try to be quiet. Please don't wake up my mom.'"

"Oh," I moaned again, "I heard things going on. I should have gotten myself up."

"No, I think that would have upset him. His only concern was for you. He said you were very tired and you needed to sleep. I mean it, he kept saying, 'Please don't wake up my mom.' I think it is good that you did not."

"But if he needed me, I wouldn't have cared about being awakened."

"He said you were very tired, that you had not slept well since he had been here in the Transitional."

"Yeah, I know, but, it's so odd for me not to have gotten up. I'm such a light sleeper and I'm fully awake as soon as I open my eyes..."

"I think it was better this way for both of you." She said, "You have something special between you, don't you?"

"Yes. Very special." *A very special blessing from above,* I thought and I now understood why and how I had laid there so still through all the night's activity. It was what Dawson wanted.

By the time Bill arrived, Dawson was awake and seemed to be doing fairly well. His temperature had gone down which had helped a lot. He was still on the oxygen, but it was just through the nasal cannula, so he was able to take it off and on when he wanted to. He told Bill of the trouble he had during the night and how glad he was that I had slept through it all.

After Bill left for work, Dawson wanted to get up and sit in the chair. The nurse helped him and he did fine. When his breakfast arrived, he ate a little bit of it and shared some with me. He said, "Mom, look at the bear. Do you see where he is looking? Up past the sun." I looked over at the bear and he was facing the window and his head was tilting upward. I was telling him that he was right that it sure did seem like that was where he was looking, when Laura came in.

"How are you guys doing?" she said.

"Pretty good," I said. "Dawson, I was supposed to call Grandma this morning, so I'm going to go call her now." Looking at Laura I nodded, "I'll be back." I knew Dawson liked Laura and he liked talking to her and I wanted to give him that opportunity. When I got back to his room, I looked in and Laura saw me. She motioned that she was just leaving, so I waited outside for her. When she came out to meet me, I said, "What did he say?"

"Not too much. He seems a little anxious, but that is understandable. But I heard that you were quite upset yesterday."

"Oh, you heard that? Did your associate tell you she had seen me?"

"Yes. She thought you might need to talk."

"Well, I really can't explain what went on yesterday, but it just seemed like he had some kind of an awareness. It was both beautiful and scary. I don't know. It sounds crazy. He spoke of a light and a place up past the sun and a day that would be perfect. And he seemed so at peace. I am really worried. His fever and other problems just are not getting resolved."

"I can understand your concern. But are you feeling more comfortable in this unit now?"

"I guess a little."

"I told everyone here that you might have some anxiety being in new surroundings and with Dr. Wiviott and Dr. Harris not here."

"And Bill worked the weekend."

"Oh, I'm sure that didn't help. Anyway, I had made recommendations that they have consistent nursing care for Dawson to foster trust and a feeling of safety and I suggested that they bring in a cardiac chair that might work well for Dawson. I know how he prefers to be in a sitting position and the cardiac chair could recline if he wanted. These are just some things that I hoped would help to make your transition a little less stressful."

Our transition. "Thank you, Laura. I really appreciate all you've done for us."

Later, I talked with the nutritionist. She said that they had decided to take Dawson off all dairy products. I was so glad that Bill had brought Dawson the frozen yogurt the day before. I was glad for Bill because he had talked about wanting to do that for such a long time and he would be unable to now. This was not progress.

In the afternoon, the nurse came in to do a CVP, checking for any pressure on his heart. Dawson did not like it when they did this because it required lowering the head of the bed. The nurse was just leaving when Bill arrived. She said she was going to tell Dr. Harris of Dawson's CVP. I thought I heard her say it was twenty-four. I did not know the significance of that, but she seemed concerned.

Dr. Harris came in shortly after and said, "I'm thinking of calling for an echocardiogram to be done tonight. We're suspecting there is some fluid collection around his heart."

"Didn't we think that before, a while back?" I said.

"Yes, we did."

"I remember at that time, the risk of going in and draining it outweighed the benefits."

"Yes, that's right, but we have to see what is going on now. It may be causing some compression of his heart. If that is so, we would have to drain it."

"So the echocardiogram, what does that involve?"

"It's the transesophageal echocardiogram like we had done before. We go down through the esophagus. We will take him back into ICU and do it there."

"Will he come back to this room?"

"No, he'll have to stay in ICU tonight."

"Then will he be back here?"

"We're going to have to reevaluate his overall condition. There seems to be a lot going on here, along with his fever and rash returning. We'll talk about that later. I'll be back. We probably won't get started for a few hours."

I looked over at Dawson and he was looking quite drowsy. He seemed unaware that anything was wrong. I guessed that was good, but it concerned me, too. Bill looked worried and stood as close to Dawson as he could get.

When Dr. Harris returned, he said that Dawson was scheduled at eight o'clock that evening. He said that we should pack up Dawson's things to move out of the room. I quietly said to Bill, "Maybe we can wait to pack until after they take him, O.K.?"

"Why?"

"I can't do it now," I said almost whispering. "I can't have him see us packing. I can't." I was feeling quite upset and it was obvious.

"Andrea, get a hold of yourself," Bill said in a voice so low that Dawson could not hear. "Dawson seeing you like this would be worse than seeing you packing."

"You're right," I said as Dr. Hunt and Dr. Harris walked in.

Dr. Hunt said, "Dawson, how are you feeling?"

"Good," Dawson said.

I looked at Dr. Harris and shrugged my shoulders. Dawson began to talk to Dr. Hunt about the VAD "holster" that he had heard about.

He had been told they were experimenting with something that you could wear that would hold and support the VADs. Dawson had said that he would like to try it and give his opinion and suggestions for it. It had been Dr. Hunt's associate who had talked to Dawson about it, but Dr. Hunt seemed not to know what Dawson was talking about. Although I knew what he was saying and he certainly was making sense, his soft voice and slow speech was making it seem as though perhaps he did not. There was a fuzziness to what he was saying and an odd nonchalance about the upcoming procedure. Dr. Hunt seemed to dismiss it and asked him if he had any pain. Dawson said that he did not. They did not mention that he would be moving back to ICU. Neither did I. I could not say it.

Not long after, they came in to take him. As they wheeled him out in his bed, I ran after him and tucked his Saint Jude card in his hand. I followed him until they reached ICU. On my way back to his room, I saw Dana, one of the transplant doctors who had been following Dawson's case very closely. I said to her, "Does he really have to go back to ICU?"

"Yes," she said.

"Couldn't they just monitor him in the TICU?" A few days ago, I wouldn't have believed that I would be trying to keep him there.

"No, he will be better off in ICU. He needs to be watched."

"I know, I know. I'm sorry. It's just … so much was made of his big move … into that nice room … when he wakes up back in ICU he's going to know he's worse. Will he still be listed?" I asked with tears running down my face.

"Not at this time."

"Oh, no. See, that was his chance the other night."

"He can get back on the list when he gets better. If we find fluid, we'll drain it. Perhaps it is an abscess and that may be the cause of his fever and other problems. We are doing what is best for him."

"I know," I said, wiping my eyes, "but it's just too much."

"I understand," she said. But did she? Did she really?

I got back to Dawson's room as Bill was just finishing packing Dawson's things. The room looked so empty and the expanse of black sky that had once sparkled beyond the windows now only looked bleak. Bill put the last few things into a box and placed the little bear on top. I sat down and cried.

Bill said, "Andrea, c'mon. He's going to be all right. He'll be better off there. They can watch him. He didn't mind it over there. He liked the nurse being right outside his room and he liked it that he could see all the activity going on."

"Yeah, that's true," I said, wiping my tears. "It is really secluded here, especially this room tucked into the corner. But it is nice and he knew it meant he was getting better."

"Andrea, he'll be all right. C'mon, let's take his stuff over there."

"O.K. Maybe we just weren't ready. Maybe when we come back here, we will be." We went into ICU and the nurses greeted us. We were told what room he would be in. It was room 315, right next to where he had been before. Dr. Harris came in and said they did see some fluid near his right atrium. He said, "But he's doing fine right now. He's comfortable. There were no complications. He should sleep well tonight. He's sleeping now, but you can go in and see him. He's in that first room. I'll talk to you tomorrow when we decide if we need to do anything. Good night."

"That's the room he was in when he was put on the ECMO," I said to Bill. We entered to see him back on the monitor with all the green numbers. He did appear to be sleeping comfortably. And the ICU nurse was right there. Bill and I quietly said good night to him.

We rode the elevator down and walked out into the night. I said, "Bill, today Dawson told me that I would not have to stay in the hospital with him anymore. He was right, but it is only because he is no longer in the Transitional." Crying, I said, "Oh, Bill, that was our stay in the Transitional? Three nights and then right back to where we'd been? That's not a transition."

Transition: The passage from one state into another. We had not made an obvious passage in the physical sense as we had anticipated, but as for our state of awareness ... our state of devotion ... of trust, faith and love, all of which would never again be the same for us ... had we not made a transition, a passage? In the truest sense of the word, we surely had.

Chapter Twenty-Seven

Tuesday, September 24....Days in Hospital:49....Days on VADs:44

MSICU. Medical/Surgical Intensive Care Unit. We were back. The anguish was back, that awful fear was back and so was Dawson's fever, again nearing one hundred and four. Bill and I were now back on the schedule we had been on prior to our move into the Transitional. I was back to sleeping on the couch and getting up at five in the morning. We'd leave at six, get to the hospital around quarter to seven and Bill would stay about forty-five minutes, then he'd leave for work. I'd have the entire day with Dawson. Bill would arrive from work at four in the afternoon. We'd stay with Dawson until about nine o'clock in the evening and usually we'd get home by ten. This became our standard schedule. Although these were long days, they were quite short in respect to how quickly they were passing.

Throughout those weeks when Dawson was first hospitalized, when he had "The Fever," he'd also had the added complication of being sedated and on the respirator. Those factors had contributed to his anxiety and agitation and had made his terror uncontrollable.

Now that he was awake, the fever still made him anxious and agitated, but now he could verbalize it. Though this fever was not causing him to be out of control, it was causing him to be somewhat confused and slightly disoriented. At times he was cooperative with the nurses, but at other times, he was not. When they tried to put the cooling blanket on him, he told them that he hated it and did not want it. He refused to let them put it on him. The nurses said that he was being disagreeable. Considering my past experience of having witnessed how a fever could affect him, it seemed logical to assume that this behavior must be due to his fever. I knew he was not just trying to be mean or difficult. Though it was disturbing to see his demeanor changed so dramatically, and I would have been absolutely despondent had I not understood it, I was not overly concerned about it. Since I had seen a glimpse of his healed, enlightened soul, I was able to find consolation and some comfort in the belief that the only healing that he needed now was strictly that of his ailing body.

Though the previous night's echocardiogram had shown fluid collection near his heart, the opinion today was that it was not obstructing nor compressing his heart. However encouraging this conclusion had sounded, it unfortunately had supplied no explanation for his lowered blood pressure, raised CVP, or his shallow, rapid breathing. In search of answers, they did a CT scan. The findings were insignificant. No doubt we were back.

His digestive problems had improved only slightly on the new medication. Because there had been no significant improvement after having been taken off of citrus and dairy products, now they had taken him off of, literally, everything. He was allowed ice. He did not seem to mind and he actually looked like he was enjoying his ice chips, though he was appearing a little dazed from time to time. It was especially noticeable to me when each time he asked me for more ice, he simply said in an almost childlike voice, "Ice chips, Mom? Ice chips?"

He seemed drained of energy and when the physical therapist came by, he told her that he could not do any exercises. It broke my heart to see him unable and uninspired to work with her as I was remembering how enthusiastic and optimistic he had been just a week earlier. This was all heading us in the wrong direction. All I could do was pray that this would turn around soon.

I spent the day talking with the doctors, the nurses, Joyce from transplant social services, Laura, the psychologist, and tending to

Dawson's needs. The fever had made him lethargic and was causing him periodic chills and sweating. Helping him on with more blankets when he was shivering and off with them when he was too hot kept me busy. Bill took over the blanket and ice duties when he arrived. Dawson was appreciative of the care and attention we were giving him. I knew this was not the way he wanted our days to be, but we were glad to be with him and happy to do anything we could for him. We stayed later than usual, hating to leave him knowing that he needed us. Reluctantly, we said good night to him and he responded with a phrase that we had never heard him use before, but was to become the words that he would say to us every night from that night on. As we were about to leave, he looked at us and said, "I love you guys. I really love you guys."

"We love you, too, Dawson. We love you, too, so very much." It was obvious that, emotionally, we *were* moving in the right direction, getting closer to each other every day.

When Bill and I arrived home, there was a phone message from Deacon Joe. He said he wanted to talk to me about starting the RCIA group and making my confirmation and he left his number. "Should I call him?" I asked Bill.

"What would you say?"

"That I'm not going to join that group."

"Would you ask him for some books?"

"I don't know. It seems like if you want to learn anything you have to go to that class."

"But just looking at a book would be so much better. We wouldn't have to get involved with anyone."

"Yeah, I know and if I call him, I feel like I'd have to explain our situation. When I talked to the woman at the church, I told her about Dawson, but that's as far as I went. What would I have to do, tell him that I'm not really living here, that I'm just staying here at my ex-husband's because I moved out of my boyfriend's house, and the only other place I could stay was at my mother's, but she got a cold?"

"I don't know," Bill said, rolling his eyes. "It's up to you. If you don't want to call him, that's fine."

"So *you're* not going to call him, I guess, huh?" I quipped.

"Me? No way. I can't talk to a deacon. Well, it's getting late and I'm tired. I'm going to bed."

"O.K., good night, Bill. I'll see you in the morning. See you, Harley." They went upstairs and as I made up my bed on the couch, I was thinking of the tender good nights Dawson and I had shared those precious days in Transitional. *Good night, Dawson,* I whispered to myself. *I love you, hon. Sleep well.*

Wednesday, September 25....Days in Hospital:50....Days on VADs:45

"It would be good if you could get Dawson a calendar," the nurse said. "I need to keep reorienting him as to what day it is."

"O.K., I'll see about getting one," I said.

Dawson still had a fever and he was still lethargic, but he was alert and did seem to be feeling slightly better. He seemed up to a little light conversation, so I said to him, "Remember I told you that I had called St. Anthony's church to get some books? The deacon called me again last night. He left a message that he wants to talk to me about taking that class. He sounded really nice, but I don't know, I just didn't want to call him back. I guess I should." Dawson nodded. I said, "I'll just have to take the time to do that."

It was midmorning when I told Dawson I was going to go buy a calendar. "I'm going to look for a notebook, too," I said, "so we can write those things down that you wanted to remember and maybe we can start making some notes for your story."

"O.K., that would be good. You know, Mom, I still think my story is going to help someone."

"Oh, I know. It will."

"And not just help people I know, but strangers, too … I can see myself being somewhere, like a coffee shop or something … and I'm talking to some people, people I don't even know … and I tell them my story … and somehow it just helps them … I don't know exactly … but I know it is going to help someone. O.K., Mom, you'd better go shopping. How long do you think you'll be gone?"

"Gee, I'm not sure. I'm going to walk down to Fillmore Street. That's one block down. There are shops on that street, but I don't know how far I'll have to go before I find a stationery store. It will take me a little bit to walk there and back, but I'll be as quick as I can." I left and walked down the hill, turned the corner at the Mexican restaurant we had gone to weeks earlier, and proceeded down the street. There were some nice shops along the way, but they were mostly of the boutique variety, so I kept walking. Just when it looked like I was coming to the end of the shopping area, I came upon an office supply store. I felt so lucky. When inside, I found it to be very well stocked with a wide selection of notebooks. I chose a nice tan one with black binding. The pages were lined paper and on the top of each page was *No.* and *Date.* It looked like it would work for what we wanted, so I continued on through the store looking for a calendar. I soon discovered that late September was not the time to buy the current year's calendar, for all the calendars were for the following year. I did find one that was just what I wanted, but it was for the upcoming year. I liked it because it was not a monthly calendar. It was daily. Each sheet had the month with the day's date in large, bold numbers. I thought it would be perfect because I could tear off the old sheet each morning to reveal the new day. It reminded me of ones that I had seen in old movies where the pages blow off in the wind representing the passage of time.

I took it to the clerk and asked her if she had one like it for the current year. She said, "I don't know if I have any of those left. I'll have to check." She went to the back and returned with one.

"Oh, thank you," I said. "That's wonderful." Knowing I must have been looking slightly overexcited, I almost explained to her why I needed it and why I was so grateful that she had found one, but I did not. I paid her, thanked her again and took it back to Dawson. "Look what I have," I said as I took it out of the bag. "It wasn't too easy to find one this time of year." When I showed the calendar to him, he responded with a smile and I said, "We can hang it up on the wall, but first I have to get it up-to-date." I removed all the past days, leaving the day's date on top. "See, Dawson. This is today's date."

He looked at it. "September twenty-fifth," he said. "It's Claudia's birthday."

"Yeah," I said, "it is."

"She's twenty-nine," he said, raising his eyebrows and giving a look that showed it was hard for him to believe that his sister could be that old. Then I took out the notebook and showed that to him. He said, "That's great. I know some things I want you to write in it. Can we do it now? I want you to make a list of some things I want, O.K.?"

"Sure, it's for whatever you want to use it for."

"O.K., first, I'd like a picture of the VADs and some information about them. You know, a description of them and how they work."

"I think I can get that."

"Good. And, you know how I've met so many doctors here. There is always a different doctor coming in to see me. Do you think I could get a list of them?"

"Yeah, I could do that. I think I know them all. And it seems that when they come to see you they record their visit onto your chart, so I would think that it would all go into the computer. If I needed it, maybe someone could get the information for us."

"O.K., I'd like a list of all the instruments and equipment they've used on me. Maybe there's a book with diagrams. They are always working on me with weird and interesting-looking things."

"O.K., I'll see what I can do."

"I'm trying to figure out where I am now in relation to my room in the Transitional. I thought maybe I could get a floor plan."

"They might have one here, but if not, I can draw one for you."

"O.K., thanks."

I dated the page 9-25-96, made the list and numbered the items one through four.

He said, "You know, a lot of nurses have come in to see me and they keep saying how awful it is that I had to leave that nice room."

"Really? You're kidding. That's what they said?"

"Yeah, why do they have to say that?"

"I guess it's because they were so happy for you and they care and they just want to …"

"I know, but I wish they wouldn't say it. I really liked that room, but I know why I'm back here."

"You do? Why?"

"I just wasn't ready. I mean, I wasn't going along with the hospital program the way I should've been."

"How do you mean? There's nothing you could have done differently."

"Yeah, I think there was. All those sodas and, oh, I don't know, it's kind of hard to explain."

"Well, when you *are* ready, we'll get back there."

"Yeah, but, Mom, I really don't mind it here."

"That's good. I know we like the nurses here a lot better, huh? Speaking of nurses," I said as his nurse came in.

"Dawson," she said, "still no food today, but Dr. Brown is going to discontinue one of the antibacterial drugs that may be contributing to some of your stomach problems. So that might help."

"Can I have ice chips?"

"Sure."

"Can I have some now?"

"Yes, I'll get you some," she said and left.

I said, "Dawson, would you like to call Claudia and wish her a happy birthday?"

"Yeah. Would you dial her number for me?"

"Sure." As it started to ring, I handed the phone to him.

He listened for a moment, then he looked at me and said, "She isn't home." Then, obviously speaking into her recorder, his voice hoarse and his speech slow, he said, "Hi, Claudia. It's Dawson. Happy birthday. Call me." He shrugged his shoulders and smiled at me.

"That's good," I said. "She'll like hearing from you."

His nurse came in with his ice and he looked quite pleased. It was surprising to me how ice chips could satisfy him and that was gratifying to me, but I wondered how long this was going to go on and how long he would be content with it.

Bill arrived with Dr. Walker, the gastroenterologist, following right behind him.

"Dawson, how are you feeling?" the doctor asked.

"O.K."

"Keeping you off of food has helped slow down your volume of output. I'd like to continue like this for at least another day and I'm going to try another medication, tincture of opium."

"O.K.," Dawson said again.

"Do you know what's causing this problem?" I asked.

"Well, I doubt that it is inflammatory. I greatly suspect that its origin is in the small intestine."

"Do you think it is a reaction from one of his medications?" *How many times am I going to ask this question?*

"The medications he is on are not commonly known for causing this, so I'm not sure about that. Let's just see how he is tomorrow."

Tomorrow. Why is it always tomorrow? Why can't it be today that we see these problems resolved? … Oh, to see a good tomorrow … and beyond … to see an eventual tomorrow when all is cured … to be able to just live for each beautiful day … to be able to stop yearning for some desired, elusive, perfect tomorrow.

Thursday, September 26....Days in Hospital:51....Days on VADs:46

No matter how much I longed for that day in the future, that tomorrow, when Dawson would be well and no matter how often I imagined that wonderful day in my mind, I did not overlook the importance of appreciating each today. I was living for every moment that I could share with Dawson and I was living them fully. My mind, my heart, my soul and all my senses were acutely aware of each day as it unfolded.

My days began before dawn, and we arrived at the hospital while it was still dark outside. When approaching Dawson's room, I'd feel somewhat relieved when I'd see the light from his TV flickering within his dimly lit room. Today, as always, Bill walked in first then nodded to me to come in. Dawson was awake, sitting up in bed.

"How're you feeling, hon?" I asked.

"O.K.," he said, "but my tongue hurts."

"Your tongue? What's wrong with your tongue?"

"It's all cracked. It was bleeding last night and I told the nurse."

"What did she say?"

"She said it was a yeast infection from all the antibiotics and she gave me some medicine I have to swish around in my mouth."

"Is it helping?"

"Yeah, it's a little better."

"That's good."

"They wanted to put that cooling blanket on me again last night."

"Did they?"

"No! I hate that!"

"But if it works … "

"No, it feels terrible."

Bill said, "Yeah, I can imagine it would. Are you too warm now, Dawson? Do you want me to take one of those blankets off?"

"O.K., just leave the white one on," Dawson said. "Thanks. Dad, could I have my ice? Could you hold the cup for me? My fingers hurt." His fingertips had peeled through so many layers of skin that they had become quite sensitive. His skin was peeling everywhere on his body where the rash had been, but his fingertips and toes had peeled the most.

Today, Dr. Walker arrived as Bill was leaving. "How are you this morning, Dawson?" Dr. Walker asked.

"My tongue hurts," Dawson said.

"Oh, yes, I see that here on your chart. It's a yeast infection. O.K., they're treating you for that. Dawson, I have you scheduled for an abdominal ultrasound this afternoon. We'll be looking for a possible abscess."

"If there is an abscess that means draining it, right?" I asked.

"Yes." This was sounding all too familiar. "We're continuing with just ice chips today," he said, "and I'm trying another antidiarrheal medication. We'll start it today and I'll try to get back to see you later."

When he left, I said, "You had that test before, Dawson. It's not too bad, is it?"

"No, I guess not." He said, "Mom, do you want a hot chocolate? You should go down to the cafeteria and get one for yourself."

"No, that's O.K., I don't want to have one when you can't. I wouldn't feel right drinking it in front of you."

"Oh, I don't care, really. I know you like to have a cup in the morning. Go down and get one."

"Are you sure you don't mind?"

"Yeah, I'm fine. Really. I have my ice."

"All right, then, I'll go. I'll be quick."

On my way back from the cafeteria as I was stepping off the elevator, Laura was there, about to get on. She stopped and said, "I just saw Dawson." The elevator doors closed, but she seemed not to care that she had missed it. She smiled and said, "He seems a little better today. His spirits are up a little from yesterday and he says he slept well with no nightmares. He views his current situation as only a temporary setback. He has not lost hope."

"That is very good to hear."

"He wanted to talk more and we would have, but he was having trouble breathing."

"He gets short of breath," I said. "I don't know what's causing that."

"Well, try not to worry. Call me if you need me."

I thanked her and went back to Dawson. He seemed a little apprehensive about the upcoming ultrasound, but was glad when the nurse told him that they were going to bring the equipment to him and would be doing the test in his room.

It was late in the afternoon when they wheeled the equipment in. I left and went to the waiting room. I sat there until I became restless, then I went and stood by the elevator. I expected Bill would be arriving soon. When he did, I was not surprised, but I was surprised to see Matt with him. Though Matt had been coming every day on his way home from work, they usually did not arrive together.

I told them that Dawson was having the ultrasound in his room. "We can't go in yet," I said, so we stood there in the hallway, waiting together. Matt and Bill leaned up against the wall and I said to Matt, "It's so nice of you to come by every night like this."

"Hey," he said, "Dawson and I go way back."

"I don't know if I ever told you how much I had appreciated your going to see Dawson when he was first sick. It always made me feel so much better when I'd go to the house and see that you were there with him." Matt was looking slightly uncomfortable from my praises. "I mean it," I said. "And I really appreciate your coming here every day. I know Dawson does, too. You really are a good friend. You know, when Dawson told me he was going to Hawaii for your wedding, I was so upset. I really didn't want him to go. I'd have done anything to keep him from it. But as it turned out, I know he had a good time and being your best man meant a lot to him."

"Dawson means a lot to me," he said, "and he really did fine there. Everyone looked out for him, too."

"He was with good friends."

"Yeah, we all care about Dawson. My mom was there, too, and she really likes him. And he took it easy."

"Oh, that's so good to hear. It seemed like he had, but I worried about him so much when he was there. Does Jenn mind that you're late getting home every night after stopping here?"

"Oh, no, she's fine with that."

"That's good. Some new wives might resent their husband coming here every night. I'm glad she's understanding. You know, I always wished Dawson would find a nice girl."

"Well," Matt said with a little laugh, "Dawson never wanted a nice girl." He laughed again. "He doesn't like the *nice* girls."

"Hmm, I see. Well, I guess they don't like him much, either."

"Yeah, they do. *All* the girls like Dawson."

"Oh, really? Even with that attitude of his?"

"Yeah. We'd go to a party and he'd stand there giving his look. A girl would come up to me, and looking over at Dawson she'd say to me, 'Who's the asshole? Does he have a girlfriend?'" Matt laughed and so did I.

"Well, we can probably go in and see him now. They should be through."

We all went in and Matt stayed a little while. When he was leaving, he clasped Dawson's hand and said, "Take it easy, Dawson."

"Thanks, man. I will." Matt said goodbye to us and left. Dawson said, "I had asked the nurse for some ice and she said she'd be right back, but she hasn't come back yet. They say that all the time, 'I'll be right back.' They just say that, though. They don't mean it."

I said, "They probably do, but they just get busy with other things and other patients. I think I'll write that in our book. It's our quote of the day." I took out the notebook and wrote, "9-26-96." Then I wrote, "Right back." I did not say to Dawson what I was thinking, that it was possible that the nurses might be deliberately avoiding getting back to him because he was pestering them with his frequent requests.

By evening, his fever was on the rise and he was shivering with chills. I put an extra blanket on him and pulled it up under his chin with his arms tucked under the blanket. His lips were parched and dry, so I put some lotion on them. Then he said his face was itchy and I scratched it for him and he closed his eyes. He remained comfortable for only a short while, for not long after, he was sweating and wanting all the blankets off. Bill took them off for him. These were the kind of things that a nurse could not be expected to do, but we certainly did not mind doing them. How could we mind? He was so ill. He'd been through so much. We'd do anything to make him comfortable and we were glad to be there to do it. We certainly did try and we were more than rewarded for our efforts when he looked at us and simply said, "I love you guys."

Friday, September 27....Days in Hospital:52....Days on VADs:47

From outside Dawson's room, we could see that he was sitting up in the chair waiting for us. *He must be better,* I thought. Bill went into his room and I asked the nurse, "How's he doing?"

"He still has the fever," she said.

"How high is it?"

"Last time I took it, it was 39.8, but one good thing, the new medication for his stomach problem seems to be helping a little."

"That's good. Hi, Dawson. You're up! How do you feel?"

"O.K., a little shaky, though."

"You mean when you were standing and getting to the chair?"

"Yeah, two nurses had to help me. My hands are shaky, too."

"That might be because of the fever. How did you sleep?"

"Off and on. They come in all night to do stuff to me. They keep waking me up and then tell me I should be sleeping more. These lines and wires get all tangled and uncomfortable. It's just hard to sleep here."

Bill asked him if there was anything he could do for him and I said, "Dawson, I'm going to go see Lacy, the girl at the desk, and ask her about that floor plan. I'll be back. You know, like they say, 'I'll be right back.'"

Lacy was not at her desk, so I walked out to the hall. One of the nurses from the Transitional was walking by and when she saw me, she asked, "How's Dawson doing? Is he still having the stomach problem?"

"Yes, but it's a little better," I said.

"Oh, that's good. In all my many years of nursing, the only case I have seen that severe was when I had a patient with cholera."

"Cholera?" I said, raising my voice.

"I'm not saying that he has cholera. I'm just saying that it was that bad."

"Well, it has improved a little, but it has not been resolved. He has not eaten in days and they've tried a different medication on him every day and I'm worried that when they do let him eat, it'll get worse again. It's still pretty scary."

"I can imagine. Well, good luck."

"Thanks," I said. I was thinking of a conversation I'd had with Elissa. She had told me of only one patient in all *her* years of nursing that she had with a case this severe. I had asked her if they knew what caused it and she said it was a drug reaction, but that they did not use that drug anymore. I then had asked her if they had been able to treat it and she told me they hadn't and the patient had died. I was understanding more fully that what was happening to Dawson was quite out of the ordinary and serious and I felt very frightened. I walked back, hoping Lacy would be at her desk. She was, and I asked her about the floor plan. She said she was sure there was one around somewhere and she'd have to look.

I got back to Dawson's room as Bill was leaving. Dawson and I were alone and I was watching him enjoying his cup of ice chips. I said, "Dawson, I really think it's something how well you're handling all of this."

"But, Mom, I'm not."

"I think you are, Dawson, considering all you're going through."

"Yeah, I know if someone told me I'd have to go through all this, I would have told them that I couldn't do it. But really, Mom, I'm not doing it all that well."

"Well, you seem like you are."

"Yeah, when *you're* here, but when you're not, I'm like yelling n-n-u-r-r-s-s-e, n-u-r-s-e!" He said this to me in a high-pitched shrill, making his head and voice quiver and giving me a wide-eyed frantic look.

It was so funny, I had to laugh. "Oh, Dawson," I said.

He laughed, too, then he said, "But I'm not kidding, Mom." Then looking a little less serious he said, "I'm getting kind of hungry. I wonder if they're going to let me eat anything."

Dr. Harris answered the question soon after. "Just ice today, Dawson," he said. "But things are looking better, so you'll probably get to eat tomorrow."

"Well, tomorrow, Dawson, at least that's something," I said. "What about the ultrasound?" I asked the doctor. "What did it show?"

"Nothing. No abscess. And all cultures continue to come back negative, as well."

"So still the same story then, huh?"

"Looks that way."

"So whatever was causing the reaction before is still with him," I said, "and we still don't know what it is." But I was thinking that the good thing was that if they believed again that there was no infection, Dawson might get back on the transplant list. I decided not to ask the doctor if that were so. We'd know soon enough.

He said, "I'm considering restarting the steroids. This fever is causing him too many problems." He left without saying when he thought he might be doing that.

I told Bill of that possibility when he arrived in the afternoon and he thought it would be a good idea. I did, too, but it was so disheartening to know that the steroids were not a cure-all. Still, it would improve how Dawson felt and that was important. It would work again to eliminate that fever the way it had worked before, wouldn't it?

At six o'clock in the evening, they started him back on the steroids. His fever was at 39.1 and by the time we were ready to leave for home at nine o'clock, his temperature had dropped to 38. It was only one degree, but it appeared that the steroids were working. I had been anticipating this and hoping for it, but it still amazed me when I saw it happening.

The nurse said, "You're not as grumpy now, Dawson." Then looking at me she said, "It's quite obvious how much that fever affects his disposition." She looked over at Dawson and gave him a smile.

"I know," I said. "Dawson, we're going to get going now, so you be good to your nurse, O.K.? Don't give her a hard time tonight." He gave a little laugh and I carried the sight and sound of his chuckle home with me.

Saturday, September 28....Days in Hospital:53....Days on VADs:48

Claudia had the day off and was coming up to see Dawson. With her work schedule and her living three hours away, it had been a few weeks since she had visited, but I talked to her almost every day. She was following Dawson's mysterious course and had researched some things on the internet. She said it sounded like endocarditis, which was inflammation of the heart lining. That didn't sound good and we hoped it wasn't that.

Today, she planned to get to the hospital around ten in the morning. Because this was a Saturday, Bill did not have to get up and out of the house by six in the morning. He wanted to sleep in a little and take care of some chores around the house, so we planned to get to the hospital around eleven.

Months earlier, I had bought Claudia's birthday present, but I had not wrapped it yet. Bill stopped on the way to the hospital so I could buy wrapping paper and a card. I bought a card that said, "Happy Birthday to our Daughter," and one from Dawson that said, "For my Sister." I wrapped her gift as I rode in the truck on the way there.

Claudia was in Dawson's room when we arrived and he was sitting up in the chair. They were talking and they both looked quite upbeat. It warmed my heart to see them smiling and obviously having a pleasant time.

Dawson said, "Look what one of the nurses brought me." He puckered his lips and mimicked a pout. He said, "See, it says, 'Poor beebee.' She bought it just for me. Pretty nice of her, huh?" He handed the jar to me. Turning its wide lid, I opened it and saw a creamy, pure white lotion.

It had a pleasing scent and I said, "This is really nice, Dawson."

"I know. She was my nurse the night before last and she saw how dry and peeling my skin was, so last night she brought this to me."

"That was very nice of her. It's French. 'Pour Bebe' means 'for baby.'"

"No," he laughed, "poor beebee."

"O.K. Do you want some now?"

"Yeah," he said and I handed him the jar.

Claudia was talking to Bill and I took the opportunity to show Dawson the card that I had bought. He nodded and smiled his approval and I said in a low voice, "Do you want to sign it?"

"My hands are pretty shaky," he said.

"It's O.K. You don't have to sign it. She'll know who it's from," I said.

When I gave Claudia her cards and gift, she asked, "Can I open them now?"

"Sure," I said. My gift to her was a photo album and scrapbook supplies for making a unique and personal album. A friend of hers was making albums for her children's pictures and Claudia thought it would be fun to make one, also. She decided to do an album of her vacations. Bill's mother and sister had taken Dawson and her on special trips each summer from the time they were quite young and she had continued the tradition as she'd gotten older and traveled on her own. She was going to start the album with the very early vacations she and Dawson had taken as children. She and Dawson started to reminisce and they shared their memories and some laughs. Claudia said there were some trips she had only a few pictures from. Dawson told her he had some.

Claudia said, sounding surprised, "You have pictures from our trips?"

"Yeah."

"You still have them?"

"Yeah."

"You know where they are?"

"Yeah," Dawson said, kind of chuckling at the tone of Claudia's questions. "When I get home, I'll get them for you. You can look through them and take whatever you want to put in your album."

"O.K., great. Thanks."

"Or if you want them now, I can tell you where they are. You could go in my room and get them."

"No, that's all right. I'll wait. I don't have to have them today."

Bill's mother and sister came by for a visit later in the day. They brought Claudia a birthday gift and Dawson a little stuffed toy gorilla. "He's wearing motorcycle leathers just like you do when you ride your bike," they said.

Dawson was smiling and seemed happy with this little brown gorilla. The gorilla had a funny grin and big, wide eyes looking off to the side. Dawson made a face to look like the gorilla's. We all laughed and I marveled at how, with all that he was going through, he still could make us laugh.

When everyone left, Dawson was looking quite sleepy. No doubt he had enjoyed the day, but it had tired him out. When he dozed off, Bill and I went to the cafeteria. When we came back, we ran into Laura who had just been to see Dawson. She said, "He looks good. He said he was 'worn out,' but his spirits remain high and he is feeling quite optimistic."

I was, too. It had been a good day. His fever was down, he was feeling better and he had been able to eat a little. He had enjoyed the day and he had entertained us in his unique and special way. Perhaps, for just a few, short hours we had been able to forget. We had been able to put our fears aside and feel hopeful once again.

Sunday, September 29....Days in Hospital:54....Days on VADs:49

It was a sunny Sunday morning and already quite warm. I was playing with Harley on the front porch while waiting for Bill to get ready. Glen was outside, too, washing his truck. I thought of that day that we had gotten into Glen's truck for that heart-wrenching ride to the hospital. *God, that was almost two months ago,* I thought. *It was still summer then.*

Although today may have seemed like a summer day, for it was very warm, there was no mistaking that feeling in the air that told me it was no longer summer.

"Indian Summer" is what I've always heard these days called and Indian Summer days had always made me feel sad. Years ago, I used to lie out in the hot, summer sun for the purpose of getting a tan, but when the day came when there was that feeling of autumn in the air, no matter how hot it was, I would not sunbathe. Friends of mine still did, savoring every last day of sunshine, but I could not. For me, it was over and there was something about that interval, that transition, that stretch of warmth with barely a hint of autumn that saddened me.

What was it about these days that gave me such a melancholy feeling at this time every year? Why did I feel that a few more warm days at the close of summer were something to be sad about? Was I just sad to see summer coming to a close? Did I simply dislike winter? Or was it because an Indian Summer day was a pretense? Because it could fool you into avoiding the fact that winter was close? I didn't know, but whatever it was, even if everything in my life was going well, a warm day with that unmistakable look and feel about it caused an unexplainable sadness to come over me.

Today, I was remembering years of summer's endings. I was remembering feeling sad as I stood on this porch waving to Claudia and Dawson as they went off to school or waiting here for them after school, watching for the school bus that stopped at the corner. And today, standing on this same porch so many years later, I was feeling sad again. But I was truly sad today, not just an indefinable Indian Summer kind of sad.

Bill came outside and Harley jumped up and down with excitement.

He followed Bill into the pen as Bill carried a bowl of water and a bowl of doggie treats. Bill locked the gate when he came out and Harley began to whimper. I hated that he had to be locked up, but there was no fenced-in area around the house. There were three acres that he could roam, but Bill worried that he would wander off down the road and get picked up by the Humane Society. It was safer to lock him up. It was a nice sized pen with a doghouse and a shade tree and a view of the road. And, at least, today he would not have to be in there for as many hours as he did on the weekdays.

Dawson was watching a Raiders football game on television when we arrived. He looked well and said he was feeling "pretty good," too. "How's Harley?" he asked. "I miss him."

"He's good," I said. "I got to play with him a little bit this morning before Dad put him in the pen."

"I hate it that he has to be locked up. If I were home, he wouldn't have to be."

"Oh, but he probably doesn't mind it in there and it's a nice day."

"Well, it is better than him running around. I would be worried about him. Does Glen let him out when he's home?"

"No."

"That's too bad. Gee, I wish I had a picture of Harley here. I have the ones you took when he was real little."

"Maybe I could take some pictures of him to bring to you. Do you have a camera?"

"No."

"I have one," I said, "but it's, well, I don't have it at the house. I guess I could get it, maybe next week."

"O.K., whenever. That would be good."

"So are you eating today?" I asked him.

"Yeah, I ate a little, but I got kind of sick. It might have been because I was coughing so much, but the nurse gave me something and I felt better."

Bill and Dawson watched football most of the day. Bill in a chair and Dawson in bed, they each dozed off from time to time. I read the Sunday paper and worked a crossword puzzle. Bill was asleep when Dawson looked over at me and in a low voice he said, "It's good that Dad's getting some sleep. He must be tired."

"Yeah, but I hope he wakes up before we have to leave for church. I hate to have to wake him," I said.

"You know, Mom, when you guys go to church, I kind of hate

to see you leave. But it's something, by the time you get back, I feel better than I did before you left. It's like when you are in church, I get better."

"Really? Well, you know we do light a candle for you every time we're there."

"I know."

Later, after we'd returned from church, Lacy came into Dawson's room carrying a piece of paper. "I finally found this," she said as she handed it to me, "I knew we had one somewhere."

"Oh, great. Thanks. Dawson, here's your floor plan," I said.

He looked at it for a moment and said, "Where was my room in the Transitional?"

Bill stood and went to Dawson. "Let's see," Bill said. Looking at it, he said, "It doesn't show it on here. Hand me that pen. I'll write it in." He placed the paper on Dawson's table where Dawson could see what he was writing. I went and stood by his bed so I could see, too. The last room shown on the plan was room 319. In the rectangle representing that room, Bill crossed out 319 and wrote, "End Room, 337." Then in the rectangle numbered 301 he wrote, "First." He said, "This is the first room you were in." He then proceeded writing and saying, "302 was second, 314 was third, 337 was fourth, 301 again was fifth, and 315 is sixth, where you are now."

Dawson watched and listened intently. I said, "That's good. We've got one thing off our list of things you wanted, Dawson."

"Yeah, that's great. Thanks," he said looking at us both. It had been a pleasant day of warmth and togetherness.

Unlike those dwindling days of summer that I had refused to savor, I embraced these bright moments I had with Dawson. I would not allow myself to believe that these were like those warm Indian Summer days that could only lead to a cold, dark winter. No, these sunny days would go on forever. These warm days could never turn cold. Surely, God would see to that.

Monday, September 30....Days in Hospital:55....Days on VADs:50

"I think Dr. Wiviott gets back today," I said to Bill on the early Monday morning ride in to the hospital.

"That's good," Bill said. "I hope you're right. I miss him. I trust him."

"Yeah, me, too." When Dr. Wiviott had told me that he was going to be gone for ten days, I had it figured out that he would be back on the last day of September. I did hope I had figured right. I missed having his input and I wanted him back. A little after ten o'clock, Dawson and I were watching *The Price is Right* and Dr. Wiviott came in. It was very good to see him.

"Good morning," he said.

"Welcome back," I greeted him.

"You look good, Dawson, but what's going on here?"

"I don't know," Dawson smiled.

"So the fever came back, huh? The rash, too, somewhat. Your skin is sure peeling. Are you itchy?"

"A little."

"Hmmmm," he sighed.

"What do you think?" I asked him.

"Well, all his cultures are still negative and his white blood count is O.K. today." He sighed again. He was, after all, the infectious disease control doctor and he was trying to treat an infectious disease that still was eluding everyone.

"So he had been NPO, I see." I had heard that phrase many times from other doctors, nurses, and the dietitian. I did not know what the letters actually stood for, but I knew it meant that he was not allowed to eat anything. Dr. Wiviott continued, "He started back to eating yesterday and he did O.K., but he has not been able to handle it today. Hmmm. You've been coughing, Dawson?"

"Yeah."

"Quite a bit?"

"Yeah, my sides hurt sometimes from coughing." He was quite hoarse and his cough did concern me. At times it was just a dry, hacking cough, at others, it was what the nurses called "productive." It seemed to me that something was going on with his lungs and I worried about the possibility of pneumonia, but none of the doctors had ever used that word.

"You're getting oxygen through the nasal prongs. Are you more comfortable with that on?"

"Yeah, my breathing isn't too good."

"Hmmm," Dr. Wiviott murmured again as he looked deep in thought. He also looked disappointed. I knew he so wanted to have resolved these problems for Dawson. "O.K., Dawson," he said, "I'll see what I can do." He left, giving me hope that he would find a way to help us.

Dr. Jordan Shlain came by to say that he was going to change Dawson's lines a little later in the day. Dr. Shlain was a young, attractive man with blonde hair and a stylish haircut. He was friendly and down-to-earth when talking with Dawson. In fact, he had told Dawson to call him Jordan. They had joked with each other from the first day they met. As they were getting acquainted, he had told Dawson that he had grown up in Mill Valley. Mill Valley was not far from where Dawson lived and had grown up, but Mill Valley was less rural, quite upscale and more "preppie." Dawson's answer to Jordan when he told him where he was from, had been, "I can tell," and he said it with his sly grin. Jordan had responded, "And you're from Novato. I can tell." They both laughed. From that day on, it was obvious Dawson respected this young doctor and the doctor was respectful and considerate of Dawson's needs. Dr. Shlain did come back in the afternoon to change the lines in Dawson's neck and I left the room.

When I returned, Dawson was sleeping. When he woke up, he looked over at me, then looked at the clock. It was four o'clock. He said, "Dad should be here soon." Five minutes later his dad walked in. Dawson smiled at me and I knew he was thinking what I was thinking. Now we never had to worry about Bill being late. He was there promptly every night.

Right after Bill said his hellos and asked Dawson how he was, Bill said, "I was talking with an engineer on the job today. We were just talking and he said he lived in Novato."

"Oh, yeah?"

"Yeah, he was talking about his family and stuff."

"Does he have children? Are they grown? Maybe Dawson knows them," I said looking over at Dawson.

"They're a little younger. I told him about Dawson being in the hospital. Then this engineer that I don't even know said to me, 'Is your wife's name Andrea?'"

"What?" I said. "He's someone I know?"

"Not exactly."

Bill had an odd look on his face. "Bill," I asked, "who is he?"

"You're not going to believe it. He's Deacon Joe."

"What? Deacon Joe?" I looked over at Dawson. We were both stunned. "Bill, you met Deacon Joe? At work?"

"Yeah, do you believe it?"

"No. How did he know who you were? How did you know it was him? How did he know to ask you if your wife was named Andrea? Bill, this sounds strange."

"I know. It is weird. Well, when I told him that I lived in Novato and that I had gone back to church because my son was in the hospital, and he knew what the lady at the church had told him about you, he put two and two together. He said, 'I've been trying to get a hold of her.'"

"What did you say?"

"I told him everything, how we're divorced and how we hadn't been to church in so many years and how things at mass are so different now and that you weren't ready to think about making your confirmation because you're here every night. I told him we just wanted a book. He said he's going to get me some."

"You're kidding!"

"No. He's really a nice guy."

"So it was easy to talk to him?"

"Oh, yeah. He's just a regular person."

"God. This is so weird. I can't believe that you just happened to meet him. What are the odds of that? And that you'd even be talking to him and that he'd figure out who you were. So he just says to you, 'I'm Deacon Joe?'"

"Yeah, pretty amazing, huh?" Bill looked over to Dawson and said, "Deacon Joe said he's going to pray for you, Dawson."

"Dawson, see?" I said. "This is the kind of thing I was telling you. Like the lady on the bus and that lady here in the hospital after church and that guy that Dad knows is having his whole congregation pray for you. So many things like that."

It was the many times like this, when Dawson and I would just look at each other amazed, and say, "That's going to go in the book."

We had not talked specifically about the story Dawson wanted everyone to know, the story he believed would help someone. Often we were just too busy with hospital procedures and trying to get through each day. I knew if he wanted to he would tell me, so I did not probe. I did not ask him to tell me how and why and what he had done. I did not ask him about his regrets. I only knew he had them and wanted others to learn from them. And it was not the time for looking back. It was time for living each day and looking toward tomorrow and telling his story gave him something to hold on to and many days the mere mention of "the book" seemed to uplift him. I wanted to keep it that way. I was afraid that perhaps if he told me his whole story, he would say to himself, "O.K., I did what I came here to do in my lifetime. I'm done. Now I can go." I could not let that happen.

"Something big and very special is going on here," I said. "How these people and their prayers just keep finding us are all special blessings, Dawson, sent just for us."

"I know," he said. "I know."

Chapter Twenty-Eight

Tuesday, October 1....Days in Hospital:56....Days on VADs:51

The pages of Dawson's calendar had not blown symbolically off into the wind, but their removal each day was dramatically marking the passage of time, just the same. I had not removed any of the pages, myself, as I had assumed I would. His morning nurses had been doing it before I arrived and I had no complaints with that, in fact, I was pleased to see they were using it to help him.

This morning, I had not noticed until after Bill had left, that it had not been updated. I said to Dawson, "Your calendar hasn't been changed." I walked over and removed the page dated September 30, revealing the page dated October 1. "There," I said as I looked over at him.

His eyes were fixed on the calendar. "It's October!" he said, sounding surprised. He appeared to have been struck by the realization of just how long he had been there in the hospital. Seeing that it was October must have been a visible reminder of the length of time he had been away from home and he looked worried and somewhat sad. His expression reminded me of when we were in the Transitional and he had asked me, "Do you think I will be home by Christmas?" But he did not ask that question today. With his expression unchanging, he only repeated, "It's October." October obviously held significance for him and I hoped this would be the month we would finally make a breakthrough.

So far, there were no major signs of that. Although his intestinal problems were slightly better, it seemed obvious that it was just because he was still not allowed to eat. His fever remained down, but no doubt that was only due to the steroids. I was grateful that these two conditions appeared to be stabilizing, but having acquired the results by these somewhat drastic measures made them tentative. But Dawson seemed to be feeling all right and when the doctors came in and asked him how he was, he consistently answered, "O.K."

When Laura came by to see us, Dawson was sleeping. She did not want to disturb him, so we stepped outside his room. She said, "His chart looks good and you do, too. You seem a little more relaxed today. That's nice to see. I know this is rough for you. You've been coming here every day for quite a while. It must be quite difficult."

"Yeah, I guess, but I can't imagine *not* being here. In fact, I'm happy that I'm getting here earlier now." I wanted to continue to arrive early, but I had been wondering how long I could expect to stay at Bill's. I took the opportunity to talk to Laura about the apartments that Joyce had told me about, the ones that were close by and available to patients' families. She said she would find out if there were any vacant.

When I went back into Dawson's room, he was waking up and he asked me if I could get him some ice. His nurse was not around, so I went to look for her. When I found her, I asked her for some and she went into a locked room across from the nurses' station. I could see her through the windows as she retrieved the ice from the machine. She came out and handed me the paper cup filled with ice chips.

When I returned with his ice, I told him I was thinking of going to buy a game or a puzzle, something for us to do. He liked the idea, so I left and walked to the shopping district. I went directly to the bookstore that I had remembered seeing on my previous excursion. I bought a puzzle, a trivia game, a book of games, a book on origami and origami paper. It felt like I was Christmas shopping and that feeling was decidedly bittersweet.

Dawson was quite happy with my purchases when I returned, but he said, "You've spent a lot of money. When you go home, I want you to take the money I have in my wallet."

"Oh, no," I said, "I don't want to do that."

"Please, Mom," he said, "I want you to have it." He was so insistent that I finally agreed I would take it. We spent the afternoon looking over all the stuff and when Bill arrived, Dawson was anxious to show it all to him.

That evening when the doctors made their rounds, Bill and I went to the cafeteria. While we were there, an alarm went off and over the loudspeaker came the words, "CODE BLUE ... MSICU ... CODE BLUE." We had heard this alert on other occasions and I did not understand the reason for alerting those in the cafeteria, but each time we heard it, it was terrifying. What it meant to me was that someone in ICU was in cardiac arrest or something just as horrible. I said to Bill, "They would come looking for us here, wouldn't they? I mean if something happened to Dawson? Wouldn't they try to find us?"

"I think so," Bill said. "I'm sure they would, but do you want to go back up?"

"Yeah, I do. I just can't sit here." When we got back to ICU, the doors were locked, which was standard procedure in a Code Blue situation. I took a deep breath.

Bill said, "Don't worry. He's O.K." And when the nurse unlocked the doors and greeted us with a smile as she let us in, I knew it was true. Dawson was O.K.

"Hi," Dawson said, casually, as we entered his room. His simple "hi" had always been good to hear, but good could not come close to describing it at that moment.

One just could not live with this kind of fear day in and day out, minute after minute and not grasp on to and deeply appreciate the simple things of life. Hearing someone you love say hi was such a simple thing and yet undeniably precious.

Wednesday, October 2....Days in Hospital:57....Days on VADS:52

On the ride in, I told Bill of the conversation I'd had with Laura the day before. I told him she was checking on the availability of those apartments for me. He said, "Andrea, I don't have a problem with you staying at the house. You can stay as long as you want ... and even after Dawson comes home ... they said he'll need someone with him ... I'm sure he'd want you there ... and it would be fine with me." He paused a moment, then he added, "You'll always have a place at the house."

His words were comforting and I knew they were sincere. "That's really nice to know, Bill," I said. "Thanks."

We arrived at Dawson's room to learn that his fever was back up.

Dr. Wiviott informed us it was because they had tried lowering his dose of steroids. It was quite evident that maintaining the level of solumedrol was the only way his fever was going to be controlled, but the reason for the fever still remained not much more than an educated guess. He also told us he was discontinuing the gentomyicin, one of the antibiotics. The juggling of medications continued, but there was also some good news. They were going to let Dawson have some dinner.

Meanwhile, Dr. Thompson had some unexpected information for me. She said they were going to do another ultrasound, but this time it would be of his gall bladder. "Gall bladder?" I said.

"Yes, we think he might have gallstones."

"Gallstones?" All I seemed able to do was question her, for this seemed so odd. "Do you really think he could have gallstones?"

"Yes, we think it is possible."

"And if he does?"

"We may have to operate. We'll just have to wait and see what we find."

"This is crazy," I moaned.

"It seems Dawson wants to go for the full hospital experience while he's here," she quipped.

I suppose her statement was humorous, but I found nothing funny about Dawson's condition. When I called my mother and told her, she said, "He doesn't have gallstones."

"You don't think so?"

"Definitely not. I know he doesn't have gallstones."

Dawson had the ultrasound later in the afternoon and, sure enough, my mother was right, no gallstones. The test was negative as all tests for everything he'd ever been tested for previously had been.

When his dinner came, on the tray was a container of chicken, rice, bread and canned fruit. There was also an empty glass on the tray and Dawson seemed most pleased with that. He said, "Oh, keep this glass. I don't want them to take it. I've been wanting a glass for my ice because I don't like those plastic ones they give me or those paper or Styrofoam cups. This will be good to have." He seemed so pleased. I guess we all had come to appreciate the simple pleasures of life that could still be ours.

Thursday, October 3....Days in Hospital:58....Days on VADs:53

"Today's Papa's birthday," Dawson said as he looked over at his calendar.

"He's eighty-one," I said. "Hard to believe, huh?"

"Yeah, he sure doesn't look it."

"What time did you get up to the chair this morning?"

"Oh, I just did. And I marched ten steps by my bed."

"Oh, that's good."

"Yeah, Scott helped me." Dawson liked Scott as much as we did and appreciated the care he was giving him, for Scott always washed his hair and helped to make him comfortable. "I feel better today," Dawson said.

"Your fever is down. You always feel better without that darn fever."

"I feel like having a fried egg."

"We'll have to find out if you can have that," I said and when the doctor came by, Dawson asked him.

The doctor was slightly hesitant, but he decided to let him have it and he told the nurse to order it for him. "We're going to start him on Benadryl," he said, "so that may help the situation."

When the nurse brought his egg, she also had some yogurt for him. I said, "Is it all right for him to have that?"

She said, "Yes, the dietitian ordered it."

Dawson ate the egg and then he pulled the foil cap off of the yogurt container. "Look at this, Mom. I might win forty-thousand dollars!" He showed me the sticker that he was about to peel off to reveal if he were an "instant winner." Looking at me, he said, "Mom, wouldn't it be something if I won?"

"It sure would, Dawson." But what was even more amazing was that he still must have considered himself lucky, lucky enough to be an instant winner.

He peeled it off. "Oh, I guess not this time," he said. He ate the yogurt, enjoying every bit of it.

When the nurse came back with his dose of benadryl, I said to her, "I know benadryl is an antihistimine and can be used to treat allergic reactions, like bee stings, but how would it help his stomach?"

She said, "It may be that his intestines are releasing histamines as a reaction to one of the drugs." That made it clear.

Unfortunately, what also became clear to me, was the reason why they had thought that Dawson might have had gallstones. His liver function was being compromised and when they had seen signs of that, they had considered gallstones as a possible cause. The test showed there was some "sludge," but since there were no gallstones causing it, the logical conclusion now was that it, too, was due to one of the medications. I felt so helpless and at the mercy of the doctors' capabilities and their suppositions. I was primarily at the mercy of God, so I continued to pray for His divine intervention and there was nothing else I could do except to be with Dawson and to let him know we were in this together.

"Mom, can we try one of those games you bought?"

"Sure. How about the trivia one?"

It was *The Nick at Nite Classic TV Game*. We did not set up the playing board. We simply read each other the questions. We had gone through about forty cards when Laura peeked in on us and waved. I knew it must have looked like we were just pleasantly passing the time, waiting for the day when he was well enough to go home. That was how I prayed it would eventually be, but my innermost fear was that the day that we could all go home might never come. I refused to let myself believe that, so looking ahead with optimism, I said with a smile in my voice, "I guess when you get home, we're going to have to watch a little more *Nick at Nite*, Dawson. We'll be able to answer these questions a lot better then."

Everything will be better, Dawson, when you get home. When you get home ...

Friday, October 4....Days in Hospital:59....Days on VADs:54

"You know what I feel like having today?" Dawson asked.

"No, what?"

"Thanksgiving dinner; turkey, mashed potatoes and stuffing."

"That sounds good," I said. When Bill called, I told him and he said that maybe we could go out and get him a dinner. I said, "Like maybe at that hof brau place. Could we go there?"

"Sure," Bill said. So when Dawson saw the doctor later, he asked him if it would be O.K. for him to have that. The doctor said it would, so that was our plan for when Bill arrived.

Dr. Wiviott came in to see Dawson and he informed me they were holding off his dose of the Vancomyicin. I said, "I've been worried about that drug. I've always felt that it was the one that Dawson was reacting to. But what do I know?"

Dr. Wiviott said, "Maybe a lot. I trust a mother's instinct."

"You do?"

"Oh, yeah. Mothers have a sense about their children. I always pay attention to what a mother thinks."

"That's nice," I said. I knew I liked this man.

"We're holding off on the Vanco because we're seeing diminished renal functioning."

"What? His kidneys?"

"Yes, but we're watching it closely. It's good that you are here. You are so in touch with Dawson's condition. I must say, I am impressed with your whole family. You are all very strong and it's not often that I see a family so close."

"Thank you," I said, and although I was aching over the news, as Doctor Wiviott left, I wondered if he knew or would be surprised to hear that Bill and I were divorced.

The benadryl was making Dawson quite drowsy. We tried to play some games, but he kept falling asleep. One of the nurses' aids, Terry, who was extremely nice to Dawson came by. She said, "Dawson, do you want to take a ride up to the terrace? I can get a wheelchair and call a VAD tech to come with us. What do you think? Do you want to go for a ride?"

I said, "Dawson, that would be nice."

"Oh, I don't know," he said, sleepily, "I think I'm too tired today."

I said, "Well, maybe another day."

"Sure," Terry said. "Whenever you want to go, Dawson, let me know." I felt sad that he didn't feel up to going and I was sorry she had been denied the opportunity to do such a thoughtful deed. I admired her, for she was kind, very energetic and conscientious. I never saw her walking slowly or, in fact, walking at any pace slower than quick. She practically ran from chore to chore. Despite how hard she worked, she always looked neat in her pressed, navy blue scrubs with her clean and shiny dark hair. She had fair skin, a crooked smile and a youthfulness about her. I was surprised when I heard that she was into her second career and that she had already been successful in another field. I decided that she must be older than she appeared. I knew she liked Dawson and was concerned for him. She had told me once that while she was off for a few days that she had a dream about him. She said, "I can't help thinking about him. I hope he gets better soon."

By the afternoon, the doctors' decided to put him back on NPO. There would be no Thanksgiving dinner that night. But with the benadryl making him so drowsy, he would not have been able to enjoy it anyway. Thanksgiving would have to come another day.

It seemed to me that Dawson's desire to have a Thanksgiving dinner should not have been too much to ask for. When he could not have it, I was so saddened that I could have cried. I knew that I must not let those feelings show, so I told myself there would be a day when he would have that dinner, and I promised that I would give thanks whenever that day came. In a desperate attempt to think positively, I told myself that perhaps there was a chance that we all might have a real Thanksgiving dinner at home this year. I knew, however, that it was more likely that we would spend it here in the hospital. And that, only with God willing.

Saturday, October 5....Days in Hospital:60....Days on VADs:55

How quickly the days were adding up, one after the other. Dawson had been in the hospital sixty days now. How could that be? How could we be no closer to his recovery after two months?

Although I was spending more time in Dawson's room with him, there were still some days that I spent time in the waiting rooms. When I did, often there were other patients' families there. Usually by the time they had been coming there for a day or two, they'd want to talk. They'd ask me about my circumstances and when I'd tell them, their response was always the same. "You've been coming here every day for how long? How can you do it?"

My answer was always the same, "How can I not?"

The Middle-Eastern women whose mother was waiting for a transplant were still coming every day, as well. We had not talked much lately, for they, like me, were spending less time in the waiting room. We saw them briefly this morning and they said, sadly, that their mother was not doing well. I told them that I was sorry to hear that, but did not ask them any questions and I wished them well. I said to Bill, "I know beautiful things can happen here, miracles even, but mostly this is a terrible, scary place to be."

We spent the day with Dawson, but he was still on the benadryl, so remained quite sleepy. He was not allowed to eat, but he did not mind. He had his ice chips. We watched baseball on TV, which I much preferred to football. When it was time for us to leave, we said good night and Dawson blew me a kiss. "I love you guys," he said and though I was getting used to hearing him say those words, I never took them for granted. When you've spent two months in ICU, nothing can ever be taken lightly.

As we walked down the hall to the elevator, I saw the two sisters waiting there. One of them was holding a maroon pillow. It was the kind with armrests that one uses for sitting up in bed. The other sister was carrying a large, clear plastic bag that appeared to hold their mother's belongings. I gasped out loud. As we approached, the elevator came, the doors opened and we all got in. I looked directly at one of them, my eyes searching hers. She shook her head slowly and bowed her head. We did not speak a word. The elevator doors opened and we all walked silently through the lobby to the front door and out into the dark, cool night and I never saw them again.

Sunday, October 6....Days in Hospital:61....Days on VADs:56

Bill and I decided to go to the hospital earlier than we usually did on the weekends. We knew how much Dawson looked forward to having us there and he had become accustomed to having us there early. But we were not going to go in before dawn as we did on those weekdays.

As we were riding in, the rising sun was illuminating the clouds, turning them a pale, golden-orange. There were vapor trails forming a huge amber X in the sky over the San Francisco skyline. "Look," I said to Bill. "Look at that! Isn't that something? I wish I had my camera."

"That *is* something," Bill said

As we moved along the highway, I watched as the X changed its position as my perspective changed. "There," I said. "That's the picture right there with the X directly atop the Transamerica Pyramid. Look, Bill." Bill had been working at the Transamerica building for a few months installing an emergency generator system.

He said, "X marks the spot."

"The spot in the sky?"

"I guess."

"What would that spot in the sky be?" I asked out loud, but in my mind I imagined Christ descending from Heaven through that spot, here to save us all. *Or was it the spot where those of us who were chosen would ascend into Heaven?* I did not know, but I believed it was a sign of something. We entered the tunnel and when we emerged, the X had already faded and was nearly gone.

Dr. Walker was with Dawson when we arrived. He said, "The benadryl is making Dawson too drowsy. I'd like to take him off of it, but we are seeing some improvement. So I am going to lower the dose somewhat and continue with the tincture of opium and the octreotide."

"With all those different medications, do we know which one is working?" I asked.

398

"Not exactly, but most likely they are all doing their part."

"Do you know yet what is causing his problem?"

"I'm having another culture sent out and we will get the results tomorrow. I suspect that the results will support a diagnosis of an internal edema due to a drug reaction."

It's these damn drugs. I know it. All his problems are due to the medications. And they continue to add more. One's affecting his liver, one's affecting his stomach, one's affecting his kidneys, and one's causing a fever and a rash. It just goes on and on with no remedy.

Our Sunday "family" time consisted of Dawson and Bill watching sports and me doing the crossword puzzle in the pink section of the Sunday paper. Dawson slept off and on, perhaps a little less drowsy than he had been, but not much. But he seemed to be comfortable and made no complaints.

With Bill sitting on the opposite side of the bed, I could look over and see the two of them as they were looking up at the TV. Dawson really looked nothing like Bill. It wasn't just their coloring that was different; Bill with his white hair and beard and Dawson's hair and eyes so dark. Their features were different, as well.

Bill was no longer heart-throb handsome as he had been in his younger days, but he was still quite attractive. A few nurses had remarked how much he looked like Kenny Rogers. And age had not diminished his shyness. It was obvious how remarks about his looks could still embarrass him.

Despite the physical differences between them, it was surprising how much Dawson reminded me of Bill, simply by his mannerisms. I sat there looking at the two of them, my heart breaking thinking of all those family times we should have had, but didn't. But I dared not dwell on the should-have-beens, for I had to be forever mindful of the beauty that was. And certainly father and son side by side was something beautiful to see.

Monday, October 7....Days in Hospital:62....Days on VADs:57

"I slept through the weekend," Dawson said to Dana. Dana was a doctor on the transplant team. She reported on Dawson daily. I worried about what she wrote in her report because I felt she had a big influence on whether Dawson was considered ready to be listed or not.

She said, "No other complaints, Dawson?"

"No," he said.

She said nothing to us about the growing concern over Dawson's kidney function. Dr. Harris was the one to tell me that they were scheduling a nephrology consultation to determine the need for possible dialysis.

His white blood count was up and they were also considering doing a CT scan of his abdomen and chest. More blood cultures were going to be done and I was becoming overwhelmed by the increasing number of problems that had to be resolved. By the time the nephrologist arrived, I could barely hide my concern.

Dr. Harris gave me the nephrologist's conclusions later in the day. He said, "She feels he has a need for dialysis, but we can wait a day or two to see if it improves. If his electrolyte, fluid balance, or metabolic disturbances worsen, we will proceed with dialysis."

"You can wait to do that?" I asked. "And you do think that he might not need it?"

"Yes. I'm going to wait in the hopes that he will resolve it on his own."

"And he could?"

"He's done it before."

That's right, I thought, *and was it not still true, if anyone could do it, Dawson could?*

Tuesday, October 8....Days in Hospital:63....Days on VADs:58

"Today's CT scan was not helpful," Dr. Harris said. "It showed nothing that would explain his fever or elevated white blood count." Could anyone actually be surprised by this? It was the same old story. The source of Dawson's symptoms continued to escape detection.

The nephrologist checking on Dawson's kidneys said that his renal function was "unchanged." I was relieved that, at least, it was no worse.

The gastroenterologist ordered Dawson to continue on "just ice" while he added another medication, Questran.

Dana, of the transplant team, mentioned that his "bilirubin was still climbing," and I learned that was an indication of his compromised liver function. She said that it could be due to an obstruction. They had already checked for gallstones and had found nothing. Wouldn't they have detected an obstruction?

Dr. Wiviott said, sounding surprised, "Dawson looks good."

"I know," I said. "Everyone comments on how good he looks, but what does it mean when his chart looks so bad?"

"Oh, I think it means a lot," he said. "You can tell quite a bit by a patient's appearance and he does look good. He actually does not look sick."

Nina, head of the VAD team, said, "I'm just wondering if there is something simple here that we are missing. Something that he is allergic to that we are not recognizing." She asked me, "Is there anything you can think of?"

"Maybe aspirin. I never knew for sure, but there were times he'd break out in hives on the bottoms of his feet. There seemed to be a connection to aspirin, but it wasn't definite."

Nina seemed to feel as strongly as I did that Dawson's condition was due primarily to one thing, an allergic reaction. If only they could just take him off everything, he might have a better chance of fighting this on his own. The doctors did not think so and as I had said before, "What do I know?"

The day had been spent between caring for Dawson and talking with several doctors, but it was one nurse who said it all.

Cara, his first nurse, and I were alone in the hallway when she said, "I don't know why they don't just list him and give him his heart. All this fooling around with trying to find an infection, keeping him on hold. They should just let him get his heart! He's certainly earned it."

Chapter Twenty-Nine

Wednesday, October 9....Days in Hospital:64....Days on VADs:59

If it were up to the nurses," Cindy said, "Dawson would get his heart today. We want him to be next and then, just wait and see. When he does get his heart and comes back to visit us, the whole unit will practically shut down just to see him. It'll be a big day here."

"It *will* be a big day," I said and I could see that day in my mind. I could see us walking into the unit together. He'd be walking beside me, walking unrestricted by the constraints of tubes and lines and VADs. The nurses would see him dressed and looking handsome, no longer in those old, faded hospital gowns. I imagined him looking at me, sharing his smile and triumph with me. Though it was heartening to think about such a day, I had to think about today. We had today's challenges to face and perhaps some small triumphs to savor, as well.

"You seem to be in good spirits today, Dawson," the nutritionist said. "Are you feeling better?" Dawson said that he was and asked her if he were going to be able to eat. She said, "No. Are you hungry?"

"Not really, but I was thinking that some fruit sounded good."

When Dr. Harris came by, he said, "Well, Dawson, you did it again."

"What?" I asked.

"Bounced back. His renal functioning is improving on its own. If it continues like this, he will not need dialysis."

"I knew you could do it, Dawson," I said and he gave me his best smile, the one that came from his heart and touched mine.

Dr. Steele came in with his report. He said that the medications for Dawson's stomach problems were working, and that they were going to start slowly coming off the "individual agents" to determine which one was the one that was helping. He said, "We were considering an endoscopy, but I'm not sure now that we'll need to do that."

By midmorning, there was a lull in visitors and Dawson said to me, "Can we try doing some origami?"

"Sure," I said. "Did you see anything in the book that you would like to make?"

"I don't know. Let's look."

"Why don't we see if we can find something to make for Nina. She's leaving tomorrow for her vacation and she'll be away on her birthday. If we can make something today, we could give it to her before she goes. What do you think?"

"Yeah, I'd like to do that."

We started at the beginning of the book looking through the animal section, the bird section, then fish, insects and flowers. "How about these, Dawson? These tulips look cute. Let's try these." We followed the instructions and worked together. I chose the color of the paper. He used his ruler to mark the fold lines and he asked me to do the folding because his hands were too shaky. When we finished, I said, "It looks pretty good. Do you want to give it to Nina?"

"No, let's try making something else," he said.

"Maybe we can find something to make out of that wrapping paper I bought. Would you want to do that?" The wrapping paper was a wood burl pattern. When I had brought it to him for our origami, I had said, "It's for woodworking, hospital style."

"Yeah, that would be good."

"Hey, how about this?" It was a mobile with an origami goldfish hanging in the center of a diamond shaped frame.

Though Dawson was starting to look a little tired, he seemed to want to continue, saying, "I like the frame. Let's make that, but not the fish."

"O.K., we'll do the frame in the wood paper and we'll keep looking... hey, how about this? A heart. How perfect for Nina. We could do a heart in place of the goldfish. We have nice red paper we could use."

"Yeah, let's do that," he said. We worked quite diligently on it, but I could see it was an effort for him as he tried to make it perfect. His hands were so shaky and he was trying so hard to stay awake, but when we finished, he was quite pleased with it.

I said, "Maybe you could take a nap now and I'll go buy her a birthday card." He laid his head back and I stroked his eyebrows and he went right to sleep. I walked to the card shop and found a card I liked. It showed a drop of water landing in a pool of blue water with the words circling like ripples. *There are those whose lives affect all others around them, quietly touching one heart, who in turn touches another, reaching out to ends further than they would ever know ... leaving all of us a little richer than we were before. Happy Birthday to a very special person.* Nina had touched our lives and had shown us compassion at a time when we needed it most and I believed that I would always remember fondly her openness and her natural, unaffected kindness and understanding.

When I brought the card back and showed Dawson, he said he liked it. I was surprised by how much he seemed to like it, remembering how particular he was about the greeting cards he gave.

The nurse said, "Dawson, do you feel up to having a visitor?"

"Who?"

"A man who had a heart transplant a few years ago. He's here for a checkup. He said he'd like to visit with you, if it's O.K." I was so pleased when Dawson agreed to see him, for though the nurse had said Dawson had slept while I was gone, he was looking tired and rather pale. I was encouraged by his willingness to meet this stranger.

Dawson was sitting in the chair when the man and his wife slowly entered. He was an older man neatly dressed in a sport shirt, slacks, and polished shoes. He told Dawson he had received his heart five years earlier and that he felt great. "A transplant is a wonderful gift," he said. The man's name was Jack Donner. He and his wife had been taking trips to Europe and Hawaii since his transplant. He said, "It is so important that more people become aware of the need to be organ donors," and he said that he'd been working on recruiting donors through the Lions Club.

I looked over at Dawson and he appeared quite interested in what this man was saying. He had an expression on his face that showed respect and admiration as he listened, never taking his eyes off of him. But for the first time, I became sadly aware that his husky build was beginning to show the ravages of his ordeal. Perhaps I had not seen it before, for I had been looking at him only through my own loving eyes, but today, I may have been seeing him as this stranger was. Dawson was sitting with his elbows on the armrests, leaning slightly forward. His gown was hanging low on his shoulders, exposing his collarbone. I told myself that maybe it was only because of the way he was sitting that made his upper body look almost frail.

Jack Donner and his wife did not stay long, for it was obvious that Dawson was tired. But it was a pleasant visit and he had given Dawson some encouraging words. As he left, he said, "I hope you get your heart real soon, Dawson."

"Thank you," Dawson said, not hiding his gratitude for this man's sincere good wishes. When he left, Dawson looked at me and his eyes told me that he had learned something very important. He said, "Mom, that's what I'm going to do when I get my heart. I'm going to visit people waiting for theirs and maybe I'll be able to help them. I want to make it easier for someone else, maybe someone who doesn't have a family like I do to help him through it. That's what I'm going to do, just like that guy."

"That'll be wonderful, Dawson. What a special gift you'll have to share with others."

"Yeah, that's what I'm going to do when I get my heart," he said again and dozed off to sleep. I watched him as he slept, in awe of his optimism and bravery.

Thursday, October 10....Days in Hospital:65....Days on VADs:60

Many of Dawson's friends were calling the hospital wanting to find out how he was doing and hoping to talk to him. The calls came through the nurses' station, and sometimes he took a call, but most often he did not. He said he knew they would ask him if they could come visit him and he told me that he didn't want them to see him "like this." Once, when he did take a call, I heard him say that he was "just waiting for a heart." *If only it were that simple.*

Though he discouraged his friends from visiting, he was always pleased when Bill's friends came to see him. Wes, who had kept Bill and me company many nights during those first weeks, now came by from time to time see Dawson. Bob Coffee, a friend of Bill's came to visit as did Carlos, another old friend and his son, Larry. Dawson enjoyed their visits and they had entertained him with their stories and had made him laugh.

Butchie, another of Bill's friends, came by several mornings on his way to work. The first day he had come by, I hadn't recognized him, for the last time I had seen him was when Bill and I were still married. Butchie had brought Dawson a poster that I had taped to the window. It was a colorful poster announcing, "The Blue Angels Parade of Ships and Air Show."

This morning, Butchie said, "Well, The Blue Angels tomorrow, Dawson. They're going to fly right over here."

"I know, and one of the nurses said she'd take me up to the terrace to watch."

"Hey, great!" Butchie responded.

"I guess they're going to be loud, huh?" I said.

"You won't believe it," Butchie said. "Well, I've got to get going, Daws. Take care. Enjoy the show."

Dawson was feeling stronger today, and while he was still not allowed to eat, he continued to appreciate his ice chips. In fact, he was enjoying them so much, he was frequently asking the nurses for more. One of the nurses had said to me, "If you want to, you could get his ice. Do you know where it is?" I had told her I did, but that I thought the room was locked. She told me that sometimes it was, but not always. I had questioned whether it would be all right for me to go in there. "Oh, sure," she had said, "we know you."

Dr. Jordan Shlain came in to tell Dawson they were going to change the line in his neck. He said, "I'll be the one to do it." Dawson was glad to hear that because Dr. Shlain had the least problems finding the right place in Dawson's neck to insert the line. All the other doctors had trouble, and Dr. Shlain had discovered it was due to an unusual asymmetry of Dawson's jugular veins. I realized that must have been the cause of the difficulty Dr. Burke had on that day we had come so close to losing Dawson. That day so long ago.

I had to leave the room while Dr. Shlain did the procedure, and when I returned, Dawson said it had been "easy." But suddenly he said, "Mom, Nina hasn't come by. What if she already left? How will we give her her present before her birthday?"

"Don't worry," I said, but I was worried. "We'll get it to her." And I knew I had to. I went to the tiny office just inside the entrance to ICU. I did not know what that office was, but the lady who worked there was very friendly. As far as I knew, she did not have a medical title, but she was knowledgeable and caring and had been capable of answering many of my questions. She wasn't there every day, and when she was not, the door was locked. I decided to go talk to her, hoping I would see her office door open. It was, and I told her I needed to contact Nina and I explained why. I said, "I'm afraid she may have already left for her ten-day vacation."

Joann said, "I'll call her office for you and see if she's there." She wasn't, but she was expected back before she left for the day. Joann said to me, "You could take it to her. Do you know where her office is?" She explained that it was in the other building and how to get there. I must have been looking confused, for she said, "I can take it there, if you'd like. I pass her office on my way out and I'll be leaving soon."

"Oh, that would be wonderful. You don't mind?"

"No, not at all."

I went back to Dawson's room, then took the mobile and the card to Joann. I thanked her again, but I was thinking that perhaps I should have taken it myself. Maybe I would have seen Nina and that way I could have known she had received it. I was concerned that she might not. What a shame that would be, for Dawson had worked so hard. I hoped that if she did get it before she left that she would let us know. I knew it would mean so much to Dawson.

Friday, October 11....Days in Hospital:66....Days on VADs:61

Dawson was smiling when he said to Dr. Shlain, "My fingernails and toenails are too long and they're bugging me. My mom said I couldn't use the nail clippers. My dad cut a little bit off my fingernails, but she was kind of freaking out when he was doing it."

I said, "Well, we were told he had to be very careful with things like that because of the blood thinner. I didn't want anything to happen."

"Your mom is right, Dawson, you do have to be careful, but I'm sure we can do something."

When he left, Dawson said, "He's really a nice guy."

"Yeah, I think you told the right person."

Not long after, Dawson looked over at me in amazement. He certainly had told the right person. A young man in a white lab coat had entered the room saying, "Mr. Bell, Dr. Shlain has asked that I give you a pedicure." He examined Dawson's feet and remarked at the extensive peeling. The skin on his toes was coming off in thick chunks. He massaged his feet with lotion and carefully clipped his nails. Dawson thoroughly enjoyed it.

This was starting out to be a good day. His kidneys had continued to improve and there would be no need for dialysis. His intestinal problems were also improving, so he was allowed clear liquids. He had some broth and a popsicle, which seemed a magnificent treat and when the physical therapist came by, he worked with her.

It was just after noon when we heard a rumble and I felt a vibration. In the next instant, there was a thunderous roar and a huge shadow passed over the rooftop across the street. The Blue Angels had arrived. The next moment, we heard the power of their engines again, and this time, we saw the underside of the jets just outside our window as they flew by.

When Bill arrived in the afternoon, he said that he had seen them fly over downtown. He said, "Man, they fly low. They are so close and the speed and power are incredible. It just gave me chills."

"We've got two more days of them," I said. "They're scary. It feels like they're going to come right through the building."

Dawson said, "Dad, you'll be here tomorrow when they fly over, right?"

"I sure will, Dawson. We'll watch them together."

Saturday, October 12....Days in Hospital:67....Days on VADs:62

I got up early, went to Rusty's and got my camera, bought some film and went back to Bill's. We used the entire roll in front of the house to take pictures of Harley before we left for the hospital. Soon after we arrived at Dawson's, I left to take the film in for development. It was on the same block I had shopped before. As I was about to enter the photo store, I heard screaming and I turned around as a young man sped past me, blood running down his forehead. Several people were chasing him. I quickly ducked into the store and left the film and hurried back to the hospital, a little unnerved. I was glad I got back before the Blue Angels flew over because I found them unsettling, as well.

We did not have a good view of them from Dawson's window, but we could hear them and feel them, which was enough for me. And Bill and Dawson still found it quite exciting to catch a glimpse of the awesome, low flying jets. I said, "Wasn't there a time, or was that only in cartoons, when there were signs posted that said, 'Quiet. Hospital Zone?'"

When the exhibition was over, I walked back to get Harley's pictures. Dawson was anxious to see them and picked out the one he liked best to put on his bulletin board. He had room for it there only because Bill's sister, having seen his board overflowing with get well cards, had brought in a card line. It was a string, like a clothesline, with tiny clothespins that were designed to hold Christmas cards. Bill and I had hung the string across one corner of Dawson's room. It was now almost full of cards, for he had received so many. One that he was especially touched by was a handmade one from Andrew, a young boy who lived next door to him. It had been left on Bill's doorstep with a handmade, painted and glazed clay box. When we had brought it to Dawson, he'd seemed astounded at the kindness and concern of this boy.

As I tacked Harley's picture up next to Saint Jude, Dawson said, "I sure miss Harley. I wish I could see him."

By evening, ICU had run out of their limited supply of popsicles. The nurse said to me, "If you want to, you could go up to pediatrics. It's on the next floor. They always have them up there. Just tell them why you want it and they'll give you one." When I walked through the doors of Pediatric ICU, I was struck by the sight of the cribs with babies and children hooked up to the familiar IV bags. One little boy was crying. I went to the nurse and told her my son was in ICU and had been NPO for days. I said that he had started back on clear liquids and was enjoying the popsicles, but they had run out and did she have any. She said, "Oh, sure. We have some. What color does he like?"

"Red."

"Here. Take two. He might like to have one during the night."

"Oh, how nice. Yeah, he just might. Thank you," I said. She must have understood how a mother's son was her baby no matter how old he was.

Sunday, October 13....Days in Hospital:68....Days on VADs:63

"Oh, my God! What happened?" I asked when I walked in the door. Dawson was sitting up in bed and his nose was wrapped in a bandage. A large wad of gauze was over his nostrils and another strip was taped to both sides of his nose, looped under it like a sling.

"I have a bloody nose," he said.

"When did it start?"

"A couple of hours ago."

"A couple of hours?" That seemed like a terribly long time, but in fact it was only the beginning, for his nose continued to bleed for eight more hours. Several times throughout the day, they repacked it and were considering cauterization.

Though it did not hinder him or Bill from watching and enjoying the football games on TV, I could not enjoy my Sunday crossword puzzle. I was so focused on how he was and how he was feeling, that I could not get interested in anything else. Though a nosebleed was certainly not the most awful thing that one would have to endure, I could not keep from asking, *Just how much does he have to go through, Lord? Tell me. How much?*

Monday, October 14....Days in Hospital:69....Days on VADs:64

His nose was still packed with gauze when we arrived the next day and we were told there had been some fresh bleeding. Dawson said he would like to get out of bed, so the nurse helped him to the chair. As he stood, blood began to run down his leg from a raw spot on the back of his left thigh. His skin was breaking down from the months of lying in bed and the weeks of sitting in the chair, hours at a stretch. The nurses had been trying to get him to spend more time in bed lying on his side, but he had a difficult time staying comfortable in that position. Now the front of his hospital gown showed there was also some bleeding from the VAD site.

The previous day, I had quietly asked, "How much, Lord?" Today, I wanted to scream, "Tell me! Lord! How much does Dawson have to go through!"

He did not look well. His eyes had a yellowish tint, which worried me. He said he felt, "O.K.," but he refused physical therapy when his therapist came by. She could see that he wasn't up to it, but she had been getting discouraged with him in the past week. He'd had several days when he had told her that he could not exercise. His reasons had been, "I'm swollen and I can't move. My legs hurt. My feet hurt. I took some cough medicine this morning and it made me sleepy. I'm eating my Jell-O. I'm watching football. I'm just too tired."

All of this was true, but seeing that she was disappointed, as she was leaving he said, "I will do some exercises this afternoon." She smiled at him, winked at me and was gone. He said, "Mom, when does Nina get back from her vacation?"

"I'm not sure. Let me think. She left on the tenth. I think she's going to be gone about ten days. I would say she could be back next Monday." He looked like he felt that was too long to wait. I felt that way, too.

He said, "We don't even know if she got her present. I hope she did."

"Oh, I'm sure she did," I said, trying to reassure him.

"Thank you for getting that card for her. That was a really nice card."

"Oh, I'm glad you liked it," I said, wishing that Nina were coming back today, for an awful feeling had come over me. I tried to put the dreadful thought out of my mind. *What if "something" happens to Dawson before she gets back?*

Tuesday, October 15....Days in Hospital:70....Days on VADs:65

I could see Bill was feeling as apprehensive as I was when we arrived at the hospital this morning, for we did not know what we would see. The one thing we knew for certain was that we could never know what to expect to find upon arrival. The shock of seeing Dawson's nose in a sling the other day certainly had confirmed that. We both took a deep breath and entered. Dawson was awake, sitting up in bed.

"How are you feeling, hon?" I asked.

"O.K.," he said, "but last night ..." Bill and I looked at each other afraid of what he was about to tell us. Dawson proceeded, "Little Bo Peep and Little Miss Muffet..." *My God! He's hallucinating!* Bill was frowning, obviously concerned. Dawson went on, "The two of them were on one side of me and The Jolly Green Giant and Too Tall Jones were on the other." He was smiling, but Bill and I were speechless. In his condition, I could not imagine that Dawson was anything but delirious. "They were going to give me a new mattress," he said. "They said the new one would be better for my sore butt and legs. They wanted to lift me off my old mattress, so each of them held a corner of the mattress pad, and when they lifted me they almost dropped me! It was so stupid. With Little Miss Muffet and Little Bo Peep on one side and Too Tall Jones and The Jolly Green Giant on the other side of me, duh! The two big ones lifted me up about four feet and the two little ones barely lifted me at all. I'm completely slanted, almost rolling right off. I'm about this far from hitting the floor!"

Bill and I looked at each other again, but this time, we burst out into laughter. "Oh, Dawson!" It certainly was true. We could never know what to expect. Bill and I had arrived filled with anxiety over how Dawson would be. We could not have imagined he would have had us laughing.

Dr. Walker informed us that they were going to do an upper endoscopy later in the day. "I want to do a few biopsies, but I am concerned about bleeding," he said. "I've asked if they could hold the heparin before the procedure, but they won't, so I will have to make the decision whether or not to take samples depending on what I see." It didn't sound good, but if it could give us answers, they had to try.

Dawson said he was hungry, but was told he could not have anything until after the endoscopy, so it was good they had him scheduled early.

When it was over, Dr. Walker said, "He tolerated the procedure well. I was able to take two biopsies with minimal bleeding."

"Did you see anything that explains what's causing his problem?"

"Well, his stomach and esophagus looked normal, but there was some whitish secretion in the duodenal area."

"What does that mean?"

"Not too much. We could have expected to see that with what's been going on with him. We really will know nothing until we get the results of the biopsies."

So far, another inconclusive test. *Would we ever have an answer to the mystery of Dawson's condition?*

Wednesday, October 16....Days in Hospital:71....Days on VADs:66

"Dawson's in a very good mood this morning. He said he's feeling stronger and he's hungry."

"Well, that's sure good to hear," I said to his nurse. "You look good, too, Dawson."

"Maybe we can do some more origami today," he said, "or play some of those games out of the book you bought."

After Bill had gone, we started looking through the origami book. We decided to make a boat. We worked in the same way we had before. I picked the paper, he precisely marked the folds and I folded. We worked well together just the way we had done when we had worked on stamping or woodworking. When we were through, I said, "Let's see if it floats." I took Dawson's toiletries out of the plastic rectangle pan they were in, then I filled the pan with water from his sink. "O.K., Dawson, give it a try."

He carefully put our tiny, blue, paper boat into the water. "Hey, it does float," he said.

Just then, Cindy was passing by the room. She stopped, looked in and said, "Oh, look at that! You guys are too much. I love origami. I learned it when I was a child." She gave us some pointers and we thanked her.

His physical therapist came in and she, too, liked our little boat, but Dawson was reluctant to work with her because the VAD site had been bleeding and was worse when he stood. She managed to coax him into doing some exercises while he remained in bed. She looked discouraged when she left, and I went outside with her. I said to her in a low voice, "Do you have any charts or calendars you use for your patients so they can check off what they've done in a day? I thought maybe it would be an incentive for Dawson."

"I do have a calendar and stickers I use with my young patients. Would you want that?" I told her I would and she brought them to us a while later. Dawson seemed interested and slightly amused with the whimsical stickers, especially the one that said, "Awesome." He had been called, on occasion, "Awesome Dawson."

I slid my chair to where the sun was shining in and I sat there and wrote out a program we could follow. I began to feel quite sleepy and I laid my head back, then I turned my head to look at Dawson. He was looking at me with an expression so gentle and loving. He said, "The sun feels good on you, huh, Mom?"

"Yeah."

"You know the things I said in the Transitional? About how I feel and about the sun and stuff?"

"Yeah."

"You probably think I don't feel that way anymore because I haven't said anything like that lately, but I still do. It's just hard to talk about. Sometimes, it's even hard to think about."

"I know, Dawson. I understand."

"You look sleepy, Mom. Maybe you should take a nap."

"Yeah, maybe." I closed my eyes and went into a light sleep for a short while. When I awoke, I heard Dawson's voice.

"You had a little nap. That's good. Mom, is that a new watch or did you have it a long time?"

"It's new. I got it when you came here."

"Oh, because it looks like something you could've had back in the seventies."

"I never thought of it looking like that. You're right, but no, it isn't old."

"Mom, could you get me some ice?" There were many times now that his nurse was not around and I had gone into the "locked" room for ice, feeling uncomfortable about it every time I did. Some nurses seemed O.K. with my doing that, but others did not. When his nurse returned, I told her that I had gotten his ice and I told her how I didn't feel right about doing it. She said that I could go into the nurses' lunchroom and get ice there if I preferred. It was right in ICU and she showed me where. I wasn't sure how comfortable I would feel doing that either, but some of the nurses and doctors had joked with me that I should be on the payroll for I was there so many hours.

Bill and I were becoming standard fixtures. In fact, we were now allowed to stay in the unit and in Dawson's room when the doctors made their rounds. I thought that was quite an exception to their heretofore stringent rule. I felt it was a special privilege and we all appreciated it.

When Bill and I got home, the phone was ringing. It was Deacon Joe. He had given Bill some literature and had wondered if we'd had a chance to read it. I told him I had and I thanked him. We talked about how incredible it was that he and Bill had met. We talked for almost an hour. I told him Dawson's story and mine, telling him of Dawson's triumphs, his struggles, my fears and our faith. He said, "My prayers are with all of you. May God bless you."

Thursday, October 17....Days in Hospital:72....Days on VADs:67

The duodenal biopsy results were due today and I anticipated the possibility of an answer to Dawson's condition.

Dr. Walker came in with the report. "It is quite a dilemma," he said. "We have no evidence to show an infectious etiology. The major possibilities at this time include an allergic/hypersensitivity reaction, perhaps to the Vancomycin. Another possibility is ischemia."

"What is that?"

"A condition caused by low blood flow. I've scheduled a colonoscopy for tomorrow in the hopes I may find something more conclusive."

"What does that procedure involve?"

"He'll be mildly sedated." Dawson asked if they were going to perform it in his room, but was told they were not.

When Dawson and I were alone, I said to him, "You know, Dawson, if I could change places with you, I would."

"Mom, don't say that."

"I just want you to know that there isn't anything in this world that I wouldn't do for you, Dawson, to make it better for you if I could. I mean it. If I could take your place and spare you all of this, I would."

"I know you would. I do know, Mom, and I appreciate all that you do for me. I couldn't have come this far without you."

There was nothing I could do for the discomfort he was experiencing from the blood that was continuing to drip down the back of his throat, causing him to gag. The doctors and nurses seemed unable to help, as well. They all noted it down, but did nothing to relieve it.

Was anyone going to help us out of this? I noticed Dr. Hunt, the cardiac surgeon, at the nurses' station. I seldom saw him, so I decided to take this rare opportunity to talk to him. I nervously approached him and said, "I know Dawson has been on hold for the transplant because of the concern that he has an infection. No tests have concluded that. It seems that his problems are due to an allergic reaction. If that's true, couldn't Dawson be listed? Wouldn't getting his heart and being off of those medications solve the problem?"

He stood facing me, his arms folded. Looking quite serious he said, "I'd like to think that was true, but I feel that giving him a heart in the condition he's in would only be a disservice to your son. We must resolve his problems, so we can give him the best opportunity to accept a new heart. That is what we want for him. When he's stronger, we'll transplant him. It will be at a time when it is best for him." I wondered how many times he had said this to others and how many times it had worked out. I wanted guarantees and promises, but there was no one who could give me that.

Friday, October 18....Days in Hospital:73....Days on VADs:68

Dr. Jordan Shlain told Dawson that the colonoscopy was scheduled for eleven that morning. Dawson said he wished they did not have to take him out of his room to do it. He said he was worried about the nurses moving him and he told Jordan how they had almost dropped him. He told the story of the two little nurses lifting one side of him while the two big ones lifted the other. He said, "Wouldn't you think it would have made sense to have put one short one and one tall one on each side?"

Jordan agreed and he laughed when I told him how Dawson had told us the story, naming the nurses "Little Miss Muffet," "Too Tall Jones" and such.

Jordan said, "Dawson, would you feel more comfortable if I went with you?"

"Yeah. Could you?"

"Sure, and I'll definitely see to it that they don't drop you."

Dawson smiled at him and simply said, "Thanks," but I saw a tremendous amount of admiration and gratitude in his eyes. I had seen that expression before. It was when Jack Donner had visited.

After Jordan had gone, Dawson looked at me and said, "That is sure nice of him to do that for me. He's pretty cool."

Dawson had discovered a new definition of what cool looked like. It looked like Jordan, a young man who had spent years in medical school learning how to make people well, yet had also learned how to make someone feel better just by his presence. And it looked like Jack Donner, an old man who visited a twenty-seven-year-old kid he did not know, just to give him some encouragement. Yes. Dawson had learned what it took to be cool.

Dawson was given a mild sedative in preparation for the colonoscopy, but I could see he was a little anxious waiting for them to take him. His eyes looked frightened. I stood close to his bed and held his hand. Jordan arrived just before they wheeled him out. Jordan was upbeat with Dawson, kind and considerate. He talked with him as he walked alongside. I walked with them all the way down a hallway where I had never been before, to a large elevator. I waited there while Jordan, the nurse, and the VAD tech tried to maneuver Dawson, all of his equipment, and themselves into the elevator. They finally managed to fit and I waved to Dawson as the doors closed. "I'll see you in a little bit, Dawson." This was nearly unbearable for me, watching him go through this. Yes, I would change places with him. I would. I wanted to spare him. I wanted him to be well. I wanted him to come home. I wanted him to have a life. And it would be a new, meaningful life, for I had seen that Dawson had learned what life was all about. He knew it was not about how many risks you could take or how many crazy things you could do or how much fun you could have. It was how you could help someone else. It was how you could open your heart to care for a stranger.

I was relieved when, from the waiting room, I saw him being wheeled back to his room. I hurried to meet him there. I was so glad it was over. Now he could relax without a pending procedure to worry about. Now he could have some broth or a popsicle. And maybe we were about to find the cause of his digestive problems and the doctors would go on to remedy it. Maybe we would know something soon.

When Dr. Walker arrived, I was waiting with nervous anticipation thinking about what he was going to tell us. "Well, we found nothing significant," he said.

Oh, God! Not that again.

"You saw nothing?"

"Well, there were some signs of ischemia."

"I heard that word before. What does it mean again?"

"It is an indication of low blood flow."

"So what can you do about that?"

"I'm going to discuss it with the team of doctors on Dawson's case. I'll get back with you later."

When Dawson's nurse came in, Dawson said, "I can have something to eat now, right?"

"No," she said. "You'll have to wait because Dr. Walker told me they might be doing an angiogram."

"What?" I said. "An angiogram? Why?"

"To check his blood flow."

But when Dr. Harris and Dr. Thompson came by, they seemed reluctant to order the angiogram. They felt it was quite unlikely that Dawson could have low blood flow while on the VADs. Dr. Thompson finally said, "Well, we've checked everything else." Dawson was looking at her when she said, "Let's go ahead and do it today."

"Today?" So much for thinking we were done with procedures. And we had thought he was going to be able to eat. So much for that, too. Trying not to show how disappointed I was that we were not through for the day, I casually said to Dawson, "Papa had that done before." I didn't tell him how much my father had hated it. The procedure involved inserting a catheter into the artery in the groin and injecting it with a dye that would show under x-ray. The flow along the blood vessels can then be studied. After the procedure, it was vital that the patient lie flat for several hours. It was that which my father found unbearable and I knew Dawson would, too. They both had difficulty breathing in that position.

The nurse informed us that the angiogram was scheduled for late in the afternoon. In one respect that was good, for Bill would be with me this time when they wheeled Dawson out of his room. It was also good that there would be no long wait for the results, for the doctors would immediately see on the screen what it was they were looking for.

When it was over, as I had expected, Dawson was quite upset at having to remain flat. He tried to coax the nurse into letting him sit up, but she explained the necessity for staying on his back. In addition to his breathing discomfort, he said the clamp they had on his groin was the most painful thing he had ever felt. And this was all for nothing. The angiogram, of course, was negative. There was no indication that he had low blood flow.

Periodically, an intern or a nurse came in to examine the entry site for a possible hematoma or excess bleeding. They said it was looking fine, but the intern said that he could understand why Dawson was experiencing such pain. The clamp was tightly pressed against a nerve. One nurse became quite upset with him because he insisted that she raise his head slightly. She did it though she did not want to and she told us that she would not be responsible if anything happened.

Nurse Suzann came in and was talking with me and joking with Dawson like she always did. She lifted up the sheet to check the site and screamed, "Oh, no!"

I gasped and Dawson looked terrified. "What is it?"

"Nothing," she said. "It looks fine. I was just kidding with you, Dawson."

Dawson did not laugh, neither did I. It appeared we had lost our sense of humor. *Was it any wonder?*

Chapter Thirty

Saturday, October 19....Days in Hospital:74....Days on VADs:69

Bill, look. I have never seen those before. Have you?" Bill and I were walking past the nurses' station on our way to Dawson's room when I noticed a row of binders on a bookshelf. They had the patients' last names on them and obviously contained their hospital records. Each patient had one binder with their name handwritten vertically down the spine, except there were four extra-wide ones labeled "Bell." "That just shows how much he's been through," I said, "and how long he's been here. He's gone through so much, Bill, things just have to start shaping up soon. How much more can his body take? I am getting so scared."

"I know, but it'll start getting better. You'll see. He'll be O.K."

"Do you believe that?"

"Yes," he said with assurance. He took a quick glance back at the binders, a visual representation of the last several weeks of our lives. "C'mon," he said, "let's go see him."

Dawson's fever was up and he looked a little flushed, but he greeted us with a smile. His nurse said, "I was just telling Dawson that we have a VCR available on this floor. If you have any movies you want to bring in, you can use it."

"Thank you. I had heard that," I said, "but we have not used it yet. Dawson, would you want to see a movie?"

"Yeah, I'd like that." I asked him if there were any in particular that he'd like to see and he said he couldn't think of any at the moment. "Whatever you want," he said. "You decide."

That afternoon, Bill and I went to the video store and bought three movies. When we returned, the nurse went to find the VCR and when she came back with it, Bill moved the VAD unit aside so she could wheel it into the room. She pushed the cart over to the corner, in front of the sink and asked if we'd like the curtains closed. She turned off the lights and slid the glass door shut. Bill put a tape into the VCR and the words "Coming Attractions" appeared on the screen, just like we were at the movies.

But we were not at the movies and there was no forgetting that fact. By the time the second coming attraction had come on, I was acutely aware that whatever I was about to see would be uniquely affected by the circumstances under which I was watching. The attractions for a movie had come on with the words, "Year: 2022." I could not help but wonder what our lives would be like in the year 2022. I would be seventy-eight years old. Dawson would be fifty-three, the same age Bill was now. I picked up the jacket from this movie that I had seen years earlier trying to remember just what it was about; a father battling a crime boss for the life of his son.

The life of his son. The movie began. Against the backdrop of a night sky and a somber tune, the young man spoke. I was viewing every scene and hearing every word from my new perspective. Sitting with Dawson and Bill in our own private world, I listened and watched … the playful mischief of a dark-haired, nine year old boy … the father and his young son spending a day together talking about baseball and the Yankees. And though years ago when I had seen this movie I had found the characters intriguing, today, all I could think about was *my* son.

Scene after scene, dialogue with what seemed like personal messages for us. As the movie ends, the son, now grown, recounts the lessons he had learned. He had learned to give love and to get love and that the saddest thing in life was wasted talent and that the choices that you make will shape your life forever.

Sunday, October 20....Days in Hospital:75....Days on VADs:70

The little gorilla that Bill's mother and sister had given Dawson was now hanging in his window. He said he liked it there because it wouldn't get lost and he could always see it. And we could see it, too, as we drove up to the hospital. Now it was easy to tell which room was Dawson's and I still imagined that one day I would look up and see him standing in the window waiting for us.

"I feel better today," Dawson said.

"That's good and we have the first game of the World Series to watch today," Bill said. "The Braves and the Yankees."

"Maybe we can watch a movie, too. The VCR is still here."

"Sure, we can do that."

"How about *Babe?*" Dawson asked. We were all ready for a little lightheartedness.

Lightheartedness? This was lighthearted? ... A baby pig's mother is taken away for slaughter and the little pig whispers sadly, *"Goodbye, Mom"* ... Then he is taken away to be a prize in the state fair ... frightened, he's squealing until the tall, quiet farmer says soothingly, *"That'll do, pig."* ... As the farmer holds the pig and they look at each other eye to eye, the narrator tells us, *"The pig and the farmer regarded each other and for a fleeting moment something passed between them, a faint sense of some common destiny."* ... The farmer wins the pig, brings him home and puts him in the barnyard ... alone, the little pig cries, *"I want my mom."* ... The farmer's dog comforts the young pig, telling him, *"You've got to be a brave boy, now."* ... The farmer soon discovers the innocent pig's talents, but the pig gets sick and will die if he doesn't eat, so in an attempt to encourage him to eat, the farmer sings to him ... *"If I had words to make a day for you, I'd give you a morning golden and true ... I would make this day last for all time, then fill the night deep in moonshine."* ... The pig recovers and has the opportunity to help the farmer win a coveted trophy ... when the pig accomplishes an unprecedented feat for a pig and is awarded a perfect score, they look lovingly at each other, and the farmer, a man of few words, simply says, *"That'll do, pig. That'll do."*

"If I had words to make a day for you, my son ... "

Monday, October 21....Days in Hospital:76....Days on VADs:71

"Everyone should have their mother, their sister or their grand-mother as their nurse," Dawson said. "What I mean is, even though the nurses here are really nice and take good care of me, there is nothing like having someone who loves you and is with you because they want to be. You know, Mom, I always feel better when you're here."

"And I will always be here, Dawson. This is where I want to be, with you."

"I love you, Mom."

"I know. I love you, too, Dawson."

"Mom, can I have a hug?" He was sitting in the chair and I went to him and put my arms around him and he laid his head against my chest. As I stroked his hair, he said, "I get scared sometimes, Mom, 'cause it doesn't seem like I'm getting any better."

"I know. I get scared, too, sometimes, but I know you're going to be all right, Dawson. I know you are."

In a soft voice, he said, "Mom, sometimes I think I'm not going to make it." I held him tight, kissed the top of his head, and told him not to worry, and I assured him that everything was going to be all right. And I tried to assure myself, as well.

His stomach problems had worsened with the discontinuation of the antidiarrheal medications and his fever was up slightly. His ankles seemed more swollen than they had been, but when he asked me if I could get him some ice, I did. I did not debate whether I should get it or not, only where to get it. I had already gone to the cafeteria twice to get ice from there, and once from the locked room, so I decided to go to the nurses' lunch room, as I had been doing for the last few days. It was a very small room with a table and a couple of chairs. I knocked on the door, and when no one responded, I went in. I quickly got his ice from the machine and left.

As I was handing it to him, I saw that he was looking past me and a smile had come across his face. I turned around to see what he was seeing. "Nina! Welcome back. How was your vacation?"

"It was good," she said. "I want to thank you guys! I love my mobile. I'm sorry I didn't get to tell you sooner. My last day here got quite hectic."

"Oh, that's O.K.," I said. "We understand."

"Dawson, did you make the mobile?"

"Yeah, and my mom. We did it together."

"You did a great job. I have it hanging in my office."

"Oh, I'm so glad you like it," I said.

"And the card! It was so beautiful and it came at a time," she paused, "well, when it meant a lot to me." Dawson just beamed with pleasure hearing how much she liked our gift. When she left, I walked out of the room with her. She explained to me that on her last day before her vacation, she had been having quite a rough day. She said, "I had just broken up with my boyfriend of many years and I was questioning everything in my life, including my work here. When I got that card from you guys, it made me feel that what I'm doing is worthwhile. It could not have come at a better time. Thank you so much."

I had just finished telling Dawson what Nina's gift and our card had meant to her when Dr. Wiviott came in. He said he had reviewed the events of the weekend and was concerned. He had learned that Dawson's fever was up, the diarrhea had increased, and he was retaining fluid. Dr. Wiviott said, "His body is reacting, despite the steroids. What is troubling is that while the steroids did control the fever and rash for a while, his stomach problems persisted. But the fact that the endoscopy, the colonoscopy and the biopsies revealed nothing makes it appear that his problems must be a reaction to a medication. But I have never encountered this type of reaction to Vancomycin, and even if it is what he is reacting to, I am hesitant to discontinue it. We must take some action, but I am not comfortable taking him off the Vanco, for I know what will happen if he does have an infection that goes untreated. What I don't know is what will happen if he stays on a drug that he is allergic to."

"So what can we do?" I asked, desperate for a solution.

"I do have an idea, but I'm not sure about it. First, I want you to understand that I am not totally convinced that his problems are all due to the Vanco. But assuming they are, I checked into a new drug that has been shown to work on the same type of staph infection that the Vanco does. This new medication is in the trial stages and I am not even sure I can get it. We would have to apply under a 'compassionate use' protocol. Do you know what I mean?"

"Yes, I had hoped to get Dawson in on a compassionate use study a couple of years ago for his enlarged heart. I had talked to Dr. Thompson about it."

"How would you feel about trying it, Dawson?"

"O.K.," he answered.

I said, "Well, I know we have to try something. What is the drug called?"

"Synercid. I will continue to investigate it and confer with the others and I'll keep you informed. Dawson, you and your mom and dad discuss it, too, because if we decide to do it, we'll need your

permission. My opinion is that we should start as soon as we can."
When Bill called, I told him and he said if Dr. Wiviott recommended
it, that was good enough for him. He would agree to it.

The nurse informed us that because Dawson was retaining fluids,
his water and ice intake was going to be monitored and restricted to a
few ounces per hour. I looked over at Dawson and without a word we
shared our mutual feelings of discouragement. It had been bad enough
that he could only have ice and water, but he had accepted that. In
fact, he enjoyed his ice and I liked it that I could get it for him. Now,
that was taken away from us, too.

When Bill arrived, I told him of the new development. Dawson
said, "Now I can't have my ice anytime I want."

"And it had been working out so well, too," I said, "with me getting
it for him. We didn't have to wait around for the nurse to get to it."

Scowling at me, Bill said, "I can't believe you didn't see that he
was swollen."

"Well, I did."

"Then how could you have let him have all that ice? Andrea, I can't
believe you would do that!" Bill was not shouting at me, for he was not
one to shout, but he was looking and sounding quite upset with me.

Then, Dawson, more stern than I had ever seen him, said, "Dad,
don't talk to her like that. It's not her fault. It's mine."

I said, "But I should have known better."

"It's O.K.," Dawson said, and we all let the issue pass.

Matt arrived in time to watch the second game of the World Series
with us. The Yankees lost again, but the game was an enjoyable and
needed diversion. When we said good night to Dawson, he said, as
he had been saying every night, "I love you guys." And he blew me
a kiss.

Tuesday, October 22....Days in Hospital:77....Days on VADs:72

This morning, as soon as we entered ICU, I said to Bill, "The extra
VAD unit isn't here. You know, it's always right here in the hallway.
Why would it not be here? I wonder if they had to use it to replace
Dawson's unit for some reason. What else could have happened to
it?"

"I don't know, but I'm sure it's fine," Bill said, reassuringly.

I wasn't so sure, so it was the first question I asked Dawson's nurse
before I entered his room. She said, "A new patient was admitted last
night and he was put on the VADs. He got that one."

"So there will be another spare one available, though, right?"

"There should be."

Dawson was quite sleepy. He said he hadn't slept well during the night. "The nurses helped me lie on my side, but everything they do to me hurts."

Dr. Wiviott came in to tell us that he had applied for the Synercid. "We are hoping for approval tomorrow."

When he left, I said, "You know, Dawson, this could be the answer to our prayers."

"I know," he said.

Nina entered the room and I said to her, "I heard that someone else is on the VADs. Now there's no backup unit. I know there's supposed to be one. I had been told that in case there was an emergency with the one Dawson was on, there would always be a backup."

"That's true, but I don't think we have one," she said, "but I'll go check on that for you right now. I'll be back."

Dawson said, "Mom, would you scratch my back with the loofah? It's really itchy." I had bought a loofah to use on his itching, peeling skin, but the loofah was much too rough. So I bought a buff-puff which was gentler on his skin. He knew the puff was not a loofah, but he liked to call it that anyway. He liked the sound of the word and he kind of chuckled when he said it.

He had peeled so extensively that his skin was baby-soft and tender, so even the puff left pink scratch marks on his new skin. "Maybe some lotion would help the itching, Dawson. Do you want me to put some on your back?" After I rubbed his back with lotion, I said, "How about your feet? They're looking pretty dry." He carefully maneuvered himself from his side to his back, wincing.

As I rubbed the lotion into the cracked skin on his feet and toes, he said, "It tickles." I was pleased that, unlike the nurses, I could do something for him that did not hurt him.

"How are you today, Dawson?" Christy, the VAD tech, asked as she came into the room.

"O.K. A little tired."

"We might be starting on a new medication tomorrow," I said. "We've already applied for it. We're thinking it will be the answer to our prayers."

"That's great. I hope your prayers will be answered."

"Well, they have been so far. Just getting on the VADs was obviously a blessing from God."

Christy said, "It is so important to have faith. My boyfriend is very sick and I've been trying to get him to believe in prayers, but he is so … "

"Oh, I know what you mean. But prayers do work and they've proven it scientifically. I have a book that tells of all the studies and tests that have been done in scientific environments with believers and nonbelievers and they have proof that prayers do work."

I looked over at Dawson. He raised his eyebrows and Christy said, "That sounds like something that my boyfriend could relate to. Maybe if he heard that, he would be more open to going to this prayer group I've been trying to get him to."

"What is his illness?" I asked.

"He has a brain tumor."

"Oh, God, how awful. Would you want to borrow my book? I can bring it to you."

"Well, if you don't mind. Yes, I would like to read it. Thanks."

Nina returned to tell me that she had checked with the doctors about the VAD backup unit. She said, "They told me that they were not planning on getting one."

"What? I was told there had to be one."

"I know, and when I reminded them of that, they just kind of shrugged it off, but when I said, 'Mrs. Bell was asking about it,' they quickly changed their attitude. A unit will be here this afternoon. You know, every hospital patient needs a bird-dog looking out for him. Dawson has you. You are his bird-dog."

Wednesday, October 23....Days in Hospital:78....Days on VADs:73

"We got our approval. We can start the Synercid," Dr. Wiviott said, sounding excited. "We're going to get him on it this morning and stop the Vanco. And then we'll see. This should tell us something. If his symptoms subside off the Vanco, we will finally know that is what he has been reacting to."

I signed the permission for him, hoping desperately that this would prove to be our salvation. We so needed a blessing and this seemed to have come just in time. I could imagine a miraculous turnaround. It seemed truly possible now. I believed that his symptoms could just quickly come to a halt, we would have our answers, a solution and we would be on our way to his recovery.

Dawson was still feeling tired and his blood pressure was quite low. He had been requiring larger doses of the Neo to keep his pressure up. The nurse asked him if he felt light-headed and he said that he didn't. I was thankful for the Synercid and I already considered it a blessing, for it had given me real hope. And what seemed like the greatest blessing of all, was that I knew it gave Dawson hope, too. I could see it in his eyes. We had shared so much and had exchanged so many glances between us over the past months that I had come to know what was in his heart by looking into his expressive eyes.

When the nurse came in and hooked up the Synercid to his IV, she said, "This is pretty special stuff, Dawson."

"Yeah, I know. I'm feeling pretty hopeful about it."

A while later, a nurse came in who had been assigned to Dawson on other days. She was very nice and said, "I hear you're on a new medication, Dawson. I hope it works well for you." She was still smiling when she looked at me, but was looking rather sheepish. She said, "Mrs. Bell, I hope you understand what I'm going to tell you. I don't want it to sound mean." Dawson and I flashed a questioning look at each other. She said, "You really should not be going into the nurses' lunch room. It really is just for the nurses and when we take our breaks there, we sometimes discuss patients and things and we need to know it is our private place."

I was embarrassed, but I certainly understood and she was trying to tell me in the most tactful way. I said, "Oh, I understand. I never felt comfortable going in there, but one of the nurses told me I could. I guess I should have known better, though." I looked at Dawson and he looked guilty and apologetic.

She said, "I'm glad you understand. You take care, Dawson."

When she left, Dawson said, "I'm sorry, Mom. It's my fault. You told me you didn't think it was right. I should never have had you do that."

"Oh, Dawson, it's O.K. She was nice about it." We shared a smile, camaraderie, and so much more. We knew in the realm of things, how bad? We certainly could forgive ourselves.

He said, "She did seem like she was really trying to be nice. You know, Mom, I kind of give the nurses here a bad time. Sometimes they get upset with me 'cause I get kind of impatient and I ask for a lot of stuff."

"Oh, I'm sure they understand, Dawson. They know it's hard for you being here."

I had thought that they had understood, but that was until his afternoon nurse came on duty. She brought one of his medications in for him to take. It was in powder form and came in a small foil packet. She went to his sink and got some water in a paper cup and was about to shake the powder into it.

Dawson said, "Can I have ice water, instead? That medicine is pretty awful tasting, but if the water is really cold, it helps."

She looked annoyed by his request, but he went on to say, "Just the ice *"water ."* Without a word, she quickly turned and left. When she came back, she handed the cup to him and he said, "Oh, I didn't want the ice. Just the ice water, no ice chips. The powder gets stuck on the ice and then it's really hard to take."

"You said ice water. I can't get ice water without ice," she snapped.

"I'm sure I can do it," I said. "If you could just bring me another cup, I'll work it out."

She left in a huff and came back with a cup of ice-cold water, no ice. She poured the orange powder into the cup, gave it a stir, handed it to Dawson and turned to leave.

"Thanks," I said, but I could have lunged at her and ripped her eyes out. How dare she take an attitude with Dawson when all he'd had for days was rationed water and ice and foul-tasting medicine. Was it too much to ask for to try to have the medicine easier to take? Was that really too much to ask for? *Sometimes it feels like you and me against the world, Dawson.*

We were both back into our hopeful frames of mind by the time Bill and Matt arrived. We all enjoyed the fourth game of the World Series. It was the Yankees' second win, tying the series at two games apiece. I was glad, for that meant more games might be played. Because Dawson looked forward each day to watching them, I did not want the World Series to be over any sooner than it had to be and I felt unexplainably sad when I thought of it coming to an end.

Thursday, October 24....Days in Hospital:79....Days on VADs:74

I handed Dawson two cards in sealed envelopes. When he opened the first one and read it, he said, "Oh, I didn't realize that's what day it was." The front of the card showed a little man in a yellow raincoat, walking under a large, gray cloud, raindrops falling all around him. It said, *"You can't see it now"* ... and inside, the clouds were gone, the rain had stopped, and there was a sun shining in the blue sky. It said, *"but it's there."* I had written below it, *"Happy ½ Birthday! Love, Mom. Our prayers will be answered."*

I had always acknowledged the kids' half-birthdays when they were young. Claudia had said she was the only one of her friends who got gifts and cards for a half-birthday and I had continued through the years, somewhat. At times, when I had a little something to give them, I would give it as a half-birthday present. This was a tradition I had learned from my mother. Or was it the other way around? Hadn't I been the one to call my mother's attention to my half-birthdays and hadn't she simply responded? I had not only been a birthday brat, I had been a half-birthday brat, as well.

He then opened the second card. It had cupcakes on the front and my mother had added "½" in front of *"Birthdays are Magic."* Inside, it said, *"They cause wonderful things to happen."* She had written, *"To Dawson from Papa and Grandma."* I said, "They will be coming to see you tomorrow, but Grandma wanted you to have your card today."

Though there had been no magical improvement in Dawson's condition overnight, the doctors all agreed that it was too soon to expect any major changes. They felt it could take at least a week or more of being off the Vanco to see if it had any bearing on his condition.

The sun will come out, Dawson, and wonderful things will happen.

He was feeling about the same as he had the day before, maybe a "little bit stronger," he said, but still tired. He did not work with the physical therapist. He told her "everything hurts." She seemed to understand and left quietly.

We spent a relatively quiet day ourselves. He slept off and on. When he was awake, I willingly tended to his needs; blankets on, blankets off, ice packs on, ice packs off, slippers on, slippers off. I rubbed his back, brushed his hair and kept track of his rationed cups of ice. He said, "Mom, I'm sorry I make you do so much for me."

"Dawson! Please don't be sorry. I want to do everything I can for you."

"I know, but I feel like I ask too much of you."

"No, you don't. I'm glad that you ask. Dawson, I am so very happy that there are things I can do for you. That way, I know that my being here helps."

The most serious expression I had ever seen on him came over his face, he looked directly at me, his eyes intense, yet gentle and he said slowly and emphatically, "Mom, don't ever doubt it."

Friday, October 25....Days in Hospital:80....Days on VADs:75

"Hi, Grammah. Hi, Papa. Thanks for the card."

"I'm glad you liked it," my mother said. "How are you feeling?"

"O.K., but my voice is almost gone."

It was not unusual for Dawson to be hoarse and to speak in a breathy whisper, in fact, my mother had told him that he had sounded like the "Godfather." He had thought that was quite funny, but today he was more hoarse than usual.

My father said, "What's this, Dawson?"

"Oh, it's my loofah."

"I brought it to scratch his back with," I said.

"Do you want your back scratched, Dawson?" my dad asked. "I'll scratch it for you."

Dawson looked at me, smiled and said, "Yeah, O.K." and moved carefully onto his side.

"I'll be right back," I said. As I stood, my head began to ache and I was uncomfortably warm. I went to the waiting room and while there, I could feel a sore throat coming on. *I've got a cold!*

My mother came looking for me. "Are you all right?" she asked.

"No, I'm not. I'm feeling kind of lousy. I think I'm coming down with a cold! How can that be? I can't have a cold! What am I going to do? Not see Dawson? I can't do that, but I know I can't expose him to it. How could this happen?"

"I don't know. What are you going to do?"

"I guess I have to stay away from him. He can't afford to get it. I just can't believe this! I'm glad that you guys are here today and can help him with things, so I won't have to get too close to him."

"Sure, whatever he wants, we'll do it."

"I'm going to go back and tell him," I said, heading back down the hall. "Dawson, I think I'm getting a cold. I don't want you to get it, so I'm not going to get near you and I'm going to ask the nurse to give me a mask to wear." When he needed anything, my mother and father helped him. It was good they were there and they stayed until Bill arrived.

Dawson said, "Mom, if you don't feel well, you should probably stay home tomorrow and take care of yourself. And that way, too, Harley won't have to be locked up in the pen. You can take care of Harley tomorrow, and I'll be O.K. Dad will be here."

"And Claudia will be here, too," I said, "but I hate not to come."

"Mom, it's all right. You don't feel well. It will be good for you to take it easy tomorrow."

I had no choice but to agree. For though today I merely felt a cold coming on, I imagined that by tomorrow I would be much more contagious, coughing and sneezing. He seemed sincere in his desire to have me take care of myself and Harley, but I did not want to stay home and not be there with him. Trying not to show how upset I was, I changed the subject, saying, "There's no baseball game on tonight. They play tomorrow night, so do you guys want to watch *Forrest Gump?*" They said they would and Bill put it on.

For all the things that the movie was and for all the years and events it covered, the only scenes that had any meaning for me were the ones with Forrest and his mother. It seemed they had a special kind of relationship, a special kind of love and when his mother became ill, he went home to be with her. She was sitting up in bed and he was at her bedside, just like Dawson and me, only reversed.

"What's the matter, Mama?"

"I'm dying."

"Why are you dying?"

"It's my time. It's just my time. Don't you be afraid, sweetheart. Death is just a part of life, something we're all destined to do. I didn't know it, but I was destined to be your mama. I did the best I could."

"You did good."

"I will miss you, son."

"Mama died on a Tuesday."

When the movie was over, Dawson said he'd like to get up and sit in the chair and Bill and the nurse helped him. He asked that they slide the chair as close to the window as it could go. He was sitting as far from his bed as he could, which was a mere two steps, tethered as he was to the machine that was keeping his damaged heart pumping. Yet as I watched him gazing wistfully out at the magnificent sunset, I could see that he was, indeed, very far away. Was he somewhere in the what-could-have-been future, or perhaps, in the what-should-have-been past? I did not know. I did not ask him. I did not have to. I knew he was where he was seeing the true beauty of life and I could see he had found comfort in that iridescent peach and turquoise sky.

Chapter Thirty-One

Saturday, October 26....Days in Hospital:81....Days on VADs:76

I knew my decision to stay home because of my cold was the right one, but it definitely did not feel right. This was the first morning in more than eighty days that I had not awakened to prepare for a day at the hospital. It was the first day that I would not be with Dawson to take care of his needs and I would be forced to rely on others' assessment of his condition, rather than my own observation. I would have to count on Bill.

I was glad when I heard his shower running, relieved that he had not slept late. I had been hoping that he would get to the hospital before noon and when he came downstairs, I asked him what time he was leaving. I said, "I want to call Dawson. I'd like to tell him what time you'll be there."

"I should be leaving in a little bit," he answered.

I dialed the hospital and a nurse answered, "ICU."

"Hi, I'd like to talk to Dawson Bell. This is his mother."

"Hold on."

Waiting to hear his voice always filled me with such apprehension.

It was almost as if I stopped breathing until I heard his, "Hi." Today, an unusually long time passed before I heard, "Mrs. Bell, this is Elissa. I'm Dawson's nurse today."

"How is he?" I asked anxiously. "Is he all right?"

In her soft voice, she answered, "Well, he's having some problems this morning."

"What kind of problems?" I asked, as I looked to Bill shaking my head.

"Respiratory. His breathing is quite rapid and it is tiring him out, but I'll see if he can talk to you. Please hold on."

Placing my hand over the receiver, I said, nervously, "Bill, it doesn't sound good."

Finally, I heard Dawson say, "Hi." He was extremely hoarse and breathless.

"Hi, hon. You're having kind of a rough time this morning, huh?"

"Yeah," he said, sounding distressed.

"Well, I just wanted to let you know, hon, that Dad is on his way."

"O.K."

"You know I'm not coming today because of my cold, right? I wish I could be there, but I don't want you to get it."

"I know. It's O.K.," he said, sounding more out of breath with each word. Then he said, slowly, "Mom, I've gotta go."

"O.K., hon. You take care. Dad will be there soon." I hung up and said, "Bill, I should be going with you." I knew it would probably not make a difference in his condition that I was not going to be with him this one day, but for my own sake, I had a profound need to be there.

"You can't see him with that cold."

"I know, but maybe I could just sit in the waiting room. At least I'd be there to know how he was doing."

"Andrea, that wouldn't work. You'd want to go in to see him, and you know that you shouldn't. I'll keep you posted."

"All right. Are you ready to leave? You really should get going."

As Bill drove off, it just did not feel right that I was not going with him. But I was sure the nurses would actually think my staying home was a good idea, for they had been telling me to give myself a break and take a day off. "You shouldn't feel that you have to be here every day," one nurse had said. It wasn't that I *had* to be there, I *wanted* to be there. I guess she didn't understand.

There was no doubt Juana, the chaplain, had understood. I had been stunned to learn that her teenaged son had died waiting for a bone marrow transplant. But even she had stressed that I take care of myself. She had said to me, "I know that your only concern is for Dawson, but all of this can take quite a toll on you, too." Everyone's concern for me was reasonable and obviously well intended. However, that could not change the fact that being with Dawson was where I would always choose to be. Today, that choice was taken out of my hands.

Bill called shortly after he arrived at the hospital. Claudia was already there. He said Dawson was sitting up in the chair and he was somewhat out of breath, but otherwise he seemed fine. I was not feeling fine and I spent most of the day on the couch dozing off from time to time between saying rosaries and worrying about Dawson.

I did not hear from Bill again until six-thirty, but this time he said, "He's not doing well."

"What do you mean?"

"They're thinking about putting him on dialysis."

"That must mean his kidneys aren't functioning. Did they say that? Are his kidneys failing?"

"I'm not sure."

"Oh, Bill, this isn't good. You'd better get back to him."

An hour and a half passed until Bill called back. This time he said, "Now they're talking about putting him on the respirator."

"Oh, no. What is happening? Bill, what are they telling you?"

"Well, he's having a hard time breathing."

"Yeah, but why? What is going on?" *God, how could this be happening to him on the one and only day that I am not there!*

"They just told me that he needed to be on the respirator and that they had talked to him about it, but he doesn't want it."

"He doesn't have a choice, does he?"

"Well, he has to give his permission. They can't do it without it."

"I understand that he hates that thing, but he has to let them do it."

"I know."

"Oh, God, they'll have to sedate him and then it will be that same thing again, trying to get him off the sedation and the respirator."

"I know."

"Bill, if they say he needs to be on it, they have to do it."

"I know, but the doctors talked to him for a long time and explained that to him and he refused to agree to it."

I knew he hated the respirator, but aside from that, I knew he didn't want to be sedated. I did not say it, but Dawson had told me he didn't want to ever be sedated again. He had said he felt if he were, he would never wake up.

"I'm going to go talk to him," Bill said.

"O.K., call me back as soon as you can."

I knew Dawson must agree to this, for it did not seem likely there was any chance that he could get by without the assistance of the respirator. This seemed far more serious than the time, a while back, when Dr. Harris had come quite close to putting him back on it. That day, soon after he had told us what he might have to do, Bill and I had left for church. When we had returned to Dawson's room, Dr. Harris had said to us, sounding surprised and looking slightly puzzled, "He seems to be looking better." Appearing to be finding this hard to believe, he asked me, "Does he look better to you?" He asked Dawson, "Do you feel better?" Then he turned and looked at the monitor. "He is better!" he said. "Dawson, you're fine now. We won't have to put you back on the respirator, after all." Dawson had looked at me as if to say, "See, you went to church and now I'm better." I was wondering if, perhaps, I should go to church now, but not wanting to leave the house, I said a rosary and sat nervously waiting for Bill to call back.

When he did, he said, "I told Dawson that he had to let them put him on the respirator and he said to me very clearly, 'Dad, I don't want it.' Then I said to him, 'Please, Dawson, do it for me,' and…"

"And what, Bill?"

"And he said, 'O.K.'"

"Oh, Bill. So they're going to do it?"

"Yeah."

"Dawson is doing it for you, because you asked him."

"I know. I'm going to stay here with him tonight."

"Oh, you are? He'll be sedated, though, right?"

"Yeah, but I promised him that I would be right outside in the waiting room. I told him I wouldn't leave."

"Oh, that was good. O.K., O.K. That's good that he knows you're there. Oh, Bill."

"Try not to worry. Claudia is going to be leaving soon and she's going to the house to stay there with you."

"O.K., good. Has she left yet?"

"No, she's getting ready to. Why don't you and Claudia sleep in my bed? There's no sense in you having to sleep on the couch."

"O.K., thanks. So she's leaving soon?"

"Yeah, right now."

When I hung up from Bill, I called my mother. She tried to console me, reminding me of how things always had a way of working out for Dawson.

"Yeah, I know that's true and he always does bounce back … when they had been worried about his kidneys before, they did improve … and his failing liver function, that turned around. And you know that lady I met who had been on the VADs, she had to go back on the respirator and she made it through. Yeah, Dawson can do it, too," I said, trying to believe my own words. I heard a car pull up. "Ma, Claudia just got here. I better go. I'll talk to you later."

When I opened the door, Claudia was coming up the front steps, carrying a big cardboard box. I recognized the box. It was the one that had been in Dawson's room that we had kept all our stuff in. As she came in and put it down, she said, matter-of-factly, "They needed room for the respirator, so they told us to take this." She didn't seem to know what this box and the things in it meant to me, but she must have seen something in my expression, for she added in a comforting tone, "Mom, you can always bring the stuff back when he gets better." I could not respond. I could only stare at that box and its contents; our origami book, our book of games, our notebook, the puzzle we had not yet worked on. This was our box of dreams and hopes.

"Mom, are you O.K.?"

"I'm just so worried, Claudia."

"He'll be all right, Mom. You know Dawson."

"How did he seem today?"

"He seemed O.K., but when Dad put his slippers on him, I could see that it was hurting him just to barely lift his feet. But when he saw that I had been watching him, he made a funny face, you know how he does, rolling his eyes. It was as if to say, 'Whew, that was a rough one.' Then he kind of smiled at me."

"I should have been there," I said.

"He understood and after he got back in bed, he slept a lot, so it was pretty quiet there. I just knitted all day."

"Dad said that if we wanted to, we could sleep in his bed. Do you want to do that? He said there's clean sheets in the linen closet."

"Yeah, that's fine." We went upstairs, changed the sheets, and got into bed, Claudia, Harley and me.

Sunday, October 27....Days in Hospital:82....Days on VADs:77

I woke up several times during the night thinking about calling the hospital. I was able to refrain from doing so because I was sure Bill would call me if there were any changes. I told myself that not hearing from him must be a good thing.

By morning, I was quite anxious for his call and I expected he would be calling soon. I was lying in bed saying a rosary, Claudia and Harley were still asleep when suddenly, Harley began to bark, jumped off the bed and ran to the door. I sat up and saw Bill's truck coming down the driveway. Claudia was now awake and I said to her, "Dad's home," and I quickly got out of bed, went downstairs and met him at the front door. "How is he?" I asked.

"He's still sedated."

"But is he O.K.?"

"He's about the same. I just came home to shower and I'm going right back."

"I'm going with you."

"What about your cold?"

"It's not that bad. I'm a lot better than I was yesterday and I have to be with him."

Riding to the hospital, I said to Bill, "I have been waiting for the day when we would arrive to see him standing in the window watching for us. Even though he hasn't been able to do that yet, at least he had been awake and waiting for us. But now ... oh, Bill, I can't bear to see him sedated and on that respirator again. This is a horrible setback. This is just too awful. I am so scared."

Bill said, sternly, "Andrea, don't give up."

Walking into his room and seeing him hooked up to that respirator made it nearly impossible to remain optimistic. Though the respirator tube was taped to his mouth, I could see blood around it. "Are his lips bleeding?" I asked his nurse.

"No. Evidently when they were intubating him, he bit his tongue."

"His tongue is bleeding? He must have been fighting that respirator, even sedated."

"Yes, but he's calm now. We're keeping him comfortable."

"What happened to cause all this?"

"Well, he's quite acidotic." I knew that was what the lady on the VADs had experienced and she had recovered from it. "What causes that?" I asked.

"It's partly due to his failing renal function."

"But he's on dialysis, now, right?"

"Yes."

"He's had renal failure before," I said, "and it came back. It could come back again."

"Yes, it could."

"What caused it to fail?"

"Most likely, his ongoing sepsis."

"What is that? I've heard 'systemic' in reference to his condition. What is sepsis? Is that the same?"

"Systemic means affecting the entire bodily system. Sepsis is bacteria in the blood."

"He has bacteria in his blood? Does that mean that he does have an infection? The doctors were just about convinced that his symptoms were due to an allergic reaction. There was only the suspicion of a *contained* infection on the VADs. So why did he all of a sudden get worse? Was it taking him off the Vanco?"

"I don't think so. He had already started in this direction before switching him to the Synercid. I think that's why they tried it."

"I just don't understand how he got so bad so quickly."

"Well, everything about his condition has been quite a mystery all along. But we are aggressively treating him for all of this. We are transfusing him right now." I was grateful for all they were doing, but I could see that when the nurses tended to him, he grimaced in pain. He only appeared comfortable as long as no one touched him, so I sat quietly beside his bed feeling inconsolably helpless.

My mother, father, and Claudia arrived later that morning. It seemed they soon sensed that not only was there nothing they could do for Dawson, there was little they could do for me, as well. They stayed outside his room most of the day, looking sad, worried and unsure.

Claudia was scheduled to work that night and since there was no change in Dawson's condition, she said, hesitantly, "Mom, I think I'm going to leave. I don't know what else to do. Is that O.K.?" I told her that it was, but when she left, I felt uneasy that she was going to be three hours away from us. My mother and father left soon after and Bill and I went to five o'clock mass. For the first time, this magnificent church did not seem quite so vast. Something had changed. It was as if its immenseness had been dwarfed by the absolute enormity of what I was facing. And as I knelt and prayed, I found that my prayers were changed, as well. Unlike my prayers that had previously burst forth from my soul, these now lingered there and remained deep within my heart.

When we returned to the hospital, the doctors and nurses encouraged us to go home and try to get some rest. They were aware that Bill had stayed in the waiting room the night before and likely had not had much sleep. Reluctantly, we decided to leave.

When we said good night to Dawson, it was the first night in weeks that we did not hear, "I love you guys." But we knew. We knew.

Monday, October 28....Days in Hospital:83....Days on VADs:78

It was dark when we drove up to the hospital. I looked up at Dawson's window. The lights in his room were on and I could see his little gorilla. As we took the elevator up, that familiar anxiety was coming over me. Every time I had approached ICU over these past three months, I had felt fearful of what I would find, but today I was feeling nearly paralyzed by that fear. I took a deep breath, let out an audible sigh, looked at Bill, then managed to walk through ICU's double doors. We were not yet near his room when a nurse came over to me and said, "You're here. That's good. We called you. I guess you were already on your way."

"You called us?"

"Yes. He's worse."

"No. No," I moaned, backing away from her.

"He's much worse," she said.

'No! Don't say that! Please don't say that," I cried. "Oh, Bill. No, he can't be worse. He can't be."

"You must go to him," she said as she put her arm around me, gently leading me to his room.

"Dawson. Oh, Dawson." He was lying still, but he looked the same as he had yesterday. His mouth was still bleeding, but he didn't look worse. *Maybe he's not worse. Maybe it's not true. Oh, God, please make it not be true.* Bill and I went and stood beside his bed. I knew Bill was crying, though he was not making a sound and I saw no tears. He had begun to wipe his eyes, continually stopping the tears before they ran down his cheeks.

When Dr. Harris arrived, he confirmed what the nurse had said, "He seems to have taken a turn … for the worse."

"There must be something you can do," I begged.

"Well, we will do everything we can. We are continuing his medication and we are still transfusing him."

"So there is still hope," I pleaded.

"Not much. It is looking very bad."

"No. No. Oh, God, no."

"Well, let's just see how he does today. I'll check back with you later."

I said, "Bill, I think I should call my mother." He agreed. When she answered, I cried, "Ma, he's not doing well."

"Oh, no. What should I do?'

"I think maybe you should come down."

"Your father isn't here. He already left for golf. Remember Rusty had invited him a while back? It's that fire department tournament."

"Oh, I don't know. Yeah, now I remember. Where is it, Redwood City?"

"Yeah, I think so. What should we do?"

"I think I should call Daddy. I can get him on Rusty's cell phone. Do you know their starting time? Oh, I guess I can't worry about that," I moaned, "but I hate to have to do this."

"I guess you have to. Call me back."

I called Rusty and told him how things were looking, apologizing for having called. "I wasn't sure what to do," I said. "I'm just so scared."

"Don't worry about it, Andrea. It's O.K. I'll bring your dad home. We'll leave right away."

I called my mother and asked her to call Claudia. My mother called me back to tell me that she hadn't been able to get a hold of her. She had gotten her answering machine, but had not left a message. I knew she had worked the midnight shift the night before and must be sleeping, so after I had tried calling her two more times and she still had not answered, I called Tracy at work. I told him I was sorry to have called him there and I tried to explain my urgency. He said that he would go right over to Claudia's and wake her and that they would be at the hospital as soon as they could.

O.K., I said to myself. *O.K., I'm taking care of things. That means that my mind is still working. That's good.* And that was good to know, for I was terrified that I might lose my mind. That terror was real. It was not some, I-think-I'll-go-crazy, off handed expression. No. I felt it could happen to me in the true sense of the word. I was fearing that this decline in Dawson's condition was going to be too much for my mind to handle. After living in a controlled state of panic for the past three months dreading every day that his condition might worsen, now that it was actually happening, I was afraid of what it would do to me. But I knew that I should not be worrying about myself, for I believed Dawson still needed me and he needed to sense my strength beside him.

Bill and I were sitting close to him, Bill on one side of the bed, me on the other, like we had done so many times before. The nurse came in from time to time to change his IVs and hang bags of blood to transfuse. It was encouraging to see they were still treating him. Surely, that meant there was still hope. After all, he was alive. And as long as he was alive, there would always be hope. That hope and my desperate need to be strong for Dawson helped me to stay in control of my mind and by doing so, I was able to control my emotions, as well as my sanity. *I will stay strong, Dawson. I will do it for you, hon. I can do it for you.*

I put my hand into my jacket pocket. *My rosary beads.* The mother who I had seen praying her rosary while her daughter lie dying, came to my mind. I had not, as yet, said a rosary, openly, as she had, but I was struck by the fact that, today, I had not said a rosary at all. I thought, *How can that be, at a time like this? Why am I not praying? After all we have been through, after all the blessings we have received and all the prayers that have been answered, how can I now be unable to pray? Have I turned my back on God?*

Searching my soul for answers, I realized it was precisely because I did believe in God, that I was not praying. I had not turned away from Him, to the contrary, I had turned and faced Him and had lain our fate at His feet.

"Bill, I think we should call a priest." Bill looked startled. "I just want a priest to see Dawson. Maybe we can get Father Cassidy. What do you think? Can I call St. Dominic's?"

"Yeah, do that."

Father Cassidy was not available. I was told that Father Xavier would come to see Dawson and he arrived shortly after in his long habit, carrying a bible. I told him how serious Dawson's condition was and I said he had not seen a priest nor had he received communion, but he had talked to the chaplain. I said, "We all have renewed faith since coming here and Dawson seems to have been enlightened." He went to Dawson, stood beside his bed and prayed, *"Lord, relieve the sufferings of our brother, Dawson, on whom we lay our hands in your name."* Then he was silent as he placed both his hands on Dawson's head and held them there. Then he reached into his pocket and took out a small vial of oil. *"God of mercy, ease the sufferings and comfort your servant, Dawson, whom the church anoints with this holy oil."* Then he touched Dawson's forehead and Dawson's hands, saying, *"Through this holy anointing may the Lord who frees you from sin save you and raise you up. Father, with your love and mercy look upon our brother, Dawson. In the midst of illness and pain, may he be united with Christ, who heals body and soul; may he know the consolation promised to those who suffer. We ask this through Christ our Lord, Amen."*

"Thank you, Father. Thank you."

"May the Lord be with you," he said as he left.

"I think that was good, Bill, don't you?" I said, my heart breaking, but feeling so thankful that I had thought of doing that.

"Yeah," Bill said, wiping his eyes, which were now very red, "it was good."

Dr. Wiviott came in looking quite serious and sad. He said, "We're going to stop the Synercid and restart the Vanco."

"Was it taking him off the Vanco that made him get worse?"

"It's hard to say. He was headed in this direction before we stopped it. He was already showing signs of the metabolic acidosis. His condition is very guarded." My mind seemed to be closing down on me and I asked no more questions of him. I was so afraid of the answers.

Bill called his mother and sister. Soon after they arrived, my mother and father also arrived. Dr. Harris said, "We're going to open up Dawson's room to the room next door, so you can have it for your family." The nurses moved the hospital bed out of the connecting room and brought in chairs and a stool. Shortly after that, Claudia and Tracy arrived. We took turns sitting or standing by Dawson's bedside and sitting in our private waiting room. When Matt arrived, he sat alone with Dawson, close to him.

It had been a long day and by early evening, one by one, everyone started to leave. Bill's mother and sister left, then Matt and then my mother and father. Claudia and Tracy stayed, but decided to get some dinner. They came back with slices of pizza and found Bill alone with Dawson, and me asleep, sitting atop the stool. They thought it amazing that I had not fallen off and they gently woke me. Bill and

I tried to eat, but we had no appetite. Claudia and Tracy stayed with us until almost nine o'clock.

Once alone, Bill and I sat quietly beside Dawson. He seemed to be resting comfortably. It wasn't until after ten when Bill, looking exhausted, said, "Andrea, what should we do? Should we go home and come back early in the morning?"

My mind was numb. All I could do was nod. We said good night to Dawson and to the nurses and slowly walked out of ICU. We were almost at the elevator when I stopped. "I can't leave," I said. "I'm staying."

We turned around and Bill walked me back to Dawson's room. I told his nurse that I just could not leave him. "We'll get a cot for you," she said. "We'll put it in the adjoining room."

"Oh, you don't have to do that," I said. "I can just sit in the big chair."

"No, no, no," she insisted.

Bill said, "Are you going to be all right?"

I nodded that I would. "I just have to be with him. You'll be here early, won't you?"

"Yeah, I will. Good night, Andrea."

"Good night, Bill." I quietly said to Dawson, "Mom's here, Dawson. Mom's here." I wanted to touch him, but I was remembering how he had grimaced when the nurses had touched him and I did not want to hurt him. "Oh, Dawson. I love you, hon. I love you."

I went to the nurse and asked her if she would call Juana. I knew if he could hear her voice, it would bring comfort to him and she would want to see him. Juana was not on call, so another chaplain came and I asked her to be sure to tell Juana that we had called and had requested her to come to see Dawson. "She has to know," I said.

I could not believe this was actually happening. After all that we had been through; the miracle of him surviving long enough to get here, all those tests and all those prayers and everyone trying so hard to get him well and how brave and how strong he had been and how he had found new meaning to his life ... after all of this ... how could this happen?

As the nurse wheeled in the cot, I was reminded of the night Tammy had wheeled one into our room in the Transitional. I remembered how happy Dawson had been to have me there with him ... how we had waved good night to each other ... and how he had hugged me and had told me he loved me … and how I had promised God that I would be forever grateful for all the beautiful days Dawson and I had shared, no matter what else happened. *Forever grateful, no matter what. That was what I had vowed, wasn't it? … And I am grateful,* I cried, *but Dear God, Dear God! Tell me! Is this the end?*

Chapter Thirty-Two

Tuesday, October 29....Days in Hospital:84....Days on VADs:79

It was 4:00 A.M. when Dana, the doctor from the transplant department, came in to see Dawson. I sat up and watched as she stood by Dawson's bed, writing her notes, making her report for the day. Previously, her reports had worried me the most. I used to hope that whenever she would come by to see him that he would look strong for her and that he would tell her he was feeling well. Now, there was no possibility, no hope of that. I no longer felt vulnerable to her stringent assessment of his condition. There was no fear of what she might report, for there would be no transplant evaluation to consider today. Nothing she could say could hurt Dawson now. "How are you doing?" she asked me, stopping between Dawson's room and mine.

"I don't know. Terrible, I guess."

"I'm so sorry," she said. "You know, it isn't looking good. We had continued the aggressive treatment on him yesterday in the hopes that he would respond." I was looking at her, waiting, but I knew what she was about to say. "He has not responded."

"He still could, though, couldn't he? Couldn't he respond today?" I asked, pleading for the answer I knew I would not hear.

"It is not likely. We could continue with the support as we did yesterday. You know, we want to give him every chance, but at this point, I feel it is quite futile. You are going to have a decision to make. You and your husband will have to discuss it."

"What are you saying, that we'll have to make the decision to discontinue his treatment?"

"Yes."

"Oh, God. I can't ... how can I ... I can't do that to him ... after all these months of trying so hard ... I can't."

"I understand how difficult this is for you. I can imagine what you are going through."

"I don't think you can possibly imagine what this is like for me. Dawson and I have struggled so hard for so long."

"Because I see so much of this here," she said, sighing, "I have often wondered what I would want, whether I would want to have time like Dawson had, or would I rather avoid the prolonged pain and struggle and just go quickly."

"Though some of these days here have been the worst days of my life, I would not give them up for anything, for others have been the most beautiful I have ever known. Since his heart condition, I always knew there was the possibility that I could lose him suddenly. And before that, he could easily have been killed without warning on his motorcycle. I know that would have been easier for him than spending these past three months in ICU, but we both would have missed the most precious moments of our lives. So as difficult as these months were, I believe he would not have given them up either."

"Then I'm glad for both of you that you had that time. Well, I'll be talking to you later and I know Dr. Harris will be, too. Take care."

When Bill arrived a couple of hours later, I told him what Dana had said. He put his hands to his eyes and began to wipe them and continued wiping and wiping, but was unable to keep up with the flood of tears. His entire face was wet with sorrow. He went to Dawson and leaned over him and put his arm across Dawson's chest, holding him, then he laid his head next to Dawson's. The sight was too painful to watch. I went back to my cot and sitting on its edge, I put my face in my hands and cried for Dawson, for Bill, for myself and for all the things that should have been, but were never going to be. It was over. It was all over. Dawson's precious life. My life.

Dana came in and talked to Bill and me around eight o'clock that morning. When she left, she said, "I know you will need some time to think about this. Take all the time you need."

"Thank you," I said, but Bill said nothing to her. He had not spoken a word while she was there.

Bill and I went to Dawson and we sat on each side of him, as we always did. We were both quiet. I was looking at Dawson, at his arms, his hands, his fingers. I was looking at his face, his eyebrows, his eyelashes, his goatee, his shiny hair. When I looked up, I saw that Bill was looking at me. He extended his hand out to me, reaching across Dawson. I reached out to him and our hands joined and rested on Dawson. Crying, but still looking at me, Bill said, "I'm sorry. Andrea, I am so sorry." I could see the anguish in his eyes and the regret and remorse in his heart. I knew he was telling me he was sorry I was losing Dawson, but I knew he was saying much more than that. I knew he was saying he was sorry for the part that his own behavior had played in influencing the choices Dawson had made in his life. I knew he was saying he was sorry for the heartache he had caused me during our life together and I knew, upon all that was sacred as Dawson lay there between us, that he was saying he would never hurt me again.

By noon, my mother and father, Claudia and Tracy and Matt had arrived. I could see how terribly upset Matt was, so I told him that if he would like to have Jenn with him, he should call and ask her to come. Bill's friend, Carlos, came by and stayed a short while, but I was incapable of visiting with anyone. I needed to talk to Dr. Harris and I went to find him. He motioned me over to the small desk to the side of the nurses' station. He rolled the chair out for me and he sat casually on the desk. I said, "Please tell me, do you think there is a chance that Dawson could come through this? Any chance at all?"

"Yesterday, I thought it might be possible, but today, no. His blood is so acidotic … it isn't even blood."

I was silent for a moment, then finally I asked, "What do we do?"

"Well, even if we stop all medications and the respirator, his heart will continue to beat indefinitely because of the VADs."

"So what are you saying?"

"We will have to shut off the VADs."

"Oh, God," I moaned. "Turn his VADs off?" *How can we do that? The miracle that had saved his life? How could we ever do that?* I was remembering how horrific I had thought those VADs were when I had first seen them and how worried I had been that Dawson would not be able to accept them. But he had accepted them so well and had come to protect them and revere them. He had even come to joke about them. I was remembering the day Dawson was sitting in the chair and he said to Dr. Harris, "Hey, Doc, how're my VADs hangin' today?" It had taken the doctor quite by surprise. "Good, Dawson," he had answered, laughing, "very good." They were *his* VADs. They had become part of him and it was almost as if he had come to feel proud of them. He had eagerly welcomed a doctor from China who was interested in examining them. And Dawson had his plans to make a pad for them so that they would be more comfortable for someone else. He had come to learn how to unkink them if they started to beep. He knew they were his lifeline and he respected them and all those who were involved. *How could we ever turn off his VADs? How could we do that to him? God, help us.*

Dr. Harris broke into my thoughts. "You must prepare to say good bye to him," he said. "It is time to say good bye."

"I know. I know."

"It should be today. It can be later today, but it should be today." I nodded, stood and walked back toward Dawson's room. Suddenly I felt an unexplainable tightening, almost a burning sensation around my wrist. I had become uncomfortably aware of my watch and I began to rub my arm ferociously. I had to get it off and when I got back to Dawson's room I quickly removed it and threw it in my purse.

Bill was alone with Dawson and I told him what Dr. Harris had said. He said, "I want to hear it from Dr. Wiviott. I won't do anything until I hear it from him."

"I'll see if I can find him," I said, trying hard to be brave. I felt I had to be strong because I wanted to be sure to do everything right for Dawson and I wanted him to be proud of me, the way I was so proud of him for his bravery. I was hoping that I could do all this with dignity, yet I was amazed at how calmly I was behaving. It really was true, I could do anything for Dawson. I went to the phone and called Nina. I asked her if she could give Dr. Wiviott the message that we wanted to see him. Then, as if someone else were uttering the words through me, I heard my voice asking, "What will happen when we turn off his VADs?" She did not answer right away and I stammered, "I mean ... will he ... will he ... continue to breathe ... will he make any sounds ... will his heart ... beat on its own ... for anytime at all ... or ... will it ... happen right away?"

"He may gasp a little, but most likely he will be quiet and it will not take long."

"O.K., thank you, Nina." I hung up the phone and leaned into the wall. Dr. Harris came over to me and I moaned, "In the realm of human suffering, this must be the most..."

"He isn't in any pain now," Dr. Harris said, assuming this would console me. "We are keeping him comfortable."

"I don't mean his suffering," I groaned. "I mean mine."

I went back to Dawson and sat beside his bed. The nurse who had reprimanded me for having used the lunchroom came by. She said, "Mrs. Bell, I am so sorry. Here, I've written down the name of a book that helped me when I lost my mother. I hope it will help you."

Another nurse came in to see me. She said, "We were all feeling so terrible that day Dawson wasn't doing well and you weren't here. We were saying, 'Why did this have to happen to him on the first day his mother didn't come?' After you had been with him every day, we felt so bad for both of you. We were all thinking of you. We are so sorry." Many nurses came by throughout the day. They all told me how sad they felt and they all hugged me, some cried.

When back in our adjoining waiting room, I began to pace and ramble out loud. "Why did this happen when I wasn't here? Why did I get a cold now? Did he get my cold? Is that what made him so sick? Is this my fault?" I had expressed that fear yesterday and everyone had assured me that there was no connection, but I could not get that thought out of my mind. After all, he had touched my hand that day. "Oh, Dawson, how did this happen?" I continued pacing and circling the room. I was vaguely aware there were others around me, but I was the only one speaking. I began to drone out the story of a documentary I had seen where an elephant's baby had died. Standing over his lifeless body, the mother had unfurled her huge trunk, extended it up into the air and had wailed, trumpeting her pain to the heavens. "I feel like that mother," I wailed. "I want to scream to Heaven. I want Heaven to hear my cries of pain. There can be no greater pain than this. In all the earth's animal kingdom, the loss of a mother's baby ... it is universally supreme ... a mother and her child ... no greater bond exists." Still, no one spoke, for there was nothing anyone could say to me. Nor was there anything anyone could do.

Dr. Wiviott arrived, having received my message and went directly into Dawson's room. Bill was with Dawson and I went in to be with them. Dr. Wiviott, looking directly at Bill, said, "I have reviewed Dawson's chart and I'm sorry. I have to agree with Dr. Harris. We have done all we can. I am so sorry." He shook Bill's hand and mine, then left.

My father came in and sat by Dawson. He said to me, "He knows I'm here. When I tell him, 'Papa's here' and I hold his hand, I can feel his hand move."

I said, "Yes, he does know." I believed that Dawson did know we were all there with him, but unlike my father, I could not touch him. I knew God was calling him and I believed my touching him would be holding him back, making it harder for him to go. I did not want to make it harder for him. I wanted to ease his struggle. Despite the fact that Bill had told me earlier that he had opened Dawson's eyes and, in Bill's mournful words, "Dawson wasn't there," I felt that he was still with us. I saw my touch, not as a comfort to Dawson, but as a restraint. I would be holding on to him and I knew I must let go.

Bill's eyes were red and his face flushed. He went to the sink and turned on the cold water and splashed his face. He looked at me and said, "We have to take his get-well cards down."

"No, I can't. I can't take them down."

"Andrea, would you rather take them down *after?*"

"No, Bill. No."

"Then, Andrea, please. Please help me. We have to do it."

I proceeded to take the little clothespins off the cards that I could reach and stacked them neatly on Dawson's table. Bill took the others and did the same. I took Harley's picture and the Saint Jude card off of his bulletin board and his gorilla out of the window and the tiny pumpkin Claudia had brought him off the shelf, then I took his calendar off the wall. I held the calendar, looking at the date, Tuesday, October 29, 1996, then I placed it on top of the stack of cards.

"Oh, Bill," I cried, "he didn't get to tell his story."

Without a moment's hesitation, Bill responded, "Well, Andrea, then you're just going to have to do it."

When we had all the cards down and put away, I went out to Dr. Harris and I said, "We know it's time, but I'd like to have a priest here."

"Sure. Just let me know when you are ready."

I went back and told Bill that I was going to call the priest. Everyone then took turns going in to Dawson and saying their good byes. Dr. Harris came in and speaking to Bill and me he said, "I wish it could have worked out better." I looked over at Bill and he looked as though he could have punched the doctor. *Worked out better? Better? Isn't better the comparative of good? As if this had worked out good, but it just could have been better? What could he have meant? This was the worst possible way it could have worked out. God, it couldn't be worse.* Then he said, "I have to ask you..." I knew what he was about to ask and I was prepared for his question. He said, "I would like permission to do a limited autopsy. Would you agree to that? It would not delay or interfere with any plans you make."

"No," Bill said.

"Bill, it might help someone else. Maybe if they could finally discover what happened they could save someone else from having this happen to them. Dawson would want that. You know how he wanted to help others in his position." Bill finally nodded his reluctant consent.

Dr. Harris said, "I'll get the papers for you to sign."

I followed him out of the room, then in a quiet, almost weak voice, I asked him, "Did you think that this was the way it was going to go?"

"No," he said, emphatically, "I always thought we would transplant him."

"Oh, you did?" I didn't know if I could have heard anything more sad and yet somehow so gratifying. Just to know that while Dawson and I had such faith and were trying so hard to be optimistic that Dr. Harris, too, believed that Dawson would get his heart. "He wasn't such a bad patient, was he?" I asked.

"No! He's a great guy."

I went back to Dawson's room and when the priest came, we all gathered in our waiting room. He stood in the middle of the room and opened his bible and read in part, "We know that if our earthly dwelling, a tent, should be destroyed, we do have a building from God, a dwelling not made with hands, that is eternal in heaven. Therefore, we are not discouraged; rather, although our outer self is wasting away, our inner self is being renewed day by day. For this momentary light affliction is producing for us an eternal weight of glory beyond all comparison, as we look not to what is seen but to what is unseen; for what is seen is transitory, but what is unseen is eternal."

When he had concluded all of his readings, I left to find Dr. Harris. To tell him what? That we were ready? How could I tell him we were ready when what I wanted to say was, "We will never be ready. Please tell me we don't have to do this." But I spoke calmly to him and after I had, he went into Dawson's room and turned off the respirator and the monitor. *Could this really be happening?*

Bill and I sat on the same side of Dawson, sitting close to each other. I glanced around, trying to see everyone, but their faces were out of focus to me. I looked at Dawson lying so still. I curled my fingers gently around his, then I took my hand away. I wanted to hold his hand, to grip it, but still I could not. Now, it was for myself that I could not hold his hand. I was afraid that if I were holding his hand on the last moment of his life that I would somehow feel his hand leave my grasp. I could not bear to have that happen. As if anything could make the reality of that awful moment any more unbearable. But isn't that one of the basic fears of a mother, that her child will let go of her hand and run off into harm's way? But isn't it just like a child to run on ahead? I told myself that was what Dawson was doing, just running on ahead of us and he would wait there for us to catch up.

Dr. Harris had told me that when I was ready, that I should just nod to him. *How can I do it? How can I? How can I?* I turned quickly around to the priest who was standing silently behind Bill and me, and I implored him, "Say a prayer. Please, say a prayer."

He started, "Our Father who art in Heaven..."

I looked to Dr. Harris, gave barely a hint of a nod, then quickly put my head down. *Dawson. Dawson. May you go in peace. A part of me goes with you and will always be with you. I love you, Dawson, my son.* The VADs went silent. The clicking had stopped. We were all quiet. And Dawson so quiet. My baby, Dawson. That moment that I had feared had come to pass.

Dawson died on a Tuesday.

Part Four

"I call on the Lord in my distress, and He answers me."

—Psalm 120:1

Chapter Thirty-Three

I closed my eyes, lay my head on Dawson's bed, my cheek lightly resting on his hand, knowing from that moment on, nothing in the world was ever going to be the same for me.

"We will take care of things…" the nurse was saying as she softly touched my arm. "If you would like to leave for just a short while you can come back and be with him … we'll wash his face … we'll change his gown…"

"No," I said, "don't put another gown on him. Put his sweatshirt on him. It's in that bag." It was a gray sweatshirt I had brought him when he was having chills. I had cut it up the back so he did not have to put in on over his head and have it interfere with his lines. He always looked comfortable in it and I think he felt more like himself when he had it on.

"I will do that," she said as she gently coaxed me to stand and guided me from the room. Speaking in a nearly trance-like monotone, I said to my mother, "I should call Rusty and tell him." I went to the phone and when he answered, I simply said, "He's gone."

"Oh, Andrea, I am so sorry," Rusty responded. "Thank you for calling."

We went back to see Dawson and my mother said, "He looks peaceful." He had found peace, but I felt defeated and stunned.

I sat beside him, my mind caught between colliding worlds. The reality was that Dawson was gone. He would never open his eyes again, or smile at me, or laugh, or say, "I love you guys." Not ever. But in contradiction to those unbearable truths was the overwhelming belief that he was, in some unexplainable real sense, still very much with me.

I had no idea how much time had passed when Bill said, "I don't want to leave him, Andrea. How can we leave him here tonight?"

"Bill, this is the first night that we will not be leaving him. He's coming home with us. Bill, he's finally coming home."

Bill hugged him and I did the same as I whispered, "I love you, Dawson." Then we all slowly walked to the elevator. I was carrying the hospital bags containing Dawson's belongings as we rode down in the elevator for the last time. There would be no ride up in the morning. *Oh, Dawson, how could this have happened to you? How can I go on living? God, please help me.*

When Bill and I returned home, Harley was happy and excited to see us. I grabbed him and squeezed him. I was thinking of how much Dawson had wanted to see him and how much he had missed him. *Is it really true that Dawson will never see Harley again? How could that be? How will I ever accept that Dawson will never be walking through the door, that I will never be able to hug him, that I will never see him smile or hear his laugh?*

My mother, father, Claudia and Tracy arrived not long after. I was sitting in Dawson's chair, the one my father had given him. I sat slowly rocking back and forth and quietly moaning. I could see everyone around me and hear their voices, but I felt beyond their grasp. My mother's eyes told me she wished there were something she could do to take away my hurt. My father kept his head down, his eyes never meeting mine. Bill sat at the kitchen table not moving and not speaking. Claudia was sitting closest to me, her eyes and voice more sympathetic than I had ever known them. "Are you all right, Mom?" she asked. I had suddenly stopped rocking and tears were rolling down my face. She came over and sat with me in Dawson's big chair. She put her arms around me and I lay my head on her shoulder. She said, "I know it hurts now, but not every day will feel like this," words I had used many years earlier to comfort her.

Bill and I, evidently having finally reached our limits of exhaustion, fell asleep sitting in our chairs. Claudia woke me, saying quietly, "Mom, we're going to go. O.K.? You and Dad are tired. We'll see you tomorrow, O.K.?"

"O.K., hon. Thanks." She hugged me tightly, letting me know how much she cared. I hugged her back, holding on to her, hoping she knew how much I loved her and how grateful I was to have her for my daughter.

My dad gave me a hug. My mother merely nodded to me. We needed no words between us. Mother to mother, mother to daughter, we knew each other's pain and that pain was unspeakable.

I closed the door, went to the couch, wrapped myself in a blanket and sank into the familiar cushions. Bill, now standing, said, "Andrea, you shouldn't have to sleep alone tonight. Come upstairs with me." He took my hand and I followed him with Harley right behind us. We got into bed and Bill put his arm around me. I lay my head on his chest and we fell asleep talking of Dawson and shedding quiet tears.

I awoke a short time later crying aloud, moaning and sobbing. My own cries of anguish had awakened me and I quickly got out of bed. Still crying as I went down the stairs in the near darkness, I was thinking that I might see Dawson, for I was sure he had come home with us. But I did not see any glimpse of him and I lay on the couch and opened my heart to the grief and sorrow I could no longer contain. When I heard Bill coming down the stairs, I stopped crying and sat up.

"Why are you down here?" Bill asked.

"I didn't want to wake you with my crying."

"You don't have to worry about that. I understand. Andrea, don't ever feel that you have to hide your tears from me."

"Oh Bill, how are we ever going to get through this?"

"Together," Bill said. "We'll do it together."

Wednesday: The innocent yet intrusive light of an uninvited dawn invaded my dark world, quietly announcing the arrival of morning, the first morning Dawson was not alive to see. Though daybreak had always brought me hope and promise, today it brought me disbelief, disbelief that a day could dawn upon the earth where Dawson no longer walked, making this a day unlike any other. How was I to greet such a day?

Bill and I needed to talk about making the necessary arrangements, but Bill appeared to be in his own state of disbelief and when I tried to discuss these things with him, he looked detached from the reality of having to face what we must do. There were so many things we had to take care of. We had not yet begun when Fran, an old friend and neighbor, stopped by. Her husband, a good friend of Bill's, had died a couple of years earlier. She had also lost her grown son many years before, so there was no doubt she understood our pain. Today, she spoke of the first time she had met Dawson. He was about eight years old and she remembered him as being shy and quiet. She said, "I can still see him standing so close to Bill, looking up at me with those brown eyes of his." She asked us if we had been to church to talk to the priest about planning the services. When we told her we had not, she said, "Then let's go." She knew the priest at Our Lady of Loretto personally and he greeted us warmly when she introduced us.

I asked him, "Would it be possible for us to have the funeral mass at St. Dominic's in the city? Even though we don't live there, that is the church we have been attending for the past three months. Dawson had said to me that when he got out of the hospital, he wanted to see the church his Dad and I were going to. It was our plan to take him there, so I want to do that for him."

"That should be no problem," Father O'Neill said. "We can do the rosary and vigil at the funeral home across the street in the evening and you can have the mass the next day in the city. What day are you planning?"

"I want the funeral on Saturday."

He called St. Dominic's and I spoke with Father Xavier. He confirmed Saturday noon would be fine and that he would officiate. He asked me, "Do you want to have the mass in the side altar?"

"I wasn't thinking that," I said. "I was hoping to have it in the main altar."

"Certainly we can do that, but it is so large that sometimes it is better with a small group to be in the smaller area. It is just more intimate."

"I can understand that, but it is the beautiful main altar I had described to Dawson and it is that sight I had always imagined sharing with him. So could we have it there?"

"Yes, of course."

We discussed the music and Father Xavier gave me the name of their guitarist. He said to ask Father O'Neill to give me the book from which to choose the passages to read. When I hung up the phone, I asked Father O'Neill about it and he took a small, white book out of his desk drawer and handed it to me. I read the title, *Through Death to Life — Preparing to Celebrate the Funeral Mass.*

When we were through there, we walked across the street to the funeral home. After sitting with the funeral director in his tiny office, discussing our plans, he led us to a room full of caskets. I stopped short at the door, not wanting to enter. But in that one brief moment I had caught sight of it. "The shiny, black one," I said abruptly and quickly turned and went to the lobby. When Fran and Bill rejoined me, we went back to the office and finalized our plans.

On the ride home, I began looking through the book. Under the heading, *A Message for the Family,* I read, "I naturally don't know who you are or where you are. But I do understand that right now you feel confused, sad, stunned, even overwhelmed by your loss. The Roman Catholic funeral ceremony presented in this book should offer both comfort in this present sorrow and great hope for the future." *Great hope for the future? What hope could there be for the future? Dawson has no future. How can I?* I read on, "In the past you have loved others, comforted them and shared their losses. During the hours ahead it will be your turn, your time to be loved, to be comforted and to let others share your grief. What will surprise you is the wonderful support and uplift you receive from others. The words and embraces of friends and relatives, their prayers, their phone calls and written notes, their silent presence at the family residence or in the funeral home will raise you from the depths and help you carry on. I know. They did it for me and I promise it will be the same for you." *How could this stranger make that promise to me?* He went on to say, "That is the primary purpose of wakes and calling hours. They make it possible for others to share your sorrow, to lend you support, and to pray for your departed loved one." *My departed loved one? Dawson? Dawson.* I read on, "Christians, however, find bright rays of hope in the midst of their many tears. We believe that death is not an end, but a beginning; that a beloved has passed through death from this present, temporary life to a perfect, permanent one; that he who saw God in faith on earth now sees the Lord face to face in heaven; that while death separates us now, it is but for a time only. Soon we will be reunited, as God tells us in the Bible, with those we love in a dwelling provided for us by God, a dwelling in the heavens."

That was what I had to believe, though it would have been easy to discard any notion of a God who had done this terrible thing to Dawson and me when we had such faith in Him. But faith was something Dawson and I had shared and because of that, I would never let go of it. It was ours and it would always be a part of me as it was a part of Dawson. To give up my faith now would be rejecting the beauty of what Dawson and I had experienced together. And when I thought of the precious moments we had, I was reminded they could only be described as blessings, as prayers answered and at once my faith was restored.

We thanked Fran for her help and as we hugged good-bye, she said she would bring food over on Saturday for after the services.

Not having given that any thought before, I said, almost as a question, "Oh, everyone will come back here."

Bill said, "Yeah, I'm sure they will." That made sense, for the cemetery was just down the street from the house.

When we had bought our property twenty years earlier, some friends had questioned how we could live so close to a cemetery, but it had not bothered me. The cemetery was in a beautiful, peaceful, country setting. I could not have known when we built our house here it would turn out to be a blessing. It was a perfect place now. Dawson would always be near.

My next thought was, *How could we have guests?* I was looking around, seeing a house that appeared not to have received any attention in the ten years I'd been gone. This was obviously a house where a couple of men lived who did not have housekeeping and decorating on their minds. The cushions on the window seat were completely worn out, the lace curtains needed washing, the hardwood floors needed polishing, there were tools everywhere and my boxes and suitcases now added to the disarray of the family room. Something had to be done.

I asked Bill, "Do you think we could do some straightening up before Saturday?"

"Yeah, I guess," he said.

It was a large, two-story house with too many rooms to clean in just a few days, so I decided to concentrate only on the rooms on the main floor. I knew there was no hope of ever having it look like a normal home, for, after all, I had designed it that way. And surely Dawson's friends knew the house was not your usual house, for they had seen Dawson work on his motorcycle in the kitchen.

We went from briefly discussing that insignificant task, to the monumental one of going to the cemetery to choose Dawson's grave site. Before we were shown the available spaces, we were informed that interment could not take place on Saturday. It would have to wait until Monday. This disturbed me at first, but when I realized it meant interment would be private, for only our family would be there with us on Monday, it seemed right.

Bill and I had no preconceived ideas of what we wanted for a grave for Dawson, but when we were shown the crypts, we both knew that was what we preferred. He would not be buried in the ground. He would be placed in a white marble enclosure. We were told there would be a bronze plaque placed on the front and we were to think about what we wanted it to say. "There will be his name and dates, of course," the funeral consultant said, "and any special inscription you want. Take your time to think about it. There is no need to decide right away." That would come later. Now we had to decide upon a site. There were many to choose from and we agreed on one at ground level. It was in an area not far from the entrance, facing the house and from that spot we could see a glimpse of Dawson's bedroom window.

When we arrived home, Claudia and Tracy were there. They were waiting to take me to the local newspapers to post the notices in the obituary columns. The schedule that was to appear was: Thursday night, October 31, Halloween, was what the funeral director called, "viewing," but what I preferred to call, "visiting." Friday night, November 1, All Saints Day, was visiting and rosary. Saturday noon, November 2, All Souls Day, was mass at St. Dominic's. The announcement would also read that interment was to follow at Valley Memorial Park in Novato, although that was not quite true. We would be going there after St. Dominic's, but it would be for a final blessing only.

While telling the woman behind the desk at one of the newspapers the notice was for my son, I was thinking how this all seemed so unreal. *I have a son who died? I have to face that I am a mother who lost her son because nothing can ever change that. For as long as I live, that is what I'll be.*

From the newspaper offices, Tracy drove us to the shopping mall so I could find something to wear to the services. On the way, I called Juana to ask her if she would like to speak at the mass. I was shocked to discover she had not received the message that I had called her that night Dawson was so ill. She said, "No one told me. I had no idea his condition had worsened. I went to visit him this morning. What a dreadful shock it was for me to find him gone." She sounded quite upset.

I said, "Oh, Juana, I had told the other chaplain to tell you. I told her how much I wanted to talk to you and that I wanted you to see Dawson. I thought she would tell you. I'm so sorry."

"It was not your fault. She should have given me your message. And yes, I would love to speak at Dawson's service. Thank you for asking me. It will be an honor."

I bought a simple, black pantsuit and hoped to find something for Dawson to wear, but found nothing. When we returned home, I asked Bill what he would be wearing and he seemed unwilling or unable to discuss it. But he did make the call to Deacon Joe to ask him if he would officiate at the rosary. When he said he would, Bill thanked him and told him I would like to talk to him.

The first thing Deacon Joe said to me was, "Andrea, I had planned to go to the hospital and meet Dawson and spend some time with him. I am so sorry I did not get there."

"Oh, I'm sorry, too. That would have been so nice, but I understand."

"Tell me again about Dawson."

"Well, he was very brave and courageous during these past two years since his illness. He never complained about what he was going through. Even these past three months, the doctors and nurses all marveled at his strength and how he accepted and met each challenge. Everyone said he should have received his heart, that he had earned it. But my opinion is he had earned *more* than a heart. I believe he had earned true peace. I do wish you could have met him. He had such faith. He told me he understood that his trip to the emergency room was just the first step on his journey and that 'the day' was already set and whatever happened would be 'perfect.' Bill and I had found comfort and hope in our visits to St. Dominic's and St. Jude's Shrine and Dawson was aware he felt better after we had been there. Even the doctor had noticed it. Dawson told me that St. Dominic's was the first place he wanted to go when he left the hospital. That is why we're having the funeral mass there."

"I am so sorry I did not get to meet Dawson. Andrea, that is a beautiful story. I will mention these things at the service Friday night."

From sharing these special thoughts of Dawson with Deacon Joe, I went out to buy fabric to cover the window seat cushions, the same cushions I had covered more than ten years earlier. I also bought a black silk shirt for Dawson to wear. All the while, I was wondering how I was able to do these things. How was I? How could I be calmly shopping for the shirt Dawson would wear ... in his coffin? I wondered, as I looked around at the others in the store, if they would believe it if I told them my son had just died. I knew I looked like everyone else there, but I was not like them. I was buying the shirt my son would soon be buried in. No one else was doing that.

Thursday: The funeral director called to tell us they were unable to have the viewing that evening as we had planned because Dawson had not arrived. I called the hospital, irate because Dr. Harris had promised me the autopsy would not delay our plans. I was told Dawson was on his way.

Many of Dawson's friends were coming by the house. Several had expressed the desire to be one of Dawson's pallbearers. Larry, Carlos' son, had called and said that if we hadn't decided on the pallbearers he would like to be considered. He and Dawson had spent many weekends together as children when Bill and Carlos would take them on hunting trips. They enjoyed being together and over the years whenever they saw each other, it was the same. Bill told him immediately that, yes, he could be a pallbearer, that Dawson would like that. The others were soon decided upon, as well. Matt, of course, who had been with Dawson to the end. Then three old friends of Dawson's, Tom and two Ians were chosen. Eric, another friend, who had been working on a fishing boat in Alaska when he had received the news about Dawson, called and said he had managed to have the boat take him back to dock and he would be home in time for Dawson's funeral. He asked if he could please be a pallbearer and he told me of the most beautiful sunset he had ever seen on the night Dawson had died. Dawson had his six pallbearers, six loyal and loving friends.

An idea came to me. Though I did not know how possible it was, I called Rusty to ask him about its feasibility. I said to him, "You know, Dawson really loved that project we started him on, the shadow box with all the little fire department symbols. In his room he has the materials he used to make the different pieces. They're in a tool case with all the compartments labeled. It is so neat and organized and he has one shadow box ... he was in the middle of working on. It's all assembled and painted. It's really obvious how much he enjoyed that project. You saw how closely he checked out the trucks at your firehouse so that he could make everything just right. Anyway, I was just wondering … if it would be possible … since your firehouse is so close to the church … maybe a couple of the guys on duty Saturday … while on their way to buy groceries … I don't expect them to make a special trip, but just while they're out shopping … maybe they could just stop for a little bit at the church … just so Dawson … oh, I don't know exactly … I guess I sound crazy … but … I just think he would really like … a fire truck there." Rusty said he wasn't sure he could arrange it, but he would see what he could do.

Bill's family arrived that evening to discover there would be no visitation. Bill took them out to dinner, but I declined going. I was exhausted and felt I had done all the "acting normal" I was able to do. I stayed home, went into Dawson's room, sat on his bed and wept. I had placed my rosary beads on his pillow the night before. To my disappointment, that morning when I had checked, they were unmoved and now they were still in the exact position I had left them. I had truly believed Dawson would have been there and would have moved the rosaries ever so slightly, but just enough to let me know he had seen them and was with me.

When I went to bed, I still expected that if I awoke during the night, I would see Dawson standing in the hallway watching over me. Though I did not, I decided that just because I did not see him, it did not mean he wasn't there.

Friday: When I woke, I knew this was the day I would be seeing Dawson and he would be wearing the new shirt I had bought him. Bill had taken Dawson's clothes to the mortuary and was told we could visit him later in the morning. I finished my cleaning and sewing and proceeded to get myself ready. I put on the suit I had bought and waited for my mother and father, so we could go over together. When we arrived, my cousin Leah, a floral designer, was bringing in beautiful floral arrangements. Two young women were already with Dawson. They were sitting in the front row and both were crying. I did not know who they were, but they smiled at me and I smiled back. Bill went right up to the open coffin and stood looking at Dawson. When he came back to me, I asked him, "How does he look? Does he look O.K.?"

"He looks fine," Bill said.

"Mommy," I said, "will you go look at him and tell me what you think. Can you?"

She nodded that she would. She went to see him and when she came back, she said, "He looks O.K."

"He does?"

"Yes," she nodded. "Go see him."

"Come with me." We walked up to him and I could barely do more than take a quick glance, but what I saw was Dawson looking unnaturally pale. It was so difficult for me to look at him, life gone from his body. It was an image I had to put out of my mind and my heart.

Claudia and Tracy arrived with Ian, one of Dawson's pallbearers, and his wife, Sally, Claudia's close friend who had sat with her the night Dawson was taken to the hospital. Ian immediately went to see Dawson, but Sally could not. I told her I understood.

The more friends and relatives that arrived, the more surprised I was that I was able to talk to them without being overly emotional. Some visitors were crying more than I was. It was strange what was happening. I was conducting myself so normally and I was actually having conversations while Dawson ... Dawson lay there. And as flowers were delivered, I promptly and with unexpected enthusiasm opened the little cards that were attached. Reading the sympathy and love expressed was amazingly consoling. Bill was so touched when flowers arrived from his friends, some of whom he hadn't seen in quite some time.

I went and sat in the front row and I was beginning to realize what I had read in the booklet from the church was true, it was surprisingly comforting to have others lending their love and support. I sat looking at all the beautiful flowers surrounding Dawson. I had never realized before how much these thoughtful expressions of caring could mean to grieving families.

All the flowers were beautiful, but one amazed me. It was a striking, yellow arrangement from my mother and father. I went over to my cousin. "Leah," I said, "you did that one, the standing yellow one, didn't you?"

"Yes, I don't usually do yellow, but ... "

"I know. Yellow isn't my color either, but that arrangement ... it ... " It had two spherical groups of yellow lilies and yellow roses high in the arrangement with extending streams of yellow orchids and spikes of unusual plants. "It reminds me of the light Dawson talked about. The light that goes around and around. He said that when it was perfect, it would come and take him to that place up past the sun. That one ball is like the sun and the other the light."

"Really?" Leah said. "I don't even know where the idea for that design came from. I have never done anything like it before."

"Well, I know where the idea came from. Dawson knows, too."

Leah had made other outstanding arrangements and one had a banner that read, "Beloved Son," from Bill and me, but it was the one that read, "Beloved Brother," that tore at my heart. Perhaps it was because I was already so well aware of my own loss, but this reminded me of the loss Claudia had suffered. Though she and Dawson had taken very different paths in their lives, he was, nonetheless, her brother. Claudia had lost her little brother.

Leah's children, Kirsten and Jason, whom Claudia and Dawson had grown up with, were also floral designers. Jason made a beautiful and poignant broken heart composed entirely of perfect, red roses and Kirsten made an adorable little basket from her young son, Jared.

We spent the day in this small visiting room, but in the late afternoon they moved Dawson and all his flowers into the chapel-like room. More friends and relatives arrived and to my surprise, Joyce, the social worker from transplant services came by.

"Joyce! How nice of you to come."

"Well, I was up this way and I wanted to tell you how sorry I am. Everyone is. We all hoped Dawson would get his heart."

"I know and they did try. I don't understand what happened. Will I ever know? Do the doctors know?"

"Well, they have the results of the autopsy."

My first thought was, *What if it shows that something very simple was the cause of Dawson's problems? What if it shows that Dawson did not have to die?* I knew I could not bear to hear that, however, I did ask the question, "And what did the autopsy show?"

"Nothing really," she answered.

"There was no infection around the VADs?" I asked, surprised.

"No, I don't think so."

"Well, that's where they thought the infection must have attached itself. If that wasn't it, then what did they find?"

"It was rather inconclusive."

"Oh," I sighed. "I guess I should have expected that."

She nodded that she understood my cynicism. "But," she said, "it is just a preliminary finding. They should know more when they get the results from the cultures."

Yeah, right, sure they will, I thought. But even if they did, it no longer mattered. It could not make any real difference to me or to Dawson now, whatever it was.

The other Ian, who was to be one of Dawson's pallbearers, arrived with his mother. She expressed her sympathy to me, then glancing over at Ian, she said, sadly, "Our boys have been friends for so long."

"Yes," I said, "they were just children when they met." I could see Ian was hurting terribly. His eyes were red and swollen. I thanked her for coming and as she hugged me I said to her, "I know how hard it must be for you to see your son so sad. Take care."

By evening, the chapel was filled with an abundance of flowers and plants and so many friends. There were many of Dawson's friends, but there were also a large number of Bill's friends, some of whom I had never met. When Bill introduced me to each one of them he said, "This is Dawson's mother. She was with Dawson every day, all day, the whole time he was in the hospital."

"I feel so lucky," I said, "to have had that time with him." And every time I said that, I wondered how it was possible to feel lucky while at the same time be feeling so unlucky.

Deacon Joe came over to me and introduced himself and his wife. He said he would be changing into his vestment for the prayer vigil. When it came time to start the service, everyone was seated and our family sat in the first row. Deacon Joe led the prayers and then told of the incredibly fateful way he had met Bill. Then he spoke of Dawson, telling some of the things I had told him. He said, in conclusion, "Dawson's mother told me of his faith and of his amazing journey. I deeply regret I had not met him. He must have been a remarkable and very loved young man. If any of you present would like to share your special memories of Dawson with us, I invite you to do so."

I considered getting up and walking to the podium and describing to everyone the beautiful moments I had shared with Dawson and how much I loved him and how much I was going to miss him and how I believed with all my heart that by the unexplainable power of God, he was in a better place, yet still very much with me. But I could not seem to make the move. I looked around and no one was making a move to speak. There was a long and awkward silence. My eyes met my aunt Elmy's eyes and she was frowning, looking painfully uncomfortable and she quickly looked away. I knew she was thinking how embarrassing and sad it was that Dawson had no one who had anything to say about him. But I knew that wasn't true. I knew the others just felt as I did. There was so much to say, so many heartfelt emotions to express and it was just too hard to do. I understood that, but Deacon Joe was looking uneasy when out of the silence, a young man dressed in black motorcycle leathers stood and in a voice so emphatic, yet shaking with emotion, he said, "That boy could ride and I'm gonna miss him!"

Dawson must have loved that. I was sure to Dawson that was the greatest thing anyone could have said about him, "He could ride!" But I was not to discover the full extent of what that meant until after the funeral service the following day when so many of Dawson's friends wanted to share with me, personally, their favorite stories of Dawson.

Chapter Thirty-Four

Saturday: The limousine was scheduled to pick us up at ten o'clock to take us to the funeral home. It was almost nine o'clock and I was nearly ready, but Bill was still outside working around the pond, digging and watering. As I watched him from the window, I was reminded of days from our past. Bill had always seemed so relaxed and content when puttering outside. I was sorry I had to call him in and when I did, he acknowledged that he had heard me, but he did not stop what he was doing. A short while later, when I called to him again, I said, "Bill, please come in and get ready. The limo will be here soon."

When he finally came in, he said, "Andrea, this just can't be true. I just don't believe that this happened. He can't be gone."

"I know. I can't believe it really happened either. It doesn't seem possible. Bill, I wanted to ask you, I have the picture of Harley that was on Dawson's bulletin board, what do you think about putting it in with Dawson?"

"Yeah, do that."

My mother and father and Claudia and Tracy arrived soon after. I knew I could count on them to be prompt and we were all ready and waiting, including Bill, when the limo drove up. When we arrived at the funeral home, Leah was there removing the flowers to take them to the church. We went into the room, now empty, where Dawson had spent the night alone. The pallbearers were there and Eric had placed a rose on Dawson. I knelt at the casket, silently expressing my love to Dawson and thanking him for the love he had given me. The funeral director approached me and said, "We must get going. I have to close it now."

"O.K., but wait just a minute," I said. "I have a picture I want him to have with him." Bill stood beside me as I placed Harley's picture on Dawson's folded hands. I turned away as the coffin's lid was closed. Leah then placed a large, impressive spray of beautiful, red anthuriums on Dawson's coffin, which was then taken out to the hearse. Our limo then slowly followed the hearse carrying Dawson out of the parking lot. I was reminded of the day we had followed the ambulance carrying Dawson out of the hospital parking lot just three short months ago. So little time we'd had, yet in many ways it was a lifetime for Dawson and me.

I prayed silently, *Lord, I will keep my promise to be grateful for the days Dawson and I have shared. How could I not be thankful to you for having given them to me? Without them, I know I could not live through this day. It was such a miraculous gift to have witnessed Dawson's enlightenment and it is that which gives me the hope and strength to carry on.* As if by the grace of another miracle, I was able to say on this most sorrowful of days, *"Thank you, Lord."*

We were all quiet as we started on our way. We crossed the Golden Gate Bridge and made our way through the city, taking the same route we had taken daily to see Dawson at the hospital. I held back my tears as my heart ached at the thought that I would never see him again. As long as I lived, I would never see him again. But what pained me more was thinking of all the things Dawson would never see again.

As we approached the church, we saw a great number of people gathered outside waiting for Dawson's arrival. But the first thing I saw was not the mourners, but the big, shiny, red fire truck parked directly across the street from where we would stop. "Oh, my God. Look at that!" I cried. "It's for Dawson. It's for you, Dawson! It's for you." We were helped out of the limo and the hearse's door was opened. Dawson's young friends took their positions and removed him from the hearse and carried him toward the church steps. And there, lined upon the steps were two rows of firemen standing three abreast. "I have never seen anything so touching in my whole life," my mother exclaimed as Dawson was carried up the steps, passing between the uniformed men. As he slowly passed between them, they saluted him. I was completely overwhelmed by the sight. My mother quickly went to Rusty to thank him and we then followed Dawson into the church. The priest in his white and gold vestment greeted us in the entry saying, "May the Father of mercies, the God of all consolation, be with you." He sprinkled the casket with holy water, saying, "In the waters of baptism Dawson died with Christ and rose with him to new life. May he now share with him eternal glory." The flowers were removed from the casket and a white cloth was draped over it. Father then began to lead our procession. I was struck by the sight of so many people standing and watching us and nearly filling the huge church. I thought about how Father Xavier had said this main chapel might be too big for a small group. He had not known the many who would mourn Dawson and would come to pay their respects.

As we slowly walked down the long aisle of this magnificent church, I was looking beyond the sad faces of friends and family. I was seeing the beauty and grandeur of the church, the sight I had imagined I would share with Dawson. I had envisioned so many times that on the day Dawson walked out of the hospital we would come here and open its huge doors, enter, and I would say, "This is it, Dawson. This is where my prayers were heard and answered." I had imagined the look of gratefulness and awe in his eyes. We would have fallen to our knees to honor our Savior.

As we reached the altar, Father Xavier placed a large, standing, gold crucifix near Dawson, saying, "In baptism, Dawson received the sign of the cross. May he now share in Christ's victory over sin and death. Lord Jesus Christ, you loved us unto death. Let this cross be a sign of your love for Dawson and for the people you have gathered here today." The guitarist's hymns and the scent and sight of the burning incense were filling the air. I felt surrounded by a powerful love and I embraced the extraordinary significance and magnificent beauty of the moment. Father prayed, "Lord, in our grief we turn to you. Are you not the God of love who opens your ears to all? Listen to our prayers for your servant Dawson, whom you have called out of this world: lead him to your kingdom of light and peace and count him among the saints in glory. We ask this through Christ our Lord. Amen." Father Xavier ascended to the altar then spoke of how we as Catholics believe that the dead do not die and that in death our life is changed, not ended. He said that was the belief with which Dawson had been baptized and I recalled the baby Dawson as the baptismal waters had been poured over his head. I remembered the priest saying he was baptized into death. Father Xavier was saying the same thing now, only now he was saying that Dawson was passing through death into life, eternal life with Christ. He said he understood how we would mourn Dawson whose life had passed so quickly, but that we now could entrust him to the Lord who would have mercy on him and who would welcome him to his heavenly dwelling and would grant him the happiness of everlasting youth. "Today we are here to pray for Dawson and for Dawson's family. We ask Christ that he grant them comfort and consolation and that he heal their pain and dispel the darkness and doubt that come from grief."

Juana was invited to the altar. "I am honored to be here," she said, "and to have had the opportunity to know such a beautiful young man. I will never forget the night I met Dawson. As I sat with him in his hospital room, he spoke to me of his love for his family and God. I saw his eyes glistening with adoration and his face seemed aglow when he spoke of that love. He told me of the amazing changes he felt within himself and wanted to express to God the gratitude that was in his heart. We can take comfort in knowing Dawson has most assuredly been welcomed into God's heavenly kingdom. May I say to Dawson's family and, in particular, to his mother whom I have come to know, be ever thankful for the precious years you had with Dawson and know that he truly loved you."

Father Xavier walked over to us in the first row as we stood to receive communion. As he placed the holy Eucharist in my hand, he said, "Always remember, whenever you receive this, you are closer to him." When he had completed serving our row, he went back to the front of the altar and invited everyone to receive communion. He said, "If any of you do not want to receive the Eucharist, I welcome you to come up, cross your hands over your chest and you will receive a blessing."

Those who came forward to the priest stopped to acknowledge us when returning to their seats. One by one, they hugged us, spoke consoling words, sharing our grief. Then a man, and a woman who was wiping tears from her eyes, were in front of us. Before I realized who they were, Bill said, "Scott!"

"Suzann!" I said. "Oh, how nice of you to come!" I was so surprised and touched by the visit from two of our favorite nurses.

Scott hugged me and said, "I'm so sorry."

Suzann said, "Everyone feels terrible. We all wanted Dawson to get his heart." It was true, the hospital staff had cared about him. Dawson had touched their hearts in his special way.

Then a man wearing a motorcycle policeman's uniform was passing us. Bill said to him, "Rene, good to see you. Thank you for coming."

He had been a friend of Bill's for years, but I had not known him very well. I was thinking he must have come from work, since he was still in his uniform. Though I had told him it was nice of him to come, I could not have imagined to what extent.

When the entire congregation had returned to their seats, Father Xavier placed his hands on Dawson's casket, bowed his head and said, "Into your hands, Father of Mercies, we commend our brother Dawson in the sure and certain hope that, together with all who have died in Christ, he will rise with them. We give you thanks for the blessings which you bestowed upon Dawson in this life: they are signs to us of your goodness and of our fellowship with the saints in Christ. Merciful Lord, turn toward us and listen to our prayers: open the gates of paradise to your servant and help us who remain to comfort one another with assurances of faith, until we all meet in Christ and are with you and with our brother Dawson forever." The music started and Father Xavier began walking up the aisle. He was slowly swinging the brass censer from its softly-clinking brass chain, swinging it rhythmically, its aromatic curls of smoke leading the way. As Dawson's casket was somberly carried past us, Bill and I walked from our pew and took our place following behind him. Suzann was to tell me when I spoke to her the following week, that she had never seen anything so sad in her whole life as Bill and me walking behind Dawson's casket. We followed Dawson out to the foggy, windy San Francisco day, a day much like those we had spent in San Bruno when Claudia and Dawson were little. It was much like those days when I had insisted they wear their knit hats to go outside and play. Very much like those days I had bundled Dawson up in his warm jacket, pulling his hat down over his ears. *Oh, Dawson, Dawson,* my heart cried out.

I could see the fire truck was gone as was expected, but through my tears, I was seeing what? What was this? Rene, Bill's friend, was sitting on his police motorcycle, but there were others. There were many other policemen on motorcycles gathered in front of the church. Our limo driver escorted us to the limo and Dawson was placed in the hearse as I was asking myself what all those policemen could be doing there. From the limo, I watched as Rene began to direct us and all of the other cars leaving the church. Then the motorcycles paired up and began to lead the way to Geary Boulevard. They were ceremoniously leading our motorcade. They continued to lead us down the boulevard. We watched out the window as two officers broke away from the procession and rode ahead to block the intersection. They repeated this at every intersection along the way, enabling us to pass the stopped traffic and drive through the red lights. We were all watching in astonishment. Claudia and my mother, in utter amazement, kept saying, "I don't believe this! I just don't believe this!" Our mood that had been so solemn as we had left the church, had now been uplifted to almost lighthearted. We were all smiling. Strangers on the street were stopping and watching as we went by. They must have been thinking, "I wonder who that is?" and wanting to ask, "Who is that?" I wanted to open the window and shout, "It's Dawson! It's Dawson! It's my Dawson."

What Rusty had done for Dawson had far exceeded my expectations, and what Rene had done for him I could not have dreamed. Though Dawson was not a heroic fireman or policeman killed in the line of duty, it seemed the honors bestowed upon him had been a testament to his courage and it was a most fitting celebration of his magnificent journey which was now nearing its end.

We were escorted as far as the Golden Gate Bridge and then we proceeded on to Valley Memorial Park in Novato. We arrived and entered the small, peaceful chapel. When everyone was seated, Dawson's casket was carried in by his pallbearers and placed on a stand. They removed their white gloves and laid them upon the casket. Deacon Joe spoke briefly and Claudia read from a card we had received from a friend that week. It had touched my heart as though it were Dawson's own words telling me he was "Safely Home." Mostly maintaining her composure, she read:

"I am home in Heaven dear ones;
Oh, so happy and so bright!
There is perfect joy and beauty
In this everlasting light.
All the pain and grief is over,

Every restless tossing passed;
I am now at peace forever,
Safely home in Heaven at last.
Did you wonder I so calmly
Trod the valley of the shade?
Oh, but Jesus' love illumined
Every dark and fearful glade.
And He came Himself to meet me
In that way so hard to tread;
And with Jesus' arm to lean on,
Could I have one doubt or dread?
Then you must not grieve so sorely,
For I love you dearly still;
Try to look beyond earth's shadows,
Pray to trust our Father's Will.
There is work still waiting for you,
So you must not idly stand;
Do it now, while life remaineth
You shall rest in Jesus' land.
When that work is all completed,
He will gently call you Home;
Oh, the rapture of that meeting,
Oh, the joy to see you come!"

We all sat silently as she read, then Deacon Joe told everyone they were invited back to our house. I sat quietly for a few moments, then I stood and went to Dawson. I put my fingertips to my lips then touched his casket with my kiss. I whispered, "I love you, Dawson," and tears fell quietly. I was telling myself, *Don't scream. Don't wail. Make Dawson proud. Show dignity and make my mother proud.* I stood there a moment then walked from the chapel out to the tree-lined courtyard. Everyone then filed past Dawson, stopping, then joining me outside.

When back at the house, friends and family hugged me and told me how sorry they were. What seemed to console me most was the obvious admiration Dawson had from his many friends. So many of them came to me and wanted to tell me their funny Dawson stories. Their eyes lit up when they recalled the humorous things Dawson had said. Some felt as I did that Dawson's quick, spontaneous wit defied retelling and one such friend just said, "He always had us laughing. We'd never know what he was going to say or how he could come up with such funny stuff all the time." It made me feel good to see so many young men who, while appearing so sad, were smiling and laughing remembering Dawson. They stood around me, all talking, saying, "There was this one time when … and how about the time … and remember when he … " and on and on with their fondest memories. It was wonderful to hear the delight in their voices. "Dawson was definitely unique," one of them said and they all agreed.

That Dawson had so many friends may not have surprised me, but the extent of their admiration did. What surprised me even more was when Dawson's female friends wanted to share their feelings for Dawson with me. One told me how, when her husband had died, Dawson had been the friend who helped her the most. She said, "He'd come by and take me out for a ride and just let me talk and cry. He was a very special person."

"Sheri loves Dawson," her friend, Anita, said. "She came down from Washington to be here." Then looking very serious, Anita said, "I had called the hospital a few times trying to find out how Dawson was doing, but it was very hard to get any information. How was he? I mean, you know, most of the time while he was there, how was he?"

"He was Dawson," I said. "He was totally Dawson … and so much more."

A twinkle came into her eyes taking away some of the sadness and she said, sighing, "Oh, I am so happy to hear you say that. I had such visions."

"Well, I'm not saying that he did not go through a lot, a lot of rough times, but through it all … he was still Dawson … funny, sharp, sarcastic … but he was even more … he truly had found faith … he was loving and so wise … it was as if he had learned the meaning of life. He had made an incredible journey."

"It sounded that way. When the chaplain was talking, it seemed like something really special had happened to him."

"Yes, it had and she found it so extraordinary that she had written a paper about that meeting and submitted it for her ministry's thesis."

"Really? Well, what she said was so beautiful. So it seems he was at peace. You know we all would have gone to see him … "

"I know. He knows, too."

"Thank you for telling me all this," she said. "I feel much better. We all loved him."

"Thank you," I said. "It means a lot to me to see how much Dawson was loved. I didn't know. I only knew how much I loved him and how very special he was to me."

Another young woman I did not know had joined us. Her name was Victoria. "He cared a lot for you, too," she said. I may have looked surprised to hear her say that, for she added, "He did. He always spoke well of you and his whole family. He used to tell us how creative you were. He was very proud of you and his sister, too. He said she was really smart."

"Really?"

"Oh, yeah. I am so glad to finally meet you. I understand now why Dawson was so special."

I said, "I don't think anyone has ever said anything nicer to me. Thank you."

A young woman named Tanya said, "I know Bill is sure proud of you."

"What makes you say that?" I asked, taken by surprise.

"I saw it in his eyes as he was looking at you while he was introducing you as Dawson's mother and telling how you were at the hospital with Dawson every day. It's obvious he admires you very much."

"We've been through a lot together these past months and he knows how important it was that we were with him. I am so grateful to have had that time. Dawson was incredible, so brave and he took responsibility for everything that had happened to him. He blamed no one."

"I believe that," Tanya said. "It doesn't surprise me at all. No matter what Dawson had gotten himself into, you know, drinking or whatever, what always impressed me about him was that he never lost his integrity. Never. You could always trust him."

"That is very nice to hear. It is wonderful to see that Dawson had so many loving friends. In the end, you know what he hoped for most," I said, "was that his friends would benefit from his mistakes."

These loving friends of Dawson's all hugged me and throughout the day, they and other good friends took care of things, clearing the tables, doing dishes and such.

Tom, one of the pallbearers came to me wanting to tell me what had happened when we had arrived at the cemetery. He said, "When we got there, the driver of the hearse told us to put Dawson's coffin on the cart so we could just wheel him into the chapel." Tom paused, then looking directly at me, his bright blue eyes sparkling, he said emphatically, "We told him, 'No way! We're not wheeling him in. We'll *carry* our buddy Dawson. We're going to carry him.'"

If I ever had any doubt, I had none now. I was not the only one who thought Dawson was special and it was not just because I was his mother. Dawson was special, unique and loved and now I had discovered he was also respected.

Ian said, "There are so many stories we could have told about Dawson last night at the service, well, some of them may not have been too appropriate, but there are a lot of funny and great stories of things Dawson has said and done, but it just was too hard to speak. I'd like to spend a day with you and Bill and share some of the stories with you guys."

"Yeah, anytime. We'd love to hear them. Come by anytime. I certainly understand how hard it was to get up and speak last night. I wanted to say some things, too, but couldn't. Well, that guy Mike saying, 'That boy could ride and I'm gonna miss him,' said a lot."

"Hey, it was true. Dawson could ride!"

They began to tell me the Dawson bike stories, most of which I was glad I had never heard before. "One time, we're on the freeway," his friend said, "this guy cuts Dawson off and he's forced into the guardrail. Man, anyone else but Dawson would've lost it!"

I said, "He always loved to ride."

"Well, just because you like to ride doesn't mean you *can* ride."

"Oh, so if someone has a bike and rides it, it doesn't mean he can ride?"

"No!" they all agreed. "You can ride or you *CAN RIDE!* Dawson could definitely RIDE!"

Sunday: Claudia and Tracy came over and we spent most of the day talking about Dawson's funeral service and how beautiful everything had been. As everyone who had attended expressed to us, it was not just the gorgeous flowers or the magnificent church. It was much more than that. There was a feeling, an atmosphere, an aura of spiritual splendor. It had been a glorious acknowledgment of Dawson's life. And beyond that, it had acknowledged the beauty of Dawson's journey into death. It had magnificently honored the reality that Dawson had done something none of us had done and he had gone to a place where none of us had been and we were awed. I could see it in the eyes of all those who had attended as they spoke of how amazed they had been by the Deacon Joe meeting story, how impressed by the beauty of St. Dominic's Church and how inspired by Father Xavier's words. We were told how moved they had been by Juana's experience with Dawson and how encouraged by his faith. Claudia, too, seemed surprisingly impressed. Some friends even expressed their inspiration to return to church, which was the greatest thing anyone could have said. I knew that pleased Dawson.

That evening, Bill and I planned to go to five o'clock mass. Tracy had left for home, but Claudia planned to stay the week with us. Claudia had not been to Sunday mass in a very long time and I said to her, "You'll come to church with us, hon, won't you?" I was pleased when she seemed quite willing.

This was our first mass at Our Lady of Loretto parish. Its architecture was plain and modern, quite a contrast to St. Dominic's. We were all standing when the priest said, "Let us pray for our departed brothers and sisters and especially Dawson Bell." Claudia and I both gasped. We had not expected to hear Dawson's name here and the words had taken us quite by surprise.

"Oh, Mom," Claudia said as she hugged me. This was just our first mass here and though St. Dominic's still felt like our church, I knew then Our Lady of Loretto was going to be home for us. After mass, as we lit a large candle for Dawson I knew this would be home for him as well.

Monday: I awoke to the fact this was the day we would say our final good byes to Dawson. My mother and father, Claudia, Matt, Jenn, Bill and I drove down the street to the cemetery. No, it was no longer the cemetery. It was now, as its name stated, the memorial park. Dawson was at the memorial park.

Dawson's coffin had been placed in front of his crypt. The marble slab had been removed from the front and a blue velvet drape had been placed over the opening. We stood there several minutes quietly praying to ourselves. I touched his coffin for the last time as I said, "I love you, Dawson and I will always be with you. Nothing can separate us. I am with you, hon, and you are with me in my heart, safe and so very, very loved."

Chapter Thirty-Five

A week had passed since Dawson's life had come to an end, but our lives had to continue on and one week after Dawson's death and one day after his burial, Bill went back to work. Work would be good for him, but being alone would not have been good for me. Claudia must have known that when she had decided to stay.

After having cared for Dawson for so many months, it seemed I had only managed to survive my first week without him because I had the funeral arrangements to take care of. Planning Dawson's services, in addition to keeping me busy, had enabled me to continue to do for him. But now, what purpose could I find to my days?

Everything was changed for me and for everyone, including Harley. He no longer had to spend fifteen hours a day locked in his pen and he certainly seemed to have enjoyed the past week with Bill home. Bill let him outside each morning and as long as Bill was home, Harley was allowed to come and go as he pleased. His life had definitely changed, but it was about to change again and so was mine.

Before Bill left for work, I said to him, "I don't feel comfortable letting Harley out on his own like you do to roam wherever he wants."

"But he's pretty good," Bill said. "He doesn't go far. He really stays on the property most of the time."

"But I would worry about him. He could get hurt if he went out in the street."

"You have to let him out sometime. He has to go."

"I know, but … I just can't have anything happen to him … and especially when you're not home."

Bill thought a minute, then he said, "Dawson has a leash for him. You could take him out for a walk."

"Take him for a walk?" With some hesitation, I said, "O.K., I guess I could do that." As amazing as it seemed, I had never taken a dog for a walk in my whole life. As a child we only had cats.

Bill found Harley's leash in Dawson's room and as he left for work, he said, "I'll call you later."

I put Harley's leash on him and bundled myself up to face the cool November morning. I wrote a quick note for Claudia and I said to Harley, "We're going for a walk." We headed out the door and started down the road, Harley happily trotting along, a dog with a purpose. "Where are we going?" I asked and I answered, "Dawson's. We're going to Dawson's." Thus began our tradition, our daily routine with a purpose for us both.

It was an easier walk than I had expected. We walked down to the corner, turned and walked past the large eucalyptus trees, then through the black iron gates of the memorial park. I instantly saw the many funeral flowers covering the front of Dawson's crypt. When I reached his place, I said, "Mom's here, Dawson, Mom's here." I stood there, tears streaming down my face. "I love you, hon," I said, believing that somehow he could hear me, but finding it hard to believe I was standing where Dawson had been laid to rest.

We stayed a short while and when we returned home, Claudia met us at the door. It was a great comfort to know she would be with me to help me through the remainder of the week. And what a tremendous help she was. She started right in getting us busy working on a thank you card list, which involved going through the gift cards from all the flowers, the sympathy cards we had received in the mail and taking and deciphering the names from the guest book. She began an efficient list with codes denoting whether a person had visited, sent flowers, sent a card or telephoned. I had to do a little detective work in order to supply her with some current addresses and along with that, in my mind, I designed the thank you cards. I wanted them to be special, something different than the ones given to us by the funeral home. I wanted to send thank yous as unique as Dawson.

Bill called me from work as he had said he would. In fact, he called me twice. Each time he said, "I just wanted to see how you were doing." Claudia seemed pleased, but somewhat surprised by his concern and attention for me, but I was not surprised. Bill and I had shared an extraordinary experience that would undoubtedly leave us forever changed and it had created a sense of protectiveness for each other and a special kind of bond between us.

Claudia asked, "Mom, do you think you'll stay here? Are you and Dad back together?"

"It's hard to say. All I know is, for now, being here feels right. I can't imagine being anywhere else right now."

Throughout the week, Claudia and I worked on the thank you list, all the while continuing to add to it. We were receiving cards daily and hearing from those who had attended Dawson's service telling us it had been the most beautiful and most inspiring funeral they had ever seen.

Just as planning the funeral had helped me get through my first week without Dawson, occupying myself with the thank you card project helped me get through the second week. It made me feel there were still things I could do for Dawson, still ways I could make him proud, still ways I could show my love for him.

Claudia's stay had been both comforting and productive and the time for her to leave came much too soon. It was an unusually warm afternoon for November as we stood on the porch hugging goodbye. "Are you going to be O.K., Mom?" she asked.

I really wasn't sure I would be, but I said, "Yeah, I'll be fine, hon. Really. Thanks so much for being with me and for all the work you've done. It was so good to have you here."

"I'm glad I could do it. If you get any more addresses or figure out some of those names, give me a call," she said as she walked to her car. She waved goodbye, got in and drove down the road. I stood on the porch watching her as a warm breeze touched my face and sadness filled my heart. It was one of those days, one of those warm autumn days, but the sadness I felt had nothing to do with the weather. It was seeing Claudia leaving and knowing she would be three hours away when she returned home. I felt a burning sensation in the back of my throat, a now-familiar signal that tears would soon follow. I was still watching her as she turned at the corner where the school bus used to stop. The tears that had been welling up inside me began to run down my face as I mourned not only for Dawson, but for the years that had also passed away. I was overcome with pangs of regret thinking of the irreplaceable loss of precious days that were gone forever, days that had not been fully appreciated and now it was too late. It was that which wreaked upon me the sorrow that I could not suppress. This day was as sad as any I had ever known. Was this the Indian Summer day I somehow always knew I was to live? The overwhelming sadness that I felt as I walked back into the empty house, had it always been with me just waiting for this day?

Feeling more alone than I ever had, I crumpled to the floor next to Harley and wrapped my arms around him, sobbing into the thick, gray fur on his neck. He turned his head and licked my ear. "Oh, Harley," I said, both crying and laughing, "what a blessing you are. I'll bet Dawson knew I was going to need you." Harley tilted his head looking at me. "Maybe we should go for a walk," I said. "What d'ya think?"

We had not taken an afternoon walk before this and before we left, I touched up my makeup, changed my shoes and called my mother. I did not want her to worry, in case she called me while I was out. "We're walking down to Dawson's," I said.

The timing was perfect. I knew Bill stopped there every day on his way home from work and we arrived to find him sitting on the bench in front of Dawson's crypt. He looked up, pleased and surprised to see us. "Hey, you guys," he said, smiling as Harley wagged his funny little tail at the sight of Bill. Then Bill looked at me with an expression that seemed to foretell he was about to say something important. But when he spoke, all he said was, "I'm going to be starting on a new project at work next week."

"Oh?" I said, wondering why he had such an odd expression on his face.

"It sounds pretty interesting," he said.

"What is it? Will you be leaving the Transamerica job?"

"No, I'll still be at the Pyramid. In fact, I'll actually be working *in* the pyramid."

"What do you mean? Doing what?" He still had that odd look on his face and I asked, now with great interest, "Bill, what is it you'll be doing?"

"They're putting in a new light at the top of the spire, which is eight hundred feet high. They're calling this light "The Crown Jewel" because it will have huge prisms that will give it an unusual, gem-like effect. They say it is going to be so beautiful and so powerful it will be visible for miles and will shine in the sky like nothing anyone's ever seen."

"Bill! It'll shine to the heavens."

"Yeah, I know and I'm going to be in charge of it."

"Bill, do you realize?"

"Yeah. Dawson will see that light."

"He will. I know he will."

"Now while he's out there roaming the cosmos," Bill said, "he will never get lost. He will have this light to guide him. It will show him the way home."

"Oh, Bill. It will be Dawson's light," I cried.

"I don't know, but it just seems like something, that I should be the one to put this light in at this particular time."

"It *is* something. It really is something to have been given such an opportunity. It will be like the candles we light for Dawson. It will be like a giant candle with its light burning just for him. And you'll be the one to light it."

"Yeah," he said, wiping tears from his eyes.

"This is a gift, Bill."

"I know. And it will be my gift to Dawson."

The following Tuesday, two weeks from the day Dawson died, Bill started work on "Dawson's Light."

Though it had been a couple of weeks, sympathy cards continued to come in and Bill and I cried as we read each one. Crying had become a daily experience for me. But the tears Bill and I shed as we read the cards were not just tears of sadness, they were also tears born out of awe and appreciation for the love that was expressed. There were some that, along with expressing their sympathy for us, shared their remembrances and thoughts of Dawson.

Despite my own feelings of love for him and despite that I had seen such admiration and respect for him from his peers, I was amazed when I read the glowing accounts of him from the most unexpected sources.

One from an electrical foreman read: *Dawson was my apprentice a while back. I just want to tell you that he was the nicest young man I had met in a long time. I have a son also in the trade. I can only imagine your pain. My son ran into Dawson some time ago and told me of his illness, but I am still shocked. All I can say is that my prayers are with you and your family.*

Another electrician wrote: *Bill, I think a lot of you and Dawson. After working with and getting to know Dawson, I can honestly say he was the most polite and well-mannered young man, plus being a great electrician and person, that I have come across. My heart goes out to you.*

These sentiments for Dawson filled my heart, for they told me he must always have been the young man I thought he was. Some of what I had seen in Dawson, others had seen, as well. How I ached to see Dawson again and however hopeless and impossible it was, I longed to see his smile. It must truly have been a special smile, that smile of his, for so many of his friends had remarked about it to me. A card from Bill's cousin, Tim, and his wife, Lorraine, seemed to confirm that. She wrote in part: … *I hadn't seen Dawson in some time, but I always remember how handsome he was. And Tim said that even when he was little he always had a cute, little smile on his face. I hope that all the wonderful memories he gave you stay clear for you and help you through this very difficult time.*

Then we received a card quite unexpected and undeniably precious. It read: *Dear Andrea and Bill, my heart goes out to you, as though words might ease your grief. Dawson was such a wonderful young man, wise beyond his too few years. His warmth, his incredible smile, his courage gave the many days in ICU meaning. The pain of losing a child so deeply loved is unimaginable. You gave him everything. He gave so much back. With deepest sympathy and love, Elissa (ICU nurse.)* The incredibly tiny writing was so fitting, for this was from the tiny nurse with the soft voice, the nurse Dawson had so admired for her strength and kindness. I had told Dawson she liked him and it was true. *Dawson, it was true.*

These expressions of sympathy from those who knew Dawson spanned from his childhood to his young adulthood to his very last days. He had obviously touched others' lives and he had ultimately found meaning to his own life. He had so much to live for, it would have been understandable for me to be angry with God and to shake my fist at Him and demand an answer as to why He took Dawson. But I did not demand that from Him and I was not angry. There were times when I found my mind wandering close to asking in a quiet, undemanding way, "Why, God?" but I decided there was no point in asking. Some days I truly believed the day would come when I would have the answer, though many days I felt there was no answer that could ever satisfy me.

It seemed that every minute of every day my thoughts were filled with memories of Dawson. That was especially true while on my walks, as I relived my days in the hospital with him, the many, many days—yet far too few—that we had shared. I thought back to the day I had not gone to see him because of my cold. I had not known it then, but I was never to see him awake again. I relived the last time I had spoken to him, when I had called him and Elissa had told me he wasn't doing well. When he got on the phone, it was to be the last time I would hear his voice. *Oh, my, God,* I thought, *the very last words I heard him say to me were, "Mom, I've gotta go."* He had to leave me and he had told me so.

Dawson, I do not know why you had to die and as long as I live, I may never know, but I do believe it was something you had to do. I may have to wait until I see you again and until I come face to face with God before I have the answer, but someday, Dawson, I believe I will know why. Until that day, I will trust in God's wisdom.

I also thought about the last conscious act Dawson did upon this earth. The very last thing he did before he fell into the sleep from which he would never awaken, he did for Bill. All the times over the years when Bill had asked Dawson to do something for him and all the times that Dawson had not done it, the very last thing Dawson did he did because Bill had asked him to. Dawson did not want to be put back on the respirator, but he agreed to it when Bill had begged,

"Please, Dawson, do it for me." Dawson had spoken to me about how everyone would know what a changed person he was when the first time someone asked him to do something for them, he would do it.

You were true to your word, Dawson, may God bless you.

God certainly had blessed me and I thanked Him every day for my loving friends and family and Harley. Harley gave me a reason to get up in the morning and a reason to go out. He had become my partner. We now walked every afternoon, in addition to our morning walks. Each morning after we returned home, I called my mother. Just knowing she was there to listen helped me through each day.

Sympathetic friends and family had all told me I could call them anytime.

"If you need anything or if you just need to talk, you know you can call," they had said to me. I knew they were sincere, but I seldom called anyone other than my mother. I hated to call someone just to tell them how sad I was, but when anyone called me and asked, I did tell them.

My friend, Sheila, who had lost her daughter in an automobile accident several years earlier, just days before her daughter's twenty-first birthday, called one afternoon. We talked a long while and it was comforting to talk to someone who really knew what I was going through. She told me how after her daughter had died, she had gone right back to work. She said it had been good for her. But she told me how she would have to plan what she was going to wear to work each day and then lay her clothes out the night before because this simple task would take her hours, for she was unable to keep her mind focused. She said she cried a lot at work and often got lost driving there. Despite how it sounded, she said having to get up and go to work had helped her, and she suggested I think about getting a job. Though I had a great need to keep busy, I felt I was incapable of going to work and especially starting a new job. Beyond that, there seemed to be something else I had to do. The days I had spent with Dawson had such a profound effect on me, I knew whatever I did, it had to be something that would be meaningful for me and for Dawson.

Sheila told me she had been unable to find any comfort in faith, so I was surprised when she said to me, "Andrea, I believe they have a way of reaching us. Stay open to receiving little signs, little messages from Dawson." She went on to tell me how she had been taking a nap one afternoon and she had heard her daughter say, "Mom, I'm O.K.," and she awoke to the scent of her perfume. She also told me of the day she and her husband were visiting an old "ghost" town and she felt her daughter's hand grasp hers.

"Oh, Sheila," I cried, "I have hoped that something like that would happen to me, but I was afraid to believe that it actually could."

"Well, it won't be just like that, but there will be something, maybe even something small, but there will be something. A bag of groceries rolled off the table on one of her birthdays. I hadn't said 'Happy Birthday' to her yet and it was as if she were reminding me. There have been lots of little things. I know some of the things could seem silly to other people, but when they happen to you, you'll know."

"I hope so. Hearing this really helps me because I have been thinking Dawson would find a way to let me know he was still with me. You have given me hope it could happen."

"I'm glad," she said. "Andrea, take care. It will get easier. It never gets easy, but it does get less hard. It just takes time. Right now, he is probably all you can think about, but someday you'll find yourself thinking less about what happened. Maybe it will be for just a few minutes, then one day maybe an hour or so will go by and, in time, well, like I said, it will get less hard. One day you'll be able to smile and even laugh again. When that happens, don't feel guilty. I remember the first time I laughed. I caught myself and thought, how can I be laughing when my daughter ..."

"But she would want you to," I said.

"Yes, and Dawson wants you to, too."

I thought a lot about our conversation after we hung up. I thought of the joy I would feel if I received a sign from Dawson and I wondered how he would choose to let me know he was with me. I decided he would not appear in a vision before me nor would he speak to me, for he would know I would seriously question my sanity if his presence were overtly supernatural. So he would be subtle. He would be clever. He would do something that would have special meaning to me. It would be something little that I could choose to explain away if I feared my grief was taking me over the edge. But a part of me had to wonder, *Will I really get a message from Dawson? Will I really?* And I worried, *What if I don't?*

She also had spoken of how difficult it was for others to know how to deal with our grief. I agreed that no one really knew what to say. How could anyone know, when in fact, there was nothing anyone could say. She told me it upset her when someone would say, "I know how you must be feeling." She said that no one knew. I told her that was probably true, but even though they did not really know, they did know it must be horrible to lose your child. And that was true. It certainly was.

Of all the friends that had told me to call anytime, it was Elaine who did not wait for me to call her. She called me almost every day. She was not what I would have thought of as a close friend, though I had known her for several years, but she was there for me as close as any friend could be.

I had met her through Rusty. He and her husband worked at the same firehouse and were good friends. Over the years, we had gone out with them to dinner, to the firehouse Christmas parties, to the racetrack and we always attended the annual bocce ball party she and John gave at their home. She was one of the nicest people I had ever met. I never saw her cranky or heard her say anything unkind about anyone. Whenever we were at a gathering, we usually ended up sitting with each other, talking, but she and I had never gotten together on our own.

Our circumstances were much different now. I was no longer working and we now lived in the same town. Although I had always known her to be a kind person, I was somewhat surprised how she had so naturally taken me under her wing. Many days she would call and just say, "Let's go out to lunch today," or "Come shopping with me. I need your help choosing some fabric." And although many days I did not feel like going out, she gave me a reason to. Being out with her did help to take my mind off of my sorrow. Sometimes it amazed me how that was possible. It was not that I would forget my sadness, I never did. It was always there, but I was able to function and do things in spite of it. When my grief did surface, Elaine was sympathetic and understanding. She cried herself as she told me of her young brother who had died many years earlier of an enlarged heart. She told me how on the night before he died, he spoke of seeing their late grandfather standing at the foot of his bed. She said that was a sign that our loved ones will be there to greet us when we reach Heaven. She told me it was important for us to pray for those we loved who had died. "The more prayers that are said for them," she said, "the sooner they get to Heaven."

Elaine was known for making beautiful lamp shades and one day when she called, she said, "Do you want to make a shade? I'm going to this great shop in Sonoma tomorrow morning. Why don't you come with me and get a frame and I'll show you how to cover it and we can work together."

I had covered lamp shades many years before. I had sewn them all by hand and it was a lengthy project, but Elaine had a method that required no sewing, so it was much quicker. I decided to make a small shade for Bill's mother for her birthday, which was two days after mine and less than a week away. Elaine assured me I could have it finished in time.

The next morning she picked me up and drove us to this incredible shop in a little old cottage where the owner lived. There were dozens of the most fabulous lamp shades I had ever seen and stacks of frames in various shapes and sizes and rolls and rolls of luxurious hand-dyed and beaded fringe.

Elaine was in the next room when the owner said to me, "I'm

sorry about the loss of your son." I was taken by surprise and must have shown it, for she explained, "Elaine told me. When she called yesterday to tell me she was coming by today, I told her that I was going to be closed because I had some things to do. Elaine asked me if I could wait for her if she got here early. She said, 'My friend just lost her son. She needs a project and I want her to get started right away.'"

"That sounds like Elaine," I said. "She is a very special person."

"Yes, she is. How long has it been since you lost your son?"

"Three weeks today," I said. "It's hard to believe he's been gone that long."

Elaine bought some supplies and I bought a small frame, a base, some mauve brocade fabric and beaded fringe. Thanks to Elaine, I had a project. When we arrived at her house, she said, "This is where we'll work, here on the dining room table. I always do my lamps here."

"I guess that is Mario's," I said, seeing a model car in progress.

Mario was Elaine's sixteen-year-old grandson who lived with her and John, and I had seen him several times over the years. I did not know him very well, but I had always felt kindly toward him. He had reminded me of Dawson. He had dark hair, was nice looking, and was quiet and subdued in a way much like Dawson was when he was younger. Though he was never openly affectionate to Elaine, whenever he looked at her, his eyes lit up and I could see the love and admiration he felt for his "nonna." When Elaine spoke of him, it was obvious he had a special place in her heart.

"Yes, we work here together," she said, smiling. "I do my lamps and he does his cars."

"Dawson had a paint organizer just like that," I said, staring at the orange plastic, tiered swivel rack holding the little bottles of model paint. "Dawson always liked making model cars, too." Remembering how much I had enjoyed those days when Dawson and I would sit side by side working on jigsaw puzzles together, I could have stood there and cried wishing Dawson and I could be sitting at our dining room table working on our projects. That was the way it was. I might manage to find some pleasure in an enjoyable task, but it was always with the sorrow never far away.

The following morning, just as I was about to leave for my walk, the phone rang. It was the neighbor next door, Jennifer, the mother of the boy who had made the thoughtful card and clay box for Dawson when he was in the hospital. She said she had seen me walking many mornings and asked if she could join me. I did not know her, for her family had moved in after I had left, but she knew Bill and Dawson and she sounded quite sincere as she expressed her interest in wanting to talk to me. I told her I was leaving in a few minutes and I would meet her at the end of her driveway. Instead of walking down to Dawson's, I decided we should take another route. It was a much longer walk, but it went quickly, for we talked the entire time. She told me she had been thinking of Bill and me and was feeling so bad for us. She said, "This is just not the way it is supposed to be. It is not meant for the child to go before the parents."

"That's true," I said. "Yes, had I gone first, I would have been spared this terrible pain, but if I had died before Dawson, I would not have been there for him when he needed me. I would rather endure my agony, than to have had Dawson go through his suffering without me by his side. He was not too old to need his mother and I am just thankful I was there for him." As we continued to walk, I told her Dawson's story, my story, our story, the story of our faith and what we had experienced on our journey. I told her how Dawson had wanted everyone to know his story because he thought it would help others. I told her how on the night we had to say goodbye to him, I had cried that Dawson had not been given the chance to tell it. Then I told her what Bill had said to me, "Well, Andrea, then you'll just have to do it."

"You will, won't you?" she asked.

"I don't know. I'd love to do that for him, but I don't know if I can. He never really told me what he wanted to say. It was something we were going to do together when he got well. I can't tell his story the way he would have told it. I can only tell it from my perspective, so I don't know."

"Oh, Andrea, you should do it. Just what you've told me today, you've told beautifully. I'm so glad I called you and we had this chance to talk. I feel much better seeing how strong and brave you are." She was wiping tears from her eyes as she said, "I really admire you."

I was humbled by her words and felt undeserving. "Thank you," I said, "but I'm really not very strong. I do have faith and it is only because of Dawson and what we had experienced that I can still hold on to it. I feel very blessed."

"It is so wonderful you are able to feel that way."

"I know. That is exactly why I see what Dawson and I went through as a miracle. That is the miracle, feeling blessed even after the worst has happened. Seeing Dawson's enlightenment is the *only* thing that could have helped me through this. Had he died without it and without ever having opened his heart to me, I would not be here talking to you like this today. Our experience instilled in me the belief that Dawson's life and death was meaningful in a way beyond our imagination and though I suffer over my loss, I know he is in a better place. Had he survived, even that would not have been as miraculous. It would have been a wonderful medical miracle, but this blessed feeling and realization can only be described as a miracle of God."

"Andrea, I'm Catholic and I fell away from my religion, too, but I'm going to go back to church. Thank you," she said and we hugged goodbye.

As I walked down the road, I could hear Dawson's words, "I want everyone to know my story. I think it will help someone."

Dawson! Has it already, just this morning, made a difference in someone's life? Was what we experienced going to help guide her back to her faith?

Though I had seemed strong to her and it was my faith that kept me going, the truth was that my heart was still broken, that I cried every day and that I missed Dawson terribly. At times, I was able to console myself with the belief that Dawson was at peace, but I could not keep my heart from aching for all the things Dawson had hoped to do and never would.

As I went into the house, I was thinking about one thing he had wanted to do, what we had planned to do together, to tell his story. Was it possible I could do that for him?

Throughout the day, I thought about how there could be no greater gift I could give Dawson and no more meaningful endeavor I could pursue, than to tell his story and have it help someone.

By Thursday, I had Bill's mother's lamp shade completed. I had finished it in time, just as Elaine had promised. Bill and I were going to give it to her when we went out to dinner Saturday night. Claudia and Tracy would be coming up for the occasion and I was looking forward to seeing her.

Thoughts of telling Dawson's story continued to stay in my mind, but I was filled with doubt. I questioned Bill, "Did you really mean it when you said that I'd have to tell Dawson's story for him?"

"Yes."

"You really think I can?"

"Yeah."

"But he really didn't tell me … "

"Andrea, you were with him every day. You know everything he went through better than anyone. You know all you need to know. And I think Dawson would want you to do it."

"Oh, Bill, you do?"

"Yes, Andrea, I really do."

"But Bill, can I? Can I do it?"

"Yes, of course you can."

"Oh, Bill. I'd be doing it for Dawson. It would be my gift to him. I want so much to do that for him, but I just don't know."

"Well, I think you should do it."

"Bill, I want to order Dawson's plaque. We have to decide what we're going to put on it." We had been discussing what we wanted to say and the simple words that expressed what was in our hearts were, "We love you," and we had decided that was what we'd put on the line above his name. But we could also choose to put a line below the dates if we wanted to, but we had not yet decided upon that. I said, "I was thinking about the second line and you know the phrase that keeps coming to my mind is what Mike had said, 'He could ride.' I think Dawson would like that. And I guess it really was something how well he could ride. I had never realized before how much that must have meant to him."

"I like it," Bill said, without hesitation.

"You do?"

"Yeah."

"So do you want to put that on it, then? 'He could ride.'"

"Yeah. What else is it going to say? What did we decide?"

"Above his name, 'We love you.'"

"We love you," Bill repeated. "Yeah, that's good. We love you."

I was noticing that though Bill may have lost that twinkling, devil-may-care look in his eyes that I had found so seductive long ago, what had replaced it was far more charming. His eyes now told of the kindness and the gentleness that was in his heart.

"Then I'll go ahead and finish filling out the form," I said, "and take it in to the office when Harley and I go down for our walk tomorrow."

Tomorrow. My birthday. *Oh, Dawson, tomorrow is my birthday.*

Chapter Thirty-Six

Moonlight was streaming through the uncurtained window. I sat up in bed to look at the clock on Bill's night stand. The illuminated, red numbers told me it was 12:35. A little early, I thought, not only because I had barely been asleep more than an hour, but also because it was a little earlier than I had awakened the past four nights. Even though each of those nights, I had awakened at the exact same time, it was that I had awakened at precisely 1:42 that had astounded me. 1:42 A.M. was the time Dawson and I had both been born.

It would have been significantly appropriate to awaken at that time this night, fifty-two years to the minute of my birth. Undoubtedly, it was anticipating my birthday that had made me restless and had aroused me from sleep. For as I lay awake in the quiet, moonlit darkness, I was thinking, *If it's true that Dawson is able to get a message to me, he will certainly do it on my birthday.*

I had taken my friend, Sheila's, words quite to heart. "Stay open to receiving little messages from Dawson," she had said. And though at the time, I had already begun anticipating a sign from Dawson, her words had given me added reason to hope.

So far, I had not received any to speak of, but over the past few weeks, there were many times when I had called upon Dawson to help me and I felt he had. Those otherwise insignificant occasions were when I had misplaced various items, when the lock on the front door had jammed, and when I had decided I should reset the clock in my car. Daylight Savings Time had been over since two days before Dawson died, but I had put off changing the clock in my car because I didn't really care what time it was, but mostly it was because I could not remember how to do it without getting out the handbook. I knew there were three buttons I had to push, but I could never remember in which order. When they were done out of order, the clock display went crazy. Now I did not even want to try, for I was remembering the day when Dawson had been with me and I had asked him to do it for me. I told him the handbook was in the glove compartment. He said he didn't think he needed it, because he doubted it was that difficult to figure out. I told him that it was for me. After he had looked at all the buttons, he pushed the three in their correct order. "See," he had chuckled, "It was easy." Why did I mix it up every time?

So here it was, time to change the clock again and as before, I had forgotten how to do it and this time I did not have Dawson to help me, or did I? As I drove down the driveway, I said, "Dawson, could you help me, please, so I don't have to bother with the handbook? Just help me so I can get it right on the first try." I took a deep breath and pushed "reset," "clock," and "set." It worked! It was easy. "Thanks, Dawson!"

Whenever I talked to Dawson as if he were with me, I was reminded of Rusty's mother and the stories she told of her late husband. I thought she was silly when she said, "There is this intersection that is very busy. I always worry when I have to drive through it. I'm afraid I will not be able to get across. When I get there and the traffic clears for me, I say, 'Thanks, William.'" It sounded a little ridiculous to me at the time, but now whenever I asked Dawson for help, it did not seem ridiculous at all. It seemed quite natural to think of Dawson being somewhere where he could hear me and could help. These little things had comforted me these past weeks, but on my birthday, it would take something more.

I was lying there, feeling wide-awake, my anticipation soon turning to anxiety, as I thought, *What if I do not get a sign? What if there is no message from Dawson? What if he doesn't say "Happy Birthday?" How will I console myself if that should happen?* It would mean that Dawson could not hear my words nor my prayers and that he had no way of telling me that he loved me. It would mean he was truly gone. It would be like losing him a second time.

If Dawson were with me in the way I thought he was, he would want me to know and he would want to tell me he was thinking of me on my birthday. I had no doubt of that and that, in itself, was quite a blessing. But I begged for more and I reached over to my night stand for my rosary beads. I fell asleep praying for something, however small, but something I could interpret as a birthday wish from Dawson. I prayed for something to happen that would be one of those things that, as Sheila had said, "When it happens to you, you'll know." I prayed, fell asleep and awoke at dawn.

Friday, November 22, 1996, my first birthday without Dawson was upon me. This could have been the first birthday in a very long time I would not have had to worry or wonder if I would hear from Dawson, for I now knew he loved me. What a wonderful birthday this could have been. It could have been one of the happiest of my life. Instead, it was the saddest.

Bill wished me a happy birthday before he left for work, then Harley and I walked down to Dawson's. I cried all the way. "Mom's here," I said, as I had said every day when I arrived. It wasn't that I believed he was there waiting for me, but I believed when I was there, he was, too. With tears streaming down my face, I began the prayer I had been saying every day.

"Dear Lord, thank you for welcoming Dawson into your Kingdom of Heaven

Thank you for surrounding him with the beauty of your everlasting light

Thank you for comforting him with your love

Thank you for letting him know how much we love him

Thank you for letting us know how much he loves us

Have mercy on his soul, dear Lord, and on us all

That we may be rejoined with him

And dwell together with you

In the House of the Lord forever and ever. Amen."

As part of my daily ritual, I said, "I love you, Dawson. You know that. And I am with you, hon, and you are with me in my heart, safe and so very, very loved." I then clutched my arms across my chest in a mock hug, saying, "I've got your hug, Dawson, I've got your hug, the one you told me I would have forever." That hug comforted me often whenever I needed it. Harley and I walked home and again I cried the entire way, but there was nothing odd about that these days and crying was not at all unusual for me on my birthday.

I called my mother when I got home. "Happy birthday," she said, "I guess."

"Yeah, I guess, but how can it be happy?"

"I don't know," my mother said, sounding as forlorn as I had ever heard her. "Andrea, I don't know how this could have happened to us. I did not believe my God would ever do this. He has always answered my prayers. Things like this just don't happen to me. God has never let me down before."

I understood that her mourning was not only over her loss of Dawson, for in addition to having lost her only grandson, she had lost her faith in God. She said she did not understand how He could have turned His back on her when she needed Him the most. It was understandable how sorrowful she must have felt, for are they not said to be the saddest words in the Bible, "Lord, why hast though forsaken me?"

I did not want her to feel betrayed. "Mom," I said, "there is a reason for this. We cannot expect to understand it now, but someday we will. And I know Dawson is O.K. He's in a better place. And you know how you always say things are 'a pattern set'? Well, you probably didn't think this could happen to Dawson because his pattern was always to luck out. But if you believe in your 'pattern set' then we must believe Dawson did luck out. We just can't see it, but maybe getting his heart, trying to live up to the expectations he had, I don't know, maybe it would have been too much. Maybe God knew."

"I hope so."

"I have to believe that. After everything Dawson and I experienced, I must. I will never stop believing God was listening and answered our prayers. But today, I have to hear from Dawson. There has to be something I can determine is from him. If there is nothing, then there will be only one conclusion I can come to and it won't be that he doesn't love me. Mommy, do you think there will be something?"

"I don't know," she sighed.

"If I don't hear from him … what will I do? … how will I reconcile that within myself, for if he really is somewhere like I think he is… and if Sheila's daughter could … there would be no reason why he wouldn't …"

I did not know if it was because my mother could hear the desperation in my voice and was just trying to console me or if she suddenly believed it, but she said, "You probably will."

"Hear from him?"

"Yes," she said confidently.

"Oh, God, I hope so. I guess I'll just have to wait and see. Ma, what do you think I ought to do about telling his story? I mean, should I try? Should I just try to write it as best I can? Just tell his story through my eyes?"

"Yeah, I think you should."

"And you think I can do it?"

"I know you can."

"You do?"

"Of course."

Claudia called to wish me a happy birthday. We talked briefly and she said, "I'll see you tomorrow, Mom." I told her how much I was looking forward to it. I hoped she had not been able to tell I'd been crying and when we hung up, I went back to working on what I had thought would be a simple project. There was an antique, oak side-by-side cabinet with a glass door that had been in Claudia's room when she lived here, and when I had found it empty in an unfinished room upstairs, I had told Bill I wanted him to bring it down so we could use it in the kitchen-dining area. He had looked at me incredulously. "You want me to carry that thing down here? Why?" I told him I thought it would be useful for putting some things in and it would make more sense than having it sitting up there doing nothing. With a deadpan expression, he looked at me and said, "Ooooh, yeah, I remember you." Maybe Dawson *had* gotten some of his humor from Bill.

So now that it was downstairs, I had filled the shelves and it proved to be quite useful. But the glass door made everything I put on its shelves visible and I did not like the way that looked, so I decided to gather a piece of lace behind the glass. That was the project I planned to finish today.

I had the lace measured and the piece cut when my cousin, Leah, called. She said, "How are you?"

"I don't know. It's pretty tough."

"Well, I just wanted to wish you a happy birthday ... but it just doesn't ..."

"I know," I said. "It doesn't really make sense to wish for a happy anything. Nothing can ever be happy. It just hurts too much. Sometimes I wonder how I can go on. I know there must be a reason for this happening to Dawson, but I still wish it hadn't." I began to cry. "I'm sorry," I said.

"It's all right. I just wish there was something I could do for you."

"I know. Thanks."

"Have you given any thought to writing Dawson's story?"

"Yeah, I've thought a lot about it. I'm just not sure. So you think I should do it? Do you think I could do a decent job of it?"

"Yeah, I do, but I don't think you should wait too long."

"It just seems so big. Where do I start?"

"It doesn't matter. What is important is that you do start. Write something down. Anything. Write something today."

"Today?"

"Yeah, why not?"

"My birthday? Hmm, my birthday."

"Yeah, that seems like a good day to start. Don't you think so?" Then she said emphatically, "Just start by writing *something* today, O.K.? It doesn't have to be a lot, even just one page, one paragraph. Just write. Will you do that?"

"O.K., I will. I promise."

When we got off the phone, I debated whether to go back to my lace project or start what might be my next project, writing. Because I had made that promise to Leah, I sat at the table and with pen and paper and tears, I began: *"As far back as I can remember, I have always cried on my birthday. Today is no exception. What were those silly things I had found to cry about in the past? When did I discover how trivial they were? I guess I've known for a long time now, but never more than I know it today."* It seemed the word "cry" could not even apply to what I had done on past birthdays when compared to the tears I shed today.

I went on to write about how in the past, I had to hear from Dawson in order to have a happy birthday and how, though I usually did hear from him, I was never sure that I would. But this year would have been so different, for he had become the son I had always known he could be. I wrote, *"Please let me hear from Dawson. I cry out as I have never cried out before."*

My cries were desperate and bittersweet, for without a doubt, I knew if he were alive I would hear him say to me, "Hi. Happy birthday.

I love you, Mom." I was drowning in tears as I wrote those words and I could not go on, but it was a start.

I needed to keep busy so as to not dwell on the fact I had not received a greeting from Dawson yet, so I went downstairs to work on attaching the lace. I did not have the right tools for the job. I needed tacks or staples or brads. If I had to hammer nails into the wood frame I was sure I would break the glass. I could have waited for Bill and had him help me do it right, but I wanted to do it myself and I wanted it done before he got home. I decided to try using straight pins. I knew that was a stupid idea, but it was all I had. I proceeded to stick the pins through the edges of the lace and into the hard wood frame around the glass as best I could. All the while, I was thinking how Dawson must be amused and, at the same time, appalled at my haphazard technique. I was sure he knew a better way and I was thinking perhaps I should go look in his room for some tiny nails he might have used for his woodworking projects. The pins were working, so I persisted with them, but the feeling that I should go and look in Dawson's room also persisted. I was nearly finished when I was compelled to go up to his room.

I had been in his room several times over the past weeks to borrow things like tools or glue and sometimes just to look around and to touch the things he had touched. I felt I knew everything in his room.

Today, I went in, went directly to his worktable and reached over to his tool chest with the small compartments, thinking there may be some tiny nails in one of them. As I reached across the table, I knocked over something he had been working on. It was one of his projects halted in progress. He had been in the process of repairing the leg of one of the dining room chairs. He had removed the leg from the chair and had set it on top of something. I had looked at the chair leg many times over the past several days and on some occasions, I had run my hand across the smoothly-sanded oak thinking of the last time he must have touched it and how he had not known he would never be working on it again. I had never noticed what it had been sitting on, not until this moment when I bumped the leg and knocked it off. There sat a brand-new toolbox. I stood there a moment, stunned. *A toolbox! Dawson, a toolbox!* I had reminded him in the hospital I had wanted a small toolbox for Christmas or my birthday. *My birthday, Dawson. You led me to my birthday present. You did! I know you did. Thank you, Dawson. Thank you, God.* I picked up the small, gray plastic toolbox.

It was empty, but it was more precious than any treasure chest might have been. I held it to my breast, sobbing, for this was the most magnificent gift I had ever received. It was not just a toolbox, it was not just a birthday present, it was an affirmation that Dawson was not gone. He was with me. And what I had written that morning was true! He would say those words to me. It was true!

Oh, Dawson, I knew you would want to let me know you were with me today. I knew our love was so strong nothing could separate us. I will never forget that. Thank you. You are a most loving son.

I called my mother and told her what had happened and what I'd found in Dawson's room. I said, "It's from Dawson, isn't it? Mommy, he led me to my present, didn't he?"

"Yes, he did," she said.

"You do believe that?"

"Yes, I really do. It has to be."

"Like Sheila said, when it happens to you, you'll know. Well, I know. I know Dawson made sure he gave me my gift. He did that for me. I know it," I said, crying. He had as much as spoken the words, "Happy birthday, Mom, I love you."

When I saw Bill that afternoon at Dawson's, I told him. He did not seem quite as awed as I was, but he was definitely thinking about it. He said, "I always ask him, 'Dawson, give me a sign. Please give me a sign.' But he hasn't."

"He will," I said. "This was a sign for me, just like I had asked. I know it was. When it happens to you, you'll know, too. It's when you know it in your heart." And only I knew how hard I had prayed for just something, anything, that would satisfy my need to hear from Dawson on my birthday and I had definitely received that. That was something no one could deny and that, in itself, was an extraordinary gift.

We opened the mail when we returned home and there was a card from Dawson's friend, Anita. It said: *"Dear Bill, Andrea and Claudia – It has been a few weeks since Dawson's funeral and we miss him so much, talking about him all the time. The vigil and funeral were beautiful. I was very touched by the chaplain as she spoke. The talk I had with you, Andrea, meant so much to us. (I relayed it, word for word, to Mike.) We hold on to those images ... of his spiritual healing, his encouragement to his family even in his own suffering, his humor. I truly believe that he was a far more mature and serene man at the end than he was when he entered the hospital. What he gained is priceless.*

To know God for even an instant is far better than an entire lifetime without Him. I know this because I had a similar revelation in 1982 in the hospital with systemic lupus. I thought I was dying, but instead, I had a divine appointment … I really appreciate your sharing all of those stories with me. And I am so grateful that you chose to share good news at his funeral along with the sad. I think it meant a lot to many others besides us. Dawson is so special to us. I'm not sure if I told you this, but Mike and I are very active in AA, being recovering alcoholics. Last Saturday, I was asked to speak to a group of us about any subject I wanted. I spoke about miracles and how much Dawson's life and death affected me. I didn't use his name, but spoke of the deep love and courage he showed and what I'd learned from my talk with you. Many people listening had tears in their eyes and you could hear a pin drop. I said that we need to follow his example like his mother wants to and that the miracles Dawson experienced and the growth can still be experienced by us, even if Dawson isn't here to tell us. He proved to me that it is true. He increased my faith! Now that we've met Dawson's family, we realize why he's so special! Anita and Mike."

I immediately called her and, crying, I thanked her for her beautiful letter. I said, "It was a wonderful birthday present for me. It meant so much to hear that Dawson's story was told to help others. That was just what he wanted." I thanked her again. It seemed so right that I had started writing this morning, for now I was sure that telling Dawson's story was something I must do.

Saturday arrived and we were to give Bill's mother her gift at dinner that evening. I was not feeling nearly as heavy-hearted as I might have been had I not heard from Dawson, yet my heart still sadly wished that he could really be with us. Claudia and Tracy arrived early in the afternoon. I showed her the lamp and told her I had not wrapped it because I did not have a box it would fit in. She suggested we go and buy one. Tracy drove us to the shopping center and while Claudia and I were in the box store, Tracy went to the video store. We found the perfect size box and as we were walking to the car, we saw Tracy walking toward us. Claudia and I looked at each other and then back at Tracy.

Claudia said, "Where did you get that?"

"At the video store."

"You bought it?"

"No, they were giving them away."

"What?" Claudia and I both said in unison.

"That's weird," Claudia said, as she looked at me. "A gorilla!"

"They had several different animals, but this is the one the man handed me," Tracy said. "Here, Andrea, I want you to have it. It's for you."

When Bill's mother had given Dawson the little gorilla in the hospital, she saw how much he liked it. From then on when she gave him get well cards, they had gorillas on them. Gorillas had come to symbolize Dawson to us and it had all started with Bill's mother. So to see Tracy carrying a gorilla that he had been given while Claudia and I were shopping for Bill's mother, astounded us. In fact, that's all we talked about as we rode home with the lamp in its box on the seat next to me and the furry toy gorilla on my lap.

I wrapped the present on the dining room table as the little gorilla sat there looking on. There was no doubt in my mind Dawson had found a way to tell me not to be sad that we were going to dinner without him, for he was with us. Claudia seemed as awed by the irony as I was. Then to my surprise, she said, "Mom, I've been going to church."

Claudia had not attended church for years, so this took me by surprise. I knew she had seemed impressed when the priest spoke to us at the hospital, but this seemed quite a turnaround for her. For when Dawson was first sick, I had given her the book about the healing power of prayers and after reading it, she had asked me why I had given it to her. She obviously had been uninspired.

"So do you mean you are going to mass on Sundays?" I asked.

"Yes."

"That's wonderful, Claudia. I'm so pleased to hear that."

"But I think I need to do more."

"What do you mean?"

"Well, they have this RCIA group ..."

"Oh, I know about that. Deacon Joe wanted me to go so I could make my confirmation."

"Yeah, well, you know, I haven't made mine either. I'm thinking of starting the class. I was told I could just go and see how I liked it and if at the end of the session, I did not want to get confirmed, I didn't have to. So I could just go to learn some things. It's been so long since I've been to church that I don't really understand what's going on. It's all so foreign. I don't know exactly what I hope to learn, but it is like I have a calling to go."

"Oh, hon, I think that is wonderful."

"Well, I haven't decided for sure, yet, but I am thinking about it."

That was a beautiful birthday gift from Claudia. I would be so happy if she returned to church. Dawson would be, too. His life and death had truly made a difference in others' lives.

Monday, Rusty called. He had told me he was going to hire someone to do the bookkeeping and now he called to tell me she was working out quite well. He said she was making progress in getting the books back in order. He said she could definitely see where I had left off and she was trying to continue with my system. He asked, "If she has any questions, can she call you?"

"Sure," I said. "I'd be glad to help her if I can."

"Thanks. How are you doing?"

"I don't know. I'm just so sad, but I still have faith and things do keep me believing. And you know how I told you that Dawson wanted everyone to know his story? Well, I've decided to try and do that for him. I started writing on my birthday, not much, but it's a start. And … well … you know once I start something … "

"Yes, I sure do. You will not quit. Andrea, I think it's great you're going to do that. Are you doing it on a computer?"

"No. I'm just writing freehand."

"Does Bill have a computer?"

"No. He hasn't had a need for one and I don't think I'd want to use a computer anyway. I would want something simpler, something that the only thing I could do on it was write. Nothing else to distract me."

"You know what would be good," Rusty said, "is a word processor."

"How is it different?"

"Well, it's between a typewriter and a computer. You can only type on it, but it has a monitor and it does its own printing. And it's easy. No frills."

"That sounds just like what I'd want. Do you know how much they cost?"

"Oh, I don't know. A couple of hundred or so, I think."

"That's sounds pretty good."

"I'll check them out. Andrea, I'd like to get it for you."

"Oh, no. You don't have to do that."

"I want to. I believe in what you're doing. I'd like to get it. Please, can I do that for you?"

"I don't know. That would be very nice of you, but … oh, I don't know …"

"Andrea, I really believe it is important for you to write."

"I do, too. I have to do it for Dawson."

"But it will be good for you, as well."

"Oh, I don't know about that."

"Well, I think it will be and I think Dawson thinks so, too. You know when he said his story was going to help someone, maybe that someone is you. Andrea, this is going to sound odd coming from me, but as I was passing your exit on the freeway the other day, there was this one cloud in the sky. Only one. And it was right over where your house is. Andrea, it looked like an angel. I can't explain exactly the way it made me feel, but I knew. I just knew it was Dawson's way of watching over you that day. Now if *I* can say that, you know it must have been a very powerful feeling."

"That's true. I never thought I'd hear you talk about believing in angels."

"Me either."

"I do know Dawson is with me."

"I know it, too. Well, I'm going to check on those word processors for you, O.K.?"

"O.K. thanks."

"Happy birthday, Andrea."

Chapter Thirty-Seven

During periods of optimism, Bill and I had talked of how life would be after Dawson received a heart. We had agreed I would stay here at the house when he came home to recover. We had never spoken of what I would do if Dawson did not come home.

Now we had to. We talked casually about my being there "for as long as it felt right." And it definitely did feel right to be together after what we had been through. Bill, wanting me to know I would be welcome to live there as long as I wanted, said, "Andrea, this will always be your home." I did feel very much at home in this house I had designed, and in ways it was still my home, both emotionally and physically. The fact that no one had come in and redecorated after I left helped justify that feeling.

The day I went in to look around at the unfinished guest room and found Claudia's side-by-side there, I saw something else. There, amidst the tools, fixtures, boxes, sawdust, and cobwebs, sat two chairs. They were antique chairs I had purchased while Bill and I were still married. And there they were, with the fabric I had planned to recover them with, draped over the seats, just as I had left them nearly ten years earlier. I remembered having cut the fabric into two pieces, folding it, laying it over the seats, then standing back to view them. That was as far as I'd gotten on that project before we divorced, but there they were sitting with ten years worth of dust, waiting patiently for me to return. It was as if they knew I would.

Friends and family were telling us they were glad to see us "back together." It seemed no one had ever doubted I was home to stay, not even Rusty. He called to tell me he had gone to look at word processors. He said, "There were a few different styles to choose from. I didn't know which one you would want. But any of them would be fine, I'm sure. Since Bill does not have a computer, you're going to need something like that. You know, this is a very big project you're starting."

"I know," I said. "I think it will take me about a year."

"At least a year," Rusty said. "You should go and look at them and pick out the one you want. Then let me know."

"I really appreciate your help. I would never have known about them and it sounds like it will be just what I'll need. But, Rusty, maybe I should just buy it."

"Andrea, you get it and I'll pay you for it. Please, I want to." Knowing Rusty, I knew it meant a great deal to him to do this for me and he let me know he expected nothing in return. He said, " ... and, Andrea, I don't want you to worry about moving your stuff. I'm getting it together for you. I have some wardrobe boxes for your clothes and I'll do the packing and there is no rush. Whenever you want to come and get your things, you can. But your priority now is getting that word processor and getting on with telling Dawson's story."

Bill had told me he wanted me to have all the time I needed and a place where I could write. He, too, believed in me and it was understood now that my life was with Bill. It was walking Harley and being close to Dawson. I was almost ready to embark upon that new phase of my life, writing.

The holidays were upon us and although I did not plan to be busy with holiday festivities, I decided I would wait until after the first of the year to devote myself fully to telling Dawson's story.

Thursday was Thanksgiving, but Claudia had to work, so she would not be coming up. My mother offered to cook Thanksgiving dinner so we could have a quiet holiday with just the four of us. As we sat down to turkey and dressing and all the trimmings, I could not help but think soulfully of the Thanksgiving dinner that Dawson had hoped to have.

When Bill and I arrived home that evening, there was a message from Dawson's friend, Eric, calling from Alaska. He asked us if we would bring a rose to Dawson the next day, Friday, November 29, the one month anniversary of Dawson's death.

As I placed Eric's rose at Dawson's crypt the following afternoon, feeling sadder than usual, Bill drove up, parked his truck and got out. Harley ran to greet him and I followed. As Bill walked toward me, he said, "I saw Dawson today."

"What?" I gasped.

"Well, not really saw him, but he was with me."

"Bill, what do you mean?" I begged, wanting to hear more.

"I was working up in the spire. You know, inside the pyramid, but all the way up to the top. I was working alone, but I turned around, as if someone had come up the ladder behind me. When I turned around there was this … I can't really describe it, but there was this shape … but it was like a mist moving between me and the steel wall. I thought it was my eyes, so I closed them, then looked in another direction. I didn't see it, but when I looked back to where I had seen it before, it was still there. I knew then it was not my eyes and I said, 'Dawson, is that you?'"

"It was!" I said.

"I kept saying, 'Is that you, Dawson?' I did not get an answer … but …"

"But what?"

"But I do believe it was him."

"In your heart, do you know it?"

"Yeah."

"Me, too. Oh, Bill, he is not gone," I said, crying, "and he loves us and he knows how much we love him."

How would I be coping if it were not for those little signs from Dawson that kept me believing? I was coping, but nothing could entirely take away my sorrow. Some days were more difficult than others, and though I cried every day, I thanked God for the support and encouragement of loving family and friends.

As Elaine and I grew closer, her friendship became one I cherished. She called on Sunday and asked, "Do you want to go to the city on Tuesday? I need some fringe. How about you? Do you need anything for the new shade you started?"

"Yeah, there are some things I was thinking I'd like to look for."

"Good," she said, "because this lamp I'm working on now, I want to finish it before I get too busy with my Christmas shopping. I'll see you Tuesday then."

When we hung up, I thought, *Christmas shopping. Oh, my God, I can't think about Christmas shopping.* Remembering my happy Christmas shopping jaunts with Dawson, I could not bear to think that we would never experience them again. But how lucky I was, I quickly reminded myself, to have had them at all, to have seen the pleasure they had brought Dawson and to know now they must have meant as much to him as they had to me. In my heart, I think I always knew it. This would have been just about the time we would have been starting. It was the first day of December.

Two Christmases earlier, Claudia thought a nice gift for me would be a portrait of Dawson and her. Rusty, who was a good photographer, volunteered to take their picture. They arranged to have him take them while I was at work one day. Rusty used several rolls of film outside amongst the trees. Claudia had the best one framed and along with it, she had given me all the pictures Rusty had taken that day.

Now, thinking about how we were told we could put a picture on Dawson's crypt, I remembered those pictures. They were all of Claudia and Dawson sitting next to each other, so whichever one I chose, I would have to have it cropped to include only Dawson and enlarged to make it a close-up. Many of the pictures were quite similar with just subtle differences and slight changes in expression. It was hard to decide which one I preferred. There were some where he was obviously smiling broadly, others where he appeared to be almost laughing and others where he looked like he'd had just about enough of this photo session. I was hoping to find one with just a little smile. I finally decided on the one I thought might be it, though I was not sure if he were smiling or sneering. I realized I would not know until I saw it enlarged.

That day, my mother came with me to the photo shop that had a machine where I could do it all myself. I put the picture in the machine, manipulated it until it was how I wanted it. Then I pushed the "start" button. In a few minutes, out came an 8x10 Dawson, smiling at me. "Oh, Mommy," I said. "It's it. He's smiling." I felt he was there with me, smiling just for me and I clutched the picture to my chest.

A friend of Dawson's came by that evening and when I showed him the picture, he seemed to like it so much I decided to have one made for him. And since I knew exactly how I wanted it, I would be able to show the picture to a film developer and have them do the work professionally.

The next morning was cold and rainy. As I watched out the window, waiting for Elaine to pick me up, I was thinking of how she had said to me, "In the spring, you can come with us to the garage sales." She said they started out early Saturday mornings and went to as many as they could. She looked for Victorian style lamp bases for her shades. I had thanked her for wanting to include me. I imagined waking up early on a bright, spring morning with a plan of something enjoyable to do, but I was ashamed when I had found myself feeling envious of my friend. She was so full of enthusiasm, she had such a positive approach to life and she could look forward to a spring without sorrow.

She drove up and I went quickly out to her car. I asked her if we could drop off the picture at the express photo shop on our way to the city. When we arrived at the shop, I told the young clerk what I wanted and she said it would be ready that afternoon. Elaine and I did our shopping in the city, then we stopped at our local craft store. I wanted to look for some wooden beads. As we started down the aisle where I thought the beads would be, I halted suddenly. The aisle was stocked with wooden dowels and small woodworking supplies. An overwhelming feeling of anguish washed over me. I was remembering so clearly the day Dawson and I had enjoyed shopping there for the supplies he needed to make my shadow box and how we had enthusiastically checked the items off his list. I thought I might fall to the floor, right there in the middle of the store and wail out in pain as my heart grieved over my loss. "I can't go here," I said. "This is Dawson's aisle. I mean where Dawson and I picked out the stuff ... I can't. It hurts too much."

"I'll look for the beads for you," Elaine said. "I think I know what you want."

As I waited near the counter, she brought me a couple of bags of assorted beads. I bought them and as we left the store, she said, "Let me buy you lunch. How does Chinese sound?"

She drove us to a small, quiet Chinese restaurant in town. As we waited for our food, she said, "I have a doctor's appointment tomorrow. It is my annual checkup with the cardiologist. You know they keep watch on my valve. One of these days he's going to tell me it is time to have it replaced."

"Are they sure you will eventually need a valve replacement?"

"Oh, yeah, but I've managed to put it off. They'll tell me if it becomes necessary." Then she said, "Mario said to me the other day, 'Nonna, I don't know what I'd do if anything ever happened to you.' Andrea, I just have to live long enough to get him grown."

"Well, of course you will!" I said emphatically. She smiled as I said, "Let's see. How old would he have to be for you to consider him grown?"

"Oh, maybe twenty-five, twenty-six."

"Well, then you only have to live ten years more. You can do that. I'm sure you have a good ten years left in you!" She laughed and I held up my water glass and she hers with its standard slice of lemon and we clinked glasses. "To friendship," I said.

"To a very special friendship," she responded.

After lunch, we went to pick up my finished print. I was so glad Elaine was with me, for when I looked at it, I shrieked, "That's not it! That's the wrong picture!"

"What?" the girl asked, looking startled. "It's from the negative you gave me."

"But he's not smiling!" I wailed.

"But that's the picture you wanted."

"No! I mean, I know, but he was smiling before."

She looked at me like I was crazy. She took out the picture I had done and compared the two. "Well, yes," she said, "there is a slight difference, but … " She checked to see that she had made the print off the correct negative. She had.

"You see it, don't you?" I asked. "It's not the same! He's not smiling like he did for me."

"Do you have the other negatives and pictures off this roll?" she asked.

"Yes, they're in the car. Do you want me to get them?" She nodded. Feeling confused and frustrated, I went to the car. When I went back in, we looked at every picture and negative under a magnifying glass. After checking each one, we had to conclude that the two pictures in question were made from the same negative. She printed it again, and he was definitely not smiling. Elaine said the difference was so slight you could almost say neither one was smiling. But there was a difference, slight or otherwise and I could see it. No one could explain how it could be that when I needed to see him smile for me, he had.

When we left the shop, I said to Elaine, "She must be wondering why I reacted the way I did. I guess she thinks I'm nuts."

Elaine said, "No, it's O.K. I explained to her that he had died. She understood." I felt so fortunate to have her as my friend and when she left me off at my house, I said, "I'll see you Thursday. Remember, I'm taking you to lunch for your birthday."

"Mexican, right?"

"Right. We'll really celebrate and have a couple of Margaritas."

The next day, the mailman knocked on the door. He had a package too big for the mailbox. I knew what it was and I had been anxiously awaiting it, but before I opened it, I opened an ivory colored envelope with a card inside. On the front of the card was a faint image of a sage-green Christmas tree with one bright, red light on it. Written across the tree in the same soft green was, *"Each light on this tree will burn brightly during the Christmas season as a silent sentinel in the darkness. Together, perhaps they will stir our hearts to kindness and caring that will 'light up' our lives and the lives of others in our community.* I opened the card and read, *"There is a light shining on a Hospice Tree for Dawson Bell donated by and with love from Jack and Sheila."* I wept as I read on, *"Light Up A Life is an annual community celebration of cherished memories. For four weeks, three majestic evergreen trees are illuminated by hundreds of bright, clear lights. Each light symbolizes the life, hope and dreams of a loved one.* What a thoughtful and beautiful thing to do for us, I thought. What dear friends. I immediately called Sheila and told her how her gift had touched me. "I do one every year for my daughter," she said.

Her daughter, and now, my son. "It's a beautiful thing to do," I said. "Thank you so much."

When I hung up the phone, I opened the box which I knew contained the thank you cards I had designed and ordered from Bill's sister. She and her husband had a printing shop and had offered to make the cards to my specifications. It had taken a while for me to decide on the exact design and wording and then even longer to get the paper I wanted. But it was worth the extra wait. I was very pleased with them. They were shiny black with a silver "Thank you" on the front. They opened horizontally and inside on the upper flap was imprinted:

"Perhaps you sent a sympathy card,
   Or sat quietly in a chair.
Perhaps you sent a funeral spray,
   If so, we saw it there.
Perhaps you spoke the kindest words,
   As any friend could say.

Perhaps you were not there at all,
Just thought of us that day.
For what you did to console our hearts,
We thank you."

The lower half of the card was left blank so we could write our own personal messages. Imprinted along the bottom was, *The Family of Dawson Bell.* Included were bookmarks of the same shiny black paper with the poem, *"Safely Home,"* imprinted on the back. Below the poem it said, *"Read by Claudia at Valley Memorial on Nov. 2, 1996 as a tribute to our faith in God and our undying love for Dawson."*

On Thursday, when I arrived at Elaine's for her birthday outing, I said, "How did it go at the doctors?"

She said, "It's time."

"Time for you to have the valve replacement?"

"Yes. My doctor wants me to do it soon, but I told him I had to get through Christmas first."

"What did he say?"

"He said he would rather I didn't wait, but if that's what I wanted to do, it was up to me. He told me just not to overdo it." This time, as we clinked glasses, I toasted to her birthday and many, many more.

Claudia came up on Friday to spend the weekend helping Bill and me write out the thank you cards. We started soon after dinner on Friday night. She had her completed, efficient list from which we worked. Claudia's job was to address the black envelopes in silver ink in her neat, legible handwriting. She kept track of the list as Bill and I shared the duties of personally writing out the cards. In addition to the special message imprinted on the card, we wanted to express our gratitude, personally, to all who had offered their sympathy. The three of us sat at the dining room table. Claudia was writing out the envelopes and reading the names to us. When it was a friend of Bill's, he took a card and wrote in it. When it was one of mine, I took it. We discovered this was going to be one of the most emotionally wrenching tasks we had ever encountered. As Bill began to express his feelings in his personal notes, tears poured down his face. He handed me what he had written and as I read it, I cried, too. I gave him what I had written and I went upstairs and brought down a box of tissues. We soon progressed from the tissues to napkins to paper towels, for we were both openly sobbing over every card we wrote. This went on until bedtime and we resumed the daunting, heart-stirring task the following morning after breakfast. We continued like that throughout the day. Bill and I poured out our emotions as we opened our hearts to thank our loving friends and family. We worked into the night and went to bed exhausted and drained. We could never have accomplished what we had without Claudia. She held us together through our heartbreak with her encouraging words and her organized approach.

Sunday morning we went to church and when we returned home, we finished up the last few remaining cards. We had one hundred and ninety cards ready to mail. Together, we had accomplished what we had set out to do; express our appreciation to all those who had been there for us when it meant so much. And for me it also had been a way of doing something for Dawson. I imagined I would forever have that need.

It seemed Bill did, too, and had found a way to fill it. At Dawson's the following afternoon while we were standing in front of his crypt, Bill said, "I try to say as many prayers as I can for him every day. I say some when I stop here in the morning and continue to say them all the way to the freeway. Some days I say *Our Fathers* all the way to the bridge."

"That's great. Elaine said that the more prayers you say for him the sooner he'll get to Heaven."

"I know. That's why I do it. I like to imagine that every time I say a prayer, he moves up a notch."

"He does. And he looks down and says, 'Thanks, Dad.'" I thought what a precious gift Elaine had unknowingly given to Bill. It obviously comforted him that he could do something for Dawson. And what greater thing to do than to help him into Heaven?

Bill said, "How many prayers do you say when you're here?"

"One."

"One?" he asked indignantly.

"Well, mine is a different kind of prayer. It's like parts of different prayers that I combined and say just for Dawson."

"What is it?"

"Well, I thank God for all the blessings He gave Dawson and me. Do you want to hear it?" I then recited what I said every time I went to Dawson's, beginning with "Dear Lord, thank you for welcoming Dawson into your Kingdom of Heaven," and finished with, "Have mercy on his soul, dear Lord, and on us all that we may be rejoined with him and dwell together with you in the House of the Lord forever and ever. Amen."

"Hmmmm," he said when I finished. Then half-seriously and half-smiling he said, "I don't know if that counts." He kind of chuckled, a Dawson-like chuckle.

It was not unusual that I did not hear from Elaine over the weekend. She and John were going out with friends to celebrate her sixty-first birthday on Saturday night. I expected I'd hear from her on Monday. When I had not heard from her by Wednesday, I thought it was odd. I had just decided to call her, when she called me. She said, "I've been in the hospital."

"No! What happened? Are you home now?"

"Yes. You remember we went out to dinner Saturday night? Well, on Sunday, I just didn't feel well. I thought it was something I ate. When I started having pains on Monday, I went to the doctor. My cardiologist wanted to do an angiogram, so he put me in the hospital."

"God! So what is he saying?"

"He wants to do the valve right away. You know, he never wanted me to wait until January anyway."

"So are you going to do it?"

"I guess I have to. I just didn't want to do that to my family, be in the hospital at Christmas."

"Maybe your family would rather that you take care of this. I really think they would prefer to have you in the hospital recuperating, than at home, because they know you. If you were home, and hadn't had the surgery yet, you might try to do too much, with Christmas dinner and everything. I think that would worry them more. They just want you to take care of yourself."

"You're probably right. I know I should do it. The doctor is talking about maybe next week. Oh, I received your thank you card. It's beautiful. It is really beautiful. I have it sitting out, so everyone can see it."

Elaine scheduled the surgery for the following Thursday, December 19. She was trying to take it easy, so we did not get together to go on any shopping trips. I put my lamp shades on hold and concentrated on Christmas. Had it not been that Claudia would be coming up, I would not have even gotten a Christmas tree. But with her able to share Christmas with us, for her, I wanted to make sure it felt like Christmas. My mother offered to have us get together at her house as we always did, but I knew I could not bear to be there with the vivid reminders of the last, happy Christmas. I could see Dawson sitting in the big, gray chair smiling while Claudia enforced her gift opening rules. So I decided we would have Christmas Eve at our house and we all agreed we should not do our usual extravagant gift giving, but would keep it to one meaningful gift each. Christmas would, no doubt, be different this year, not only because Dawson was not with us, but because we would be celebrating the true meaning of Christmas, the birth of Christ. Christ, who I believed had blessed us with the faith that had sustained me.

Our church had a Christmas tree decorated with paper stars, each with a needy person's age and size on it. Parishioners were asked to choose a star and buy a gift for that person. I told Bill I wanted to do that. After mass, many people went up to the tree and were spending time reading the stars before selecting the one they wanted. As Bill and I walked down the aisle toward the tree, I told him I was going to choose a star from a distance. It would be the first one that caught my eye. As I approached the tree, there were several people milling around and examining the stars, but I was focused on a yellow star on one of the upper branches. I went directly to it, reached up and took it off the tree and read it. "Bill! It's for an adult male, size extra-large. That could be a description of Dawson!" With Christmas shopping having been kept to a minimum, it was no problem adding this man to my list. I bought him things I would have bought Dawson, warm sweatshirts, size XL. Bill was quite busy with his job on the pyramid. They were working overtime, for the goal was to have The Crown Jewel completed in time to light for Christmas.

Elaine called me on Wednesday, the day before she was scheduled to go in for her surgery. She said, "I guess I'm ready," sounding understandably apprehensive. "You are on the list I'm giving to John of people for him to call. So he'll call you and let you know how I'm doing."

"Oh, thank you," I said. "I really appreciate that."

Sighing, she said, "I'm trying not to think about the operation. It's kind of hard to do, but thinking about our trip to Reno helps. I'm really looking forward to it, more than ever. I can't wait for May to get here."

"Yeah, and we'll be going to the garage sales then, too. I'm really looking forward to that. I'm glad you called. Take care. And I'll be hearing from John real soon and it will all be over. Now try not to worry."

Friday, the day after Elaine's surgery, John called. "She's off the respirator, sitting up and eating Jell-O," he said.

"Oh, John, that's wonderful. So everything went well?"

"Yeah, we're on the road to recovery now."

"That's great. Thank you for calling."

"Well, she made very sure you were on the list. She'll call you when she gets home."

"Well, tell her not to worry about that. She needs to take it easy. Thanks again, John."

"John called today," I said to Bill when I met him at Dawson's that afternoon. "Elaine was sitting up eating Jell-O. I know she was scared, but now that is all behind her. She must be so relieved. Are you going to have to work tomorrow?"

"Yeah, we're going to do a few more things to the light and then we should be ready to test it," Bill said, his eyes widening with anticipation.

"What are you expecting when you test it? Are you worried?"

"Oh, no. I don't think we'll have any problems. I'm just anxious to see how the light will look."

"Dawson's light. I wish I could see it."

"When we're finished and it's all working, I'll take you to see it."

When Bill left for work the following morning, Saturday, I said, "Good luck. I hope it goes well." When he came home that night he told me they had worked on the light all day and were ready to run the test around dusk. I could see Bill's excitement as he said, "We fired it up. No problem. Jack, the superintendent on the job, said he was going to take a ride up the street to take a look at it. There was some fog laying over the city, so I didn't expect he'd see much, but Andrea, when he came back he said it was awesome. It was just starting to get dark and the light was shining up through the mist into the clouds. He said it looked like a stairway to Heaven!"

"Bill!"

"Yeah, I know. Dawson's light does reach Heaven."

"Bill, just like you said it would. It *is* his pathway home."

Sunday, the phone was ringing as we walked in the door from church. I ran to get it. It was Sheila. "Andrea, have you heard from John?"

"Oh, yeah. He called Friday. Elaine was doing well."

"Andrea, sit down. Elaine died."

"No!" I screamed. "No, Sheila, No! God, no! What happened?"

"I don't know. She was doing fine and then they had to take her back into surgery for some reason. I don't know what happened."

"Oh, Sheila, how could this be? This is too terrible. Oh, my God. Wait a minute. I just noticed there's a message on my answering machine. I'm going to check it and see if it's John. Sheila, it's Bernadette! She's asking me to call her." Bernadette was Elaine's daughter-in-law. "Oh, Sheila, this is so awful. I can't believe it. I guess I better call her. Oh, God. Well, thanks for letting me know. If I hear anything more, I'll call you."

Bernadette and Elaine were extremely close. Although they were mother-in-law and daughter-in-law, their relationship reminded me of mine with my mother. Bernadette was sure to be devastated. "Have you heard?" she asked when I called.

"Yes, Sheila told me. What happened?"

"I don't know. She seemed to be doing fine. They said it might have been a blood clot."

"Oh, Bernadette, this is just too terrible. She was such a wonderful person, so loving and giving. She has been so good to me," I said, crying.

"She really cared about you, Andrea. She spoke of you often. She had such sympathy for you."

"Oh, God. I am going to miss her so much and I know how close you two were. I'm so sorry."

"I don't know how I can be without her. She has been like a mother to me."

"She was such a beautiful person. I have never met anyone like her in my whole life."

"We've started thinking about making the arrangements," Bernadette said. "I'm thinking ahead to when we will send out thank you cards. I wanted to ask you, well, I was wondering how you would feel if ... would it be all right if I used the wording you had on Dawson's thank you cards? It was so beautiful and Mom loved that card. Of course, the card would have to be green."

"Oh, yes. It has to be green." Green was Elaine's favorite color. Her home was decorated in deep hunter green and she often wore green to match her sparkling green eyes. "I don't mind your using the wording. It's for Elaine. How could I mind? She has been so good to me! It's the least I could do. Oh, Bernadette, is there anything I can do for you? Can I help you with the cards? You know, I had those made up by Bill's sister. Would you want me to see about ordering the paper and have her do the printing?"

"Andrea, could you? That would be such a help. Thank you."

"O.K. I'll wait before ordering them until you can let me know how many you'll need. Call me if there's anything I can do for you."

"Thanks, and I'll let you know when the services will be."

Remembering how so many people, including myself, had wanted to speak at Dawson's service, but had not and had regretted it afterwards, I decided I did not want to have that happen again. I did not want to miss the opportunity of telling everyone what a wonderful person and friend she was. Feeling it was something I must do, I sat down and wrote:

Speaking in front of so many people is not something I am comfortable doing, but because of my feelings for Elaine, I felt compelled to do so tonight. Though I will be reading these words, they come from deep within my heart.

Some of you know and some of you may not know that eight weeks ago I lost my adored son, Dawson. Up to that time, Elaine was a friend, I could have even called her a good friend, but after I lost Dawson, Elaine became the dearest and most beloved friend I have ever had. All of you who knew her, knew her to be kind and generous and giving. So I know it won't surprise anyone to hear how wonderful she was to me in my time of great suffering. I needed comforting, I needed distractions, I needed understanding and she gave me all that and more. The greatest thing of all was that I never had to ask her for them. She knew and she was always there. She helped me more than anyone could ever know. I will be forever grateful for her friendship and her help.

Because of the circumstances that brought us closer together, we had many conversations about death, faith and prayers. She told me, "The more prayers that are said for someone the quicker they get to Heaven." So I know she will appreciate all of your prayers. She told me many stories (with tears in her pretty, green eyes) of incidences that had inspired her faith and had confirmed her belief that our loved ones are not gone. She believed in a Heaven from which our loved ones watch over us. And so I know in my heart she is there … still caring and loving and watching over us. May God bless her.

On the night of her service, I folded up the hand-written paper and put it in my pocket. It was pouring rain when I arrived at the same funeral home where Dawson's service had been held just two months earlier. I walked up to her forest green coffin. It was closed, but there were pictures of her from happy times. I offered my condolences to her family; John, her children and Mario. Mario looked past me as if he did not know me. He had a blank stare on his face and I understood, but I had hoped I could reach out to him. I knew how much he must be hurting and I wished he could know I understood his pain. I then went and sat next to Sheila. She put her arm around me and I could not suppress my tears. The priest spoke and then read the loving words from Elaine's children. Had I known he was going to read, perhaps I could have given him my words to read, as well. Since I hadn't, I would have had to get up and walk to the front and make it known that I wanted to say something. I was so emotional by this point and there were so many people, I just could not do it.

When I returned home, I was filled with regret and I could not believe I had not told all those people how wonderful Elaine had been to me. I should have done that for her. She had done so much for me. I berated myself for not taking the opportunity to do this for her.

Dawson, I cried, *I should have learned. I saw how so many from your service had wished they had spoken. Why didn't I say what I felt for Elaine? I had wanted so much to do something for her. I should have done it.* Suddenly, I stopped crying. I hadn't thought of it before. Why hadn't I realized it? Why had I not made the connection? I guess Elaine's death had been such a shock ... *She died when? Saturday? And was it not around the time... Oh, my God. Dawson, your light! The stairway to Heaven! Oh, Dawson. Your light must have been the pathway for Elaine.*

Elaine was safely home.

Chapter Thirty-Eight

There is very good reason why we cannot see into the future. Many years ago, as a young mother, I went to astrologers and psychics. Today, I can't imagine why. Assuming they had possessed supernatural powers, if I had looked into a mystic's crystal ball and saw myself on a Christmas Eve of the future saying, "Bill, it arrived just in time for Christmas!" would I not have peered deeper into that magical orb? And if I had, could I have gone on living when I looked closer and saw that I was standing at Dawson's grave referring to a bronze plaque newly placed upon his crypt?

On my birthday, when I had ordered the plaque, the woman in the office asked me if I wanted to put a rush on it for Christmas. At the time, it seemed like an odd question and an even odder thing to want, but I had answered, "Yes, I guess if I could, it would be nice to have it by Christmas."

Harley and I, having walked down to Dawson's, found Bill already there, standing, looking at the plaque. Its four lines read:

We Love You
Dawson Bell
Apr. 24, 1969 – Oct. 29, 1996
"He Could Ride"

It was just as we had ordered, yet seeing it was a shock. It made it all undeniably true. Dawson had lived and had died. My son's life on earth had ended. I dropped to my knees, leaned forward, my hands touching the cold, white marble of his crypt as I kissed his name embossed on the new bronze plaque. *Merry Christmas, Dawson. Merry Christmas.*

When I stood, Bill put his arm around me and said, "The Crown Jewel made it in time for Christmas, too. They're going to light it tonight at eight o'clock. Do you want to go down and see it?"

"Yes! Of course, I do." I was quite anxious to see it and I was glad it would give us something special to do on Christmas Eve. Claudia had to work and was not coming up until the next day, so we had chosen to start our Christmas then. But now we had our short trip to the city to see Bill's gift to Dawson. How perfect that it should be on Christmas Eve.

Around seven-thirty, Bill said, "Harley, you want to go for a ride?" Harley jumped up and down, barking excitedly. "We're going for a ride!" Bill said.

I got my coat and Harley's leash and we stepped out into the crisp December evening. We climbed into the truck and Bill said, "I hope it stays clear like this. If it does, we'll be able to see the light from this side of the bridge." Fog will often lie over the bay, but as we approached it, we could see there would be none this evening. Bill said, "There it is! See it?" He took the next exit off the freeway and pulled into Vista Point where tourists go to see the view of the Golden Gate Bridge, the San Francisco Bay and across the bay to the San Francisco skyline.

Every building along the Embarcadero was decorated for Christmas, outlined in lights. There, amidst, but above all the other buildings, the pyramid stood and atop it was Dawson's light, sparkling like a magnificent diamond against a black velvet sky. Bill parked the truck and we got out. There were sightseers who were out of their cars, looking at the spectacular view and I wanted to tell them, "See that light? It's Dawson's. It's his Christmas gift from his father. It's his guiding light, his way home." I looked over at Bill. A breeze off the water was blowing his white hair back off his forehead as he stood with his arms folded, gazing across the bay on this beautiful, clear, winter night. The light looked like a star that had come down from heaven and landed there for us. "Dawson must be very pleased," I said. "That's quite a Christmas present you've given him. Merry Christmas, Bill."

We tried to make Christmas, if not merry, then at least as pleasant as we could. But for me it did not feel like Christmas. We had the tree, we had the presents, but we did not have Dawson. I did not outwardly show how my heart was aching throughout the holiday celebrations and we managed to have an enjoyable, but quiet time with my mother, father, Claudia and Tracy. As we opened our presents, I was thinking of Elaine's family opening theirs, the ones Elaine had bought and wrapped before she went into the hospital just days before Christmas.

"Hi, Andrea. It's Bernadette.

"Oh, hi. How are you doing?"

"Terrible. Christmas was too awful."

"I can imagine. I was thinking of all of you."

"So how are *you*?" she asked.

"Today's the twenty-ninth. It's been two months. It seems impossible that he could have been gone that long. I know two months is not a very long time, but to have so many days separating me from the time I had been with him, just hurts."

"I know I'm going to hurt for a long time. I can't imagine ever getting over losing Mom. But the reason I'm calling is, I have a picture I thought you might like to have. Are you going to be home today?"

I told her I was and later that morning, she came by and brought me the picture. It was of Elaine and me as we were leaving the church at Bernadette and Jeff's wedding several years earlier. It wasn't a great picture, but I was quite happy to have it. It was the only picture I had ever seen of the two of us. We were walking side by side against the wind and we were smiling.

As we talked of how difficult Christmas had been, I told her that though it had been hard having a family holiday without Dawson, it was New Year's I dreaded. I did not have any poignant memories of past New Year's, as I did Christmas, I told her, but it was the new year's arrival that was going to be heartbreaking for me. The fact this year would be one Dawson would not see made it unwelcome and I did not want to live in a year that Dawson had no part of.

When she left, we hugged and wished each other well, and that afternoon I took the picture to the same photo shop I had taken Dawson's picture. The same girl waited on me. It was hard to believe it had been just weeks earlier Elaine had been standing by me as I requested Dawson's picture to be cropped and enlarged. Here I was asking the same thing be done with Elaine's. Elaine had told this girl that Dawson had died and now I was telling her that Elaine had died. Life and death, both unexplainable mysteries.

It was becoming clear that grieving was not a neat, organized process. It did not progress in an orderly fashion. It was not a path on which you steadily improved every day or even every month. It was an unrelenting rise and fall of intense emotions with no predictable order.

The days, the weeks, and the months would go on like that; a combination of moments of great sorrow intertwined with beautiful and inspiring ones. If I thought it hurt when two months had passed between me and those last days with Dawson, I would not be surprised if six months hurt more. I was dreading what one year would feel like.

New Year's Eve, Bill and I stayed home and went to bed before midnight. I could not ring in nor welcome this new year. I suppose I should have wanted to celebrate the end of the outgoing year that had taken my son and my friend, but it had also been the extraordinary year they had been near me, making it a year I wanted to hold on to forever.

Our friend, Fran, invited us to her house for her family's New Year's Day dinner. Bill and I did not want to go and we told her we wouldn't be there. We were both too sad to be sociable, but she urged us to come. We thought she understood how we felt, for after all, she had lost a son. But when, at the last minute, she asked us again, we agreed to go. I wore red, trying to look festive and not somber like I felt. Her three children were there with their children. When we arrived and my eyes caught sight of her young grandson, I had to swallow my tears. He was wearing a cowboy hat and cowboy boots and I could not help but remember Dawson in his. He was very young when he had gotten his first tiny cowboy boots. He was so thrilled with them he wanted to wear them to bed. He loved it when we dressed him up in a cowboy outfit for Halloween that year. Then he did not say, "Boy named Dawson." He said, "Me cowboy. Me Dawson. Cowboy hat, cowboy shirt, cowboy vest, cowboy boots." I did not outwardly show my anguish, but Bill knew. He said, "Are you all right?" I assured him I was and I got through the evening and cried on the way home. *Happy New Year.*

I knew it was not always going to hurt this badly, but I also felt that nothing ever again could be truly happy, nor would there ever be the expectation of a holiday or celebration being perfect. Perhaps realistically, nothing ever could have been perfect, but there was always the anticipation that it might. I felt I would never anticipate that again.

The holidays now over, I had my word processor, and hadn't I said, "After the first of the year, I will devote myself to writing Dawson's story?"

Though I had officially started writing on my birthday, I had not gotten very far, but I could no longer ask, "Where do I start?" Now I was asking, "Where do I go from here?" Over the next few days, I added writing to my routine and within a month, it was very much a part of my weekly schedule. On the days I was home all day, I wrote. When Bill came home, I stopped and went downstairs. I did no writing in the evening.

I was writing about Dawson's early years, my feelings for him, and how I had always worried about him even before I had reason to. I sobbed openly over every word I wrote. This was undoubtedly going to be the most difficult project I had ever attempted. Writing and remembering opened a floodgate of emotions that spilled over into all areas of my life. But it was not just the emotions of sorrow and grief that flowed from my heart, it was also the love and gratitude. I was surprised how my heart seemed open to everyone close to me. It was not what I would have expected.

I thought as a wound in its healing will form a scar, so must the heart. In that process, I could imagine my heart turning cold and tough, protecting itself from the agonizing loss of a love too dear. I did not want that to ever happen to my heart because it had to be open and loving, for it was where I now held Dawson. So I had to keep the wound unhealed and bleeding, raw feelings and emotions continually flowing from it. There were times when I thought Bill just might shut down his heart to avoid the feelings he was finding too painful. But that, I believed, would sacrifice the love that was also there. When I told all this to my mother, she said she could easily understand Bill's choice. For she told me that the description of my heart was the most horrible thing she had ever heard. "If my heart ever felt like that," she said, "I think I'd want to kill myself."

Writing certainly did keep it all flowing as I poured over the words describing Dawson and my life with him. When I had written more than fifty continuous pages, I gave them to my mother and to Claudia to read. My mother encouraged me to continue. "How do you write about these things?" she asked. "Through my tears," I answered. "Through my tears." Claudia called me after she had read them and said, "Mom, you have to divide it up into chapters. I went ahead and made suggestions where the sections should end. You have six chapters there! I also went ahead and made other suggestions and some corrections. I hope that's O.K."

"Yeah, that's good. I appreciate it. Thanks, hon." And thus began our working relationship. Claudia and I, together, embarking on our own new journey.

I had taken Dawson's picture to the memorial park in January and ordered the bronze-framed-weather-proofed picture that would be attached to his marble crypt. I was told it would take about eight weeks. I was thinking, even if it took longer, there should be no problem having it arrive before his birthday. *How could a mother want to give this to her son for his twenty-eighth birthday?* I left the office, went to Dawson's crypt, placed fresh flowers in the urns mounted on his plaque, reading its words. As I read, *April 24, 1969 – October 29, 1996*, I remembered having heard somewhere that it was not the dates that were important; it was the dash between them.

His picture came well before his birthday and when I arrived to see it on his crypt, to see him looking back at me, it was as great a shock as his plaque had been. *Dawson, how is it ever going to be all right that the only smile I'll see of yours is in this picture?*

I stood there gazing at him, the sun warm against my back. I noticed how in his picture the sun was shining on his hair. It made it seem like he was there with me, as if the sun were shining on us both. Looking at his thick, dark hair with just a hint of curl made me smile as I thought of how he and Claudia had liked joking with me about how glad they were they had not gotten my extremely curly hair. And I remembered a day in the hospital when he said he needed a haircut. His hair was getting unruly. Bill called his barber and he came and cut Dawson's hair as he sat with his legs dangling over the side of the bed. He was so happy with his new haircut. Dr. Harris had said it was a good sign when a patient begins to care about his hair.

I was crying when Bill arrived and after he had stood there a long while looking at Dawson, I said, "See how the sun is shining on his hair?"

"Yeah, I saw that," Bill said. "How it looks like *Touched by an Angel?*" I was looking at him questioningly and he said, "Isn't that what you meant? How his hair looks like the angels' hair when the light shines on them?"

"That wasn't what I was thinking, but you're right. It does look like that. He looks like one of the angels. Bill, we've been touched by an angel."

Winter was coming to an end and the days were dawning earlier and brighter. On those cool, but sunny mornings, I thought of Elaine and the spring I thought we would share.

In March, Claudia started in the RCIA group at her church. She found it enjoyable and enlightening and she made wonderful new friends there and seemed to be finding something she had been seeking.

In my grieving, I was still searching. My faith helped me cope, but nothing could ease the sorrow. My memories of Dawson remained quite painful. In my mind, I saw us during our days in the hospital. I saw how frightened, yet hopeful we had been and I cried for that mother and her son. The hurt was like nothing I'd ever known. Surely one could die from a pain this intense and I wondered why I didn't. There were times when I wished I would. But the days continued to find me. I did not seek them out.

A week before Dawson's birthday, in April, my next-door neighbor, Jennifer, called to tell me she wanted to do something for him. Because the natural pond on our property was situated in the middle between both our properties, I understood when she said, "When I think of Dawson, I see him down by the pond. I thought I'd like to put a statuary or something there in remembrance of him, but I wasn't sure what. I wanted to talk to you first to find out if that would be O.K. or if you had any other ideas. I was hoping to do it for his birthday. Do you want to go look at some things? Can you go tomorrow?"

"That would be great. It really is a very nice idea. It means a lot to me that you would want to do this."

We did not like any of the statuary we saw. They did not seem appropriate with the naturalness of the pond or Dawson. "How about a big rock?" I suggested.

"That sounds good. Maybe with a plaque on it."

"Yes, we could put his initials and the date of this year's birthday, the day we'll dedicate it to him."

I ordered the plaque engraved with *D.B. 4-24-97.* I selected a rock I liked and her husband picked it up in his tractor and placed it near the pond. On Dawson's birthday, Bill affixed the plaque and my mother and father came down. Fran came by later and when she saw what we had done, she said, "You're making it harder on yourselves. Doing things like that is just too painful."

"Yes, it is," I said, "but to do nothing in honor of Dawson's birthday would hurt me more. There is no way I could not acknowledge the day Dawson was born. It will always be a special day to me."

I understood that everyone had their own way of grieving and I already knew hers was quite different from mine. Soon after Dawson died, she had told me that when her son had died she immediately packed all of his things and emptied his room. She had suggested we do that with Dawson's. Bill and I had discussed it, but neither one of us wanted to do that. We wanted to leave everything as it was. If anyone thought that was wrong, we didn't care. We both felt the same and it was our decision to make. When, and if, the time ever came when we felt the need to do something with his things, then we would. But as long as we didn't and we were in agreement, then who could tell us what we should do? Yes, it was painful to enter his room and see his life as it had been and was no more, but to pack it up and remove everything as if he had never been there would have shattered me.

There did not seem to be any one way to grieve that was right for everyone. I had bought the book that Dawson's nurse had recommended that had helped her when her mother died, in the hopes it would help me, too, but it did not. I did not know if any book could help, but when I was at the bookstore, I had seen another one that seemed like it might. So when Claudia asked me what I'd like for Mother's Day, I told her the name of the book. While talking to Leah later that day, I was telling her how hard this first Mother's Day was going to be for me.

Leah said, "I'll never forget the terrible thing I did to that poor woman on Mother's Day years ago. Do you remember?"

"Yes. I sure do." Leah had a floral shop and over her years there, she had seen an old woman walking by almost every day. She looked lonely and sad. Whenever Leah saw her, her heart went out to her. One Mother's Day when Leah was busy with orders, surrounded by beautiful flowers as she made floral arrangements for other mothers, she saw the woman walking by the window. She looked sadder than ever, walking slowly with her head down. Leah had a strong impulse to do something for her and she quickly grabbed up a bunch of flowers and ran out to the woman. Leah handed her the flowers. "These are for you," she said. "Are you a mother?" The old lady looked up at her and answered sadly, "I was."

Leah was saying now, "I'll never forget how horrible I felt. What a terrible thing I did to that woman."

"I thought it was terrible, too, at the time," I said, "but you know what? Now I don't think it was at all. I know we probably felt you had reminded her she was no longer a mother, but that was not true. She had never forgotten it. Not for one minute. But beyond that, I'm sure it meant something special to her to have gotten those flowers."

Leah, knowing how I could find messages from Dawson in small incidences, said, "Oh, Andrea, do you think she felt maybe they were from her child?"

"Yes. And maybe they were."

At the card shop buying a Mother's Day card for my mother, I was looking in the "From Daughter" section. I glanced over to the "From Son" section and one card seemed to summon me to pick it up. I thought, *Is that the one from you, Dawson? Is it the one you have picked out for me?* There was nothing about this card that was extraordinarily eye-catching and the only wording I saw was *On Mother's Day from your Son.* My heart was anticipating a message from him, and I was praying it would sound like something Dawson could feel. I took it off the rack, opened it and read: *Mom - you always saw the best in me ... And your support made all the difference in the world. Happy Mother's Day. XOXO.* It was so perfectly Dawson! It was not mushy. Its message was unique and so appropriate for us. I bought the card. "Thank you, Dawson," I said. Then I went grocery shopping. When I got home, I put the grocery bag on the counter and took out my Mother's Day card. I said, "Are these really your words, Dawson?" As I was reading the card, the bag of groceries rolled off the counter. "Yes," he had answered. "Happy Mother's Day, Mom. I love you."

I thoroughly believed our loved ones remained connected to us and one Sunday in his sermon, Father O'Neill was speaking of our need to believe we all have a place with the Lord when we leave this life and how the need was even greater when we think of the ones we love. I thought of how true that was. There are times when we can think of our own mortality and are able to say, "I'll live my life and then I'll die and that will be the end of it." But when we think of our loved ones, our hearts will not allow us to say that. We cannot even think it, for the pangs of sorrow are too great. They cannot die and then it's over! They were here and now they cease to exist? No. We must believe they are somewhere, in a better place.

I did not hear where Father O'Neill was going with his sermon, for my mind had taken me through a maze of many questions about *my* beliefs. I asked myself if that was *why* I believed, because it was too painful not to. *Is it just so hard for us to accept that when a loved one dies he is gone forever, that we must find a way to reconcile that? The death of someone we love is so enormous, is this belief just our way of bringing it within our realm of acceptance? Our realm of acceptance, perhaps, but still not our realm of understanding. Which was harder to comprehend? Dead and gone or dead and gone to some beautiful afterlife? Was the idea of leaving this world for another world just too hard for some to fathom, as Dawson being gone forever, was to me? I could not understand death, but I could not understand life either. So what was the difference? Life in this world was every bit as unexplainable to me. Life was no doubt a wonder. Wasn't life-transforming-itself just another wonder?* To me it was, and as the sermon was over, I knelt to worship the Lord I believed had made this wonder possible.

The day-to-day sorrow was eased by my faith and my little messages from Dawson, and I wondered, *If I can feel this badly, despite these blessings, what would I be doing without them?*

The most difficult days were those of events or celebrations and gatherings of families. Bill and I were invited, and we bravely attended, a christening, an awarding of an Eagle Scout honor and a wedding. I tried handling them in different ways, but the result was always the same.

At the christening of twin boys, I relived Dawson's in my mind. I remembered the hope a mother holds for her babies. There were friends there with whom I spoke of Dawson, who openly cried with me … and I wept on the way home.

At the Eagle Scout presentation, I remembered Dawson's Cub Scout days. Personal tributes were made to my friend's son receiving the honor. A mention was made of him having handed down his small cowboy boots to a younger boy years earlier. I did not speak of Dawson to anyone there … and I wept on the way home.

At the wedding, a second marriage for the bride, her two grown sons walked her down the aisle. There were friends there to whom I spoke of Dawson, but I would not cry … and I wept on the way home. There seemed no way to avoid it. I had lived it three different ways, but all ways, the result was the same; I cried when the event was over.

Along with the sadness, was also envy. I was ashamed how many times this feeling came over me and I knew I must seek reconciliation in church. These social events had all been painful reminders that others still had their precious sons and I did not have mine, but socializing, in general, was always painful. Being out with others whose hearts did not carry the heavy weight of sorrow, just seemed to throw a spotlight on mine. I came to the conclusion that having a broken heart was in some way very much like having a broken leg. If your leg were broken and you sat at home just watching television, it might not matter that your leg was in a cast. For a moment or two, you might even forget that it was. But if you were to go to a party and saw everyone dancing, you would be reminded. There would be no denying that you could not enjoy what others were. The same with your heart. Sitting in your home, so what if you are sad, so what if you want to cry? But at a party where no one else is sad and no one else is crying, and in fact they are laughing, it becomes quite obvious that you are not like the others that you see. I was aware my heart could no longer dance.

So at home it was easier. I had my routine. I still cried every day and always on my walks, as I relived in my mind the events I would write about that day. I came home, talked to my mother, discussed with her what I was going to cook that day for dinner, for all the years I was with Rusty, he had done all the cooking. Firemen all cook. While with him, I had become very intimidated with my lack of cooking skills and had gladly taken over the duty of doing dishes instead of cooking. But now, with Bill working all day while I was at home, it seemed the least I could do. And it was good for me to have something that took my concentration away from my grief. And planning what to have for dinner and how to cook it did take my concentration. I'd go off to the market, trying to be normal and not sorrowful, but even the grocery markets were often a difficult place for me. I so desperately longed to have been shopping for Dawson the way I had imagined I would do one day. Had the markets always played such sad music over their speakers? I had never noticed before. Everything on the shelves reminded me of Dawson. Anything that was salt-free, of course, broke my heart, and peach Jell-O, well, the shelves were full of memories. Some days I expected I would be grocery shopping and would become weak and drop to the floor. I imagined someone coming over to me and asking me if I were all right. And I would simply tell them, "No."

One day leaving the market, I saw a man who had been a customer of mine who I had seen working at the hospital. He was driving out of the parking lot and when he saw me, he stopped and rolled down his window and shouted, "How'd your son do?"

I shook my head. "He didn't make it," I said.

"Oh, I'm so sorry."

"Yes, it's pretty terrible." He nodded and drove off.

The same thing had happened to Bill one day at work. He came home overwhelmed by the sad truth he had to speak.

Sheila had warned me how difficult it could be when someone you've just met asks if you have children. "What do you say?" I had asked her.

"I used to say I had two daughters and one died. Then seeing how that affected people, I just said I had two daughters. Now sometimes I just simply say I have one daughter."

"I think I will always say I have a daughter and I have a son who died. If people were asking, I'd assume they wanted to know. To say I only have a daughter is not telling what is true. I still have a son. Dawson will always be my son."

That discussion had not prepared me for when the first time the question was actually asked of me. I became paralyzed. The truth of how many children I had and that one was dead strangled me and I could not speak. I tried, but the words would not come out and, nearly gasping for air, I ran from the room. I apologized later to the stunned, unsuspecting woman.

Throughout the year, friends of Dawson's went by to visit him and left flowers. Sometimes they would leave cards and I would know who had been there, but often they did not. I always knew when Tanya had been there, for she left doggie biscuits for Harley, Victoria always left mini roses and Eric, on his trips home from Alaska, left fishing lures. On Dawson's birthday, there were several arrangements and cards when I arrived. It touched me deeply to know how much he was still thought of and loved.

When the year anniversary of Dawson's death was coming up, I was sure there would be friends who would stop by to see him and others who would bring flowers and many who would be thinking of him. I wanted to be able to thank them all, for I was so grateful for their love. I had to do something to thank all those who remembered Dawson. I thought I might write a thank you note and leave it down at his place so anyone who went to visit him would see it. Then I thought of all those who may not go by, but would be remembering him in their own way. How could I thank them? I decided to put a thank you letter in the newspaper in the obituary section. I sat down to write a thank you. It turned into a rather simplistic, but nonetheless heartfelt poem. It appeared in our weekly newspaper dated October 29–November 4, 1997. The front page had color pictures of small children choosing pumpkins. I remembered our annual visits to the Pumpkin Patch when Claudia and Dawson were little and I thought, too, of the tiny pumpkin Claudia had brought Dawson in the hospital. *Was that really one year ago?*

The poem appeared with his picture. Above it were the words, "In Loving Memory," and below were his name and dates and then my humble attempt to express my thanks.

> The saying goes, he is not gone
> He is just away
> But I know that those of us who love him
> Just wish he were here with us today
> But I believe he's in a better place
> And it isn't far from here
> For though I cannot see him
> I feel that he is near
> Still I miss his funny ways
> His laughter and his smile
> And I am so sad he only stayed with us
> For such a little while
> But the moments he did share with us
> I treasure in my heart
> And there will be more for I believe
> We won't always be apart
> The day will come I'll join him
> We'll be together once again
> So to see him waiting for me with a hug
> I'll just have to wait 'til then
> I thank the Lord for blessing me
> With family and friends who care
> For your love and understanding
> Have made my days less hard to bear
> For it is true there has not been
> One day this sorrowful year
> That I have not cried for Dawson
> That I have not shed a tear
> But as his mother I must tell you
> What I really want to say
> Is how moved and proud I feel
> To know you think of him today
> My heart is touched and Dawson's too

By the special love you give
I know-for my heart truly is one place
Where Dawson will always live

As I walked home from Dawson's, I was remembering a day several months earlier. I had been walking home that day when a car pulled up beside me. A woman I did not know was driving. She stopped the car and leaned over and rolled down the window. She said, "I live across the street. Are you Dawson's mom?" I told her I was and she got out of her car and came around to me and said, "I just want to tell you how sorry I was to hear about Dawson. How are you doing?"

"It's pretty tough," I said, "but my faith keeps me going and Dawson and I shared some pretty amazing experiences that keep me believing. And one of the greatest gifts is to have discovered how loved Dawson was … his friends call us often and tell us how they talk of Dawson all the time and so many days there are flowers left for him."

"Oh, that must be so wonderful," she said. "My daughter died two years ago."

"Oh, no. Oh, I'm so sorry."

"Katie was only four. She doesn't have any friends who will always remember her."

"But you will never forget her. I'm sure she will always be in your heart."

"Oh, yes. She will. Well, if you ever want to come over, just come by anytime."

We were both crying and I thanked her as we hugged. I went home thinking of little Katie. I cried for the little girl I had not known and wished I had. I felt so blessed to know that Dawson would always be remembered by so many. I was thinking how it was hard to know which was worse; losing a child so young or losing a child you've loved for so long. I realized that though I had said no one could possibly know what grief felt like to the parent who had lost a child, it went far beyond that. I knew now that I did not know what it felt like to lose a young child. In fact, I did not know what someone felt who had lost a daughter. Or even a son. All I knew was what it felt like to lose Dawson.

Chapter Thirty-Nine

My poem had served its purpose, thanking all who had remembered Dawson, and there were many. There were flowers and plants and cards left at his crypt and one floral arrangement was delivered to the house addressed to Bill and me. The card said, "Just want you to know we are thinking of you. We loved Dawson, too. Anita and Mike."

Everyone understood the sorrow of a grieving family at a funeral, but how many think of that family on the anniversary of the death a year later?

Was that because we assumed the grieving was over? And in some cultures was it not the official ending of the grieving period? Why was there such a custom? Was it because it was assumed to be the length of time it took for one to heal? Was it considered necessary to grieve for at least a year out of respect? Or was it because if you did not have that specified time period, you would grieve forever? I believed I would.

I had not imagined that in some ways the pain would be worse a year later than it had been at the funeral, but I learned I was not the only one to have that experience. One morning at Dawson's, I noticed a lady walking through the memorial park. When she saw me, she walked over to me. She told me she often walked past Dawson's crypt. She said, "Is he your son?" When I told her he was, she said, "He was very handsome and so young." I asked her if she were visiting someone there. She said, "Yes, my husband, Eddie." She began to tearfully tell me the story of his illness, his death and his burial. She said, "When I arrived here for his grave side service, everyone was standing around his light blue coffin." Then smiling and almost jokingly, she said, "I shook my fist at him and I said, 'Eddie, how could you do this to me?'" Then suddenly wiping tears from her eyes she said, "But the way I hurt today, if I were standing there now next to his coffin, I would throw myself on top of it and tell them to bury me with him."

I put my arms around her, and crying myself, I tried to console her. I told her I knew how she felt.

"I don't want to live without my Eddie. It hurts more than I could have believed possible."

"I know," I said. "I know."

The year anniversary of the day I started writing was approaching, which would also be my second birthday without Dawson. I was writing most days, but still no nights. I had thought it was going to take me a year to write this story. Though Fran had told me, "More like two," I hadn't believed it. She may have been right, for I was nowhere near finishing and it appeared it would be at least another year before I would even be close.

While on the phone to Leah, I told her how far I was from finishing the book and she asked me if I had an ending for it yet. I told her I did not and I worried about not having a preconceived plan for one. The fact was, I did not know where it would end, but I knew it did not end when Dawson died. Our story had not stopped there. I was not about to fabricate an ending, so when Leah said, "Why don't you have it end on this birthday? It seems like a good place. It would include your first year of writing and grieving." I liked the idea. I liked the orderliness of starting and finishing on the same date, but nothing had happened that told me the story was complete. Something would have to happen that said, "That's it!" and so far nothing had.

I went to bed thinking of the enormity of the project I had taken on. I awoke in the middle of the night and as I rolled over, I felt slightly dizzy and my ears were ringing. Our bedroom light was still on, but

I did not bother to reach over to turn it off and went back to sleep. I awoke again a short time later. Harley was crying. Bill was sleeping. I sat up to look at Harley and as I did, it was as if someone had yanked me by my ankles and had hurled me off a cliff and I was spinning out of control in mid-air. "Bill!" I screamed. "Bill! I'm dizzy! I'm really dizzy!"

He reached for me and laid me back down. "You must have sat up too quickly."

"No! No!" I screamed as I lay in his arms. "It's not going away! I'm scared. This is more than dizzy! If I move at all, there's this horrible sensation! I can't stop it."

"Just relax," Bill said. "Just lie here. It will pass."

"It's not. This is really bad. Bill, call 911."

"Really?" Bill asked disbelieving.

"Yes. I mean it. This is terrible! Bill, I can't move. It's my inner ear, I think. I can't do anything! Call them! Bill, can I have my rosary beads, please."

"What makes you think it's your inner ear?"

"I don't know," I said frantically. "My ears have been plugged up for the last few days. I thought maybe it had something to do with all my crying. Maybe just too many tears. I don't know."

Soon after, three paramedics were entering the bedroom. Harley was barking and as they approached, he jumped up on the bed and began to bark frantically. It felt as though the bed was rising and dropping fifty feet with every bounce. Bill put Harley in another room and they carried me out on a stretcher and slowly down the outside stairs. It had been raining and the stairs were wet and slippery. Bill said, "I'll meet you at the hospital." As they put me into the ambulance I heard Bill say, "She's been under a lot of stress. Our son died."

They closed the doors and the paramedic asked me when my son had died. If he were surprised when I said, "It's been a year," he did not show it. I said, "But in some ways it feels like it was yesterday. The heartache is still very intense."

The emergency room doctor confirmed that it was my inner ear. I was lying flat as I tried to take the pills he gave me. He said I should be feeling better soon and he left. Bill arrived and tucked the blanket under my feet the way I had seen him do for Dawson. The nurse came in and told me they get at least one case of this a day. She said it was positional vertigo. It can be caused by a virus or an infection she said.

She periodically came in and checked on me, but I was not getting any better. I could not sit up without the room spinning around me, so she gave me more pills. She said it was taking me an unusually long time to get over it. "Most people are ready to leave in an hour or so," she said. "Your attack must have been quite severe." She added that I was lucky, in most cases it was accompanied by nausea. I was lucky, but I was there for four hours before I could get up and leave.

The experience was so frightening, it left me with a constant feeling of anxiety that I could not shake. I feared that awful feeling returning. I did not believe it was caused by an infection or virus, so I did some researching. There was a theory about some kind of crystallized formation in the inner ear that spontaneously breaks loose and disrupts your equilibrium. That seemed more like what I believed had happened to me. I learned it was something that could recur at any time or it may never happen again. But I became acutely aware of every slight sensation that seemed to warn of its onset.

I told Leah, "That certainly wasn't the experience I'd want to have as the ending of the book. That definitely wasn't it." In general, I was having a difficult time writing. Whenever I sat down to write, a feeling of panic came over me. I brought the word processor downstairs and I set it up in the family room/kitchen on a small table next to Dawson's chair, thinking I could be more relaxed there. I thought perhaps if I felt panicky it would help to get up and do other things and yet still be close enough to get right back to writing. I didn't know what was wrong with me. Was I going crazy?

I came across an article that listed the signs of depression. I had almost every symptom. Was that what was wrong with me? Was I not coping? Was this all just too much for me? Right from the beginning I did everything as if I were normal. I functioned. But I was aware that though I did everything, I felt like I was the saddest person anyone would ever see doing them. Would anyone understand how sad I still was, how much my heart continued to ache? I was keeping busy and that helped, but there remained seemingly simple things that I found quite difficult to do like watching the Discovery channel. It seemed every nature program showed a mother animal with her baby and more often than not, the stories were of strife and struggle and babies who did not survive. Mothers of all species, it appeared, anguished at the loss of their offspring. "Bill, please, let's not watch these programs anymore," I cried as I watched a lemur baby jumping playfully in the trees, his mother intently watching close by. The baby, in his exuberance, slipped and fell from the branches to the ground. The narrator informed us this happens often without harm. The mother scurried quickly down the tree to her baby, who lay motionless. The narrator then told us that though ordinarily the baby would have survived this fall, this playful baby had hit his head on a rock. The mother tried to pick up his lifeless body in her little paws. She stroked his head as he draped from her arms. She looked up. She looked frantic, screaming and confused and frightened. Her mate came to her side and tried to coax her to leave her baby. She would not leave him. She tried to carry him, to drag him, to take him with her. Sobbing, I said, "Bill, please turn it off. I can't watch this." How could I ever wonder what was wrong with me? A mother cannot be expected to lose her child and ever get over it. It was just too much to ask, but I prayed to God I would find some peace in my heart.

On the morning of my birthday, after Bill left for work, I was remembering my last birthday and how much Dawson's gift had meant to me. How blessed I was to have received his message and so many more throughout the past year. I told myself I should not be afraid to hope to hear from him today. But it seemed everything made me fearful these days and I wished I could rid myself of the anxiety that had persistently lingered.

I began to go about my chores. My mother and father were coming down when Bill got home from work and we were going out to dinner. *If only Dawson ...* I thought, as I picked up a catalog that was on the kitchen table. It was a catalog of woodworking supplies that had arrived for Dawson. It was from the company where I had ordered the "Handcrafted by Dawson Bell" wood-burning tool I had given him on his birthday. The catalog had been on the table since it arrived in the mail at least a week earlier. I had been reluctant to do anything with it, though usually I put them in his room when they arrived. Sometimes, I had put them in the recycle bin. This one, I had been unable to do anything with until this morning, when I picked it up and looked at the cover. I didn't know why I was standing there reading it. But then I read, *A Gift to You, Every Day of the Year.* I stood there a moment and thought maybe Dawson was trying to say he had a gift for me for my birthday. Maybe that was it. Maybe there was something in this catalog that I would see and know was something he would have made for me. I began to look through it. Would I know it if I saw it? I wondered. I went through the entire catalog. Nothing. I was about to put it down when I thought, *Seeing these catalogs is so painful for me. Maybe I should call and cancel them.* I had never thought of that before. It seemed an odd thing to do, but I went to the phone and began to dial. *I'm actually going to tell them to take him off their mailing list?* As the phone was ringing, I was staring at the cover. I read again, "*A Gift to You, Every Day of the Year.*"

"Dawson, what are you trying to say to me?"

A voice at the other end of the phone said, "Thank you for calling. A representative will be with you shortly. Please stay on the line." Then the usual mind-dulling music came through. I stood there holding the catalog wondering what the heck I was doing. Then suddenly I became aware of the male voice singing. The words he sang were: "*Don't be afraid my love, I am watching you from above. I would give anything to be with you tonight, but just think of me and I'll be there.* "Dawson!" I said aloud. "Oh, Dawson. I will think of you and you will be with me tonight for my birthday."

I could not explain these messages. I believed they were from Dawson, but if they were not, there was no denying that some beautiful force was answering my prayers. The power of faith and love was truly awesome.

In December, I was quite touched and surprised when we received the card that told us that Dawson would have a light on one of the trees in the town square again this year. The lighting ceremony was to be held on the coming Friday and, though we had not gone the previous year, I wanted very much to go this year.

We bundled up and took Harley with us. As we arrived on the lawn surrounding the giant trees, we were handed candles and song books. There were at least three hundred people gathered there, and on this starlit, crisp, winter evening, all of us holding flickering candles sang Christmas carols. I was thinking how far I'd come from the Christmas Rusty and I had turned out the lights so the carolers on the street would not stop at our house.

As I sang from my heart *O Holy Night, the stars are brightly shining, it is the night of our dear Savior's birth ... Down on my knees, I hear the angels voices ... O Holy Night,* I felt close to the angels and Dawson. I continued singing, *Come and behold him, born the King of Angels. Oh come let us adore Him. Oh, come let us adore Him ...*

"Andrea, Dawson's here," Bill said.

"I know," I said.

"I mean, really. I felt like he was with us and I said, 'Dawson, if you are here blow out my candle.' It instantly began to flicker wildly and went out. Andrea, I know Dawson did it. I asked him to show me he was here and he did."

"But Bill, there is a breeze."

"Your candle is still lit. So is everyone else's."

Yes, my candle had not gone out. In fact, when we left the park and I walked to the truck carrying my burning candle, it still did not go out. I did not want to blow it out, so I carried it all the way home in the truck. I walked from the truck to the front door and still no breeze had blown it out. Bill's candle had told us Dawson was with us and my candle's flame, which came home with us was my sign that Dawson had, too. *Sleep in heavenly peace.*

With all my blessings, I wondered why my grief and sorrow persisted, as did my nervousness. I was angry with myself for indulging in such selfishness. It appeared to me to be a sign that I was dwelling too much on my own pain. I had to remind myself that mine was not the only sorrow in the world. That, joined with the memory of Dawson's desire to help others, led me to think there was something more I should be doing. I considered the idea of volunteering to visit patients awaiting heart transplants to give them encouragement as Dawson had wanted to do, but I did not feel I could be of help to anyone. Just the thought of walking into an intensive care unit nearly brought on a panic attack. *There must be something I can do, Dawson, to honor your desire to help others.* I prayed to God to show me the way.

One Sunday, I was reading our church bulletin. This announcement appeared: *LITA, Love Is The Answer, needs volunteers to visit lonely, nursing home residents at Novato facilities. Since 1975, LITA has been matching volunteers in one to one friendships with nursing home residents. Volunteering may be done any day and any time that is convenient. Share yourself.*

The following day, I called and made an appointment for an interview. I went in the next day and spoke with a kind and understanding woman. She explained how conscientiously LITA members worked at matching the volunteer with a resident. She wanted to know about me and how I came to want to do this.

I said, "My son was in intensive care for three months while waiting for a heart transplant. A man came to visit him who had received a heart five years earlier. He wanted to give Dawson encouragement. When he left, Dawson told me that was what he was going to do for others when he got his heart. He did not get the chance and I did not want Dawson's hopes to have been in vain, so I've been considering ways I could carry out his plan for him. But when I imagined myself entering a hospital's ICU, seeing someone going through what Dawson had gone through, I did not believe I could be of any help. But every day I hear Dawson's words of how he wanted to help others and how important it was for people who were confined to have someone with them who cared, someone who was there because they wanted to be. When I read your announcement, it seemed to speak to me."

She said, "Well, I am very happy you came to us. Some residents in assisted-care homes are very lonely. They need someone who will spend time with them and give them something to look forward to. We like our volunteers to visit on a regular basis to give their friend the comfort and security of someone they can count on. We hope our volunteers will visit as they would visit a friend, because they want to. It seems you certainly understand the importance of that. I think I have just the lady I'd like you to meet." The following week I met a volunteer coordinator who introduced me to Mary.

Mary was a very sweet little lady. The three of us chatted for a short while. She seemed nervous and did not seem to understand what I was doing there, but when I told her I would be back to visit her again, she took my hand and thanked me. The coordinator smiled and nodded at me. A match had been made.

When I arrived the following Thursday, she did not remember me. We had a short visit and she seemed to enjoy the company, but when I was leaving she asked if she could pay me. I told her, "No, no. This is not my job. I'm here to visit you because I want to." I told her I would see her next Thursday at the same time.

When I met with her the next week, again she did not remember me. Though she was in very good physical condition, her memory was failing her and she was often confused. She remembered things from her long ago past and talked to me of those things. I listened with interest and one day I suggested we go to the arts and crafts class given on Thursdays in her facility. She was reluctant, but I convinced her that I would help her and we would work together. And we did. From that day on, when I arrived to pick her up, she knew me. Each week, I met her in her room and we walked hand in hand to class. She did not always know it was the day I would be coming, but when I arrived, she was happy to see me. I always asked her how she had been and told her I had been thinking of her. Most often, with tears in her eyes she would answer, "Oh, I'm all goofed up. I get so confused." Every week she asked me to look at her calendar with her and tell her what day it was so that she could cross off the previous day. She was frightened and her hands trembled. I sympathized with her nervousness and fear and I forgot my own and when sitting side by side working on our projects, we were able to forget our sadness. We laughed and we shared. When it was time for me to leave, she no longer said goodbye to me at the door, she began walking outside with me. I could see she did not want me to leave and I wished that she could have someone with her all the time. Many days I stayed longer than I planned.

One day, she walked me to the curb and we hugged goodbye. As I walked to my car, we waved and blew each other a kiss. A lady stopped and asked Mary, "Is that your daughter?"

"No," I heard Mary answer, "but I love her very much. And she loves me. She is my sunshine." Smiling, she said, "I always feel better when she's here."

As I drove away, watching her wave to me until I was out of view, tears flooded my eyes. *She feels better when I'm there!* I had heard those special words before. She knew I was there because I truly cared for her. And I believed Dawson knew his life had all the meaning he had hoped it would have. For there was no doubt it was because Dawson had lived that Mary had a friend. I drove directly to church, entered and walked down the aisle and knelt before the altar and thanked God for His many blessings.

Claudia, in her faith's journey, had continued in the RCIA program and had made the decision to be confirmed. Her confirmation would take place on Easter. I was quite proud and pleased. Along with her spiritual quest, she was doing well in her career. She received a promotion that made her the first female Lead Forecaster in the Western Region, which encompassed eight states.

I told her how very proud I was of her. She said, "Now, it's your turn, Mom. You have to start RCIA classes, so you can make your confirmation."

"I know," I said, "I will, but not just yet. I am just so busy with trying to get the book written."

"O.K. Well, I'm glad you will be able to go to communion with me. I'm waiting to go until I'm confirmed. It will be a very special day for me."

"I'm so glad I'm able to go, too, and I'm so happy you have gotten back to church. It really means a lot to me, hon."

"Do you think Dad would go to communion, too?"

"I don't know. We've talked about it, but he doesn't want to go to confession. I'll ask him about it."

I mentioned it to Bill and his eyes opened wide. "What?" He said, "I'm not going to confession. It's been too many years."

"Well, Claudia thought it would be nice and she knows we go to church every Sunday. It would be a wonderful thing to do for her, to show her how happy we are for her."

"Oh, I don't know," he said, shaking his head.

When I told my mother, she said, "I would like to do that for Claudia, but how many years has it been for me? Bill should do it. At least he's going to church now. I'm not even doing that."

"Are you thinking you might go to confession?"

"I don't know. I'd like to do it for her, but ..."

"What about Daddy? Would he?"

"It's been even longer for him. I'm going to think about it, but don't say anything to Claudia."

"O.K. Have you forgiven God for taking Dawson?"

"Well, I still don't understand it. Dawson should have had the chance to be the person he wanted to be."

"But, Mom, there must be a reason why he had to go. Maybe God even gave him the choice."

By the time the four of us went to Monterey for Claudia's confirmation, I was the only one who had gone to confession. In the motel, I looked in the phone book for Catholic churches. I called them to find out their reconciliation schedules. The Carmel Mission was hearing confessions that day in an hour from the time I called. When I hung up the phone, I said, "O.K., we can make that one. Who's going?"

My mother and father and Bill all exchanged frightened glances. My mother said, "Bill, if you go, I'll go."

Bill said, "I'll go if Frank goes."

My father said, "Hey, don't look at me. I'm not going."

"You guys are terrible," I said.

My mother said, "I know it would mean a lot to Claudia. O.K., I'm going."

"You are?" Bill said, "O.K. let's go. Frank, you're coming, too."

Confessions were being heard in the small chapel on the Mission grounds. We all entered. There was no one else there. My mother went into the confessional first and when she came out, she said, "It wasn't too bad." My father was next and came out quite choked up. Then Bill came out crying.

That night, we all watched as Claudia, in her white robe, came down the procession. I was so moved and proud of her. The priest poured the holy oil over her and she was confirmed. When it came time for the administering of the Eucharist, Claudia filed out of the pew. She looked back at me as I followed her and then her eyes widened as Bill followed me and then my mother and father behind him. She was looking like she could not believe it. She looked back at me questioningly, with tears in her eyes. I nodded. "Yes, they have done this for you, Claudia." Tears escaped from my eyes, as well.

After the ceremony, she asked, "Did you all …"

"Yeah."

"Even Papa?"

"Yes. We are with you, hon. We are all with you and Christ is with us." We had all made a commitment to our faith. It was quite an extraordinary event. And what added to its beauty was that we had done it as a family. I felt blessed when Claudia introduced Bill and me to her new friends and we were there as a couple. It was the way it should be. And in the eyes of the church, we were a *married* couple. Certainly in the eyes of God we were. *What God hath joined together …* I reached over and touched Bill's hand, yes … *until death do us part.*

The following week, Claudia called and said, "Sister Teresa has asked each of us in our RCIA group to write something telling of our experience. She said they will appear in our bulletin next week."

"Are you going to do it? If you do, I'd love to see it."

"Yes. I'll mail a bulletin to you."

"I'll be anxiously awaiting it," I said. "I want you to know I'm very proud of you, Claudia; starting that class, sticking with it for the year and making the commitment to follow your faith. You've made me very happy."

When it arrived, I read: *Reflections RCIA 1998. Sit down, stand up, kneel here, say Amen there. That's all I needed to know, or so I thought. After all, I was raised Catholic and had gone through my first communion. Even though I had not been back to church since then, I never missed it. That is, until* the moment I was in the hospital room watching the doctor turn off my brother's life support system. As I was sitting there, Jesus came to me and said, "Your brother will be all right. Don't be afraid. I am with you." I had been called. It was time to go back to church.

I knew it was something I had to do, but I was quite scared. Since my religious education ended when I was seven years old, I had no idea what to expect or what was expected of me. I remember the first day I walked into St. Angela's. It was so foreign. This was before the church went through its remodel and the pews were at a strange angle with the altar on the side wall, not what I thought a church should look like. The lighting was so dim and yellow. I was definitely in unfamiliar territory. Only the power of God could have made me come back another day. And I did and joined RCIA shortly after.

What I was looking for was a list of rules and regulations, what I had to do to be Catholic, but what I found was something quite different. I found friends, family, community and a place where I belong, a place where I am welcomed. I discovered a stronger love for God, compassion for others, and the deeper meaning of prayer. Like the old church, my life was dim and without color, but now it is as bright and sunny as the church is today.

Through the process of my renewed education, I learned many things about Jesus, religion and the Catholic church. Since my family members were fallen-away Catholics as well, they asked me many questions over this past year. Not only did this help me to better understand what I was learning, but it must have had an effect on my family. Though my father and grandparents had not been to church more than sparingly in the last twenty years, on Holy Saturday they were inspired to go to reconciliation and stood with me and my mother in the communion line. You welcomed back one Catholic at the Easter Vigil, but you gained four.

Thank you for opening my eyes, expressing your love and giving me a place to belong. I pray I am able to take this love you've given me and someday give it to someone else and change their lives the way you've changed mine.

I immediately called Claudia. Crying, I said, "I got the newsletter today. It's wonderful. You did a beautiful job of writing. You know, we've never really talked about what made you decide to go back to church. Claudia, what was it that happened when you were in the hospital?"

"It is hard to explain, but Jesus was there. I was looking out the window. I didn't actually see Him, but I knew He was there. He was telling me though Dawson was going to die, he was going to be O.K. and I believed it. What struck me was that up until then I'd always thought in terms of God. But it was Jesus there in the hospital, so it had to be real. The moment when they turned off his VADs, it was so horrible. We were all sobbing and the pain was excruciating, but then I felt this peace and calm come over me and I knew everything would be O.K."

Jesus had not appeared to me that awful day in the hospital. Whenever I thought of the moment when I had nodded to the doctor to turn off Dawson's VADs, I felt the anguish of those horrifying minutes as I sat beside him knowing life was leaving his body. But now, believing as I did that he was still with me, there were times when I could think of that moment and not see his life coming to an end. I saw life transforming into a new and miraculous form. I imagined a whole and beautiful spirit that was Dawson having ascended from his ailing body.

I knew now what I wanted to do for Dawson's birthday. I wanted to thank him for having led us all to Jesus. I thought if I could have mass intentions said for him on his birthday that would be a wonderful gift to him. I went to church not realizing that mass intentions were reserved almost a year in advance. The secretary informed me of this and I must have looked so disappointed that she suggested I talk to Sister Jeanette.

Sister Jeanette had kind, friendly eyes and a warm smile. She asked me to have a seat in her tiny office. She sat across from me and I proceeded to tell her why I was there. She was very attentive and I continued to tell her our whole story. She reached for her box of tissues and offered me one and took one for herself. She said, "I am not crying because it is sad. I am crying because it is so beautiful."

"Oh, thank you for saying that. I am trying to write his story, but there are times when I worry that someone will read it and say, 'Whoever told this woman she could write a book?'"

"Well, Andrea, just don't let anyone tell you you can't! I'll talk to Father and have him say a special prayer for Dawson on his birthday. Good luck on your book. I can't wait to read it."

"Thank you," I said. "Sometimes I just can't believe one day I will actually have a book."

In the mail, professionally imprinted in bold letters on a business-sized envelope was: *A remarkable new book is about to be published-and* **you,** *Dawson Bell are in it!* When I saw this, I was stunned. It was a solicitation to buy a book that was soon to be released on the history of Bells in America that would include a directory of every Bell household.

But that did not matter. *A remarkable new book is about to be published—and you, Dawson Bell are in it!* Amazed by the wording, I concluded it was a message for me. I was not to doubt that I could write a book, Dawson's remarkable book.

"Happy Mother's Day," Claudia said. "I didn't know, but I saw it and I just bought it." *Why I Believe in Life Beyond Death,* was the title of the little book I had just unwrapped. The book I had requested last Mother's Day, like the book I had bought earlier had done nothing for me. I didn't know exactly what I was looking for, but whatever it was, I had not found it.

"Oh, it looks interesting," I said. "And you never know where you might find something you need."

That certainly was true. You never know. The next day, I began to read the little book that Claudia had picked out on her own. It was a book of individual stories about the connection between this life and the next. They were all lovely stories, but there was one that told me what I needed to hear. As in the way we grieve is an individual matter, so, too, is the way we find solace. This story was mine.

I was reading a story by Cecil B. DeMille, at one time one of the greatest motion picture geniuses in the United States, a very sensitive, spiritually minded man. He said that one summer day he was in Maine, in a canoe on the lake deep in the woods. He was all alone. He wanted to do some work on a script, so he let the canoe drift idly while he worked. Suddenly he discovered that he was in low water, about four inches deep, near the shore, and he could plainly see on the lake bottom a number of water beetles. One of them crawled out of the water onto the canoe and sank his talons into the woodwork of the hull and there he died.

Three hours later, still floating in the hot sun, DeMille observed a wondrous miracle. He suddenly noticed that the shell of the water beetle was cracking open. A moist head emerged, followed by wings. Finally the winged creature left the dead body and flew in the air, going farther in one half second than the water beetle could crawl all day. It was a dragonfly, its beautiful colors shimmering in the sunlight. The dragonfly flew above the surface of the water, but the water beetles down below couldn't see it.

Do you think Almighty God would do this for a water beetle and wouldn't do it for you?

The little dragonfly story had given me a real picture of what, until then, I had only imagined. Now when I thought of that painful moment of Dawson's death, I could easily see him emerging from his tired, cumbersome body. He could soar to greater heights than had ever been possible. I saw him able to see us still struggling below. I saw him free. I saw him beautiful.

I understood how it could be possible that he was there, yet we could not see him. And someday we would crawl out of our habitats and soar with him. This was no longer just a creation of my own imagination.

I called Claudia immediately and thanked her, telling her she had chosen the perfect book with the perfect story written just for me. When I met Bill that afternoon and told him the story, he cried.

It was spring and our pond was alive with many beautiful dragon-flies. Bill and I loved seeing them there. Since the story I had read, they had come to have great meaning to us. They were a welcome reminder of the power of God and the beauty of life and rebirth.

Bill and I were working around the pond one warm afternoon, when Rob, the teenage boy who lived next-door and shared the pond, came over. "Hi, Rob, how're you doing?" Bill asked.

"O.K.," he answered. "I've been working on my truck." They talked a while about engines and transmissions and then he said to me, "A friend of mine knows you."

I said, "Really? Who?"

"Mario."

"Mario?"

"Yeah. He said you were a friend of his grandmother's."

"Mario! Yeah, Mario. How is he?"

"O.K."

"How did you find out he knows me?"

"He was over the other day and he noticed Dawson's Camaro. We were looking over at it when he said he recognized your car."

"He should have come over! I would love to see him. If he comes by again, will you bring him over? Tell him I'd like to see him, O.K.?"

"Yeah, but he's kind of shy."

"I know, but tell him he has to."

I went inside and a short time later Bill came in to tell me about a dragonfly he saw. He said, "It flew over to me and landed right next to me. It was sitting right there so close that I said, 'Dawson, are you here?' and I reached over to the dragonfly and touched its wing."

"It let you touch it? It didn't fly away?"

"No, it stayed there. I couldn't believe it. I said, 'Dawson?' and I reached over and stroked its other wing."

"You're kidding! I can't believe that. Was it hurt?"

"No, it was fine. It stayed around, skimming over the pond and then flew into the sky. I couldn't believe it let me touch it!"

"Dawson must have been holding him for you."

Chapter Forty

Over the months, writing became no longer just a part of my weekly schedule. It developed into a major part of my daily routine. Previously I had waited to write until I was going to be home all day, now I wrote whenever I had the chance. If I found I had an hour or so, I spent it writing. With my word processor more conveniently located downstairs, I began to write in the evening, as well. I was comfortable and relaxed in Dawson's chair and there was hardly a day when I did not spend some time on "the book." It had become an integral part of my life and my grieving.

When I ran into friends I had not seen in a while, the most common question they asked me was, "Are you working?" My answer was, "I'm writing." Writing was a full-time job. When I told them *what* I was writing, their first response was always, "Oh, that must be good for you, so therapeutic." I did not know if it were or not and Bill certainly questioned that theory. He said, "It really doesn't look like it's good for you. I sure know I couldn't do what you're doing. It would rip my heart out if I had to relive that whole, sad ordeal day after day. It's hard enough for me whenever I just think about it."

One evening, I was writing about the shadow box Dawson had

made for me and I had it sitting in front of me. Bill looked over at me, the tears pouring down my face, my heart obviously breaking, and he said, "Andrea, maybe you shouldn't be doing all this writing. It looks like it's tearing you up." *A little late for that,* I thought. He was right, it was difficult, but it was something I had to do. And I knew I would be reliving it all every day anyway, even if I were not writing about it. At least this way, it was serving a purpose. I was not just indulging myself for the sake of my own pity. I had a good reason. I was doing it for Dawson. Reliving my memories had become a way of life and reliving them for the sake of the book had given my life purpose. If I had to be sad and cry every day to do it, I accepted that. Crying was akin to brushing my teeth; something I routinely did and then got on with my day.

When I explained to others about my writing, many asked, "Are you writing a *book*?" "Yes," I said, but I felt compelled to qualify what might appear to be arrogance, by explaining, "I have a tremendous will to do it for Dawson." Then I would tell them what Bill had said. When he had said them, I had no idea how important those words would become. Now I used them, not only to bolster confidence in myself, but also as an explanation to others. I felt so fortunate to have them so I could explain that I was not writing just because I wanted to or thought I could. It seemed Bill's words were a gift, for they helped me express the humbleness I felt at taking on such an ambitious task.

The fact was, though Dawson had told me he wanted to tell his story and we had discussed how we would write it together, he had never told me what it was he wanted to say. I knew he felt it would help others who were making the wrong choices as he had. I imagined he would have told how and why he had made them. His message would have been for young people, but now all I could do was write my version of his story, his story from the mother's perspective. Despite my own insecurities, I thoroughly believed in Dawson's story. I was sure Dawson knew it was true when he said it was going to help someone. I believed it would prove to have a power that was all its own that had little to do with my writing abilities. The sheer telling of it was what was important.

Armed with a sense of purpose and faith, I proceeded on. Caring friends offered suggestions. "Make an outline, tell it into a recorder, write the whole story as a rough draft and then go back and refine it." They were all worthwhile ideas to consider, but I did it the only way I could. I chose to write it just as I had lived it; minute by minute, chapter by chapter, never moving ahead until each chapter was complete, not taking notes, not knowing exactly what the next minute would hold for me — and having no knowledge whatsoever of how the story would end. I just kept writing and hoping that something would happen that would tell me, "This is the perfect ending." If nothing ever did, I could imagine writing forever. That worried me, for if I did that, it would be my personal journal, not a book, and that would not accomplish what Dawson wanted. When I expressed my fears over still having no ending, Bill told me not to worry. He said, "You must have faith" and my mother assured me, "Something *will* happen." But what? And when?

As I continued to write, telling the story of our eighty-plus days in ICU, I was not only immersed in living it all again, the agonizing days of frustration and fear and hope as Dawson battled for his life, I was also living with the truth that he had not survived and I was missing him terribly. When the time came to write about the pain and intense sorrow I was feeling, would I be able to express it? Would I find the words?

Words. Authors find them powerful. They revere them. They live by them. The words they choose and how they arrange them enable writers to portray whatever they can imagine. Am I then not an author, I asked myself, for when I tried to find the words, they were but flat, emotionless, black specks pressed upon a stark white page— humbly summoned to attempt a task beyond their capabilities. How could they possibly express the feeling that burned within my heart? How could they evoke the pain that wrapped around it and welled up in my throat that begged for relief, that pleaded for tears to cool the burning, to soothe the ache and wash away the unbearable hurt within my soul? No words I knew could impart this. No phrasing I was capable of could express this. No description I could give would make a reader actually feel the physical sensations of sorrow. How could I expect anyone to feel the kind of agony that encompassed me when I thought of what Dawson went through and his hopes and plans, his faith, his fears, his love. "May your memories be a comfort to you," they said. Did anyone know the pain that, not only sad, but also beautiful memories could bring? Could the memory of the laughter in his eyes bring *comfort*? Would I be capable of describing what those memories did to me? Could any words describe that? Was I asking too much of myself and those specks, those innocent, little specks we call words that sit still and lifeless upon the page?

The more I wrote and the more I grieved, the more I believed

Dawson's death was something that was meant to be. Did I believe it was his destiny? And if so, did that mean no amount of prayers could have changed the outcome? As I pondered over these questions, I was reminded of a legend from the Middle East.

A rich merchant's servant in Baghdad came to his master one day in great consternation. "Master," he cried, "someone bumped into me in the market place this morning. When I turned around, I saw it was Death. I caught his eye and he gave me such a strange and terrifying look that I am now in fear of my life. Master, please lend me your horse so that I may flee. With your help I can be far away in Samara by nightfall." The merchant was a generous man and, lending the servant a fine horse, he sent him forthwith on his way. Later, the merchant himself went to the market place and saw Death standing in the crowd. "Why did you frighten my servant this morning and give him such a threatening stare?" "I did not threaten him," said Death. "It was a look of surprise. I was astounded to see a man this morning in Baghdad when I have an appointment with him tonight in Samara."

Was the merchant's servant fated to die that night, or could he have exercised his free will and remained in Baghdad and avoided Death? But perhaps Death would have changed his traveling plans and kept the appointment anyway. What would have happened if the servant had confronted Death instead of running away? Perhaps he could have negotiated a delay in the timing of the appointment and enjoyed a longer life.

If Dawson had exercised his free will and had made different choices in his life, would he have avoided his early death? Or would it have happened in some other way? We had confronted death and had we not, with our prayers, tried to negotiate a delay? Was praying a way of bargaining? But did prayers really have that kind of power? With all that I had lived through, I believed they did, for I continued to believe the glory surrounding Dawson's death had come about through our prayers. Nothing would ever convince me our beautiful experiences were not God's gift to us in answer to them.

With my birthday approaching on Sunday, I began to wonder how he would say "Happy birthday" to me this year. It would be two years since the day I started writing. That seemed like a noteworthy milestone, if only for the fact that my sorrow had not lessened, my pain was just as deep, my tears were just as frequent and my longing to hug Dawson just as strong. At times I became angry with myself when my faith could not uplift me. In my weakest moments, I questioned everything I believed in.

It would be two years in December since Elaine had died and I still missed her, too. She was in the same memorial park as Dawson and I visited her often. She was in an area where the deer ate the flowers, so I had made an artificial flower arrangement for her. It was now looking quite weather-beaten and I brought it home to replace it with a fresh one. On Saturday, I brought it to her. I cleaned and shined her green marble headstone and trimmed the grass around it. I was pleased her place was looking neat. Kneeling at her grave site, I looked toward the gray, overcast sky and seeing a glint of light breaking through the clouds, I said, "I pray you are in that place up past the sun that Dawson spoke of. You deserve a beautiful place, my dear friend." I stood, and with tears streaming down my face, I said, "Elaine, please give Dawson a hug for me." I made the sign of the cross and said The Lord's Prayer for her as I walked to my car.

That night, Claudia came up from Monterey and my mother and father came over to celebrate my birthday. I was sitting by the fireplace with everyone around me and I was about to open my presents. There was a click of the latch at the front door. Bill heard it and looked at me. Harley got up and went to the door, but he did not bark. He stood there for a moment then came back and laid down. Bill said, "I guess it was the wind." I shrugged my shoulders thinking, *No, it was Dawson letting me know he's here for my birthday.*

That would be enough for me, I thought. This was one way in which this birthday was different than the past two had been. I would not despair if I did not find a message from Dawson. I was confidant he was with me.

The following morning, Claudia came to church with Bill and me. Because she had to work that evening, she left for home right after mass. Bill took me to breakfast and on the way home I thought, *We celebrated it last night, but today is actually my birthday. Will Dawson do something for me today?* I was struck by how calm I was about it.

When we arrived home, I went upstairs and changed into casual clothes. I put on my black leggings, black turtleneck, a sage-green sweatshirt and my Uggs. I was about to come down when I heard Bill open the front door, and then I heard voices. I thought, *Wouldn't you know it? Someone's here and I just changed out of my better clothes. If I had just waited two minutes.* I was thinking it was probably somebody for Bill anyway, and then Bill yelled up to me, "Andrea, there's somebody here to see you. It's Mario."

"Mario?" It had been months since I told Rob that I'd like to see him. That was last spring! I hurried down the stairs and went to the front door. Rob and Mario were standing there. "How have you been?" I said.

"Good," he said with a smile.

"Oh, I'm so glad. I think about you and wonder how you're doing. Where are you living?"

"With my dad," he said. He looked well. We shared some small talk, then Rob showed him Dawson's Camaro up close and under the hood. He was awed and excited. I imagined it was much like Dawson's reaction when he first saw it. We walked to the pond and he told me he had a job and had bought a car. He said he had a lot of responsibilities that he never had when Elaine was alive. He said, "Nonna was always so proud of me, even when I did little things. I can imagine how proud she would be of me now."

I said, "Not *would* be. *Is.* She *is* proud of you. Trust me, she knows. Are you still in school?"

"Oh, yeah."

"How are you doing?"

"O.K., but my dad doesn't even care how I do." He didn't say it with anger or sadness, he just stated it as a fact.

"So what are you guys up to today?" I asked.

"We've been working unloading Christmas trees," Rob said. They began to tell the humorous story of their experience with this rather odd Christmas tree lot owner. Their imitations of him were quite amusing. It reminded me of the kind of story Dawson enjoyed telling.

We came back in the house so I could show him Dawson's motor-cycle. I found myself smiling hearing their oohs and aahs and Rob's stories of how impressive Dawson had been on his bike. Rob described in his words the way "Dawson and his bike were one." He said to Mario, "He could really ride!" I told the story of Dawson's funeral service and how one of his friends had stood up and said that. I told him that was on his plaque. They both agreed, "What could be better to say than that!" It was nice sharing the many Dawson stories and Mario appeared to truly enjoy them.

I said, "Some of those 'He could ride' stories make me glad I had not heard them before. I worried about him enough as it was."

"That's the way Nonna was with me," Mario said. "She was always afraid of me getting hurt." His eyes glancing around, he said, "You know, Nonna had described this house to me. She said she really liked it. Now I know why. It's really cool."

I showed him the picture of Elaine and me I had framed and displayed on the side-by-side. He looked at it closely. The lamp I had made with Elaine's help was beside our picture. I said, "I made that shade with your grandma." He reached over and touched its fringe.

I said, "Do you still make model cars?"

He looked surprised and said, "Yeah, sometimes."

"I used to see your projects on the table. You had the same orange organizer with all the little compartments that Dawson had."

Smiling, he said, "Yeah. And it swiveled?"

"Yeah. It was the same one." I told him that when I had seen it, it had made me sad. "It reminded me that Dawson had a brand new model I had given him for his last birthday and he had not gotten to do it. It had lights that worked and all kinds of special features. It is still in his room in the box and it breaks my heart when I see it. Last Christmas, I thought of donating it, but I was not ready to part with it. Hey, if you need a winter project … " I said as the three of us walked to the front door and out onto the porch.

Remembering his special days with Elaine, he said, wistfully, "Yeah, Nonna and I used to work on the dining room table together. I'd work on my models and she'd work on her lamps."

"It's hard to see projects now of Dawson's that he didn't finish. Everything in his room is just as he left it. It hurts to see his things, but packing them away would hurt more."

"I would've left everything of Nonna's just like she had it. But Grandpa got rid of it all. I just couldn't understand how he could do that. All her clothes, all her projects, her car. As if she had never been there. I hated that."

"I don't really understand that. I couldn't do that with Dawson's things. But I guess there is no right or wrong way. You just have to do what seems right for you. Maybe seeing her things was just too painful for him. You never know. Everyone grieves differently."

"I didn't like Grandpa's way. I wanted to keep her things there. I liked smelling her perfume in the house. And he didn't like it when I talked about her, either. But I wanted to."

"Yeah. I know. I would hate it if I were with someone I couldn't talk to about Dawson."

"Sometimes I would talk about her as if she were still there and sometimes I would just talk about things in the past. I just missed her."

"I know. I still miss her. I think of her a lot, well, every time I see something green I think of her!"

Laughing, he said, "Yeah! I know!" He said to Rob, who had been standing on the steps listening quietly, "She loved green. She always wore green." Looking at me, he said, "You know, you remind me of her today. You're dressed like her. She used to wear those kind of pants."

Elaine and I were the same height and of similar coloring, except for her green eyes. I looked down at my clothes and said, "That's true, and my shirt is sort of green."

"It's been a long time since I've been with one of Nonna's friends and talked about her."

"Is it O.K.?"

"Yeah. I like it."

"I don't ever want to not think or talk about Dawson. But that's one thing that will never happen as long as I'm writing." I looked at Mario and said, "I'm writing Dawson's story. It is two years ago today that I started. I started writing on my birthday. Today is my birthday."

"It is?" Mario said. "Today is your birthday?"

"Yeah." Smiling, I said, "Oh, but you knew that. That was why you came over today, right?"

"Yeah! Right!" he said. We both laughed and he reached out naturally to me and gave me a warm hug. "Happy birthday," he said.

"Thank you." We walked down off the porch and I said, "Come by anytime, O.K.?"

"I will," he said.

"Come by and we'll take some flowers to your grandma. Come by if you just want to talk. Hey, come by with your report card!"

"O.K., I will," he said, smiling broadly.

As they walked down the road, I called to him, "Be good. Make your Nonna proud."

I walked back into the house, my heart stirring. I sat quietly in Dawson's chair. When I finally spoke, I said, "Bill, yesterday when I brought that arrangement to Elaine, I asked her to give Dawson a hug for me. Bill, think about this. Yesterday, I asked Elaine to give my son a hug and today, her grandson comes here and gives me a hug. Today, on my birthday!" Tears welled up inside me and flooded my eyes. I was overwhelmed by the unsuspecting message I had just received.

There was no mistaking the fact Dawson had received my hug from Elaine and they had worked out a way I could receive mine from Dawson. I definitely had heard from him on this birthday in an incredible way. It was in an undeniably real, physical sense and I had not searched to find it. His wish to me was as clear as if I had heard his voice saying, "Hi. Happy birthday. I love you, Mom."

How could I ever doubt the power of a love so strong it could transcend beyond what we could imagine? We could not see Dawson, but he was there and he could see us. Just like the beautiful dragonfly who could skim across the water and see where he had been, knowing that those left below could not imagine the beautiful new life he had.

Death was not the end! How could I not believe?

"Bill," I cried. "Do you know what just happened?" Awed, I said, "Bill, I just lived the last chapter of the book. And it ends on my birthday! Just as I would have wanted! And with a hug! What a wonderful thing for him to do. He knows how much getting a hug from him has meant to me. This is more than I could have ever hoped for! Bill, I'll be right back," I said as I got my keys.

I went out to my car and drove down to Dawson's. With the car still running, I rushed to him. Letting the tears run freely down my face, I said, "I love you, Dawson." I grasped my arms around me the way I always did, but this time it was so different. With new found meaning, I said the words I had said so many times before, "I got your hug, Dawson, I got your hug!" The tears I was shedding were no longer bitter tears of sorrow, they were sweet, long-awaited tears of joy.

Epilogue

When I embarked upon this writing journey, I had not imagined it would span five years. I encountered many unknowns along the way, but from the beginning, there was one constant; this book was to be my gift to Dawson. Now, looking back, I realize having this extraordinary story to write about was Dawson's gift to me.

There were many times I grew impatient with how long it was taking me. I so wanted to have this book completed for Dawson. Many days as I was writing and promising him that one day I would finish, I made him another promise. I told him that "everyone" would know his story, just as he had wanted. My gift to him would not be complete until I accomplished that.

I know now that the time I spent writing was a blessing, a special gift for me. I don't know how I would have managed without it. Writing had enabled me to experience and explore the depths of my love and my faith and along the way, I discovered that the combination of love and faith is quite a powerful one. But when love and faith are joined with sorrow, the kind of sorrow that reaches to the core of one's soul, the infinite, unimaginable power of that combination makes all things possible.

After living what I considered would be "the last chapter of the book," my writing routine continued on, but it was then with a clear path to where the story ended, or so I thought.

Harley and I continued to walk at about the same time every day. Many of the same cars passed us on the street. Strangers I did not know began to wave to me as if they knew me. Neighbors also waved. Many days I was so engrossed in formulating and reliving what I would be writing that day, through my tears, I did not notice who had driven past.

My next-door neighbor, Jennifer, drove by many mornings on her way to and from taking her boys to school. Some days she passed me when I was on my way down to Dawson's and some days it was when I was on my way back. Some times I would notice her in time to wave, some, I did not. And there were many days I did not see her at all.

It was a cold and dreary morning in the middle of January as I was on the last stretch of my walk. I was approaching Jennifer's driveway. I saw her driving up the street and she turned into her driveway at the exact moment I reached it. I anticipated her acknowledging me, for I was only a few feet away from the driver's side window. I nodded to her, and she stopped and rolled down her window. "How are you doing?" she asked.

"O.K.," I said.

"Are you writing?"

"Oh, yeah. Every day. I can't believe it's been over two years and I am still not close to finishing. How are things with you?"

"Not very good," she said.

"Oh, what is it?" Seeing she was upset, I urged, "Jennifer, what's wrong?"

"It's Rob. I'm so worried." She appeared on the verge of tears as she stepped out of her van.

I gave her a hug and asked again, "What is it?"

"He is so angry. He seems depressed or something and I don't know why. I'm so worried about him and I'm frightened. He is terribly angry at me. It really scares me. I'm sorry to burden you with this, but, Andrea, I just don't know what to do. I really can't talk now. I'm already late! I have to drive Trevor to school … I'm sorry … I just … "

"I understand," I said. "It's all right. You'd better go. Take care." As I walked home, I was wishing there were something I could do for this mother in such despair.

Once home, I began my daily morning chores, but I could not get Jennifer and Rob out of my thoughts. If only there were something I could do for them. Dawson had so wanted to help others and right next door was a young man, troubled, and there was nothing I could do. Or was there? *Dawson, you said your story was going to help someone. Is Rob that someone?* It was as if Dawson was telling me, yes, and he wanted me to try. *I don't even know what the problem is. What can I do?* I had spent the past two years saying how Dawson believed his story was going to help someone, and now I found myself feeling utterly helpless, but I kept hearing Dawson's words.

I was putting laundry into the washing machine, and then I stopped. Suddenly, I was compelled to tell Dawson's story to Rob. I sat down at the word processor and began a letter, planning to tell Rob of all the things Dawson had learned and how he had discovered life was too precious to waste. *But is that what Rob needs to hear?* I didn't know. *What am I doing? Maybe I should take my shower first before I get into this. And go to the market. I have nothing to cook for dinner. Maybe I should stop and take care of these things, and then write. What am I going to do with a letter anyway? Am I actually going to give it to him? But how can I? Wouldn't he then know his mother had talked to me? And wouldn't that make him even angrier? Maybe I should just stay out of it.*

But there I was. Writing. I did not stop. I did not take a shower. I did not go to the market. I did not finish the laundry. I did nothing but write. Finally, I had written and rewritten it enough times to where I felt I had said everything I wanted to say. I looked at the clock and could not believe it was going on four o'clock in the afternoon! I had nothing for dinner and it was now too late to shop, if I was to meet Bill at our usual time, four-thirty. I had this letter, but what was I going to do with it? *Maybe I could give it to him tomorrow. Maybe I should at least wait and show it to Bill and see what he says. Maybe he would think I should mind my own business. Maybe he would be right. But Jennifer had come to me. Hadn't she?* Well, certainly fate had, literally, placed us in each other's path. *What am I going to do? Maybe I should forget about this letter for now and maybe if I hurry I could go to the market and make it back in time to meet Bill.* It was almost four. But then without another thought, I suddenly picked up the phone and called her.

"Jennifer, it's Andrea. How are things going?"

"Terrible."

"Oh, no. What is it? Is he home?"

"Yes, and he is so angry!"

"I'm sorry ... I ... I just couldn't get you guys off my mind. I was wishing there was something I could do for you, but I didn't know what. Dawson had told me his story was going to help someone and I thought, who could he want to help more than Rob? I know how much Rob admired Dawson. Something just told me I should try. I tried to condense his story into a letter for Rob."

"Oh, Andrea. How sweet of you."

"But I'm not sure what I should do with it."

"I'd like you to give it to him."

"I really don't know if it will mean anything to him."

"Rob loved Dawson. Idolized him. I'd like him to read it."

"But I have to read it to you first. He's *your* son. You have to know what it is I'm saying to him."

"Andrea, I trust you."

"No, I have to read it to you first. O.K.?"

"O.K."

I began, "Dear Rob. You know I am writing a book about Dawson. I don't know if you know how it came about that I would take on such a task." I then went on in the letter to explain how, when Dawson finally awakened after having been sedated for a month, one of the first things he said was he wanted to tell everyone his story and how he believed it was going to help someone. I continued to read my words to Jennifer, "Rob, I want you to know Dawson's story. There is no greater gift I can give Dawson than to tell it to someone and have it help. And there is no greater gift I can receive. It is true I do not know exactly what Dawson thought, did, or felt that got him to where his life ended, but I do know what he had learned. And I know he wanted others to benefit from it." The letter went on to tell how awed he was by the doctors' and nurses' dedication to helping others and how he had said to me, that in his twenty-seven years, he hadn't done anything for anybody. I read, "Of course, that wasn't really true, but in the realm of life, I suppose it was. He meant he had not given of himself for the sake of someone else. He had lived his life doing what he felt like, doing what was fun. He didn't worry about how it affected anyone else. Hey, he was cool." I wrote of his visit from the elderly man and how Dawson's eyes had told me he had learned what being "cool" was really all about and how he had the same look when he talked with the young, compassionate doctor. I wrote, "He looked at this doctor with such respect for what this young man had made of his life, for the road he had chosen and for the efforts and sacrifices he must have had to make. Dawson obviously had regrets not only for what his choices had done to his health, but also for the opportunities he had missed because of his choices. He saw that young man's life had purpose and meaning. He could have been that man." I wrote of the night he sat gazing wistfully at the peach and turquoise sunset and how I could see he knew the true beauty of life. I wrote how I had said, "Dawson, at twenty-seven you know things some people who have lived to be seventy-seven don't know" and how he had looked at me with such profound wisdom and said, "Oh, but they will." "He knew the day would come in everyone's life when 'they would know.'" I finished the letter by writing, "What Dawson knew was that life is a gift. And that we must always choose to do good. Though Dawson felt he had not done that with his life, he knew if he shared his story with others, ultimately he would do something very good. Rob, his life had purpose. It mattered. And he wants you to know that yours does, too. Do only good things, Rob, please."

When I finished reading, we were both crying. Jennifer said, "Andrea, that is beautiful. I can't believe you would do all that for Rob. Thank you so much. You must give it to him."

"He'll know you discussed him. Won't that make him even madder at you?"

"Andrea, at this point, I don't think that matters. From the first time I talked to you … I don't know … I just trust you. Give him your letter."

"So how should I get it to him?"

"Call him. I'll give you his personal number."

I nervously dialed, thinking, *What am I doing? What am I going to say to him?*

He answered, "Hello."

"Hi, Rob?"

"Yeah."

"This is Andrea, next door. I was wondering if you could come over for a minute."

"Oh, right now?"

"Yeah. Are you busy?"

"Kind of. Did you need something?"

"Oh, I just had something I wanted to talk to you about."

"Oh. O.K., I'll be over."

I hung up the phone, folded the letter and in a couple of minutes he knocked on the door. I let him in and asked him how he was. He said he was O.K. and I said, "I was kind of worried about you today."

He looked surprised. He said, "Oh. I thought you probably wanted to ask me something about Mario."

"No. That's not what I wanted to talk to you about. You know I'm writing Dawson's story. I thought maybe it … I don't know … maybe it might help you."

"Help me? Did my mother talk to you?"

"Not really. I saw her this morning on my walk and she seemed so upset. I was hoping there was something I could do. I could maybe talk to you about Dawson and what he had learned and what he had wanted to share with others. I wanted to share it with you. I wrote it down." I handed him the letter and said, "I hope you'll read it, but … whatever… if you want to talk to me about anything… Well, just take care, Rob."

"Thanks," he said and left. I looked at the clock. It was almost time to leave to meet Bill. I had a few minutes, so I called my mother and told her what I'd done.

"I hope I did the right thing. I told him if he wanted to talk to me … I don't know what he'll think about it." We were talking when Harley began to bark wildly and in an unusual frenzy ran to the back door.

My mother heard him and asked, "Why is he barking?"

"I don't know. He must have heard something. It's a weird bark. It seems like something must have frightened him to be barking like this, but I don't see anything." He finally stopped and we resumed our conversation. I said, "I'm not sure I should have gotten involved. What if he gets mad? I don't know, but something just told me I should do it." We were discussing this when Harley startled me by barking again, but this time he ran to the front door. *What is it? What's got him so spooked?* Then I heard frantic knocking. "Oh, God. Mom, someone's here! It must be Rob! I hope he isn't mad at me." I was still on the phone when I opened the door. Rob was not standing there. Quicker than I had time to question in my mind why Andrew, Rob's younger brother, was there at my door crying, he screamed, "Rob shot himself! My mom told me to come here!"

"Oh, my God! Andrew! Oh, my God." Into the phone I cried, "Mom, Rob shot himself! I've got to go!"

She screamed, "No, Andrea!"

As I ran with Andrew down the road and around the pond to their house, I was pleading, "Andrew, tell me what happened! Did he read my letter? What happened?" *I'm responsible for this tragedy,* I thought. *My God. It's my fault. What was I thinking to impose my words on someone else? What have I done? God, why did I do it? God, why did you let me do this?*

Jennifer was standing on their front porch. She was covered with her son's blood. *It's true! My God, it's true.* I ran up the steps to her and tried to hold her and console her, but she had turned to stone. "Jennifer, oh, Jennifer. I'm sorry. I'm so sorry. My God, was it my letter?"

Dazed and unmoving, tears trying to roll from her wide-open eyes, she said quietly, "No, Andrea, it was not you. He was already planning to do it."

The sheriff arrived, then the paramedics and other neighbors. "It's going to be all right," I told her. "It's going to be all right." I knew she didn't believe me. This mother who, only minutes ago, had said she trusted me, now could not believe my words. How could she? How could I? How could anyone ever again? I ran down the grassy slope, running back around the pond and into my house and grabbed Harley's leash and ran out the door with him. I ran down the road as another neighbor was coming up. "Andrea, my God! You are so pale! What happened?"

"Rob shot himself," I said. "I talked to him just before he did it. *I talked to him!* I have to go meet Bill. I have to go meet Bill." I continued running down the road and down the street. As I approached the memorial park, I was alarmed to see policemen at the gate. A small crowd was standing outside. A red, emergency helicopter was landing near the grass in front of Dawson's place. *Oh, my God! What has happened?* In my panic, I thought something must have happened there. No one was ever there at that time except Bill and me. *If something had happened it must have been … Oh, my God! Bill!* I saw the manager at the gate, a very nice man who knew us because we were there so often. I ran to him, questioningly. "No," he shook his head. He knew what I was asking. "It's something else," he said quietly.

Then I heard someone in the crowd say something about "a kid was shot."

It's Rob. Of course. It's for Rob. The helicopter could not land on their property, so the paramedics had to bring him there to be airlifted to the nearest trauma center. *Well, then he's still alive! He's still alive!* I realized Bill would be arriving soon and he would come upon this scene. I had become alarmed at the sight, so I imagined how it would look to Bill. I saw his truck as he came up over the knoll. At first, he did not see me. He saw the crowd and the flashing lights. I waved to him. He pulled over and we jumped in.

"What's going on?" he asked. "At first I thought something happened to *you guys*."

"It's Rob! He shot himself! And I talked to him just before he did it! I talked to him and I gave him a letter I wrote! And then he shot himself!"

"What? Why did you write him a letter? What did you say to him?"

"Jennifer was worried about him. Oh, Bill. She told me he had already planned to do it before he got my letter, but I still feel like it's my fault. Bill, she trusted me. She hoped I could help. I only wanted to help."

"What did you say to him?"

"I just told him Dawson's story. But he was already mad at Jennifer. She told me this morning. I think he must have gotten angrier when he found out she had talked to me. God! I should have stayed out of it."

"Oh, Andrea. Why did you do that?"

"I told you. I wanted to help!" I cried.

As we went into the house, I said, "I have nothing for dinner. I'm sorry. I never made it to the market."

"Don't worry about it," Bill said. "I'll find something."

"Bill, I'm so scared."

"Maybe he'll be all right. He was alive if they took him by helicopter."

"I know, but … what if he isn't? Bill, why would God have put me in the position to have done this? If I didn't have Dawson's story to tell him, I would not have gotten involved. Bill, it was like it was fated. I don't see Jennifer every day. It was so perfectly timed. Like she was meant to talk to me this morning. But, why? If I could have helped, if Dawson's story could have helped then I would understand, but why would I have been meant to bring on this tragedy or be a part of it? Why, Bill?"

"Well, we don't know that you did. Didn't you say Jennifer said he had already planned to do it?"

"Yes, but … then why couldn't I have stopped it? Dawson believed his story would help someone! I just don't understand. It's just too terrible. I know what those people are going through. That drive to the hospital, not knowing if … Oh, God. Could he possibly be all right?"

"Well, anything's possible," he said.

Bill made a sandwich for dinner and I did not eat. I couldn't. Over the next couple of hours, I went over and over in my mind lamenting the events of the day. When the phone rang, I said to Bill, "Do you think they'd call and tell us anything? Maybe that's them. Oh, God." But it wasn't. It was Leah. I told her what had happened and she gasped. I said, "I know. It's horrible. If I had not talked to Jennifer or Rob and I heard that this had happened, I would undoubtedly feel terrible. But now, I have these questions that will drive me crazy. Why did God involve me? Only to have me fail? Leah, everything I believed in, everything I've been working toward, every word I've written has been with the belief that it will help someone. If at my first attempt, it has done just the opposite, how can I go on writing? How can I go on believing? How can I go on?"

"Andrea, don't do this to yourself," she said. "I know you believe in the story, but you can't expect it to help everyone. If it doesn't work this time it doesn't mean it never will."

"No, that's not it. I mean, I know, but … this was the first time. It had to work. Otherwise, why did God involve me? It was so fated. I was so compelled. I don't know why He would bring me this far and put me in that place and then take everything away."

"Well, you don't know that he has. O.K., you say that you stepped in and caused something to happen, right?"

"Yeah, it happened right after he had been here."

"Well, timing is everything. You take an extra minute to do something and your whole life can be changed. And Rob was still alive. Right? Well, maybe that was what was changed. Maybe he wouldn't have been if you hadn't stepped in. We don't know. What we do know is that you altered the timing of the events in one way or another, perhaps even indirectly just by having called him and having him come over … and he is alive."

"Oh, God, Leah. He just has to live."

When we got off the phone, the phone rang again. I answered it. It was Rob's father. He said, "Andrea? I just want to tell you that Rob is stable. He's doing well. There are some injuries, but it appears he will be all right. Thank you."

"Oh, God," I cried. "Thank you for calling. Thank you so much."

"Thank *you*," he said.

When I told Bill the news, I broke down and sobbed. "Thank you, God," I said out loud. I called Leah. I called my mother. I thanked Dawson. I praised God.

Over the next few days, I learned that after he had left my house with my letter in his pocket, yet unread, immediately upon returning home, an argument had ensued with his mother and he had rashly put a gun under his chin and fired. A week later, Jennifer called me from the hospital. I was so pleased to hear that Rob was off the respirator. It was like a miracle. She said, "I just wanted to tell you that I told Rob that God had saved his life. Rob said, 'God saved me twice.' He said the first time was when you phoned. He said, 'When Dawson's mom called, I had the gun to my head. I put the gun down to answer the phone.' Andrea, I want to thank you."

"It wasn't me. It was God. It was Dawson. They told me what to do. I just did what they told me. Oh, I'm just so glad he's O.K."

"Thanks. He seems so different. I don't think he's angry anymore."

He was soon out of the hospital with no permanent injuries. It was absolutely amazing. And not long after, on my morning visit to Dawson, I arrived to see something taped to the white marble. As I got closer, I read in bold letters. "My Gratitude to Dawson." It read in part:

To this wonderful man, my life is in great debt. From the moment my young eyes first fell upon him, I had wanted to be just like him in every aspect of his unique person. In my eyes, Dawson was my idol, but now with my age and experiences, it is evident he was and is something so much more than just my idol. He is an angel. There is no doubt in my mind he helped me through my hardest time. I felt his presence constantly by my side while recovering in the hospital. He was in my dreams every night with encouragement to carry on. Dawson bared a deep love and understanding for life, which I feel he tried to bestow in me. There is not a day goes by without Dawson in my mind and in my prayers.

So to you, Dawson, I write this in thanks for your handsomely unselfish support for me and my family.

P.S. I got a "Hog" and someday I hope to learn to ride it half as good as you rode yours.

Bill and I went to early morning mass on Easter Sunday and were on our way home from church when I said to Bill, "I'd like to go by St. Dominic's today on our way to your mother's. Could we do that? There won't be a mass at that time. I just want to stop in. O.K.?"

Bill had been to St. Dominic's since Dawson's funeral, but I had not. Working in the city, there were times when he found himself close by and he would stop in, light a candle and say a prayer for

Dawson. I had not had a real opportunity, but yet I had not made any effort either. I had been hesitant to return, for I was not sure I could bear the emotions being there might evoke. But today, I wanted very much to go.

It was a pleasant spring day and Bill spent the remainder of the morning and early afternoon working outside. He had come in to get ready and was in the shower when Ian, Dawson's friend, came to the door.

It was nice how his friends still dropped by from time to time. Over the past months, three of them had wives who were going to have babies. I was told a discussion had been going on about what they would name them, for if they were boys, they all had considered "Dawson." But after they had deliberated with many of their friends, they came to the decision they could not do it. "Because," they had concluded, "there was only one Dawson."

Ian had come by to wish us a Happy Easter. He looked good and said his life was going well and I told him how glad I was to hear that.

We engaged in the usual type of small talk. Then he said, "I had this dream … " He hesitated.

"What was it?" I asked.

"Oh, maybe I shouldn't … maybe I shouldn't tell it … I don't know. It was really strange."

"Like what? Was it bad?"

"No! No, it was good. But it was just so real."

I said, "It's all right if you don't want to tell it. You don't have to. I understand."

"I would like to tell you, it's just that … well … In the dream, I was at this friend's house … with these people … people I knew I shouldn't be with … you know … doing things I knew I shouldn't be doing." He walked over to the windowseat and sat down. "I was sitting like this," he said. "I was sitting at a table, leaning over like this … everyone was doing coke." I nodded to him to go on. He said, "I leaned over this mirror to snort a line of coke and as I did, I looked into the mirror. I looked right into the mirror and I saw … I saw Dawson! He was in the mirror looking back at me. I mean it was Dawson. His eyes just looking straight at me. It was so real. I could see his face. I could see his eyes. He was looking at me and, man, I stopped right there. I woke up and I knew I'd never do that again. And I haven't. It changed my life. Since that night, I've had more ambition, more energy, more hope than I have ever had. My outlook on life has completely turned around."

"That is so wonderful, Ian. I am so glad for you and so happy you shared that with me. Dawson is watching out for us. He loves us and he helps us. I know that." With tears in my eyes, I hugged him and thanked him.

Driving into St. Dominic's parking lot, I was remembering the many times we had done this while Dawson was waiting for us in the hospital. My heart ached that he was not waiting for us today. But perhaps I was not hurting quite as much as I would have been had I not just heard the inspiring story from Ian. But I was wondering if it was such a good idea to come here. I took a deep breath as I entered, but I was immediately filled with peace and awe. Bill seemed to be, too. He said, just as he had said years earlier, "This church is so beautiful." But I knew it was not just the beauty of the structure, as always, it was much more than that.

We went directly to St. Jude's shrine and lit a candle for Dawson as we had done so many times before. I knelt and prayed and thanked God for the blessings we had received and for sending Ian to share his dream with us. I stood and walked toward the main altar taking in the magnificence. I was surprised when I saw Father Cassidy coming down the center aisle. Father Cassidy was special to me because he was the priest that always said the St. Jude mass. He was gentle and soft-spoken. For that reason, I had chosen to say my first confession to him. When he noticed me, he came right over. In his quiet voice, he greeted me.

I told him how glad I was to be visiting. "It's been two and a half years since I have been here," I said. And assuming he did not know anything about me, I said, "Father Xavier had anointed our son, Dawson, while he was in the hospital and he had said his funeral mass here."

"Oh, I remember," he said. "So how are you?"

"Well, I still miss him."

"I know," he said. Then he looked upward and he smiled and nodded as if to say, "But he's up there and he's all right."

I nodded, knowing that was true. I said, "I've missed this church, too. St. Dominic's will always be special to me."

He smiled and in a quiet, reverent manner he proceeded to tell me about St. Dominic. He said, "St. Dominic was the founder of the Dominican Order. You see, he had this great idea." I was listening intently as he spoke of the Bishop's role versus the priest's role in the Roman Catholic Church of the 1200's. He told how St. Dominic had a plan for The Order and had gathered support and enthusiastic followers. He said, "These men had great respect and confidence in him. He was barely into his mission when he became gravely ill and his followers were devastated. They loved him and they loved his ideas and they did not believe they could carry out his wonderful plans without him. They were saddened, discouraged and despondent at the thought of his impending death. St. Dominic tried to console them. 'Do not be sad,' he told them. 'Do not worry. You must not despair, for this is the way it must be. And you'll see, I can do more good from up there.'"

When Father Cassidy had spoken those words of St. Dominic, he had looked upward just as he had done when he had spoken of Dawson. The words he had said then echoed in my mind. "I can do more good from up there."

He could do more good from up there! I could have sworn I heard the church bells tolling from the tower as I realized the events of the day, the year, had led me to this one, revealing moment. The glorious moment when He had answered what until now I believed to be the unanswerable question, "Why, God, why?"

And though I had not asked it of Him, nor demanded it, God had given me the answer. "Dawson could do more good from up there!" Dawson must have known that all along.

... As it was in the beginning, is now and forever will be, life without end. Amen.

Acknowledgments

To all of you who have shown such interest in this work and in my journey, I thank you.

In particular, I want to thank Rusty for all he did for Dawson and me, and, too, for the word processor which helped me get started writing. My thanks go to my editor, Leslie Keenan, who was the first "outsider" to read my work. When I handed it over to her, she understood my reluctance and said reassuringly, "Don't worry. I will take good care of it." And she did. My gratitude also goes to Michele Caprario, my final editor and consultant, for her spirit, compassion and enthusiasm in helping me to get this book ready for print and beyond.

Writing is quite a solitary venture in which many hours are spent alone with one's own thoughts and memories. I believe the reason I was able to spend these long hours working on this book was because I knew that no matter how deeply I found myself immersed in my sorrow, my loving family would always be there for me when I needed them.

My father eagerly offered to do things for me, wanting to comfort me and help me in any way he could. I thank him for being the strong, caring, sensitive man he is.

My mother was, and continues to be, my most earnest supporter. She gave me the encouragement I needed whenever I doubted myself. Although we spoke to each other every day, I never discussed with her the chapter I was working on until I finished it. And when I did, I would immediately give it to her for her approval. She was always touched by what I had written, finding nothing to be corrected or changed and this gave me the confidence to go on. She had faith in me and understood me—just as she always had. I am so lucky and thankful to have her for my mother.

The same chapter would then go to Claudia. She was the perfect balance to my mother. From her, I received the chapter returned, emblazoned with her neat, red marks, comments, questions and suggestions. She was honest and efficient and took her duties of First Editor quite seriously. She kept me in check when I went on too long. When something I wrote did not make sense to her, she did not hesitate to question me. We had a perfect working relationship, for through my attempts to satisfy her, she invariably got a better chapter out of me. The painstaking time she spent on this book cannot be measured in hours and I am so grateful to her, my special daughter. She has always been my blessing.

The love of my family helped me to pursue this project. But it was Bill who gave me the time, the place, the security that I needed in order to write. With his generous and loving heart, he supported me in all ways possible. He encouraged me to take my time, to do my best to complete my gift for Dawson. He shared my pain, my sorrow, and my love. He understood my endless tears and I thank him, my officially-no-longer-ex husband, for his desire to make it all a little easier for me.

And my thanks also go to my sweet, funny and adorable Harley. He is my partner, my buddy.

And, of course, with all my heart, I thank Dawson and God. Without their love, there would have been no story to write.

If you enjoyed this book and would like to give one to someone else, you may obtain a copy at your favorite bookstore, online bookseller, or fill out a copy of the form below.

Name _____

Address _____

City _____ St ____ Zip _____

Please send me:

____ copies of *Dawson's Gift* at $24.95 $ _____

California Residents please add Sales Tax
        of $1.81 per book: ____ books x $1.81 = $ _____

Shipping*: ____ books x $4.75 = $ _____

Total enclosed $ _____

Send order to:

    Odonata, LLC.
    P.O. Box 1533
    Novato, CA 94948-1433

    Fax: 415-897-9957
    Toll free: 1-866-251-4460
    Order on-line: www.dawsonsgift.com

For more than 5 copies, please contact the publisher for multiple copy rates.

*International shipping costs extra. If shipping to a destination outside the United States, please contact the publisher for rates to your location.